Property of

James Knight

Essentials of Marketing: Text and Cases
Second Edition

Essentials of Marketing:
Text and Cases
Second Edition

Geoffrey Lancaster
Chairman
Management Development Centre Ltd
Durham Associates Ltd
University of Newcastle-upon-Tyne

Lester Massingham
Principal
MTMS Ltd
Managing Director
Charles Massingham Consulting Pte Ltd,
Singapore, Kuala Lumpur & Hong Kong

McGRAW-HILL BOOK COMPANY

London · New York · St Louis · San Francisco · Auckland
Bogotá · Caracas · Lisbon · Madrid · Mexico · Milan
Montreal · New Delhi · Panama · Paris · San Juan
São Paulo · Singapore · Sydney · Tokyo · Toronto

Published by
McGRAW-HILL Book Company Europe
Shoppenhangers Road, Maidenhead, Berkshire, SL6 2QL, England
Telephone 01628 23432
Fax 01628 770224

British Library Cataloguing in Publication Data

Lancaster, Geoffrey A.
  Essentials of Marketing: Text and Cases. –
2Rev.ed.
I. Title II. Massingham, Lester
658.8

  ISBN 0-07-707728-8

Library of Congress Cataloging-in-Publication Data

Lancaster, Geoffrey.
  Essentials of marketing: text and cases / Geoffrey Lancaster,
Lester Massingham.—2nd ed.
    p.   cm.
  ISBN 0-07-707728-8
  1. Marketing. 2. Marketing—Case studies. I.Massingham,
Lester. II. Title
  HF5415.L2625 1993
  658.8—dc20   93-19905
                                                  CIP

56 CL 95

Typeset by Alden Multimedia, Northampton

Printed and bound in Great Britain by Clays Ltd, St Ives plc
Printed on permanent paper in compliance with the ISO Standard 9706

CONTENTS

PREFACE

The importance of marketing in a dynamic business environment is now more fully appreciated. Those organizations that have not been prepared to look to the needs of their customers first have found it increasingly difficult to survive in today's competitive business climate.

This contemporary marketing text synthesizes marketing knowledge and does not purport to break new ground. It is highly readable and does not assume previous knowledge of marketing. It is unique in that it contains a number of longer marketing cases previously written by one of the authors and used by the Chartered Institute of Marketing, and is brave enough to suggest solutions to the questions asked. The text is, therefore, 'different' in that it is not merely a distillation of theoretical knowledge, but it is practical through the medium of 'real-life' cases and their solutions. It thus translates theory into practice.

It has been written by two of the Chartered Institute of Marketing's senior examiners as the fundamental text that underpins any introductory marketing course. Throughout the text, other specialists' texts are referenced and recommended for more advanced and specialist reading. In terms of Chartered Institute of Marketing studies, it is appropriate to purchase this text at Certificate level, in the knowledge that it will not become redundant as the Diploma stage case study is catered for in terms of advice on how to tackle marketing case studies. Most case study texts tend to concentrate more upon business policy and are thus not generally applicable to the area of marketing. This text is relevant, as the cases are the actual or modified ones used in recent examinations. Indeed, some of these cases are now used on university MBA and postgraduate programmes.

The text is attuned to the needs of both students and tutors and contains supporting references and end-of-chapter questions. It is appropriate to the needs of all basic marketing courses from higher national to postgraduate levels. It is also appropriate for marketing courses where case study analysis forms a component of that course.

With the increasing application of the marketing concept by marketing-oriented organizations, this second edition of the text is indeed timely. Specifically, large sections have been added on marketing research, portfolio analysis and logistics. The subjects of selling and buyer behaviour have been reworked and updated. Business institutions are changing rapidly—evidenced particularly in modern retailing—and this makes the text all the more relevant. It is particularly relevant to modern marketing; and unlike most comprehensive marketing texts it is written by British authors, who, being Chartered Institute of Marketing senior examiners, can concur with the Institute's logo, 'Marketing means business'.

MARKETING PERSPECTIVE

ONE

MARKETING—ORIGINS AND DEVELOPMENT

INTRODUCTION

The marketing way of management is not a particularly complex or original notion; indeed, the saying 'the customer is always right' is as old as business itself. Marketing is really a business orientation based on this principle, which has grown and developed into a management discipline over the years. Marketing is not narrowly confined to a particular office or department: it is an attitude of mind, an approach to business problems that should be adapted by the whole organization, from the chairman and chief executive down to the lowest levels.

Marketing is based on the concept that the customer is the most important person to the company. In order to prosper or even survive, every company must work hard to retain its existing markets and continually strive to secure new and profitable customers. The marketing concept puts the emphasis on *customers* and the identification and satisfaction of customer requirements. Such an orientation to business consequently results in the customer becoming the focus of the company's activities, and most successful companies in the world owe their prosperity to the adoption and application of this marketing concept.

In starting our discussion of marketing, it must be stated that, although the concept of marketing is relatively straightforward, the term 'marketing' often means different things to different people. This confusion is not restricted to the ordinary person in the street. There are still many business people who have not fully grasped the importance of the marketing concept. The objective of this first chapter is to explain clearly what the marketing concept is all about and to compare and contrast it with less sophisticated approaches to business which, even today, are still practised by many business firms.

A DEFINITION OF MARKETING

It was explained above that the marketing approach to business is really quite straightforward and that the basic principles of marketing have been used to a greater or lesser degree for as long as mankind has engaged in trading activity. In this sense, marketing is a rather old subject, although the name 'marketing' is relatively new.

As far back as 1776, Adam Smith,[1] the father of modern economics, wrote the following passage in his famous work, *The Wealth of Nations*:

Consumption is the sole end and purpose of all production and the interests of the producer ought to be attended to, only so far as it may be necessary for promoting that of the consumer.

In the above statement Adam Smith has given the essence of what modern marketing is all about. The very word is *consumer*, as it is the identification and satisfaction of a *consumer's requirements* which forms the basis of modern marketing.

Although the essence of marketing is as old as trade itself, marketing emerged as a serious subject of study and has been accepted as a major management discipline only since the middle of the present century. In this sense, marketing is a very new subject concerned with the analysis of conditions and forces that make for successful commercial exchanges.

In certain commercial subjects, for example accountancy, it is possible to give a reasonably accurate definition of the scope of the subject in a few lines. Such a straightforward, simple definition is however more difficult to find in the case of such a wide-ranging subject to marketing. This is not because a definition of marketing does not exist. On the contrary, the problem is choosing the most appropriate one as there are so many definitions.

Because marketing is such a wide-ranging topic, different people often look on the subject from different viewpoints or give the subject a particular emphasis. To some extent such different viewpoints result from the academic background or the area of employment of the person giving the definition. For example, many people often go into marketing after studying economics, and tend to give the subject an economic slant. Others have worked for many years in a specialized area of marketing, e.g. market research or advertising, and hence tend to regard their particular area as the most important facet of marketing.

The following list is a sample of the wide range of definitions given for the subject:

Marketing is a social process by which individuals and groups obtain what they need and want through creating and exchanging products and value with others.[2]

The marketing concept is a philosophy, not a system of marketing or an organizational structure. It is founded on the belief that profitable sales and satisfactory returns on investment can only be achieved by identifying, anticipating and satisfying customer needs and desires.[3]

Marketing is the delivery of a standard of living to society.[4]

Marketing is the primary management function which organizes and directs the aggregate of business activities involved in converting consumer purchasing power into effective demand for a specific product or service[5] [and] . . . in moving the product or service to the final consumer or user so as to achieve company set profit or other objectives.[6]

Marketing is the process whereby society, to supply its consumption needs, evolves distributive systems composed of participants, who, interacting under constraints—technical (economic) and ethical (social)—create the transactions or flows which resolve market separations and result in exchange and consumption.[7]

The generally accepted UK definition is the one given by the *Chartered Institute of Marketing*, which reads as follows:

Marketing is the management process which identifies, anticipates, and supplies customer requirements efficiently and profitably.

The reader will appreciate that, although there are many generally accepted definitions of marketing, there is no one unified definition. All of the definitions given above are correct while at the same time all are slightly different. Because of the difficulty of incorporating all the facets of marketing into a simple definition, let us instead look at a number of key points which will help clarify the situation:

1. Marketing focuses the firm's or individual's attention towards the *needs* and *wants* of the marketplace.
2. Marketing is concerned with *satisfying* the genuine needs and wants of specifically defined target markets by creating products or services that satisfy customer requirements.
3. Marketing involves analysis, planning and control.
4. The principle of marketing states that all business decisions should be made with a careful and systematic consideration of the *user*.
5. The distinguishing feature of a marketing-oriented organization is the way in which it strives to provide *customer satisfaction* as a way of achieving its own business objectives.
6. Marketing is *dynamic* and operational, requiring action as well as planning.
7. Marketing requires an improved form of business organization in order for it to be able to lead and catalyse the application of the marketing approach.
8. Marketing is both an important functional area of management and an overall *business philosophy* which recognizes that the identification, satisfaction and retention of customers is the key to prosperity.

This last point is particularly important, as much of the problem of definition and misunderstanding over the term 'marketing' stems from the confusion between the *function* of marketing and its *philosophy*. The term 'marketing' is used to describe both the techniques used by the marketing department and the overall marketing orientation of the firm. Marketing is in fact both a functional area of management and a business philosophy. Let us look at these two views of marketing in a little more detail.

MARKETING AS A FUNCTIONAL AREA OF MANAGEMENT

One of the main sources of confusion for someone approaching the subject for the first time is the fact that marketing is a complex phenomenon that combines both the *philosophy* of business and its *practice*. Hence marketing consists of two interrelated phenomena:

1. A basic concept that focuses on customers.
2. A set of management techniques.

Many organizations have a marketing department made up of both marketing generalists, e.g. the marketing manager, and specialists, e.g. the sales manager or marketing research manager. Such a marketing department will obviously be based in a physical location within the organization in the same way as, say, personnel or purchasing. The people involved with the day-to-day running of the marketing department will have at their disposal a range of management techniques often referred to as the marketing spectrum or mix. These techniques cover such areas as sales and sales management, advertising and promotion, pricing, packaging, product development, marketing research, planning, distribution and after-sales service. The concept of the marketing mix will be discussed further in Chapters 2 and 4. Many of the functions of marketing offer separate career opportunities and are often undertaken by specialists, with the marketing manager responsible for coordinating all the separate but interrelated activities.

Looked at from this point of view, marketing is indeed a functional area of management which is usually within the firm and which uses a number of highly developed techniques in order to achieve specific objectives. As a function, an important part of marketing's role is to identify correctly both the current and future *needs* and *wants* of specifically defined target markets. This information is then acted upon by the *whole organization* in bringing into existence the products and/or services necessary to satisfy customer requirements. It is the marketing function that forms the interface with the firm's existing and potential customers. Marketing provides entrepreneurship by identifying customer requirements, and through marketing the rest of the firm is able to mobilize resources to capitalize on them.

In fact, the process of marketing management is no different from any other functional area of management in that it essentially comprises of four key tasks.

Analysis

The starting-point of marketing management decisions is analysis. Customers, competitors, trends and changes in the environment, and internal strengths and weaknesses must each be fully understood by the marketer before effective marketing plans can be established. Analysis, in turn, requires information using systematic marketing research and marketing information systems.

Planning

The second task of the manager is the planning process. The marketing manager must plan both long-term marketing direction for the organization (strategic planning), including, for example, the selection of target markets, and the marketing programmes and tactics that will be used to support these strategic plans.

Implementation

Both strategic and tactical plans must, of course, be acted upon if they are to have any effect. The implementation tasks of marketing management involve such activities as staffing, allocating tasks and responsibilities, budgeting, and securing any financial and other resources needed to translate plans into action.

Control

The fourth, and sometimes neglected, task of the manager is measuring and evaluating progress against objectives and targets established in plans. Control of marketing plans can be problematical, with difficulties associated with both measuring marketing performance and pinpointing cause and effect. For example, market share—a frequently used measure of marketing performance and hence a basis for marketing control—needs very careful analysis and interpretation if it is to provide a useful basis for controlling the effectiveness of marketing strategies and plans. Both qualitative and quantitative techniques of control should be used by the marketing manager and include budgetary control, control of marketing mix effectiveness and, from time to time, a full marketing audit. In fact, the control task of marketing management, in turn, forms part of the analysis function discussed earlier, thereby completing the essentially circular nature of these four interrelated tasks.

Although it can be seen that marketing has a very important functional role within the organization, the influence of marketing should not be restricted to the marketing department. A marketing-oriented business has implications for the way people *throughout the organization* respond to the initiatives that are forthcoming from marketing.

MARKETING AS AN OVERALL BUSINESS PHILOSOPHY

Many successful companies see marketing as the keystone of their business. Such firms do not see marketing simply as yet another functional area of management but more as an overall business philosophy, a way of thinking about business, and a way of working which runs through *every aspect* of the firm's activities. Hence, marketing is viewed not as a separate function, but rather as a profit-oriented approach to business that permeates not just the marketing department but the *entire business*. Looked at from this point of view, marketing is seen as an attitude of mind or an approach to business rather than a specific discipline.

The holistic view of the role of marketing within the firm has been expressed by a leading authority on management thinking, Peter F. Drucker,[8] who stated:

> Marketing is not only much broader than selling, it is not a specialized activity at all. It encompasses the entire business. It is the whole business seen from the point of view of its final result, that is, from the customer's point of view. Concern and responsibility for marketing must therefore permeate all areas of the enterprise.

This marketing-oriented business philosophy is referred to as the *marketing concept*. It is a philosophy that puts the customer at the very centre of the firm's corporate purpose. Marketing cannot exist in a vacuum. To be really effective it must permeate the whole company. What is needed is an integrated approach, not just the creation of a marketing department. It is the company's whole approach to business problems that is the key issue. It is the adoption of a business philosophy that puts customer satisfaction at the centre of management thinking throughout the organization that distinguishes a marketing-oriented firm from other less enlightened companies. Such an approach to business propels the marketing-oriented company into new activities and new opportunities and away from the narrow preoccupation with selling existing products to existing customers. Marketing cannot begin to be effective within a company unless it has the firm support of general management and penetrates every area of an organization.

The question we must ask ourselves is why, if the marketing concept is so simple and straightforward, has it been only relatively recently that firms have adopted it as a serious business philosophy? To answer this question, and to see how the marketing concept has evolved over the years into the form accepted today, we need to take a historical perspective and look at the development of trade.

MARKETING IN A HISTORICAL CONTEXT

Marketing is principally concerned with exchange or trade. Trade in its most basic form has existed ever since mankind has been capable of producing a surplus.

In historical terms surplus was usually agricultural produce, which would then be traded for other goods such as pots or cloths. This early process of exchange brought about the existence of the local market and later the village fair to facilitate trading. The emergence of trade allowed people to specialize in producing particular goods and services and to exchange them in markets for other goods they needed.

THE ECONOMIC ROLE OF EXCHANGE

If individuals and organizations within our society were totally self-sufficient and could survive without the need for exchange, there would be no need for marketing. However, in a modern society, virtually everyone depends upon exchange for economic welfare. An organized system of exchange, based on formalized procedures and an explicit legal framework, is fundamental to the working of any modern industrial economy.

Exchange is the act of obtaining something of value, usually a product or service, from another party, an individual or organization, by offering something of value to the other party. The thing of value offered can be another product or service resulting in a simple barter agreement, although in modern exchange transactions money is usually used as a medium of exchange. The act of exchange is an important economic process because it actually *creates value*. The act of production creates wealth, but the value of this wealth is greatly enhanced through the exchange process, which allows an individual or organization a greater range of consumption possibilities, resulting in greater satisfaction and utility all round.

Hence the exchange process is central to the subject of marketing, which, broadly speaking, can be said to be concerned with how, why and when consumers choose to satisfy needs and wants through exchange.

THE INDUSTRIAL REVOLUTION

Before the Industrial Revolution the production and distribution of goods tended to be on a small scale. Producers generally sold their products to a very localized market. The period 1760–1830 saw the British economy transformed from its dependence on agriculture with a dramatic increase in industrial production. With industrialization and the development of machines, production became more geographically concentrated, carried out in purpose-built mills or factories. Enterprises were now on a much larger scale and manufacturers produced relatively large volumes of products, not only for a localized market but for a national and even an international market. Although this period brought many social problems, economic activity and production expanded dramatically, particularly from the end of the eighteenth century. The development of the heavy industries such as iron and coal, the availability of steam power to drive machinery, the greater use of machines in all industries, particularly textiles, and the equally dramatic developments in communications, transport, agriculture and commerce transformed the economy, resulted in the growth of the factory system and saw the migration of the population from the countryside to the new industrial towns.

During this period trade flourished, but because consumption had now become more dispersed over greater geographical distances, producers no longer had immediate contact with their markets. In order for producers to be able to manufacture goods and services that would sell in such markets, it became necessary for them to *analyse* carefully and *interpret* the needs and wants of customers and to manufacture products that would 'fit in' with those needs and wants.

This process of matching the resources of a firm to the needs and wants of customers was termed 'entrepreneurship'. Generally, the entrepreneur was the individual who 'carried' the firm; for example, Josiah Wedgwood epitomizes the traditional entrepreneur. In a sense, the entrepreneurs were practising an early form of marketing although they did not actually call it such.

This period also saw advancements in production techniques based on job specialization and the division of labour. Prior to industrialization, production was carried out by the craft industries. In the craft industries, work was based on specialization in the production of a particular product, with the producer engaged in all the processes of production. The craftsmen would then trade their specialist product in order to obtain goods and services produced by other craftsmen, who of course also specialized in the production of a particular product. A skilled craftsman, e.g. a blacksmith or a cobbler, develops a high degree of skill in carrying out a particular activity. The craft industries were based on an early form of division and specialization of labour, productivity and output.

Industrialization saw the process of specialization and division of labour taken even further. The process of producing a product was broken down into stages or activities. Individuals then specialized in a particular operation. This resulted in a higher level of skill and speed and a greater amount of output than was possible when individuals had to carry out all the operations in the production of a product. The increase in job specialization increased the need for *exchange*. Specialization resulted in greater productivity, which in turn reduced costs and hence the price of products. Larger-scale production meant that channels of distribution had to be created to enable the effective demand from a much larger market to be met. The period of the first Industrial Revolution laid the foundations of the modern industrial economy, in which we now have a sophisticated system of institutions and economic organizations carrying out specialized activities in manufacturing, distribution, communication and finance to facilitate modern-day commercial activity, which of course is still based on the fundamental concept of trade or exchange.

THE MID-NINETEENTH CENTURY TO THE PRESENT DAY

From the middle of the nineteenth century to almost the beginning of the twentieth century, Britain was a dominant force in the world's economy. Throughout the nineteenth century both Britain's industrial output and the world's demand for that output had dramatically increased. The main factor underlying this industrial growth was the development of international trade. Britain was still seen as the 'workshop of the world' and held a virtual monopoly in the supply of manufactured goods to the relatively underdeveloped countries of the British Empire.

The latter half of the nineteenth century saw the emergence of other countries as competing industrial powers, most notably the United States of America and Germany. The rapid development of industry in these countries resulted in a significant increase in total output. Although Britain faced fierce competition in the areas of coal, steel and textiles, the period up to the First World War continued to be one of industrial expansion. Although Britain's share of world trade declined, the actual value of her trade increased as the incomes generated in other countries resulted in an increase in total demand.

During the First World War Britain's economy was concerned with the war effort. After the war Britain discovered that many of her previous overseas markets were now trading with her new industrial *competitors*. The financing of the Second World War resulted in Britain selling off many of her overseas investments. As a result, trade was even more important to the country's future. The period since 1945 has seen a decline in the importance of the traditional Empire and Commonwealth countries as overseas markets. Attention is now focused on the United States, Japan, and particularly countries in the European Community.

Despite an overall growth in world demand, the increase in world productivity has resulted in the excess supply of many products, e.g. steel and textiles. The international situation has changed from a sellers' market, where there was once a virtually insatiable demand for everything produced, to a buyers' market. Today we have a large number of producers competing to supply a finite market. Modern industry, as we have seen, is based on the process of mass production which necessitates *mass consumption*. Today, in order for a product to be commercially successful, it must be produced in sufficient volume. In order for producers to achieve a sufficient level of demand, they must produce products that that the market *wants to buy*. Simply to produce is no longer enough. To be competitive, firms not only have to take the needs and wants of the market into consideration: they have to *start with them*.

Today's modern organizations have become larger and more complex to manage. Markets too have changed and consumers' tastes have become more sophisticated. In the modern firm the entrepreneurial function is rarely left to one individual, but has developed into a management function and overall business philosophy that we now term marketing.

It can be seen then that marketing has its historical roots in trade and entrepreneurship. Marketing to a greater or lesser degree has always been practised by successful firms, albeit in a rather unsophisticated manner. It is only in modern times that it has developed as a formalized business concept with a codified philosophy and set of techniques. The realization by producers that they needed to take the buyers' points of view into account has slowly developed since the onset of industrialization. However, it has only been over the last 30 years that this growing realization has matured into the ideological breakthrough we now call marketing. Manufacturers eventually realized that, not only must they take the buyers' needs and wants into account, but these were the starting-point in the production of goods and services. This 'marketing maturity' did not happen overnight, but was a gradual process. Even today there are many firms that really only pay 'lip service' to the marketing concept and have still some way to go before they can truly claim to be *marketing-oriented*.

THE PRODUCTION-, SALES- AND MAKETING-ORIENTED FIRM

Many organizations pass through programme stages of business orientation before fully adopting the marketing concept. Broadly speaking, even today there are three types of company:

1. Production-oriented.
2. Sales-oriented.
3. Marketing-oriented.

Most marketing-oriented companies have evolved over the years, passing through the first two stages before reaching the third. Let us look at these various stages in a little more detail.

Production orientation

We saw earlier that in the nineteenth century and early part of the twentieth century the fundamental role of business was seen as production. Manufacturers were in a suppliers' market and were faced with a virtually insatiable demand for goods and services. Firms concentrated on production and productive efficiency in order to bring down costs. Product decisions were taken first and foremost with production implications in mind. Firms tended to manufacture and offer products that they were *good at producing*, with customers' requirements and satisfactions of secondary importance. Firms tended to be 'production-oriented', and the production man was the most important person in the organization, as it was thought that he held the key to the firm's prosperity. This production mentality was a workable philosophy as long as a sellers' market existed. However, many firms had to change their attitude as the world economy drifted into recession in the 1920s and 1930s and to produce was no longer enough.

Manufacturers who focus their attention on existing products and pay little or no attention to the changing needs and wants of the marketplace are in danger of one day discovering that they have no customers. Such firms suffer from what is often termed 'marketing myopia'. This is a very shortsighted viewpoint where firms are so busy concentrating on their products that they fail to take customers' requirements into account.

It is strange that even today firms can be found who pay little regard to the needs and wants of their customers and still have the production concept as the guiding philosophy of their businesses. Such firms take the attitude that they produce excellent products and common sense dictates that people will want to buy them.

Naturally, consumers have to be informed and convinced of the superiority of the company's products, and this task is entrusted to the salesforce. If consumers are not buying the firm's products, then as far as the company is concerned there can only be two possible reasons:

1. The customer is ignorant and does not appreciate a good product.
2. The salesforce is inept.

Figure 1.1   The organization of a production-oriented firm

Many firms have, in their own opinions, produced excellent products, but not necessarily of the type customers want to buy. The British motorcycle industry produced fine-quality machines, but consumers preferred the styling and range offered by Japanese manufacturers.

In a production-oriented company senior personnel such as the chairman and managing director are likely to have production backgrounds. Such companies are likely to have a small sales department which handles traditional marketing functions such as advertising. The greatest importance is placed on production. Under the production concept the salesperson's task is a relatively minor one; he or she has to sell what the firm has produced. Such a firm is typically organized as shown in Fig. 1.1. The sales area is viewed as a service function, and so the sales manager is not part of top-level management.

Sales orientation

The world economic recession of the early twentieth century concentrated the minds of business people. Many firms failed and fortunes were lost. Unemployment was high and effective demand slumped. Production capacity was underutilized and there were many unsold goods. Gradually business people began to realize that it was not enough simply to produce goods as efficiently as possible. For profits to materialize, such goods had to be sold.

The guiding business philosophy of many firms switched from production to sales orientation. The salespersons and the sales manager now became the most important people in the organization. The firm could manufacture the goods, but these goods still had to be *sold*. The sales concept stated that effective demand could be created by sales techniques, and it was thought that the sales department held the key to the firm's future prosperity and survival.

In a sense, sales orientation was a conceptual step forward because, although goods and services were still produced with little regard to customer requirements, at least it was realized that products did not sell themselves as a matter of course.

This period saw the development of a number of techniques that are still used today in modern order to achieve a competitive advantage, greater importance was attached to differentiation and branding. Advertising, sales promotions and other sales techniques increasingly used to achieve a 'sales angle'. These techniques were still used to *sell* the product rather than to communicate and inform or to increase customer satisfaction. Although these methods are still used today, it was the ethos with which they were used that distinguishes the sales approach from modern marketing practices, with the emphasis on the *hard sell*.

Even today many people think of marketing as being synonymous with selling and promotion. Although personal selling forms an important part of a firm's marketing programme, especially in industrial markets where personal contact with customers is of particular importance, it is not necessarily the most important element of marketing. In fact, selling is only one of several functions for which the marketing department is responsible. Personal selling is but one of an array of marketing tools, each of which has a particular part to play in the overall scheme of things. Individually, such tools are only part of the firm's overall 'marketing mix' or set of marketing tools which must be finely tuned to achieve maximum impact in the marketplace.

This is not to say that selling is of no importance: rather that, if the firm has applied the concept and techniques of marketing, i.e. identified consumer needs, produced appropriate products, priced, packaged, promoted and distributed the product correctly, then consumers should *want to buy* the product rather than the firm having to rely on intense selling. At the extreme, Peter Drucker,[9] one of the world's most respected management theorists, has stated:

> There will always, one can assume, be need for some selling. But the aim of marketing is to *make selling superfluous*. The aim of marketing is to know and understand the customer so well that the product or service fits him and sells itself. Ideally, marketing should result in a customer who is ready to buy. All that should be needed then is to make the product or service available . . .

In a sales-oriented firm its whole business philosophy is centred around sales. Often these firms believe that with some young, highly motivated salesmen, hungry for success and with a well worked out incentive scheme, they can sell anything. Sales volume is the most important criterion, and planning horizons tend to be relatively short-term. The actual customer, and how customers might perceive the value or utility of the goods being 'sold', is of secondary importance. Philip Kotler[10] defines this selling concept as:

> a management orientation that assumes that consumers will either not buy or not buy enough of the organization's products unless the organization makes a substantial effort to stimulate their interest in its products.

From the above definition, the implicit premises of the selling concept are as follows:

1. Consumers can always be induced to buy more through various 'sales techniques'.
2. Consumers tend to resist purchasing and it is the salesperson's job to overcome this.
3. The firm's key task is to organize an effective salesforce.

In a sales-oriented company the sales function is given equal seniority with finance and production. Such a firm is likely to be organized as shown in Fig. 1.2.

The basic asssumption of firms practising the selling concept is that their goods and services are 'sold' not *bought*. The aim of these firms is to get the sale and not worry about post-purchase satisfaction; customer satisfaction is considered secondary to getting the sale.

Examples of such selling situations are:

1. Certain double-glazing, burglar alarm, loft conversion, cavity wall insulation and other home 'improvement' companies: once they have a 'lead' from an unsuspecting target, they send round a high-pressure salesman with a 'foot in the door' approach.

```
                        ┌─────────────────────┐
                        │  Managing Director  │
                        └─────────────────────┘
                                   │
        ┌──────────────────────────┼──────────────────────────┐
┌───────────────┐          ┌───────────────┐          ┌───────────────┐
│ Production    │          │ Financial     │          │ Sale.         │
│ Director      │          │ Director      │          │ Direc         │
└───────────────┘          └───────────────┘          └───────────────┘
```

Figure 1.2   The organization of a sales-oriented firm

2. Many insurance companies, which search out potential customers and 'hard sell' them on the benefits of life insurance.
3. Encyclopedia companies, which often disguise their real intention through an 'educational survey' and other devious methods.

A sales approach to business is all very well to those companies that are 'here today and gone tomorrow', but not to firms that want to remain in business and build their business on the basis of trust, respect and genuine *customer satisfaction*. A good high-power salesperson can sell virtually anything to anyone—once! For repeat business over the long term, however, the typical selling mentality of many firms is not enough: a more 'customer-' or market-oriented approach is necessary for long-term success.

Marketing orientation

As discussed earlier, the modern marketing concept is a twentieth-century phenomenon. The concept has evolved from the rather myopic production and sales orientation of earlier times as a direct response to the obvious shortcomings of these less sophisticated business philosophies. The concept started to be seriously put into practice in the United States during the 1950s and has, since that time, been adopted as the central business philosophy by many firms throughout the world.

The marketing concept is sometimes referred to as a 'marketing' or 'customer' orientation. Simply stated, the marketing concept suggests that in order for a firm to survive in the *long term* and make a profit it must ascertain the genuine needs and wants of specifically defined target markets and then produce goods and services that satisfy customer requirements.

Under the marketing concept, it is the customer who takes the central place on the business stage. It is the satisfaction of customers that is seen as the key to prosperity, growth and survival. A marketing-oriented firm produces goods and services that customers *want to buy* rather than what the firm wants to make. The emphasis is put on the customer buying rather than on the firm selling the goods.

The management of a sales-oriented company tends to be short-run-oriented and preoccupied with achieving current sales. In such a company customer considerations are often limited to the sales department. To progress from this position to a marketing orientation, the firm must be able to cultivate a 'company-wide' approach to customer requirements. Marketing cannot begin to be effective within a company unless it has the full support of general management and penetrates every area of an organization, from the lowest to the highest levels.

Levitt[11] has drawn a sharp contrast between the selling and the marketing concept:

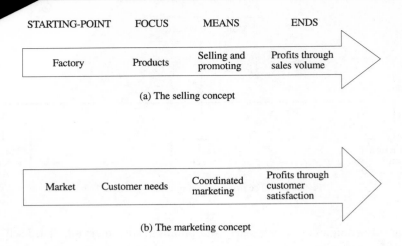

Figure 1.3 The selling and marketing concepts contrasted

Source: P. Kotler, *Marketing Management: Analysis, Planning, Implementation and Control*, 7th edn, Prentice-Hall International, Englewood Cliffs, NJ, 1991, p. 17

Selling focuses on the needs of the seller; marketing on the needs of the buyer. Selling is preoccupied with the seller's need to convert his product into cash; marketing with the idea of satisfying the needs of the customer by means of the product and the whole cluster of things associated with creating, delivering and finally consuming it.

The contrast is illustrated diagrammatically by Kotler[12] and shown here in Fig. 1.3.

To change from a sales- to a marketing-oriented company, the firm will have to become long-run oriented and preoccupied with planning the right products, the right channels, level of service and marketing strategy to meet the customer's long-run needs. The marketing approach challenges every member of a company, whatever his or her specialist function, to relate his or her work to the needs of the marketplace and to balance it against the firm's own profit needs. Nowhere is this more important than in the area of product design, where customers' views, rather than the views of production, should be the starting-point.

It was shown in Fig. 1.2 that a sales-oriented company is likely to be organized in the form of specialized departments charged with carrying out different company tasks; each department directly or indirectly will have an impact on customer satisfaction through its own activities and decisions. Under the marketing concept, it is desirable to coordinate these activities because the ultimate satisfaction gained by the customer is a function of the *totality* of all company departments acting in *unison*.

Changing from a simple sales to a more sophisticated marketing orientation will mean that marketing will have much more influence and authority over other departments to bring about *integrated* coordinated marketing. The sales department and other functional management departments may resent having to bend their efforts to the will of the marketing department. The major departmental differences or organizational conflicts between marketing and other departments are summarized in Table 1.1.

Table 1.1

Department	Emphasis	Marketing's emphasis
Sales	Short-term sales	Long-term profits
	Sales most important	Customer satisfaction most important
	One department	Whole organization
Purchasing	Narrow product line	Broad product line
	Standard parts	Non-standard parts
Finance	Hard-and-fast budgets	Flexible budgets
	Price to cover costs	Market-oriented pricing
Accounting	Standard transactions	Special terms and discounts
Manufacturing	Long runs	Short runs
	Few models	Many models
	Standard orders	Custom orders
	Long production lead time	Short production lead times

The main problem facing the sales-oriented firm in progressing to a marketing orientation is the management of organizational change. Marketing will set the strategies and plans in consultation with the departments concerned, but these departments will retain the authority to execute the agreed programme in the way they think best. The human implications of this organizational change should not be underrated, bearing in mind that it will involve a reallocation of power within the company. Functions previously carried out by other departments will become the responsibility of marketing, and every part of the firm will have to conform to a plan drawn up by marketing in consultation with other departments.

In a marketing-oriented firm, the chairman and managing director are likely to come from a marketing background. In addition, there is likely to be a marketing director with a position of equal status to that of the production and financial directors. Such a firm is likely to be organized as shown in Fig. 1.4.

Although the proper organizational structure is an important element in a firm becoming marketing-oriented, such an orientation is not achieved simply by adopting an organizational chart. Management must also adopt and use the marketing concept as a business philosophy. Hence in a marketing-oriented firm marketing is not confined to the marketing director and the marketing department. To be really effective, it must permeate the whole company. A change of management labels and titles will not achieve the necessary fundamental change in company attitudes. It is the company's *whole approach* to business problems that is the key issue. It is the adoption of a business philosophy that puts customer satisfaction at the *centre* of management thinking throughout the organization. It is this that distinguishes a marketing-oriented firm from a production- or sales-oriented firm.

Although the main thrust of this chapter has tended to reflect tangible products, its should also be remembered that the marketing concept should equally apply to the marketing of services. The theme of services is covered in more detail in Chapter 8.

DEVELOPMENTS IN THE CONCEPT AND PRACTICE OF MARKETING

Like most areas of management and business, both the marketing concept itself and, as a result, the practice of marketing management have continued to evolve and develop and no doubt will

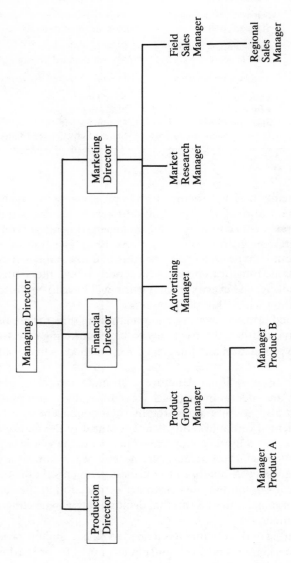

Figure 1.4 The organization of a marketing-oriented firm

continue to do so in the future. It is impossible to trace all of these developments and changes in this chapter, but among some of the more important are the following.

Ecological/environmental and consumer welfare issues

Recent years have witnessed an increased interest in protecting the environment, together with a recognition of the complex and potentially fragile nature of the ecological system of our planet. Coupled with these developments has been an increased emphasis on protecting consumers against marketing malpractice and dangerous or unhealthy products. Effective and aware marketers have responded to these developments by, for example, producing recyclable products and packaging, reducing the pollution that the use of their products causes, and even protecting consumers against their own worst excesses by stopping the selling of certain products. The consumer movement and so-called 'green' issues are considered further in Chapter 15, but there is no doubt that these developments have had far-reaching effects on marketing practice. There are some that argue that the marketing concept itself needs to change to reflect this increased concern for consumer and environmental welfare, calling for a societal-based marketing concept.

Not-for-profit/non-business marketing

A second important development in marketing practice has been the increasing use of marketing tools and techniques in not-for-profit and non-business organizations. Traditionally, marketing was conceived as a means of generating and sustaining profits. However, many organizations have objectives other than profits, and many are not business organizations in the conventional sense. Examples of such organizations include churches, charities, political parties and 'public' organizations such as local authorities, police and fire services and government departments. Once spurned by such organizations, or at the very least thought of as not being relevant, marketing is increasingly being used as part of their plans. Again we shall consider the special issues of marketing approach and application in these types of organizations in more detail in Chapter 15.

Services marketing

Unlike not-for-profit and non-business marketing, many providers of services have long recognized the value and importance of marketing and of being marketing-oriented. As mentioned earlier, the marketing concept applies just as much to service products as to physical products; however, probably because of the growth in importance of services in the economies of many developed countries, more and more attention has focused on the special issues and problems of applying marketing in this area. As we shall see in Chapter 8, the characteristics of services compared with tangible physical products gives rise to additional considerations in their marketing.

Global marketing

Business and trade, and hence marketing, have become more and more global in nature in recent years. As with services, the application of marketing—in this case by companies trading across international frontiers—is not new, but again, the growth in activity in this area, and particularly the spread of the global marketing organization, has focused more and more attention on this aspect of marketing. International and global aspects of marketing are considered in more detail in Chapter 14.

CONCLUSIONS

This chapter has traced the development of the modern marketing concept, and compared it with less sophisticated approaches to business. These approaches tended to put the product or product sales, rather than customer requirements, at the centre of business thinking. Even today the marketing concept is still often misunderstood by practising business people and, as a result, is often criticized as a mangement 'fad' or nothing more than rhetoric. If modern marketing principles are to gain acceptance by the senior managers who must put them into effect, the need is not for more elaborate marketing techniques, but for better communications between the marketing specialist and the general manager.

Unless the marketing way of thinking and caring about the business is practised at a level where effective action can be guaranteed, then the most up-to-date and sophisticated marketing techniques in the world will not succeed. Marketing can provide policies for profitable action, but top management must give the authority to form these policies into action.

Marketing is not narrowly confined to a particular office or department: it is an attitude of mind, an approach to business problems that should be adopted by the whole organization, from the chief executive downwards.

Every person working in an organization should realize that without customers there is no business and hence no jobs. If a company cannot attract and retain customers' business, it will eventually be forced into liquidation or merger. All departments within the organization should be *working together* as an integrated unit with a common purpose—the satisfaction of customers' needs and wants. They should strive to carry this out more effectively and efficiently than competitors and, in the case of profit-making organizations, to make a profit out of the whole operation.

The marketing concept acknowledges that a business geared to serve the needs and requirements of customers will achieve better results over a longer period of time than a company whose orientation is along different lines. When a company is said to be 'marketing-oriented' it puts the customer at the very centre of its corporate thinking. It sees its mission in life and its very purpose for existence as being the identification, satisfaction and retention of customers.

The philosophy of marketing was once viewed as being most relevant to the organization seeking profits, but increasingly the marketing concept and tools of marketing are being applied in the not-for-profit/non-business organization. Other developments that are continuing to shape the future of marketing include the growth in services marketing, the consumer movement and green issues, and global marketing. Marketing is a dynamic subject and management function, and one that must respond to these sorts of developments.

APPLICATION QUESTIONS

1. How does marketing differ from selling?
2. 'Marketing is often said to be concerned primarily with an exchange of relationships.' Elaborate on this statement, illustrating your answer with examples.
3. Define briefly the marketing concept. Explain how a thorough understanding of this concept enables an organization to ensure that it is responsive to changes in consumers' needs and wants.
4. Give examples of three firms that you feel are very marketing-oriented. State clearly, using examples, on which basis you made your selection.
5. 'Consumption is the sole end and purpose of all production' (Adam Smith, *The Wealth of Nations*, 1775). What do you think this statement means?

6. 'Marketing thinking and practice have to evolve in order to meet the challenges of the future.' What are some of the most important developments that will shape the future of marketing?

REFERENCES

1. A. Smith, *The Wealth of Nations*, Random House, New York, 1937.
2. P. Kotler, *Marketing Management: Analysis, Planning and Control*, 5th edn, Prentice-Hall, London, 1984, p. 4.
3. C. Barwell, 'The marketing concept', in: *The Marketing of Industrial Products*, A, Wilson (ed.), Hutchinson, London, 1965, p. 3.
4. P. Mazur, 'Does distribution cost enough?, *Fortune*, November 1947, p. 138.
5. M. Christopher, M. McDonald and G. Wills, *Introducing Marketing*, Pan, London 1980, p. 9.
6. L. Rodger, *Marketing in a Competitive Economy*, 4th edn, Associated Business Programmes, London, 1974, p. 47.
7. R. Bartles, 'The general theory of marketing', *Journal of Marketing*, XXXII, January 1968, pp. 29–33.
8. P. F. Drucker, *The Practice of Management*, Harper and Row, New York, 1954, p. 56.
9. P. F. Drucker, *Management: Tasks, Responsibilities, Practices*, Harper and Row, New York, 1973, pp. 64–5.
10. P. Kotler, *Principles of Marketing*, Prentice-Hall, Englewood Cliffs, NJ, 1980, p. 21.
11. T. Levitt, 'Marketing myopia', *Harvard Business Review*, July–August 1960, pp. 45–6.
12. P. Kotler, *Marketing Management: Analysis, Planning, Implementation and Control*, 7th edn, Prentice-Hall, Englewood Cliffs, NJ, 1991, p. 17.

TWO

THE MARKETING ENVIRONMENT

INTRODUCTION

We saw in Chapter 1 that the marketing-oriented firm places the customer, and the satisfaction of customers' needs and wants, at the very centre of all corporate thinking. Rather than establishing what the organization can produce and then going out and 'selling' it, the marketing-oriented firm first finds out the genuine needs and wants of consumers and then attempts to produce products and services that satisfy these requirements. It was also shown that, in a wider sense, the marketing concept is more an attitude of mind or a customer-oriented business philosophy, rather than merely a functional area of management.

Although a clear understanding of consumers' requirements is of paramount importance in putting such a business philosophy into practice, there are also other factors to consider. The marketing firm operates within a complex, dynamic, external macro-environment. It is the task of the marketing-oriented firm to link the resources of the organization to the requirements of consumers within the framework of opportunities and threats presented by this macro-environment. Hence, the marketing firm not only has to put consumers' requirements at the top of its list of priorities, but it also needs continually to adjust to environmental factors.

The objective of the first part of this chapter is to develop an understanding of the factors making up the marketing macro-environment. Firms cannot usually control their environment, but they can understand, and to a certain extent anticipate and react to, environmental forces.

In order to place the macro-environment in its proper context, one should realize that the general term 'marketing environment' is often used to denote both *internal* organizational forces and forces *outside* the control of the firm. For example, Kotler[1] defines the general marketing environment as follows:

> A company's marketing environment consists of the actors and forces that affect the company's ability to develop and maintain successful transactions with its target customers.

Such a definition includes *all* environmental forces outside of the firm's marketing management function. This would also include inter-departmental influences. Although the marketing concept is a customer-orientated philosophy that should permeate the whole organization, marketing as a *function* invariably has both to compete and to cooperate with other functional areas of management.

Firms are blessed with finite resources. The marketing function often has to compete with other management functions in order to obtain the resources it requires to carry out its job. For example, it needs to spend on employing sales personnel, advertising and marketing research. Other management departments such as production or purchasing may feel they are equally deserving. The marketing function also *cooperates* with other departments within the firm. For example, the marketing research department may establish a 'gap' in an existing product market. Marketing would then work in conjunction with research and development, production, finance and legal departments in developing a possible new product.

Russ and Kirkpatrick[2] call the interaction between the marketing department and other functional areas of management the *intra-firm environment*. It is important, in order to understand the influences of external environment forces, to appreciate that, although the marketing function is the channel through which the firm adapts to changes in external conditions, marketing's ability to carry out this role is also influenced by internal factors. Marketing managers make decisions that have a bearing on other functional areas of the firm. Likewise, the decisions made by other departments have a direct effect on the marketing department's ability to carry out its job. The role of marketing in the company setting and the interaction between marketing and other functional areas is discussed later in this chapter.

The *general* marketing environment, therefore, consists of *all* the factors and forces influencing the marketing function. This includes both internal and external forces. Internal forces, i.e. the intra-firm environment, are largely within the control of the firm. It is the generally uncontrollable forces outside the firm in the macro-environment that pose the most important sources of opportunities and threats to the company.

As mentioned earlier, Kotler divides the general marketing environment into two distinct categories, which he terms the *micro-* and *macro*-environments. Using this classification, the micro-environment consists of people and organizations in the company's *immediate environment* that affect its ability to serve its markets. As we have seen, this includes inter-department influences within the company itself, but it also includes suppliers, market intermediaries, competitors and other 'publics'. Kotler reserves the term 'macro-environment' to denote other external forces such as demographic, economic, political, technological, and socio-cultural forces.

The term 'micro-environment' would seem a somewhat inappropriate term when used in this context. The *Collins English Dictionary*,[3] for example, defines the term 'micro' as 'small or minute: indicating abnormal smallness or underdevelopment'. While intra-firm relationships and forces could rightly be called micro-environmental influences, it would not seem appropriate to use this term to denote environmental forces outside of the firm. While it is true that certain markets are relatively small, and hence involve a limited number of suppliers, distributors and competing firms, this is by no means always the case. Many markets are extremely large and often operate on an international scale. In such markets, the number of suppliers, distributors and competitors may be legion.

In the context of this chapter, the term 'macro-environment' denotes all these forces and agencies *external* to the marketing firm. Some of these outside factors and forces will be somewhat 'closer' to the firm than others, for example immediate suppliers and competitors. We will term this the *proximate macro-environment* (proximate meaning 'close', as in the word 'proximity'). This will serve to distinguish between the environmental influences close to the firm, and the wider external forces such as economic or political forces, which of course also affect the people and organizations in the firm's proximate macro-environment as well as the firm itself.

THE MACRO-ENVIRONMENT

The only really certain thing in this world is change. Sometimes change occurs so slowly that it is virtually imperceptible. We are often unaware that change is occurring until it is too late to do anything about it. At other times change is so rapid that, even though it is obvious, we find it difficult to react quickly enough. Although none of us possess the power to foresee the future, we can be sure that it will be *different* from today, and that change is a fact of life. We have little power to stop it, and the sensible course of action is to welcome change and attempt to adapt to it. However, one can attempt to predict such changes through forecasting, a subject dealt with in more detail later.

Charles Darwin,[4] author of *On the Origin of the Species*, put forward the theory that many living organisms have been able to survive in a changing and hostile world because they were able to adapt successfully to changing conditions. Fossil records indicate that long ago there existed many forms of life that for some reason no longer exist today. Although many theories have been put forward to explain the demise of prehistoric animals, the main factor seems to have been their inability to adapt.

Firms also operate in a changing, and at times hostile, business environment. They too, in order to survive and prosper, need to take account of, and adapt to, changing environmental conditions. Firms that fail to do so are likely to end up as extinct as the prehistoric mammals.

In order for a firm to be able to adapt successfully to changing circumstances, management needs to have an understanding and appreciation of the factors and forces influencing such changes. Ideally, a firm should be in a position to adapt to changes as they are occurring, or even in advance. Firms should attempt to capitalize upon change rather than merely reacting to it. By identifying environmental trends soon enough, management should be able, at least in part, to anticipate where such trends are leading and what future conditions are likely to result from such changes.

Unless firms are able to identify and react to changes quickly enough, they are likely to be dictated to by circumstances beyond their control. Instead of being part of the changes occurring, and *leading* the market, they will, of necessity, be forced into being market followers. Instead of adapting to change and even going some way towards *influencing* events, events will instead influence them, perhaps in an unfavourable way. The 'Mars' company not only makes Mars bars; it makes pet foods, convenience foods, computer software, etc. It makes no secret of the fact that its intention is to be market leader in all its operations.

In terms of its speed of response, and its ability to react to changing conditions, we can generally classify three types of firm:

1. Firms that identify and understand the forces and conditions bringing about change. Such firms adapt and move in line with such changes. To a certain extent, such a firm may itself play a part in influencing events.
2. Firms that fail to adapt to changes early enough to become part of that change. Such firms have little opportunity to influence events, but are usually forced to react to changes eventually, out of the necessity to survive.
3. Firms that fail to realize change has occurred, or refuse to adapt to changing circumstances. Such firms are unlikely to survive in the long term or, if they do, are unlikely to prosper.

Controllable marketing variables and the macro-environment

In a mixed economy, such as that to be found in the United Kingdom, firms enjoy a considerable amount of autonomy. Not only does the management of a firm have control over how it organizes and integrates its management functions, but generally it is free to decide what and how to manufacture as well as matters concerning pricing, packaging, advertising and distribution. Generally speaking, the management of a firm is free to carry out its business affairs in any way it

Figure 2.1   Macro-environmental forces influencing the marketing organization

pleases, and so a number of marketing variables like price are directly under its control. Collectively, we call these controllable marketing variables the 'marketing mix', and this concept is discussed in detail in Chapter 4.

While marketing firms control much of their operations, they do not plan strategies in a vacuum. As we have seen, all organizations are influenced by a number of macro-environmental factors which are broadly outside their control. These environmental forces, and in particular changes in these forces, give rise to marketing opportunities and threats. Stanton *et al.*[5] suggest that the ability of a marketing decision-making executive may be measured by the skill with which he or she can carry out the following tasks:

1. Adjust to the external elements in the changing environment.
2. Forecast the direction and intensity of these changes.
3. Use the controllable variables at his or her command (the marketing mix) in adapting to this external environment.

The most important factors making up the firm's marketing macro-environment are shown in Fig. 2.1.

We shall look at each of these sub-environments in more detail, starting with those macro-environmental forces closest to the marketing firm.

The proximate macro-environment

The proximate macro-environment consists of people, organizations and forces within the firm's immediate *external* environment. Of particular interest to marketing firms are the sub-environments in which we find:

1. Competitors
2. Suppliers
3. Intermediaries (e.g. distributors)

The people and organizations making up the above sub-environments all have a *direct*, and at times *immediate*, effect on the commercial well-being of the marketing firm.

The competitive environment

There are very few firms that are fortunate enough to have no competitors. While it is true that certain industries such as gas or electricity are near-monopolies, even these industries face competition, if only from each other. For example, gas is a substitute for electricity in many areas of energy use. In fact, nearly all firms face competition from other firms within the same industry or from firms in other industries which offer *substitute* products or services.

The competitive environment can often determine the success or failure of a product. Boone and Kurtz[6] discuss the case of 'Corfam', a leather substitute introduced in the United States during the 1960s by Du Pont. The cost of leather in the United States at this time was very high and Du Pont was convinced it had produced a 'winning' product. Years of research had managed to produce a synthetic leather nearer to the real thing than anything else on the market. The new product had many of the attributes of real leather, including 'breathability' and the ability to absorb foot moisture. Du Pont was so convinced that Corfam would succeed that it even confidently cut back on advertising the product because it was thought unnecessary. Corfam had to be withdrawn from the market eventually because foreign competition flooded the United States footwear market with real leather shoes which could be sold at a lower price than shoes made from Corfam. Du Pont's Corfam was an excellent product, but the firm failed to judge correctly the reaction of foreign competitors to its introduction. As a result, Du Pont spent millions of pounds on research and development only to end up with a commercial failure on its hands.

The Corfam story illustrates how factors in the competitive environment can affect the commercial prosperity of any firm. It also shows how marketing management must be *alert* to the potential threat of firms marketing product substitutes of both domestic and foreign origin. Many British manufacturing industries such as steel and textiles have been experiencing heavy competition from substitute products, often produced overseas. For example, the UK carpet industry has traditionally had a reputation for producing high-quality Axminster and Wilton carpets. Today foreign imported carpets have captured a large share of the market. Many of these carpets are made from synthetic materials instead of the traditional wool pile with jute backing. They are also produced using the cheaper 'tufting' process instead of the traditional 'weaving' process. Many carpet manufacturers have been forced into liquidation over the past 10 to 15 years as a result of these heavy competitive pressures.

In some industries, such as textiles, there may be hundreds or even thousands of manufacturers worldwide to pose a potential competitive threat. In other industries, such as car production, there may be only a few dozen, although the level of competition is likely to be just as fierce. Whatever industry the marketing firm is a part of, it will be necessary for management to identify its competitors. Management will also need to establish exactly what benefits competitors are offering consumers if its firm intends to compete effectively. Having done this, management should then establish how its own firm compares in relation to competition. Only when management has a clear understanding of the factors and forces making up the competitive environment can it hope to compete.

Supplier environment

Suppliers are other business firms and individuals who provide the resources needed by the marketing firm to produce goods and/or services. Nearly every firm, whether engaged in manufacturing, wholesaling or retailing, is likely to have suppliers. Large firms such as Marks and Spencer or the Ford Motor Company are likely to have numerous suppliers. For example, Ford must obtain glass windscreens, headlamp units, brakepads, tyres, steel sheet, fabric for interior upholstery and a number of other materials in order to produce cars. While some of these product constituents will come from major manufacturers such as British Steel, Pilkington's Glass, Lucas and Dunlop, other components, ranging from industrial fasteners to engine gaskets, will often be supplied by a large number of smaller, less well known companies.

As you will appreciate, Ford depends on possibly hundreds of suppliers for its manufacturing capability and commercial prosperity. In the same way, hundreds of firms depend on Ford for orders. The firms that supply Ford with finished components are also likely to be supplied with raw materials or semi-processed goods by a host of other suppliers.

Purchasing is regarded as a very important management function in many organizations. The reason for this is that firms must be able to purchase products and services at an acceptable price and quality. The firm must also ensure that its suppliers are capable of offering an acceptable level of service on such matters as delivery, reliability, stock availability, servicing arrangements and credit facilities.

Manufacturing firms have to decide what proportion of their products actually to make themselves and what parts and components should be sub-contracted out to other manufacturers who are often specialists in their field. For those materials that have to be bought in, purchasing personnel will have to obtain detailed product specifications from engineers and designers, search for suppliers that are capable of producing or supplying materials to specification, rate them on potential suitability, obtain tenders and arrange contracts.

The buyer–supplier relationship is one of economic interdependence. Both parties rely on each other for their commercial well-being. Changes in the terms of the relationship are usually based on negotiation rather than on *ad hoc* unilateral decisions. Such relationships are usually long term, with each party realizing its dependence on the other. Both parties are seeking security and long-term stability from their commercial relationship. This is not to say that factors in the supplier environment do not change. Suppliers may be forced to raise their prices and may also be affected by industrial disputes which, in turn, will affect delivery of materials to the buying firm. Some suppliers may find themselves in financial difficulty and be forced into liquidation. In an attempt to limit the effect of such factors, many buying firms use a 'multiple sourcing' purchasing policy. This avoids over-dependency on any one supplier and reduces the vulnerability of the buying firm.

Since the illustration has been taken from the motor industry, it is appropriate to discuss the fact that the trend is now for car companies to hold as little stock of components as possible. This trend has been established by the Japanese, and it is not unusual to hold only four hours' stock of certain components. The aim is for 'zero defects' and is an extension of a school of thought called 'just-in-time management'.

The advantages to the car company are that it saves on working capital in that stockholding is minimal. However, the implication is that there must be absolute reliability on suppliers in terms of quality and delivery. The implication to companies marketing to large car firms is that quality and reliable delivery are as important (if not more important) than price.

Marketing firms are also buyers of specialist marketing services. For example, although the larger firms are likely to have their own 'in-house' marketing research department, they will often commission surveys, and test marketing programmes and product facilities, from outside specialist agencies.

Whatever the product or service being purchased by the marketing firm, developments in the supplier environment can have an immediate and possibly serious effect on the firm's commercial operations. Marketing management should be continually monitoring changes and trends in order to plan ahead.

The distributive environment

Many firms, particularly in industrial markets where products are often buyer-specified, market and deliver their products direct to the final customer. Other firms use some form of intermediate distribution system. The distribution system is then made up of one or more 'middlemen' who can be individuals or other organizations. They range from agents, distributors, factors and wholesalers to retailers.

Because of the seeming permanence of the distributive environment at any point in time, many firms make the mistake of thinking it is static. In fact, distribution channels change and evolve just like any other facet of business life. As Davidson[7] explains:

> Distribution channels resemble the hour hand of a watch. They are always moving, but each individual movement is so small as to be invisible in isolation. The cumulative movement over a number of years can, however, be massive.

Because distribution channels change relatively slowly, it is easy for manufacturers to respond too slowly to their evolution. Existing channels may be declining in their popularity or efficiency, while new potential channels of distribution may be developing, unnoticed by the marketing firm. These important considerations concerning the dynamic nature of channels of distribution are considered further in Chapter 10.

At this stage it is sufficient to appreciate that factors in the distributive environment are also likely to be subject to change, especially in the legislative field—a subject taken up later in Chapter 15. As with all the other elements of the macro-environment, the distributive environment is also a source of potential threats and opportunities to the marketing firm. The marketing firm needs to monitor events closely and take appropriate action in order to adapt to changing conditions.

Wider macro-environmental forces

Up to now we have been looking at those macro-environmental factors and forces that are closest to the marketing firm. We termed this the 'proximate macro-environment'. Other macro-environmental forces have a wider influence and affect not only the marketing firm, but also those organizations and individuals (e.g. suppliers) that make up the proximate macro-environment.

Socio-cultural environment Of all the elements in the marketing macro-environment, the socio-cultural environment probably presents the greatest challenge. People's basic beliefs, attitudes and values are shaped by the society in which they grow up. Their general behaviour, including their purchasing behaviour, is influenced by social conditioning. A more detailed and academic discussion of consumer behaviour is given in Chapter 3.

The main factor influencing a society's attitudes and behaviour is its culture. Core cultural values are firmly established within a society and are generally difficult to change. Such beliefs and values are passed on from generation to generation through the family and other social institutions such as the church, schools and government. Because core cultural values are difficult to change, they act as relatively fixed parameters within which marketing firms have to operate. Kotler[8] states that in addition society has a set of secondary cultural values. These values are less persistent than society's core values and tend to undergo changes over time. Social and cultural influences are so interrelated that it is extremely difficult to evaluate the effects of one factor without the other.

Before we look at the role of culture in more detail, let us first summarize some of the major changes that have occurred in the socio-cultural environment that can have affected marketing.

Changes in social values The 1960s saw the birth of the so-called 'permissive society'. Over a period of about 10 years, society's values went through a period of dramatic change. Society's attitude towards marriage, divorce, sex, religion, drugs, economic and social institutions and authority changed and the values of the previous generation were radically altered. People in general became more responsive to change; in fact they welcomed it. This was the period of 'individualism', 'do your own thing', and 'anything goes'. Today we have seen a reversal of many of the attitudes and beliefs of the permissive society. Today people value health, economic security and stable relationships and in many ways have returned to a lot of the social values and norms of the pre-1960s. In addition, as we saw in Chapter 1, individuals and society have become much more conscious of the need to protect the environment.

Changes in attitudes towards credit Over the past 20 years society's general attitude towards credit has dramatically altered. As recently as the 1960s, borrowing was generally frowned upon, except for major purchases such as cars and houses. Hire-purchase agreements were usually signed in the store manager's private office, and there was something of a social stigma attached to buying something on the 'never never'. Today, credit availability has become an intrinsic part in the marketing of many products. Credit has lost its social stigma, and many people carry Access, Visa, American Express or individual store credit cards. Credit transactions are now conducted openly, and it is the person who never buys using credit who is considered to be unusual.

Attitudes towards health Twenty years ago people who went jogging or ate specific 'health' foods were regarded as being a little eccentric. Today people are more aware of the health implications of what they eat and drink, and regular exercise is an important part of many people's lives. Smoking, which was once considered the height of social sophistication, is now thought of as an anti-social habit. Changes in society's attitude to health have resulted in a multi-million-pound industry developing and supplying health foods, clothing, books and exercise equipment.

Change in attitudes towards working women Not so very long ago, society's attitude towards working women tended to be chauvinistic. A woman's place was thought to be 'in the home' and the 'career woman' was viewed with a certain amount of suspicion. Today, such attitudes have changed and a high proportion of workers are women. This fact has doubtless contributed to the acceptance of convenience foods as a normal part of everyday life as well as to the widespread adoption of such products as home freezers and microwave ovens. The high proportion of working women has also contributed to the development of 'one-stop shopping'. With both spouses working, leisure time is at a premium. Many couples now do a major 'shop' once a month, buy in bulk, store in the freezer, and cook mainly in a microwave oven.

The changes in society mentioned here do not form an exhaustive list, but are illustrative of the sort of changes that have influenced, and will continue to influence, marketing firms. Although social change is not occurring at the speed that it was in the 1960s, it is nevertheless in evidence. Marketing firms need to monitor social trends and to be prepared to adapt to social changes if they intend to serve their customers effectively and remain competitive. As mentioned earlier, one of the major factors influencing changes within our society is changes in cultural beliefs and norms. It is to the subject of cultural influence, and in particular cultural change, to which the discussion now turns.

The role of culture

A society's culture is a completely learned way of life which is handed down from generation to generation. Cultural influences give each society its own peculiar attributes. Although the norms and values within a society are the result of many years of cultural conditioning, they are not static. It is cultural change, and the resulting revised norms and values within a society, that is of particular interest to the marketing firm. Nowhere is the aspect more poignant than when the company is marketing internationally, a point discussed in detail in Chapter 14.

The English anthropologist, E. B. Taylor,[9] denied culture as:

> that complex whole which includes knowledge, belief, art, morals, law, custom, and any other capabilities and habits acquired by man as a member of society.

Taylor's definition is an accepted classic in defining some of the major facets of culture, and in emphasizing that culture is very much a learned phenomenon. British culture has historically been largely materialistic, derived as it is from the Protestant work ethic of self-help, hard work, thrift and the accumulation of wealth. Arguably, other Western cultures such as the United States, West Germany and Japan are even more materialistically oriented. This factor is often thought to be one of the reasons for these countries' superior economic performance. Cultural values do, however, change over time, and a number of Western core values are currently undergoing major changes. Adler[10] describes some of the changing cultural values which are particularly prevalent among the young:

—A questioning of materialistic pursuits at the peak of our affluence.
—Increasing pressure for social justice.
—A decline in respect for authority and the law.
—A belief in the rightness of militancy and confrontation.
—A love of novelty.
—A passion for style and format—paralleled by a loss of interest in content.

Sub-cultural influences

Within each culture are numerous sub-groups with their own distinguishing modes of behaviour. In the United States black Americans represent the largest racial/ethnic sub-culture. They account for 11 per cent of the total population.[11] While American marketing firms realize that it is impossible to treat such a large group of consumers as a homogeneous mass, a number of studies indicate that their consumption habits are significantly different from those of the remainder of Americans. As a result, American firms are now designing products and advertising campaigns aimed specifically at this large minority market.

Although the UK is more culturally homogeneous than the USA, firms can no longer ignore the cultural differences of the ethnic populations. Ethnic heterogeneity is slowly being recognized by more enlightened firms as potential source of marketing opportunities. Cannon[12] highlights a number of interesting examples of marketing opportunities and problems:

—Products may need to meet special religious needs (e.g. kosher foods).
—Marketing intermediaries may be different (e.g. the importance of small, Asian-run, shops).
—Consumer tastes may differ (e.g. Cadbury Typhoo's Poundo Yam, aimed mainly at consumers of Caribbean origin).
—Language can be a problem in marketing communications (e.g. in the UK, 77 per cent of Pakistani-origin women and 43 per cent of Pakistani-origin men cannot speak working English).

The culturally aware marketing firm will recognize that sub-cultures represent distinct market segments and will seek to increase their awareness of the needs, attitudes and motivations of sub-groups.

Culture and marketing awareness

An understanding of cultural values is of particular importance to a marketing firm involved with overseas markets. Many countries are geographically distant, but culturally close, while others that are geographically close are culturally distant. For example, France is geographically closer to the UK than, say, the United States or Australia, although both of these latter countries are 'closer' to the UK from a cultural point of view.

Often, because of cultural differences, a marketing programme that has been successful in the UK cannot be applied directly in international markets. Cultural differences exist between different countries, and the differences must be known and evaluated by the marketing firm. A number of factors contribute to a country's overall culture including religion, education and aesthetic appreciation. For a full understanding of a country's culture, management will have to have an understanding of the factors influencing that culture, a point that is taken up in Chapter 14.

Political environment

To an increasing extent, the operation of business firms is being influenced by the political framework and processes in our society. Marketing management must be alert to changes in the political attitudes or 'climate', which depend on the policies of the government of the day. The political environment cannot be examined in a vacuum. Political philosophies on their own are nothing without action. The outcome of political decisions can be seen in the legislation and economic policies of government. In this sense, you will appreciate that, although for clarity of exposition we are examining the various macro-environmental forces in isolation, in reality they are very much interrelated. Many of the legal, economic and social developments in our society and other countries are nothing more than the result of political decisions put into action. For example, in the 1980s the Conservative Party favoured a monetarist approach to the management of the UK economy. It attached great importance to the control of money supply and hence government public expenditure. The general philosophy of the Conservatives is one of 'self-help' and free enterprise, preferring to see business in the hands of private shareholders rather than being owned by the state. Its main concern is with the reduction of the level of inflation which is seen as being vital to long-term economic growth and stability. Expenditure on services such as education and social services has generally been reduced as a percentage of total expenditure since 1979. Business, entrepreneurship, private ownership and profit are seen as being a good thing, vital to the country's future prosperity.

This discussion does not purport to make any normative statements about the running of the country or to proffer political ideologies. The important thing to realize is that the political climate is of great significance to the marketing firm and is likely to have a direct bearing on many aspects of the economy and society in general.

To put the opposite political view, it is a fact that the Labour Party is based on a radically different political ideology. Moderates within the party favour Keynesian economic policies which involve larger expenditure on public works programmes. They see social programmes and a reduction in the level of unemployment as their prime objective. While they appreciate that profit is a necessary economic propellant, they look unfavourably upon what they would consider to be 'excess' profits. The Labour Party would prefer to see large sections of the economy under state control, rather than in the hands of private ownership. Under Labour, the country is likely to see an increase in public expenditure, a reduction in unemployment and a rise in the level of inflation as a result of such policies. Wages and prices may be controlled by use of a prices and incomes policy.

Although developments in the domestic political scene are likely to be of prime concern to the majority of companies, many will also be affected by international political developments. Many British firms import from, or export to, foreign countries and may even have subsidiary companies or divisions overseas. In the UK, political change is brought about through the democratic process. The UK enjoys a high degree of political stability which instils confidence in overseas buyers and suppliers, and this is good for business. In some overseas countries the political situation is more volatile. Change and political power are often obtained through force rather than the democratic process. Companies operating in such a climate have to monitor the local political situation very carefully.

The political environment is the starting point from which many other macro-environmental forces originate. Firms themselves can go some way in influencing the political climate through their trade associations or organizations like the Confederation of British Industry (CBI). Organizations such as these are often looked to by the government for advice, or may themselves act as 'pressure groups' in lobbying the government over political or economic issues. Whatever industry the marketing firm is involved in, factors in the political environment at both national and international levels should be carefully monitored and understood.

Economic environment

Marketing management must understand the effects of the many economic variables that are likely to affect their business operations. We see in the mass media that inflation is rising or falling, that exchange rates are affecting the value of the pound or influencing the level of interest rates. We hear discussions on the level of unemployment, industrial output, or the current state of the balance of payments. Such economic factors are of concern to marketing firms because they influence costs, prices and demand.

Marketing firms have had to adapt to significant economic changes over the past 10 to 15 years. The most dramatic of these changes has been the lengthy economic recession originally brought on by the oil crisis sparked off by the Middle East war of autumn 1973. The dramatic increase in oil prices affected the cost of energy (e.g. transportation, power and heating) as well as the cost of many oil-based products like synthetic fibres and plastics.

The oil crisis was not only an economic factor, but also a political one. In fact, development in the economic and political environments are often closely interrelated. As Wilson[13] explains:

> What the oil crisis really signified was the end of the age of certainty, the upsetting of traditional structures and balances in the world and especially in the business environment. For the oil crisis demonstrated that any group possessing resources that were needed by others had much more power than traditionally had been recognized or wielded.

The overall economic picture is perhaps not quite as black as it has been painted. Although many British firms have lost their battle against recession and have been forced into liquidation, much of British industry remains highly competitive, particularly in the more sophisticated and technologically advanced markets.

A further important economic development for the UK was her joining the European

Community on 1 January 1973. The 'Common Market', as it is often called, is essentially a customs union. A customs union implies two things: first, that all tariffs between members on industrial products be abolished; and, second, that a uniform tariff be adopted for other nations' products imported into the customs union area. Membership of the European Community has subjected British firms to new economic pressures to which many companies are still adjusting. The pressure to adjust became even greater with the passage of the so-called 'Single European Act' in December 1992. Set into operation in 1987, the objective of this Act was to abolish all barriers to trade between the member countries of the Community by the deadline referred to above. Technically, after this date, goods, services, capital and labour should all enjoy freedom of movement between all member countries—the culmination of a process of moving towards a genuinely 'common' market.

The Single European Act has posed both opportunities and threats to business in each of the member countries. Companies that adapted to the new competitive conditions should thrive; those that did not may flounder. Changes in economic policy and legislation are continuing developments and it is essential for marketing firms to monitor continually all business facets affected by the Community's actual or proposed economic policies.

On a wider scale, recent years have witnessed dramatic changes in trading practices and patterns in other areas of the world. Perhaps some of the most notable of these changes are those brought about by political changes in the Eastern bloc countries. *Perestroika* and *glasnost*, the policies of Mikael Gorbachev in what was previously the Soviet Union, have resulted in what were once centrally planned economies becoming more market-driven.

Other important developments include the continuing success of Far Eastern competitors—not only Japan but also Singapore, Malaysia, Thailand and China—in world markets; the harmonization of East and West Germany; the near breakdown of the most recent round of GATT (General Agreement on Tariffs and Trade) talks. In short, the international economic environment is dynamic, and needs to be constantly monitored and adapted to in marketing plans.

Although world economic forces are of paramount importance to marketing firms, particularly those involved with either importing or exporting, domestic economic forces usually have the most immediate impact. The level of domestic unemployment affects the demand for many consumer products, especially those classed as 'luxury goods'. This in turn affects the demand for many industrial products, particularly manufacturing plant such as machine tools. The rate of inflation and the cost of borrowing capital affect the potential returns from new investment and inhibit the adoption of new technologies. Governments of every persuasion attempt to encourage economic growth through various policy measures. Tax concessions, government grants, employment subsidies and capital depreciation allowances are some of the measures that have been used.

The marketing firm needs to monitor continually the economic environment at both the domestic and international level. The 'ebb and flow' of economic forces and the policies that governments use to attempt to manage their economies could have a significant impact on a firm's business operations. As with all other environmental factors, economic factors can be viewed as a source of both opportunities and threats to the marketing firm. By carefully monitoring and understanding the economic environment, a firm's management should be in a better position to capitalize upon the opportunities and to do something about reducing the threats.

Technological environment

Technology is a major environmental influence upon the marketing firm. It affects not only the firm's operations and products, but also consumers' life styles and consumption patterns.

Management must be aware of the impact of technological changes. As Wilson[14] explains in relation to electronics:

> The development of the microprocessor and its large scale production has revolutionised information collection, processing and dissemination which in turn is affecting the whole spectrum of marketing activity.

The impact of new information technology has been particularly marked in the marketing research area. For example, it is now possible to design and administer questionnaires via computer terminals. At present this method is used on a limited basis, but it is likely to become more frequently used in the future. Computer assisted telephone interviewing (CATI) has revolutionized the speed with which surveys can be completed. Responses are fed immediately into a computer and a report 'hard copy' can be available immediately after the final interview is completed. As Thomas[15] explains:

> On-line interviewing is now in widespread use in the larger data gathering market research firms. Interviews, using telephones, work from a questionnaire which is displayed on a VDU and responses are keyed straight into the computer.

Sales forecasting has always been, and always will be, an important marketing activity. Until recently, the majority of firms tended to use subjective or judgemental sales forecasting methods. The development of computers and available software programs has brought the use of sophisticated forecasting techniques within the reach of all companies. The role of sales forecasting is discussed in greater detail in Chapter 6.

Technology also affects the way in which goods are distributed and promoted. Containerized freight and automated warehousing have increased the efficiency with which products can be distributed. Sales representatives can now use audio-visual equipment for presentations and demonstrations. Technology is also affecting marketing at the retail level. Electronic point-of-scale (EPOS) data capture is now used by the major retailers. The 'laser checkout' automatically records consumer purchases and is used to analyse sales and to control and re-order stock. Operation of the laser checkout system depends on the electronic reading of codes. Many fast-moving-consumer-goods (FMCG) manufacturers have responded to these developments by incorporating 'bar codes' on their product labels.

Technology has influenced the development of products themselves. Calculators, aerosol cans, televisions, compact disc players, video-recorders, word processors and instant cameras have all come into widespread use over the past few decades. While older industries are in decline, whole new industries, sometimes referred to as the 'sunrise industries', have developed and grown to take their place. These new industries have capitalized on developments in the technological environment (e.g. information technology, biotechnology and aerospace).

The rate of technological change would appear to be accelerating. Marketing firms themselves play a part in technological advancement and must make use of current technology. They must ask themselves what products or processes are likely to be demanded and technologically feasible to produce in, say, the next 10 or 20 years that are not available now. Management must anticipate the impact of technological change not only on the firm, but also on all other elements in the macro-environment.

Scanning and adapting to the environment

Our discussion so far has concentrated upon reviewing the range of macro-environmental factors and their potential importance to marketing management. Because of this importance, it is vital that the marketing function regularly scans the environment so that trends and changes can be spotted and adapted to by the organization. This task of marketing management, however, is both difficult and complex. A full review of environmental scanning and appraisal systems is beyond the scope of this text, though interested readers may consult *Marketing Management*, by Lancaster and Massingham,[16] for a more detailed discussion. The essential stages in an environmental scanning and appraisal system, however, are outlined below.

—*Identifying key environmental factors*   First, the key environmental factors must be identified. Not all environmental factors are equally important to all organizations. Indeed, the effect of external environmental factors varies with the type and purpose of the organization; for example, a multinational organization is obviously affected more than a purely domestic firm by such factors as international regulators and trade. Senior management, therefore, just identify the key components of the environment which are critical to their particular organization and its plans.

—*Monitoring and forecasting trends and changes in key environmental factors*   Having identified key environmental factors, the next step is to monitor and forecast any trends and changes. For example, a manufacturer of luxury products may need to forecast trends in personal disposable income to which sales of the organization's products may be sensitive. Similarly, most firms will need to monitor trends in those regulations that affect their particular product markets. A systematic and continuous system of scanning and forecasting is essential. More sophisticated modern forecasting techniques now make it increasingly possible for managers to anticipate changes in technology, government regulations, social/cultural factors and so on.

—*Assessing the likely/potential impact of environmental trends and changes*   The third step in coping with the external environment is the assessment of the likely/potential impact of trends and changes in key environmental factors. Put simply, some trends and changes will have a potentially adverse effect on an organization, for example a predicted new technology from a competitor. These are normally and understandably referred to as *threats*. On the other hand, some trends and changes will have a potentially positive effect and hence can be referred to as *opportunities*. Both opportunities and threats must be identified and appraised for their likely impact on the organization.

—*Planning to adjust to the external environment*   The final step in coping with the external environment is adjusting to the trend and changes in the external environment and the opportunities and threats that are potentially posed. Sometimes the organization can influence the environment in order to reduce threats and maximize opportunities, for example by taking over a new competitor who is posing a threat. Often, however, the environment must be treated as a given and adaptations made within the organization. Controllable or uncontrollable, however, the most important way that organizations cope with the external environment is through the development and implementation of marketing plans. In other words, the environment needs to be managed through the marketing planning process; threats must be minimized and opportunities maximized. In developing these plans, however, equal care needs to be paid to the relationship of marketing with other functions in the organization, i.e. the intra-firm environment. It is to this aspect of the environment that we now turn our attention.

THE INTRA-FIRM ENVIRONMENT

Implementing the marketing concept

An essential element of implementing the marketing concept is the need for the marketing function, or rather the managers in it, to develop effective working relationships and systems for ensuring coordination and cooperation between marketing and the different functional areas. In practice, implementing the marketing concept often gives rise to conflict between marketing and other functions. A company needs to understand the sources and issues of such conflict, and also needs to look for ways to convert potentially damaging dysfunctional conflict into more functional forms of management behaviour. In other words, the marketing manager needs to consider the intra-firm environment in marketing plans.

Perhaps one of the best ways to appreciate the range and nature of the types of problems encountered when translating the marketing concept into practice is to reflect for a moment on the following problems:

1. Suppose that you wanted to gauge the extent to which a company had implemented the marketing concept: how would you assess this; what would you look for in the company; what would be the signs?
2. Alternatively, and now that you know what the marketing concept is, if you were made responsible for turning the production- or sales-oriented company into one that is marketing-oriented, what steps would you take?

How problems are approached, and indeed the identification of the problems themselves, is not just one more academic exercise. These questions go right to the heart of the very practical issue of moving from what seems to be a statement of fundamental common sense—the marketing concept—to a position where a company can rightly be judged to be 'good' at marketing. After all, for many years now politicians, academics, industry pundits and so on have extolled the virtues, indeed the necessity, for British companies to improve in this respect. Further, and interestingly, not many practising managers, from whatever function, would deny the central importance of the customer and his or her needs. Fewer, but perhaps still not an insignificant number, of these same managers, including those directly involved in marketing management, would be willing to admit that there is still plenty of room for improvement.

It appears, therefore, that for some reason translating a concept into practice poses problems which some companies find insurmountable. To explore this further, let us return to the first of our hypothetical problems—that of gauging the extent of implementation.

A doctoral thesis completed at the University of Bradford as long ago as 1969 remains one of the most thought-provoking and, therefore, useful frameworks for judging the extent to which a company has moved from marketing concept to marketing practice. In his thesis, Saddik[17] suggested that in order to make this judgement we should look to seven key areas or aspects of a company's operations:

—Company philosophy/managerial attitudes
—Organizational structure
—Planning procedures—particularly as they relate to marketing planning
—New product development activities and decisions
—Intelligence and information-fostering activities and decisions
—Promotional activities and decisions
—Distribution activities and decisions

Using these seven areas of measurement, Saddik investigated the extent to which companies in two of the important local industries in the area—engineering and textiles—had implemented the marketing concept. With so much time now having passed since Saddik completed his findings, there would be little point in detailing them other than to note that at the time he concluded that the marketing concept was far from being fully accepted and implemented in the industries studied.

Nevertheless, his framework for measurements is still relevant, particularly if we reclassify some of his seven criteria. This reclassification is shown below:

—Company philosophy/business definition
—Managerial/workforce attitudes
—Organizational structure
—Planning and information gathering
—Processes and procedures for decision-making

We shall examine each of these in turn in order to clarify their significance to the implementation issue.

Company philosophy/business definition

We have already seen that the marketing concept is an idea or rather a philosophy of the essential purpose and conduct of a business. This philosophy is based on the notion of *consumer sovereignty*: that the purpose of a business is to create customers, and unless a business satisfies the needs of its customers it will not, in the long run, and under normal competitive conditions, survive and prosper. In order to begin the process of implementation, it could be argued that the first step is the acceptance of this philosophy. In the context of the measurement problem, which was posed earlier, we could perhaps gauge the extent to which a company had implemented the marketing concept by examining its philosophy. But where in a company would we look to for evidence of its having accepted this philosophy? How could we measure it? Although there is no doubt some difficulty in such measurement—after all, companies as such do not have philosophies: rather, it is the people in them who have—there are a variety of signs which would indicate the extent to which a company had passed this important first test. For example, an indication of company philosophy can often be gleaned from a company's annual report; alternatively, one might look to a company's Articles and Memorandum of Association. Perhaps the clearest, and certainly the most important, indication (and therefore the best measure) would be found in how the organization defined its business.

The importance of business definition in the context of implementing the marketing concept was perhaps most clearly highlighted by Levitt.[18] In his article 'Marketing myopia', Levitt illustrates that failure to define what business a company is currently in is a clear indication of a failure, or an unwillingness, to implement the marketing concept. An incorrect business definition, in Levitt's terms, is one is too narrow and/or is based on a false premise. For example, how would you define the business of the following companies?

—General Motors
—Max Factor
—IBM

Even with no particular or detailed knowledge of any of these compenies, no doubt you could at least guess what business they are in. Certainly you would think that the companies themselves would have little difficulty answering Levitt's question. But would you, or they, be correct? More specifically, would your or the companies' answers indicate that progress had been made towards implementing the marketing concept? Let us take one of the companies mentioned above to explore this further.

IBM represents the initial letters of a company called International Business Machines. Founded in America in the early 1920s, this now large and very successful multinational company currently produces a range of products primarily for use in the business office. IBM is probably best known for its computer products, both hardware and software. In fact this is a market which it has come to dominate. The answer to the question 'what business is it in?', therefore, would appear to be straightforward. After all, the company name itself gives us the answer. Surely this is a company that is in the business of making machines for business; or, alternatively, given the prime focus on computing, this company is in the business computing market.

Perhaps your thoughts were moving along the same lines in terms of defining IBM's business. If so, you may be accused of suffering from Levitt's marketing myopia. If IBM were to define its business in this way, it would be a strong indication that the company had not begun to implement the marketing concept.

The reason for this can be found in Levitt's original article. Here Levitt proposed that a company which defined its business in terms of the products it produces is invariably suffering from what was termed in Chapter 1 as production or product orientation. In our terms, its company philosophy—as represented by business definition—would imply that it has not begun to implement the marketing concept. Such a company, Levitt argues, would have a shortsighted and blinkered view of its markets and customers and would, therefore, tend to miss both marketing opportunities and marketing threats. Because of this, a business definition based on products or production would in most cases eventually lead to the long-run decline of a business.

In contrast, Levitt suggested that market-/customer-based business definitions should be used to condition company philosophy. Using our earlier example, a customer-/market-based business definition for IBM might be represented by the following:

> IBM is in the business of meeting the needs of businessmen for speedy and economic systems for data production, handling and interpretation.

Remember of course that the definition is only hypothetical; business definition is not easy. Some companies have spent considerable time and effort arriving at a meaningful definition. The purpose of this hypothetical definition for IBM is to demonstrate the difference between a marketing philosophy and a product or production philosophy. Our second IBM business definition is based on customer/market needs rather than being couched in terms of what IBM predominantly produces, i.e. computers. There are many advantages to be gained from such a market-/need-based definition; for example:

—It helps to identify competitors, present and potential.
—It acts as a guide for strategic decision-making.
—It forces the company to consider what the customer is actually purchasing and why. Customers buy benefits not products.

Because of these and other advantages of properly defining the business, we shall return to this aspect again in Chapter 4 when we consider marketing decisions. At this point it should be noted that the redefinition of a business from a product- to a customer-based one represents a fundamental shift in company philosophy and would represent a key signal to the effect that a company had begun to implement the marketing concept. An indication of the significance of such a shift is illustrated in the following extracts from a leading UK management publication:[19]

> . . . British Airways of late has made the astonishing discovery that an airline's success, in this age of overcapacity, might actually depend on pleasing its customers . . . [now] the focus has shifted squarely to the market and how to please it—a 'quantum leap', according to [BA's] head of marketing . . .

Managerial/workforce attitudes

It has been suggested that one of the difficulties of assessing company philosophy stems from the fact that companies do not have philosophies: rather it is the people in them, and in particular their senior management, who do. A customer-/market-based business definition is thus in itself a reflection of a certain attitude on the part of management. Perhaps, then, in gauging the extent to which a company has begun to implement the marketing concept, we should focus on the predisposition of the managers in a company, particularly as they relate to marketing in general and customer needs in particular. In fact, an essential second step in implementing the marketing concept is the recognition and acceptance throughout a company, in every function, and at every level from shopfloor to chairman, of the importance of satisfying customer needs. The point is that redefining the business alone is not sufficient to ensure that a company has become marketing-oriented. After all, such a redefinition may reflect an acceptance of the marketing concept by only the senior management of a company or even by only the marketing team itself. Neither of these is sufficient. Implementing the marketing concept requires that the whole of a company and the people in it be oriented towards the needs of the customer. But what are the practical issues and problems to which this assertion gives rise, and in particular what steps can a company take to instil this attitude?

One of the critical issues to which this need to change attitudes gives rise is the possibility of conflict between marketing and other functional areas. For example, the production or accountancy departments have their own jobs to do, their own set of specific problems to solve and activities to perform. Their task is not to take account of customer needs—this is the responsibility of the marketing function. Again, few of these other functional managers would deny the importance of customer needs, but they often find it difficult to relate this to their own activities. If not carefully managed, attempting to instil a customer-oriented attitude throughout a company can result in antagonism, and often open hostility, to the ideas of marketing in general and towards the marketing function in particular. A carefully planned, and above all diplomatic, programme of activities is essential in achieving this second step in implementing—instilling the right attitude.

To achieve this, some companies have taken the step of organizing seminars, teach-ins, familiarization programmes, etc., for company personnel designed to acquaint them with customer needs and their own role in meeting these. The limited evidence available on the success of such schemes would appear to suggest that they can contribute significantly in turning a concept into a practice. After all, most of us respond well to being kept informed and to being able to see how we can contribute to the achievement of objectives. Some of the best examples of this sort of practice leading to positive attitudes and improved company performance have come from the Japanese companies, many of which hold regular meetings with representatives of the workforce to discuss consumer-related problems. We shall return to some of these ideas in this chapter when we consider the issue of conflict. You should realize by now, however, that in redefining the business—the first step in implementation—we should not expect, as if by some process of osmosis, for this to filter automatically through the different layers of the company. We need to take steps to ensure that it does.

Organizational structure

As we saw in Chapter 1, the development of the marketing concept can be viewed as a series of evolutionary changes, from production to sales orientation, and so on. We saw also that accompanying these different steps of evolution may be changes in the organizational structure of a company. Again, redefining the structure of a company is often seen as being essential to the implemention of the concept. Stanton[20] encapsulates this notion in his two suggestions for translating the philosophy of marketing into action:

. . . the marketing activities in a firm must be better co-ordinated and managed . . .

[and]
the chief marketing executive must be accorded a more important role in company planning . . .

In implementing the marketing concept, various activities that traditionally may have been the province of other management functions, for example sales, product planning and inventory control, should come within the remit and control of the marketing function.

Stanton's ideas about the organizational requirements for implementing marketing are not unique; indeed, they are broadly representative of most marketing authors on this topic. Not surprisingly, then, a frequently used indicator of the extent of marketing commitment in companies has been the organizational chart. After all, can a company be said to have implemented the marketing concept if the marketing function and the managers in it occupy a very lowly position in the company hierarchy? More extreme still, can the company that does not have a marketing department at all be said to have implemented the concept? It may surprise you to learn that the answer to both these questions can be yes! In other words, it is possible for a company to have implemented the concept fully without this being accompanied by changes in its organization chart. More importantly, and again reinforcing what was said earlier, you should understand that it matters little what we call it, or where it appears in the organization chart—if at all—so long as someone is responsible for representing the customer and his or her needs to the rest of the company, and for coordinating those activities necessary to meet those needs.

This should not be interpreted as meaning that organizing for marketing and assessing its overall role or position in company structure is unimportant. Equally, implementing the concept will often necessitate changes in company structure. All that is being said is that the organizational chart alone is not sufficient to judge the extent to which a company has implemented the concept. Nor, therefore, are exercises in chartmanship, changing job titles, elevating the status of marketing in the hierarchy, etc., of themselves sufficient to bring about marketing orientation.

If anything, if we want to look organizational factors in assessing the extent of implementation (and if we want to ensure that our company is taking the right steps in its programme of implementing), we would be better advised to look at *what activities are performed*—by whom; involving what relationships and authority; and to what purpose—than simply looking at the job titles in a box on the organization chart. It is to some of these 'activities' parts of marketing that we now turn our attention.

Planning and information gathering

There is no doubt that implementing the marketing concept requires that planning, and the gathering of information on which such plans are based, assumes a greater importance in overall company activities. In addition, in the marketing-oriented company the focus for planning and information-gathering activities centres around the hub of company decision-making—customer needs and satisfaction.

These implications of implementing the marketing concept provide yet another basis for gauging the extent to which a company has in fact become marketing-oriented. To return to our earlier measurement problem, if we look at the extent to which a company plans for its future, and in particular the procedures and information on which such plans are based, this will enable us to assess the extent to which the marketing concept has been implemented. In order to appreciate this, consider the following example:

. . . your company has just completed its annual marketing plan for the forthcoming year. The planning process commenced with the preparation of a sales forecast based on the pattern and trends of the previous five years' sales. On the basis of this forecast, a sales budget has been prepared and translated into production and operating budgets for the company as a whole. The plan includes a detailed schedule of activities and decision-making required to implement the plan including product, pricing, distribution and promotion decisions . . .

The question is, to what extent is your company marketing-oriented?

The answer is that we cannot tell without knowing on what basis the plan was prepared, and in particular with what knowledge of the facts about the market and the customers. To continue our example:

> . . . your company has recently acquired a new managing director who was previously employed in the capacity of marketing director by a fast-moving consumer goods company. Her experience in marketing is substantial. After considering your company's proposed marketing plan, she calls in the marketing manager responsible for preparing it. Specifically, she is worried that the plan contains no details of the information and market facts on which the plan is based . . .

The marketing manager explains again that the plan is based on his sales forecast. When asked what market research has been carried out in recent years, he replies that this expensive luxury has never been considered necessary. After all, both he and most of his staff have worked in the industry for some twenty years.

The newly appointed managing director then proceeds to ask the marketing manager the following questions:

—Who are our customers?
—What do they buy?
—How do they consider value?
—How do they buy?
—When do they buy?

To the marketing manager's consternation, he finds these questions difficult to answer. The simple fact is that he has never before considered them.

The evidence suggests that planning is not customer-based. No attempt has been made to gather the necessary information and facts on which to base effective marketing decisions. In short, the company has a long way to go in implementing the marketing concept.

The example illustrates that an essential step in implementing the marketing concept is the establishment of planning based on an accurate, factual understanding of customer needs. This, in turn, requires that a company has adequate sensing mechanisms for analysing and interpreting these needs. In most companies this sensing mechanism is provided by the marketing research function. However, you should be careful not to interpret this as meaning that implementing the marketing concept will always require the establishment of a marketing research function. The smaller company may not be in a position to afford this. What matters is not how much a company spends on it, nor who does it, and certainly not what we call it, as long as a company is basing its decision-making on an adequate and accurate mechanism for sensing market and customer needs. It is to these decision-making aspects of implementation that we now turn our attention.

Processes and procedures for decision-making

Perhaps the clearest indication of the extent to which a company has implemented the marketing concept is contained in its processes and procedures for decision-making, and in particular how decisions are made with regard to products, prices, distribution and promotion. Again, an example will serve to illustrate this:

... your company spends some 2 per cent of its annual turnover on developing new products in its research laboratories. On average, over the past ten years the company has launched four new products every year. Only three of the last 25 products launched have been successful, but these have earned good profits. The research and development team is given a free hand to develop any products which the company is technically and commercially able to produce and market. Once the technical and production problems have been overcome for a new product, it is passed over to marketing for commercial evaluation and possible launch. This year the company has only two products which it feels are worth launching; these products have reached the stage where a decision has to be made with respect to their market price. In fact, the pricing of the company's new products presents few problems. All products, including new ones, are priced on a cost-plus basis. The procedure is that the accountancy department calculates the variable costs of producing the product (raw materials and labour costs) and adds to this a proportion of the fixed costs of factory overheads (rent, rates, etc.). To this 'total cost' is added a percentage profit margin according to the estimated life of the product and the investment required to develop and launch the product. This result is the final price of the product . . .

At first glance the company does not appear to be doing too much wrong—certainly, its success rate for new products is low, but this is not unusual as new product development is risky. But to what extent is the company a marketing-oriented company, and what clues are there in the example which would enable us to assess this?

In fact, on the basis of the relatively small amount of information given in the example, it is almost certain that the company has not implemented the marketing concept to any given extent. The evidence for this conclusion lies in the processes and procedures for decision-making. There appears to be little communication between research and development and marketing, at least in the early, and most crucial, stages of new product development. Similarly, the procedure for pricing of products is distinctly non-marketing-oriented. Demand considerations appear to play little part in this decision-making process.

What the example illustrates is the fact that perhaps the most fundamental change that is required to implement marketing in a company is an often subtle, but nevertheless vital, change in how decisions are taken. There are two related aspects to this.

The first change in decision-making required to implement the marketing concept is for every department or function—and not just marketing—in the company to place the customer and his or her needs at the very centre of its decision making. This is a question not only of what was referred to earlier as education, but also of the establishment of a system of processes and procedures for functional decision making which is customer oriented in every department of the company and one which is based on adequate and accurate market facts.

The second aspect of changed decision-making in the company that implements the marketing concept is that the different areas of functional decision-making, however customer oriented they may be individually, must be effectively *coordinated* to achieve a concerted and consistent, company-wide marketing effort. This is a key function of marketing management, but again, if misunderstood (by other functions) and/or badly managed (by marketing or senior management), can give rise to problems and further hostility.

In effect, it is in its decision-making that a company evidences the extent to which it has been successful in all of the previously discussed facets of the implementation issue. But what of marketing's role in this process, and more specifically, what are the functional responsibilities of the marketing department in a company?

The function of marketing and its responsibilities

Our discussion of the requirements of implementing the marketing concept points to a number of key roles for the marketing function in a company. First, the marketing function must act as an intermediary between the company and its customers' needs. In fulfilling this boundary-spanning role, marketing acts as a sort of representative for the customer, interpreting his motives for purchase and ensuring that the company comes closest to satisfying the customer's requirements. This notion is shown in Fig. 2.2.

In addition to this boundary-spanning role for the marketing function, and because of the importance of planning referred to earlier, a further key role for marketing in a company is the formulation of company and marketing plans based on market facts and information. This notion is shown in Fig. 2.3. The planning role or marketing management is discussed later in Chapters 4 and 13.

Finally, the marketing function must attempt to ensure that decision-making throughout the company adequately reflects both company and marketing plans, and the assessment of market and customer needs on which these are based. This is shown in Fig. 2.4.

These three broad areas of responsibility for the marketing function must be translated into a specific set of responsibilities and activities for marketing personnel—a job description, in other words. Some marketing textbooks go further than this and list what these are likely to be in the typical company. An example of this approach is that given by Buell.[21] Unfortunately, such 'lists' often do not take account of the fact that there is no such thing as the typical company. All companies are different and we should expect to find that, within the three broad areas of responsibilities for marketing described above, specific responsibilities and activities for marketing will differ between companies. We should also remember that, as in other functional areas of business, marketing may comprise of a hierarchy of management levels, each of which will have its

Figure 2.2   The boundary-spanning role of marketing
Source: Adapted from P. Kotler, *Marketing Management Analysis, Planning, Implementation and Control*, 7th edn, Prentice-Hall, Englewood Cliffs, NJ, 1991

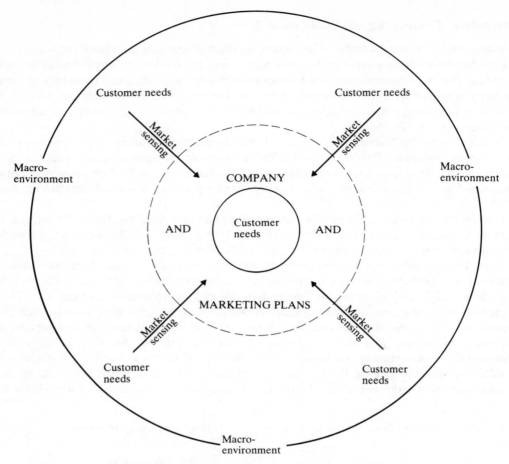

Figure 2.3 Planning and information gathering

own set of responsibilities and activities. The product or brand manager level of the marketing hierarchy, for example, faces a very different (if interrelated) set of issues from those facing the senior marketing manager in a company.

Achieving marketing orientation

We have seen that becoming more marketing-oriented may entail an enlarged role for marketing in overall company decision-making. Functions and responsibilities that had previously been the province of other functional areas in a company may, under the marketing concept, come within the remit of the marketing department. Although it is not inevitably the case, both enlarged responsibility and increased status are often the outcome of this process. This can give rise to conflict between marketing and other departments. Some of the possible issues of such conflict were discussed earlier; you will recall, for example, that marketing and production may have very different notions as to what constitutes effective management and decision-making within each of their respective functions. So too may marketing and research and development, and marketing and scales, and marketing and finance. In fact, it would not be an exaggeration to suggest that the potential for inter-functional conflict is at its greatest when we consider the relationship between

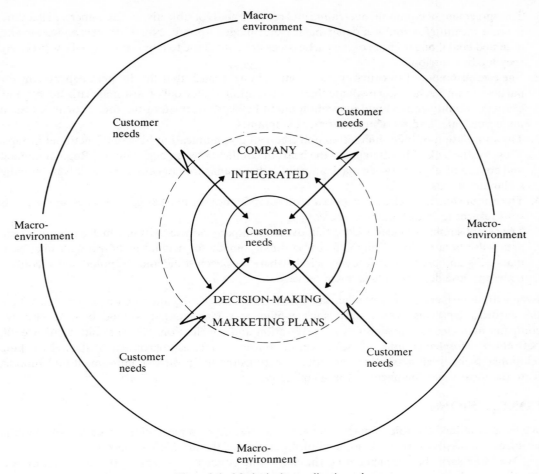

Figure 2.4 Marketing's coordinating role

marketing and virtually every other functional area of a business. Of course, conflict in itself is not always undesirable, as Shapiro points out;[22] not unlike market competition, conflict can ensure effectiveness and efficiency. However, conflict can reach such levels as to be dysfunctional; it can effectively disable the participants and reduce efficiency. Unfortunately, some companies have attempted to minimize the potential for conflict between marketing and others (or, rather, have provided a mechanism for reducing the outcome of such conflict situations) by increasing the power and authority of one of the protagonists—marketing. The usual result of enforcing 'agreement' in this way is more, not less, conflict. The reason for this is that simply increasing the authority of marketing over other functional areas does not remove the basic issues which probably gave rise to the conflict in the first place. On the contrary, the nature of marketing's authority and power relationships will often be at the heart of it.

What is required is a mechanism whereby there are no 'losers'. Handy[23] suggests a number of procedures which a company might use to achieve this, and which may bring about more effective coordination between the various functional groups. Some of these and their relevance to marketing's relationships in a company are as follows:

1. The agreement of common, overriding and realistic goals or objectives. 'Customer satisfaction' is not a meaningful goal if a department is not judged upon it. Nor is it likely to become an accepted goal if one or more of the parties does not contribute to it or is unsure of how precisely they might contribute.
2. The establishment of information and control systems such that the different departments or parties can appreciate and evaluate their contribution to the goal of customer satisfaction. For example, quality control and inspection might be kept informed of the role of their efforts in increasing sales and reducing customer complaints.
3. The stimulation of high interaction and frequent communication between functional groups. Trust, or the lack of it, often lies at the heart of conflict between departments. Regular contact and communication between marketing and other managers can help considerably in building a climate of trust.
4. The establishment of clear *and agreed* terms of reference for marketing and other departments with respect to duties, authority, etc.
5. The establishment of clear and explicit overall company policies within which each functional area will operate. For example, if it is company policy to produce a full product line, both marketing and production know precisely where they each stand and the potential for conflict between these departments is much reduced.

Even with these mechanisms, conflict can arise between marketing and other departments. Where the parties themselves cannot settle such conflict in a manner that is conductive to effective company management, procedures for arbitration and conciliation will be required. Above all, both effective implementation of the marketing concept and the establishment of effective working relationships between marketing and other functions require positive commitment and support from the most senior management in a company.

CONCLUSIONS

We have examined the role of marketing in various settings. In particular, we have looked at the problems and issues surrounding the implementation of the marketing concept.

We have seen that implementing the marketing concept will require that a company pay attention to business definition, managerial and employee attitudes, and the systems and procedures for planning and information gathering. Sometimes, but not always, adopting the marketing concept may also give rise to changes in organizational structure. Perhaps the clearest indication of the extent to which attention to these factors has resulted in increased marketing orientation is in a company's processes and procedures for decision-making. To have fully implemented the marketing concept requires that all business decisions, and not just those concerned with marketing, adequately reflect customer and market needs. Furthermore, a company must ensure that individual/functional decision-making is coordinated so as to achieve a concerted and consistent marketing effort. In implementing the marketing concept, a company must be prepared to face and deal with potential conflict and hostility towards the ideas and activities of marketing. Regardless of the specific mechanisms for improving the relationship between marketing and other departments, an essential requirement is the commitment and support of senior management to improving marketing practice.

APPLICATION QUESTIONS

1. To what extent do you consider that factors in the economic environment are the result of decisions taken within the political environment?

2. For a company of your choice suggest:
   (a) a product-oriented business definition.
   (b) a market-oriented business definition.
3. What types of individuals or organizations make up the proximate macro-environment? To what extent are these individuals or organizations affected themselves by wider macro-environmental factors?
4. What do you understand by the term 'boundary spanning' in the context of marketing's role in a company?
5. In implementing the marketing concept, careful attention must be given to the relationships between marketing and other functions. Outline the nature of these relationships and discuss what can be done to minimize any conflict.

REFERENCES

1. P. Kotler, *Marketing Management: Analysis, Planning Implementation and Control*, 7th edn, Prentice-Hall, Englewood Cliffs, NJ, 1991, p. 129.
2. F. A. Russ and C. A. Kirkpatrick, *Marketing*. Little, Brown & Co., Boston, MA, 1982, p. 24.
3. *Collins English Dictionary*, William Collins, London, 1983, p. 931.
4. C. R. Darwin, *On the Origin of the Species*, 1859.
5. W. J. Stanton, M. S. Sommers and J. G. Barnes, *Fundamentals of Marketing*, McGraw-Hill, New York, 1977, p. 27.
6. L. E. Boone and D. L. Kurtz, *Contemporary Marketing*, 2nd edn, Dryden Press, Hinsdale, IL, 1977, p. 30.
7. J. H. Davidson, *Offensive Marketing*, Pelican Books, Harmondsworth, 1979, p. 232.
8. Kotler, op. cit., p. 107.
9. E. B. Taylor, *Primitive Culture*, Murray, London, 1971, p. 1.
10. M. Adler, 'Cashing-in on the cop-out: cultural change and marketing potential', *Business Horizons*, February 1970, p. 21.
11. Boone and Kurtz, op. cit., p. 163.
12. T. Cannon, *Basic Marketing, Principles and Practice*, Holt, Rinehart and Winston, New York, 1985, pp. 38–9.
13. M. Wilson, *The Management of Marketing*, Gower Press, New York, 1980, p. 5.
14. Wilson, op. cit., p. 7.
15. M. Thomas. 'World of research', *MRS Newsletter*, no. 174, September 1980.
16. G. A. Lancaster and L. C. Massingham, *Marketing Management*, McGraw-Hill, Maidenhead, Berks, 1993, pp. 22–42.
17. S. M. A. Saddik, Marketing in the Wool Textile, Textile Machinery and Clothing Industries (PhD thesis, University of Bradford Management Centre, April 1969).
18. T. Levitt, 'Marketing myopia', *Harvard Business Review*, July–August 1960, pp. 45–6.
19. 'BA's new flight path', *Management Today*, July 1984, p. 44.
20. W. J. Stanton, *Fundamentals of Marketing*, 5th edn. McGraw-Hill, Tokyo, 1978, pp. 11–15.
21. V. P. Buell, *Marketing Management in Action*, McGraw-Hill, New York, 1966, pp. 23–7.
22. B. P. Shapiro, 'Can marketing and manufacturing coexist?' *Harvard Business Review*, September–October 1977, pp. 104–14.
23. C. B. Handy, *Understanding Organisations*, Penguin, Harmondsworth, 1976, p. 236.

MARKETING AND CUSTOMERS

INTRODUCTION

It might seem obvious, but if the essence of marketing centres on identifying and satisfying customer needs, then it is vital that marketers understand these needs. Moreover, they need to understand what influences these needs and how consumers go about satisfying them. In short, marketers need to understand the buying behaviour of existing and potential customers. Unfortunately, however, this behaviour can be extremely complex and multifaceted. Partly for this reason, marketers have increasingly called upon the knowledge and techniques of the behavioural scientists in order to gain insights into buyer behaviour. In this chapter we shall examine some of these insights. Specifically, we shall be looking at the way in which customers purchase and the behavioural forces and factors that affect this choice process. We shall also be looking at some of the implications of this process for marketers.

Because it is felt that there are fundamental differences between the way individuals buy for their own purposes and the way they buy on behalf of an organization, we shall refer to the former as *consumer buyers*, and to the latter as *organizational buyers*. Each type of buyer will be considered separately below. Clearly, in a single chapter we are not able fully to discuss all the behavioural concepts relevant to understanding consumer and organizational buyer behaviour. For a more detailed treatment of the subject area, readers are advised to consult one of the specialist texts in this area such as Engel *et al.*[1] Louder and Della Bitta[2] or Schiffman and Kanuk.[3]

CONSUMER BUYER BEHAVIOUR

The distinguishing feature of consumer buyer behaviour as opposed to organizational buyer behaviour is the fact that consumer buying consists of the activities involved in the buying and using of products or services for personal and household use, whereas organizational buyers purchase primarily for organizational purposes. As we shall see, this seemingly obvious difference in fact gives rise to further major differences between the two types of buying.

As stated earlier in this chapter, consumer behaviour is complex. An illustration of this complexity can be seen if we examine some of the questions that relate to consumer buyer behaviour, the answers to which, therefore, the marketer must seek. Kotler[4] suggests that the following questions need to be answered. He refers to them as the 'seven Os' of the marketplace:

—Who is in the market?	Occupants
—What does the market buy?	Objects
—When does the market buy?	Occasions
—Who is involved in the buying?	Organizations
—Why does the market buy?	Objectives
—How does the market buy?	Operations
—Where does the market buy?	Outlets

Answers to these questions will give a company an added advantage over less aware competitors. They will enable the company to fit its product offerings to the customer more closely and therefore to satisfy customer needs more fully than competitors. Marketers will also need to know whether their controllable variables, e.g. marketing mix variables, will affect buying behaviour.

However, as mentioned earlier, understanding consumer buyer behaviour in order to address these questions raises complex issues. In order to investigate these in detail, it is advantageous to break down the purchase process into a framework so as to simplify the process and factors influencing purchase behaviour. Figure 3.1 shows a simplified framework of consumer behaviour. As can be seen, environmental influences that are external to the consumer have an effect on purchase behaviour. The consumer also has influences that are individually determined. Both types of influence are carried, consciously or subconsciously, within the consumer's memory. The third box in the diagram shows the decision-making process an individual goes through when purchasing a product. The directional lines show that at any stage, information can be fed back and the purchase process can be stopped and resumed at an earlier stage. The framework will now be discussed in greater detail.

Environmental influences

Consumer buyer behaviour is influenced by a range of outside stimuli.

Cultural Culture is the broadest environmental factor and can be defined as:[5]

> Norms, beliefs and customs that are learned from society and lead to common patterns of behaviour.

So, as behaviour is learned, culture determines the broad values and attitudes an individual holds. Culture can be investigated by using an inventory of values. A child growing up in a certain culture learns its cultural values from the people with whom it socializes. So family, school and friends have a large impact on the cultural values with which the child grows up. Some aspects of culture— for instance, freedom in the UK—have not changed over time. Other aspects are, however, dynamic; for example, the role of women in society has changed over the years. So, even though culture is a basic foundation of society, in the strategic management process it has to be monitored for changes. In addition, culture is often assumed, and this has meant that many mistakes have been made when companies have tried to market their products abroad, where there are cultural barriers to entry. Other aspects of the socio-cultural environment include sub-culture, social class, and group and family influences.

'Sub-culture' refers to groups in society that have distinct cultural differences. This includes nationality groups such as Indian, West Indian, Italian or Irish, who may have individual life styles and values. Religious groups, such as Jews, Muslims, Christians and Hindus, are another sub-culture within the larger cultural group. Blacks, whites and Asians are examples of broad racial groupings, and geographical groups can include northerners, southerners or Scots as distinct groups. Sub-cultural groups can vary in the products they wish to buy, the outlets they buy from, the prices paid, the media they watch, etc.

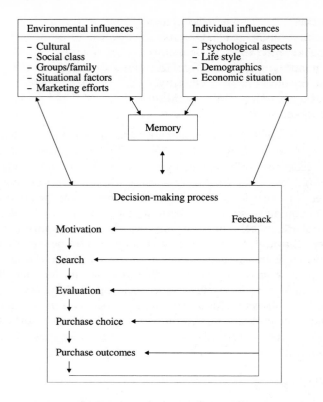

Figure 3.1 A framework of consumer buyer behaviour

Marketers ignore cultural factors, including sub-cultures, at their peril, especially when they operate in different cultures such as in international markets. Take, for example, the case of a UK company planning to launch a new consumer product in France for the first time. What questions pertaining to cultural factors would need to be considered by this company? For example:

—What needs does our product fulfil in the French culture? (relevant motivations)
—What broad French cultural values are relevant to this product? (e.g. attitudes to work, health)
—What are the characteristic forms of family (or household) decision-making in France?
—Are there any characteristic French behaviour patterns that are relevant to this product? (e.g. shopping habits)
—Through what type of marketing institutions would we be expected to market this product in France?

We could go on listing relevant questions, but we can see that cultural factors are very important to marketers. Indeed, in the widest sense cultural factors shape many of the elements of individual behaviour that we shall consider later. The marketer, too, must be aware of cultural trends and changes, for these give rise to new marketing opportunities and threats. True, cultural changes tend to be relatively slow (although the pace of cultural change is quickening), but cultures do change. For example, in many societies cultural attitudes towards sex, religion, and family and marriage, health, youth and leisure have changed dramatically over the past 20 years. The successful marketer must keep abreast of these changes and anticipate them.

Social class 'Social class' refers to the grouping together of individuals or families who have certain common social or economic characteristics. Members of the same social class exhibit similar patterns of behaviour and have similar values and interests. Criteria used for this type of grouping can be occupation, education or income. People from the same social class are supposed to be more alike than people from differing classes. Social class is seen in terms of higher or lower classes (although individuals can move from one class to another), but this does depend upon the rigidity of the social system in the society in question. Social class is a major influence on buyer behaviour because classes show different product purchase behaviour in certain product categories. Examples include cars and holidays, where social class is a determining factor of the types of product purchased. The 'best' measures of social class have a number of factors included in them rather than just one, for example income. Social class may determine not only the products people choose to purchase but also the store type chosen. For example, department stores, market stalls, mail order or independent retailers may be favoured by certain social classes.

Groups and family Group and family influences can also affect purchase decisions. *Reference groups* are all the groups that an individual is exposed to that have a direct or an indirect influence on behaviour and attitudes. *Primary groups* are those with which the contact is continuous, and can include family, neighbours, friends and colleagues or peers. *Secondary groups* are groups that have less contact with individual members, for example a football team. People also have aspirations and may then be affected by group pressure from an *aspirational group*. For example, this is used quite often in the marketing of cosmetics, where advertisements show women from the aspirational group of beauty, wealth and desirability using the product. Reference groups affect individuals in three ways:

1. They influence self-image and attitudes.
2. They expose individuals to new behaviour.
3. They create pressure to conform.

Of course, reference group importance will depend greatly upon the product in question. If group influences are strong, it is worth while for the marketer to identify opinion leaders in the group. Opinion leaders have influence over members of their reference group. For instance, if a friend you know is interested in computers and you wish to purchase one, you may ask your friend for advice. Then the friend is an opinion leader. The family group also has an influence on purchase behaviour. Indeed, some purchases are made by the family as a group—for example houses, holidays, cars and furniture. In family decision-making, individual members may assume different roles. Depending on the purchase and individuals involved, they may perform one or many roles, such as:

1. Information gatherer
2. Influencer
3. Decision-maker
4. Purchaser
5. Consumer

So for the purchase of a holiday, say, a mother and daughter may go into a travel agent's and pick up brochures; all the family will influence the decision; the final decision may be made by the father; but the mother books the holiday and is then the purchaser; all the family are consumers. Some products within family decision-making are dominated by the husband or wife; others are made jointly.

Situational factors These may also determine a purchase or consumption situation, and may be a major aspect in purchase behaviour. If you were asked about your favourite food, it would be quite acceptable to state that it depends upon the situation. At times you may prefer a snack, at others a meal with the family and at other times a special meal, perhaps in a restaurant. The consumption situation will directly influence consumer brand perceptions and purchase behaviour—that is, where precisely the product is going to be consumed. The purchase situation is also important. Product availability, change in price and the existence of queues may have an effect on purchase behaviour.

Marketing efforts The final environmental factor affecting consumer buyer behaviour is the marketing effort of organizations. Much of this text concentrates on the planning of decisions aimed at influencing buyer behaviour. For example, as we shall see, the marketer makes decisions concerning products, prices, distribution and promotional campaigns aimed at influencing consumers to purchase the marketer's brands. A good example is in the area of marketing communications.

Marketing communications from companies are always around us. Some of these are retained in memory, and we then have an image of companies and the goods and services they provide. This may lead to a motivation to purchase the product or to be aware of the product and provide for future use. Recent television campaigns promoting personal pensions have stimulated a perceived need in this area.

Marketing efforts, therefore, are—at one and the same time—both a cause and a result of buyer behaviour.

Individual influences

The second major group of factors that influence a consumer's purchase decisions are those that are personal or individual to the consumer. The major ones are outlined below.

Psychological factors A number of complex behavioural factors come under this heading. They include perception, motivations, attitudes and personality. Again, we must stress that the full complexity of each of these factors cannot be explored here; but as an indication of the relevance of some of these psychological factors to marketers, and the way they are interrelated, we can briefly consider perception and attitudes.

Perception is the way in which individuals select, organize and interpret stimuli. This includes how they see and interpret a company and its products. When a message is perceived, it is modified by the individual's interpretation. Each person selects (subconsciously) the exposure, attention, comprehension and retention of stimuli. This information is then organized so that it can be easily understood. This can be effected by placing information in categories or combining these into brand images. It is therefore important that marketers build up brand awareness so that a personality for the brand is developed in the minds of existing or potential buyers.

Attitudes are specific. An attitude is held about a certain good or supplier in the context of consumer behaviour. Attitudes are very difficult to change, so companies finding that certain products are associated with a poor attitude would, if at all possible, be better advised to change the product than to try to change consumer attitudes.

Life style variables These encompass an individual's activities, interests and opinions. (Indeed, as we shall see in Chapter 7, it is often called AIO research.) A person's life style describes how a

Figure 3.2 Maslow's hierarchy of needs

person interacts with his or her environment. This again will have consequences for purchase behaviour.

Demographic variables These describe individuals according to age, sex, income, education and occupation. Demographic factors will have a bearing on the types of product individuals want, where they shop and how they evaluate possible purchases. For instance, a teenage girl will want, in the main, different products from her mother. A concept similar to age is the life cycle stage. Throughout life, people go through stages—single, married, married with children, children left home, and retired. At each of these stages their product needs will be somewhat different.

The economic situation This factor encompasses not only how much income individuals have but whether they have borrowing power, and their attitude towards spending. Clearly, the economic situation of individual consumers is of prime concern to marketing managers when planning their marketing strategies.

The decision-making process

A further aspect of consumer behaviour is the decision-making process involved in a purchase. In Fig. 3.1 this is shown in the lower box and encompasses five stages. In the first an individual feels a need which a certain product will satisfy and is motivated to evaluate the goods on offer. People have many varying needs; if a need is intense, then they become motivated to purchase the good that will satisfy it. Maslow[6] described the different needs of human beings as being hierarchical. Figure 3.2 shows Maslow's hierarchy of needs. This shows, at the bottom of the pyramid, physiological needs. These are the most basic and important of human needs. When needs lower in the pyramid are met, individuals move up the hierarchy to fulfil 'higher' needs. Motivation to satisfy such needs can be stimulated by marketing. For instance, when people see an advertisement for a burger they may then feel hungry and purchase one. Alternatively, they may search for alternatives to fulfil the need to satisfy hunger—they could, perhaps, go to a restaurant, or have a pizza or a sandwich in a café. This searching for alternatives may be *external,* that is a physical search for alternatives, or *internal,* i.e. searching the memory for what a person knows about products and suppliers. Marketers, then, need to research (a) how they can stimulate a need for their products and (b) the type of information consumers want on their products.

There are many sources of information on products. Friends and relatives can be used as information sources in addition to company information such as advertising. There may be some public media sources of information, for example press articles about product areas. Another source is the actual handling of the products. When information has been assimilated by the individual, he or she can then make judgements about the brands that are available. Marketers then, as well as building awareness, need to ensure that their products have *unique selling propositions* so that they stand out from competing brands.

When consumers have enough information, they will evaluate the alternatives in the market place. The criteria on which products are evaluated vary depending on the products and on how many brands are available. The evaluative criteria used will depend on what need is being fulfilled by the product. Most often discussed are the role of price and the brand image. Again, it is imperative that marketers know on what basis their products are being judged. If there are common themes from consumers for the evaluation of alternative products and the ideal product offering, this has implications for marketing management. It means that products can be tailored to suit consumer needs and marketing communications can respond to the evaluating criteria they use. Evaluating products often coincides with the search for such products.

When products or brands have been evaluated, one product is selected for purchase. However, purchase intention can be affected by unforeseen factors; for example, the price may rise. Also, other people can have an effect on purchase choice even at this late stage. There may now be no purchase at all.

Purchase outcomes or *post-purchase behaviour* will be either satisfaction or dissatisfaction with the purchase choice. Again, the product will be judged against the needs that were to be fulfilled by the product and by the criteria on which alternative brands were judged. Satisfaction occurs when expectations of the product are either met or exceeded. This is remembered the next time the product is purchased. Also, the satisfied consumer may tell friends about the product. If expectations have not been met, the consumer experiences some *post-purchase dissonance.* There are many ways in which consumers try to reduce such dissonance. They can find information to support their product choice, or avoid information that will not confirm their purchase. If dissonance is strong, the consumer may take action either with the company directly, perhaps asking for a refund, or indirectly, for example by telling friends about the problems with the product.

Of course, whether all these stages are experienced and the amount of time spent at each stage depends on the individual and the product purchased. Some products require extensive problem-solving where a great deal of information is required in order to make a decision. This type of product is usually expensive, complex to understand, and/or has not been bought previously, for example a house, a personal computer or a car. Limited search and evaluation would be used when there is some knowledge of the products on offer, for example a small item of furniture for the house, or a car radio. When customers know quite a good deal about the products, then there is little search and evaluation. The purchase may be habitual, for example the repeat buying of the same brand of toothpaste or washing powder. This 'low-involvement' decision-making causes some problems for marketers. Should they try to make such decisions higher-involvement? Are consumers being brand-loyal to products in an active way, or are they displaying inertia? What is the best way of promoting the product in low-involvement market? Ways in which marketers try to increase involvement of consumers include:

1. Link the product with an issue; a recent example here is the marketing of relatively mundane products being described as environmentally friendly or 'green'.
2. Use advertising that involves consumers, e.g. 'Try the Pepsi challenge'.
3. Change product benefits; for example, Radion advertisements emphasise the 'new' benefit of clean-*smelling* clothes.

For a more detailed investigation of the marketing strategies that are successful for low, medium and high-involvement purchasing, see Assael.[7]

A framework such as Fig. 3.1 shows the marketer how to break down consumer behaviour into aspects that can be analysed for effective strategic marketing planning. However, as acknowledged earlier, this framework is very much simplified and therefore understates the full complexity of the range of factors affecting consumer buyer behaviour and the interrelationships between them. Because of this, marketers and behavioural scientists have turned to developing more comprehensive (and complex) models of consumer buyer behaviour.

Models of consumer buyer behaviour

The use of models has been a fairly recent development in the study of consumer behaviour. They reflect an effort to order and integrate the various components of information that are known about consumer behaviour. Models are useful in aiding research design to give a deeper understanding of consumer behaviour. Chisnall was one of the first UK authors to document and discuss such work in the mid-1970s, and his *Marketing: A Behavioural Analysis* provides a detailed discussion of such models.[8]

The Howard–Sheth model[9] (Fig. 3.3) Howard and Sheth have provided one of the most comprehensive models of consumer behaviour. Their model uses the concept of stimulus–response to explain brand choice behaviour over time, using four major components:

1. Input variables
2. Output variables
3. Hypothetical constructs
4. Exogenous variables

Input variables Input variables are those stimuli that come from the environment. There are three types:

1. *Significance stimuli* These are actual elements of a brand which the buyer confronts, for example price.
2. *Symbolic stimuli* These are generated by manufacturers representing their products in symbolic form, for example in advertisements.
3. *Social stimuli* These are generated by the social environment, for example in reference groups.

Output variables The five positions shown in the right-hand portion of Fig. 3.3 are the buyer's observable stimulus–response inputs. They consist of

—Attention
—Comprehension
—Attitude
—Intention
—Purchase behaviour

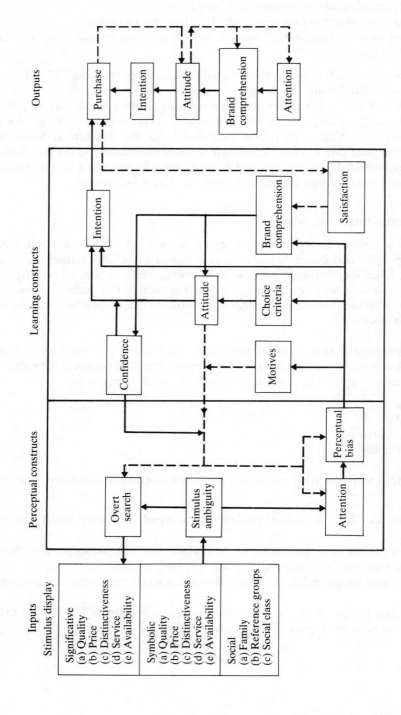

Figure 3.3 The Howard–Sheth model of buyer behaviour

Source: J. N. Sheth and J. A. Howard, *The Theory of Buyer Behaviour*, John Wiley, Chichester, Sx, 1969

Hypothetical constructs These are intervening variables which can be categorized into two major groups: perceptual constructs and learning constructs.

1. There are three *perceptual constructs;* these deal with information processing:

    (a) Sensitivity to information—the degree to which the buyer regulates the stimulus information flow.
    (b) Perceptual bias—distorting or altering information.
    (c) Search for information—active seeking of information about brands or their characteristics.

2. There are six *learning constructs;* these deal with the buyer's formation of concepts:

    (a) Motive—general or specific goals impelling action.
    (b) Brand potential of the evoked set—the buyer's perception of the ability of brands to satisfy goals.
    (c) Decision mediators—the buyer's mental rules for matching and ranking purchase alternatives according to his or her motives.
    (d) Predisposition—a preference towards brands in the evoked set expressed as an attitude towards them.
    (e) Inhibitors—environmental forces such as price and time pressure which restrain purchase of a preferred brand.
    (f) Satisfaction—the degree to which the consequences of a purchase measure up to the buyer's expectations.

Exogenous variables These external variables can significantly influence buyer decisions. Because such variables are external to the buyer, they are not as sharply defined as other aspects of the model.

The process of operating the model begins when the buyer confronts an input stimulus and it achieves attention. The stimulus is then subjected to perceptual bias as a result of the influence of the buyer's predisposition as affected by his or her motives, decision mediators and evoked set. The modified information will also influence these variables, which in turn will influence the buyer's predisposition to purchase. The purchase will be influenced by the buyer's intentions and inhibitions which are confronted. After the purchase, the buyer evaluates satisfaction, and satisfaction increases the buyer's predisposition towards the brand. More information means that the buyer engages in less of an external search for information and exhibits more routine purchasing behaviour.

The Howard–Sheth model made an important contribution towards the understanding of consumer behaviour. It identifies many of the variables that influence consumers and details how they interact with one another. The model also recognizes that there are different types of consumer problem-solving and information search behaviour. There are, however, a number of limitations to the model: there is no distinction made between exogenous and other variables; some variables are difficult to measure because they are not well defined; and its greatest limitation is its complexity.

The Engel–Kollat–Blackwell model[10] (Fig. 3.4) This model considers consumer behaviour as a decision process concerning five activities which occur over time:

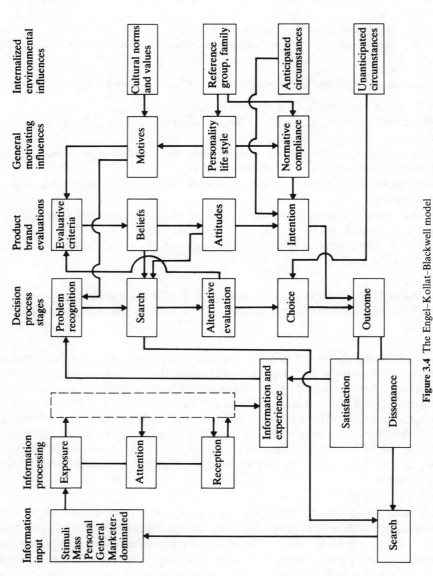

Figure 3.4 The Engel–Kollat–Blackwell model

Source: J. Engel, D. Kollat and R. Blackwell, *Consumer Behaviour*, Dryden Press, NY, 1978

1. Problem recognition
2. Information search
3. Alternative evaluation
4. Choice
5. Outcomes

These steps provide the basic core. The model also takes into account a number of other variables that influence the decision process. These variables are grouped into five general categories:

—Information input
—Information processing
—Product brand evaluation
—General motivating influences
—Internalized environmental influences

The arrows in the model show the direction in which the influence is exerted.

Problem recognition The consumer detects a difference between his or her actual and an ideal state of affairs. This may occur through external stimuli, for example an advertisement, or the activation of a motive, for example hunger. In order for action to occur, the consumer must perceive a sufficiently large discrepancy between actual and ideal states.

Information search The initial information may consist of beliefs and attitudes the consumer already holds. If more information is needed, a consumer may look to friends, salespeople or the mass media. The processing of this information is carried out in a number of stages. The individual is first exposed to stimuli which may be attention-catching. The information is then received and stored in memory. Information processing is highly selective, and individuals may distort information depending on their predisposition to accept what they perceive.

Alternative evaluation The standards by which products are judged are derived from the consumer's underlying goals or motives. The consumer also has beliefs about which brands possess which characteristics and hence will respond positively or negatively towards a particular brand.

Choice The consumer's attitude will influence his or her choice. Other influences will comprise normative compliance and anticipated circumstances. *Normative compliance* is the extent to which the consumer is influenced by others, for example friends or family. It considers their attempts to influence, and the susceptibility of the individual to influence from anticipated circumstances— that is, factors a consumer expects (e.g. availability of funds for purchase). At this stage a purchase is likely to occur. However, a barrier to purchase would be *un*anticipated circumstances, such as a drop in income.

Outcomes If the outcome is perceived as positive, the result is satisfaction. The alternative to this is dissonance—a feeling of discord brought about by doubt about the chosen alternative relative to another, or a range of, unchosen alternatives. The consumer may require more information to support his or her choice.

The Engel–Kollat–Blackwell model considers a number of variables that influence consumers, and its emphasis is on the conscious decision-making process that consumers adopt. The flow of the model is fairly easy and relatively flexible, recognizing that in some purchase decisions many of the detailed steps are passed through very quickly or are bypassed, for example in repeat purchases.

One weakness in the model, however, is the inclusion of a number of variables whose effect on behaviour is not well specified, for example environmental variables and motives.

The Sheth model of family decision making[11] (Fig. 3.5) This model depicts separate psychological systems, which represent the distinct predispositions of father, mother and other family members. These lead into 'family buying decisions', which may be either individually or jointly determined.

The right-hand side of the model depicted in Fig. 3.5 lists seven family and product factors that influence whether a specific purchase will be autonomous or joint:

1. Social class
2. Life style
3. Role orientation
4. Family life cycle stage
5. Perceived risk
6. Product importance
7. Time pressure

The model suggests that joint decision-making tends to prevail in families that are middle-class, closely knit and with few prescribed family roles, and among the newly married. In more specific terms of product purchasing, it suggests that joint decision-making is more prevalent when there is a great deal of perceived risk, when the purchase decision is considered to be important, and when there is ample time to make the decision.

The models of consumer behaviour that have been outlined above are three of the most comprehensive models that describe the decision-making of choice processes of consumers. As yet, such models tend to be theoretical, and are not of direct practical use to marketing practitioners. The Howard–Sheth model is the only one that has been subjected to specific testing. The models will need to be developed and tested for them to become useful devices for synthesizing behaviour in further studies in consumer behaviour.

Theory versus practice in consumer behaviour Research into the behaviour of consumers continues to evolve, and as it does it is likely to become more relevant. Consumer researchers are having to justify the relevance of their search, not only in terms of cost, but also in terms of how useful it is to marketing practice and theory.

Researchers are less willing to accept the conclusions of an investigation merely at face value. More frequently research strategies are being questioned, resulting in replications and critiques of prior research studies. Furthermore, research investigations tend to have a strong theoretical basis and are part of ongoing research programmes. These factors point towards a discipline that is becoming mature, with more valid results and realistic findings.

There has been an increase in awareness about what can and cannot be achieved through consumer research. Part of this increased awareness is the result of better training and tuition in the subject. A number of colleges, particularly in the United States, offer specific courses in consumer behaviour, and many institutions run professional seminars. In the United States in the 1970s, the Association for Consumer Research was founded, as was the *Journal of Consumer Research*.

With increased awareness, consumer researchers have had to consider how they should approach investigations. For example, questions that have been asked of the consumer have mostly been determined by the marketer or researcher; yet many of the product characteristics determined in this way may not be the most relevant to consumers in their purchase decisions. A number of researchers have overcome this problem by using consumer-originated questions when

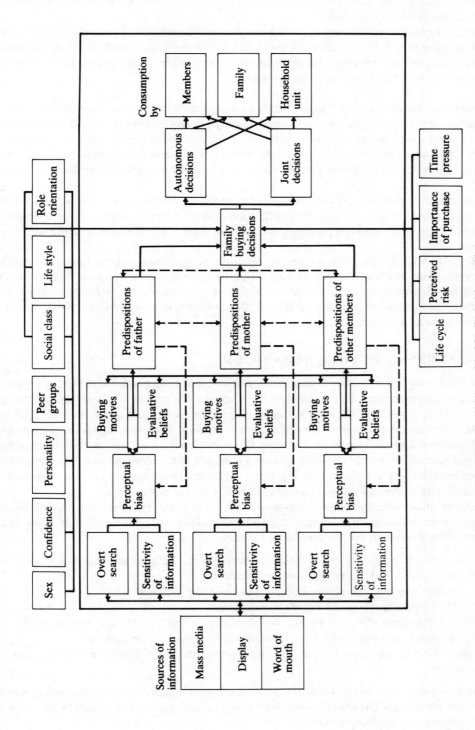

Figure 3.5 The Sheth model of family decision-making

Source: 'A theory of family buying decisions,' in J. N. Sheth, *Models of Buyer Behaviour*, Harper & Row, NY, 1974, pp. 22–3 investigating product attributes. This has been achieved through using group interviews and such techniques as the repertory grid test.[12]

Researchers are also recognizing that the wrong questions may have been asked of consumers because those questioned did not always know what they wanted in a product. Since consumers are generally not creative enough to be of direct assistance in designing new products, it is often more productive to find out what they do *not* want.

Future trends in consumer research There is likely to be a continuous re-evaluation of the concepts, data and techniques being employed in consumer research investigations. Standard approaches to the study of consumer behaviour will continue to be evaluated and if necessary refined or eliminated. Consumer research is likely to come under more interactive examination concerning its managerial implications. Hence studies should become more relevant for decision-making purposes.

As consumer research expands, it is likely that expenditure on this subject will increase. While increased expenditure may be the rule, more attention also needs to be given to the cost/benefit of such projects. This will increase attempts to use the most cost-efficient research tools and techniques.

Finally, it is hoped that more integrated research programmes will be initiated, tracking consumer behaviour over time and monitoring trends in behaviour and attitudes. Despite the fact that integrated research programmes require a high level of commitment in terms of effort, time and resources, the need for them seems to be critical for yielding more valid and reliable data than have previously been available.

ORGANIZATIONAL BUYING BEHAVIOUR

Consumer behaviour relates to the buying behaviour of individuals (or families) for products for their own use. Organizations buy to enable them to provide goods and services to the final customer. This has implications for marketing management, as we shall see later. Organizational buying behaviour has many similarities to consumer behaviour. Both encompass the behaviour of human beings, whether individually or in groups. Organizational buyers do not necessarily act in a more rational manner than individual consumers. One study in Canada[13] showed that only 30 per cent of buyers followed a rational buying style. Organizational buyers are also affected by environmental and individual factors, as outlined in the previous section.

One of the main differences from consumer buying is that organizational buying usually involves group decision-making. In such a group individuals may have different roles in the purchase process. These can be categorized as follows:

1. *Users* These are the people in the organization who will be using the product. Sometimes they will also be involved in devising product specifications.
2. *Buyers* Buyers have the formal authority to purchase the product.
3. *Deciders* Deciders actually make the buying decision.
4. *Influencers* Influencers affect the buying decision in many different ways. For example, they might be technical personnel who have developed the product specifications.
5. *Gatekeepers* Gatekeepers control the flow of information to and from the buying group (or 'buying centre').

One person may play all the above roles in the purchase decision, or each role may be represented by a number of personnel. The salesperson trying to sell to an organization should be aware of the roles people assume in the buying centre.

Need recognition
↓
Determine specifications (general)
↓
Determine specifications (specific)
↓
Search
↓
Evaluation
↓
Selection
↓
Post-purchase evaluation

Figure 3.6 Organizational buying process

Another difference in organizational buying is that products tend to be more complex and require specialist knowledge to purchase. As many products are changed according to the specifications of the buyer, there has to be more communication and negotiation between buyers and sellers. After-sales service is also very important in organizational buying, and suppliers are often evaluated quite rigorously after purchase. In general, organizational markets have fewer, larger buyers who are geographically concentrated. Another aspect of organizational buying is the nature of *derived demand*; that is, demand for organizational (especially industrial) goods is derived from consumer markets. If demand for the end-product consumer good falls, then this has an effect along the production line to all the inputs. So in organizational marketing the end-consumers cannot be ignored, and trends should be monitored.

Organizational buying decisions can also be categorized as to how complex they are, similar to the low high-involvement decision-making in consumer markets:

1. *Straight re-buys* These occur often, are relatively cheap and are usually a matter of routine. If the supplier is an 'in-supplier', that is if it is on the company's approved list of suppliers, then it has to perform so as not to get taken off the list. If it is an 'out-supplier', it has to try to get on to the approved list.
2. *Modified re-buy* This situation requires some additional information or evaluation of suppliers. It is usually the case that specifications, etc., have been modified since the last purchase.
3. *New task* A new task or new 'buy' situation is the most complex purchase decision when the company has not bought this product before. Search and evaluation procedures are extensive here.

The process of organizational buying The process involved in organizational buying has many similarities to consumer buying. Both go through a form of need recognition, search, evaluation, choice and post-purchase evaluation. Figure 3.6 shows the specific stages that organizations go through when buying. Need recognition occurs when the company has a need that can be fulfilled by the purchase of a product. Need can be stimulated internally from within the organization or through external means (for example if a salesperson visits with a new product). The company will then draw up general specifications. This can be done in consultation with the prospective seller. Then more detailed specifications are assimilated. Value analysis can be used to reduce the costs of components in the production process. In the search stage, buyers can use numerous sources of information. They may advertise for tenders for certain products, investigate trade journals or directories, speak to salespeople, look at their own records or visit trade shows.

For suppliers, marketing considerations would lead them to aim for a good reputation in the marketplace, attend trade shows, maintain a certain level of advertising, and try to identify prospective customers. By so doing, the purchasing company can be considered early in the decision process and may even be involved in the formulation of specifications.

Evaluation may be systematic, involving some form of supplier evaluation technique. These can be very detailed, covering quality, price, delivery and after-sales service, for example. The buying centre will evaluate the proposals and alternative product offerings and decide upon the most suitable purchase choice. At this stage there may be further negotiations to alter the price on certain product specifications. The buying centre may choose to have a number of suppliers so as to protect it from being too dependent on one source. The selection stage may also incorporate some form of reordering system, and evaluation of the product after purchase is often formalized.

Again, the time spent, resources committed and, indeed, whether or not all the stages are passed through depends on the type of product bought. A 'new task' product will mean that all the stages will probably be passed through. A straight re-buy situation will be a relatively quick process, missing a number of stages; indeed, this type of purchasing is often accessed by computerized buying.

The people involved in the decision-making process can also change over time, although it is still very important for marketers to be aware of the process and the ways in which they can develop marketing strategy around this. Cardozo[14] stated that it is very important for the seller to be involved in the buying process at an early stage.

Members of the buying centre are influenced by both rational and emotional factors in their decision-making. Marketers should be aware of the different influences on the buying centre, although emotional factors are much more difficult to predict and interpret. Hutt and Speh[15] discuss the different types of motivation in the following buying process:

Rational motives	*Emotional motives*
Price	Status and rewards
Quality	Perceived risk
Service	Friendship
Continuity of supply	
Reciprocity	

These motivations for purchase are not the only influences on organizational buyers of which strategic marketers should be aware. We will now examine other factors that influence organizational buyer behaviour.

Influences on organizational buying In consumer buying behaviour we discussed two main influences on purchase behaviour: environmental factors and individual factors. In organizational buying we have a more complex environment for buying decisions. Figure 3.7 shows the main influences in the purchase process.

Environmental forces on buyer behaviour include economic, legal, political, cultural, physical and technological factors, so the general economic trends of the area in which the buying organization is located are important, as are the economic trends of any areas in which it trades (owing to derived demand). Increasingly, as world trade expands, when evaluating economic trends the marketer should take a global perspective. The political and legal environment, which includes government spending, taxation and import and export controls, should also be evaluated for their influence upon buying decisions. In the developing global markets for goods and services,

Figure 3.7 Influences on organizational buying

it is easy to disregard cultural differences; however, there are still many different cultural climates in the world, and they do not appear to be diminishing in importance. Physical influences involve the geographical location of the organization. The changing technological environment also influences buying decisions.

Marketers must take account of group force purchasing influences:

1. Who is involved in the buying decision?
2. What influence does each member have?
3. How does each member of the buying centre evaluate alternative products?

The type of information that is needed on group forces is the type that becomes available only when close contact is maintained with the buyer. This reinforces the role of the salesperson in the buying decision process. Members of the buying centre were outlined earlier in this chapter, when the roles that various individuals carried out were described.

Organizational forces, such as the organizational culture of the business, also have an effect on the buying decision. For instance, marketing to an organization that has a highly centralized structure, including the buying function, needs a different marketing approach from that of companies that have a decentralized structure.

It is easy to assume that organizational buying has little to do with individual factors. However, in any buying centre it is individuals who make the buying decisions, not the organization. Different members of the buying centre may evaluate products using different criteria, which complicates the issue for the organizational marketer. Some of the motivations of individual buyers were outlined earlier in this chapter. Individuals will also try to reduce the level of risk they are exposed to in the purchase decision, for example by using multiple sources or making use of an extensive information search.

Models of organizational buyer behaviour

Just as in consumer buyer behaviour, attempts have been made to capture the full complexity of organizational buyer behaviour by developing comprehensive models of the process. Each model incorporates a number of variables and processes and attempts to show how these interrelate. Some of the concepts in organizational buying already discussed in this chapter directly derive from some of these models—for example, the concept of a buying centre, types of buying decisions, and the range of factors affecting these decisions. Two of the more influential of these models are outlined below.

The Webster–Wind model (Fig. 3.8) This model is concerned with environmental, organizational,

Figure 3.8 The Webster-Wind model of organizational buying behaviour
Source: W. Webster and Y. Wind, *Organisational Buying Behaviour*, Prentice-Hall, Englewood Cliffs, NJ, 1972

interpersonal and individual buying determinants.[16] The model implies that these determinants affect individual and group decision-making processes and final buying decisions. The environmental influences in this model are seen to act as constraints on the buying goals of the organization. Although the marketer cannot control any of these factors, an understanding of the parts they play may be critical to success.

An explanation of the organizational influence relies upon four elements of the buying organization: people, technology, structure and task. The concept of the buying centre is one example of how the model uses these elements. The buying centre concept discussed earlier recognizes that a number of people participate in the buying decision, including individuals and groups from various departments in the organization.

The model also suggests that within the decision-making unit there are a number of roles that people play. These roles were outlined earlier in our discussion and are a valuable contribution of this model.

Although this model is a valuable contribution to the theory of organizational buying behaviour, in that it indicates a whole range of factors that can directly or indirectly influence the outcome of a buying decision, it still provides only a static representation of a dynamic situation.

The Sheth model (Fig. 3.9) This model was proposed by Sheth in 1973[17] and was developed from the earlier Howard–Sheth model of consumer behaviour. The model concentrates on information sources and portrays a more dynamic situation. The buying centre consists of purchasing agents, engineers, users and others. The actions and expectations of the individuals are influenced by previous experience, and the information received by the individuals is subject to their own perceptual distortion.

The Sheth model is dynamic in that it considers time and acknowledges that any future decisions that are made will use continually updated information. It is successful in four ways:

1. It demonstrates the complexity of industrial buying behaviour.
2. It depicts the most important variables in a systematic way.
3. It is a generalized stimulus–response model of the behaviour of industrial buyers.
4. A number of theories and concepts are brought together and are supported by empirical research.

The two major weaknesses of the model are that it does not elaborate much on the process of industrial buying and on how the relationships of the variables might change during that process; in addition, it does not look closely at the various methods of conflict resolution that may be involved in decision-making.

The models outlined are only a sample of the theories that have contributed towards the study of organizational buying behaviour. For a fuller discussion, readers are directed towards one of the specialist texts in this area.

Theory versus practice in organizational buying behaviour

Over the past 20 years, attempts have been made to advance knowledge on this subject. Although there has been a considerable output of literature in this area, it has still received little attention in comparison with consumer buying. The majority of research, particularly in the United States, has centred on the industrial buying approach and has concentrated on two main areas. First, there have been studies of the process of industrial buying behaviour and the factors that affect the choice of supplier. Second, there have been studies of the effect of individual elements of the marketing mix on industrial markets.

To some extent, industrial marketing practice has not kept pace with the conceptual development of organizational buying behaviour. Initially, models were developed from research carried out in the 1960s which focused on identifying variables that influence behaviour. The framework provided by the models supported the variables, and this represented the most advanced thinking in this area. However, the evidence presented by these theoretical models was not backed up by sufficient research to show that this was how organizations bought. In addition, the industrial marketer was not encouraged to implement these concepts. Sheth comments that the

Figure 3.9 The Sheth model of industrial buying behaviour

Source: J. N. Sheth, 'A model of industrial buying behaviour', *Journal of Marketing*, **37**(4), October 1973

work carried out within the area of industrial buying seems to have had little impact on marketing thought and practice. He also considers that marketers may have been led to believe that little is known about industrial buying behaviour. Hence there has been reluctance among practitioners to move in the direction suggested by conceptual developments in organizational buying.

Another reason for the gap between theory and practice is that data on organizational buying can be more problematical to obtain in industrial markets, and as a result the usefulness of such data in formulating marketing strategies has not been demonstrated. The difficulty of obtaining reliable data has caused a number of problems. Consumer behaviour has been researched in greater depth than industrial buying behaviour, because consumers are more accessible, more numerous, more identifiable and generally more cooperative than participants in industrial buying decisions. In addition, organizational buying decisions tend to be more complex, as do the products purchased.

Finally, we should note that organizational purchasing itself is changing. Indeed, this is one of the most dynamic areas of commercial practice. Some of the most important trends and developments within organizational purchasing include the following:

1. Purchasing is more specialized and professional.
2. There is more centralized purchasing.
3. Computerized purchasing has increased.
4. There are new philosophies of purchasing and manufacturing, e.g. just-in-time, zero defects and materials management.
5. There is more, and improved, supplier capability and performance analysis.

These trends have meant that there have had to be closer links with buyers and sellers. If just-in-time purchasing is to work successfully, close contact has to be maintained between buyers and sellers. There has been an increased emphasis on product quality and delivery schedules. The emphasis is not now on single-product attributes but rather on the overall 'profile' of the good in question. The sales force of organizational marketing has a great responsibility through the purchase decision, and there is much greater emphasis on its role and specific training requirements. This has meant an increased profile of what is termed 'relationship marketing'. This is where, over time, a close relationship is actively built up between the seller and the buyer. This is often on a social level and has been called 'lunch', 'golf', or 'dinner marketing', but relationship marketing requires extremely close co-operation and trust between suppliers and customers, which can often be established through such social contacts. It is only really worth while on high-value accounts, as a relationship marketing strategy can be very expensive.

CONCLUSIONS

This chapter has sought to provide an overview of buyer behaviour and a study of buyer behaviour from the point of view of the contemporary marketer. It has been shown that there are significant implications from a marketing point of view in the analysis of buyer behaviour. The concept of fulfilling consumer needs is central to successful marketing strategy. The study of buyer behaviour is a relatively new discipline and has become a specialist area of marketing, owing to its complexity. It covers questions concerning who is in the market, what they buy, when they buy, how they buy, and where. Marketing mix variables—price, product, place and promotion—have effects on buyer behaviour, so the marketer should be aware of the impact of these controllable variables.

Buying behaviour does not simply encompass the straightforward decision process, but also covers the underlying influences and motives for purchase. These are difficult to measure but are none the less very important in a thorough understanding of purchase behaviour. The principles of buyer behaviour theory can be applied to the commercial sector (both consumer and organizational), to non-profit-making institutions and to service providers. A simple framework has been used in this chapter to describe the factors that might influence purchase behaviour, but more complex models of both consumer and organizational buyer behaviour have also been introduced. They are useful in providing a framework for study.

In organizational decision-making, additional influences were included. These included group influences and organizational factors. The actual decision-making process will depend on whether the purchase is a new task, a modified re-buy or a straight re-buy for the organization. The process involved is similar to the consumer decision-making process. Within organizational buying, motivation is not simply rational: *emotional* motives for purchase also play a part in the decision to purchase. Recent trends in organizational purchasing have implications for marketing management. For example, just-in-time purchasing, computerized purchasing and centralized purchasing have meant that salespersons' roles and responsibilities have changed.

APPLICATION QUESTIONS

1. What are the major differences between organizational and consumer buying decisions, and why should they be treated as separate and distinct?
2. Do you believe that organizational purchase decisions are made on a more rational basis than those for consumer purchase decisions? Why?
3. How do you think that sellers can be assisted as a result of a knowledge of buyer behaviour?
4. Do you believe that consumers or industrial buyers behave in a sufficiently consistent manner so as to enable marketers to study them? Give reasons and elaborate on your opinion.
5. List some of the recent trends and developments in organizational purchasing. What are the implications of these for the marketer?

REFERENCES

1. J. F. Engel, R. D. Blackwell and P. W. Miniard. *Consumer Behaviour*, 5th edn, Dryden Press, Hinsdale, IL, 1986.
2. D. Louder and A. J. Della Bitta. *Consumer Behaviour: Concepts and Application*, 3rd edn, McGraw-Hill, London, 1988.
3. L. G. Schiffman and L. L. Kanuk. *Consumer Behaviour*, 3rd edn, Prentice-Hall, Englewood Cliffs, NJ, 1987.
4. P. Kotler. *Marketing Management: Analysis, Planning, Implementation and Control*, 7th edn, Prentice-Hall, Englewood Cliffs, NJ, 1991.
5. H. Assael. *Consumer Behaviour and Marketing Action*, 3rd edn, Kent Publishing Co., Boston, MA, 1987.
6. A. Maslow. *Motivation and Personality*, Harper & Row, New York, 1954.
7. Assael, op.cit., Chapter 12.
8. P. M. Chisnall. *Marketing: A Behavioural Analysis*, 2nd edn, McGraw-Hill, London, 1985.
9. J. N. Sheth and J. A. Howard. *The Theory of Buyer Behaviour*, John Wiley, Chichester, Sx, 1969.
10. J. Engel, D. Kollat and R. Blackwell. *Consumer Behaviour*, Dryden Press, New York, 1978.
11. J. N. Sheth. 'A theory of family buying decisions', in *Models of Buyer Behaviour*, Harper & Row, New York, 1974, pp. 22–3.
12. G. A. Churchill. *Marketing Research: Methodological Foundations*. Dryden Press, Hinsdale, IL, 1976, pp. 17–21.
13. D. T. Wilson. 'Industrial buyers' decision making styles', *Journal of Marketing Research*, November 1971, pp. 433–6.
14. R. N. Cardozo. 'Modelling organisational buying as a sequence of decisions', *Industrial Marketing Management*, **12**, February 1983.
15. M. D. Hutt and T. W. Speh. *Business Marketing Management*. Dryden Press, London, 1989.
16. W. Webster and Y. Wind. *Organizational Buying Behaviour*, Prentice-Hall, Englewood Cliffs, NJ, 1972.
17. J. N. Sheth. 'A model of industrial buyer behaviour', *Journal of Marketing*, **37**, October 1973, pp. 50–6.

FOUR
MARKETING DECISIONS

INTRODUCTION

We have seen that being marketing-oriented requires that all activities of a business, and not just those related to the marketing department, must be focused on customers and their needs. This in turn is a reflection of the importance of satisfying customer needs if a company is to enjoy long-term success.

Becoming more attuned to the needs of the market almost inevitably means that the marketing function is required to play a more central role in overall company decisions and plans. Specifically, what this means in organizational terms, and the problems and issues it can give rise to, are those that have been discussed in the second section of Chapter 2. In stressing this role for marketing, we must be careful not to forget the distinction between marketing as a concept—as an overall philosophy for the conduct of a business—and marketing as a function.

In its functional role, marketing stands between the company and its customers. It must anticipate, analyse and interpret customer needs into specific action programmes designed to achieve company objectives. The objectives themselves, and therefore marketing activities, are derived from a broader context of overall company planning. Put simply, marketing decisions should be placed into a framework of corporate planning within a company.

This chapter examines the nature of corporate strategic planning from the identification of environmental opportunities and threats to the determining of specific overall company objectives and plans. We shall look carefully at the important, indeed essential, role that the marketing function plays in this process and what this role means for marketing management. We shall also be appraising some of the techniques of strategy appraisal and selection, ranging from the relatively simple Boston Consulting Group's two-dimensional matrix to the empirically based approach of the Strategic Planning Institute. In the final part of the chapter, we will focus on the framework of marketing decision-making with an emphasis on those controllable decisions referred to collectively as the 'marketing mix'.

CORPORATE STRATEGIC PLANNING

It has been suggested by Henry[1] that corporate planning is essentially an *ad hoc* process. What he means by this is that the steps in corporate planning, and the procedure through these steps, are not fixed. Every company is unique and must decide for itself on the appropriate approach to, and sequence for, corporate planning. Having said this, if we are to make sense of the notion of

Figure 4.1 The elements of corporate planning

strategic planning, and if we intend to use it to improve organizational effectiveness, we need some formalized framework of the essential steps. This framework is shown in Fig. 4.1.

The outcome of corporate strategic planning, and therefore the centrepiece of Fig. 4.1, is the formulation and selection of company strategies. In arriving at these strategies, we need to consider the following aspects:

—What is our corporate mission? (What business are we in?)
—What are our relevant strengths and weaknesses?
—What are the relevant opportunities and threats?
—What are our corporate objectives?

The broken lines in Fig. 4.1 indicate that, although we shall deal with these factors sequentially, in practice, to arrive at strategic plans we need to consider all these factors in combination. Rather than being a step-by-step process, corporate planning is iterative in nature. Determining what business we are in requires us to look at both our environment and our capabilities as a company. In turn, our assessments of what contributes 'relevant' opportunities and threats, and 'relevant' strengths and weaknesses, is determined by our business definition.

With these considerations in mind, we will now examine each of the constituent elements of Fig. 4.1 in turn.

Corporate mission

One of the most pervasive distinguishing characteristics of the formal organization is that it exists to serve a purpose. This purpose may take a variety of forms and may be classified in a number of ways according both to our viewpoint and the particular organization. For example, in the context of the overall economy of a country, the purpose of the business organization could be said to be the 'creation of wealth'. The purpose of a trade union might be said to be 'the furtherance of the interests of its members'.

In the context of corporate planing, however, generalized statements of purpose such as these have little value. We need something that will provide a clear focus for direction and decision-making.

In fact, most companies do have a statement of purpose or mission. Normally this purpose is enshrined in a company's Memorandum and Articles of Association, which specify at the inception of the business what its broad programme of activities shall be. In most instances, however, this broad statement of purpose is again too general to be of use in corporate planning. What is required as a basis for corporate planning is an up-to-date and relevant statement of corporate mission or purpose. This statement should reflect the essential characteristics of the company, its current environment, its resources and the preferences of the owners and managers of the business.

Determining a corporate mission that fulfils the requirements outlined above is by no means easy. Some companies have spent two or three years redefining their corporate mission and have still managed to produce a corporate mission statement that is not particularly useful or relevant. But what precisely is the nature of such a statement?

The corporate mission statement is perhaps best thought of as a *definition of the business*, of the order of 'Our business is . . .'. To be useful and relevant, a business definition should ideally fulfil a number of criteria. The following represents the more important of these criteria when thinking about how to define a business:

1. The definition should be neither too broad nor too narrow . . . Definitions such as 'we are in the business of making profits' or 'we produce pens' are not really useful.
2. Ideally, the definition should encompass the three dimensions of what Abell[2] refers to as the 'business domain'. These three dimensions are, respectively:

   (a) Customer groups to be served
   (b) Customer needs to be served
   (c) Technologies to be utilized

An illustration of how these dimensions might be incorporated into a corporate mission statement is:

> . . . The business of Acme Trading plc is in the provision of *beauty aids* [customer need] to *female students* [customer group] based on *non-allergic, animal-free products* [technology] with the aim of . . .; etc.

This notion of a business domain is a useful extension of the much-wanted need to avoid 'marketing myopia' advanced by Levitt[3] in the early 1960s. To avoid a narrow, shortsighted view of one's business, Levitt argues, it is necessary to define the business in terms of what customer needs a company fulfils, rather than in terms of what it provides. For example, Austin Rover Group would, in Levitt's terms, be said to be in the business of fulfilling the need for transport rather than being in the business of producing vehicles. There is little doubt that this apparently simple piece of 'common-sense' advice from Levitt was instrumental in bringing about an increased marketing awareness in countless boardrooms throughout the United States and later in Europe.

The additional dimensions added by Abell may perhaps have a similar long-term effect on corporate planning in that they add substantially to the relevance and, therefore, usefulness of the corporate mission statement.

Figure 4.2 Achieving a strategic fit: SWOT analysis

Analysing strengths and weaknesses, and opportunities and threats (SWOT analysis)

It might seem logical to conclude that we can move directly from the corporate mission statement to the determination of corporate objectives. However, in setting objectives we need to appraise both external (environmental) factors, and internal (company) resources. This is essential if a company is to ensure a marketing fit or, as it is sometimes referrred to, a 'strategic fit', between itself and the environment. This matching process is essentially one of relating external opportunities and threats to internal strengths and weaknesses and is often referred to by the mnemonic 'SWOT', as shown in Fig. 4.2.

It is important to remember that the external appraisal of opportunities and threats and the internal appraisal of strengths and weaknesses should be considered together. For the time being, however, we shall consider first external (environmental) analysis.

External analysis In Chapter 2 we considered the macro-environment which surrounds and affects each and every company. This macro-environment consists of those factors that are broadly outside the control of the individual company and includes social, political, economic and technological forces. In the context of corporate planning, the macro-environment has a number of significant features, in particular:

1. The macro-environment is changing constantly. Some of these changes are long term and relatively predictable, others occur rapidly and often without warning.
2. It is primarily these changes in the macro-environment that cause the most significant opportunities and threats to a company.

One or two examples will serve to illustrate these points.

—Long-term forecasts of world oil reserves suggest major profit opportunities for the developer of alternative energy sources and major threats to those oil exploration companies that do not diversify.
—Sudden revaluations of a nation's currency can represent a significant threat to would-be exporters from that country.
—An unexpected technological breakthrough by a company can represent a significant opportunity for the developer of the technology and a significant threat to his or her competitors.

One significant point you should note from these examples is that any given environmental change can represent a threat to one company and an opportunity for another. A particularly important aspect affecting this is the particular strengths and weaknesses of each company.

For example, a period of particularly rapid technological change and development can provide a substantial opportunity to a company with the technological and market skills to exploit it and a significant threat to the company lacking these necessary resources.

Similarly, a company may pride itself on its 'strength' in being able to produce top-quality 'premium' products, and yet find itself threatened if economic trends depress levels of disposable income and, therefore, market prices. In addition to external analysis, therefore, the marketing planner must also make a careful internal appraisal of organizational strengths and weaknesses.

Internal analysis As mentioned earlier, achieving a 'strategic fit' is essentially a matching process between the opportunities and threats presented by trends and changes in the organization's environment and its strengths and weaknesses. There are a number of steps in this process.

First, the marketing planner must determine what activities and/or resources of the organization should be included in the internal analysis. A simple checklist can be assembled for this purpose, although care should be taken first to establish what are critical strengths and weaknesses. Only strategically significant strengths and weaknesses should be assessed. Examples of attributes that could conceivably form part of an internal appraisal include:

—Marketing strengths and weaknesses
—Financial strengths and weaknesses
—Manufacturing and physical resource strengths and weaknesses
—Personal strengths and weaknesses
—Research and development strengths and weaknesses

It is important to note that these are only examples. Which attributes are vital to assess are company-specific. We should also note that a simple checklist approach ignores the fact that the attributes are interrelated. A combination of seemingly moderate strengths in all of the attributes may result in a company that is in fact very strong when it comes to competing in markets or dealing with opportunities and threats from the macro-environment.

Having identified the key attributes for an assessment of strengths and weaknesses, the next step is to determine the *degree* of strength or weakness. Are we, for example, *very* strong with respect to our channels of distribution, or only reasonably so? Are we *extremely* weak when it comes to research and product development, or simply not very adept in this area? In other words, we should distinguish between where we are particularly strong or weak and where we are moderately so.

Third, we must assess strengths and weaknesses in comparison to our major existing, and potential, competitors. It is dangerous to develop plans and strategies based on own-company 'strengths' when the competitors are even stronger in these areas.

Finally, remember that we must assess strengths and weaknesses in relation to environmental opportunities and threats. As our earlier example showed, only by comparing strengths and weaknesses with the challenges posed by an ever-changing marketing environment can the marketer determine if what were once assessed as key strengths, and on which competitive strategies were built, remain so.

The conclusion we may draw from this is that the appraisal of company strengths and weaknesses and an assessment of possible opportunities and threats make sense only if we consider both internal and external factors together. Furthermore, every company will have its own particular and different SWOT profile. As with the overall corporate planning process itself, SWOT analysis requires an iterative approach. This is illustrated in Fig. 4.3, together with some of the more important elements to be appraised.

Clearly, SWOT analysis involves a company in the process of what Argenti[4] has termed

Figure 4.3   SWOT analysis

'environmental scanning'. This involves not only keeping abreast of changes in the environments but also, more specifically, attempting to forecast or predict them. This in turn raises a number of questions for the managers of a business. For example, on what external factors should information be obtained? By whom, and at what cost? To what use will this information be put? What forecasting techniques can be used?

These are not easy questions to answer, and once again the answers are company-specific. In addition, forecasting is made difficult by the possibility of unanticipated events and the fact that the various environmental factors interact one with another. Recent years, however, have witnessed the growth and development of much more sophisticated forecasting techniques to aid management, and some of these are elaborated in Chapter 10.

Because it is difficult for incumbent managers to be totally objective, especially as regards the assessment of weaknesses, if often helps if external consultants are used to conduct the internal assessment. Where this is not possible, or appropriate, an inter-departmental team of assessors should be assembled from within the organization.

Setting objectives

Both overall company mission statements and SWOT analysis input to this stage of the corporate planning process. The importance of objectives to the planning process cannot be overstated; indeed, many texts on planning cite objective-setting as being the starting-point in the process.

Broadly, setting objectives involves a company in considering the following two questions:

—Where do we wish to go?
—When do we intend to arrive?

Without an answer to these questions, a company can be likened to a ship without a compass; it can move, but it lacks a clear sense of direction. More specifically, among the more important functions that objectives serve in a company are the following:

1. Objectives provide for a *sense of purpose* in a company. Without objectives, companies lack the means to focus and organize their efforts.
2. Objectives help a company to *achieve consistency* between the various levels of decision-making, and between the different functions.
3. Objectives help to *stimulate effort*; they provide a basis for motivating individuals to achieve them.
4. Finally, objectives provide the *basis for control* in a company. Unless we know precisely what is required, it is difficult, if not impossible, to know the extent to which we have achieved it.

In order to fulfil these important functions, objectives must have a number of characteristics. Again, among the most important of these are the following:

—Preferably, objectives should be *quantified*. Quantitative objectives with respect to both levels of performance and time reduce the risk of their being vague or ambiguous.
—Ideally, objectives should be *acceptable* and *agreeable* to those charged with the responsibility of attaining them. It is pointless setting objectives if they are not acted upon—or if the effort to achieve them is given grudgingly.
—A frequent reason for objectives being unacceptable is that they are felt to be too difficult or impossible to achieve. Objectives should be *realistic*, pitched neither too high nor too low.
—Finally, objectives should be *consistent*. As we shall see shortly, often companies have a variety of objectives as opposed to a single one. It is important that these multiple objectives do not conflict one with another in such a way that the achievement of an objective in one area is inconsistent with the achievement of objectives in others. For example, an objective of improved profitability may be inconsistent with an objective of maximum sales.

Having discussed the functions of objectives, and the characteristics that objectives ideally should possess if they are to serve these functions, we can now turn our attention to the variety of corporate objectives that a company might set.

In economic analysis it is often asserted that a firm has one, and only one, objective: namely, 'to maximize its total profits'. We shall examine this notion of profit maximization in more detail in Chapter 13, which is concerned with pricing. At this stage it is sufficient to note that profit-maximizing does not in fact reflect the reality or richness of objective-setting in most companies. Clearly, for many companies profits are enacted for long-run survival, and because of this they will normally formulate objectives in this area. Usually, however, these profit objectives are set in terms of some satisfactory level of profits, often couched in terms of a specified rate of return on the assets employed.

In addition to profit objectives, it is now recognized that companies may have a variety of objectives encompassing a spread of activities. Among some of the most frequently encountered objectives in companies are:

—Profit objectives
—Sales objectives
—Market share objectives
—Growth objectives
—Technical and market standing objectives
—Survival objectives
—Social responsibility objectives

Whatever the mix of objectives, it must be remembered that the objectives themselves relate to

Figure 4.4   The planning gap

some point in the future, hence the importance of specifying a time-scale for their achievement. For an existing business there will also be a past. It is possible, therefore, to measure the past and current performance of the company with respect to those areas in which it has objectives for the future. Management can then compare where it wishes to be (objectives) with where it is likely to be on the basis of a projection from past performance. Any difference constitutes what Ackoff has referred to as a 'planning gap'.[5] This notion of a planning gap is illustrated in Fig. 4.4. The gap stems from the difference between future desired profit objectives and a forecast of projected profit based on past performance.

In the face of such a planning gap, a number of options are available; the intention, however, is to close the gap. For example, the gap could be closed by revising objectives in a downward direction. Such a step might be taken where the initial objectives are unrealistic. Alternatively, or in addition, the gap could be closed by actions designed to move the company off the projection curve and towards the desired curve. In fact, any movement towards a point at some time in the future requires action decisions—even if the action decision is of the order of 'do nothing', i.e. continue much as we have done in the past. More frequently, these action decisions require the exploration and evaluation of a variety of options, the selection of courses of action from these options, and the commitment of resources. This next step in the process of corporate planning is the formulation of strategies.

Strategy formulation and selection

If objectives relate to the 'where' and 'when' of planning, strategy formulation and selection are concerned with the 'how'.

This idea of strategy is essentially a military one, but it has increasingly been applied in a business context. One of the major difficulties with its application in this context is that the full range of strategic alternatives in business is virtually unlimited and is certainly extremely complex.

Market \ Product	Present	New
Present	1. Market penetration	3. Product development
New	2. Market development	4. Diversification

Figure 4.5   Ansoff's product/marketing scope

In an effort to reduce this variety and complexity to manageable proportions, a number of conceptual frameworks have been developed to aid the company in the delineation and choice between strategic options. We shall outline two of the more important of these.

Ansoff[6] has proposed the idea of 'product/market scope' to aid in the formulation and selection of strategies, particularly for those companies with growth objectives. The basic framework of this approach is shown in Fig. 4.5. The matrix comprises 'markets' on the vertical axis, and on the horizontal axis 'products'. In turn, each axis is subdivided into 'existing' and 'new'. Each cell of the matrix so formed represents a different strategic alternative for achieving growth.

Strategic alternative 1, *market penetration*, is a strategy of expanding sales based on existing products in existing markets. Where the total market is still growing, the strategy may be achieved, for example, through 'natural' market growth. In markets that are static or declining, a market penetration strategy can be achieved only by increasing market share at the expense of competitors.

Strategic alternative 2, *market development*, is a strategy of expansion based on entering new markets, i.e. markets not previously served by the company, with existing products. A good example of this would be a company entering an export market for the first time.

Strategic alternative 3, *product development*, entails developing and launching new products for sale in existing markets.

Strategic alternative 4, *diversification*, involves a company expanding on the basis of new products *and* new markets. This diversification can take a number of forms. For example, a company might choose to diversify into new product markets by moving through the channel of production and distribution. A car manufacturer taking over a component supplier and both using and marketing the components to other companies would be a good example of this. Alternatively, the diversification may be into an entirely unrelated form of business activity—for example, a tobacco company moving into the production and marketing of children's toys.

Ansoff's product/market matrix is probably one of the best known frameworks for delineating overall corporate strategies.

A second and increasingly popular group of techniques aimed at the identification and selection of corporate strategies is also based on analysing appropriate marketing strategies. For an extensive evaluation of these techniques, the interested reader is advised to consult more specialized texts in this area. Excellent reference sources to both texts and techniques are those by Greenley[7] and Chisnall.[8] Together, these texts provide an indication of the range of strategy selection techniques available to the decision-maker. However, some of the more influential of these are outlined below.

Boston Consulting Group's (BCG) growth/share matrix   In the mid-1960s, the Boston Consulting

Figure 4.6 BCG's growth share matrix

Group (BCG) was founded to provide advice to strategic marketing planners. BCG developed a simple but useful strategic planning technique based on an analysis of a company's product portfolio. The technique entails assigning each individual product (or strategic business unit) of an organization to one of four possible cells in a simple matrix according to the relative market share and rate of market growth associated with that particular product/business. An example of a completed matrix is shown in Fig. 4.6.

The steps in completing the matrix are as follows:

1. For each product or strategic business unit, determine the annual growth rate in the market. Normally, annual growth rates of 10 per cent or more are considered 'high' and anything less than this, 'low'.
2. Determine the relative market share of each product or strategic business unit by comparing with the share of the largest competitor, and express as a ratio. In order to qualify for the 'high' relative market share category, a ratio of 1.0 or above is required. So, for example, if the market share of the product is 20 per cent and the largest competitor has only 10 per cent, the ratio is 2:1. Clearly, in order to qualify for the 'high' relative market share category, the product or business must be equal to the share leader in the market or above.

We now have all the information we need to position products or businesses in the matrix. We can also indicate the relative values of the turnover of each product or business by using a circle, where the area of each circle is proportionate to this turnover.

According to which cell of the matrix the products or businesses are calculated to lie, they are classified as being 'dogs', 'cash cows', 'problem children' or 'stars':

—*'Dogs'* These are products with low market share and slow market growth. Such products are sometimes referred to as 'cash traps', in that they do not generate a significant cash flow to a company and what little is generated is normally required to be reinvested simply to maintain the sales of the product.

—*'Cash cows'* These, on the other hand, are products with high market share and slow market growth. This combination typically means that a product in this category generates large amounts of cash over and above that required to keep the product in this sector.

—*'Problem children'* (sometimes called question marks or wildcats) These are products with low market share but in high-growth markets. These products can consume cash resources at alarming rates. The overall net drain on cash with these products is greatest when a company is attempting to increase its market share.

—*'Stars'* These are products in high-growth markets with a relatively high share of the market. Stars can generate a relatively large cash inflow, but this is more often than not matched or exceeded by the outflow of cash necessary to maintain market share. In net terms, therefore, such products provide, at best, modest net cash flows and often are net cash users.

In using and interpreting the product portfolio, a number of factors are important.

1. The portfolio is *dynamic*; i.e., in the absence of any action on the part of a company, products will move their position in the portfolio. Principally because of the product life-cycle effect, products have a tendency to move downwards in the portfolio; i.e., 'problem children' become 'dogs', and 'stars' become 'cash cows'. This tendency is indicated by the arrows in Fig. 4.6.
2. The notion is to achieve a certain balance in the portfolio. A balanced portfolio would ideally contain few or no 'dogs', some 'problem children', some 'stars' and some 'cash cows'. The balance between 'problem children', 'stars' and 'cash cows' should be such as to ensure that the company has sufficient net positive cash flow from its 'cash cows' to fund its 'stars' and turn them eventually into 'cash cows'. Funds from 'cash cows' are also used to turn products that are currently 'problem children', because of relatively low market share, into 'stars'. Not all 'problem children' can be moved in this way, and eventually some of them will fall to become 'dogs'. In the long run, all 'dogs' are potential candidates for elimination from the product range.

As a consequence of these two factors, a company must take steps to ensure that the future portfolio mix is as the company wishes it to be. In other words, it must select appropriate strategies in order to achieve in the future a balanced product portfolio. As with most of these techniques, the basic idea of the BCG's product portfolio analysis is to delineate the range of strategies required. The technique, however, is not without its problems and limitations.

Problems and limitations Some of the more frequent criticisms of the problems and limitations of the BCG matrix are:

—Oversimplification
—Problems of classification
—Assumptions
—Application
—Incomplete coverage

Each of these is considered further below.

1. *Oversimplification* Many critics have argued that the BCG matrix is an oversimplification of product markets and can lead to insufficient management attention to the range of factors that are important in marketing strategy. For example, the matrix is based on only two key factors—market growth and relative market share.

2. *Problems of classification* There are severe conceptual and practical problems associated with defining what comprises a strategic business unit, a concept essential to the analysis. Similarly, there is some doubt as to precisely where the line should be drawn between what constitutes a high/low relative market share, and what constitutes high/low market growth.

3. *Assumptions* In common with all the strategic portfolio approaches, the BCG model is derived from a number of key underpinning assumptions. If these assumptions are misplaced or wrong, then the subsequent value of the technique is reduced or removed completely. For example, a central assumption of the BCG matrix is that higher rates of market share are associated with higher profit rates. While there is some considerable evidence to support this assumption, it is by no means invariably the case that higher share equals higher profits.

4. *Application* The BCG approach implies that managers of different products/strategic business units will cooperate by, for example, not objecting to cash surpluses from their 'cash cows' being used to fund other parts of the business, or by withdrawing certain products in the 'question mark' or 'dog' categories. While it is true that the technique itself makes no claims to address such problems, there is a danger that management may overlook those problems of application.

5. *Incomplete coverage* The axes used on the BCG matrix mean that this technique effectively ignores new products at the introductory stage of their life cycles and markets that are in the decline stage and hence exhibit negative growth. Later in this chapter we shall examine a product portfolio matrix that is specifically designed to deal with these problems.

McKinsey/General Electric's multifactor portfolio matrix Partly because of the limitations and criticisms of the BCG growth share matrix, a number of product/market portfolio techniques now use several factors to analyse strategic business units instead of only the two found in BCG's approach. Working in conjunction with McKinsey & Co., General Electric USA (GE) has developed one of the more popular of these multiple-factor screening methods.

In the GE matrix, strategic business units are evaluated using the two dimensions of *market attractiveness* and *competitive position*. In contrast to the BCG approach, each of these two dimensions is, in turn, further analysed into a number of factors that underpin each dimension. In order to use this technique, the strategic planner must first determine these various factors contributing to market attractiveness and business position.

GE's product/market attractiveness factors The original GE matrix used the following factors to assess product/market attractiveness.

—Size
—Growth rates
—Competitive diversity and structure
—Historical profit margin
—Technological requirements
—Social impacts
—Environmental impacts
—Legal impacts
—Energy requirements

GE's competitive position factors For assessing competitive position, the GE matrix uses the following factors:

—Market share
—Share growth rate
—Product quality
—Brand reputation
—Distribution network
—Promotional effectiveness
—Productive capacity
—Productive efficiency
—Unit costs
—R&D performance
—Managerial personnel

GE believe that these are the key factors for their businesses, which, taken together, influence return on investment. (Note that the BCG approach uses cash flow.) However, this list of GE factors can be modified for each company according to its own particular circumstances. Indeed, many of the alternative multiple-factor matrices simply use different checklists of attributes.

Compiling the GE matrix The five steps in compiling the GE matrix are:

1. Identify strategic business units.
2. Determine factors contributing to market attractiveness.
3. Determine factors contributing to business position.
4. Establish ways of measuring market attractiveness and business position.
5. Rank each strategic business unit according to whether it is high, medium or low on business strength; and high, medium or low on market attractiveness.

The final two factors (measuring and ranking) require that some numerical rating be given to the relative importance of each factor used to assess market attractiveness (assuming they are not all equally important) and in order to assess competitive position. Multiplying these together and totalling them for each strategic business unit (SBU) then gives an overall composite score which in turn enables the matrix to be compiled. In addition, the total market size for each SBU can be represented by the area of a circle, with the share of the company's SBU in each product market being indicated by a segment in the circle. The approach typically results in a visual portfolio similar to the one shown in Fig. 4.7. As with BCG's matrix, the visual presentation enables a considerable amount of complex information to be presented in an easily digestible form.

Interpreting and using the GE matrix Having completed the matrix, again as with the BCG approach, the marketing planner can then assess the balances of SBUs in the organization and determine appropriate future strategies for each.

Strategy guidelines Of itself, the GE matrix does not purport to establish detailed strategies for each SBU. Clearly, this is a task for the management of the company and will require a consideration of many factors. However, according to an SBU's position in the matrix, we can distinguish between three broad strategic guidelines. These are indicated in Fig. 4.8.

Clearly, SBUs that score high or medium on competitive position and market attractiveness are those in which a company should seek at least to maintain investment, and preferably to grow. SBUs that score a combination of low/low or low/medium on competitive position and market attractiveness are candidates for (at the very least) no more investment. Wherever possible, as much cash should be harvested from them as is feasible. SBUs scoring either high/low or medium/ medium combinations on competitive position/market attractiveness should be examined to see if some degree of selective investment to maintain or increase earnings would be appropriate.

Figure 4.7 Illustrative presentation of a GE Matrix

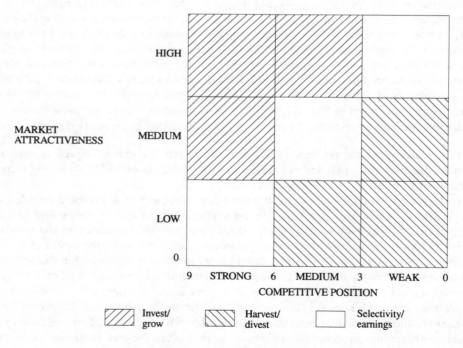

Figure 4.8 Strategy guidelines from the GE matrix

		PROTECT POSITION	INVEST TO BUILD	BUILD SELECTIVELY
	High	– Invest to grow at maximum digestible rate – Concentrate effort on maintaining strength	– Challenge for leadership – Build selectively on strengths – Reinforce vulnerable areas	– Specialize around limited strengths – Seek ways to overcome weaknesses – Withdraw if indications of sustainable growth are lacking
		BUILD SELECTIVELY	SELECTIVITY/ MANAGE FOR EARNINGS	LIMITED EXPANSION OR HARVEST
MARKET ATTRACTIVENESS	Medium	– Invest heavily in most attractive segments – Build up ability to counter competition – Emphasize profitability by raising productivity	– Protect existing programme – Concentrate investments in segments where profitability is good and risk is relatively low	– Look for ways to expand without high risk; otherwise, minimize investment and rationalize investment
		PROTECT AND REFOCUS	MANAGE FOR EARNINGS	DIVEST
	Low	– Manage for current earnings – Concentrate on attractive strengths – Defend strengths	– Protect position in most profitable segments – Upgrade product line – Minimize investment	– Sell at a time that will maximize cash value – Cut fixed costs and avoid investment meanwhile
		Strong	Medium	Weak

COMPETITIVE POSITION

Figure 4.9 Prescriptive strategies for cells of a GE matrix
Source: George S. Day, *Analysis for Strategic Market Divisions*, West Publishing Co, St. Paul, MN, 1986, p. 204

A more detailed breakdown of prescriptive strategies for businesses in different cells suggested by Day[9] is shown in Fig. 4.9.

Criticisms and limitations Because the GE matrix uses several dimensions to assess SBUs instead of only two, and also is based on return on investment rather than simply cash flow, many believe that it offers a substantial improvement over the BCG approach. However, the approach is not without its limitations and problems:

1. The approach offers only very broad strategy guidelines, with no indication as to precisely what needs to be done to achieve the strategy (e.g. selective growth).

2. There is no precise indication as to how to weight the various elements of market attractiveness, or how to score business strengths against these.
3. Evaluation and scoring is subjective, as are the points of division of the matrix into high, medium and low segments.
4. The technique is much more complex than the BCG approach, and requires much more extensive data gathering and processing.
5. The approach does not explicitly take account of possible relationships between various SBUs or product market areas.
6. The GE approach has been criticized on the grounds that it is not supported by empirical evidence or research; what evidence is there, for example, to support the notion that market attractiveness and business position are related to return on investment?

Industry maturity/market evolution models A number of strategic marketing planning tools are based on the notion that different strategies are required at different stages of the evolution of an industry. We shall outline two examples of this type of strategic planning tool.

Porter's model of industry/market evolution Michael Porter's model[10] is based on the following three broad stages in the evolution of an industry/market:

—Emerging industry
—Transition to maturity
—Decline

According to Porter, each of these stages has its own particular characteristics, some of the more important of which are listed for each stage:

1. Emerging industry
   (a) Uncertainty among buyers over:
      —Product performance
      —Potential applications
      —Likelihood of obsolescence
   (b) Uncertainty among sellers over:
      —Customer needs
      —Demand levels
      —Technological developments
2. Transition to maturity
   (a) Falling industry profits
   (b) Slow-down in growth
   (c) Customers knowledgeable about products and competitive offerings
   (d) Less product innovation
   (e) Competition in non-product aspects
3. Decline
   (a) Competition from substitutes
   (b) Changing customer needs
   (c) Demographic and other macro-environmental forces and factors affecting markets

Porter then uses the characteristics of each stage to suggest the following strategies as being appropriate to each:

Stage of industry development

		Growth	Maturity	Decline
STRATEGIC POSITION OF ORGANIZATION	Leader	– Keep ahead of the field	– Cost leadership – Raise barriers – Deter competitors	– Redefine scope – Divest peripherals – Encourage departures
	Follower	– Imitation at lower cost – Joint ventures	– Differentiation – Focus	– Differentiation – New opportunities

Figure 4.10   Industry life cycle and strategic position
Source: M. E. Porter, *Competitive Advantage: Creating and Sustaining Superior Performance*, Free Press, NY, p. 192

1. *Emerging industry* strategies developed to take account of industry competitive structure characteristics, i.e.:
   —Threat of entry
   —Rivalry among competitors
   —Pressure of substitutes
   —Bargaining power of buyers and suppliers
2. *Transition to maturity* Strategies focused on:
   —Developing new market segments
   —Focusing strategies for specific segments
   —Developing a more efficient organization
3. *Decline*
   —Seek pockets of enduring demand
   —Divest

Clearly, this approach is similar to the conventional concept of product life-cycle analysis in identifying the stage, specifying the characteristics of each stage, and suggesting appropriate strategies for each stage. Porter has developed the notion of industry life cycle further by linking it to the 'strategic position' of the individual organization. Strategic position is categorized in terms of whether the individual organization is a leader or a follower. This approach is shown in Fig. 4.10.

Arthur D. Little's industry maturity/competitive position matrix A similar approach to that developed by Porter is the one used by the business consultants Arthur D. Little.[11] A summary of this approach is shown in Fig. 4.11. As can be seen, the matrix comprises the 'stage of industry maturity' on the horizontal axis and 'competitive position' on the vertical axis.

The stages of industrial maturity are broken down into four categories:

—Embryonic
—Growth
—Maturity
—Ageing

Company's competitive position	Stage of industry maturity			
	Embryonic	Growth	Maturity	Ageing
Dominant				
Strong				
Favourable				
Tentative				
Weak				

Figure 4.11 The A.D. Little competitive position/industry maturity matrix

Which of these four the industry is in is determined by assessing eight key descriptors:

—Rate of market growth
—Industry potential
—Product line
—Number of competitors
—Market share stability
—Purchasing patterns
—Ease of entry
—Technology

A 'mature' industry, for instance, is characterized by slow or negligible rates of growth; little or no further growth potential; few changes in breadth of product lines; stable or declining numbers of competitors; stable market share positions; established buying patterns; high barriers to entry; and process and materials innovation in technology.

Criticisms and limitations The major criticisms of this type of model are the lack of empirical evidence to support the underpinning notions, and its simplistic approach to strategy selection. Certainly there is little doubt that industries do pass through different stages and that individual companies in these industries do have different competitive positions. However, these models tend to suggest that analysing just these two factors enables the 'right' strategies to be identified and selected. Needless to say, strategic decisions are much more complex than this implies.

Shell's directional policy matrix A similar approach to the GE business screen is the Shell directional policy matrix.[12] This approach also has two dimensions—company's competitive capabilities (vertical axis) and prospects for sector profitability (horizontal axis), as shown in Fig. 4.12. The firm's products are plotted into one of the nine cells in the figure and subsequently there is a suggested strategy for each of these cells.

There now follows a brief description of how to complete the matrix and what each of the horizontal and vertical axes in the model means.

The horizontal axis: sector profitability This includes the criteria of market growth rate, market quality, industry situation and environmental considerations. On each of these factors, a product is given from one to five stars. For instance, the factor of 'market quality' might be judged on the

PROSPECTS FOR SECTOR PROFITABILITY

	Unattractive	Average	Attractive
Weak	Disinvest	Phased withdrawal	Double or quit
		Custodial	
Average	Phased withdrawal	Custodial	Try harder
		Growth	
Strong	Cash generation	Growth	Leader
		Leader	

COMPANY'S COMPETITIVE CAPABILITY

Figure 4.12 The Shell directional policy matrix

Source: Shell Chemicals UK, *The Directional Policy Matrix. A New Aid to Corporate Planning*, November 1975

basis of several criteria such as pricing behaviour, or past stability in the profitability of that sector. The qualitative or quantitative evaluation of market quality is then converted into a rating from 0 to 4. The same procedure is followed for each of the other three factors, so that the overall score on sector profitability is the total of the ratings on all four factors.

The vertical axis: competitive capabilities The same approach is used here, except that the company's capabilities are assessed on the basis of market position, product research and development, and production capability. These are further divided into sub-factors applicable to any particular industry.

The strategy recommendations contained in the nine cells of the matrix are shown in Fig. 4.12. Shell emphasizes that, whatever strategy is eventually selected, the aim is that it should be 'resilient', i.e. viable in a diverse range of potential futures. Hence, each strategy ideally should be evaluated against all future possible scenarios; the results in all of these should be acceptable, and no potential 'disasters' should result.

Limitations The directional policy matrix has been criticized on the grounds that, like the BCG approach, it assumes that the same set of factors is universally applicable for assessing the prospects of any product or business. Many critics believe that the relevant factors and their relative importance will vary according to both the firm's products and the individual characteristics of each company. In addition, like the GE technique, the matrix does not provide any guidelines on how to implement the strategies suggested in each cell of the matrix.

Barksdale and Harris's portfolio analysis/product life cycle matrix Developed by Barksdale and

Harris,[13] the product life cycle portfolio matrix is specifically designed to deal with the criticisms that the BCG matrix (a) ignores products that are new, and (b) overlooks markets with a negative growth rate, i.e. markets that are in decline. Because of this, the product life cycle portfolio matrix includes a specific focus on the growth and maturity stages of the product life cycle in developing the portfolio technique.

We shall be looking at the product life cycle concept in detail in Chapter 8. At this stage, however, it is sufficient to note some of the key underpinning assumptions on which the Barksdale–Harris technique is based.

1. Products have finite life spans. They enter the market, pass through a period of growth, reach a stage of maturity, subsequently move into a period of decline, and finally disappear.
2. Strategic objectives and marketing strategy should match the market growth rate changes so as to take advantage of the challenges and opportunities as the product goes through the different stages.
3. For most mass-produced products, costs of production are closely linked to experience (volume). Hence for most types of products, the unit cost goes down as volume increases.
4. Expenditures—investment in plant and equipment and marketing expenses—are directly related to rate of growth. Consequently, products in growth markets will use more resources than products in mature markets.
5. Margins and the cash generated are positively related to share of market. Products with a high relative share of their market will be more profitable than products with low shares.
6. When the maturity stage is reached, products with a high market share generate a stream of cash greater than that needed to support them in the market. This cash is available for investment in other products or in research and development to create new products.

Building on these assumptions, Barksdale and Harris also highlight the additional issues that arise out of pioneering new products, which they label *infants*, and products in declining markets, which they label as either *war-horses* (high-share products in declining markets) or *dodos* (low-share products in declining markets). The result is a combined PLC/product portfolio model as shown in Fig. 4.13.

This approach is based on the notions that both the initial and the decline stages of the life cycle are important; more specifically, it recognizes that product innovations as well as products with negative growth rates are important and should not be ignored in strategic analysis. The result is an expanded (2 × 4) portfolio matrix, as shown in Fig. 4.14. The eight-cell matrix is composed of the usual four BCG categories plus the following new categories:

1. *'War-horses'* When a market begins to exhibit negative growth, 'cash cows' become 'war-horses'. These products still have a high market share and hence can still be substantial cash generators. This transition might require reduced marketing expenditure, or it may take the form of selective withdrawal from market segments or the elimination of certain models.
2. *'Dodos'* These are products that have low shares of declining markets with little opportunity for growth or cash generation. The appropriate strategy is to remove them from the portfolio, but if competitors have already removed themselves from the market it may still be profitable to remain. Timing is thus critical.
3. *'Infants'* These are pioneering products that possess a high degree of risk. They do not immediately earn profits, and they consume substantial cash resources. The length of the innovative period can vary from a short time with consumer packaged goods to an extended period with a product that is innovative enough to require a shift in buying habits.

Criticisms and limitations Barksdale and Harris, the developers of the matrix, claim that it is more

Figure 4.13 Combined PLC/product portfolio concepts

Source: H. C. Barksdale and C. E. Harris, Jnr, 'Portfolio analysis and the product life cycle', *Journal of Long Range Planning*, **15**(6), 1982

comprehensive. Regardless of the level of analysis—corporate, business division or product/market categories—they suggest that the expanded model provides an improved system for classifying and analysing the full range of market situations. Classification of products according to this expanded model is meant to reveal the relative competitive position of products, to indicate the rate of market growth, and to enable the configuration of strategic alternatives in a general sense if not in specific terms.

The key here is that it is only 'general'. Barksdale and Harris admit that the new matrix does not eliminate the problems involved in defining, say, products and markets, or rates of growth. As with the other strategic planning tools, the benefits a company can achieve are only as good as the inputs upon which they are based.

It is claimed, however, that the matrix does provide an improved framework that identifies the cash flow potential and the investment opportunity for every product offered by an organization. In addition, it helps to conceptualize the strategic alternatives of all product/market categories of an organization.

The Strategic Planning Institute's PIMS databank In the early 1970s the Marketing Science Institute and the Harvard Business School established a joint study to investigate the relationship between management strategies and company profitability. Usually referred to as the PIMS project (Profit Impact of Management Strategies), the study looked at the return on investment (ROI) of a large sample of American and European businesses and compared this with information on the various strategies these businesses were using.

The essence of PIMS is the use of empirical evidence to establish which strategies are associated with higher levels of profitability in an industry and thereby to advise managers in these industries towards better (more profitable) courses of action.

RELATIVE MARKET SHARE

Figure 4.14   Product life cycle portfolio matrix

Some of the basic questions that PIMS seeks to answer include:

—What is the typical profit rate for each type of business?
—Given current strategies in a company, what are future operating results likely to be?
—What strategies are likely to help improve future operating results?

In order to obtain this information for a particular company, the company must subscribe to the PIMS project and provide detailed information, including, for example:

—Competitors and market information
—Balance sheet information
—Assumptions about future sales, costs, strategies, etc.

This information is then compared with the PIMS database and a series of reports prepared for the subscribing company as follows:

1. A 'Par' report—showing the ROI and cash flows that are 'normal' for this type of business given its market, competition, technology and cost structure. Also included is an analysis of strengths and weaknesses that are regarded as explaining high or low par figures compared with other businesses in the database.
2. A 'Strategy Analysis' report, which computes the predicted consequences of each of several alternative strategic actions, judged by information on similar businesses making similar moves, from a similar starting-point and in a similar business environment.

3. A 'Report on Look-Alikes' (ROLA), which examines possible tactics for achieving strategic objectives, such as an increase in market share, by analysing strategically similar businesses more closely.
4. An 'Optimus Strategy' report, which is aimed at predicting the best combination of strategies for that particular company, again based on the experiences of other businesses in 'similar' circumstances.

The advantages of PIMS to the individual businesses are obvious. Not only can the management of that business assess the likely outcome of its proposed strategies, but it can also identify those strategies that would yield the highest return on investment.

If this is the case, then one is bound to ask, why doesn't every company subscribe to PIMS for its strategic planning? There are a number of reasons why not every company can, or will, subscribe. First of all, there is the question of cost. The full range of PIMS services is expensive and not every company can afford them. Second, the amount of data required to be supplied by a company for a PIMS analysis is extensive. Again, this can be not only a costly process but also a time consuming one. Finally, and perhaps most important of all, there are limitations to PIMS itself. For example:

—PIMS data are historical and may be misleading in conditions of rapid change.
—The underlying assumptions of the PIMS model are not clarified and therefore must be taken on trust.
—The statistical basis of PIMS can give rise to problems of interpretation and understanding.

In short, then, PIMS is not a panacea for strategic decision-making in the individual company and is best used as another aid to managerial judgement. In this respect, some of the general findings of PIMS are useful and are much less expensive than an actual subscription.

In general terms, analysis of the PIMS database has shown that some 37 variables together account for almost 80 per cent of the variations in return on investment. These, therefore, are the key factors that most strategic company planners will need to consider in their decision-making. Fortunately, however, the analysis has also shown that, of those 37 variables, some are more significant than others. The key ones appear to be:

—Market share
—Investment intensity
—Market growth
—Life cycle stage
—Marketing expense–sales ratio

For example, PIMS indicates that on average a difference in 10 per cent on market share is accompanied by a difference of about 5 per cent in pre-tax return on investment. Similarly, a low or medium market growth rate combined with low investment intensity gives rise to high positive net cost flow and increased returns on investment.

In conclusion, we can see that the PIMS study offers managers access to one of the most comprehensive empirically based strategic planning tools. The full information, and therefore advantages, of PIMS are available only to a company that subscribes to the PIMS database and is therefore prepared and able to bear the potentially high costs and time commitment involved. However, even for the non-subscribing company, the general and published findings of PIMS regarding key determinants of return on investment have proved to be a useful guide to strategic marketing planning decisions.

Criticisms and limitations Although PIMS is useful, there is some criticism. The findings are given as conclusions from empirical research, but many of them are self-evident. O'Shaughnessy[14] has suggested that 'the findings cannot distinguish between causal factors and factors in a state of mere co-existence'. He goes on to say: 'Without supporting explanations and appropriate tests, the findings can be misleading in tempting management to deal with symptoms rather than causes.'

Day[15] to some extent agrees with O'Shaughnessy when he states three basic limitations of PIMS:

1. *Interpreting and utilizing PIMS findings* PIMS has been used to predict profitability; this should not be so because the model does not tell us about causality.
2. *Specification problems* These concern whether the regression models have omitted any important variables and have been properly structured.
3. *Measurement error* This happens because of eliminating outliers, standardized inputs, etc.

Abell and Hammond[16] suggest that PIMS does not enable the user to assess the impact of future changes in the market (except for sales, prices and costs) on business strategy. The strategic changes that can be investigated are restricted to modifications of current strategy. PIMS is most useful in assessing the viability of current strategies in the current environment and in suggesting ways to improve it. In this respect, it falls short of some of the other portfolio techniques, such as the GE matrix, which does at least provide the user with a qualitative way to consider the future.

STRATEGIC PLANNING TECHNIQUES: PROBLEMS AND LIMITATIONS

In summarizing strategy selection techniques, we can state that they are becoming increasingly popular and widespread in use. There is little doubt that they do represent a substantial step forward in management aids to strategic decision-making. Having said this, great care must be exercised in the selection and use of the techniques, with particular attention being paid to assumptions, evidence and so on. Above all, the techniques represent a supplement to managerial judgement not a replacement for it.

Overall, it must be recognized that corporate planning is as much judgemental as scientific in nature. Further, it should be noted that the *outcome* of corporate planning—corporate objectives and strategies—provides the framework for functional objectives and strategies, including marketing. We shall examine the nature of marketing planning itself in some detail in Chapter 13. In the remainder of this chapter we shall consider the relationship between marketing and corporate planning and, in particular, the important *input* that marketing is required to make to this process. The chapter concludes with a look at the range of marketing tools available for the achievement of corporate objectives.

THE ROLE OF MARKETING IN CORPORATE STRATEGIC PLANNING

A considerable degree of confusion and controversy surrounds the precise nature of the relationship between marketing and corporate strategic planning. At one extreme, there is a view that marketing and corporate planning are synonymous. If, as has been suggested in this text, a company stands or falls on its ability to satisfy customer needs, then planning on the basis of these needs becomes the focus of all company planning: marketing and corporate planning are one.

On the other hand, there is a view that marketing's role in corporate planning is no different from that of other functional areas in a business. Viewed in this way marketing becomes more of a passive recipient of plans and strategies determined at a higher level in the company. These, in turn, become the framework within which marketing activity takes place.

The view taken here is somewhere between these two extremes. There is no doubt that functional plans—including those for marketing—are part of a hierarchy of plans; a hierarchy that is led by corporate strategic planning. This is illustrated in Fig. 4.15.

Nevertheless, markets, customers and competitors are so important to the development of overall corporate plans that marketing must play a key role in their development. Because of this, marketing should contribute to the process of corporate planning and in particular to the SWOT analysis stage, and the selection of appropriate corporate strategies. Among the most important of these contributions by the marketing function would be, for example:

—Information on *past performance*: sales and market share analysis; product life cycle analysis, profit analysis; etc.
—Information on *current market position*: competition analysis; major market segments; product portfolio analysis; customer satisfaction; etc.
—Information on likely *future trends/changes*: sales and market forecasts, new competition, factors affecting likely future patterns of demand; etc.

In this way, marketing and corporate strategic planning interact to produce a clear set of guidelines for overall company and marketing activities. The tools available to a company for the achievement of company objectives, however, are very much marketing-based. Collectively, these tools are normally referred to as *the marketing mix*.

The marketing mix

We have seen, both earlier in this chapter and in Chapter 2, that a company is affected by, and therefore must take account of, factors that are environmental and hence outside its control. In order to accommodate these factors, the company must use those elements over which it does have control. The most important of these elements are those that comprise a company's *marketing mix*.

The term 'marketing mix' is attributed to Neil H. Borden[17] and refers to the set of marketing ingredients a company can use to achieve its objectives. In the same way as a cook can select from a wide range of ingredients and combine them in different amounts to bake a successful cake, so too the marketer is at liberty to pick and choose from an extensive set of marketing components in

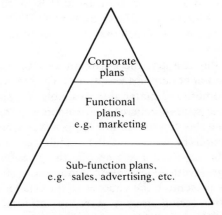

Figure 4.15 The planning hierarchy

order to find the right combination. Because of this, it has become conventional to refer to the main elements of the marketing mix as the 'four Ps':

—*Product*
—*Price*
—*Promotion*
—*Place*

As we shall see in later chapters, Borden's four Ps can usefully be extended to seven Ps for the marketing of services, but for the time being we shall restrict the discussion to a brief outline of the conventional elements of the marketing mix. Within each of these four broad categories of marketing decision variables are innumerable subdivisions, for example:

1. Product
   —Product range: breadth, depth, and mix
   —Product features
   —Product quality
   —Packaging
2. Price
   —Price levels
   —Price discounts
   —Credit policy
   —Price strategies
3. Promotion
   —Advertising: spend, copy content, media selection and scheduling
   —Sales promotion
   —Publicity
   —Personal selling
4. Place
   —Channels of distribution
   —Stock levels
   —Delivery

The marketing manager must combine these various elements of the marketing mix in order to achieve both a competitive advantage in the marketplace and company objectives. Decisions in these elements, over which the company has control, must also accommodate those factors in the company's environment over which it has little or no control. This is illustrated in Fig. 4.16. The importance of marketing mix decisions is such that the whole of Part Three of this text is devoted to examining each element in turn.

As a final corollary to this chapter, the importance of coordination between the various elements in marketing mix cannot be emphasized enough. The breakfast cereal manufacturer must ensure that point-of-sale promotional material is available to support a television advertising campaign and not only that the goods are there for customers to purchase, but that they are *seen* to be there. An example of when this clearly did not happen was when the *Amateur Photographer* magazine linked up with a famous high street retailer to undertake a promotion of 50 pence off the retailer's own brand film. This involved a reference to the promotion on the front cover of the magazine and then a one-page advertisement inside containing a '50 pence off' cut-out voucher to be exchanged for film. Upon presenting the voucher to the retailer's photographic staff towards the beginning of the redemption period, not only were the staff totally unaware of the promotion, but they had no 'own-brand' film in stock!

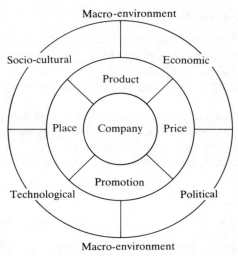

Figure 4.16   The marketing mix and the environment

CONCLUSIONS

This chapter has considered the process of corporate strategic planning from setting objectives to the identification and selection of overall company strategies. Understanding the steps in corporate planning is important, for this sets the framework for functional marketing decision-marking.

The contemporary marketing planner needs the right tools if marketing strategies are to be effectively developed and implemented. Recent years have seen significant developments in analytical concepts and frameworks of marketing analyses and decision-making.

Recent years have also witnessed the growth of a number of frameworks to help the marketer in analysis and planning. The so-called 'portfolio' planning tools range from the simple, but useful, BCG framework based on growth-share to the multi-factor matrices of which the General Electric and Shell directional policy matrices are prime examples. Yet other approaches are based on the notions of industry/market evolution and competitive position.

We have also seen the emergence of empirically based comprehensive planning tools, of which PIMS is perhaps the best known. These are aimed at helping the strategic planner delineate and select between alternative strategies for achieving the highest return on investment.

We should remember that the tools selected and discussed in this chapter represent only some of the planning tools now available to the strategic marketer. Also, none of these tools was designed or is able to replace management judgement; nor should they.

Each of the approaches and tools discussed in this chapter has its own advantages and limitations. Ideally, the various planning tools are best used in combination when developing marketing plans and strategies.

Finally, we have introduced the notion of marketing variables through which a company hopes to achieve its objectives—the marketing mix. In the next chapter we shall examine how a company can provide a clearer focus for its marketing mix decision-making through effective segmentation and targeting.

APPLICATION QUESTIONS

1. What factors should a company consider in strategy formulation and selection?
2. Outline the role of objectives in company planning. What characteristics should such objectives possess if they are to fulfil those roles?
3. Why is it important to consider strengths and weaknessess and opportunities and threats together?
4. 'Portfolio and other strategic planning tools are an aid to rather than a substitute for managerial judgement.' Assess this statement, outlining the uses and limitations of the various strategic planning tools with which you are familiar.
5. What is the relationship between corporate planning and marketing?

REFERENCES

1. H. Henry, 'Corporate strategy, marketing and diversification', in *Perspectives on Management Marketing and Research*, Crosby Lockwood, London, 1971.
2. D. Abell, *Defining the Business: The Starting Point of Strategic Planning*, Prentice-Hall, Englewood Cliffs, NJ, 1980.
3. T. Levitt, 'Marketing myopia', *Harvard Business Review*, July–August 1960.
4. J. Argenti, *Systematic Corporate Planning*, John Wiley, Chichester, 1979.
5. R. L. Ackoff, *A Concept of Corporate Planning*, Wiley-Interscience, New York, 1970.
6. I. H. Ansoff, 'Strategies for diversification', *Harvard Business Review*, September–October 1957.
7. G. E. Greenley, *The Strategic and Operational Planning of Marketing*, McGraw-Hill, London, 1986.
8. P. M. Chisnall, *Strategic Industrial Marketing*, Prentice-Hall, Englewood Cliffs, NJ, 1985.
9. G. S. Day, *Analysis for Strategic Market Decisions*. West Publishing Co., St Paul, MN, 1986.
10. M. E. Porter, *Competitive Advantage: Creating and Sustaining Superior Performance*. Free Press, New York, 1985.
11. Concepts of market/industry evolution are contained in a series of booklets published by A. D. Little Inc., New York.
12. Shell Chemicals UK, 'The Directional Policy Matrix: A New Aid to Corporate Planning', November 1975.
13. H. C. Barksdale and C. E. Harris Jnr, 'Portfolio analysis and the product life cycle', *Long Range Planning*, **15** (6), 1982.
14. J. O'Shaughnessy, *Competitive Marketing: A Strategic Approach*, 2nd edn, Unwin Hyman, London, 1988, p. 44.
15. G. Day, 'Analytical approaches to strategic market planning', *Review of Marketing*, 1981, pp. 89–95.
16. D. F. Abell and J. S. Hammond, *Strategic Marketing Planning*, Prentice-Hall, Englewood Cliffs, NJ, 1979, pp. 112–13.
17. N. H. Borden, 'The concept of the marketing mix', in *Science in Marketing*, G. Schwartz (ed.), John Wiley, New York, 1965.

TWO

INFORMATION FOR MARKETING DECISIONS

MARKETING INFORMATION SYSTEMS AND RESEARCH

INTRODUCTION

We have examined the place of marketing in business and society, its relationship with customers and how the company can better serve the marketplace through strategic planning. Such planning involves examining this marketplace through techniques of marketing research and sales forecasting, which is the focus of this part of the text. This chapter specifically gives an overview of marketing research—its nature, its role and its limitations—followed by some practical discussion of specific techniques. For a more comprehensive and professional treatment of marketing research, the reader is directed to the work of Chisnall.[1]

Information is required to identify marketing problems and opportunities; it is also required to assist with the formation of an organization's response to problems and opportunities that have been identified. The function of marketing research, therefore, is to generate information that will assist marketers in making decisions. There are two sources of marketing research data: primary (collection of new data) and secondary (data previously collected, or data that are already there), which is the focus of a later part of this chapter.

TYPES OF MARKETING RESEARCH

Marketing research can contribute to the decision-making process in all aspects of marketing activity. The major types of marketing research that are conducted can be described as follows:

1. Market research and sales research cover:
   (a) Estimates of market size of both developed and new markets
   (b) Identification of market characteristics and segments
   (c) Identification of market trends
   (d) Sales forecasting (although this is sometimes considered to be a separate activity)
   (e) Obtaining information on customers and potential customers
   (f) Obtaining information on competitors
2. Product research covers:
   (a) The generation of new product ideas
   (b) Product concept testing
   (c) Product testing

    (d) Test marketing of products

    (e) Investigations into different types of packaging (sometimes called packaging research or package testing).

3. Pricing research is concerned with:

    The identification of the relationship between a product or service's price and demand

4. Marketing communications research covers:

    (a) Research into the effectiveness of marketing communications (sometimes called advertising research, but it is felt that that term is a rather restrictive definition)

    (b) Media selection research

    (c) Copy testing

    (d) Sales territory planning

5. Distribution research covers:

    (a) Warehouse location research

    (b) Retail outlet location research

This listing demonstrates that the term 'marketing research' implies a broader sphere of activity than 'market research'. The term 'market research' could be interpreted not to include key marketing research activities such as the generation of new product ideas and pricing investigations and tends to be restricted to research that merely looks into the marketplace itself.

THE MARKET RESEARCH SOCIETY (MRS)

The Market Research Society is the major professional body for marketing researchers in the United Kingdom. It was founded in 1947 and by 1985 had over 4500 members. Its name is perhaps peculiar in view of the fact that it has already been established that market research is part of marketing research. This is probably because in 1947 it was set up simply as a body of market researchers, and it is since then that its remit has widened to embrace the broader aspects of marketing research. Among its many activities, the society publishes, in association with the Industrial Marketing Research Association (IMRA), a code of conduct to which its members undertake to adhere.

    The following extract from Part 5.2 of the code is particularly relevant to modern marketing:

No activity should be deliberately, or inadvertently, misrepresented as being market research.

    Specifically, the following activities shall in no way be associated, directly or by implication, with market or social research intervening:

(a) Sales approaches for profit.

(b) The compilation of lists for canvassing.

(c) Attempts to influence opinions *per se*.

(d) Industrial espionage.

(e) Enquiries about private individuals *per se*.

It has already been explained in Part One that the marketing concept uses the customer as the starting-point for planning activities, and this essentially means asking customers questions through the medium of marketing research. Thus, as companies adopt the marketing concept, so more marketing research will be undertaken. At the same time, companies will explore other means of obtaining business in an increasingly competitive environment. Many less scrupulous companies have taken to conduct selling activities under the guise of marketing research with a questionnaire aimed at obtaining the respondent's name and address for future selling approaches. Examples of such companies are double glazing/patio door manufacturers and insurance companies (not, we would hasten to add, from the well-known national names, but from lesser known smaller companies whose salespeople are often working only for commission, whose products and services usually cost more than better-known companies and who often cease to trade after a short period of time). Such activity gives marketing research a bad name (not to mention reputable double glazing and insurance companies) and serves to make respondents wary when they are approached to take part in a consumer survey.

Perhaps with the above mentioned fears in mind, the Market Research Society has recently introduced a scheme whereby marketing researchers have an identification issued with the authority of the MRS. The problem is that members of the public do not generally know what the MRS is, and unscrupulous companies can still issue a letter of introduction or other form of identification pertaining to claim that the 'researcher' is conducting a bona fide survey—and then use the addresses obtained for subsequent sales canvassing.

IN-HOUSE RESEARCH VERSUS OUTSIDE AGENCY RESEARCH

Sometimes a company may choose to conduct a research study by using internal company personnel. On other occasions it may employ an outside marketing research agency. In this 'make or buy' decision, the following criteria should be considered:

1. *Cost* Many companies believe that it is cheaper to use internal personnel. It is, however, important to consider that, while these personnel are conducting research, other aspects of their company employment may be neglected. This is particularly true in the case of salespeople being used for interviewing purposes.
2. *Research expertise* Here one must consider whether or not there is the necessary expertise available internally, particularly when sophisticated research techniques are to be employed in the research project. Similarly, the analysis may call for complicated statistical analysis which might well be outside the scope of internal company personnel. The problem here is that internal personnel, who are not specialist marketing researchers, may not be aware of the existence of such sophisticated techniques in the first place.
3. *Product or service knowledge* Research requiring an in-depth technical knowledge might be more suited to an 'in-house' team, because it would be time-consuming (and expensive) to impart such information to a team of outside researchers.
4. *Objectivity* Here, outside agencies are more likely to be objective because an 'in-house' team will perhaps be too familiar with the subject under discussion, and may come to conclusions largely based upon their own prejudices and preconceptions.
5. *Special equipment* Depending upon the nature of the inquiry, it may be that the research calls for specialist computer programs or specialist test equipment, which may not warrant the expenditure by an 'in-house' team for, say, an *ad hoc* (one-off) study.
6. *Confidentiality* Although it has already been mentioned that the code of the MRS places importance upon the confidentiality of completed results, it is, nevertheless, a risk to impart confidential information about, say, new products and processes to individuals from outside the company unless it can be ensured that security can be assured. For this reason, some large retailers (e.g., Marks & Spencer, Boots and Sainsbury's) tend not to use outside marketing research agencies.

In order that a company can obtain the benefits of the optimum use of resources, it is often the case that some parts of a marketing research project are handled internally and other parts are contracted out to external agencies.

MARKETING RESEARCH MANAGER

Desk research executive — Field research executive

| Data collection | Records and statistics | Data tabulation | Outside supervisors | Training officer for part-time researchers |

Figure 5.1 Typical organization of a marketing research department

Responsibility for marketing research

Sound organization is as essential to effective marketing research as to any other area of business activity.

Companies vary a great deal, not only in size but in their own internal organization, and it is difficult to lay down a general rule as to who should be responsible for the market research operation. In practice, it varies from company to company, depending on size and resources. Here we can simply give an idea of the various alternatives available and the circumstances in which each is likely to be used. There are four generally accepted sources:

—The company's own research department.
—Outside research organizations.
—Advertising agencies with marketing research departments.
—The sales manager and the salespeople.

Each is now looked at in more detail.

Company's own research department There is no doubt that this is the ideal solution if it can be afforded, but a well organized marketing research department with a qualified manager and a trained staff is costly. It is, therefore, found only among large companies, and particularly those that are selling consumer products. Most organizations commission their market research from a market research agency.

The difficulty in laying down general principles regarding the size of a marketing research department is that each firm has different ideas about the division of responsibilities between sales, marketing and market research. In practice, the marketing department is different in each company, and so is its marketing research activity. Nevertheless, if we imagine a sizeable company of importance in the consumer products field, its marketing research department would probably be organized something like that shown in Fig. 5.1.

Generally, the marketing research manager will be responsible to the marketing director of the company, and he or she must work closely, not only with the rest of the marketing department, but also with the sales department, which, because of its specialized knowledge of the company's products, of competitors, and above all of customers, can give a great deal of invaluable information to the marketing research department.

The success or failure of the marketing research department will depend mostly on its manager. In a company, many people view with distrust a newly established marketing research department because they believe it will destroy many of the myths and prejudices that exist; but if the department has a good manager, who is tactful and shows the benefits that can be reaped from marketing research, its acceptance will be much quicker.

A good market research manager should:

—Be a good organizer.

—Be a good administrator, able to control staff.

—Have a critical mind.

—Know all aspects of marketing thoroughly.

—Be able to get on with other managers in the company.

—Have a sound knowledge of the company's products and their manufacture, and of the industry as a whole.

—Above all, be honest, in that he or she reports what has been found and does not tell the management what it wants to hear.

The advantages of an in-house research department are that it is more convenient, more speedy and more specialized than an outside agency; the work of the department can be organized according to the firm's requirements, while that done by an outside body has to be fitted in with work for other clients. Furthermore, a firm's own department is bound to have a deeper knowledge of its own products than an outside agency, and research can be more confidential if handled within the firm. Agencies should treat their clients' work as confidential, but 'leaks' can occur more easily.

Disadvantages are that there is always the danger of bias in favour of one's own products. A marketing research agency which handles a wide range of clients and products is bound to have a broader knowledge of techniques than the staff of a company's own research department, whose experience is probably more limited.

Outside research organizations Some firms are too small to justify a research department of their own, so they naturally turn to a specialist research firm if they require some specific research to be carried out. A team of specially trained people, using modern methods, with a great deal of practical experience and a completely impartial view, will produce a report for them.

The drawback is that, however well briefed they may be, such an organization will lack a depth of knowledge of the product unless it works closely and regularly with the client. Furthermore, while continuous research over a long period can be carried out with one's own staff, it is too costly to use an outside organization, which is mainly used for 'one-off' investigations.

There are often cases where a firm that has its own research department uses an outside organization as well—for instance, when a particularly large investigation is needed which requires more staff than the company has at its disposal, or when the information is needed quickly and the staff is not large enough to cope with it.

Very often, outside research organizations are used for overseas research, perhaps because of language difficulties, but also because a local agency will have a much better knowledge of the market and of its problems and can do the survey much more quickly.

Advertising agencies with market research departments Most of the large advertising agencies have their own marketing research facilities, in the form of either a separate department or an associate or subsidiary company. Therefore, much of what has just been said about specialist organizations applies here.

Agencies generally have a very sound all-round marketing background, but there is a danger that the staff doing the actual research work may be drawn from people who originated in the advertising or publicity world, and whose tendency may be more to influence people than to study their reactions impartially. This is a difficult point, and it can be overcome by enquiring first as to how closely the marketing research section works together with the advertising one. Each case will have to be judged on its merits.

Sales manager and salespeople In many smaller companies, marketing research is carried out by the sales manager and staff. This is relatively expensive and easily organized. The salesforce is in constant touch with customers, so what could be easier than to ask a few questions about sales policy, packaging, and the product itself? Indeed, there is a lot to be said for this method if resources are scarce—and provided one realizes the inherent limitations.

The weakness of this method lies in the fact that sales staff cannot be impartial. If they are good salespeople, they must be enthusiastic about the product they sell, and convinced that it is the best value for money. They will, therefore, lack the critical approach that is needed for research. So the use of salespeople for this type of work will depend on the type of research that is being carried out. If one is trying to assess the respective values of one's products against competitors', it is unlikely that sales staff will produce the really impartial information that is needed, but what they do come up with will be better than no information at all.

If such research attempts to find neutral information, such as whether dealers handle one or several brands, and if so which ones; whether they put their products on shelves or hang them on pegboards; what types of customer they supply; and what the response has been to the latest coupon offer, then this can perfectly well be obtained by the salesforce working in conjunction with marketing research staff, who will have prepared the questions in the first place.

THE RESEARCH PROCESS

Research should be conducted only when it is expected that the value of information to be obtained will be greater than the cost of obtaining it. Calculating the cost of a research project is a relatively simple matter and merely involves a calculation of interviewer time, equipment used, data processing, etc. The difficulty arises in determining the value of the information that will be obtained as a result of the research, and this involves the following considerations:

—The relative profitability of the alternative decisions.
—The likely contribution the information will make to effective decision making.

When it is decided that research value will be likely to exceed the cost of research, the research process can begin. This process usually consists of a series of nine steps, the first five of which are research design phases:

1. Definition of the marketing problem to be solved, together with a specification of the research objectives.
2. Selection of data collection method(s) to be used. In marketing research there are two basic data collection methods: secondary research and primary research. Secondary data are collected mainly for background purposes and not necessarily to solve the specific problem under consideration; primary data are collected to solve the specific problem at hand. Primary data collection techniques cover: survey research, depth interviews, observational research and experimentation.
3. Selection of sampling method to be used. In some circumstances this may not be appropriate; for instance, when the universe is small, it may be decided to conduct a census.
4. Development of an analysis plan. This step specifically involves specifying the data that will be reported together with the selection of the statistical procedures that will be employed in analysing the results.
5. Estimation of the time and resources required to complete the research.

6. Obtaining approval of the research design outlined in steps 1–5 from the individual(s) requesting the research.
7. Data collection.
8. Data analysis.
9. Research reporting.

LIMITATIONS OF MARKETING RESEARCH

While it is virtually impossible to remove all sources of error in such a behaviourally based field as marketing research, it is the aim of research design to minimize the probable occurrence of the following types of error:

1. *Sampling errors* These are errors in the specification of the target population and errors caused by the selection of a non-representative sample.
2. *Non-response errors* These include a failure to contact all members of a sample and failure by such members to respond to the survey.
3. *Data collection errors* These include occasions where respondents provide answers to please, impress or irritate the interviewer. For instance, in responding to a question (especially open-ended questions where the respondent in encouraged to give a response that is not a pre-determined one from a list of alternatives) a respondent may be unable to articulate a response accurately. Data collection errors may also be caused by leading questions, and here it is the fault of the questionnaire designer, in that the way the question is worded may lead the respondent to give a certain answer (e.g., the question 'Do you believe that children should have a good breakfast?' is almost bound to produce a positive response). Similarly, interviewers may also produce such biases by the way they read out such questions to respondents with, say, a positive or negative bias in the tone of the voice. Simple clerical errors can also be included under this category, where interviewers may record incorrect response information due to misinterpretation or carelessness in recording answers. There will, of course, be a minority of anarchical individuals among respondents who will deliberately set out to give incorrect responses. Such problems, together with the possible problem of interviewer dishonesty, can sometimes be detected statistically, wherein such answers will deviate from the 'norm' of answers, or through the use of 'check' questions, wherein a question is asked to check upon the validity of a question asked earlier, and where there is a disparity then the questionnaire may be regarded as being 'suspect'.
4. *Analytical and reporting errors*
5. *Experimental errors* Experiments are designed to measure the impact of one variable (e.g. advertising) on another (e.g. sales). Experimental error may arise if uncontrollable events occur during the experiment (e.g. if a competitor launches a new product during a test period—which is quite often done deliberately, to confuse the results!).

Before a company embarks upon an expensive primary data collection exercise, it makes sense to use information already in existence. Such data are termed secondary data and are the subject of the next section.

SECONDARY RESEARCH

The major sources of secondary data are as follows:

1. *Internal sources* These data are generated by the organization itself and include: accounting

records, salesforce reports, reports from previous marketing research studies, and customer complaints records.
2. *External sources* These data are generated by sources outside the organization including data produced by the government and publishers of directories, newspapers, periodicals and research reports.

Published data of particular interest to marketers may be grouped into social and industrial statistics, company information, media information (including miscellaneous information from newspapers and periodicals) and market reports. The following listing is a sample selection of major publications relating to the UK market, and they cover what are commonly termed 'social and industrial statistics'. A fuller listing is given in Chisnall's text.[2]

—*Business monitors* The object of individual business monitors is to bring together the most up-to-date official statistical information covering production, imports and exports relating to a particular industry.

(a) The *Production Series* covers such items such as: food, drink and tobacco; coal and petroleum products; chemical and allied industries; metal manufacture; engineering; textiles; clothing and footwear; printing and publishing; timber; furniture; pottery; glass; cement.

(b) The *Service and Distribution Series* covers: food shops; clothing and footwear shops; durable goods shops; catering trades; finance houses.

(c) The *Miscellaneous Series* covers motor vehicle registrations; cinema; insurance companies; overseas travel and tourism; acquisitions and mergers; company finance.

—*Census of Population* This is taken every ten years during the year that ends with the digit 1, with a 10 per cent sample being taken during every year that ends with a 6. It collects information on numbers in the population, including age, sex, marital status, socio-economic class, country of birth and economic activity.

The Economic Activity Tables contain statistics of the working population based on their personal occupations and the employed population classified into branches of industry. Key statistics, covering age, distribution, socio-economic status, housing conditions, housing tenure, car ownership and many others, are available for each of the 106 000 enumeration districts (i.e. precisely mapped areas containing approximately 150 households each and based on wards and parishes).

These statistics have been extensively used in the past by marketing organizations in order to evaluate potential markets and form the basis of ACORN groupings (*A Classification of Residential Neighbourhoods*).[7]

—*Family Expenditure Survey* This annual publication provides an analysis of total household income and expenditure. The analysis is based upon a postal survey of 10 500 households.

—*Overseas Trade Statistics of the UK* This provides monthly and annual import and export statistics by commodity and by country, by both volume and value.

—*Regional Trends* This is an annual publication which gives details of regional trends in the UK. Subjects covered in the statistics include current and projected population, housing, health, law enforcement, education, employment, personal income and expenditure, production and investment.

—*Census of Distribution* Although it is called a census, this series samples various retail outlets, e.g. grocers, confectioners, tobacconists, newsagents, clothing and footwear shops, furniture and electrical goods shops. It provides information on numbers, sizes, type and turnover of shops.

—*Census of Production* This series samples establishments engaged in: manufacturing; mining and quarrying; electricity; gas and water supply. It provides information on employment, wages and salaries, stocks, capital expenditure, purchases of materials and fuel, sales and work done.

—*Employment Gazette* The Department of Employment Gazette, published monthly, contains an analysis of employees in employment, employees by industrial groups, unemployment, changes of rates of wages and hours of work, and retail prices.

—*Economic Trends* This is published monthly and contains information on the value of: imports and exports, volume of retail sales, index of production, new car registrations, retail prices, gross domestic product, personal disposable income, saving and borrowing, consumer expenditure, investment, relationship of stocks and output, changes in stocks.

—*Monthly Digest of Statistics* and *Annual Abstract of Statistics* These publications are very popular and are quite often a good starting-point for a marketing researcher, before going on to the more specialist statistical publications. Statistics are provided on such matters as population trends, employment statistics, manufactured goods, external trade and shipping. As the titles suggest, these are general publications, and as such they are more useful for background information.

—*Family Expenditure Survey* This is an annual publication based upon a continuous sample survey of approximately 7000 private households on a personal interview basis. It includes data on housing, employment, education and health.

In addition to government statistics, statistics are also produced by trade associations which reflect their members' interests. It is not the purpose of this text to produce a list of such publications, because the best course of action for any researcher here is to contact the individual trade association and enquire whether or not the information sought is available. There may, however, be difficulty in obtaining such information if the sponsoring company is not a member of that trade association. There are also a number of independent research report publishers (for example *MINTEL*, published by Market Intelligence). The publication *British Statistics Index* provides a useful guide to such publications.

There are a number of statistical publications that provide information relating to individual companies and groups of companies, the principal ones of which are as follows:

—*Guide to Key British Enterprises* This is produced by Dun and Bradstreet on an annual basis. It is arranged alphabetically by company name and has a product index. The addresses, telephone numbers and names of directors are given, together with brief details of company activities, ownership of the company and its approximate turnover and its number of employees. Approximately 20 000 companies are included in this publication.

—*Kompass (UK)* is published annually by Kompass Directories. It is arranged in two volumes, the first of which is arranged geographically, alphabetically and by county, town and name of company. An alphabetical index by company name is also provided. The second volume is arranged by Standard Industrial Classification coding and by company, and this volume is probably of more use to purchasers wishing to obtain details of companies manufacturing certain types of products. The guide also gives brief details of company turnover, number of employees and names of directors.

There are also a large number of trade directories for specific industries, e.g. *The Food Trades Directory* (published by Newman Publications), which lists producers, retailers and all other potential outlets for food products. A full list of specialist trade directories is provided in *Current British Directories*. There are a number of other general directories, which, although not as ambitious as those mentioned, are useful and easy to use, e.g. Kelly's, Sell's, Stubbs' and Ryland's.

—*The Times 1000* is published annually by Times Books Ltd and it contains listings of the top 1000 UK companies by turnover plus 500 European top companies, 100 top American companies and 50 top Japanese companies.
—*Who Owns Whom (UK)* is published annually by Dun and Bradstreet and gives details of parent companies, associate companies and subsidiary companies.
—*Extel cards* provide details of company financial results and chairmen's statements.
—*Datastream*, produced by Datastream International, is a computerized database of company financial results available 'on line'.
—*Prestel* This information can be seen on a domestic television set fitted with a Prestel adaptor. Information is available 24 hours a day and it is continually updated. It works like teletext and gives such information as: stock exchange prices, commodity prices from the international commodity exchanges, advice to importers and exporters, etc.

Information can also be obtained directly from companies themselves. Such information can include the annual report and product literature. Information of interest to marketers is not limited to information on industrial and social statistics and company performance. Newspapers and periodicals contain a vast amount of potentially useful marketing information. For example, stories about mergers, announcements of new products, new personnel appointments and the opening of new premises can be useful for general background market intelligence.

To assist in the location of relevant news items, there are several indexes of newspaper and periodical articles:

—*Research Index* This is a fortnightly publication and indexes are available for the *Financial Times, The Economist, Investor's Chronicle, Marketing Week* and *Marketing*, among 120 or so other important publications. Each issue of *Research Index* is divided into two sections: the pink pages contain the industry index and the blue pages the company index. The industry section cumulates on a six-monthly basis.
—*McCarthy Information Services* This publication is useful, for example, when the researcher has identified something of interest from the *Research Index*. This information service will then provide fuller details which the client requires. Such data are reprinted on cards and indexed by company and market.
—*Worldcasts* is published by Predicasts eight times a year and summarizes over 75 000 published projections for products and markets in over 50 countries.
—*Chambers of commerce* Although this is not a publication, these establishments can sometimes be fruitful sources of information. Many large towns and conurbations have their own chambers of commerce. Some have useful libraries which contain reports on countries and area of the world, to which export missions may have been sponsored by that particular chamber of commerce. They mainly contain useful local commercial information relating to the area which they serve.
—*Market reports*. From the number of secondary sources already mentioned (and this is by no means the full listing) the reader will begin to appreciate the volume of work that secondary research can cover. Various research agencies have recognized that companies often require similar collections of published data. Such agencies undertake to collect, analyse and then sell published reports to interested companies. In essence, they perform desk research and distil whatever information is available into a concise report. Such published reports are indexed in a publication called *Marketing Surveys Index* which is a monthly publication published in association with the Institute of Marketing.

Table 5.1 Relative effectiveness of different research techniques

Criterion	Mail	Telephone	Personal
1. Ability to handle complex questionnaires	Poor	Fair	Excellent
2. Ability to collect large amounts of data	Fair	Fair	Excellent
3. Accuracy on 'sensitive' questions	Good	Good	Fair
4. Control of interviewer effects (e.g., respondent–interviewer interaction; unintentional cues from interviewer)	Excellent	Fair	Poor
5. Speech	Poor	Excellent	Fair
6. Cost	Good (but not low response rate is a problem)	Good	Poor

Most of the publications mentioned are available at major commercial reference libraries; it should be emphasized that there are often surprisingly good commercial sections in modestly sized town libraries. It is always better to investigate these local sources first before visiting one of the major commercial libraries. This is because the larger libraries tend to be more for the professional user, whereas local libraries will contain staff who are more 'in tune' with the needs of 'learners', and will personally show them how to use certain facilities and how to reference the information they require.

PRIMARY RESEARCH

If secondary data do not provide sufficient information to satisfy research objections, primary data must then be collected. In this section primary data collection methods are considered under the following headings:

—Survey research
—Depth interviews
—Observation
—Experimentation

Survey research

This is concerned with the administration of questionnaires, and is the most common method of collecting primary data for marketing decisions. When planning a survey, there are four major issues to be considered:

1. Selection of communication method (i.e., mail, telephone or personal survey)
2. Maximizing response to a survey
3. Questionnaire design
4. Phrasing of questions

Mail, telephone or personal survey The general strengths and weaknesses of these three methods are summarized in Table 5.1. An important criterion not featured in this table is 'probable response rate', which is discussed later.

Postal questionnaires The main attraction of postal questionnaires is their low cost. The cost will vary with the numbers involved—the more questionnaires, the less the cost per unit. When you take the cost of each item, i.e. paper, printing, pre-paid cards on envelopes, testing, recalls, etc., the cost per copy is much higher than might be first thought. Nevertheless, it is still possibly the cheapest method of all. Where an industrial population is geographically dispersed, the postal questionnaire has obvious attractions in time and money. If the sample to be taken is large, the postal questionnaire yields results more quickly than personal interviewing and is almost as quick as telephone interviewing, without the need for such a large staff. There can be no bias because there is no interviewer, and the respondent has the choice of remaining unknown.

There are, however, a number of disadvantages, the chief one of which is that there is no control over the person actually filling in the questionnaire. (An advantage of personal interviewing is that it can be highly structured.) Also, the respondent can read the complete questionnaire before filling it in, thus perhaps prejudicing his or her answers to early questions.

There are not many people who are prepared to sit down and complete a long questionnaire. The more questions one asks, the less response one is likely to obtain. Questions should be kept simple. Complex questions which cannot be explained should not be included. (Contrast this situation with personal interviewing.) Moreover, despite pre-testing and piloting of questions, misinterpretation on the part of the respondent does arise. A further disadvantage is that, whereas the whole essence of personal and telephone interviews is the chance to follow up leads, this is obviously impossible in the case of a postal questionnaire. Finally, non-response is a problem. You may never know why those who did not reply did not. One must also ask whether a high non-response will affect the sample.

There is some evidence to show that questionnaires mailed on Mondays and Tuesdays have a better chance of being completed and returned. When mailing interviews, certain rules should be adhered to:

1. *Personalize* Use the respondent's name. Do not address to 'The Sales Manager' or 'The Marketing Director', etc.
2. *Sponsorship* Use of the sponsor's name helps to promote confidence in the respondent's mind by allaying suspicion.
3. *Reason* State the reason for the request and explain any use that will be made of information supplied.
4. *Anonymity* If people are given the impression that they can remain anonymous, they will be more inclined to reply. This is the case when the respondent does not have to state a name or address.
5. *Confidentiality* The letter and questionnaire often display the word 'confidential' when it comes from a named respondent. However, there is evidence that confidentiality is not strictly necessary as this guarantee seems to have little effect on response.
6. *Premiums* If any premium is enclosed in order to stimulate interest and response, then its inclusion should be explained in the letter.
7. *Additional questionnaires* If you are dealing with business firms, it is often desirable to enclose a second copy so that the firm can file it for its own purpose.
8. *Stamped addressed envelope* This is an absolute necessity.

Telephone interviews When time is short, the telephone is frequently the only medium. The number of calls that can be made in a day will depend upon your luck in finding the respondent in, his or her garrulousness, and on the number of questions you intend to ask.

The cost of a call will obviously vary with the length of time and distance involved. However, research organizations have found that the telephone method costs roughly 25 per cent of the personal method for similar types of survey. Almost all industrial firms are connected to the telephone. Even in the consumer market, the majority of households in the UK now have a telephone. If certain industries are widely scattered, the telephone is the best method of contacting an adequate sample.

The interview can be run on organized, structured lines without upsetting interviewees by showing them a long questionnaire. If a person selected does not turn out to be suitable, you can ask to be transferred to someone who *can* help.

There are, however, a number of disadvantages, including the fact that you cannot readily ask questions over the telephone the answers to which require a search of company records. The questions must be limited to those that can readily be answered without resort to company records or other research. Bias can arise on the part of the interviewer in similar fashion to personal interviewing. It can also be introduced in a quite different way; for example, if the telephone directory is used as a sampling frame, bias can be introduced in selection because a certain percentage of firms will be listed more than once.

Maximizing response Error caused by a difference between those who respond to a survey and those who do not is termed non-response error. Non-response can involve the refusal to answer an entire questionnaire or just a particular question. It is one of the most significant problems faced by a survey researcher. In general, the lower the response rate to a survey, the higher is the probability of non-response error. However, a low response rate does not automatically mean that there have been non-response errors. Non-response error occurs only when a difference between the respondents and the non-respondents leads the researcher to an incorrect conclusion or decision.

In telephone and personal surveys, reply refusal and respondent non-availability are the major factors that reduce response rates. The number of 'not-availables' may usually be reduced by a series of callbacks at varying times. Refusal rates (the percentage of contacted respondents who refuse to participate) for telephone surveys have been found to range from 0 to 50 per cent.[3] Interest in the survey topic is a primary factor in the cooperate–refuse decision. Prior communication with the interviewee by letter also helps to reduce the refusal rate. Attempts to increase the response rate to mail surveys focus on increasing the potential respondents' motivation to reply. As with telephone and personal surveys, the respondent's interest in the subject matter is a key factor. Response rates may usually be increased by offering token incentives to reply and sending reminder letters, which include another copy of the original questionnaire.

Questionnaire design A questionnaire can be used to collect data on the respondent's behaviour (past, present or intended), demographic characteristics (age, sex, income, occupation), level of knowledge, attitudes and opinions. Before a questionnaire can be designed and used, answers are required to the following questions:

—What information is required?
—From whom is it required?
—Which method of communication will be used, i.e., mail, telephone or personal interview?
—Are all the questions really needed?
—Is each question sufficient to generate the required information? (Does the respondent have the information? Can the respondent find or remember the information? Is the respondent able to express his or her answer?)
—Will the respondent answer the question correctly? (Is the answer confidential or potentially embarrassing? Do the words used have the same meaning for all respondents? Are any of the words or phrases put in a leading way?)
—Are the questions in a logical sequence?

When designing a questionnaire the following guidelines should be applied:

—The overall questionnaire should move from topic to topic in a logical manner, with all questions on one topic completed before moving to the next.

—Sensitive questions, such as the respondent's income, should be at the end.

—The first few questions should be simple, objective and interesting.

—The questionnaire should be designed so as to minimize recording errors and assist analysis.

—The questionnaire should be pre-tested with respondents similar to those who will be included in the final survey.

Question phrasing There are three types of question format: direct questions, attitude questions and indirect questions.

Direct questions The direct question format may be subdivided into open and closed questions. Open questions allow the respondent to answer in his own words. Closed questions include all possible answers, and the respondent makes a choice from among them. Closed questions may be dichotomous or multiple-choice. Dichotomous questions allow only two responses; such as 'yes–no', 'agree–disagree' and 'male–female'. The two responses of dichotomous questions are often supplemented by a third neutral category such as 'don't know'. Multiple-choice questions allow three or more responses. To clarify the various types of direct questions, here are some examples:

Open	'Why did you stop travelling by train?'
Closed—dichotomous	'Do you like travelling by train?'
	Yes ☐
	No ☐
Closed—multiple choice	'What is your favourite method of travelling to work?'
	Car ☐
	Bus ☐
	Train ☐
	Walking ☐
	Bicycle ☐
	Other ☐

Open questions have the advantage that the respondent is not influenced by stated response categories. The major disadvantages of open questions are respondents' difficulties in articulating answers; interviewers' difficulties are in recording answers, introduction of bias through probing, and the complexity of categorizing answers.

Closed questions have two main advantages: they are easier for the respondent and interviewer, and they aid questionnaire analysis. Closed questions have two disadvantages: research is required to ensure that a comprehensive range of alternative responses is presented, and considerable skill is required to ensure that the presentation of alternative responses does not sometimes stimulate response bias.

To benefit from the advantages of both open and closed questions, researchers will often use open questions in preliminary research situations. Feedback from this preliminary research is then used to formulate closed questions for a final and more extensive survey.

Attitude questions Consumer attitudes and opinions help to predict their function behaviour, and for this reason collection of this type of data is of vital importance to marketers. Attitude data may be collected using direct or indirect questions. We shall discuss some of direct questioning scales used, of which there are four types, for the direct questioning of attitudes. These scales are the non-comparative rating scale, the comparative rating scale, the semantic differential scale and the Likert scale, which can be most easily explained using examples.

Non-comparative rating scale How would you rate the taste of
Furgekin Lager?

5	4	3	2	1
Probably the best	Very good, I like it	All right, neither good nor bad	Not at all good, I do not like it	Probably the worst

This scale is non-comparative, as the respondent has not been asked to compare one product with another.

Comparative rating scale How do you like the taste of
Furgekin compared to Gazekeg?

5	4	3	2	1
Vastly superior	Superior	Neither superior nor inferior	Inferior	Vastly inferior

Semantic differential scale What are your opinions of the Vega Estate car? Please tick the box that best describes your opinions.

	Extremely	Very	Some-what	Neither nor	Some-what	Very	Extremely	
Fast	☐	☐	☐	☐	☐	☐	☐	Slow
Good	☐	☐	☐	☐	☐	☐	☐	Bad
Large	☐	☐	☐	☐	☐	☐	☐	Small
Inexpensive	☐	☐	☐	☐	☐	☐	☐	Expensive

Likert scale The Vega Anglian is the best small car on the
market. Do you . . .

Strongly agree	Agree	Neither agree nor disagree	Disagree	Strongly disagree
☐	☐	☐	☐	☐

Research has shown that when the various scaling techniques have been compared the results have been similar across all techniques.[4] Therefore, the selection of a scaling technique will depend largely upon the information that is to be collected.

Indirect questions It is not always possible to use direct questioning to obtain information. People may be either unwilling or unable to give answers to questions they consider to be an invasion of their privacy or that are embarrassing. Projective methods are a group of techniques used to obtain information that cannot be obtained through direct questioning. Projective techniques are based on the theory that the description of vague subjects requires interpretation, and this interpretation can only be based on the individual's own background, attitudes and values. The major projective techniques employed are word association, sentence completion, story completion and cartoon techniques.

   Word association requires the respondent to give the first word or thought that comes to mind after the researcher presents a word or phrase. Responses are then grouped into categories of interest to the researcher. The most common use of the word association technique is for the testing of potential brand names.

Sentence completion, as the name implies, requires the respondent to complete a sentence. For example, 'people who smoke are . . . '. In this example the respondent is not required to associate with the answer, and more revealing answers can be obtained than with a direct question such as: 'What kind of people smoke?'

Story completion is an extension of the sentence completion technique. In story completion part of a story is told and the respondent is asked to complete it.

Cartoon techniques present cartoon-type drawings of people in a particular situation. One of the individuals is shown with a sentence in a 'bubble' and one of the others is shown with a blank 'bubble' that the respondent is asked to complete. This technique can show attitudes towards products, purchasing situations, etc., as depicted in the cartoon.

While projective techniques can uncover information not available from direct questioning, their results are difficult to analyse so their use is normally limited to preliminary research.

Piloting the questionnaire Before a questionnaire is ready for final use in the field, it needs to be pre-tested under field conditions. The questionnaire is piloted to discover if there are any problems in the areas we have been discussing. A small number of respondents, representative of the types of respondent to be interviewed in the actual survey, are selected and the questionnaire tried out on them.

The findings of a pilot survey regarding the product will not be included in the final report. These interviews are conducted not to test the product, but to test the efficiency of the questionnaire. The researchers are examining the ease with which the questionnaire elicits the required information:

—Are some of the questions superfluous?
—Should others be added to get a fuller picture?
—Are the questions clear enough to be understood by the public at large?

In the nature of things, it is not practicable to try out the draft questionnaire on a large and elaborately selected sample. Nevertheless, the pilot survey must be undertaken under actual conditions with people representative of those who will finally be interviewed. To try out the questionnaire on members of the Market Research Department, for instance, would give a distorted answer, as the reactions of specialists in this field are likely to be quite different from those of the public at large. Instead, interviewers will go out and put the questions to passers-by in the street, or will call on various households taken at random, with the aim of getting a cross-section of informants approximately similar to that selected for the actual survey.

Panel research A panel refers to a group of respondents who have agreed to provide information over a period of time. In effect, panel research is continuous survey research. Panels are normally operated by research agencies rather than by individual organizations. Two of the most common types of panel operated are retail audits and consumer panels.

Retail audits A retail audit (such as that produced by A. C. Nielsen Company) records sales to consumers through a panel of retail outlets. The estimate of consumer sales is based on observations. It is arrived at as follows:

$$\text{Opening stock for period (checked at last audit)} + \text{Net deliveries since last audit} - \text{Stock held at present audit} = \text{Sales to consumers during period}$$

The information obtained from such an audit is sold to manufacturers, who can see how their brands are performing alongside others. The reports issued to such subscribers are generally along the following lines:

—Retail purchases by brand and by product.
—Retail stocks by brand and by product.
—Consumer sales by brand and by product.
—Percentage of shops handling the product.
—Percentage of shops out of stock of various brands.
—Retail and wholesale prices of various products.
—Average size of retail order from average retailer.
—Proportion of retailers buying direct from manufacturers and from wholesalers.
—Display material, promotions and advertising carried out for individual brands.

The advantages of an audit of retail sales are as follows:

1. It is factual research, based on the actual stock-taking and examination of invoices. It is therefore not distorted by likes, dislikes, prejudices or the wish to please, which is so often the pitfall of interview research.
2. It provides the manufacturer with a continuous picture of a constantly changing market.
3. It shows the manufacturer its position in relation to competitors and to the trade in general.
4. Seasonal variations and other fluctuations in consumer behaviour can be observed, and the effect of such things as price changes, special offers and advertising campaigns can be assessed.
5. The manufacturer can base its selling tactics on a knowledge of the effects of various factors, not only on its own products but also on those of its competitors.

Disadvantages are:

1. A retail audit shows the picture only at those retail outlets that are taking part in the scheme, and their selection is not random. Only some shops wish to cooperate, so important types of outlet can be left out if they are among those unwilling to participate. Retail outlets that generally refuse to cooperate usually sell a high proportion of 'own-label' merchandise, and do not want their success (or otherwise) to become public knowledge.
2. Retail audits are expensive and time-consuming.
3. They tell only part of the story. An audit of retail sales will not reveal the reasons for sales patterns, and there is still a great deal of research to be carried out to ascertain such underlying factors.

Developments in retail technology and audit data   It has already been mentioned that retail audits are carried out by people from the research agency conducting a regular physical audit in a selection of retail outlets. However, new developments in retail technology are starting to have an effect on the way sales data are collected at the retail level. The development of computerized checkout points combined with the bar-coding of products, particularly in the area of packaged grocery, will mean that retail audit companies will be able to assess accurate sales figures from retail outlets via on-line computer terminals from head office, without the necessity of actually visiting the store and carrying out a physical stock-take.

These new developments will not do away entirely with the need for researchers to visit stores, as some of the information can only be recorded through human observation, but it will make the whole retail audit task more efficient and less inconvenient to the stores taking part. Such developments will also reduce the cost of such research to the end-users.

Consumer panels   Consumer panels are typically used to study media exposure and purchasing behaviour. Data are gathered using diaries (data entered by respondents), regular telephone surveys, or instruments (e.g., use of audiometers for monitoring television viewing habits).

A consumer panel consists of a reasonably permanent set of consumers, usually a sample of housewives, selected on a purposive basis to represent accurately a cross-section of housewives in the country.

In the UK, the Attwood Consumer Panel consists of 5000 housewives in Great Britain and 500 housewives in Northern Ireland. Members of the panel are defined by age, ACORN class (dealt with in detail in Chapter 7), social class and district. Each member of the panel is given a diary in which she records information.

The housewife reports the following facts concerning the product in her 'diary':

—Brand name and description.
—Number of items bought.
—Size and weight of each item and price.
—Day of purchase.
—Type of outlet.
—Full description of any 'special offer'.
—Information on flavour of product, type and colour of container, if applicable.

The housewife returns the diary to the market research organization weekly. The market research organization sells reports of this activity to individual manufacturers. The diaries are intended to reveal:

—The performance of brands.
—The total number of people buying specific products.
—Sales volume by type of shop and geographic area.
—The effect of promotions, price changes or competition.
—Consumer purchasing patterns concerning brand switching.

Probably the most important single advantage of the panel design is that it is analytical. The panel involves collecting data from the same individual over time, and from this one can note the specific individuals who change or do not change, e.g. those who switch to different brands and those who are loyal to a specific brand. From this, one can determine the kind of person who changes brands and the kind who does not change. This can suggest the segment of the population on which promotion effort can most successfully be concentrated. The timing of such changes may help in the formulation of hypotheses as to the reasons for the change.

As panels are maintained over a period of time, it enables one to introduce new products, change advertising strategy, alter the price, etc., and observe any change in behaviour and purchasing patterns on the part of the panel members. In other words, what alterations in the marketing mix can one make in order to increase sales?

Much more detailed data can be gathered about panel members than would be the case for a one-off sample of respondents. Panel members often submit to long interviews, at the end of which the research organization will have collected a large volume of classification data. Furthermore, as the same individuals are involved in the 'before' and 'after' measurements, small changes can be identified more easily than if separate studies were made using two independent but comparable samples.

In addition, if panel members record their purchases or viewing habits during or immediately after the event, the information gained will tend to be more accurate than if an interviewer inquired about the purchase or programmes a day, a week, or a month later.

Well-run consumer panels using continuous reporting diaries can yield reasonably accurate projections of total retail sales of a variety of consumer products.

With regard to the cost factor, there can be advantages and disadvantages. If data are required at frequent intervals, it is cheaper to maintain a continuous panel than to select a new sample at each interval. If the data are required less frequently, this advantage may turn into a disadvantage.

As panel members have agreed to cooperate on projects as they come along, data can frequently be obtained from them by mail with close to 100 per cent response—and, of course, it is much cheaper than collecting information by personal interview.

Panel members may be divided into control and experimental groups, e.g. those who have satellite television and those who do not. This can aid the interpretation of the effect of introducing experiment variables.

Panels are without doubt invaluable for the study of trends over time periods and for the accumulation of data over time. Casual relationships can be better studied. More information can be obtained through cooperative effort.

There are, however, disadvantages with consumer panels, the principal one of which is that membership involves cooperating with a research organization continuously or at regular intervals. As this no doubt involves some effort, many individuals will decline to serve on panels. This raises the question of whether the sample can be truly representative of the population being studied, irrespective of whether the sample corresponds with the population on certain selected characteristics. In order to offset this, panels do pay members in money or merchandise; but this raises the further question of whether or not premiums attract a special type of panel member.

It is often assumed that both the highest and lowest social classes are under-represented on panels. Furthermore, the kind of people attracted to panels, even when selected by the quota sampling method, tend to be the more intelligent, literate and expressive section of the population.

Unfortunately, panel members die, move away, or just quit. They are replaced by new members with similar characteristics as far as these are known, but the probability is always present that the replacements differ from the original group in some significant, but unknown, way. There is evidence that those who have the least interest in the subject under study are most apt to drop out.

Response errors by panel members are usually thought to result from change of habits, self-consciousness, development of 'expertise', attempts by the panel members to 'look good', the bias of boredom or annoyance from repeated interviews or continuous reporting, failure to keep diaries on a current basis, and fatigue from completing long questionnaires or diaries.

The actions of new members to the panel are often a typical in that there is a tendency to increase the activity that is being recorded, e.g. television viewing or food purchasing. To eliminate the effects of this bias, data from new members are excluded from final results for four to six weeks.

After some time as a member of a panel, the individual may begin to think of him- or herself as an 'expert' and act accordingly, at the expense of acting normally. Other panel members may try to 'look good' by buying higher priced goods or shopping at high-class stores. However, these actions are found not to be of crucial significance, as often the first report of the panel member is discounted.

Once the novelty of panel membership wears off, interest can decline and cooperation tends to become mechanical. Diaries may be filled out just before they are sent in. Regular submission of diaries and forms is often lacking.

There must be constant vigilance of the tendency to develop a 'panel sophistication'; i.e., constant interviewing may lead to specially conditioned responses. Furthermore, control must be exercised over what is known as 'socially acceptable' responses.

There is a variety of panel types available. Some of the most frequently used are the continuous consumer purchasing panels, short-term consumer purchasing panels, television viewing panels, consumer product consumption panels, shopping panels, and product testing panels.

Brand barometers This is a service offered by market research firms to subscribers on a quarterly basis. Brand barometers each cover a particular market; they include the Private Motorist Brand Barometer, the Individual Buyer Brand Barometer and the Housewives' Brand Barometer. While the subject covered by the inquiry remains the same, the informants are chosen at random for each quarterly survey.

In each type barometer, a range of products is chosen. For instance, the Housewives' Barometer covers pet foods, bread, cleaning materials, butter, cooking fats, etc. The questions basically ask informants whether they buy each commodity, and if so when, what brand, and at what type of shop. The data are analysed into regions, age groups, ACORN and social class.

Omnibus surveys Omnibus surveys are organized by a research agency on behalf of several clients rather than a single client. As clients participate in a single survey, interviewers ask different questions, but to the same sample of people. The costs of the survey are divided between them. Each client receives only the answers and analysis relating to his or her own questions, and there is exactly the same degree of confidentiality as with an *ad hoc* study.

This type of survey is particularly suitable where a client needs original research, but only needs to ask a limited number of questions, as costs are usually based on the number of questions asked. Other factors which usually govern the cost per client are the proportion of the total sample available that the client wants to access. If the whole sample is not required, and the types of questions required are open-ended, then questions are likely to be more expressive.

There are several large, general omnibus surveys available, plus quite a wide variety of specialized ones. Specialist ones concentrate on particular types of product or customer. Anyone considering using an omnibus survey is advised to look at recent issues of the Market Research Society's newsletter, as this carries advertisements to recruit clients for omnibus surveys.

Personal interviews

If it is decided to conduct a series of interviews, one should do everything possible at the desk research stage before going out into the field. There are two basic reasons for this:

1. It is desirable to have some knowledge of the background to the discussions that will take place in the field.
2. Many executives do not have time to examine trends and ascertain the state of the market in five or ten years' time, but a market researcher, with a knowledge of market forecasting, can indicate to the respondent the way he or she thinks the market is going to move.

Before embarking on the main programme of visits, it is advisable to undertake some pilot visits to test out the questionnaire, the area of investigation, which respondents in a company to interview, etc.

Interviewers' characteristics The characteristics of a prospective interviewer warrant analysis. In the industrial market, the interviewer will have to be somebody who is going to be acceptable at all levels, from foreman to managing director. In general terms (and this includes interviewing in the consumer market), he or she needs to be a good mixer and have a pleasant personality, because interviewers are likely to confront people who may be uncommunicative, hostile or suspicious.

General approach In the industrial market, it is advisable *not* to produce a tightly written questionnaire, filling it in point by point when talking to senior officials in companies. This approach can cause antagonism. One should really begin with a general discussion. The use of an *aide-mémoire*, with ten or so key areas for discussion, is advisable.

Whereas industrial interviewing has necessarily to be much more in the nature of a discussion, in consumer interviewing a structured questionnaire is often used.

There are several advantages to be gained by employing the personal interview method:

—It permits a longer questionnaire with more comprehensive questions, and the interviewer can clear up any misunderstandings as they arise.
—Complex questions can therefore be used.
—The interviewer can probe the respondent, thereby eliciting further useful information.
—It is possible to assess the validity of some answers by observation, e.g. answers on personal details—age, education, income. The researcher can check whether answers are in line with obvious visual facts.
—The rate of response to a personal interview is higher; in effect, it reduces non-response.

There are also some disadvantages:

—It can be expensive.
—It requires a great deal of technical and administrative planning and supervision.
—Bias on the part of the interviewer can arise in the interview.

Depth interviews and group discussions Depth interviews normally involve either one face-to-face respondent (individual depth interview) or a group of 5–25 respondents (group discussions).

In the individual depth interview, the interviewer has a list of subjects of interest as opposed to a structured questionnaire. He or she is free to create questions and probe responses in greater depth.

Individual depth interviews are particularly useful in the following situations:

—Where the subject matter is of a confidential or potentially embarrassing nature.
—Where a highly detailed understanding of complicated behaviour on decision-making patterns (e.g. planning the family holiday) is required. This is usually the case in industrial/ organizational research problems where executives are interviewed on a one-to-one basis.

Group discussions (or focus groups) are often used for

—Generating ideas for new product concepts and new products.
—Exploring consumer response to promotional and packaging ideas.
—Conducting preliminary research prior to carrying out a more structured survey, e.g. to establish consumer knowledge and vocabulary.

Group discussions are normally recorded (on audio or video tape) or viewed 'live' by the client (possibly behind a one-way mirror). The researcher is responsible for leading the discussion, probing interesting comments and preparing a summary of the group's major comments. The major advantage of group discussions over individual interviews is that the interaction process tends to generate more information than could be derived from individuals separately.

There are, however, two problems with both individual and group interviews. First, they can be biased, as respondents are normally given an incentive to participate. Second, sample sizes are small and often non-representative. As with projective techniques and open questions, depth interviews are an excellent tool for preliminary research, but results from them normally require validation by more extensive and structured research.

Observational research

> An ice-cream manufacturer was concerned that sales of some of its products were not achieving the levels that had been expected (based on survey research). A direct observation study in a sample of shops revealed why. The ice-cream was kept in top-loading refrigerators with sides that were so high that many of the children could not see in to pick out the products they wanted. A picture display was devised for the side of the cabinet to enable the children to recognize each product and to indicate their choice by pointing to it. Sales increased.[5]

Observational research includes viewing and listening to situations. It also encompasses recording human behaviour with monitoring instruments.

Personal observation is used when it would be impossible or expensive to obtain data through a survey. Examples include:

—Monitoring traffic flow both inside and outside a shop.
—Studying a retail outlet (e.g. display methods, prices and customer flows).
—Viewing competitors' products at an exhibition.
—Viewing product usage by, say, children.

Monitoring instruments are sometimes preferable to personal observations for reasons of accuracy, cost or for functional reasons. Examples of their use include:

—Monitoring traffic flow through a district.
—Monitoring television viewing habits.
—Monitoring physiological reactions to promotional and packaging ideas. Physiological measures are measurements of physical responses (including eye movement, brain-wave analysis, perspiration rate, eye pupil size) to a stimulus such as an advertisement.

Computer-assisted interviewing This modern technique is currently regarded as a gimmick with which to impress clients. The advantage is that results can be fed in from a remote terminal (where the fieldwork is being conducted) and an instant readout can be obtained at the control headquarters. There must be some advantage in providing the client with 'instantaneous' results, but this might be at the expense of sacrificing accuracy, in that there is little opportunity for verification in the field. In marketing terms, there is little advantage in having instantaneous results rather than receiving a considered report in a matter of a few days.

A modern variation of the above that has recently been developed is 'computer clipboards', wherein simple questions (with closed responses) can be asked, and actually 'punched' into the computer clipboard. An instant readout can again be achieved. The problem with this device is that it cannot cope with complicated (open-ended) questions.

Experimentation

Experimentation involves the manipulation of one or more variables by the experimenter in such a way that its effect on another variable can be determined, e.g. manipulating price in order that its effect on sales can be determined.

Marketing experiments may be conducted in the field or in a 'laboratory' situation.

Field experimentation is also known as test marketing. This involves the duplication of the planned national marketing programme for a product in one or more limited market sectors. Marketing mix variables are manipulated in an attempt to identify the optimal marketing mix for the national launch. Test marketing is not limited to new products. It can be used to evaluate price changes, new packages, variations in distribution strategy or alternative advertising strategies.

In laboratory experimentation, an environment is simulated (e.g. home or shopping environment) and the environment is used to test consumer reactions to new products, packaging, displays or advertising themes.

Types of errors affecting experimental results   In order that an experiment is useful, care must be taken to ensure that all sources of error are minimalized. Such possible sources of error include:

—*Motivation*   Respondents may alter their responses to a specific stimulant over a period of time, irrespective of external events. For example, in a prolonged 'taste testing' experiment, respondents may develop more sophisticated palates as the experiment progresses and this may affect their response to a particular flavour.

—*Exogenous occurrences*   These are events not controlled by the experimenter, e.g. competitive actions and macro-environmental changes.

—*Selection*   Selection error occurs when the groups formed for the purposes of the experiment are unequal.

—*Instrument variability*   This refers to changes in the measuring instrument over time. These changes are most likely to occur when the measurement process involves people, either as observers or interviewers; their interest and professionalism may cease or become better as time passes.

—*Lost respondents*   After a period of time, respondents in an experiment may refuse to continue their participation. The experimental results at a later stage in the experiment may not be representative of what might have emerged had all the original respondents been present.

—*Experiment effect*   The fact that an experiment is being conducted often has an important effect on the respondents. Even pre-measurement can, by alerting the subjects to the topic of study, cause them to change behaviour.

Rodger[6] provides a more detailed discussion on experimental design and shows how this can measure the impact of a single variable or several variables.

Once the optimum research method has been selected, the researcher must decide who and where to study. This decision process normally involves a sampling procedure. After data have been collected, the researcher must analyse and report research findings. Sampling, data analysis and research reporting are discussed in the next section.

SAMPLING, DATA ANALYSIS AND RESEARCH APPLICATIONS

Sampling

Sampling is a necessary and inescapable part of human affairs. Each of us samples and is regularly sampled. We sample the performance of a new car by a test drive, a wine by a few sips and a new acquaintance by an initial meeting.

It is sometimes possible and practical to take a *census*; that is, to study each member of the population of interest. This is sometimes the situation in industrial market research situations where the number of companies to be investigated is small. More often than not, however, a *sample* is taken because of cost, time, accuracy and research considerations. Cost and time benefits are obvious, but the last two reasons require explanation:

—*Research effect*   The purpose of marketing research is to collect data about markets: not to influence markets. Yet responding to survey questions forces the respondent to examine his or her attitudes towards the survey topic. This examination may lead to a change in behaviour. To minimize the occurrence of behavioural changes, a sample is sometimes preferable to a census.

—*Accuracy* As sample size increases, the occurrence of non-sampling errors may also increase. Non-sampling errors include errors in data collection and analysis.

Five criteria are important when evaluating *sample frames*, or target populations:

1. *Adequacy*.
2. *Completeness* All the units of population under survey should be represented, and proportionately so.
3. *Accuracy* Totally up-to-date sampling frames are rarely available. The frame may contain units that no longer exist; e.g., the Electoral Register will contain people who have moved house.
4. *Duplication* Bias will occur where names of sampling units occur more than once; e.g., some firms may have multiple listings in telephone directories.
5. *Convenience* Sampling lists should be accessible and suitable for sampling purposes.

The sampling process consists of three steps:

1. Specify the target population.
2. Select the sampling method.
3. Determine the sample size.

Specifying the target population The target population, or frame, is that part of the total population (universe) to which the study is directed. For example, for a company selling cars in the UK, the universe could be the entire UK population plus foreign visitors, and the frame might be people aged 18 or over. Elements (e.g. prospective respondents) from the target population are selected using reference material (including directories and maps) or after preliminary questioning or observation.

Selecting the sampling method Five basic choices must be made when deciding on a sampling method:

1. Random v. non-random sampling In random samples, each member of the target population has a fixed (often equal) probability of being a member of the target sample. Random samples have to be sufficiently large to ensure that all sections of the population are surveyed. In non-random (also known as *purposive* or *quota*) samples, on the other hand, respondents are selected to fit a quota designed to mirror relevant characteristics of the population, and in this way fewer respondents are required.

A random sample design has two advantages. First, a statistical relationship exists between the sample estimates and population. Second, the composition of the sample is not affected by interviewer likes and dislikes. These two benefits have made random sample designs particularly useful for surveys that are politically sensitive.

A non-random sample may be as reliable as a random sample if the following requirements are met:

—Up-to-date statistics relating to the structure of the population are available.
—Classification questions are carefully designed.
—The interviewer's selection of respondents is carefully controlled.

In a *simple random sample*, every individual in the target population has an equal chance of being drawn. Each individual is allocated a number and the sample can be drawn using random number tables. This method is equivalent to the classic lottery where names are placed in a hat and drawn out randomly.

In a *systematic random sample*, a random starting-point is selected and every Nth unit in the frame is drawn where:

$$N = \frac{\text{Population size}}{\text{Sample size}}.$$

This method is quicker and cheaper than simple random sampling as the procedure involving random number tables is avoided.

2. *Single-stage v. multi-stage sampling* If a survey population is large and widely dispersed, a probability sample will often be drawn in more than one stage. For example, a survey of voters could be sampled first by constituencies, then polling districts, then the register of electors. Multi-stage sample ensures that interview calls are not too widely dispersed.

3. *Single-unit v. cluster sampling* In single-unit sampling, each sampling unit is selected separately; in cluster sampling the units are selected in groups; e.g., a household might be a single unit but a street would be a cluster. Cluster sampling has the advantage of reducing interviewing costs, but within-cluster variability may be low.

4. *Unstratified v. stratified sampling* A stratum in a population is a segment of that population having one or more common characteristics, e.g. companies with a turnover of £5 million–£10 million annually. Stratified random sampling involves treating each stratum as a separate sub-population for sampling purposes. The reasons for stratifying a population for sampling purposes are:

—It may help to ensure representativeness (and thus reduce sampling error).
—The required sample size for the same level of sampling error will usually be smaller than for a non-stratified sample.

Stratification is commonly used in industrial marketing research. In consumer research, details of strata are not normally readily available, e.g. individuals' incomes. The ACORN[7] method (a classification of residential neighbourhoods) does enable some stratified random sampling in consumer research. It provides 11 classifications of residential neighbourhoods according to type of housing.

5. *Proportionate v. disproportionate sampling* In proportionate sampling an equal percentage of respondents is sampled for each stratum. In disproportionate sampling a small (but important) stratum is over-sampled but restored to its due weight when considering total results. Disproportionate samples are, therefore, most cost-effective.

Determining sample size In determining sample size, there are two major considerations:

—Research budget available.
—Degree of precision required.

Research budget Based purely on resources available, sample size may be calculated using the following formula:

$$\text{Sample size} = \frac{\text{Total budget} - \text{research planning, analysis and reporting costs}}{\text{Variable cost per interview (or observation)}}.$$

Precision required For random samples, there is a statistical relationship between sample estimates and population values. Using probability theory, we are able to relate precision required to sample size. The larger the sample size, the more confident the researcher can be that the results are representative of the population. If the level of precision required can be specified in advance, it is possible to determine the minimum required sample size. This sample size refers to the number of usable responses, and allowance should be made for the likely non-response level. A more detailed discussion of sampling accuracy is given by Rodger,[8] who explains the statistical methodology behind sample size determination.

Editing and coding responses After data collection the next step is to edit illegible, incomplete and inconsistent responses. There are three ways to deal with imperfect responses:

1. *Ask the respondent to clarify response* This is usually avoided except in the case of surveys with a small sample size and a high level of imperfect responses.
2. *Use responses* This approach is often used by research agencies as they are often committed to obtaining a certain number of responses. Tabulation can keep track of non-responses as a separate category. Inconsistent responses might be assumed to average out over the sample.
3. *Discard responses* The researcher may judge that the end results will be more useful if incomplete responses are discarded.

For small studies (less than 25 respondents), it is possible to conduct analysis manually, provided only basic analysis is required. Data from large studies are coded prior to computer input.

The process of coding involves converting responses to code values on coding sheets. Coding sheets are normally 80 columns wide and one or more column is allocated to each survey question. Each line (horizontal) of the sheet is devoted to one respondent. Closed questions may be *precoded*; that is, a code is allocated to each possible response before the survey. Responses to open questions are normally grouped into convenient categories and a code is allocated to each category after the survey.

Figure 5.2 illustrates a typical coding procedure. Two commonly employed conversions are used in this example:

—Possible responses are coded from left to right beginning with 1.
—Non-responses are normally coded 9.

It can thus be seen how the system works from the questionnaire to the coding sheet, and thereafter for computer punching. In this particular example, the partial toothpaste questionnaire has been hypothetically filled in, and the partial coding sheet has been filled in from the response on this questionnaire.

Data analysis

After input to the computer, it is often desirable to create new variables. Two types of new variable may be created:

—*Combination of variables* For example, data on a respondent's age, marital status and children may be combined to generate a new variable called 'stage in the family life cycle'.
—*Introduction of secondary data*

Basic analysis Marketing research analysis usually involves simple tabulation, calculation of summarizing and cross-tabulation.

Sampling tabulation involves calculating the number and percentage of respondents who choose each of the available answers. Table 5.2 provides an example of simple tabulation. In this example an adjusted frequency discards data that are missing as a result of non-responsive or incorrect coding.

QUESTIONNAIRE

Respondent No: 890

1–3

Q1   Do you use toothpaste?

☑   ☐

Yes   No

4

Q2   Please indicate your degree of agreement with the following statements by circling a 6 if you strongly agree, a 1 if you strongly disagree, or somewhere in between depending on your degree of agreement with the statement

Strongly   Strongly
Disagree   Agree
— — — — — — — — —

I am very health conscious	1 ②3 4 5 6	5
My appearance is very important to me	1 2 ③4 5 6	6
I use mouthwash often	1 ②3 4 5 6	7

Q3   How old are you?   <u>26</u>

8–9

Q4   What is your marital status?

☐ ✓   ☐   ☐   ☐

Single   Married   Divorced,   Other
Widowed, or
separated

10

Q5   . . . etc   CODING SHEET

11

Columns

1	2	3	4	5	6	7	8	9	10	11	12	13	14	80
8	9	0	1	2	3	2	2	6	1	····	····	etc		

Figure 5.2 Coding procedure

Table 5.2 Simple tabulation

Age of respondent	Absolute frequency	Relative frequency (%)	Adjusted frequency (%)	Cumulative frequency (%)
0–17	1	1.9	1.9	1.9
18–40	20	37.7	38.5	40.4
41–64	21	39.6	40.4	80.8
65+	10	18.9	19.2	100.0
Not ascertained	1	1.9	(missing)	100.0
	53	100.0	100.0	100.0

There are two kinds of *summarizing statistics*. The first provides measures of the mid-point of the distribution and is known as *measures of central tendency*. The second gives an indication of the amount of variation in the data comprising the distribution and is known as *measures of dispersion*.

Mean, mode and median are the major measures of central tendency, and the reader is again directed to Rodger[9] for a detailed discussion of their computation.

Cross-tabulation involves constructing a table so that responses to two or more questions may be compared. Table 5.3 provides a cross-tabulation example produced using the SPSS(X)[10] software package. Here the response to a question on income groups is compared to the response to a question on weekly food expenditure.

Measurement scales The various ways of phrasing questions have been outlined earlier. From an analysis viewpoint, it is useful to categorize questioning/measurement scales into four groups.

Nominal scales Nominal scales are used to categorize responses. For example, the number 1 is assigned to female respondents and number 0 to male respondents. Nominal scales may be used to calculate the number (or percentage or frequency) of items falling within each category. The calculation of median for nominal data is meaningless, but the mode may be calculated.

Ordinal scales Ordinal scales are used to rank items. For example, a consumer is asked to rank his or her performance for brands A, B and C. In this example, if the consumer ranks B as his or her preferred brand, an ordinal scale will not reveal how much more the consumer prefers brand B to brands A and C. An ordinal scale may be used to calculate frequency, mode and median, but not mean.

Interval scales An interval scale where intervals on the scale are equal distances. For example, respondents are asked to state their degree of agreement or disagreement with a statement by selecting a response from a list such as:

1. Agree very strongly.
2. Agree fairly strongly.
3. Agree.
4. Undecided.
5. Disagree.
6. Disagree fairly strongly.
7. Disagree very strongly.

Virtually the entire range of statistical analysis can be applied to interval scales, including frequency, mean, median, mode, range and standard deviation.

Table 5.3 Cross-tabulation of income versus food expenditure

COUNT Row% Col. % Tot. %	Food expenditure Less than £15	£15–29	£30–44	£45–59	£60+	ROW
Less than £10 000	33 7.1 84.6 3.5	226 48.7 70.2 24.2	149 32.1 47.8 16.0	45 9.7 23.1 4.8	11 2.4 16.5 1.2	464 49.7
£10 000– £20 000	5 1.5 12.8 0.5	73 22.0 22.7 7.8	121 36.4 38.8 13.0	102 30.7 52.3 10.8	31 5.3 47.7 3.3	332 35.6
£20 000+	1 0.7 2.6 6.1	23 16.8 7.1 2.5	42 30.7 13.5 4.5	48 35.0 24.6 5.1	23 16.8 35.4 2.5	137 14.7
Column Total	39 4.2	322 34.5	312 33.4	195 20.9	65 7.0	933 100.0

Each cell contains four numbers:

Count   The number of people in the cell (i.e. 33 respondents had incomes under £10 000 and spent less than £15 per week on food).

Row %   The percentage of people in the row who are in the column (i.e., 33/464 = 7.1 per cent of the people with incomes under £10 000 spent less than £15 per week on food).

Col %   The percentage of people in the column who were in the row (i.e., 33/39 = 84.6 per cent of people who spent less than £15 per week on food had incomes under £10 000).

Total %   The percentage of the total sample in the particular cell (i.e., 33/933 = 3.5 per cent).

Ratio scales A ratio scale is an interval scale with a zero point. Simple counting of any set of objects produces a ratio scale. Thus, sales, costs and number of purchasers are all ratio scales. Ratio scales allow, in addition to the analysis permitted by interval scales, some specialized calculations.

Interval and ratio scales can thus be subjected to more analytical procedures, and hence they are easier to analyse.

More complete analyses Most marketing research analysis is limited to the basic analytical procedures described. However, computers now enable more complex analytical procedures to be used by marketers. Many of these procedures are concerned with analysing the degree of association (or relationship) between two or more variables. Pearson's correlation coefficient is the most common formula employed.[11]

Research reporting The results of a research project may be reported in written or oral format, or both. The importance of effective reporting cannot be overemphasized. Regardless of the quality of the research process and the accuracy and usefulness of the resulting data, the data will not be used if they are not effectively communicated to the appropriate decision-makers.

For written reports, the following guidelines normally apply:

1. The report sequence is usually title page, table of contents, summary, introduction/research objectives, research methodology, findings, conclusions, recommendations (if appropriate), appendices.
2. Most report readers will not be particularly concerned with the technical aspects of the report, such as sampling procedure and questionnaire design. For this reason, technical details should be placed in the appendix section rather than in the methodology section.
3. Use terminology that matches the vocabulary of the reader.
4. Use diagrams (such as graphs, bar charts and pie charts) whenever possible.

For oral presentations, the report sequence is normally research objectives, research methodology, major findings, conclusions and recommendations; to maintain audience attention, full use should be made of visual aids.

Application of research techniques

Marketing research techniques may be applied to assist decision-making in all the functions of the marketing mix. It should also be borne in mind that 'mixed' research tactics can be used (e.g. personal interviews combined with group discussions). The application of research techniques in product, pricing, marketing communications and distribution research is now briefly outlined; sales forecasting research is discussed in detail in Chapter 6. For a fuller and more professional discussion of the techniques, the reader is again directed to the work of Chisnall.[12]

Product research This encompasses the following aspects:

—*Generating new product ideas* Sources of new product ideas include monitoring secondary sources (particularly trade journals, the competition's literature), group discussions with consumers and/or industry 'experts', studies of product use and surveys of consumer requirements.
—*Product concept testing* A product concept is a product idea that has been defined in terms of its applications and benefits. Before embarking on the costly process of developing a prototype, it is usually advisable to research demand for the product concept. Product concept testing often involves describing the concept to consumers and asking the following question:

'If this product were available, would you be likely to buy it? Would you say that you:

☐ would definitely buy it
☐ would probably buy it
☐ might or might not buy it
☐ would probably not buy it
☐ would definitely not buy it?'

—*Product testing* In product testing, consumers are asked to use or examine product prototypes. The consumers are then asked if they would buy such a product and to state their opinions of the test product.
—*Test marketing* of products in a limited geographical area.
—*Packaging research*, including laboratory and field experimentation.

A fuller discussion of product research, especially in relation to fast moving consumer goods, is given in a text by Watkins.[13]

Pricing research This includes the setting of prices for both new and current products and involves forecasting sales and estimating costs. Methods for forecasting sales are described in Chapter 6, but the estimation of costs is more the subject of accountancy. Pricing also forms part of marketing tactics, whereby prices can be manipulated in the short term to fight a tactical battle (e.g. short-term petrol price reductions) or in longer term for product positional tactics. A fuller discussion is provided by Greenley within the context of marketing plans.[14]

Marketing communications research This includes the following.

Marketing communications effectiveness research Under this heading, the effectiveness of advertising, personal selling, sales promotion and public relations activity is measured. This involves measuring its communication and/or sales effect. An assessment of communications effectiveness is concerned with measuring awareness, attitudes or 'intention to buy' before and after a campaign. A sales effectiveness measurement may be conducted by statistical analysis of past sales versus promotion expenditure. For new products, field experiments with 'control' markets are used.

Media selection research In order to select a suitable publication or medium, a marketer should aim to collect the following data:

—Media distribution (the number of copies or sets carrying the advertisement).
—Audience size (the number of people actually exposed to an advertisement, also known as 'reach').
—Audience exposure (the number of people exposed times the number of times they are exposed, i.e. reach × frequency, also known as 'gross rating points').
—Cost per exposure.

Media distribution details are normally available from the media and these statistics are normally audited by an independent organization, e.g. Audit Bureau of Circulation for the UK. Audience 'reach' and 'exposure' data are collected and published by research organizations such as Research Services Ltd. Media effectiveness can vary greatly for different products and may be measured using the techniques mentioned in the previous sub-section.

Copy testing This is concerned with determining the effectiveness of the creative aspects (headline, pictures, etc.) of advertising or promotional material. Creative ideas may be tested using physiological measures, surveys of advertising recall, field and 'laboratory' experiments.

Researching the number and location of sales representations required Two main types of research are used for sales territory planning:

1. *Statistical analysis of sales data* For current products, an analysis of actual sales versus market potential for each territory will indicate if the optimum number of representatives is being employed.
2. *Sales effort approach* This approach is particularly appropriate for new products; it involves four stages:

   (a) Compiling lists of prospective customers from secondary sources.
   (b) Estimating the number of sales calls per year required to sell to selected prospective customers.
   (c) Estimating the average number of sales calls per representative that can be made in that territory in a year.
   (d) Dividing (b) by (c) to obtain the number of representatives required.

Distribution research This includes the following:

—*Warehouse location research* Here, the marketing research function is normally required to provide data on customer location (from secondary sources).
—*Retail outlet location research* To assist with the process of planning the location of retail outlets, marketing research can provide a great deal of useful data. Useful data on a prospective site would include volume of pedestrians, number of nearby competitors, and the socio-economic profile of the neighbourhood.

Test marketing Test marketing is a research technique in which the product under study is placed on sale in one or more selected localities or areas, and its reception by consumer and trade is observed, recorded and analysed.

Performance in these test markets is supposed to give some indication of the performance to be expected when the product goes into general distribution. 'Performance' includes two aspects:

1. The likely sales and profitability of the product when marketed on a national scale.
2. 'Feasibility' of the marketing operation, by which we mean the soundness and integration of all the elements that enter into the marketing operation.

Today, it has become an economic necessity to reduce new product risk by using one or more small and relatively self-contained marketing areas, wherein the market can apply a full-plan marketing strategy in order to gain at least a reasonably reliable indication that the product can be sold profitably in the (eventual) total marketing place.

Test marketing can be expensive, time-consuming, and can give competitors a window on your activities. At best, it provides only gross measures when one would like precision. This leads us on to the question, 'Why is it used?'

Other market research methods may indicate the *likelihood* that a new product or marketing approach will be successful. These methods have their place and should be used; but something more is ultimately needed—greater assurance than an indication or more 'likelihood'. All signs may be encouraging, but one nagging question usually remains: Will it sell? This is the question to which the answer is sought. In a market test, the product is actually placed on sale in a number of stores, and this provides a decisive acid test.

Test marketing is the final and most complex of a series of marketing research techniques used to reduce the tremendous risks inherent in new product development. It tends to be largely related to consumer products (particularly products such as groceries, confectionery, alcohol and cigarettes). Industrial products, particularly large items of capital equipment, do not permit concentrated area testing as envisaged in a test marketing programme. Industrial companies obtain their new product feedback in more informal ways. With an industrial product, e.g. computers, sales representatives and technical specialists arrange for a demonstration with potential users. Reaction on the part of potential customers to this 'trial run' may require the company to alter the product in some way.

Test marketing in the industrial situation really amounts to a 'market probe' and the emphasis is very often on the product itself. Contrast this with the consumer field and the products mentioned above, where one is testing not only the product but the price, advertising, selling effort, distribution, the package, etc. Products such as office equipment are often tested at trade shows where selected clients are permitted to use them. There are many successful industrial products on the market which have, unlike most consumer goods, started life as a special order for a particular client. That is a form of test marketing.

However, as Lancaster and Jobber[15] have pointed out, test marketing proper needs to be much more carefully designed and controlled than this if it is to serve as a basis for sales and market forecasting. With consumer durables, e.g. TV sets, refrigerators, washing machines, furniture, etc., it is unlikely that a company would go into a full-scale regional test market, with £300 000 minimum spend on TV coverage, commando sales forces, discounts to the trade and everything else, unless it had every intention of marketing the product nationally. For such products, test marketing is essentially a preliminary skirmish into the marketing battlefield, designed to iron out the problems before the final product 'roll-out'.

We shall now look at the various stages involved in establishing a test market and the important factors that must be considered.

Defining objectives The market research process, whatever set of techniques is employed, starts with a clear set of objectives. The same applies to test marketing.

Some of the more frequently encountered objectives for a product test market are:

—To provide the basis for total market production, i.e. giving you an idea of potential product sales after the launch.
—To check the entire operation, including production, distribution and marketing plan.
—To check the advertising campaign.
—To check the presentation/packaging of the product.
—To check the selling method.
—To check the distribution plan.

Setting criteria for success Performance should be assessed against predetermined and agreed standards of success. There is no sense in conducting an expensive test marketing operation only to find more disagreement after the test than before it as to whether the product is successful.

Standards can be set in such areas as sales volume, level of distribution, market share, etc. If you are studying advertising, then it is necessary to determine the degree of increase in sales that would be regarded as successful and therefore indicative of the wisdom of extending the advertising campaign, say, from one or two selected regions to national level.

Integrating marketing operations The test marketing campaign must fit into the overall marketing plan; e.g., top salesmen should not be used in test areas if this is not to be repeated on a national scale because it will produce abnormal and misleading results. Furthermore, you should not indulge in excessive advertising if this is not to be repeated in the national launch.

Establishing controls This involves three aspects:

1. What is the market situation before the test campaign starts?

   —What is the level of competition?
   —How successful are competitors' brands?
   —What are the buying habits of the consumer?
   —What are the attitudes to the product type?
   —Is there brand loyalty?
   —Is there price sensitivity?
   —How do shopping habits affect the types of outlet through which a product can be sold?
   —Has there been sufficient trade research—for example, attitudes to product type, customary discount structure, quantity discount terms, merchandising practices by companies, degree of cooperation expected from the trade?

2. During the test campaign, marketing movement should be monitored so that trends may be

identified quickly, and also to assess the likely outcome of the campaign. Use of consumer panels and retail audits in test areas can be of immense help in this respect.

3. Post-test survey research should be extended to dealers so that an overall appreciation of market influences is gathered. The frank assessment of the test operation by dealers is very important.

Selecting areas The ultimate aim should be to select test areas that reflect in miniature the national market. The reasoning behind this is that management wants to project results from test markets to entire target markets. One could take the view that there are a few large 'favourite' cities/test areas that are believed to be representative of the nation, based on analysis of demographic and socio-economic characteristics. However, this selection procedure may suffer from a number of drawbacks, including:

1. Possible reduction of market representativeness owing to continual use of test market cities/ areas and to multiple tests being conducted at the same time.
2. The ease with which competition can discover that a new product introduction is being evaluated.
3. The questionable ability of a few cities/test areas to be representative of the entire country.

Selection of a greater number of smaller, more widely dispersed, cities could overcome these difficulties.

It can be seen that the choice of a test marketing area is not an easy one. Nevertheless, consider the following factors, which stand out as being the most important influence on the choice:

—*Size* The area must provide an adequate base from which to project your findings on to a national scale, e.g. 100 000–200 000 inhabitants, yet at the same time be small enough to offer coverage at a reasonable cost. The ultimate market potential will, of course, influence the size of the test market area. A new pet food aimed at the huge pet food market would require a larger test market area than a product aimed at a small specialist market.
—*Population characteristics* Clearly, the people a product is aimed at may be defined in terms of age, sex and socio-economic grouping. It is important to try to match a test area population with the national market.
—*Research services and marketing techniques that a media owner can offer the advertiser*
—*Range of different media available*
—*Isolation* The ability to isolate and observe without interference from outside variables is, of course, a precondition of much scientific research. It applies to some extent to test marketing and is certainly a point the media owners themselves like to stress. The marketing manager at Westminster Press has stated that: 'Our test towns and their newspapers have the special advantages of being isolated. You know where you are when you are researching them and have greater control. Wholesalers, for example, have much less chance to blur distribution of the product than in any other towns.'

The main point is that it is essential to have a deep and full understanding of the test area you use so that results can be adjusted to allow for known variations from national behaviour patterns, media availability, media costs, etc.

Determining the number of test markets Results may be more representative as the number of test market areas used increases, but in so doing you increase the cost. You should use a larger number of test market areas under the following circumstances:

1. If the risk of loss is great in a national launch.
2. If a number of alternative marketing plans are being tested.
3. If the opportunity of interference by competitors is likely.

In practice, it is unwise to use fewer than two test market areas.

Establishing the length of tests There is no one answer to this question. Naturally, the ideal test period is the shortest time it takes to find out what you want to know. However, *three factors* do exert an influence on the length of the test period:

1. *Average repurchase period* This can be defined as the time period that normally elapses before the consumer restocks the product. You need to observe a few repurchase periods to obtain a fair picture of attitude towards and usage of your product. This is not a problem with a product consumed as regularly as shampoo, but it may be a problem with a consumer durable such as a washing machine.
2. *The competitor situation* No business likes to tell the competition what it is doing or give the opponent the opportunity to go national first. There is plenty of justification for this fear because the first manufacturer into a market can be overtaken by another only with great difficulty or luck. The dilemma is one of testing long enough useful information, but not so long that competitors are given a chance to catch up.
3. *Cost* As the duration of the test increases, so does the cost. Thus, everyone is anxious to make test marketing short and sweet—but not too short, because the chances of correctly forecasting the national results increase dramatically with each extra week of a test.

Deciding the cost and information required As was stressed earlier, perhaps the most important rule of all in test marketing is that objective yardsticks for assessing satisfactory performance should be established in advance of the test itself. Obviously, criteria relating to sales performance and market penetration must form the basis for the ultimate 'go'/'no go' decision. However, of equal importance are the costs involved. Is it a proper decision to say that we must go ahead because it would cost too much to pull out? I think not!

In line with this, therefore, it is important to establish what information is to be collected during the test market and from what sources. Examples of different types of information that might be collected include:

—*Data on goods delivered to the trade* This is perhaps the least informative and costly.
—*Store audits* This will inform you of actual retail sales. One can utilize the services of the Neilsen Company in this respect. However, you must remember that store audits only provide you with retail sales figures; they do not tell you anything about the characteristics of buyers, such as the proportion of new buyers to repeat buyers.
—*Consumer panels* A consumer panel can provide you with information on buyer characteristics.
—*Buyer surveys* A company may wish to obtain direct data on buyer attitudes and reactions to the new product. This would involve obtaining a sample of new buyers and proceeding to interview them with a view to determining the characteristics of the buyers and reactions to using the product.

It goes without saying that test results should be evaluated properly, because on that rest important business decisions, e.g. heavy capital investment, and the setting up of volume production lines. You may have achieved a certain percentage market success in the test market, but you cannot simply deduce from that a similar performance if you were to go national. You must examine other significant factors, namely:

—Demographic structure of the population.
—Types of outlet available.
—Strength of competing brands.
—Variations among regions in competitors' activities, which may result in variations between the test area and the national market.

After this, you should attempt to make a forecast of future likely demand for the new product on a national basis.

Criticisms of test marketing There are, of course, problems with test marketing. For example, it is difficult to 'isolate' test areas in order to ensure that the experiment is controlled. Similarly, it is almost impossible to hold constant all the factors that might affect the results of competitor activity. For these and other reasons, many researchers have cautioned against the use of this technique for certain purposes. Nevertheless, used wisely and properly planned and exercised, test marketing is a very powerful and useful aid to marketing decision-making.

Motivation research Much of marketing research is concerned with the collection of statistical data and market facts including market size and numbers of competitors. It may also involve direct questioning of potential and actual consumers about their behaviour and attitudes.

However, a buyer's real motives and other behavioural influences are often unknown, hidden, or too complex to be determined by direct questioning. Marketing has thus borrowed some indirect research techniques from the behavioural science fields, especially psychology and psychiatry, to help gain a better understanding of why people respond as they do to various products, advertisements and other marketing variables. The term 'motivation research' is used to describe these indirect techniques.

In order to appreciate the need for motivation research, consider the complexity of purchase decisions that are influenced by attitudes, beliefs, motivations and environmental factors. The consumer's perception of him/herself (self-image) and the product (product image) should be appreciated by marketers. Products are bought not only for physical benefits and functional performance, but also for psychological satisfactions.

Bradley[16] has said that motivation research helps in designing the product, its package, pricing and advertising.

Certain mechanical aids also help motivational researchers, including speeded up and slowed down video recordings, traffic counters, psycho-galvanometers, scanners, eye cameras (pupilometers), tachistoscopes, people meters (for measuring TV viewing patterns), electro-encephalograms, one-way mirrors and voice pitch analysis. Some of their uses border on clinical research, and criticism has been voiced about some of the results obtained, largely owing to the fact that skill in interpreting the results is often extremely specialist. Some results have been drawn by marketers that are scientifically suspect.

We shall now examine the main techniques used in motivation research.

Projective techniques A person who is relieved of direct responsibility for his or her expressions will tend to answer more freely and truthfully Projective tests are designed to achieve this end. They are called 'projective tests' because respondents are required to project themselves into someone else's place or into some ambiguous situation.

Consider the following examples:

1. *Word association test* This type of test, also known as 'free association', involves firing a series of words at respondents, who must state immediately any other words that come into their

minds. Association tests can be used to determine consumer attitudes towards products, stores, advertising themes, product features, selection of brand names, etc. Let us look at some examples:

—The interviewer says 'soap', to which the respondent might reply 'hygiene', 'lather', 'beauty', and so on.
—The interviewer says 'margarine', to which the respondent might reply 'health', 'cholesterol', 'convenient', 'butter', 'cost', and so on.

2. *Sentence completion test* Here the respondent is asked to complete a number of sentences. The following are some examples:

—In comparing margarine with butter, one might state:
'A housewife using margarine instead of butter is _____.'
or
'The healthfulness of margarine is _____.'
—Considering a certain brand of cigars, one might state:
'A man who smokes Hamlet cigars is _____.'

This test can provide more information than word association.

3. *Story completion test* This is an extension of the sentence completion technique. Consider the following example:

—A man bought petrol at his regular petrol station which sold a nationally advertised brand. The petrol attendant, who knew the man, said: 'Mr Smith, your battery is now nearly two years old. We have just got in a new product which, when added to the water in your battery, will prolong its life by about a year. It's a bargain at £2.50.' What is the customer's response? Why?

This technique can provide the seller with data on the images and feelings that people have about a particular product.

Another example might be where a group of housewives is asked to complete a story in which the opening sentence is related to supermarket shopping.

4. *Psychodrama* Here the respondent is asked to play a role, and to do so he is given a complete description of the circumstances. This test is similar to the 'third-person' test. A famous example is the study by Mason-Haire of instant coffee usage in America in 1949. The study involved giving housewives two identical shopping lists, the only differences being that one list contained instant coffee while the other list contained coffee beans. The findings revealed that the buyer of instant coffee was seen as lazier, less well organized, more spendthrift and not as good a wife as the woman who bought the traditional type of coffee. This study uncovered the true motivations. The original reason given for disliking the instant coffee was the flavour.

5. *Thematic aperception test (TAT)* In this test, a series of pictures is shown to respondents, who are then asked to describe what conditions give rise to the situation, what is happening, and what the outcome will be. The assumption is that, in explaining the picture, the subject will tell something about him- or herself. For example:

—The cartoon might show a young housewife looking at a display of 'bargain offer' tights, or the same woman casting her eyes over a merchandising unit offering expensive 'branded' tights. The respondent would be asked to comment on the person in the cartoon and the quality of the tights.

6. *Cartoon test* This is a variation of the TAT method and is commonly referred to as a 'balloon test'. Informants are presented with a rough sketch showing two people talking. One of them has just said something represented by words written into a 'speech balloon' as in a comic strip. The other person's balloon is empty and the informant is asked what he or she is replying. Consider the following example:

—Two women are pictured outside Smith's department store and one woman is saying: 'What do you think of Smith's department store?' The respondent is asked to give the reply of the other woman.

Many marketing situations could be usefully tested by this technique. Consider the following examples:

—A chemist is pictured saying: 'This bottle of Disprin gives you 100 tablets for £1; and this bottle gives you 100 soluble Aspirin for 75p.' What is the customer's reply?
—You could show a situation between a shopper returning faulty merchandise and a store assistant.
—You could picture a husband and wife considering the purchase of an expensive product.
—Another particular example might be to use a cartoon showing a conference in progress. One of the delegates says: 'Now this is our present supplier list. We have been with them for quite some time and they have been doing a good job. There is no reason for making any changes. The next subject is . . . .' Another delegate interrupts to say: 'Wait a minute . . . . Loyalty is fine, but there are a lot of other considerations which I think are due for a change.'

The respondent is then asked with which delegate he or she is in most agreement, and why.

Issues and problems involved You should note that motivation research, like test marketing, is not without its own special problems and issues.

A major problem is the fact that all the above mentioned techniques require the use of highly skilled interviewers and analysts trained in psychology and/or sociology. This, of course, is a problem that can be overcome, albeit at a cost.

Potentially more serious issues/problems relate to the extent to which these techniques are (a) scientific and (b) ethical. With regard to *scientific status*, the controversy continues. Critics argue that the techniques are shaky to say the least, with little comparability between various research studies. On the other hand, confirmed advocates of motivation research such as Dichter[17] suggest that the techniques are powerful marketing tools. With regard to *ethical status*, critics such as Packard[18] have long argued that the use of such techniques is tantamount to an invasion of the privacy of the consumer's mind and lays the customer open to manipulation.

No doubt the debate will continue, although it must be said that in recent years the use of these techniques in marketing has probably declined somewhat.

The professional marketer would perhaps be best advised to keep an open mind, picking and choosing from the techniques available, as and where appropriate.

MARKETING INFORMATION SYSTEMS

A marketing information system (MkIS) can be defined as a system designed to generate and disseminate an orderly flow of pertinent information to marketing managers. Thus, marketing research is concerned with the task of generating information, whereas the marketing information system is focused on managing the flow of information decision-makers. This distinction is important because information is worthless unless it is relevant and effectively communicated.

This section comes at the end of this chapter because you will appreciate that it is possible to have marketing research without a marketing information system, but not vice versa.

The marketing information system of a company is a sub-system of its management information system. A marketing information system, in turn, consists of four sub-systems.

1. The internal accounting system—a system that reports orders, sales, inventory levels, receivables and payables.
2. The marketing intelligence system—the set of procedures and sources used by executives to obtain their everyday information about pertinent developments in the marketing environment.
3. The marketing research system—the systematic design, collection, analysis and reporting of data and findings relevant to a specific marketing situation facing the company.
4. The analytical marketing system—a system for analysing marketing data using statistical procedures and mathematical models.

Systems 1, 2 and 3 are all data collection methods, whereas 4 is an analytical method. The point is that it does work, and many marketing-oriented companies are already applying the technique.

CONCLUSIONS

This chapter has covered the subject of marketing research. It has been acknowledged that this subject is an involved and detailed study in its own right. The areas covered have included an introductory description of the development of marketing research followed by secondary research methods. Primary research was then examined under the headings of: survey research, depth research, observation and experimentation. Sampling was discussed followed by data analysis. This was followed by a detailed explanation of test marketing and motivation research. The chapter concluded with an indication of how marketing research techniques could be applied to the marketing function including the adoption of a marketing information system. Lancaster and Massingham[19] provide a more strategic view of marketing research when they consider the marketing research as an element of the marketing information system.

Although it is viewed separately from marketing research, sales forecasting is concerned with 'information for marketing decisions', which is the thrust of this second part of the text. This subject is dealt with in the next chapter.

APPLICATION QUESTIONS

1. What problems are to be encountered in assessing the cost effectiveness of marketing research?
2. In which research circumstances are observation techniques more suitable than other fieldwork techniques?
3. Distinguish between the universe and the sample frame.
4. What are the essential elements of a marketing information system?
5. Explain what is meant by the following in the context of questionnaire design:

   (a) Open-ended questions.
   (b) Closed dichotomous questions.
   (c) Closed multiple-choice questions.
   (d) Semantic differential scales.

REFERENCES

1. P. M. Chisnall. *Marketing Research*, 3rd edn, McGraw-Hill, London, 1986.
2. Chisnall. op. cit., p. 38.
3. D. A. Dillman, J. G. Gallegos and J. H. Fray. 'Reducing refusal rates for telephone interviews', *Public Opinion Quarterly*, Spring 1976.
4. H. H. Kassarjion and M. Nakanishi, 'A study of selected opinion measurement techniques', *Journal of Marketing Research*, May 1969.
5. J. Kitchen. 'Observation, ethology and marketing research', *European Research*, January 1981, p. 22.
6. L. W. Rodger. *Statistics for Marketing*, McGraw-Hill, London, 1984, pp. 179–86.
7. ACORN is supplied by CACI London. It is discussed in detail in Chapter 7 'Selection of Markets'.
8. Rodger. op. cit., pp. 103–22.
9. Rodger. op. cit., Chapter 2, pp. 22–39.
10. N. H. Nie, *et al. SPSS-X*, SPSS-X, Chicago, IL, 1985.
11. See Rodger. op. cit., for a fuller discussion, pp. 122–32.
12. Chisnall. op. cit.
13. T. Watkins. *The Economics of the Brand*, McGraw-Hill, London, 1986.
14. G. E. Greenley. *The Strategic and Operational Planning of Marketing*, McGraw-Hill, London, 1986, pp. 124–39.
15. G. A. Lancaster and D. Jobber. *Sales Technique and Management*, Pitman, London 1990.
16. V. Bradley. *Applied Marketing and Social Research*, Van Nostrand Rineholt, New York, 1982.
17. E. Dichter. *Handbook of Consumer Motivations*, McGraw-Hill, New York, 1964.
18. V. Packard. *The Hidden Persuaders*, Longman, London, 1957.
19. G. A. Lancaster and L. C. Massingham. *Marketing Management*, McGraw-Hill, Maidenhead, 1993, p.274.

SALES FORECASTING

INTRODUCTION

It has now been established that a company's customers are the starting point for business planning activities, and this notion lies at the very heart of marketing. In times when demand exceeds supply, it is perhaps less important that individual consumer needs are attended to: indeed, in such circumstances it is not possible to fulfil all needs and some form of rationing has to be imposed. This, however, is a rather abnormal occurrence in modern industrialized societies and generally occurs after a war or an 'act of God'. Such conditions are then only temporary until manufacturing capacity expands sufficiently to meet the extra demand.

The point that was being made is that the 'norm' is for supply to exceed demand, and this is increasingly the case in the modern world where more efficient forms of manufacturing mean that the fulfilment of consumer needs becomes easier over time. The problem is thus a matter of matching supply to demand at a price acceptable to the marketplace. Such a problem demands that companies engage in pre-planning to ascertain what share of the market they might obtain, and then plan to achieve it.

FORECASTING AS THE START OF THE PLANNING PROCESS

Individual businesses are becoming more competitive in an increasingly complex and 'inter-nationalized' environment. Competitive circumstances tend to change more quickly nowadays and strategic decisions become increasingly critical and binding.

Companies must be able not only to predict their sales, but also to plan for profits, cash flows, etc. The days are gone when companies could afford to have 'slack' in terms of working capital, labour force, raw materials and finished stocks. Such 'slack' is costly (with higher labour and interest rates), and plant and manpower must nowadays be utilized to its optimum capacity. Inefficient use of such resources is costly, and profit margins are such that a company that does not manage such resources in an efficient manner will be prey to its more efficient competitors.

Forecasting sales must thus be the starting point of the planning process as this is the 'act of giving advance warning for beneficial action to be taken'.[1]

The main problem that exists within many organizations is that forecasting has traditionally been seen as a function of the accountant for purposes of budget preparation for the budget period ahead (normally one year), and this is termed the medium-term forecast. Accountants, naturally,

139

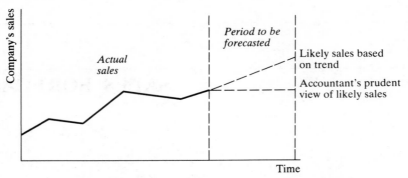

Figure 6.1 Theoretical view of a forecasting scenario

will not tend to overestimate and they will tend to forecast on the prudent side. Figure 6.1 illustrates a hypothetical situation. In this situation one might be inclined to level the accusation of excessive conservatism against the accountant. However, at the end of the day the cost/ management accountant is the one who must attempt to ensure that the organization does not over-spend in reaching its anticipated sales, and, in the absence of an intimate knowledge of what is happening in the marketplace, one can hardly blame the professional from adopting such a prudent approach.

The reality of this situation is that the market will probably grow as anticipated on the extrapolation, but the company cannot meet this growth totally because it is not prepared for it in terms of budget (e.g., there are not enough production facilities available to meet increased sales). The company will thus lose sales because it is not in a position to exploit the market. The irony of this situation is that, inevitably, production can most probably produce more than was budgeted for and sales can sell more than was budgeted for, so over-achieving on sales in this situation means that the exercise is often viewed as being successful on the basis that 'sales and production have done better than expected'! The fact that sales have in truth been lost is not considered.

One can postulate further and state that, if sales proceed better than 'likely sales based on trend', as shown in Fig. 6.1, then the capacity to lose sales will be increased even further. This leads to what McDonald calls a planning gap,[2] where action must be brought about to ensure that sales are not lost because production facilities and marketing resources are not available to meet potential demand.

We have thus established that the sales forecast is the start of the planning process and, for reasons just outlined, if the company is to achieve its maximum or optimum share of the market, then marketing must be the department that is responsible for the sales forecast. This fact is often not appreciated by many non-numerate marketing managers, and they are prepared to abrogate what is their direct responsibility to their more numerate colleagues in the finance department.

Once the situation relates to new markets or new products, it is inevitable that marketing must be involved. However, there can be a problem of what Clifton *et al.* refer to as self-protection and inertia.[3] This is where existing suppliers in a market will want to protect their own position and will tend to overstate the degree of competition and understate the market potential, when approached for information, in order to put off potential new entrants. Equally, inertia might rule inside the company, in that individuals within the firm might not want to extend themselves to addressing the problems of exploiting a new product or market. Needless to say, the problems to be overcome in this forecasting scenario rest with marketing analysts and not with cost accountants.

SENSITIVITY ANALYSIS

This is the technique of attempting to evaluate how changing various marketing inputs will affect sales. Forecasting sales for the market and the company can be done by a variety of techniques explained later in this chapter; but clearly, if, say, advertising or personal selling effort is reduced or increased during the period that has been forecasted, then sales will be affected. A forecaster, when forecasting company sales, does so with the advance knowledge that certain marketing mix inputs will take place. Manipulation of these inputs and a consequent assessment of the likely effect upon sales is known as 'sensitivity analysis'.

SHORT-, MEDIUM- AND LONG-TERM FORECASTS

Before we explain each of the above terms, it is perhaps appropriate to state that there are two methods by which forecasting data may be collected:

1. By making a forecast for the industry or total market and then determining what share of this will fall to the company (sometimes called a market forecast).
2. By forecasting sales direct using previous sales data or anticipating sales directly in some other way.

Usually the method used for market and then sales forecasts is termed a 'top-down' approach, in that the ultimate forecast is not obtained from an operational level in the organization. The opposite to this is termed 'bottom-up' forecasting, whereby the data are collected from the marketplace, usually by sales personnel who operate there. These methods are expanded upon in the next chapter.

Battersby produced the first UK written text on forecasting[4] and he differentiated between short-term and long-term forecasts. He introduced medium-term forecasts as being akin to long-term forecasts, but concerned with minor strategic decisions. Since then, the purpose of medium-term forecasting has become far more important, largely because, as has already been elucidated, it is the start of the planning process.

Briefly, each type of forecast may be said to be for the following purposes:

—Short term (for up to approximately three months ahead) Made largely for tactical reasons, e.g. to fulfil seasonal sales demands, for production planning purposes and cash flow requirements.
—Medium term (normally for one year ahead) Made principally for business budgeting. This forecast is the starting-point of the company's planning process. It is also used for predicting manning levels required to achieve these anticipated sales and for plant and machinery requirements.
—Long term (5, 10 or 20 years ahead) These forecasts are for major strategic decisions to be taken by the company. What is 'long term' is largely determined by the type of market in which the company operates. A self-evident example would be computers, where 'long term' is, say, less than five years, and steel production, where 'long term' may be 20 years. Long-term forecasts are used in areas such as management succession, company expansion and long-term financial planning requirements.

Before a company can plan, it must first forecast, as this reduces uncertainty. In this way, plans are based upon more scientific criteria. The problem is that, if the forecast is incorrect, or is based upon spurious premises, then the whole planning exercise will have been fruitless. The importance of accurate forecasts cannot, therefore, be emphasized enough. Companies can thus prepare for change by planning, in that the forecaster can predict what will happen for a set of decisions in a given set of circumstances. By taking certain actions, the planner can alter the subsequent events relating to a particular situation. A forecast may predict a fall in demand, and in this case management can make plans to counteract this fall in demand, or at least can plan to ensure that it suffers less from the fall in demand than do its competitors.

RELATIONSHIP BETWEEN FORECASTS AND BUDGETS

The forecast determines the budget, and through the sales budget sales are generated. The company sales budget is an amalgam of each individual salesperson's anticipated sales (their individual sales budgets), broken down in detail by product type, by territory and by selling area. Each individual salesperson then receives his or her share of the total sales budget which has to be sold in the period ahead, and this is then termed his or her individual sales quota or sales target.

A budget thus differs from a forecast in that the budget is what is planned to happen, unlike the forecast, which is a prediction of what is expected to happen. The forecast is, therefore, more uncertain as it is affected by external factors, whereas the budget is affected by more controllable internal factors.

One rather obvious, but sometimes ignored, fact is that the sales budget must be coordinated with other budgets within the organization. The sales budget, for instance, should not plan to achieve more sales than production has been budgeted to manufacture.

It must also be borne in mind that budgets should be flexible to allow for changing conditions or unforeseen circumstances. The budget can then be quickly changed to cover such contingencies.

TECHNIQUES OF FORECASTING

This section covers the specific techniques of sales forecasting, although not in sufficient detail to enable the reader to become a forecasting expert or specialist. For a more specialist text that starts from first principles, the reader is directed to *Forecasting for Sales and Materials Management*, by Lancaster and Lomas.[5]

Basically, sales forecasting is divided into qualitative and quantitative techniques. The first set are often called subjective or judgemental methods, as they rely heavily upon opinion in their computation. Quantitative techniques, as the term implies, rely upon mathematics, and such techniques are becoming very popular with the development of computer packages to assist in their application. Quantitative techniques can be split into time-series analysis and causal techniques. In time-series analysis, the variable that the forecaster considers is time and past events are used to predict the future. However, in applying such techniques, it is difficult to predict downturns or upturns, unless the forecaster deliberately manipulates the data. Such techniques are of little use in markets that are unstable or susceptible to sudden irrational changes. Causal techniques assume that there is a relationship between what is to be forecasted and some other measurable independent variable. The value of this independent variable is put into the equation and the forecast is produced from this. Importance must, therefore, be placed upon the choice of a suitable independent variable, and such variables should ideally precede what is to be forecast by a period sufficient to enable production and marketing plans to be implemented in good time. One should not attempt to establish the reasons behind such relationships, and there is often nothing to suppose that such relationships will hold good in the future. The fact is that a relationship has been established in the past, and part of the prediction is that it should probably hold good in the future.

It is logical to look at qualitative techniques first, because these are less scientific in their formulation; in fact, they are sometimes referred to as 'naive' methods. They often precede quantitative methods, and it is these latter that are now being taken increasingly seriously by progressive management, particularly as more sophisticated computational packages become available.

Qualitative techniques

Consumer/user survey method (market research method) This technique basically consists of asking one's customers about their likely purchases for the period it is desired to forecast and then attempting to ascertain what proportion of these anticipated purchases are likely to fall to one's company. It is quite often undertaken by the salesforce in the case of industrial products. Two problems thus arise: the accuracy of the apportionment of likely sales out of anticipated purchases; and the subjective opinion of buyers when giving their estimates to salespeople.

Sometimes it is not possible to ask customers through the salesforce, as is the case for consumer products because they are not usually sold direct to the general public. Here it makes sense to survey a sample of potential consumers through a market research survey (probably as part of an omnibus survey).[6] It is better to assess likely purchasing intentions on a graded answer basis, than on a straightforward dichotomous basis, particularly when the product is not a straightforward puchase. For instance, the decision to purchase a carpet is a complicated matter, and the purchaser goes through a number of different stages of purchasing intention before making the purchase—unlike, say, the purchase of a can of baked beans, where the decision is far simpler, based upon more immediate needs.

The method is, therefore, quite straightforward, but it is really of most value when there are a small number of purchasers who are likely to signal their intentions to purchase with a reasonable degree of accuracy. Forecasters should also be familiar with competition in the marketplace in order that they can assess more accurately what proportion of likely sales will accrue to their company out of the assessment for the total market. Consequently, its true value tends to be limited to organizational buying situations where purchasers and competitors are few—a rarity for most buying/selling situations!

Panels of executive opinion (jury method) This method is sometimes known as 'panels of expert opinion' because such 'experts' are counselled about the industry with which they are familiar with the object of producing a forecast. Such experts come from both inside and outside the company, including management consultants, professional forecasters and investment analysts. Sometimes the panel or jury can include people from client companies who will be in a position to provide advice from a purchasing standpoint.

The group meets in committee, and the committee produces a composite forecast which might mean having to average the results in the case of disagreement. The basic precept is that each member of the group should have prepared a forecast beforehand and must be able to support this forecast with hard evidence. Such evidence should be presented to the group and discussed, with any inconsistencies being overcome as they arise. As long as agreement is reached after each discussion, a similar set of forecasts should result, because each will represent the majority view; but as was stated earlier, aggregation may be necessary.

'Prudent manager forecasting' is a variation of this approach, when company personnel are asked to assume the position of prospective purchasers and evaluate company sales from a customer's point of view and 'prudently' estimate sales, taking into consideration matters like competitors' products in terms of their design, quality, price, service, etc., together with any other external factors that are considered to be of relevance to evaluating the company's sales.

Much of this type of forecasting is based upon opinion, and can be expensive in terms of the manpower involved in its preparation and discussion. It is a 'top-down' method in that a forecast is produced for the industry and it must then be decided what share of this forecast will accrue to the company. Statistics are not collected from market data (from the 'bottom up'), and there is a problem in deciding what sales will be in terms of individual products and sales territories. Such information is needed for the budgeting procedure, as was explained in the previous chapter. Thus, it has been demonstrated that there are a number of in-built problems associated with this type of forecasting, particularly the fact that it is a 'top-down' method, unlike mathematical forecasting that uses market data.

Salesforce composite This 'bottom-up' method is sometimes referred to as the 'grass-roots' approach, because it entails each salesperson in the company making an individual forecast for his or her particular sales territory. These individual forecasts are agreed with the area manager, who then takes them to the sales manager (or the divisional manager, if this stage exists in the sales hierarchy). A similar exercise is then performed between the area/divisional manager and the sales manager until the figures are agreed.

This method is quite popular, particularly in the area of setting sales quotas or targets. There can be less cause for subsequent complaint, because such figures are based on information stemming initially from the salesforce. A slight variation of this method is called 'detecting differences in figures'. Here, the salesperson prepares the figures suitably broken down by individual customers and by individual products. The area manager then produces a similar set of figures independently, and they then meet and resolve any differences that arise. The process continues in similar vein until it reaches the sales manager, when the final sales forecast is agreed.

This appears to be a good method, and, in so far as non-mathematical methods are concerned, it probably is. It does, however, fall down when the forecast is to be used for future remuneration (as it invariably is, through quotas and targets). There will thus be an inclination on the part of salespeople to produce a pessimistic forecast. This can be overcome in part by linking sales expenses to the forecast. When remuneration is not linked to the sales forecast, there might then be a tendency for the salesforce to produce an optimistic forecast. It is well known that salespeople tend to be optimists, perhaps as a result of optimistic noises made by buyers, all being part of good buyer–seller relationships. The salesforce might not, therefore, be an objective enough starting-point for sales forecasting and might produce an optimistically or pessimistically biased forecast for the reasons stated. In addition, the salesforce is not necessarily aware of the more global economic factors that might affect future sales, and may not take these into consideration when preparing forecasts.

Delphi method In this method the project leader selects the team and communicates through the post or telephone, but not in committee. He or she sends a questionnaire to members of the team (who may number 20 upwards) and they are asked to respond to questions of a behavioural nature to begin with. Such questions usually concern matters in the nature of a technological breakthrough—e.g. new processes for oil refining, new uses for glass products—that have some bearing on the products that the company makes. The answers are then collected and refined and a summary of the answers is sent out with the next round of questionnaires. This time the questioning can be more pointed, focusing on such matters as: 'If the new processes for oil refining, as predicted from the results of the first round of questionnaires, can be in production by 1990, how can this company benefit?' The rounds of questioning continue, becoming more specific each time, until sufficient useful information is to hand to make marketing and production decisions.

Because the information is not generated in committee, the danger of bandwagon effect of majority opinion is eliminated. However, this method cannot be recommended for the production of a product-by-product and customer-by-customer forecast, because it is more concerned with 'futures', and is really of value only for long-term matters like the viability of the company entering a market, or developing some new form of product or process for the future.

Bayesian decision theory This method owes its origin to an English cleric of the eighteenth century, but its workings have been refined by statisticians since that date. It is a mixture of subjective and objective material. Its detailed operation cannot be described here, and the reader is directed to more specific texts, like those described at the beginning of this chapter, for a fuller insight into its workings.

A network diagram is used, similar to critical path analysis. Probabilities are estimated by the forecaster for each event in the network. The probabilities thus represent the strength of the decision-maker's feeling regarding the likelihood of the occurrence of the various elements in the network. When making business decisions, one has to decide among alternatives by taking into account the monetary repercussions of actions taken. When one has to select among alternative investments, consideration must be given to the profit and loss situation that might result from each alternative. When applying Bayesian decision theory, this involves selecting an alternative and having a reasonable idea of the economic consequences of choosing that action.

Once the appropriate future events have been identified, and the respective subjective prior probabilities have been assigned, the decision-maker works out the expected payoff for each act and chooses the act with the most attractive payoff.

Generating the probabilities described above is a subjective business, and for this reason many forecasters reject the Bayesian approach. However, it can be useful in solving business problems for which probabilities are often unknown.

Product testing and test marketing   These methods are of most use when little or no previous sales data exist. In such instances it makes sense to anticipate likely demand for the product by testing it on a sample of the potential market beforehand.

The techniques of product testing and test marketing have already been described in Chapter 5. Since product testing involves only a small number of respondents and a summation of their opinions and attitudes towards a new or modified product, test marketing would appear to be the most appropriate medium for producing a sales forecast. Here the product is launched in a limited geographical area and one is thus able to simulate a national launch without committing too many resources in case the product is unsuccessful. Sales are measured during the test and are simply grossed up afterwards to provide a forecast.

The main drawback is that this technique is suitable only for new or substantially modified products of a consumer goods nature. There is also the problem of 'novelty', in that if the unit value is relatively small many people will purchase just to try it out and may never purchase again, which might lead one to produce an optimistic forecast for the national launch. It must also be remembered that it has been known for competitors to attempt deliberately to spoil a test marketing campaign by increasing their promotional activity in the relevant area over the test period.

Quantitative techniques (time series)

Moving averages   This is a very simple technique that smoothes the data in a time series. The longer the moving average, the greater will be the smoothing, and the principle is that one subtracts the earliest sales figure and then adds the latest sales figure. This figure is then divided by the appropriate number of data periods that have been added together to bring it back to an average. The example that follows provides the best explanation, where it can be seen that a longer moving average produces a smoother trend than a shorter moving average. The first moving average is for a three-year period, whereas the second moving average is over a six-year period and it is this one that provides the smoothest pattern of data.

The forecast is produced by extending the trend line, and it is up to the forecaster to decide

Table 6.1   Practical example of moving averages technique. Werman Duvet Company Ltd: annual unit sales of double-sized duvets, 1978–1993

Year	Number	Three years		Six years	
		Total	Average	Total	Average
1978	925				
1979	1023	3111	1037		
1980	1163	3886	1295		
1981	1700	4508	1503	8 030	1338
1982	1645	4919	1640	9 101	1517
1983	1574	5215	1738	10 510	1752
1984	1996	6002	2001	11 446	1908
1985	2432	6527	2176	11 924	1987
1986	2099	6709	2236	12 549	2092
1987	2178	6547	2182	13 356	2226
1988	2270	6829	2276	13 605	2268
1989	2381	6896	2299	13 604	2267
1990	2245	7057	2352	14 007	2334
1991	2431	7178	2393	14 156	2359
1992	2502	7260	2420		
1993	2327				

whether three-year or six-year averaging is better. In the case of a steady trend, it may not be necessary to smooth the data, and in such cases the process is simply called 'trend projection'. As a rule, the more the data fluctuate, the greater will the averaging period have to be. It is, of course, up to the forecaster to decide what averaging period to use: three years and six years have been used in the example in Table 6.1 for reasons of illustration.

In this particular example it can be seen that the three-year moving average would have been enough to provide a trend for purposes of forecasting, and even a two-year moving average would have sufficed. Longer moving-average periods are of more value to the forecaster when the data fluctuate a great deal. The graph in Fig. 6.2 illustrates this point.

Exponential smoothing   A major drawback with the moving-averages technique is that it does not respond immediately to a sudden change in sales, and if the sales trend changes it will take one or more periods before the trend is apparent in the forecast. (The longer the moving average, the longer it will take to reflect the change.) Exponential smoothing helps to overcome this by the apportionment of different weightings to earlier or later parts of the data. The skill lies in how the forecaster judges earlier or later parts of the time series to be more or less typical of the future.

The technique is relatively simple to operate, but it is essentially a technique that needs computer application, particularly if the forecaster is going to 'manipulate' the data to produce a number of different forecasts. The more precise mathematics of the technique cannot be entered into here, and the reader is again pointed to one of the more specialist forecasting or statistical texts mentioned earlier for a more detailed insight.

The technique is best illustrated by reference to the example in Fig. 6.2, annual sales of double-sized duvets for Werman Duvet Company Ltd. The sales are reproduced in Fig. 6.3, and from this it can be seen that weightings have been applied to earlier and later parts of the time series, according to how the forecaster viewed their typicality of how they would reflect the pattern for the future. In this particular example, the forecaster has a pessimistic view of the future and has

Figure 6.2   Werman Duvet Company Ltd: annual sales of double-sized duvets

apportioned a greater weighting to the downwards parts of the series and less to the upwards parts. Such weightings will produce a downward trend as the forecast, unlike the moving-average example, which produced a flattening yet still increasing trend (see Fig. 6.2).

Time-series analysis   The sales figures over a time period will fluctuate, but beneath this is a trend which the forecaster needs to know in order to apply his forecast. This fluctuation is particularly prevalent when the data contain seasonal figures or cyclical material. Bringing these seasonal or cyclical data down to a trend is called the purgative process. This technique, therefore, is of most use when there is a seasonal pattern that is repeated on a regular basis. The time-series analysis technique analyses these seasonal movements in terms of their deviations from the average trend and then adds them back into the forecast once the trend line has been extrapolated.

Using the Werman Duvet Company's quarterly sales figures over the past five years best describes how the technique works in practice. Sales are given quarterly, and it can be seen that for a product like duvets the sales fluctuate on a seasonal basis throughout the year, as one would expect. Unit sales are added for the four quarters to produce one year's data. The oldest quarterly period is then subtracted and the newest quarterly period added until the last quarter is reached. The next column adds two years' data, subtracting the oldest and adding the newest. The figure is then divided by 8 to discover the trend (because this contains four quarters over each of two years).

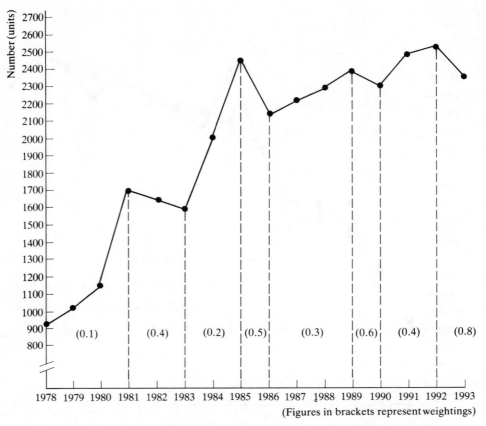

Figure 6.3   Werman Duvet Company Ltd: annual sales of double-sized duvets
(*Note:* Figures in brackets represent weightings)

Finally, deviations from the trend are calculated by subtracing the trend from the actual sales, or the actual sales from the trend, to produce a positive or negative figure in the form of deviations from the trend.

Table 6.2 gives the quarterly figures for sales of duvets for Werman Duvet Company Ltd and the appropriate calculations to provide the deviations from trend. It can be seen that when the quarterly deviations are totalled there is a positive sum of 21 remaining. The sum should equal zero, otherwise there will be a positive bias in the forecast. The sum comes equally off each quarter's figures (i.e., in this case five from three of the quarters and six from the other quarter, because to fractionalize the amounts exactly would give the forecast a spurious accuracy). In this example we have added four years, data, so the corrected deviations totals will have to be divided by 4 to bring them back to the correct average deviations. The result is as follows:

Quarter	1	2	3	4	
Deviations	−68	−207	−212	+487	=0

Again, for reasons stated earlier, the sum of the deviations should equal zero.

Table 6.2   Werman Duvet Company Ltd: quarterly sales of double-sized duvets, 1989 (1)–1993 (4)

Year	Quarter	Unit sales	Quarterly moving total	Sum of pairs	÷8 to find trend	Deviations from trend
1989	1	542				
	2	368				
	3	334	2381	4789	599	−265
	4	1137	2408	4825	603	+534
1990	1	569	2417	4848	606	−37
	2	377	2431	4676	585	−208
	3	348	2245	4441	555	−207
	4	951	2196	4417	552	+399
1991	1	520	2221	4482	560	−40
	2	402	2261	4692	586	−184
	3	388	2431	4857	607	−219
	4	1121	2426	4818	602	+519
1992	1	515	2392	4874	609	−94
	2	368	2482	4984	623	−255
	3	478	2502	5028	629	−151
	4	1141	2526	5108	638	+503
1993	1	539	2582	5075	634	−95
	2	424	2493	4820	603	−179
	3	389	2327			
	4	975				

Sum of quarterly deviations from trend, 1989–1993

Quarter	1	2	3	4	
Year					
1989			−265	+534	
1990	−37	−208	−207	+399	
1991	−40	−184	−219	+519	
1992	−94	−255	−151	+503	
1993	−95	−179			
Totals	−266	−826	−842	+1955	= +21
Corrected deviations	−271	−831	−847	+1949	= 0

The graph can now be drawn which will include the actual sales and trend line. From this, the trend line can be extrapolated. Following this, the deviations from trend should be added in as appropriate to produce the seasonal forecast which is then entered into the sales forecast. Figure 6.4 shows this information graphically.

In this particular case, the forecaster has predicted that the downward trend will continue for a short period and then turn upwards. This is where the skill of the forecaster comes in. Information for such a prediction can come from a variety of sources internal and external to the company. In fact, it is possible to apply some of the qualitative techniques described earlier, which are of more value in attempting to ascertain general trend patterns, particularly 'panels of executive opinion' and the 'Delphi' method.

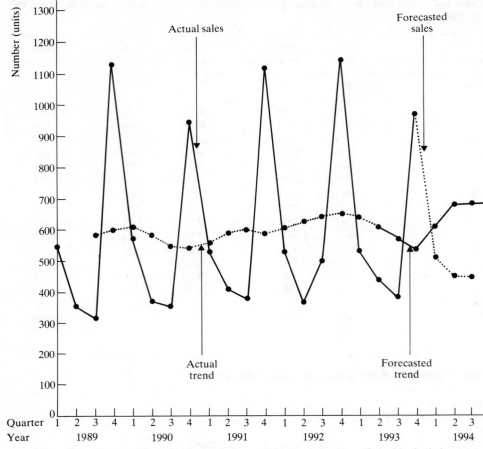

Figure 6.4   Werman Duvet Company Ltd: monthly quarterly sales of double-sized duvets

Table 6.3   Werman Duvet Company Ltd—Forecast

Year	Period	Trend	Deviation	Forecast
1993	3	565	−212	353
	4	540	+487	1027
1994	1	600	−68	532
	2	680	−207	473
	3	685	−212	473
	4	690	+487	1177

Table 6.4   Werman Duvet Company Ltd: monthly sales of double-sized duvets, 1992 and 1993

Month	Unit sales 1992	Unit sales 1993	Cumulative sales, 1993	Moving annual total
Jan.	216	240	240	2526
Feb.	136	122	362	2512
Mar.	163	177	539	2526
Apr.	149	179	718	2556
May	121	135	853	2570
Jun.	98	110	963	2582
Jul.	161	103	1066	2524
Aug.	141	111	1177	2494
Sep.	176	175	1352	2493
Oct.	328	294	1646	2459
Nov.	404	412	2058	2467
Dec.	409	269	2327	2327

Figure 6.4 shows quarterly sales and the trend line. The trend line has been extended to produce a forecast trend, and the deviations from trend have been entered on to this trend to produce an actual forecast as shown in Table 6.3.

The first two figures for 1993 quarters 3 and 4, have been given as a forecast, but these have passed, so they cannot be entered into the graph. Figure 6.4 actually produces a forecast for the four quarters of 1994 and it could, of course, have been extended further by extending the trend line and then applying the deviations from the trend.

The technique has much to commend it where there is a seasonality element in previous data. However, there must be an element of subjectivity in the extension of the trend line, and it is here that the forecaster must take most care, and apply a soundly thought-out forecast rather than merely extrapolating the general trend.

'Z' charts 'Z' or Zee charts only provide one year's data. For forecasting purposes, the forecaster must prepare a number of these from previous years and then compare them (usually merely by sight) to see whether there are any general patterns of trend that are repeated, so that a prediction can be made for the future. The technique is thus rather subjective, and its true value probably lies in the preparation of sales data, rather than as a serious medium for forecasting.

Data for two years are needed in order to produce a 'Z' chart and each line of the 'Z' represents previous sales in a different format. The bottom line is the monthly sales, the diagonal line is the cumulative sales and the top line is the moving annual total (calculated by taking off the figure 12 months ago and adding on the new month's figure). The technique is best explained by practical example from the monthly sales of Werman Duvet Company for 1992 and 1993, and this is illustrated in Table 6.4 and Fig. 6.5.

Quantitative techniques (causal)

Leading indicator This method uses the technique of linear regression to establish a relationship between an established measurable observation and what has to be forecasted. Linear regression

Figure 6.5 Werman Duvet Company Ltd: monthly sales of double-sized duvets

and its antecedent correlation are described more fully in Rodger's text.[7] Basically, Rodger states that it is possible to infer the existence of correlation (or interrelationship) between two sets of data from the visual inspection of these data on a diagram. One axis measures one set of criteria and the other measures another set. If the measurements come close together in a more or less straight line, the correlation is said to be linear, and there is then a close relationship between the two sets of data. Naturally, for forecasting purposes, if one knows in advance what the data are on one axis, then it is a simple matter to predict what the data will be on the other axis.

However, in real-life forecasting situations matters are not as easy as those just described, and in all probability the relationship between the two sets of data will be only approximately linear. We must, therefore, calculate the 'line of best fit' that runs through the data. This line is called the *line of regression*, and it describes in quantitative terms the underlying relationship or correlation between the two sets of data.

The technique needs a computer in its application, and there are a number of statistical packages available through which the technique can be used. The following simple illustration describes how the method can be applied:

The sale of children's clothes will depend upon the size of the child population. Therefore, a clothes manufacturer would use birth statistics as a leading indicator. The number of years that the indicator can precede the forecast, and for which sex of child, depends on the age range and the sex of clothing that the manufacturer caters for.

This is called *leading indicator forecasting* because the indicator precedes the forecast, but it is of course an over-simplification of how the method operates. Forecasting packages are available that combine a number of leading indicators and then provide a permutation of indicators that best fit known previous sales. It may well be that there is no logical reason why the permutation of a number of indicators relates to previous sales statistics. Such a permutation should be constantly under review as time passes the forecasted sales turn into actual sales. The permutation is then modified to take account of the most recent sales.

Simulation This is a technique that relies heavily upon the computer. It has already been explained that leading indicator forecasting seeks to establish a relationship between something that is measurable and the subject that is to be forecasted. Simulation uses trial and error (or iteration) in arriving at the forecasting relationship.

In a complicated forecasting situation the number of possible outcomes of possibilities is very large. The probabilities of various outcomes can, however, be estimated. This is known as *Monte Carlo simulation* (the obvious link being gambling on estimated probabilities). It depends upon a predetermined chance of a particular event occurring.

The technique is difficult to explain any further without going into complicated discussion and explanations. The reader is again pointed to Rodger's text for a more in-depth explanation than the one provided in this more basic marketing text.[8]

Diffusion models G. A. Lancaster and G. Wright have already provided a forecast of the video market using this technique.[9] In keeping with other causal techniques, the mathematics are complicated, and the reader should seek more specialist help before attempting to apply such methodology. The following explanation attempts to describe the thinking behind the process.

The techniques that have been explained so far have depended upon a series of past sales from the company or the industry to produce the forecast. When totally new products come on to the market there are no past sales to draw upon, and we must then rely on the application of theory called 'the diffusion of innovations'. This theory is discussed more fully in the next chapter, which deals with the product (or service), but it is appropriate to introduce it briefly here in order to describe this technique.

Diffusion theory assumes that new products have four basic elements:

1. The innovation
2. The communication of this innovation among individuals
3. The social system
4. Time

Innovations can be categorized into the following groupings:

—Continuous
—Dynamically continuous
—Discontinuous

These groupings are a hierarchical listing, with the innovations being more widely removed from previous technology as one moves further down the listing. This leads to a lower degree of likely acceptance of the innovation the further down the list the innovation is placed. In the early stages of a product innovation, knowledge must be communicated to as many potential customers as possible, particularly those who are likely to be influential in gaining wider appeal for the innovation. This process of communication is broken down into formal and informal communication. These two elements are fed into the forecasting model. As such, the model can be applied without large amounts of past sales data. The formal communication is controlled by the company and includes such data as advertising expenditure and sales support for the launch. The informal element relates to such matters as family and reference group influences.

After the innovation has been launched on to the market, a measure of the rate of adoption is needed in order to produce a useful forecast. Products are born, they mature and they die. It is important to the forecaster using this technique that the first few points of the launch sales are known in order to be able to determine the rate of adoption. The forecast can then be made using only a small amount of data points covering the early launch period. The assumption is made that the product has a life-cycle curve and that new product acceptance is through a process of imitation in that later purchasers will follow the innovators. The technique also provides a forecast of first-time users and not repeat purchasers.

MISCELLANEOUS

There are a number of further forecasting techniques, such as Box-Jenkins, spectral analysis and X-11, that are very specialized and sophisticated in their application. They are used only in rarefied circumstances, and to attempt an explanation here would perhaps imply that their importance is greater than is really the case. It is sufficient to say that they have been mentioned, and the reader should consider them only if a depth study of sales forecasting is to be undertaken. A more detailed view of these techniques, together with the part that forecasting plays in marketing planning, is provided by Lancaster and Massingham.[10]

CONCLUSIONS

The sales forecast precedes planning, and such plans are needed so that management can organize its activities in an ordered manner. Increasing competition means that businesses have to be more competitive, and this means making a more scientific approach to planning. Such an approach is through better sales forecasting.

Forecasting techniques have been split into qualitative techniques and quantitative techniques, with the latter being divided into time-series analysis and causal techniques.

Qualitative techniques have included: consumer/user survey methods, panels of executive opinion, salesforce composite, Delphi method, Bayesian decision theory and product testing and test marketing. Quantitative techniques (time series) have covered: moving averages, exponential smoothing, time-series analysis and 'Z' charts. Quantitative techniques (causal) have included: leading indicator, simulation and diffusion models.

Now that the market has been researched and forecasted, it is possible to select the market on which marketing efforts can be targeted: this is the subject of the next chapter.

APPLICATION QUESTIONS

1. As an information flow from the market to the firm, how important is sales forecasting for marketing? Why should such forecasting be the responsibility of marketing as opposed to finance?

2. Distinguish between qualitative and quantitative forecasting methods. State the advantages and drawbacks associated with each.

3. What is the relationship between the sales forecast and the sales budget?

4. How does a market forecast differ from a company forecast? How does a 'top-down' method differ from a 'bottom-up' method?

5. For a company of your choice in an industry of your choice (preferably ones with which you are in some way familiar), justify the forecasting methodology you would undertake in providing:

   (a) Medium-term forecasts.
   (b) Long-term forecasts.

REFERENCES

1. G. A. Lancaster and R. A. Lomas, *Forecasting for Sales and Materials Management*, Macmillan, London, 1985, p. 1.
2. M. McDonald, *Marketing Plans: How to Prepare Them*, Heinemann, London, 1990.
3. P. Clifton, H. Nguyer and S. Nutt, *Marketing Analysis and Forecasting*, Heinemann, London, 1985, p. 33.
4. A. Battersby, *Sales Forecasting*, Cassell, London, 1968, p. 7.
5. Lancaster and Lomas, op. cit.
6. This has been covered in Chapter 5, and it is where a company can purchase market research questions on a questionnaire shared with questions purchased by other companies. Costs are thus reduced, because it is unlikely that such questioning will take up more than one or two questions, for which it would not be worth mounting an individual survey.
7. L. W. Rodger, *Statistics for Marketing*, McGraw-Hill, London, 1984, pp. 122–32.
8. Rodger, op. cit., pp. 228–36.
9. G. A. Lancaster and G. Wright, 'Forecasting the future of video using a diffusion model', *European Journal of Marketing*, **17**(2), 1983, pp. 70–9.
10. G. A. Lancaster and L. C. Massingham, *Marketing Management*, McGraw-Hill, London, 1993, p. 297.

SEVEN
SELECTION OF MARKETS

INTRODUCTION

The central message of the marketing concept is the need for firms to identify and attempt to satisfy the genuine needs and wants of specifically defined target markets more effectively and efficiently than competitors. As a result of attempting to put this philosophy into practice, many firms have realized that, in order to relate their product and service offerings to the needs of the marketplace, it is not always possible, except in a few special circumstances, to treat the entire market as a homogeneous mass of potential purchasers. Doing this would be 'product-oriented' rather than 'market-oriented'. Market orientation means looking at the marketplace through the medium of marketing research and sales forecasting which have been considered in the prevous two chapters.

One of the most important developments in the history of marketing has been the realization that many overall markets are made up of significantly different groups or sub-markets. The people or organizations comprising each of these groups are often sufficiently similar as to be treated as a separate 'market' in terms of product offering, communication strategy, pricing policy, distribution and other marketing mix elements.

Hence, in the selection of 'markets', many firms are not so much concerned with the entire population of potential purchasers for a given product category (e.g. a motor car). They are more concerned with the most commercially attractive sectors in segments of the market for a given product form (e.g., the family saloon market or the sports car market).

This process of 'homing in' to particular segments of a given overall market is known as *target marketing*. Before one can do this, an investigation has to be made of the marketplace through various techniques already identified in Part Two. This is the logical culmination of the information-gathering process. This chapter discusses how much target markets can be identified, evaluated and selected.

THE CONCEPT OF A MARKET

The term 'market' often means different things to different people. There are many usages of the term in economics and in business in general. A market may be defined as a *place* where buyers and sellers meet, where goods are offered for sale and where transfer of ownership takes place. A market may also be defined as the total *demand* for a given product or service, for example the television market or the market for contract cleaning. Markets are also defined in *money* terms; for example, we may say the UK market for Axminster carpets is currently at around £45 million per year. Economists talk of a market as a set of conditions and forces that determine price levels.

We can see from the above examples that modern usage has given several meanings to the word 'market'. Whatever the context in which the term is used, it generally implies a demand for a product or service. Stanton et al.[1] state that, in the market demand for any given product or service, there are three factors to consider:

1. People with needs
2. Their purchasing power
3. Their buying behaviour

A market, therefore, can be defined as people with needs to satisfy, the money to spend and the willingness to spend it. From a marketing point of view, a market consists of not only existing customers but also potential customers. As Foster explains,[2]

> for marketing executives the market is not only present customers but all those persons and organisations who may be persuaded to buy the products or services they offer.

THE DEVELOPMENT OF TARGET MARKETING

The development of mass production and the mass markets of today has been discussed in Chapter 1. We saw that, as both domestic and international competition increased from the latter part of the nineteenth century, companies found themselves in a 'buyers' market' rather than a 'sellers market'. This change required greater sophistication on the part of firms in the marketing of their products and services. This eventually led to the wide-scale adoption of the marketing concept as a central business philosophy from around the middle of the present century.

The concept of target marketing is a refinement of the basic philosophy of marketing. It is an attempt by companies to relate the characteristics or attributes of the goods and services they provide more closely to customer requirements. When mass production techniques were first introduced, out of necessity they imposed a large degree of uniformity upon consumers. However, such techniques also brought an improvement in most people's standards of living. Mass production reduced unit costs and resulted in cheaper goods. Many products that were once considered luxuries of the rich became available to the ordinary people at affordable prices, and they did not really mind that their cars or sewing machines were of the same design or colour. To be even able to purchase such goods was a new experience for most people. Hence, in the early stages of mass production consumers did not really mind being treated as a homogeneous mass.

As consumers became more affluent, their aspirations also increased. They were no longer satisfied with 'a car' or 'a sewing machine', but wanted a particular type of product with *specific characteristics* that suited their requirements more accurately. Advances in production technology made a degree of product differentiation possible with little reduction in the economies of scale of the former mass production techniques. It was now possible to mass-produce a basic product such as a car, which in the later stages of production would take different routes in the assembly process. The result was different variants of the same basic model. The process was applied to many products other than motor cars.

Advancements in production techniques allowed firms to cater for disparities in consumer demand. Today, products are no longer regarded as commodities like 'coffee', or generic products such as 'cars', but are differentiated to suit the requirements of specific groups of consumers. For example, we now have a plethora of brands of coffee catering to different tastes, e.g. strong coffee, weak coffee, decaffeinated coffee, etc. Likewise with cars, we no longer have a generic Ford Escort as we did, say, with the Model 'T' Ford. Today, there is such a wide choice of Ford Escorts that it virtually amounts to buying a custom-built vehicle.

The situation today is that, while certain firms attempt to service an entire market for a particular product or service, this tends to be the exception rather than the rule. In such cases, either the market in question is very specialized and relatively small, or the firm enjoys some form of monopoly power. Many organizations operate in very large markets. Such firms recognize that the overall market is so large that it may not be possible to serve the entire population of that market effectively.

The overall market may be geographically dispersed and the firm may lack the resources to service it properly. For example, the computer 'market' is international. Very often the overall market for a particular product or service is too heterogeneous, in terms of the purchasing requirements of individuals or organizations making up the market, for any one firm to service adequately.

By targeting on to specific groups of consumers or 'market segments', instead of attempting to service the demand requirements of an entire population for a particular product category, the firm is able to develop more effective marketing programmes. To speak of the market for shampoo, audio equipment or even industrial valves is to ignore the fact that, within the total market for each of these products, there exist sub-markets which differ from one another in some commercially significant manner. This lack of homogeneity may be due to differences in the amount of money consumers are willing to pay, the way in which the product is used, motives for buying or other factors.

STAGES IN TARGET MARKETING

The process of target marketing needs to be carried out systematically and scientifically to be effective. Kotler[3] states that the process of target marketing has three distinct stages:

—*Stage One: Market segmentation* The overall market is divided into distinct groups of buyers who are likely to respond favourably to different product/service offerings and marketing mixes. The firm determines the most appropriate basis for segmentation, identifies the important characteristics of each market segment, and develops criteria for evaluating their commercial attractiveness and viability.
—*Stage Two: Market targeting* This is not to be confused with the overall process of target marketing. Market targeting is the process whereby one or more of the market segments previously identified are evaluated and selected.
—*Stage Three: Product positioning* Even within a given market segment, competitors' products are likely to be positioned in a particular 'niche' or position. Product positioning is the process whereby the product or service and all the other marketing mix elements are designed to fit a given place within a particular segment. Such a position may be more implied than real. It is how the consumer perceives the product's position relative to competitors' products that is important.

We shall now look at each of the three stages shown in Fig. 7.1. in more detail.

Market segmentation

The growth of specialized market segments has resulted in firms producing goods and services that are more closely related to the requirements of particular kinds of customers. Instead of treating all

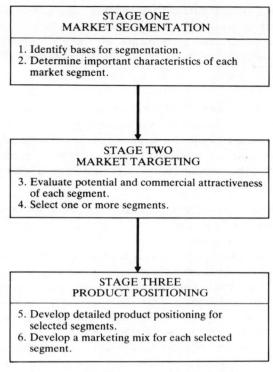

**STAGE ONE
MARKET SEGMENTATION**

1. Identify bases for segmentation.
2. Determine important characteristics of each
   market segment.

**STAGE TWO
MARKET TARGETING**

3. Evaluate potential and commercial attractiveness
   of each segment.
4. Select one or more segments.

**STAGE THREE
PRODUCT POSITIONING**

5. Develop detailed product positioning for
   selected segments.
6. Develop a marketing mix for each selected
   segment.

Figure 7.1   The three stages of target marketing

customers as a homogeneous mass, firms have identified sub-groups of customers whose precise needs can be more effectively met.

As Levitt explains,[4] the marketer should:

> stop thinking of his customers as part of some massively homogeneous market. He must start thinking of them as numerous small islands of distinctiveness, each of which requires its own unique strategies in product policy, in promotional strategy, in pricing, in distribution methods, and in direct selling techniques.

The whole process of target marketing can be illustrated schematically as shown in Fig. 7.1.

Manufacturers have always been aware that certain products were purchased by certain types of people. Rich people tended to buy fine wines and fashionable clothes, whereas poorer people tended to buy ale and more basic items of clothing. Much of this early 'segmentation' was accidental. It just so happened that products were purchased by certain types of people. Producers rarely had any particular target groups in mind, or if they did it was largely based on common sense rather than being a conscious segmentation policy.

As business people began to pay greater attention to the needs and wants of the marketplace, they began to realize that, since the people or organizations that make up a particular market are likely to be heterogeneous, they are unlikely to have identical preferences. Consequently, it was highly unlikely that one product would satisfy everyone. The outcome of this realization can be seen today in the many everyday products we see on our supermarket shelves. For example certain brands of toothpaste, such as Crest, were originally marketed with one simple flavour. However, the fact that people do not have identical preferences suggested the possibility of a number of market segments. In order to serve their customers more effectively, Procter and Gamble now market Crest in different flavours, different formulations (e.g paste and gel), and with different ingredients (e.g. regular or 'tartar control' formula). Hence the total Crest market is broken down into smaller groups or segments made up of people who may be prepared to pay a little more to obtain a toothpaste that suits their personal taste or preferences more closely than the 'standard' flavour or formulation.

Bases for segmenting consumer markets There is no 'golden rule' when it comes to segmenting consumer markets. The marketing firm may have to investigate using many different segmentation variables in order to gain an insight into the structure of the overall market. Very often it may be necessary to use a combination of variables in order to define a precise market segment. The sections that follow describe the main discriminating variables used to segment consumer markets.

Demographic variables Demographic factors are perhaps one of the more straightforward bases for segmenting consumer markets; they are also one of the most meaningful. The main demographic variables are given below.

Age For many products purchase behaviour is strongly related to age. For example, the 18–24-year age group tends to buy the latest style of clothing and a large proportion of 'pop' records, to eat a lot of 'take-away' food and to read certain magazines and newspapers aimed mainly at the 'youth market', e.g. *New Musical Express*. The 'youth market' is a specific market segment, as is the 25–35-year and 60+ year segments. Although age is one of the more straightforward segmentation variables, it is also one of the most important.

Sex Many product purchases are also related to sex. Some of these products will be obvious to the reader, e.g., dresses, lingerie, cosmetics (including mens' cosmetics) and 'women's' magazines such as *Woman's Weekly*. Some products are not so obvious; for example, certain motor cars tend to be regarded as 'female' cars; this is also true of certain brands of cigarettes.

Family size This is usually categorized as 1–2, 3–4, 5+. Obviously, the size of family will have some effect on the types of product purchased and this is especially so of pack size, e.g. family size pack.

Family life cycle In the UK the family remains the basic social unit. The demand for many products, for example consumer durables such as washing machines, refrigerators, etc., is related to stage reached in the family life cycle. These stages are often defined as:

Young	Young single, no children	Young couple, youngest child under 6	Young couple, youngest child 6+	Older couple with children 18+ at home	Older couple, no children at home	Older single

A development in the use of family life cycle segmentation is the approach developed by Research Services[5] and branded as SAGACITY. In fact, this segmentation approach combines life cycle with income and occupation to delineate different consumer groups. The approach is as follows.

First, consumers are divided into one of four possible life cycle groups:

1. *Dependent* Adults 15–34 who are not heads of household or housewives unless they are childless students in full-time education.
2. *Pre-family* Adults 15–34 who are heads of household or housewives but childless.

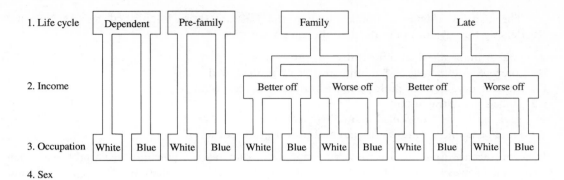

1. Life cycle
2. Income
3. Occupation
4. Sex

—*Dependent, white (DW) 6%* Mainly under 24s, living at home or full-time students, where head of household is an ABC1 occupation group.

—*Dependent, blue (DB) 9%* Mainly under 24s, living at home or full-time students, where head of household is in a C2DE occupation group.

—*Pre-family, white (PFW) 4%* Under 35s who have established their own households but have no children and where the head of household is in an ABC1 occupation group.

—*Pre-family, blue (PFB) 4%* Under 35s who have established their own households but have no children and where the head of household is in a C2DE occupation group.

—*Family, better off, white (FW+) 6%* Housewives and heads of household, under 65, with one or more children in the household, in the 'better off' income group and where the head of household is in an ABC1 occupation group (65% are AB).

—*Family, better off, blue (FB+) 9%* Housewives and heads of household, under 65, with one or more children in the household, in the 'better off' income group and where the head of household is in a C2DE occupation group (72% are C2).

—*Family, worse off, white (FW−) 8%* Housewives and heads of household, under 65, with one or more children in the household, in the 'worse off' income group and where the head of household is in an ABC1 occupation group (72% are C1).

—*Family, worse off, blue (FB−) 14%* Housewives and heads of household, under 65, with one or more children in the household, in the 'worse-off' income group and where the head of household is in a C2DE occupation group (47% are DE).

—*Late, better off, white (LW+) 5%* Includes all adults whose children have left home or who are over 35 and childless, who are in the 'better-off' income group, and where the head of household is in an ABC1 occupation group (60% are AB).

—*Late, better off, blue (LB+) 7%* Includes all adults whose children have left home or who are over 35 and childless, who are in the 'better-off' income group, and where the head of household is in a C2DE occupation group (69% are C2).

—*Late, worse off, white (LW−) 9%* Includes all adults whose children have left home or who are over 35 and childless, who are in the 'worse-off' income group, and where the head of household is in an ABC1 occupation group (71% are C1).

—*Late, worse off, blue (LB−) 19%* Includes all adults whose children have left home or who are over 35 and childless, who are in the 'worse-off' income group, and where the head of household is in a C2DE occupation group (70% are DE).

Figure 7.2   SAGACITY system and group descriptions

3. *Family* Adults under 65 who are heads of household or housewives in households with one or more children under 21 years of age.

4. *Late* All other adults whose children have already left home or who are 35 or over and childless.

These four major life cycle groups are then broken down further by a combination of occupation and/or income to produce 12 major SAGACITY groupings. These, together with a description of each group and the approximate size of each group as a percentage of the total UK adult population, are shown in Fig. 7.2. The evidence suggests that SAGACITY is a powerful discriminator between customer groups for a wide variety of products and services, ranging from package holidays to cars, use of financial services and so on.

Social class income The current convention in the UK is to use a mixture of social class and income. Classifications are based on the occupation of the head of the household.

The socio-economic groupings used in the UK are those established by the National Readership Survey, and fall into the following categories:

A   Higher managerial, administrative or professional
B   Intermediate managerial, administrative or professional
C1 Supervisory, clerical, junior administrative or professional
C2 Skilled manual workers
D   Semi-skilled and unskilled manual workers
E   State pensioners, widows, casual and lowest grade earners

In more recent years the use of socio-economic groups as a segmentation variable has been criticized. However, in 1981 the Market Research Society published the findings of a Joint Industry Working Party, entitled *An Evaluation of Social Grade Validity*.[6] The following points were reported:

—Social grade provides satisfactory discriminating power.
—No other classification variable could provide consistently better discriminatory power.
—No evidence was found to show a decline in the discriminatory power of social grade over recent years.

The use of socio-economic grade in market segmentation is discussed in more technical detail by Crimp.[7]

Geodemographic techniques Partly because of some limitations of either geographic or social class segmentation, considerable effort and research has focused on finding newer and more powerful bases of segmenting and targeting markets. Aided and abetted by the power of the modern computer, a number of approaches have been developed which are based on a combination of where the customer lives and a variety of socio-demographic variables, e.g. occupation, home ownership, size of family, etc. Not surprisingly, these approaches have come to be termed *geodemographic*, and they represent one of the most significant and potentially far-reaching developments in target marketing to date. Although a full explanation of all the geodemographic techniques is beyond the scope of this text, some of the more widely used ones are outlined below.

1. A significant recent development in segmentation studies, related to geographic, cultural, socio-economic and other factors, is '*A Classification of Residential Neighbourhoods*' (*ACORN*). The ACORN system is a method of 'mapping' geographically the concentrations of particular types of people. The assumption is that the demographic/socio-economic characteristics of people can be correlated to the housing characteristics of a particular area. The ACORN classifications are derived using a multi-variable statistical treatment of Census of Population data and are divided into ACORN groups and ACORN types. The ACORN groups are shown in Table 7.1.

Each ACORN group is subdivided further into ACORN types. By way of illustration, Table 7.2 shows the ACORN types given for ACORN Group B (Modern family housing, higher incomes).

The ACORN system has proved useful in many areas of marketing, such as retail store location and poster site location. It is of particular importance when a firm is considering using direct mail. Instead of wasting a lot of mail shots on people who are unlikely to be interested in the product, ACORN allows the firm to 'target in' accurately on the market segment of interest.

Although developed at the Centre for Environmental Studies by Richard Webber, the principal uses of ACORN are now in marketing applications. Consolidated Analysis Centres Inc. (CACI), for whom Webber now works, offers a variety of research services based on ACORN data.

Table 7.1   ACORN groups based on the 1981 Census of Population

A	Agricultural areas
B	Modern family housing, higher incomes
C	Older housing of intermediate status
D	Poor-quality older terraced housing
E	Better-off council estates
F	Less well-off council estates
G	Poorest council estates
H	Multi-racial areas
I	High-status non-family areas
J	Affluent suburban housing
K	Better-off retirement areas

Table 7.2   ACORN types for Group B (modern family housing, higher incomes)

B3	Cheap modern private housing
B4	Recent private housing, young families
B5	Modern private housing, older children
B6	New detached houses, young families
B7	Military bases

For example, 'sample plan' is a service that can be used by marketing research organizations. A computer program is used to select ACORN areas and then individual addresses which will provide the most representative sampling frame for the survey in question. Interviewers can then be provided with clear instructions as to which householders to interview and how to sample them.

Similarly, SITE is a CACI service for determining store location. Potential sites can be assessed by comparing the potential buying power and purchasing patterns of the various ACORN groups in the vicinity of a proposed location in order to find sites with maximum potential.

These are just some examples of the applications of ACORN in segmentation and targeting. The power of ACORN is evidenced by the fact that British Market Research Bureau (BMRB) now analyses the 24 000 panel data respondents in its Target Group Index (TGI) survey on the basis of ACORN groups. For a wide variety of products and services, the TGI data indicate that ACORN segmentation is very effective.

This effectiveness of segmentation based on census data and neighbourhoods has spawned a number of similar approaches.

2. *Pinpoint (PIN) analysis*, developed by a London company of the same name, is also based on analysing census enumeration districts, but a larger sample is claimed, and a system of Ordnance Survey grid referencing provides very accurate targeting. A total of some 104 census variables are used to delineate a possible 60 neighbourhood types which can be further clustered into 12 main types.

3. *MOSAIC* is, again, based essentially on census enumeration districts. This system has added data on the financial circumstances of potential target customers living within each

enumeration district, together with techniques for eliminating errors in relating postcodes to enumeration districts.

Education Many products are related, in a general way, to the purchaser's level of formal education. Classical music recordings, certain types of books, items of clothing and the purchase of more exotic kinds of food and wine are examples of this. This is very much a generalization, as there are many people with little formal education who appreciate such products.

Perhaps of greater importance is the fact that consumers' media habits are related to education. Taken as an aggregate, it would be true to say that the better educated tend to read the better-quality broadsheet newspapers such as *The Times* or the *Guardian*. Such people are also more likely to watch the more 'highbrow' commercial television programmes, such as 'World in Action' or the 'South Bank Show'.

Education is also related to social class group because, as a rule, the better educated tend to obtain better jobs. Clearly, a firm wishing to advertise a product aimed at the higher socio-economic/better educated segments of the market would be wise to use the appropriate types of media.

As a segmentation variable, education is usually expressed as terminal education age (TEA). A person's TEA is based on age on finishing full-time education. This particular classification is open to criticism, especially today, where cut-backs in full-time education provision have increased the emphasis on part-time studies. Many people today go back to education in later life to study for degrees and professional qualifications. Therefore, the standard question, 'How old were you when you finished your *full-time* education?' may not really give an indication of a person's true level of educational attainment.[8]

Benefit segmentation Benefit segmentation uses *causal* rather than *descriptive* variables to group consumers. Different people buy the same or similar products for different reasons. For example, some people buy a car purely as a means of transport, others because the shape and design of the car give them pleasure, others as a status symbol or as an extension of their personality, and others for patriotic reasons; e.g., they might always buy British.

Haley[9] first introduced this approach, based on the idea that consumers could be grouped according to the *principal benefit* sought. The now classic example given by Haley concerned the benefit segmentation of the US toothpaste market. Although this is now somewhat 'historical', the example showed that the use of a combination of different types of segmentation variables could lead to the conclusion that the main criterion for segmentation is the 'principal benefit sought'. Hence, although this approach acknowledges the fact that no single variable is likely to be of sufficient discriminatory power adequately to segment a market on its own, it regards the benefit sought as the *main variable*. As Haley himself states:

> the benefits which people are seeking in consuming a given product are the basic reasons for the existence of true market segments.

A further illustration of the principle of benefit segmentation is given by Bass *et al.*[10] An investigation into the principal benefits sought by consumers from a milk substitute allowed Cadbury Schweppes to develop the brand 'Marvel' to offer the following benefits:

1. As an emergency standby in case a household ran out of milk.
2. As a fat-free healthy substitute for conventional milk.
3. As an aid to slimming.
4. As a convenient way of using 'milk' for people who only use very little, i.e. less than a whole pint per week.

In using benefit segmentation, the marketing firm needs to determine the major benefits people are seeking from a particular product class, to identify the profiles of the people seeking each benefit, and to recognize the existing competitors' products that are close to delivering each of the benefits. Some of the benefits sought may not be serviced by existing products. This will give the firm the opportunity of capitalizing on an unsatisfied market segment.

Segmentation by usage Consumption rates for many consumer products are not evenly distributed across all households. Hence, meaningful segments could be defined in terms of usage of the product itself. As Frain[11] explains:

> Research does indeed indicate that a 'skewed' purchasing pattern often does apply—even to products intended for a mass market: 50 percent to 80 percent of the purchases of some commonly-bought products are made by 20 percent to 30 percent of all UK housewives.

If the firm can identify such heavy users, it may be able to develop a special marketing strategy aimed at winning more of them to the brand. For example, Bass *et al.* showed that heavy users of beer in the United States tended to be working-class, between 25 and 50 years of age, watched television more than $3\frac{1}{2}$ hours per day and preferred to watch sports programmes. Consumer profiles such as this are obviously helpful to the marketing firm in developing pricing and communication strategies.

Loyalty status A market can also be segmented according to the degree of consumers' brand loyalty. Kotler[12] divided consumers into four groups according to their loyalty status. To illustrate the principle, let us assume we are analysing purchasing behaviour relating to five brands of toilet soap which we will call simply A, B, C, D and E.

—*Hard-core loyals* These are consumers with undivided loyalty to one brand. Their purchasing pattern over six periods would be say, A,A,A,A,A,A.
—*Soft-core loyals* These consumers have divided loyalty between two or more brands. The purchasing pattern of such people may look something like A,B,B,A,A,B.
—*Shifting loyals* These consumers 'brand-switch' their loyalty between two or more brands. Their purchasing pattern may look something like B,B,B,A,A,A.
—*Switchers* This class of consumer shows no brand loyalty at all, but instead 'switches' from one brand to another. Their purchasing pattern may look something like B,E,C,A,D.

A company can usually attract switchers, at least in the short term, by price reductions or other forms of sales promotions. A careful analysis of brand loyalty categories can tell the firm a lot about its present marketing strategy and can point the way to improvements. For example, from an analysis of 'shifting loyals', the firm may learn about possible inadequacies in its marketing programme that are causing people to switch brands.

Geographical and cultural segmentation In Britain the indigenous population tends to be very similar culturally, although some people would argue that there are distinct regional differences (e.g. North and South of England, for beer and certain types of food). There are certainly areas of the country that are suffering more than others from declining industries and unemployment. These factors clearly act as a constraint on purchasing behaviour.

In certain parts of the UK, most notably Northern Ireland, the cultural differences are more marked. This is also true of areas of high immigrant concentration, which are often culturally distinct, and hence may be treated as a separate market segment for certain products and services.

Geographic and cultural differences are even more pronounced within certain overseas countries. This would be so of Belgium and to a lesser extent France and Germany.

Table 7.3   Life style dimensions

Activities	Interests	Opinions	Demographics
Work	Family	Themselves	Age
Hobbies	Home	Social issues	Education
Social events	Job	Politics	Income
Vacation	Community	Business	Occupation
Entertainment	Recreation	Economics	Family size
Club membership	Fashion	Education	Dwelling
Community	Food	Products	Geography
Shopping	Media	Future	City size
Sports	Achievements	Culture	Stage in life cycle

Source J. T. Plummer, 'The concept and application of lifestyle segmentation', *Journal of Marketing*, 38, January 1974, p. 34.

Life style and psychographics As we have seen, many of the more traditional bases for segmenting consumer markets, at the very least, lack a certain richness in describing consumer segments and at worst are misleading predictors of buyer behaviour. Life style and psychographic segmentation is an attempt to remedy these problems. But what is meant by 'life style' and 'psychographics'?

Life style is a term used to describe how individuals spend both their time and money, reflecting in turn their underpinning attitudes, personality, and social, educational and cultural backgrounds. One of the clearest definitions is given by Chisnall:[13]

> The concept of lifestyle refers to the distinctive or characteristic ways of living adopted by certain communities or segments of communities. It relates to the general attitudes and behaviour towards the allocation of time, money and effort in pursuit of objectives considered desirable by particular types of individuals.

Psychographics is more difficult to define—indeed, there is a lack of general agreement as to its precise meaning. However, broadly, psychographics is the process, and collection of related techniques, for measuring the life styles of individual consumers. A number of approaches and techniques have been developed for measuring and classifying life style groups.

The meaning and uses of life style and psychographics in market segmentation are perhaps easiest understood if we examine one of the earliest and best known approaches to identifying life style segments. In the early 1970s, J. T. Plummer[14] reported a life style study based on the following measures:

—How individuals spent their time on *activities*.
—Their major *interests*.
—Their *opinions* about themselves and the world in general.

Perhaps not surprisingly, this approach was referred to as the AIO framework. Respondents were asked to respond to a series of questions designed to measure their *a*ctivities, *i*nterests and *o*pinions. Information was also collected on background demographic characteristics. Table 7.3 illustrates the major elements that formed the focus of the AIO questions, together with information on demographics. Approximately 300 AIO statements were included, and respondents were asked to indicate their agreement or disagreement on a six-point scale, from 'Definitely agree' to 'Definitely disagree'. Examples of 'typical' AIO statements are:

'I like active sports.'

'I enjoy classical music.'

'I go out most evenings.'

'Sex is more important to men than to women.'

'Buying on credit is immoral.'

Using a statistical analysis of responses to such AIO statements, respondents were clustered together into distinct life style groups with descriptive labels being issued to capture the essential characteristics of each group.

Over the past few years, interest in the application of life style research in marketing has grown substantially, with many studies of life style groups being conducted in both Europe and the United States.

An example of life style research in the United Kingdom is that conducted by Research Bureau Ltd. Using AIO statements with a sample of 3500 housewives under the age of 45, the following life style groups were identified.[15] Here we can see the use of the descriptor labels referred to above.

—*'The young sophisticates' (15%)* Generally: extravagant, experimental, non-traditional, young, well educated, owner-occupiers, full-time employed, interested in new products, sociable.

—*'Cabbages' (12%)* Generally: conservative, demographically average, middle-class, average income, home-centred, little entertaining.

—*'Traditional working class' (12%)* Generally: traditional, quality-conscious, enjoy cooking but do not experiment, middle-aged, lower socio-economic group, lower incomes, sociable, husband and wife share activities.

—*'Middle-aged sophisticates' (14%)* Generally: not traditional, experimental, middle-aged, ABC1 social class, well educated and affluent, interested in new products, sociable, cultural interests.

—*'Coronation Street housewives' (14%)* Generally: conservative, traditional, quality-conscious, obsessive, DE social class, less educated, lower incomes, part-time employment, not interested in new products, not sociable.

—*'The self-confident' (13%)* Generally: self-confident, quality-conscious, young, well educated, owner-occupiers, average incomes.

—*'The homely' (10%)* Generally: bargain seekers, not self-confident, house-proud, social class C1, C2, part-time employed, some entertaining.

—*'The penny-pinchers' (10%)* Generally: self-confident, traditional, not quality-conscious, 25–35 years, social class C2DE, less education, average income, husband and wife share activities, sociable.

In the United States, the advertising agency Needham, Harper & Stears used AIO measures to identify the following male and female life style groups:

—*Male life style groups*
  1. The self-made businessman   (17%)
  2. The devoted family man   (17%)
  3. The frustrated factory worker   (19%)
  4. The successful professional   (21%)
  5. The retired homebody   (26%)
—*Female life style groups*
  1. The socialite   (17%)
  2. The contented housewife   (18%)

3. The militant mother   (20%)
4. The suburbanite   (20%)
5. The traditionalist   (25%)

We can see from these examples how life style segmentation attempts to categorize consumers into distinct groups (segments) with a clear picture of the dominant motives, habits, aspirations and so on of each group. This information can then be used to develop clear targeting and positioning strategies, with the marketing mix being formulated to the specific life style requirements of each group.

The examples shown so far of life style research fall into the category of general life style segmentation; i.e., the AIO statements, and hence the life style categories, are general and not product-specific. Product-specific life style research measures product-related activities, interests and opinions. Some believe that product-specific life style research is a much better predictor of product and brand choice. As we might expect, product-specific life style research uses AIO statements relating to the product category in question. For example, respondents might be given AIO statements relating to, say, the motor car and driving, or alcohol consumption. A number of product-related life style studies have resulted in the targeting of certain types of cigarette smokers, beer drinkers, drivers, users of financial services, coffee drinkers and so on.

It is not difficult to see the appeal of life style segmentation to marketers. Not only does it provide a means of identifying different potential target groups, but it also provides a rich tapestry of insights into the different customer types and their needs and wants, and hence provides valuable clues for planning the marketing mix. Advertising in particular can be more effectively planned with life style information. Examples of advertising campaigns based on some form of life style research include: the recent advertising for Guinness stout; Colgate Palmolive's 'Irish Spring' soaps; Schlitz beer; the British Gas share campaign; and Legal & General's insurance policies.

Life style and psychographics is not without its critics and problems. The research required can be expensive and difficult to interpret. Some doubt the validity of some of the underpinning concepts. Finally, life styles change, and hence the life style categories being used can become outmoded. However, the distinct advantages of life style segmentation stemming from the richness of the insights it gives into consumer behaviour mean that life style segmentation is here to stay.

This section has covered the main variables used to segment consumer markets. The list is not exhaustive; there are other variables which can be used depending on the situation. Many of the variables discussed here, and other less frequently used methods of segmentation, are discussed further by Frank et al.[16]

Industrial market segmentation

The concept of segmentation can also be applied to industrial markets, although the bases used are likely to be different. A more detailed discussion is given by Hutt and Speh, in their book on business marketing.[17] The following is an example of the most frequently used industrial segmentation variables:

1. *Size of firms* The criteria used could be turnover, capital employed or number of employees. Large firms tend to have different criteria for evaluating a supplier and its products than smaller firms. This is due partly to the fact that larger firms are able to employ professional buyers.
2. *Type of industry* The criteria used may be manufacturing or service industry, nationalized/ private industry, or actual type of activity, e.g. electronics or glass industry. Different industries may have different requirements in terms of product specifications, price, or after-sales service.

A firm selling, say, industrial valves may need a different marketing strategy and marketing mix for each industrial segment it deals with.

3. *Geographical region* Some areas of the UK are designated 'Enterprise Zones' or 'Assisted Areas'. The firms operating in such areas often qualify for government grants or other financial assistance. Again, a firm marketing to organizations in such areas is likely to have a different marketing strategy, especially in relation to pricing and communication policy, from that used in other parts of the country. Other geographical criteria may be urban, rural, European Community, Eastern bloc, developing country, etc.

4. *Type of buying organization* This segmentation variable is also related to size of firm. How an organization purchases its products affects the way a marketing firm negotiates and communicates with it. Larger firms tend to have a very formal purchasing procedure (e.g., British Gas). Smaller firms tend to be more informal.

Many organizations have factories or divisions located in different parts of the country or in different countries. Some of these firms will have a centralized purchasing system, where the whole company's requirements are purchased from Head Office. Other firms may have a decentralized purchasing system which allows each factory or division a certain amount of purchasing autonomy. How an organization's purchasing system is organized will have an effect on the policies of marketing to that firm.

Industrial buying situations In organizational purchasing, the following situations can be observed:

1. *New buy* As far as the buying firm is concerned, a 'new buy' situation would be:
   (a) The marketing firm was offering a totally new product.
   (b) It had never purchased from this supplier before so it was a 'new' situation.
   (c) The product had been around for some time, but this was the first time the firm had actually bought it.

2. *Modified re-buy* The buying organization had purchased a similar product before, but this one is slightly different, e.g. a new, more advanced machine tool.

3. *Routine re-buy* The buying organization had been purchasing the same product from the same firm for a number of years.

In a 'new buy' situation, the buying firm experiences a high degree of perceived risk. Marketing strategies should be aimed at reducing this risk, e.g. through a free trial, after-sales service or a guarantee. A modified re-buy is perceived as being less risky although not risk-free, and a straight re-buy is perceived as a minimal-risk situation.

Service elasticity Very often a firm will be attempting to market the same product to different industries. Service requirements, and the perceived importance of the level of service offered by the marketing firm, is likely to differ between industries. For example, a firm may be marketing industrial valves to both oil and sugar processing industries. In the oil industry price is of relatively little importance; delivery, reliability, stock availability and maintenance are very important. In the sugar industry price is likely to be one of the major purchasing criteria. The marketing firm will have to take a completely different approach in marketing these products to each industrial segment.

Price elasticity Some firms or industries are more concerned about price than others. For large successful firms, price differentials between suppliers would have to be relatively large before they would consider switching from an established supplier. Smaller firms tend to look for the cheapest source of supply they can get, although extended credit is often of more importance. A computer firm marketing hardware to public authorities would have to use a different pricing strategy than if it was dealing with, say, ICI or Ford (UK). It can be said that some firms or industries are more price-elastic or 'price-sensitive' than others.

Market structure   When a firm is dealing with a number of different industries, it may be possible to segment by market structure. Some industries may be dominated by a few large, powerful firms (e.g. the motor car industry or the defence industry). Other industries may be made up of hundreds of smaller firms. The marketing firm's approach is likely to be different between industries; i.e., it would treat large firms that virtually dominate the market differently from smaller, less powerful firms.

Decision-making unit   In industrial firms, purchasing decisions are rarely taken by one individual, except perhaps in routine re-buy situations. Very often a number of individuals are involved in the overall purchasing process. The group of people involved are known as the decision-making unit (DMU).

Again, the composition of a firm's DMU is likely to differ by type of industry, size of firm, whether the firm is a public or private-sector firm, whether the purchasing function is organized on an informal/formal basis or on a centralized/decentralized basis. The composition of the DMU is, therefore, related to some of the other factors mentioned earlier. However, when used as a basis for segmentation, it is the actual structure of the DMU that is used as the *main* discriminatory segmentation variable.

Until relatively recently, certainly compared with consumer markets, industrial market segmentation has been a neglected area by academics and researchers. However, recognition of the value of effective segmentation in business markets has led to the development of more powerful industrial segmentation models based on step-by-step, hierarchical approach. An early example of this type of approach is that developed by Wind and Cardozo[18] and illustrated in Fig. 7.3. Basically, the approach is to segment industrial markets into two successive stages. The first stage involves forming what are referred to as 'macro segments', based on characteristics of the organization. The second stage involves dividing these macro segments into *'micro* segments', based on the characteristics of the decision-making units (DMUs).

This hierarchical approach enables an initial screening of organizations and a selection of those macro segments that, on the basis of organizational characteristics, provide potentially attractive market opportunities. Organizations that may have no use for the given product or service can be eliminated. Starting with the grouping of organizations into homogeneous macro segments also provides a reduction in total research effort and cost. Instead of examining detailed buying patterns and attempting to identify the characteristics of the DMU in each organization individually, such analysis is limited to those macro segments that have passed the initial screening.

Once a set of acceptable macro segments has been formed, and the marketer may divide each of them into micro segments, or small groups of firms, on the basis of similarities and differences among DMUs within each macro segment. Information for this second stage will come primarily from the salesforce, based on sales people's analysis of situations in particular firms, or from specially designed market segmentation studies.

It is argued that the outcome from this segmentation model should include a *key dependent variable*, on which firms can be assigned to segments, i.e. the basis for segmentation; and a set of *independent variables*, which allow a marketer to predict where along the key dependent variable a particular group of customers may lie, as well as providing a greater insight into the key characteristics of the segment.

Figure 7.3   An approach to segmenting industrial markets
Source: Adapted from Y. Wind and R. Cardozo, 'Industrial market segmentation', *Industrial Marketing Management*, March 1974, p. 156

This concept of successively combining industrial market segmentation bases, giving (it is hoped) more and more precise and hence meaningful segments, is taken even further in the model developed by Shapiro and Bonoma.[19] Their 'nested' approach is shown in Fig. 7.4.

This approach identifies five general segmentation bases which are arranged in the nested hierarchy shown. Moving from the outer nests towards the inner, these bases are: demographics, operating variables, purchasing approach, situational factors, and personal characteristics (of the buyer). We shall examine each of these in turn.

Demographics This category represents the outermost nest, which contains the most general segmentation criteria. These variables give a broad description of the segments in the market and relate to general customer needs and usage patterns. They can be determined without visiting the customer, and include industry and company size and customer location.

Operating variables The second segmentation nest contains a variety of segmentation criteria

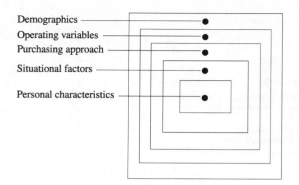

Figure 7.4   A 'nested' approach to industrial market segmentation
Source: Adapted from B. P. Shapiro and T. V. Bonoma, 'How to segment industrial markets', *Harvard Business Review*, May–June 1984, pp. 104–10

called 'operating variables'. Most of these enable more precise identification of existing and potential customers within demographic categories. Operating variables are generally stable and include technology, user/non-user status (by product and brand), and customer capabilities (operating, technical and financial).

Purchasing approaches One of the most neglected but valuable methods of segmenting an industrial market involves customers' purchasing approaches and company philosophy. The factors in this middle segmentation nest include the formal organization of the purchasing function, the power structure, the nature of the buyer–seller relationship, purchasing policies and purchasing criteria.

Situational factors Up to this point the model has focused on the grouping of customer firms. Now it moves to consider the tactical role of the purchasing situation. Situational factors resemble operating variables, but are temporary and require a more detailed knowledge of the customer. They include the urgency of order fulfilment, product application and the size of order.

Buyers' personal characteristics People, not companies, make purchase decisions, although the organizational framework in which they work and company policies and needs may constrain their choices. Marketers for industrial goods, like those for consumer products, can segment markets according to the individuals involved in a purchase in terms of buyer/seller similarity, buyer motivation, individual perceptions and risk management strategies.

These then are some of the major approaches to identifying market segments in both consumer and industrial markets. Having identified potential segments, however, the marketer must determine the extent to which these are likely to be suitable as potential target markets.

Criteria for effective segmentation The marketing firm not only has to identify potential market segments, but also has to establish whether segments are commercially viable and cost-effective. The test is whether the individuals in firms making up the segment can be serviced with a marketing mix probably specific to them. As a rule of thumb, to be commercially meaningful, the individuals or firms making up a segment must be more homogeneous in relation to some exploitable characteristic than the overall market from which they have been chosen. For this to be so, the variation of difference within each segment must be less than the variation between each of the segments. The following factors are useful in evaluating the suitability of a potential market segment:

1. *Measurability* The marketing firm should be able to identify and quantify the potential of each segment.
2. *Accessibility* To have any commercial meaning, the marketing firm must be able to reach each segment with a specific marketing programme. It must, therefore, be possible to communicate with individuals or firms making up the segment in a cost-effective way.
3. *Viability* To be viable, each segment must be large enough or commercially lucrative enough to warrant treating as a separate sub-market.

Benefits of market segmentation Market segmentation should result in benefits for both the marketing firm and its customers. If no such benefits accrue to either party, then the segmentation exercise is a meaningless waste of time. The following is an example of possible benefits:

1. Effective segmentation should result in greater sales and profitability.
2. Segmentation should allow the producer to design products and market appeals that are more 'finely tuned' to the needs of the market.
3. Segmentation should result in greater consumer satisfaction.
4. Segmentation allows the marketing firm to focus on those sub-markets with the greatest potential.
5. It allows for greater product differentiation and variety as firms seek further market opportunities by developing new segments.
6. It may result in a better competitive position for existing brands.

Market targeting

Market segmentation is only the first, albeit essential, step in the overall process of target marketing. The firm also has to evaluate each segment and decide how many of the segments to serve. It was discussed earlier that the criteria of measurability, accessibility and viability form the basis of segmentation evaluation. To establish viability, we need not only an indication of the size of the segment, but also estimates of likely turnover and profit, and an indication of where the segment is going; i.e., forecasts of future trends in demand are also necessary, which was the subject of Chapter 6.

Very often the trend in the overall market is different from that in the individual sub-markets. For example, the overall demand for cigarettes in the UK is declining, whereas the demand for 'low-tar' cigarettes is on the increase as consumers switch to less harmful forms of smoking. Many tobacco companies are now exploiting the low-tar segment of the market in reaction to consumers' changes in tastes and in order to retain their share of the cigarette market.

For a proper evaluation, each market segment must be expressed in terms of its cost and revenue implications. Buzby and Heitger[20] recommend the use of individual segmentation budgets. These can then be aggregated to form the firm's overall marketing budget.

Market coverage strategies Once market segments have been identified and evaluated, the marketing firm has to decide on its level of market involvement. It may determine that no meaningful segments exist and decide to cover the whole market with one basic product or service offering. It may establish a number of meaningful segments and decide to service all or a number of them with a differential product and/or marketing mix. It may identify a number of segments, but decide to service only one or very few of them. Hence the firm can adopt one of three market coverage strategies:

1. *Undifferentiated marketing* With this strategy, the firm focuses on what is common to all potential consumers rather than attempting to exploit differences. One product and one marketing mix are offered to all consumers without any form of differentiation. Its product features and marketing programmes are designed to appeal to as many potential buyers as possible within the overall market. The overall market is treated as a homogeneous mass, and the firm uses mass production, mass communication and mass distribution.
2. *Differentiated marketing* With this strategy the firm decides to operate in a number of market segments. The firm offers a slightly 'different' product and related marketing mix to each segment. Washing powder, toothpaste and motor car markets are good examples of this approach used by marketing firms.
3. *Concentrated marketing* Here the firm decides to attempt to cater for one, or possibly a few, market segments. It concentrates on a limited group of customers and aims to service them more effectively and efficiently than competitors. This strategy is used by the Savoy Hotel, Rolls Royce cars, and Rolex watches, which tend to cater solely for high-income groups.

Product positioning

After segments have been identified and a segmentation strategy developed, a firm needs to develop and communicate a product positioning strategy. Product positioning is the act of designing the company's product and marketing mix to fit a given place in the consumer's mind. Using marketing research, the firm should establish the position of competitors' products in any given market segment and then decide whether to compete on a 'me-too' basis (to offer a product very close to a competitor's offering) or to attempt to fill a gap in the market.

A technique that has gained popularity, especially in the 'positioning' of products, is multidimensional scaling (MDS). MDS is a term that is applied to a variety of techniques for representing brands, stores or products as points in multidimensional space. The dimensions used in the analysis are the attributes which research indicates that consumers use to differentiate products.

Tull and Hawkins[21] show how a two-dimensional scale can be used to plot the market position of soft drinks. The two primary dimensions used in the evaluation are 'cola-ness' and 'diet-ness'. This example is shown in Fig. 7.5.

Tull and Hawkins show that with the aid of a computer an 'ideal' brand position can be developed. Existing brands are ranked in terms of preference by each respondent in the test. This provides the coordinates or scores of the individual's 'ideal' brand on each dimension. The example shows a relatively simple two-dimensional map. The use of computers allows similar analysis on more than two dimensions, thus increasing the usefulness of the technique.

Product positioning is the final stage in the overall process of target marketing. Once the firm has established its product positioning strategy, it is then in a position to go on to plan the details of its marketing mix.

CONCLUSIONS

Today, companies are finding it increasingly difficult to practise mass marketing. As a result, many firms are embracing the concept of target marketing. Target marketing enables firms to focus on marketing opportunities more effectively. Instead of spreading their marketing effort too thinly,

Figure 7.5   Multidimensional space for soft drinks

Brands

1. Coca-Cola
2. Sprite
3. Fresca
4. Diet 7-Up
5. 7-Up
6. Pepsi
7. Diet Pepsi
8. Tab

target marketing enables firms to produce product offerings, pricing, advertising and distribution strategies that can 'home in' on specific groups of buyers more efficiently.

To be effective, the overall process of target marketing needs to be carried out in a logical and systematic manner. The first, and perhaps the most important, stage after suitably researching the market is the process of market segmentation. The identification of commercially meaningful market segments forms the bedrock of the rest of the target marketing programme. The remaining two stages are market targeting and, finally, product positioning.

If the process of target marketing is carried out thoroughly and scientifically, the firm should then be in a position to formulate a more meaningful strategy. Target marketing results in benefits for both the marketing firm and its customers. The firm should benefit in terms of a better competitive position for its products, resulting in greater sales and profitability. The customer should derive greater satisfaction from the goods and services purchased. This is a particularly important point as the whole rationale of the marketing concept is increased business effectiveness through the provision of consumer satisfaction.

APPLICATION QUESTIONS

1. A microwave oven manufacturer wants to develop a benefit segmentation of the microwave oven market. Suggest some possible benefit segments.
2. In what circumstances might a marketing firm use a concentrated marketing strategy? Illustrate your answer with examples.
3. Marketing firms use certain criteria in evaluating the commercial attractiveness of market segments. Discuss the usefulness of such criteria for evaluating potential segments in the shampoo market.
4. Using the two primary dimensions of expensive/not expensive and serious/not serious, plot the product positioning of existing titles of national daily newspapers on a two-dimensional scale

similar to that shown in Fig. 7.5. Discuss a possible product positioning for a new daily newspaper.

5. Show how the segmentation variables
   (a) service elasticity and
   (b) market structure
   might be useful in determining a marketing strategy for a firm producing industrial valves.

6. Explain life style segmentation and discuss its use in market segmentation.

REFERENCES

1. W. J. Stanton, M. S. Sommers and J. G. Barnes, *Fundamentals of Marketing*, McGraw-Hill, New York, 1977, p. 49.
2. D. Foster, *Mastering Marketing*, Macmillan, London, 1982, p. 151.
3. P. Kotler, *Marketing Management: Analysis, Planning Implementation and Control*, 7th edn, Prentice-Hall, Englewood Cliffs, NJ, 1991, p. 263.
4. T. Levitt, *Marketing for Business Growth*, McGraw-Hill, New York, 1974, p. 69.
5. Research Services Ltd, *SAGACITY: a special analysis of JICNARS NRS 1980 Data*, London, 1981.
6. Joint Industry Working Party, *An Evaluation of Social Grade Validity*, Market Research Society, London, 1981.
7. M. Crimp, *The Market Research Process*, Prentice-Hall, London, 1985, p. 106.
8. A. R. Wofe (ed.), *Standardised Questions: A Review for Market Research Executives*, Market Research Society, London, 1973.
9. R. I. Haley, 'Benefit segmentation: a decision-oriented tool', *Journal of Marketing*, July 1968, pp. 30–5.
10. F. M. Bass, D. J. Tigert and D. T. Lonsdale, 'Market segmentation: group versus individual behaviour', *Journal of Marketing Research*, **5,** August 1978, p. 276.
11. J. Frain, *Introduction to Marketing*, Macdonald and Evans, London, 1981, p. 103.
12. Kotler, op. cit., p. 275.
13. P. M. Chisnall, *Marketing: A Behavioural Analysis*, 2nd edn, McGraw-Hill, London, 1985, p. 92.
14. J. T. Plummer, 'The concept and application of lifestyle segmentation', *Journal of Marketing*, January 1974.
15. T. Lunn, S. Baldwin and J. Dickens, 'Monitoring consumer lifestyles', *Admap*, November 1982.
16. R. E. Frank, W. F. Massy and Y. Wind, *Market Segmentation*, Prentice-Hall, Englewood Cliffs, NJ, 1972.
17. M. D. Hutt and T. W. Speh, *Business Marketing Management*, 4th edn, Dryden Press, New York, 1992, Chapter 6.
18. Y. Wind and R. Cardozo, 'Industrial market segmentation', *Industrial Marketing Management*, **3,** March 1974, pp. 142–64.
19. B. P. Shapiro and T. V. Bonoma, 'How to segment industrial markets', *Harvard Business Review*, May–June 1984, pp. 104–10.
20. S. L. Buzby and L. E. Heitger, 'Profit oriented reporting for marketing decision makers', *MSU Business Topics*, **24**(3), 1976.
21. D. A. Tull and D. I. Hawkins, *Marketing Research, Measurement and Methods*, 3rd edn, Macmillan, New York, 1984, p. 316.

PART THREE

THE MARKETING MIX

EIGHT

THE PRODUCT (OR SERVICE)

INTRODUCTION

People who are unfamiliar with marketing often hold the erroneous view that a 'product' is a physical object with readily identifiable and tangible attributes. They would not, for example, consider an insurance policy or a package holiday to be a 'product'. Marketing practitioners must, however, adopt a very much wider view of the product. In a more abstract sense, products should be distinguished not only by their actual utilities, but also by the perceptions that consumers have of them. These can be real, or imagined by the customer, or the specific creations of the marketer. Thus, in the case of a frozen ready meal, the 'product' is not the physical food ingredients, but a convenience—a labour- and time-saving device. This is the basis for 'benefit segmentation', as explained in Chapter 7.

For the marketer, the product becomes any want-satisfying good or service that is considered together with its perceived tangible and intangible attributes. From the consumer's point of view, a product is a series or a bundle of satisfactions. It is important to realize that, whatever we as marketers 'would like' our products to be, the real nature of the product lies in the consumer's perception of it. This emphasizes the essence of marketing—a policy of customer orientation.

PRODUCT CLASSIFICATION

It should by now be clear that the product is much more than the generic 'thing' or 'object'. We can now consider the product in its widest possible context so as to obtain a complete understanding of its nature. This final consideration has been described as the 'Total Product Concept' and its understanding lies at the heart of successful marketing. In his text, *Differentiation of Anything*,[1] Levitt proposes four concepts of the product which go to make up the 'total product'.

First, as we already know, we must consider the physical product or service. This is the generic bar of chocolate, the machine tool or the two-week package holiday. Without this there can be no sale—no offer or acceptance. The customer, however, expects more than this. The expected product is, of course, wider in scope than the generic product, but it still represents the consumer's minimum expectations. Such expectations would include price, delivery or availability, after-sales service or packaging. A third dimension is the 'augmented product'; this is closely linked with the development of a policy of product differentiation, as opposed to customer-originated 'expectations'. 'Augmentations' are the creations of the marketer. One photographic film manufacturer, for example, has recently included a film development service in the purchase price of the film itself.

In the industrial sense, such things as a special 'tailor-made' delivery or storage service would 'augment' the product from its original basic parameters. Over time, there may be a tendency for customers to regard attributes of the augmented product as standard items, thus necessitating a further reassessment of the product's nature. This leads us finally to the 'potential' product, which encompasses all those things that 'could' be added to a product but which, as yet, have not been realized.

The product is, therefore, a complex idea, central to marketing and central to the consumer. It should never be viewed in the narrow terms of a physical object or service, but rather in the context of what satisfactions it brings to the consumer. In addition to this, it cannot be considered in isolation. From both the buyer's and the seller's viewpoint, the product is inextricable from the total approach that a firm adopts towards its market and customers.

We now have an insight into the scope and nature of a product. In order to aid market planning, products can be classified in a formal way. Such a classification system helps us to identify the way in which people view products, and thus why and how they subsequently purchase them.

A PRODUCT AND SERVICE CLASSIFICATION SYSTEM

Products can be divided into two main groups. 'Consumer goods' are purchased by the ultimate buyer, while 'industrial goods' are used by all the firms in the manufacturing chain. Many industrial goods, therefore, can go to make up one retail or consumer product. In other words, industrial goods are purchased in order to make other products.

Consumer goods

Figure 8.1 sets out a formal classification for consumer goods.

Convenience goods The purchase of these goods requires very little effort and more often than not they are relatively inexpensive. Most of the contents of the average weekly shopping basket fall into this category, and any planning is usually restricted to the preparation of a simple shopping list. The presence of brands may cause the shopper to prevaricate over purchases, but this does not detract from the fact that, in general, little effort is required from the shopper in order for the store to make a profit, because the store's profit is assured no matter which brand is bought.

Convenience goods can be subdivided into emergency, staple and impulse items. If sudden necessity is the motivator for a purchase, even less effort than usual will be required. Many small neighbourhood grocery shops owe their survival (faced with price competition from supermarkets) to our need for *emergency convenience goods*. *Staple convenience goods* form the bulk of everyday shopping. Items such as milk, bread, sugar or potatoes fall into this category, although it is true to say that nowadays many of these goods possess some sort of branding or other differentiation. *Impulse items* are self-explanatory—pre-planning is obviously nil; these are goods that simply 'catch the eye', and price and price comparison plays a minimum role.

Shopping goods This is the category of major, durable or semi-durable appliances. Owing to the fact that they are usually more expensive than convenience goods, their purchase is characterized by a fair degree of pre-planning, information search and price comparison. This is due not only to their relative expense, but also because these purchases are made less frequently and the consumer is less knowledgeable about the respective merits of the products that are available. As well as price comparison, place of purchase, purchase terms, service and guarantees will all form part of the purchase decision equation.

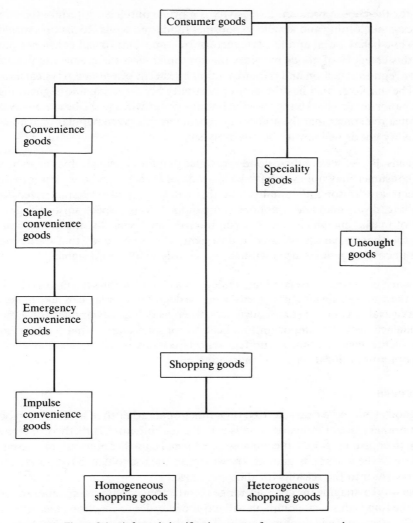

Figure 8.1   A formal classification system for consumer goods

Homogeneous shopping goods would include such products as 'white goods', prams and pushchairs or DIY equipment. Although these purchases can, in many ways, be 'special' to the consumer because of their relative infrequence of purchase, they are not classed as 'speciality' in marketing terms because the products themselves are not rare or exclusive, but are in fact almost necessities and form a part of everyday life.

Heterogeneous shopping goods are by definition 'non-standard', stylized and possess a degree of exclusivity. Price is usually of secondary importance—behavioural factors playing a more important role than for homogeneous goods. In the car market, the Porsche can be compared with the family saloon to illustrate this difference. Similarly, certain clothing labels can be classed as heterogeneous goods when compared with the more standardized ranges available from the high street multiples.

Speciality goods   These are characterized by extensive search and an extreme reluctance to accept substitutes for the chosen product. Exclusivity is a prime purchase criterion. Certain 'long-haul' holidays, designer clothing and jewellery, gourmet foods and Rolls Royce cars would fit into this category. While behavioural and lifestyle factors are important for all consumer purchases, it is likely that this category of goods provides the consumer with the greatest opportunity for self-actualization, ego-satisfaction and the satisfaction of esteem-orientated physical and psychological needs. The marketer also has the best opportunity for targeting and segmenting consumers with with a 'tailor-made' marketing effort. Although prices will usually be extremely high for such goods, we must remember that the number of consumers in a given population who will be able to afford speciality goods will always be relatively small.

Unsought goods By definition, these goods are those that the consumer does not actively seek out. Indeed the consumer may not even have been aware of them immediately prior to any purchase. New products are 'unsought' initially, but this category is also characterized by aggressive personal selling, direct mail and telephone campaigns. In this respect, unsought goods represent that aspect of marketing which is most open to criticism. Typically, insurance policies that are solicited by the above means are classed as unsought. This is not to say that sales generated in this way do not uncover a genuine need within a previously unaware consumer.

Finally, we must be aware of the fact that, while such a classification system has relevance for most consumers, there are, as always, 'grey areas' where a degree of overlap can take place. A television set may be a speciality good for some consumers, whereas Beluga caviar may, for some, represent a mere convenience item! The important implication for marketers is that for large groups of the population such a classification accurately reflects consumer behaviour and allows a firm to develop an optimum utilization of the marketing mix.

Industrial goods

Industrial goods tend to be characterized on a functional rather than a behavioural basis. This is because the primary use of industrial goods is in the manufacture, directly or indirectly, of other goods. As with consumer goods, the purpose of a formal classification system is to enable a better understanding of the market by gaining knowledge of the use to which the goods are put and by gaining an insight into the reasons for their purchase.

A simple way to imagine the complex range of industrial goods is to imagine any company and think of all the things that that company will require in order to function efficiently. Obviously, a manufacturing company will require machinery and raw materials to make the basic product, but it will also require all of the ancillary items that any company needs—cleaning materials, spare parts, stationery, typewriters, office furniture and so on. All of these items, while not being integral to the manufacturing process, are nevertheless essential to the running of the company. Figure 8.2 classifies these requirements into formal groups.

Installations These can be regarded as the 'speciality' goods of industrial markets. They are the major items of plant and machinery which a company requires for its production. Their purchase is critical and can determine the nature, scope and efficiency of the company. For a haulage company, the heavy goods vehicle would fall into this category.

Not surprisingly, final purchase is the culmination of extensive search and comparison, because that decision is essentially long-term and is likely to be the single most important capital investment at any given time. Because of the long-term implications of purchase, price, while important, is almost never the single deciding factor. A heavy reliance is also placed on expert sales advice, technical support, availability of spare parts and the general level of after-sales service.

Figure 8.2   A formal classification system for industrial goods

Accessories These comprise ancillary plant and maintenance and office equipment. A significant development of 'accessory' supply in recent years has, of course, been the increasing use of the microprocessor, which permits computer-controlled sales, production and accountancy information. Although still considered as capital items, accessories are less expensive and are depreciated over a fewer number of years. Fewer personnel are involved in the purchase decision, and this decision itself has less overall importance for the company. One only has to compare the often misguided purchase of office furniture with the implications of a similar decision involving a major piece of production machinery.

Raw materials Unlike all the other goods in industrial product classification, these go to make up the final product. How close any particular manufacturer's output is to the final product will obviously depend on the position held in the manufacturing chain. It is also worth remembering that much industrial output is not necessarily destined for the consumer market, but goes to provide products for other industries so as to facilitate their manufacturing process.

The purchase of raw materials typically makes the largest share of the expenditure of the traditional 'buying department' of a company. Efficient purchasing is of the utmost importance, because the quality of the raw materials will have a direct bearing on the quality of the product to be produced. It is probably fair to say that the importance of price diminishes, the more the raw material forms part of a commodity market. Price is, however, by no means the only deciding factor of purchase, even in the most homogeneous of commodity markets: delivery, continuity of supply, quality and the general level of service all play a vital part in the decision to deal or not to deal with a particular raw material supplier.

Component parts and materials These are similar in nature to 'raw materials' in that they go to make up the end products. A vehicle manufacturer may purchase steel as a 'raw material' while engine parts would be classed as components. Similarly, a textile manufacturer might purchase natural or synthetic fibre as a raw material, but would also require chemical finishes, dyestuffs and so on as 'materials'. Machinery would also require replacement items: these too would be classified here, and should not be compared with 'accessories'. As with raw material supply, non-price considerations figure highly in reaching the purchase decision.

Supplies If we draw another parallel with the consumer market, supplies can be thought of as the 'convenience goods' of industrial supply. Supplies represent the multiplicity of items that most companies probably take for granted. These are cleaning items—soap, brooms, cloths etc.; office stationery; as well as items for general maintenance (other than those required for plant) such as light bulbs, fuel oil and numerous 'repairs and renewals'. Purchase procedure is often routine and conducted through the medium of wholesalers. Owing to the relatively homogeneous nature of supplies, and their wide availability, price is a major influencing factor of supply.

Industrial services The supply of industrial services has greatly increased in recent years. One only needs to think of the field of marketing itself, where the opportunity to purchase the services of management consultants and market research agencies has increased many-fold during the past decade. There has been a similar increase in the use of contract cleaners and services such as 'express delivery' for urgent or fragile correspondence. The principal factor in deciding to use outside services rather than the firm's own personnel is cost effectiveness. Frequently, when such services are not required on a continuous basis, or when the long-term cost of employing expert personnel would exceed the cost of the required service, the use of outside agencies offers a convenient solution to the problem. The special issues of marketing both industrial and consumer service products are considered later in this chapter.

A classification of industrial products is an ideal aid and companion to the study of industrial buyer behaviour. Each category of products performs a different role for the firm, and this knowledge can be used by suppliers in the design of their marketing and sales strategy. It should be uppermost in the minds of both buyer and seller that the finished products can be only as good as the machinery that makes them. The product classification system also permits emphasis of the fact that, just as consumers 'perceive' benefits other than the physical form of a given product, industrial buyers are equally concerned with factors other than the immediate product and its price.

NEW PRODUCT DEVELOPMENT

The development of a new product is a component of overall marketing strategy. For most firms new products involve the effort and cooperation of the total management structure as well as a wide cross-section of the total workforce. New products involve large sums of money and higher-than-normal levels of risk when compared with many other major marketing decisions. It is for these reasons that it is thought worth while to highlight this subject as a separate element of product strategy.

What is a new product?

Most of us must be familiar with the bewildering selection of goods displayed in any supermarket. In industry, the professional buyer is consistently confronted with 'variations on themes' and occasionally with a product designed to 'revolutionize' a particular manufacturing process. Both in consumer markets and in industry, the purchaser has a tendency to adopt a 'blasé' attitude towards the latest offering from any given firm. From the manufacturer's point of view, the picture is very different—a new chocolate bar or machine part is the culmination of a vast commitment of resources, time and research. Before going on to examine in detail how this process is carried out, we should be aware of the variety of definitions that can be applied to a new product.

1. *Innovative products* These are products that are truly 'new' to the consumer: they provide totally different alternatives to existing products which serve existing markets. Among such goods can be included the television, or the motor car, which was made possible by the invention of the internal combustion engine. These new products provided an alternative to radio and cinema entertainment and to horse-drawn methods of transport. In more modern times, the microprocessor and robotic manufacturing methods would fall into this category. So too would a phamaceutical cure to an illness that had been previously thought incurable.
2. *Replacement products* These are replacements for existing products which, while not being wholly 'innovative', do provide significant differentiations from those that are currently on offer. Using a previous example, one could say that a radically new design of car offers a 'replacement' product. Similarly, the Polaroid camera 'replaced' those cameras that required films to be developed independently from the taking of the picture. The compact disc, however technically innovative, is a replacement for the conventional hi-fi system, as was the hi-fi system a replacement for the original and truly 'innovative' (in the marketing sense) gramophone.
3. *Imitative products* This final category involves all those products that are new to a company, but are already well established in the marketplace. These follow on from the replacement and innovative products which have been developed initially by individual firms. Occasionally, imitative products are perhaps disparagingly described as 'me-too' products because they imply a certain lack of imagination on the behalf of the firm launching them. It is also fair to say that all firms cannot be pioneers of product inventiveness, and thus the bulk of new products are imitative. Certainly, if a firm's financial resources and marketing expertise are strong, then it is advantageous to be an innovator rather than a follower, but in practice many firms appear content to let another take the risks of an innovative product launch, and then join the market when 'the dust has settled'. It also happens that a firm launches an innovative product and then quickly loses market share to a more powerful imitation.

   Imitative products are most often found when the technical development costs are low and are obviously launched before the initiator has had the opportunity to set up too many barriers to market entry. It is also with imitative products where the highest rate of product failures is likely to occur.

A final criterion for new product definition, irrespective of the above categories, lies in the consumer's perception. This is, of course, determined by the manner in which the product is presented to the marketplace. Thus, a relaunched product can appear 'new' if different benefits are promoted, whether or not these are tangible or intangible. Appearance or performance need not be radically altered. Provided the consumer perceives a product as being significantly different from that which already exists, then it is effectively a new product.

The importance of new product development

In his famous article 'Marketing myopia',[2] Levitt emphasizes the absolute necessity of a 'total' commitment to new product development. This is the sole medium for adaptation to change and is, therefore, critical to the continued survival of the firm. This importance is mirrored and intensified by the fact that new products are the 'rocks on which many companies founder'.

The product (and its successors) is, therefore, central to the whole being of the firm. Any efficient sales manager will maintain that without customers there is no need for production. This perfectly valid standpoint can, however, be considered in a different way by stating that without a product one has no need for a salesorce! Thus we move to the inevitable conclusion that the product is essential to the firm's physical existence, not only because a product is necessary for profit generation to take place, but also because the product is the medium through which a company fulfils the marketing concept. Taking the strictest interpretation of the marketing concept, the total ethos of the firm should be to produce goods that provide consumer satisfaction, profit being the reward of this if effectively carried out. Such a view, which may appear overly altruistic (and which is certainly complicated), is not, however, far removed from reality. Whatever company policies may be, competitive forces tend, over time, to militate against the firm whose products are not specifically aimed at fulfilling the marketing concept.

The marketing mix too is a meaningless tool without the product. It should be evident that all elements of the marketing mix are totally dependent on each other, but quite logically the core of the marketing mix is the product and new product developments. All marketing planning is based on, and must start from, the product. If that product is intrinsically weak, it will not ultimately survive, however skilfully the other elements of the mix are employed. This last factor underlines the importance of the product as the basic profit determinant of the firm. New products, moreover, should ensure that profit is sustained in the long term as well as providing the opportunity for growth and diversification.

Finally, from the strategic viewpoint, the firm must utilize new products as a means towards market leadership, rather than market imitation. The underlying trends towards a more affluent society in Western post-war history imply that the more basic of consumer needs are now, to a great extent, fulfilled. The implications of this are that firms must be increasingly aware of the need to satisfy consumers on a higher plane than was previously necessary. This requires an even more dynamic and sophisticated approach to new product development.

STEPS IN THE DEVELOPMENT PROCESS

In view of the importance of new products, and of the high rate of product failure, it is axiomatic that any development programme should be embarked upon only with the utmost care. The ramifications of a new product are numerous, but the criteria for any developments and ultimate launch can be reduced to three basic questions; no undertakings should even be considered unless satisfactory answers to the following can be supplied:

1. Is there a real consumer need?
2. Does the company have the resources and technical ability to market and manufacture the product?
3. Is the potential market large enough to generate profit?

These are the key questions, but because new products do not just 'materialize', there must be a formal method for the generation of ideas, idea evaluation and establishing practical feasibility. The following steps should provide answers to the three fundamental questions and establish a clearly defined cut-off point after which the company should feel confident in launching a new product.

Idea generation

These emanate from a variety of sources, but the source itself is less important than the system and attitude which the company has towards idea evaluation. The groundwork that leads to ideas can be described as 'opportunity exploration'. This process can be carried on by formal *research and development* departments. Here, care should be taken to avoid the syndrome of developing a product and then saying 'let's see if anyone wants it!' The *production department* can, in the course of manufacture, provide ideas for modifying and improving the existing product. The *sales team* is another source of valuable ideas: they are the people who receive direct customer feedback and who are often able to say what competitors are providing which their firm is not. *Senior management*, if product-oriented, should be responsible for creating the correct attitude towards development within the firm and for organizing formal programmes which might include techniques such as brainstorming sessions and the organization of venture teams and planning committees. Finally, and irrespective of the firm's level of sophistication in the field of market intelligence, it is possible to draw heavily on *external sources* for inspiration and ideas. These would include: trade associations, published reports, governmental bodies, middlemen and foreign competitors.

Screening new ideas

Once equipped with a set of potentially viable ideas, it is necessary to devise a method of screening these ideas so as to reduce them to a manageable number which have real market prospects. Screening should also ensure that a good product is not eliminated at an early stage, which can be equally as damaging as having to bear the development cost of a product failure.

In order to develop a screening technique, it is essential that the firm isolates a series of factors which research has shown are desirable to the consumer, and which are desirable to the firm in that they make the best use of existing strengths. The product ideas can then be compared so as to establish a short list of those that fit most closely to these criteria. Typical factors under consideration might include: raw material availability, production, distribution and product line compatibility, and the effect on sales of other products. Market research techniques such as brand mapping might provide a series of features that are thought desirable from the consumer's point of view.

The technique of screening is usually carried out by statistical weighting of the factors involved. A minimum rating score must, of course, be established and those ideas whose score is superior to this can then proceed to the next development stage. The use of 'Likert' type scales rather than numerical values is probably less effective because of the semantic difficulties in establishing what is, say GOOD, POOR or FAIR.

Business analysis

This third step concerns the financial, rather than the practical, viability of the product idea. Research and forecasting techniques are used to establish demand. Cost analysis examines not only the basic cost of production, but also such factors as capital investment, marketing costs (perhaps advertising and new distribution channels) and in some cases the engagement of new personnel. Profitability can be established in terms of 'break-even' and 'rate-of-return' analysis.

Product development

Once it has been established by analytical methods that a product idea has market potential, it is necessary to develop some form of prototype in an effort to confirm this feasibility in physical terms. This confirmation must be related both to production and marketing. Marketing activities would include motivational research and concept testing. Physical testing of the prototype by the consumer would encompass performance, packaging and comparison with products where level of acceptance is already known.

It is also necessary at this stage to ensure that production and marketing departments are working in close harmony. The marketing responsibility is to communicate immediately any reaction that would suggest that the nature of the prototype should be altered, or that whole project should be seriously called into question. The production department must be as sure as possible that the prototype corresponds precisely with any production model that would subsequently be launched. If this was not the case, all marketing research would be a fruitless exercise.

At the end of the product development stage, the firm faces a critical decision: whether to go ahead and market the new product or to 'cut its losses' by abandoning a project which appears to have an unlikely chance of success. Either decision requires considerable business competence, not to mention sheer courage! The 'go' decision involves the risk of product failure, while on the other hand the decision to abort requires that the firm must write off large expenditure and perhaps years of time spent in development. The decision must, however, be made, because this is the whole reason for having a 'planned' development programme.

Test marketing

Just as the prototype must correspond exactly to the final product, so it is vital that the 'test market' chosen for partial launch of the final product is highly representative of the total market.

Although, in practice, the test market and test marketing provide the firm with a final opportunity to withdraw the product before a full-scale launch, this is not the real purpose of the exercise. Test markets are not 'final screens'. At this stage the firm should have already made up its mind to commercialize the product. Test marketing objectives are: to predict the efficacy of the proposed marketing strategy (and refine this if needed) and to predict the effect of strategy in terms of market penetration.

The usual procedure for test marketing is to select an easily identifiable sector of the market which represents the total market in miniature and then to launch a product in the same way as a total market launch would be expected to take place, thus testing the feasibility of the full marketing programme. In the UK it is common to use ITV television areas as test marketing areas for consumer goods. As well as providing distinct geographical areas, television advertising can also be monitored area by area when experimenting with different campaigns, advertising frequency and so on. It is not uncommon to run more than one test market concurrently. In this way, different applications of the marketing mix can be experimented with, as can the attribution of marketing budgets. Market research agencies are increasingly active in test marketing, especially in the field of predictive analysis. As such predictive models increase in their level of sophistication, there is a tendency to reduce the scope of test markets in the physical sense by

Figure 8.3   The relationship between cost and product development

placing an increasing reliance on statistical hypotheses. This is less true in the industrial sense, but in consumer goods markets, 'mini' and 'micro' test markets are common.[3] For actual examples of UK test marketing procedure see Chapter 5.

Mini test markets provide one way of exercising greater control over the test itself. One danger of test marketing is that one is never completely sure that the test marketing accurately simulates the full-scale reality. This can be exacerbated by competitors who, aware that a test market is under way, can devise ways of creating artificial market conditions. An intense 'burst' of competitive advertising or a series of special offers would completely disrupt the effect of test marketing in a given area. A second danger is that, while company A is engaged in test marketing, company B can 'leapfrog' the whole process by bringing a product to market without pre-testing it. For these reasons, as well as for good statistical practice, it is always advisable to operate a 'control' test market so as to estimate the impact of a number of control variables—including competitive action.

Commercialization

The stages of product development have 'filtered' commercially viable product ideas from a wide selection of original propositions. Furthermore, a product has been chosen *and* prepared for acceptability in the marketplace. Test marketing has fine-tuned the appropriate marketing strategy, and the firm is now sufficiently confident and knowledgeable to launch and commercialize the product on a full-scale basis. New product strategy to 'skim' or go for 'market penetration' is dealt with later in this chapter and in Chapter 13.

Figure 8.3 shows a schematic relationship between product development and expenditure. The relationship is inverse in that early stages cost relatively little. At the stages of product development and test marketing, potential products have been reduced to a few, yet these are the stages where cost is highest. This underlines the importance of effective screening and business analysis. Ruthless decisions must be made to eliminate those products thought unsuitable at each stage of the process. It is also worth while re-emphasizing that, while development costs to the stage of a test market are high, the financial loss of launching a product 'full-scale' which is a subsequent failure are always considerably higher. Typically, the development cost of a new model in the car industry is between £500 and £1000 million over a time span of around five years. Imagine the cost of full production and market launch in addition to this, and the period of time required for break-even!

Despite the care and attention which goes into new product development, there exists an apparently endless list of product failures. In industrial markets, most go unnoticed by all but those who are directly involved. Consumers are, however, witness to a constant series of new products which are here today and gone tomorrow. Some estimates of failures versus successful products even go as high as 80 per cent, and evidence suggests that the figure is at least 50 per cent. Whatever the figure, failure is a feature of new products.[4] No guarantees are attached to a careful development plan, and despite the best predictions, markets have a habit of being unpredictable. On the positive side, what we can be sure of is that, like good marketing as a whole, the more thorough and professional is the development programme, the more this is likely to minimize the risk of product failure.

THE PRODUCT LIFE CYCLE

The concept of the product life cycle (PLC) constitutes an important component of product strategy. The concept proposes that, once the product or service reaches the market, it enters a 'life cycle' and will eventually fade from the market. We must remember that the PLC is meant to serve as a conceptual base for examining product growth and development, and that not every product necessarily fits neatly into all the elements of the theoretical curve (see Fig. 8.4). A study of business and economic history reveals that some predictable course of product development occurs sufficiently often for marketing planners to attach considerable credence to the concept. Thus, as well as providing a theoretical framework, the PLC can be used as a real managerial tool which is helpful in forecasting and, therefore, in strategic planning.

Figure 8.4 identifies four stages in the pattern of demand during the product's life. The cycles of two hypothetical products are shown to illustrate that the cycle concept is only a guide. The life cycles of different products will differ because they are a function of their intrinsic nature, their markets and their competitive environments.

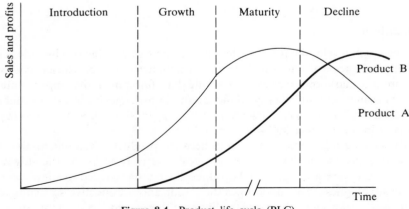

Figure 8.4   Product life cycle (PLC)

Similarly, just as the shape of the curve is likely to differ according to the type of product, the time span of the cycle may vary from as little as a few days to as much as several decades.

Whatever the shape of time span of the life-cycle curve, the implications for the marketer are of equal importance and are as follows:

1. The appropriate strategy for each stage.
2. The identification of movement from one stage to another.
3. The likely shape of the total curve.

The definition of the points where different stages in the life cycle begin is somewhat arbitrary, but each stage has characteristic phenomena which suggests a specific reaction and mode of strategy formulation.

Introduction

Characteristics This stage is, of course, typified by conditions that relate to those of a new product launch.

1. A high product failure rate.
2. Relatively little competition.
3. Limited distribution.
4. Frequent product modification.
5. Company losses at least on that product because development costs have not yet been recouped, mass production economies are not possible and promotional expenditure is usually greater than profit return on sales.

Money spent at the 'introduction' phase should be regarded as an investment in the future.

Introduction strategy Promotion is directed at creating product awareness. This may require extra effort in personal selling. For consumer goods, advertising is the most common method of promotion. In extreme cases, advertising expenditure can exceed not only profits but also sales revenue. In any case, introduction strategy requires that a firm's resources are deployed in larger than usual levels of marketing expenditure.

Pricing strategy will depend largely on the degree of distinctiveness of the product and on the length of time that this distinctiveness is likely to last. Two basic strategic options are open: either a 'skimming' or 'penetration' strategy may be adopted. 'Skimming' involves the application of a high price to a small section of consumers (the early adopters). It is appropriate when the product is unusually distinctive and demand is inelastic. Depending upon the circumstances (a critical factor being the degree of competitive activity), potential new groups of adopters are encouraged to buy the product by a planned series of progressive price reductions.

'Penetration' is likely to be appropriate where demand is elastic and the level of competitive activity is high. This is a relatively low price strategy which aims to attract the largest number of new buyers early in the product's life.

Neither strategy has an immediate profit-maximizing objective in the economic sense; rather, these are 'marketing' strategies which are designed to ensure long-term profitability, that is, profitability during the subsequent stages of the life cycle. These pricing strategy notions are explored more fully in the next chapter.

The decision to pursue a policy of market share acquisition is a matter of corporate strategy and is a highly complicated subject. Suffice it to say here that, if market share is considered as being strategically advantageous, then it is most easily accomplished during introduction while the distinctiveness of the product remains intact.

In the sense of 'market evolution' or a life cycle for markets, Hofer and Schendel[5] have identified a 'shake-out' stage between those of introduction and growth. This can be applied to individual products as well as to companies in a market, because in both cases the numbers falling 'by the wayside' can have significant implications for those that survive into the growth stage.

Growth

Characteristics

1. More competitors—less product distinctiveness.
2. Rising sales.
3. Profitable returns.
4. Company or product acquisition by larger companies.

Growth strategy Although heavy promotion is a feature of the introduction stage, advertising and promotion also feature highly in the marketing budget during growth. However, there are two important differences: one is the promotional task itself, which in growth centres its emphasis on promotion of the 'brand' or trade name, rather than on creating product awareness, as this should already have been achieved. Second, the promotional budget, relative to sales, should allow room for a profit return, whereas in introduction it is not unusual for promotional expenditure to be grossly disproportionate to sales and profit. There are, however, exceptions to these guidelines. If, for example, a large company with an extensive product portfolio is determined to ensure market dominance for one of these products during maturity, then a promotional expenditure which continues to sap profits throughout the growth stage would not be unusual.

Distribution is also a major consideration during growth, and manufacturers will fight strongly to acquire dealership and distribution outlets. Trends in the UK retail sector during the last 10–15 years emphasize this phenomenon. In many instances the key to whole markets lies within a small nucleus of retail groups. Similarly, owing to the pressure for profitable shelf space, retail groups, especially supermarkets, will rationalize the number of brands carried as soon as a hierarchy of leaders has established itself. For fast-moving consumer goods, if a product fails to be stocked by even one of the major UK supermarket chains, a large section of that market will have been lost.

You will doubtless already be aware of the strongly 'interdependent' nature of the elements of the marketing mix: growth strategy ably demonstrates this. In growth, as indeed in the other stages of the PLC, the chosen strategy will fail if either one of the key elements (in the case of growth, promotion and place) is not efficiently effected.

The opportunity to achieve maximum profits usually peaks towards the end of the growth period. This is often because brand shares have stabilized to some extent and many companies are obliged to follow the leader. This last factor, coupled with the possible opportunity for economies of scale, sometimes leads to price decreases towards the end of this stage.

Finally, for the pessimistic as well as the cautious strategist, the end of growth also heralds the beginning of decline!

Maturity

The majority of products are in this stage of the life cycle. Much marketing activity is, therefore, directed at appropriate maturity strategies. This is also usually the longest stage of the life cycle.

Characteristics

1. Sales continue to increase, but at a greatly reduced rate.
2. Attempts are made to differentiate or re-differentiate the product, and the product line may be widened.
3. Prices begin to fall as manufacturers fight to regain market share.
4. Profits fall in line with falling prices and the continued need to promote the product.
5. Inventory and brand rationalization become common among retailers and dealers.
6. Marginal producers, faced with dwindling margins and severe competition, may drop out at this stage, although it is not impossible for new entrants to appear.

Maturity strategy Promotional strategy is directed at reinforcement of the 'message' so as to encourage re-buys. Subtle differences in brands are emphasized to attract new customers as well as to reinforce the loyalty of existing users. It must be remembered at this stage actual market growth has ceased, and companies can increase their own market share only at the expense of their competitors. Such a situation implies that promotional activity must be sustained merely to hold on to the existing market share.

Price reductions (as a means of achieving the above) are often a feature of the maturity stage, but care must be taken to avoid a 'pyrrhic' victory, because very often the net result of initiating price cuts is to decrease the revenue for all firms in the industry unless sufficient increased purchases can be induced so as to offset revenue losses.

Distribution strategy must be designed to retain existing dealerships and retail outlets, because once lost, they are unlikely to be retained at this stage. To achieve this, the emphasis of promotional effort may move from consumer to distributor.

Decline

Whether because of innovation or changes in consumer preferences, a continued fall in industry sales signifies the 'decline' of the product.

Characteristics

1. Falling sales for the total industry.
2. Price cutting may intensify.
3. Producers decide to abandon the market.

Decline strategy The major strategic decision here is whether to leave the market or not, and, if the former decision is taken, when? Many firms have successfully 'hung on' in a declining market by outliving their competitors and finding 'niches' or speciality areas to serve. Cost control, although always important, becomes critical in retaining profitability when the decision to remain in a declining market is made.

On the other hand, the decision to abandon a previously profitable product is a crucial one and is the source of much 'soul searching' on management's behalf. Many firms find it difficult to accept that a product (on which the very company may have made its name) must sooner or later be abandoned. Such decisions are, however, the essence of marketing management.

Using the PLC concept

The key to successful use of the PLC concept lies in the accurate identification of where each stage

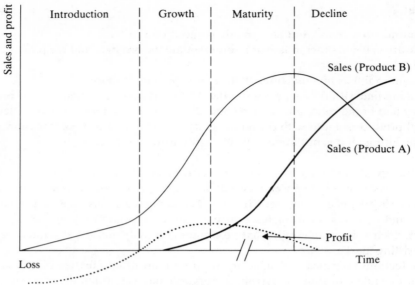

Figure 8.5 Sales/profit comparisons

starts and ends. This calls for a high degree of marketing orientation by management and thus for extensive use of marketing research and intelligence.

If we assume the above to be possible, management then has the basic medium for long-term strategic planning. As well as providing a predictable pattern of product development (during which the appropriate strategies can be planned and budgeted for), the PLC is particularly useful for planning 'beyond the life' of the existing product.

Figure 8.5 shows the likely course of profits for product A during its life cycle. Of particular importance, however, is the launch and overlap of product B.

It is essential that planning is such that companies are already beginning to receive revenue from a new product before or while the previous product is in decline. Similarly, the funding of product B must be derived from the profits of product A—and so the cycle continues.

Criticisms and variations of the concept

The value of the PLC as a strategic tool is undoubted, but, as the student of marketing should now be aware, management should not be constrained by dogmatic adherence to a theoretical course of events. Success is determined by the ability to react and adapt to 'market conditions'. The PLC provides a 'framework' for planning rather than a rigid curve that must be followed. As has already been stated, the time span of the curve can vary enormously according to the product type, but the 'actual' life of the product can in practice be modified by management. Thus, faced with difficult trading conditions or with the opportunity for a better allocation of resources, management can prematurely end the life of a product, say, in early maturity. By the same token, the product's life can be extended and re-extended by finding new end-users for it, or by applying it to totally new markets. There is the possibility of some confusion in considering the extension of a product's life, because in some cases, if the product has changed significantly, then it could be said that this is in reality a 'new product'. One must also distinguish here between the company product and the generic product. Using Levitt's example of nylon,[6] we can see that the generic life of nylon has been constantly extended by finding new end-uses for it. We must also be aware that some new end-users may themselves experience decline while the generic product lives on. The video recorder is a good example of a new product with which to study the PLC. Although a multitude of new brand videos may enter or leave the market at various stages, this will not affect the course of the video's cycle as a generic product. Provided that it remains popular with consumers, the video will not begin to decline until a radically new method of recording begins to supplant its use.

We must also consider the views of those who criticize the use of the PLC as a basic concept. It is not the intention here to engage in full-scale debate, but it is worth noting that critics of the PLC raise issues to which attention should be paid.

We have already pointed to some of the problems and limitations of the basic PLC concept. Some of the critics of this concept have gone further in their assessment of the limitations of the conventional life cycle in strategic market planning. Essentially, these criticisms are based on the extent to which the concept is, at best, irrelevant and, at worst, misleading and dangerous.

The most fundamental, and hence most important, of the criticisms of the product life cycle concept is that there is little or no consistent empirical evidence to support the notion of products following a natural and preordained life cycle with the distinct stages that we have outlined here. In short, some critics claim that the product life cycle simply does not exist.

Among the most cogent of these critics have been Dhalla and Yuspeh,[7] who have challenged the whole concept of the product life cycle. Indeed, in their influential article we are counselled to forget the concept, the use of which, they suggest, can lead to costly and potentially irrevocable mistakes in strategy.

Of course, any doubt about the existence or otherwise of both the S-shaped life cycle and the distinct stages of which it is suggested to comprise can be resolved only by an appeal to the facts. Needless to say, with such a long-standing piece of marketing theory, numerous empirical studies have been undertaken over the years designed to confirm or refute the PLC concept, including those of Cox,[8] Polli and Cook,[9] Cunningham[10] and Day.[11]

Overall, the evidence from these and other studies suggests that the classic S-shaped life cycle does indeed exist, but not for all products or for similar products on all occasions. In other words, we cannot (indeed, should not) consider the traditional PLC concept as a universal law or fact. But if this is the case, then where does this leave the marketing planner with respect to the use of the concept, and particularly with regard to the suggested application of the concepts that were outlined earlier? You will recall that we have already counselled the use of judgement and experience in interpreting the concept for marketing strategy; but does not the evidence of the lack of universality of the concept tend to undermine the wisdom of using the concept at all? Clearly, this is the Dhalla–Yuspeh view. However, the view taken here is that critics and researchers of the concept, and particularly those who have not supported the classic S-shaped PLC, have added to, rather than detracted from, the usefulness of the concept to strategic marketing planning.

The reason for this seemingly contradictory statement derives from our assertion that much of this criticism, coupled with empirical research, has helped develop and refine our knowledge of the basic concept. In particular, partly as a result of the criticisms of the basic concept and the research it has generated, it is now acknowledged that there are several possible variations on the traditional, S-shaped PLC curve. Some of these are shown in Fig. 8.6.

A number of factors give rise to these different possible shapes for the product life cycle, but there is some evidence to suggest that the shape of the PLC may be associated with the type of product/market under consideration.

For example, life cycle (a) of the figure is suggested by Kotler[12] as being frequently found in the small kitchen appliance market. Initial sales growth after a new product launch is rapid, followed by a quite severe drop in sales as the novelty wears off. Eventually, however, the decline in sales will stop and the product will enter a relatively long period of stability in sales as late adopters purchase the product and early buyers purchase again to become replacement purchasers.

The pattern shown in Fig. 8.6 (b) represents a 'truncated' pattern. The shape of this pattern

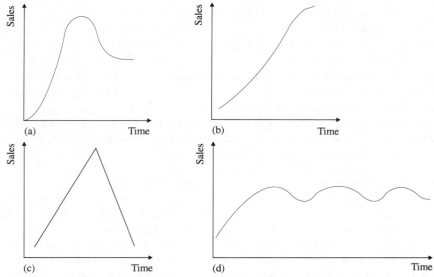

Figure 8.6   Alternative product life cycle patterns

illustrates that there is no introductory period. Sales grow rapidly right from product launch. This type of PLC curve may be associated with new products where there is a substantial market appeal and where little learning is required or risk perceived. Such products include new models of cars from the large manufacturers supported by appropriate high profile launch publicity.

Pattern (c) illustrates a rapid growth in sales, again with no introductory stage, followed by an equally rapid decline with no maturity stage. Products that exhibit this shape of life cycle are typical novelty products or fads, such as Rubik's Cube.

Finally, pattern (d) illustrates a success of PLC curves with a relatively short introductory period, rapid sales growth, a short maturity, followed by rapid decline. After this, the process is repeated. This pattern is frequently associated with fashion type products, such as clothing.

Another criticism is that, if used without imagination, the product life cycle can become a self-fulfilling prophecy. In other words, management may misinterpret market activity and think themselves into product decline and accept this as inevitable. One method of avoiding this is to extend or 'exploit' the PLC by imaginative application of the product to new markets. Thus, although the product may decline in its existing form and market, this is not to say that it cannot be profitably employed elsewhere. Such a strategy does not imply that the life-cycle concept is being ignored—rather, it is the recognition of the concept that permits such a strategy.

A further danger and cause for criticism is linked to that described in the preceding paragraph. This concerns the capacity of management to identify accurately the beginning and end of progressive life-cycle stages. This is, of course, no easy task, because each stage merges with another over a time span which may vary according to the product and its markets. In the case of a truly 'new' product, no empirical data will be available to aid decision-making: such situations will, therefore, be 'unique'. Successful use of the PLC concept is not, however, an unattainable goal. It should be the result of a coherent and long-term marketing strategy. This in turn is supported and made possible by 'continuous' marketing and market research and the employment of a comprehensive marketing intelligence system.

The PLC and the product adoption process

It is important to consider product strategy and the PLC in conjunction with the reactions of consumers who are exposed to new products. The section on consumer behaviour in Chapter 3

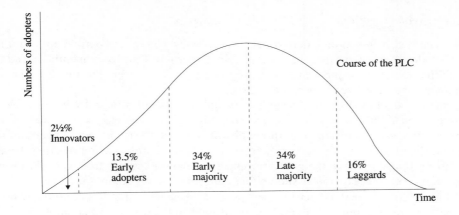

Figure 8.7   Adoption theory and the PLC
After: E. M. Roger, *Diffusion of Innovation*, Free Press, NY, 1962, p. 162

deals in detail with this subject, but it is worth while here to consider briefly the relationship that the PLC concept has with product adoption. By doing this, marketing management can appreciate the nature of the target market and its needs as the product moves through its life cycle.

Consumers can be grouped into five 'adopter categories', each of which has distinct characteristics; therefore specific strategies need to be formulated which suit the individual needs of each group at a given time. The relationship between adoption theory and the PLC concept is shown in Fig. 8.7.

This figure does, of course, present an extremely simple and logical relationship, which is based on separate research studies. However, the implication is an essential ingredient of marketing strategy. This is that the marketing of a product should be seen in as many dimensions as possible. Marketing might say that the 'early majority' will require a specific approach to advertising, pricing and distribution. The fact that competitors will be employing the marketing mix in a similar way will in turn create market conditions that require decisions and action of a strategic nature, which in this case should be relevant to the 'growth' stage of the life cycle.

PRODUCT MANAGEMENT AND ORGANIZATIONAL STRUCTURE

This section is concerned not with the total study of organizational structure, but rather with the subject as it relates to the product. As usual with marketing, the interdependent theme is strong as no one aspect of the firm can be considered in isolation. A striking aspect of product organization *vis-à-vis* the complete organizational picture is the indispensable, motivational involvement of top management.

It is the responsibility of senior executives to create the correct environment for innovation and forward thinking and thus to initiate and motivate the development of new products. The extent of their involvement is very often the only determinant of eventual product success. Vital though attitude is, this must be translated into some concrete form of organizational structure and procedure so that the communication of ideas 'top down' and 'bottom up' can flourish. One of the following formal sections is commonly found in those companies who enjoy consistent success in product innovation.

The 'new product' section

The existence of such a section or department quite obviously implies a permanent commitment to product development. Typically, the section is small, perhaps four to six members, and it is their responsibility to set up a 'new product' programme and to steer this through the stages of development that have already been described.

The new product function has the authority and credence of being a section or department in its own right and should have the ability to 'streamline' ideas, whereas a committee, for example, has a tendency to operate in a manner rather abstracted from the running of the rest of the firm. It is vital that the members of the team are drawn from a wide cross-section of other departments, thus ensuring that they have the necessary experience and expertise to cover *all* aspects of the product; moreover, this experience should facilitate constructive communication with their peers throughout the firm. A real danger for 'new product' sections is that this communication breaks down and it becomes a remote 'boffin-like' institution in the eyes of other employees.

Often the head of the section will report directly to the chief executive of the firm and will possess substantial authority. When the development stage is complete, the product will be turned over to the respective functional areas for test marketing and commercialization.

'New product' committees

In common with 'new product' departments or sections, committee members are selected from key functional areas of the firm and in this case are usually senior managers in their respective fields. Their role is not as much in the actual conception of a product, but rather more in the approval and review of existing programmes. The strengths of committees are due to the authority of their members. Thus, if a particular plan is approved by, say, the production director, it is less likely that this will meet opposition later. On the other hand, there is a danger of the committee becoming remote from its purpose because members are often more anxious to concentrate on their own existing responsibilities. Moreover, decision-making can be slow, compromising in nature, and have a tendency to impede rather than accelerate the progress of promising developments.

In some companies, committees exist side by side with 'new product' sections or departments and are the final arbiters of crucial stages of development.

The venture team

This is the newest organizational concept for product development. Its role is to manage the development of a specific product from conception to full-scale marketing. Again, members are multi-disciplinary, but, unlike the two previous examples, the venture team operates outside the mainstream of the firm—almost like a 'mini-business' in itself. Its sole objective is to bring a new product to the market profitably. Most usually, team members are relieved of their existing responsibilities so as to concentrate fully on a given project. The life span of the team can run from a few months to several years—just as long as it takes to do the job.

The essence of the venture team is entrepreneurial spirit, and companies should endeavour to choose team members on this basis. How successful venture teams really are is uncertain. The 'entrepreneur', is often difficult to identify, and it is extremely difficult to segregate a small team away from the firm and retain its effectiveness, and to free such a team from 'bureaucratic' constrains and impediments, although this is the rationale on which the team is based.

Once a product reaches market launch, the team is usually disbanded and product management is then passed back to the mainstream of the firm and its functional departments.

Product managers

A product manager is an organizational unit in one person who has responsibility for the development of a new product and for the entire management of existing products. Functional marketing areas such as sales, marketing research and advertising exist on a 'company-wide' basis, and it is up to the product manager to utilize these services as he or she thinks fit.

A major criticism of the use of product managers for new product development is that, like committees, there is a tendency for them to become preoccupied with existing products and problems rather than new ideas. This is understandable, as their performance is usually assessed on the basis of established product success rather than idea generation, although the latter forms part of their remit in many firms. Similarly, it does not necessarily follow that the skills required for established product management coincide with those required for new product development. On balance, such role duality is likely to be neither fair nor efficient, and much current thinking places the product manager's responsibility with the management of established products. For this reason, the product manager's role will be re-examined below.

There is no single 'best' method to organize for new product development. Like many other aspects of marketing, this organization is a function of the company's make-up—its managerial skills, financial resources and existing organizational structure. There are, however, distinct guidelines which, if followed, considerably increase the opportunity for success.

Whatever method is employed, development should not be harmed by bureaucratic constraints. This is the surest way to stifle progress and enthusiasm. Development should take place in an entrepreneurial atmosphere fostered by top management and permeated throughout the firm. Representatives from all functional areas should be involved in development. Finally, the importance and involvement of top management cannot be overemphasized. As long as 25 years ago, E. J. McCarthy went so far as to say that 'new product development cannot be systemized'. Organizational plans can only 'facilitate' development whose key criterion for success is a 'dynamic, innovating attitude, instilled into and felt by the whole company'.[13]

THE PRODUCT MANAGER

The product manager as an organizational unit is not really a new or revolutionary breakthrough in marketing management. What is new is its rapid acceptance and adoption by most major companies during the past two decades. The principal reason for this can be ascribed to the emergence of multi-product organizations.

Where does the product manager 'fit in'?

The particular type of marketing organization a company chooses is of course dependent on the products it markets and the markets within which it operates. The arrangements and solutions that a company decides upon are almost as numerous as the companies themselves. One major theme is

Figure 8.8   A functional marketing organization

Figure 8.9   A product manager marketing organization

Figure 8.10   Expanded product manager organization

common whatever the circumstances of the firm. They all must accommodate three basic dimensions of marketing activity:

1. Functions
2. Products
3. Markets

The most common and least complicated approach to addressing the organizational problem is to organize the company around the marketing functions that must be performed. A marketing manager or marketing director is at the head of a function that coordinates and synchronizes the marketing operation in totality. This most simple structure is illustrated in Fig. 8.8. Advertising, sales and marketing research possess their own functional specialists, but work together under the unifying supervision of the marketing director. While the system is advantageous because of its

'Personal Products Ltd' – Product Mix

Figure 8.11   The consistency of the product mix

simplicity, its appeal is considerably lessened as the number of products produced by a company begins to grow. When this happens, not only does management become physically complicated, but more importantly, there is a risk that some products will become neglected at the expense of others.

The product manager type structure offers the solution of providing each product (or sometimes brand) with someone who is directly responsible for its success, allocation of functional support and general well-being. Figure 8.9 locates the product manager in relation to the rest of the firm's marketing activities. Each product manager draws on the functional areas for appropriate support, and, because his or her activity is focused on one product only, the marketing of that product is uncluttered by dual roles and conflicting or confused product loyalties. Additionally, such a structure is higly flexible, as new managers who have very clearly defined objectives can be added as product expansion takes place.

If the product range is sufficiently large and diverse, the responsibilities can be broken down still further. A chemical company may have a manager for 'agricultural products'. Separate product managers may control 'insecticides', 'fertilizers', etc. These too can be broken down into individual 'brand managers', say, for brands within insecticides as in Fig. 8.10.

The role and responsibilities of the product manager

The product manager type company structure allows senior management to 'home in' on the progress and performance of any given product with relative ease and precision. As such, the system lends itself to marketing control and to marketing planning. Strategic planning and marketing 'audits' are, therefore, greatly improved by product manager feedback. Planning at the business level is also improved, because the product manager's primary role is to plan product objectives and strategy, ensure they are implemented, monitor their progress, take action if necessary, and coordinate budget development and control.

The responsibilities are, therefore, erroneous—in reality, the product manager runs a business within a business with direct responsibility for success or failure. Not only is the product manager a planner as well as an implementer, but a further burden is one of ensuring that the resources required to carry out a plan are readily available. In theory, as can be seen from Fig. 8.11, functional resources are shared and are at the disposal of each product. Problems arise, however, if a functional area becomes overstretched and cannot share its resources equally. Here the product manager faces the task of negotiating, perhaps even fighting, for resources that are essential to carry out the job that senior management expects. In less difficult conditions, the least that is expected from a product manager (in addition to planning and implementation) is the ability to coordinate the functional resources at his or her disposal to the best advantage of the product plan.

The 'fundamental' tasks of the product manager have just been described. The remit is so wide that it is worth detailing the various involvements. The scope of product management is as follows:

1. Planning product strategy.
2. Sales forecasting.
3. Monitoring performance and gathering field intelligence.
4. Advertising.
5. Sales promotion.
6. Marketing research.
7. Merchandising.
8. Packaging, branding, labelling.
9. New product development—product improvements.
10. Product line planning.
11. Pricing.
12. Inventories and warehousing.
13. Production planning.
14. Distribution.
15. Sales—stimulating interest and support among the salesforce.

Problems with product management

In view of the extent of the product manager's role, it is not surprising that certain problems are associated with this form of organization.

First, as has already been mentioned, the product manager, whose primary concern is the product, often extends much effort in vying for the functional resources which are shared with his or her peers. Time spent thus dilutes the amount of effort spent on planning. Such 'in-house competition' also has a psychological effect, in that the product manager is expected to be responsible for the results of, say, advertising decisions, but does not gain either personal expertise or the opportunity to be instrumental in the decision-making process. This syndrome can also be extended to profit accountability; the product manager is highly 'profit accountable', but rarely has the authority to make big profit decisions.

The product manager is, therefore, allocated great responsibility without the satisfaction of real control over the product's destiny. From the senior executives' viewpoints, the product manager's decision-making abilities are restricted because of his exclusive involvement in one product. For the product manager, this is a good reason to be afforded more executive control!

A final problem concerns organizational policy itself. At one extreme, a strictly functional structure (Fig. 8.8) is not sufficiently flexible for the demands of multi-product companies. However, there is a real danger of carrying the product manager concept too far. The structure of Fig. 8.10 shows product managers and brand managers, and here the difficulty for some companies is to know where to stop! If, for example, a product manager's time is being spent more and more on one aspect of management, an assistant may be appointed. So, in turn, a brand manager may request assistance. This process will in turn place increasing pressure on functional specialists. The end result may be an expensive and unwieldly 'superstructure' of personnel whose presence will defeat entirely the main object of product management—that of simplicity, direct responsibility and easy access to information.

Advantages of the product management structure

Much of the value of the product manager concept can be attributed to the direct responsibility and answerability that the system itself engenders. The product manager is a centre of information for planning. No single product is likely to be neglected because each manager has an obvious vested interest in obtaining the best possible level of resource support. With reference to overall product strategy, the product manager is uniquely placed as the firm's 'early warning system', giving information as to changes in the market which may require product adaptation, marketing mix modification or even the consideration of product deletion. Last, but not least, the job of the product or brand manager provides valuable experience and training to young men and women who aspire to higher managerial positions.

Despite these drawbacks, the product management structure is popular and workable in companies whose product range is too diverse to be adequately serviced by a 'functional' type of marketing organization. Any risk can be further reduced if the company clearly delineates the product manager's responsibilities, is aware of potential areas of conflict and takes steps to reduce their number, and, finally, ensures that the methods used for assessment are consistent with the product manager's responsibilities and authority.

PRODUCT STRATEGY

Many companies, while not necessarily requiring brand and product managers, do market more than one product. This is especially true of firms operating in consumer goods markets. The fact that a company has more than one product necessitates that some method be devised for monitoring and comparing their respective performances, and for enabling decisions to be made about the future. The PLC concept illustrates that, whatever the time span, the life of a product is temporary. With this in mind, the essence of product strategy is simple: the firm must manage the marketing of existing products, decide when products are of no further use, and plan the development of new profit sources by providing new products to replace those that have been deleted.

In order that firms can organize for product planning, and that their products can be easily related to each other and to respective market areas, it is useful to consider products as a series of readily identifiable groups.

The first consideration is the *individual product*. This is any product considered as a separate entity irrespective of its relationship to other products and the type of market in which it is to be found. Provided that any product differs in some way from another, through either modification or market application, the firm can regard this as an individual product.

The sum total of the products offered for sale by a firm is referred to as the *product mix*.

Finally, those products that are related in some way to one another are classed as the *product line*. The relationship could be because they are simply different models of the same basic product, or because they have marketing similarities in that they are sold in similar outlets or serve the same customer groups.

It is common to attribute the product mix with 'width' and 'depth'. This enables an analysis of the consistency of the product mix to be made. The following example illustrates the idea of the product mix and product line, and forms the basic structure of analysis and selection of appropriate line strategies. A hypothetical example best illustrates this (Fig. 8.11).

> A firm manufactures fountain pens, cigarette lighters and wrist watches. Each item is related in that they are marketed through similar channels and are targeted at appropximately the same consumer segments.
> The product mix represents the sum of the firm's products—in this case 30 products. The number of product lines is obviously three. 'Depth' refers to the number of products in each line—9, 13 and 8 with the average depth being 10. 'Width' refers to the number of product lines which a company has to offer.

By looking at its products in this way, a company is able to begin to see where existing strengths and weaknesses lie. Is there scope for adding to the product line by adding, say, digital watches to line 3? Do some products in the same line compete with each other? With respect to new products, will an addition to the line be consistent with its neighbours in terms of image, production, distribution and market segment? Conversely, is any one product so valuable in terms of image and reputation that its deletion will damage the product line or indeed the total mix? Finally, should the firm consider an addition to the width of the mix, and will these be consistent with the existing product mix and compatible with the current long-term marketing strategy?

Mix analysis is also vital to a review of marketing strategy itself. The firm is merely a representation of its products and its marketing strategy. In the case of Personal Products Ltd, the following are a few of the possible strategic options.

1. Augment product line 1 by adding ball point pens. This would remove some measure of exclusivity and represent a strategy of being 'all things to all people'—a bid to serve the whole market for ink-based writing implements.
2. Delete all but the most expensive men's lighters from line 2. This would have the effect of making the company a market specialist in men's lighters—aiming at an exclusive market segment.
3. Delete lines 1 and 2 and become a specialist in a single product line—wrist watches. In such a situation, options 1 and 2 would still be available to the company.
4. Delete all but one product and become expert in its marketing and production.
5. Add another product line. In the case of 'Personal Products Ltd' it could be a new line of pens aimed at the designer or graphics market.

Some industrial companies become expert in supplying products for special situations, such as deep sea diving equipment. This represents a decision to reduce the product mix to its absolute minimum.

Given the existing product mix and the options available, the company must begin to take product decisions that are in line with long-term strategy, and are consistent with that mix. The introduction of ball point pens by Personal Products Ltd could influence the perception the consumer has of the company as a whole. Cheaper disposable pens might not be consistent with the firm's reputation for high-quality lighters. Similarly, the firm may be technically capable of producing an industrial line, but lacking in the marketing expertise required to serve this new market efficiently.

Analysis of the product mix thus questions every aspect of the company. Any decision has financial, technical, marketing and market connotations. The critical nature of product strategy becomes more apparent when one considers the consequences of failure and the necessity for success.

We must now consider ways in which the decision to choose any of the above options is made. First, we should remind ourselves of the absolute necessity of new products. If, at any time, the rate of new product development and launch is not equal or superior to the rate of product deletion or

	Existing markets	New markets
Existing products	Improved performance Product performance Realignments of the marketing mix	New market segments Geographical expansion
New products	Same distribution channels, sales outlets and sales strategy	Diversification through innovation

Figure 8.12 A simple product strategy mix

obsolescence, the company will lose profits rapidly and ultimately will be unable to survive. A long-term view of strategy must, therefore, be taken. Still keeping the product mix very much in mind, it is possible to look at the company's future from a more abstract viewpoint, which will stimulate and aid the long-term decision-making process.

The matrix shown in Fig. 8.12 presents possible alternatives for fundamental product strategy. Of course, any decisions must be evaluated in relation to the company itself and to the market conditions that are prevalent and likely in the future. In the first case, a marketing audit is designed to establish whether the firm is currently making the best use of opportunities available in existing markets and for existing products. Market share and sales analysis should establish whether last year's objectives are being achieved, and a study of profitability by product, geographical area and market segment should be made. When an internal analysis has been completed, marketing research and intelligence systems should be brought to bear to examine whether or not any prepared action is feasible.

Armed with knowledge of itself, and present and future markets, the company can address itself to the alternatives in the BCG matrix which is discussed shortly, and go on to produce a plan for strategy realignment, new product development and possibly expansion.

Another variation of Fig. 8.12, ascribed to Ansoff, has already been provided in Chapter 4.

We now know that product strategy requires a thorough examination of the firm's own strengths and shortcomings, thorough market knowledge and an unequivocal commitment to new product development and thus long-term strategy. Product strategy must, logically, also involve methods for phasing out certain products to make way for new ones. Very often it is judicious to withdraw products from the mix long before the PLC has run its course, and such a decision is usually due to one or more of three reasons:

—A decrease in market share due to competitive pressure.
—A reduction in profitability which is deemed irreversible.
—A slowing down of sales growth which suggests that marketing resources might be better employed elsewhere.

Given available marketing information, both internal and external, and the existence of products in varying market conditions and stages of development, it is possible to classify the total product mix according to each product's potential usefulness to the company. As we have seen in Chapter 4, the Boston Consulting Group (BCG) have devised a classification technique which does this by using a matrix that rates products according to sales growth and market share. To remind you of the possible types of products in the BCG matrix, the four possible types of product in the matrix are outlined again below, together with the implications for managing each type of product.

1. 'Star' products are highly profitable, and the company should allocate them sufficient resources so as to maintain market share.
2. 'Problem children' may require a disproportionate amount of spending, relative to growth potential, in an effort to increase market share. Each case must be based on circumstances, but they are certainly candidates for divestment.
3. 'Cash cows', as the name suggests, are major sources of profit. Investment should equal that which is required to maintain market share: surplus profit can be used to finance 'stars'.
4. 'Dogs' can either be 'profit-milked' into decline, or deleted quickly so as to reallocate resources.

In using techniques such as the BCG matrix to formulate product strategies, it should be remembered that the emphasis should be on managing the total product mix (the portfolio aspect). Understandably, product managers plan what they see as the best strategies for their own products or strategic business units. As Day[14] points out, this ignores the interdependency among products and the possibility that what is optimum for each product manager is not necessarily best for optimizing the product mix for the company as a whole. In addition, as with planning other elements of the marketing mix, strategic product decisions need to be considered in the interest of the organization's business mission, company objectives, environmental forces, and corporate strengths and weaknesses. Finally, strategic product decisions must also take into account competitors and their products and related strategies. An outline of these factors and the relationship between product planning and the strategic planning process is shown in Fig. 8.13.

SERVICE PRODUCTS

At the start of this chapter, it was suggested that a product is a series or a bundle of satisfactions. It was also suggested that physical products such as a car or a machine tool include an 'intangible' service element when considered from the perspective of what the customer buys. Finally, we have seen that, when we discuss products and the planning of product decisions, a wide range of different types of products, from machine tools to office cleaning services and from baked beans to holidays, can be encompassed. All of what has been discussed throughout this chapter relating to the nature and importance of product planning decisions, plus the planning tools and frameworks, applies equally well to any category of product. We end this chapter by examining the special issues of marketing services.

The importance and nature of service products

In many developed economies of the world, and particularly the United States and the United Kingdom, service industries have outstripped manufacturing industry in terms of their contribution to gross national product. Put simply, the UK and the USA are now service economies. There are a variety of reasons for the growth of the service sectors, and many argue that the balance has tipped too far in favour of services for a 'healthy' economy. Both the reasons for the growth of services and the arguments for and against this growth are outside the scope of this text. However, the importance of service products and the special issues that surround their marketing mean that it is worth while considering them further. But what is meant by the term 'service products', and what are the distinguishing characteristics of those products that give rise to special issues in their marketing?

'A service is an intangible product involving a deed, a performance, or an effort that cannot be

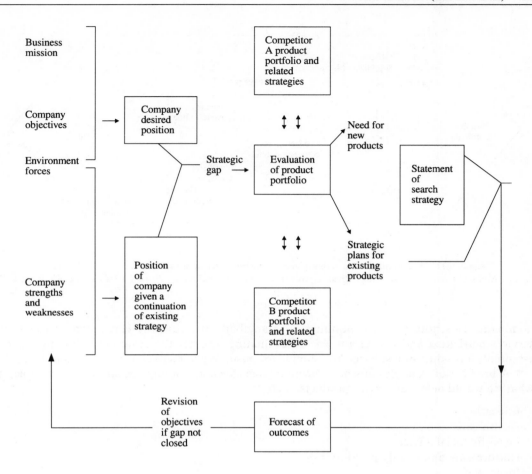

Figure 8.13 Product planning activities in the strategic planning process
Source: Adapted from G. S. Day, 'A strategic perspective on product planning', *Journal of Contemporary Business*, Spring 1975

physically possessed.'[15] This definition by Berry attempts to capture some of the key distinguishing characteristics of service products, in particular their intangibility and lack of physical ownership. For example, if we consider air travel as a service product, there is little doubt that this is a product that is largely intangible and of which the customer does not take physical possession as such. On the other hand, there is a tangible element to the product. The aeroplane itself, the seat we occupy, the meals and drinks we are served are all very much tangible aspects of the flight we purchase. In addition, we do take 'physical possession' of certain elements of the product—again, for example, the seat and the meals and drinks. In the same way as we argued that physical products usually contain an important non-physical, or largely intangible, element, so too are service products often accompanied by physical, tangible elements.

What all this means is that very few service products strictly meet the definition given earlier; rather, most products have a mixture of both tangible and intangible components. If we think of tangibility as a continuum, therefore, service products are those where the intangible element is

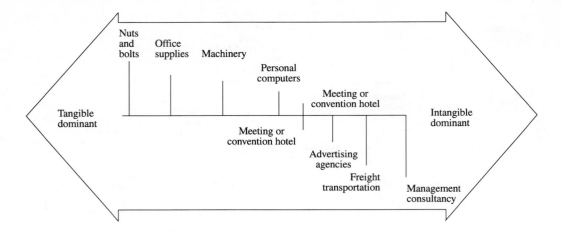

Figure 8.14 A continuum of tangibility and intangibility: business product–service classifications
Source: Adapted from G. L. Shostack, 'Breaking free from products marketing', *Journal of Marketing*, 41, April 1977, p. 177

dominant. This notion of a continuum of intangibility is frequently encountered in texts on services marketing and is a useful way of evaluating whether the customer is buying what is essentially a product or a service. An example for business product/services is shown in Fig. 8.14.

A brief list of examples of where the intangible element is dominant, and hence examples of what we would define as service products, includes:

—Education
—Health care
—Legal/financial advice
—Hairdressing and beauty parlours
—Insurance
—Hotels/catering
—Public transport

Clearly, there are plenty of other examples of service products/industries, but note that it is the customer who decides whether or not a product or service is being purchased (and hence marketed) according to the relative importance he or she attaches to the tangible versus the intangible elements.

Intangibility, then, is the key dimension that distinguishes service products; but what about the notion of 'non-possession' referred to in our earlier definition, and do services have any other distinguishing characteristics that set them apart from physical products? Briefly, the other suggested special characteristics or service products, including the aspects of non-possession (or, as we have called it, non-ownership), are outlined below. As with the degree of tangibility, you should remember that these so-called 'special' characteristics are more a matter of degree than of distinguishing between physical and service products, and are also best thought of as a continuum.

Non-ownership Many services are used rather than owned. For example, we use the services of a hairdresser rather than take physical possession of a product.

Inseparability Services are generally consumed as they are produced. For example, when we pay a visit to the dentist, normally the dentist 'produces' his services while we are there in the dentist's chair. Production and consumption are simultaneous. Because of this, the person providing the service—in this case the dentist—is very much part of the service product.

Perishability Generally, service products cannot be stored. For example, if a hotel room is not filled for the night, or if an aeroplane flies with empty seats, the room or seats for that particular night or flight cannot be 'stored' and sold later. The revenue that would have accrued had the room been let or the seat booked has been lost for ever. This characteristic makes effective matching of demand and supply for service products particularly important.

Variability Largely because service products have a high 'people content', i.e. there is a significant human element in the provision of many services, the quality of the service product may vary each time the service is provided. As consumers, we are all probably familiar with this variability of services. For example, how many of us have gone to a hotel or restaurant which in the past has provided us with good service, only to be disappointed by the level of service we get from, say, a waiter who is new or who simply cannot be bothered to give good service on that particular day?

In addition to intangibility, then, these are some of the special characteristics of service products. These characteristics in themselves would be of little impact if they did not give rise to significant implications for marketing service products; but in fact they do.

Implications for marketing service products

The characteristics of service products mean that they must be marketed in a somewhat different way from other products. Kotler[17] has argued that service businesses are more difficult to manage if using only a 'traditional marketing' approach.

For a detailed discussion of the issues and techniques of services, readers are advised to consult one of the excellent texts that are now available in this once neglected area of marketing, such as Cowell[18] or Lovelock.[19] However, some of the more important implications of the special characteristics of service products for their marketing are summarized in Table 8.1.

The marketing mix for services

As explained earlier, a full discussion of services marketing goes beyond the scope of this text. However, as mentioned in Chapter 4, it is now generally recognized that the traditional marketing mix of the 'four Ps' needs to be extended to 'seven Ps' for services. The additional three Ps for services are outlined below.

People The characteristics of services mean that an important element of marketing services are the service marketer's employees, and particularly those involved in direct contact with customers. The employees of the service marketer, therefore, must be considered in developing the marketing mix.

Physical evidence Largely because of the intangibility characteristic of services, the marketer must carefully plan and communicate the nature of the service offering, including its quality level, by managing the more tangible elements of the service mix such as physical facilities, equipment and so on.

Process How the service is provided is important to its marketing. Procedures for dealing with

Table 8.1 Service characteristics: some implications for marketing

Characteristic	Major effects/issues	Marketing implications
Intangibility	Difficult for consumers to evaluate service offerings, e.g. quality, etc. Positioning difficult to achieve/signal.	'Tangibilize' the service offering by managing the 'physical evidence' that accompanies the service, e.g. staff appearance, buildings/facilities, promotional material.
Inseparability	Direct contact with service provider. Both provider and client affect 'quality' of relationship. Market may be limited by time constraints on provider.	Selection and training of service provider's personnel is essential. Franchise/train other service providers. Develop systems/procedures for increasing customer throughput.
Variability	Difficult to ensure that service quality levels are maintained. Customer may have 'bad' experiences.	Ensure strict quality control. Staff training essential. Develop customer care programmes and systems.
Perishability	Periods of excess demand: periods of excess supply.	Manage demand and supply, e.g.: —Differential pricing —Develop complementary services —Effective pre-booking systems —Use part-time personnel
Non-ownership	Customer finds it difficult to assess advantages of purchasing service.	Stress benefits of non-ownership in promotional programmes.

customers at the point of contact, and for supplying the service itself, to ensure consistency and quality of service supply must be carefully pre-planned and managed.

CONCLUSIONS

This chapter has examined the product or service initially with a view to establishing what exactly the idea of a product or service is. The traditional, narrowly held, belief of a tangible item has been dispelled.

Product categorization has been investigated from the viewpoints of consumer and industrial goods and services.

New product development and its tactical and strategic implications have been viewed, followed by the product lifecycle concept and its practical use to marketing strategists. The adoption process was then explained as an idea to complement the PLC concept.

The management of products was posed through the 'product manager' organizational concept, as opposed to the traditional view of the organization of a marketing department.

We have also examined product strategy matrices as vehicles through which product strategies could be formulated.

Finally, we have looked at the special characteristics of services and some of the implications of those for the marketing of service products.

APPLICATION QUESTIONS

1. Define 'the product' in modern marketing terms. Give an example of a 'traditional' and 'modern' held view of a product (or service).
2. Explain and discuss the various product categorizations. What marketing approaches are normally associated with each?

3. Why is new product development so important to companies? Explain this with reference to the process of new product development.

4. How can the PLC concept be used as a tool for strategic marketing?

5. Explain the nature and role of product/brand management. Illustrate your answer with organizational structures most suited to different types of products and services.

6. What are the so-called 'special characteristics' of service products, and to what additional issues do these give rise when marketing this type of product?

REFERENCES

1. T. Levitt, *Differentiation of Anything: The Marketing Imagination*, Collier Macmillan, London, 1983, pp. 72–93.

2. T. Levitt, 'Marketing myopia', *Harvard Business Review*, **18**(1), July 1960.

3. Margaret Crimp, *The Marketing Research Process*, Prentice-Hall, London, 1981.

4. 'Disastrous debuts—despite high hopes. Many new products flop in the market'. *Wall Street Journal*, 23 March 1976.

5. C. W. Hofer and D. Schendel, *Strategy Formulation: Analytical Concepts*, West Publishing Co, St Paul, MN, 1978, p. 107.

6. T. Levitt, 'Exploit the product life cycle', *Harvard Business Review*, November–December 1965.

7. N. K. Dhalia and S. Yuspeh, 'Forget the product life cycle concept', *Harvard Business Review*, Jan.–February 1976, pp. 102–12.

8. W. E. Cox, 'Product life cycles as marketing models', *Journal of Business*, October 1967, **40**(4), pp. 375–84.

9. R. Polli and V. Cook, 'Validity of the product life cycle', *Journal of Business*, October 1969, **42**, pp. 385–400.

10. M. T. Cunningham, 'The application of product life cycles to corporate strategy: some research findings', *British Journal of Marketing*, 1969, **3** (Spring), pp. 32–4.

11. G. S. Day, 'The product life cycle: analysis and application issues'. *Journal of Marketing*, Fall 1981, pp. 60–7.

12. P. Kotler, *Marketing Management: Analysis, Planning, Implementation and Control*, 7th edn, Prentice-Hall, Englewood Cliffs, NJ, 1991, pp. 551–2.

13. E. J. McCarthy. 'Organization for new product development?' in *Product Strategy and Management*, Thomas Libery and Abe Stuchman (eds), Holt, Rhinehart and Winston, New York, 1963, pp. 384–9.

14. G. S. Day, 'A strategic perspective on product planning', *Journal of Contemporary Business*, Spring 1975, pp. 1–34.

15. L. L. Berry, 'Services marketing is different', *Business Horizons*, May–June 1980, pp. 24–9.

16. G. L. Shostack, 'Breaking free from produce marketing', *Journal of Marketing*, **41**, April 1977.

17. Kotler, op. cit., p. 459.

18. D. Cowell, *The Marketing of Services*, William Heinemann, London, 1984.

19. H. Lovelock, *Services Marketing*, Prentice-Hall, Englewood Cliffs, NJ, 1984.

NINE
PRICING

INTRODUCTION

Following the discussion in Chapter 1 on the marketing concept, it is true to say that, in general, until the 1950s price was considered to be one of the most important influences on buyer behaviour and choice. As a result of increasing competition, during the 1950s and 1960s non-price factors grew in importance, with companies attempting to differentiate their products from competitors on the bases of branding, advertising and packaging. A period of depressed demand, particularly during the early 1980s and early 1990s, combined with decreased levels of real disposable income, have meant that competitive pricing has re-emerged as an extremely potent marketing tool. As a consequence, many marketing managers are now of the opinion that price is, after the product, the most important element in the marketing mix.

This chapter covers the variety of approaches to making pricing decisions, with an emphasis on the marketing approach to pricing. In order to understand and appreciate what represents this marketing approach to pricing, it is necessary to consider first the approach and contribution to pricing decisions of the economist and the accountant. In fact, in many companies the final responsibility for making pricing decisions may, ultimately, rest outside of the marketing function. Of all the marketing mix decisions, pricing has the most obvious and clear-cut effect on company profit. Because of this, pricing is of central concern to all the managers in a company—not just marketing managers.

Given that it is logical to look first at the role that pricing plays in a company and in particular at the link between company and pricing objectives, against this background we can then consider the considerations or inputs to pricing decisions, including cost, demand and competitive considerations. Finally, we can consider pricing policies and procedures, including the important aspects of quoting and changing prices.

THE ROLE OF PRICING

It is through pricing that a company covers the costs of separate elements of its various activities: research and development, raw materials, labour and administrative costs must all, ultimately, be recovered through the price charged to the customer. Marketing costs, too, must be covered by the final price of the product, including those costs incurred in promoting, selling and distributing the product. Last, but not least, the price charged for a product is required to generate additional funds in excess of those costs to meet company profit objectives. Thus, pricing plays the following important roles:

1. Pricing fuses together the various elements of company activity necessary to fulfil customer requirements.
2. Pricing pays for their respective contributions to the final package offered to the customer.
3. To the extent that this package makes commercial sense in the marketplace, pricing generates residual profits in order to fulfil company objectives.

PRICING AS A STRATEGIC DECISION

It is sometimes asserted that, compared with decisions about the other elements of the marketing mix—product, place and promotion—pricing decisions are relatively simple. For example, if we know the costs of producing and marketing a product, and in addition have specified a percentage amount which is to be added to these costs for profit, we can 'easily' calculate the required selling price. Viewed in this way, pricing decisions become a matter of following simple rules or formulae. In addition, price is often viewed as being one of the most flexible elements of the marketing mix; that is, it can be readily changed to meet market conditions as and when required.

These notions about pricing are in fact based on a major misconception about pricing, namely that pricing decisions are tactical decisions. This is not to deny that short-term, tactical, price manoeuvres cannot—under certain conditions—be most effective; but pricing decisions are a strategic issue. This gives rise to the following implications:

1. Pricing decisions should be made in the context of overall marketing objectives and strategy.
2. To this end, pricing decisions should be related to, and be consistent with, the other elements of the marketing mix.
3. Care should be taken not to make price the overriding competitive factor. Alternatively, often more appropriate strategies for competing should not be neglected or ignored.
4. Pricing decisions should not become a matter of routine to be administered by the accounting department.
5. Pricing decisions should not place too much emphasis on cost inputs to the decision.

Some of these strategic implications of pricing are discussed more fully by Taylor and Wills, on pricing strategy,[1] and in a text by Watkins.[2] It is useful to consider some of the basic approaches to pricing decisions before turning to its strategy, in particular the contributions of the economist and the accountant.

The economist and pricing decisions

The classical economists have put forward a well-developed conceptual framework for the establishment of price levels. In fact, for 150 years economists have regarded the price variable as the most important factor in determining the level of demand. This strong, almost exclusive, emphasis on price has led to the economist neglecting the other elements of marketing effort such as advertising, product differentiation and selling efforts.

The classical economist suggests that prices should be set at that level which *maximizes short-term profits*. To maximize profit, the notion of marginal cost and marginal revenue must be introduced.

—*Marginal cost* is the addition to total costs of producing one more unit of output.
—*Marginal revenue* is the addition to total revenue of selling one more unit of output.

Using these concepts, the following pricing rule can be derived from economists' models:

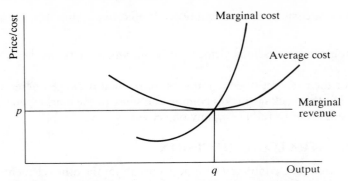

Figure 9.1 The economist's model of pricing in a competitive market

—Profits will be maximized when marginal revenue equals marginal cost.

This rule means that output should be set at a level that would imply a price at which the marginal revenue from selling one more unit equals the addition to total cost of producing that unit. This position is illustrated in Fig. 9.1. At output q, marginal cost equals marginal revenue, and the price required to sell this level of output is p.

The marginal revenue curve is a function of the demand curve facing a company, which in turn is a function of the nature and extent of competition in the market. The revenue curve shown in Fig. 9.1 is that faced by a firm in a 'perfectly competitive' market structure and is a particular, and somewhat unrealistic, type of market structure where the nature of competition condemns the individual company to being a *price-taker*. From this earliest model of market structure, economists have extended their analyses to take account of different, and more realistic, forms of market structure, including markets that are characterized by product differentiation. Regardless of the type of market structure, however, the same decision rule for pricing decisions applies; i.e., prices or output are set so as to equate marginal cost with marginal revenue. For a fuller description of the economists' model, readers are advised to consult a good basic textbook on economics, for example R. G. Lipsey's *An Introduction to Positive Economics*.[3]

This model of price-setting is appealing in that it suggests such a clear-cut decision rule for the price-setter. Nevertheless, the economists' price-maximizing theory has substantial shortcomings. In particular:

1. The assumption of the objective of profit-maximizing: undoubtedly, profits do figure very prominently in company objectives. Only by being profitable is the firm able to pay dividends to shareholders, generate the cash flow necessary to provide working capital and be attractive enough to potential investors when further capital is required. In practice, few, if any, companies set objectives in terms of profit maximization—much less do they even achieve it. Indeed, for most companies, profit objectives are couched in terms of a certain level of profitability, or return on investment (ROI). More specifically, the providers of the investment capital in a company are less interested in the absolute level of profit earned than in the percentage rate of return which they receive on their investment.
2. The assumption that price is the only factor determining the level of demand for a company's product: one only has to compare this assumption with what is known about the tools of marketing to see how restrictive this statement is.
3. The assumption that cost, and more particularly demand functions, can be measured with sufficient accuracy to be sure that the point of profit-maximizing has been reached.

4. The implicit assumption that in making pricing decisions one can ignore the trade, i.e. channels of distribution.
5. The assumption that price is set independently of the other variables in the marketing mix.
6. The assumption that the customer attempts to maximize satisfaction with respect to price alone.

These shortcomings in the economist's model are sufficient to render it of little value to the marketing decision-maker. Despite this, the model does point to one important consideration in practical price-setting; namely, *the importance of demand*. We shall return to this important contribution of the economist later in this chapter.

The accountant and pricing decisions

In contrast to the economist's focus on demand, the accountant's approach to pricing is often based essentially on costs. Such an emphasis on costs is perhaps not surprising, coming from a function that often has responsibility for their determination and control. A variety of approaches to cost-based pricing have been developed by companies. For example, a simple, and, therefore, popular method of setting prices is to calculate the total costs of producing a product or service and to add to this total cost a set percentage for profit. This *cost-plus*, or *full-cost* pricing, as it is variously termed, is justified on a number of bases. First, as previously suggested, it is relatively simple. Second, it is argued that pricing in this way ensures that a known and pre-specified level of profit is attained, with all costs being covered. Finally, it is argued that cost-plus pricing is 'fair' to both trade and final customers. In fact, like the economist's profit-maximizing model, this deceptively simple approach to pricing also has significant shortcomings. In particular:

1. Total costs are usually arrived at by calculating the variable cost per unit and adding to this an allocation of a proportion of the total fixed costs. Total fixed costs are calculated on an assumption of either a standard volume or a forecast level of output. Both the calculation of total fixed costs and the methods of allocating this total between products give rise to serious problems when using this method of pricing. For example, the amount of fixed costs that will be added to each product, and consequently the price, clearly depend upon the number of products produced. In turn, the number of products that a firm will produce will, ignoring stockholding, be a function of how many it can sell. How many will be sold, in turn, depends upon the price charged. Pricing in this way then is nonsensical; it means that, for a given production capacity, if a company finds that it is selling less, and thus cuts its production, its market prices will need to increase. This, in turn, will probably lead to fewer sales, a further cutback in production and even higher prices. To say the least, this is an unsatisfactory state of affairs.
2. A second major disadvantage with full-cost pricing is that strict adherence to a full-cost pricing policy can permit certain marketing opportunities to be passed by because the price the customer is willing or able to pay does not cover the full cost.

Clearly, then, there are problems if we base pricing decisions on total costs plus a margin for profit. In fact, we can go further and say that costs generally should not be used to determine prices. This being the case, what role do costs play in pricing decisions, and what contribution can cost information from the accountancy function play? Among the key roles that information on costs plays in pricing decisions are those that are concerned with the *evaluative* rather than the decision-making role of such information; in particular, it enables a company to:

—Measure the profit contribution of individual selling transactions.
—Determine the most profitable products, customers, or market segments.

Figure 9.2   A simple break-even chart

—Evaluate the effect on profits of changes in volume.

—Determine whether a product can be made and sold profitably at any price.

In order to fulfil these evaluative functions, it is important that the marketing manager has access to *accurate* and *relevant* information on costs.

Accurate cost information allows a company to identify costs on a very specific basis directly related to each product, activity, customer, etc. In this way, management is able to make *informal* decisions about volume mix and pricing to target market segments.

Relevant cost information is information that is presented and analysed in such a way as to be pertinent and useful in decision-making. In particular, the cost analysis should enable the marketer to distinguish between *fixed* and *variable* costs and the relationship between those and volume. Such a cost analysis and its usefulness is perhaps best illustrated in the use of *break-even analysis*. A simple break-even chart is shown in Fig. 9.2.

Fixed costs are those that do not vary with the level of output and are, therefore, represented by the horizontal fixed cost curve in Fig. 9.2. Variable costs, on the other hand, are those that are more or less directly related to production or sales. Increases in output or sales will lead to a proportional increase in those costs with any decrease leading to an overall reduction of variable costs. Taken together, of course, fixed and variable costs combine to give total costs as shown in Fig. 9.2. The remaining information contained in a break-even chart is the revenue curve. This shows the total revenue that will accrue to the company at a given price–quantity combination.

The break-even point is normally represented as that level of output where the total revenue from sales of a product or service matches exactly the total costs of its production and marketing (break-even quantity, or BEQ in Fig. 9.2). Such an analysis of cost–revenue relationships can be very useful to the pricing decision-maker.

One use of break-even analysis is to compare the break-even points associated with different prices for a product. Again, a simplified example of this is shown in Fig. 9.3.

The effect of charging a higher price is to steepen the total revenue curve and as a consequence lower the break-even quantity (BEQ). The pricing decision-maker can then assess the effect of charging different prices in terms of what these different prices and break-even points mean to the company. Specifically, the information given by a break-even chart is:

Figure 9.3 Break-even versus price (not to scale)

—Profit or losses at varying levels of output.
—Break-even points at varying levels of price.
—Effect on break-even point and profits or losses if costs change.

Break-even points can also be calculated using the following simple procedure:

$$\text{Selling price} - \text{Variable cost} = \text{Contribution}$$

$$\text{BEQ} = \frac{\text{Fixed costs}}{\text{Contribution}}$$

e.g., Selling price $= £10$
Variable cost $= £5$
Fixed costs $= £100\,000$

Contribution $= £10 - £5 = £5$

$\therefore \text{BEQ} \qquad = \dfrac{100\,000}{5} = 20\,000$ units

The notion of *contribution* is also a valuable addition to the price-maker's armoury. It illustrates that, in the short run at least, it may pay a company to sell a product at a price that is *less than the full cost* of producing it. Remember that fixed costs are those that do not vary with the level of output. If a company produces and sells nothing, it will still incur these costs. At any price over and above the variable cost of producing each product, then, the company is receiving a contribution towards those fixed costs. In the long run, of course, a company must cover all its costs through the price it sets on its products.

There is no doubt that break-even analysis, and the distinction between fixed and variable costs (and therefore contribution) on which it is based, is of much greater relevance to the price-setter than is the simple provision of total costs implied by the cost-plus approach. Nevertheless, one should note that, once again, its relevance is still more of an evaluative rather than a prescriptive one in terms of price-setting. This is because it is still cost- rather than demand-based. The total revenue curve in the break-even chart illustrates only the total revenue that would be received if we sell any given price–quantity combination. It is not, however, a demand curve. That is to say, it does not indicate the actual quantity that will be sold at any given price.

Another important and useful concept from the costing area is the relationship between costs and the cumulative volume of production, normally referred to as the *experience curve effect*.

In 1925, the commander of the Wright Patterson Air Force Base in the United States observed that the number of direct labour hours required to build an aeroplane decreased as the number of aircraft previously assembled increased. Eventually this phenomenon was explored across a wide range of industries and was found to be present in most of them. The phenomenon eventually came to be termed the *experience curve effect* (or, as it is sometimes called, the *learning curve*). Information on this effect is a vital input to pricing decisions and other elements of marketing strategy.

The basis and meaning of the experience curve effect are relatively easy to understand, and are encapsulated in the name of the phenomenon itself. Put simply, experience curve effects are derived from the fact that the more times we repeat an activity, the more proficient we become: in other words, 'practice makes perfect'. In the case of the Wright Patterson Air Force Base, the commander noticed that this led to a reduction in the time it took to assemble an aircraft as cumulative production increased. The assembly workers simply became more adept at assembling an aircraft because over time they had assembled increasing numbers. Further investigation into this effect established that, not only was the experience curve a phenomenon in most industries, but the relationship between costs and experience was predictable. The specific sources of experience curve effects are as follows:

1. Increased labour efficiency, e.g. the learning of short cuts, improved dexterity, greater familiarity with systems/procedures.
2. Greater specialization/redesign of working methods.
3. Process and production improvements, e.g. design of more effective plant, increased automation.
4. Changes in the resources mix, e.g. substitution of initially highly qualified labour for less qualified personnel.
5. Product standardization and product redesign.

The important point to note about these sources of experience curve effects is that many of them are not 'automatic'; i.e., in order to achieve experience curve effects, management must undertake the necessary steps and exercise initiative.

Experience effects provide the opportunities to lower costs, but appropriate strategies are required to grasp them.

Understandably, experience curve effects differ between industries and between companies. The basic formula for the experience curve is:

$$C_q = C_n \left(\frac{q}{n}\right)^{-b}$$

where:

q = the experience (cumulative production) to date
n = the experience (cumulative production) at an earlier date
C_q = the cost of a unit q (adjusted for inflation)
C_n = the cost of a unit n (adjusted for inflation)
b = a constant depending on the learning rate

Experience curves are normally expressed in percentage terms, e.g. an '85 per cent' experience

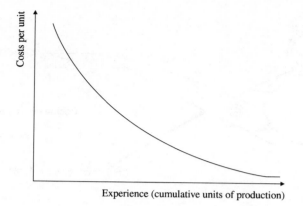

Figure 9.4   A typical experience curve

curve or a '70 per cent' experience curve. Expressing the experience curve in this way tells us the expected reduction in costs for each doubling of cumulative production. An '85 per cent' curve means that the unit cost of producing, say, 2000 cumulative units of production will be only 85 per cent of the unit cost when cumulative production had reached only 1000 units.

It is important to note that the evidence shows that this percentage impact in costs is the same across the whole range of cumulative experience; i.e., doubling experience from 4 million to 8 million units results in exactly the same percentage cost reduction as doubling experience from 100 to 200 units in the company. This, too, has important strategic implications.

A typical experience curve is shown in Fig. 9.4. Note how the curve shows that, at higher levels of cumulative production (experience), larger and larger amounts of cumulative production are required to achieve any given percentage reduction in unit costs.

Information on the experience curve effect can be used to plan pricing strategies, especially for new products. Lancaster and Massingham[4] explore these strategic uses of the relationship between costs and cumulative production in greater detail; but it must be remembered that, like break-even analysis, the experience curve is merely a useful *tool* in the marketer's armoury for pricing decisions.

It is clear that neither the economist's model of price-setting nor the accountant's contribution of cost information is in itself a sufficient basis on which to determine prices. Nevertheless, taken together, they do point to a clear-cut and universal presumption for delineating pricing decisions which can be incorporated into a more realistic and marketing-oriented approach to pricing.

The marketer and pricing decisions

Notwithstanding the shortcomings of their approach to pricing, both the economist and the accountant have provided useful, if partial, insights into this area of the marketing mix. Specifically, we can take the economist's notion of demand and the accountant's emphasis on costs, and incorporate them into the following prescription:

—The upper limit to the price of a product (or service) is determined by *demand*. Therefore, this price should not exceed what the market will bear. Put another way, the price of a product (or service) should not exceed the value of its benefit to the buyer.

—In the long run, the price should not fall below the costs of making and distributing the product (or service).

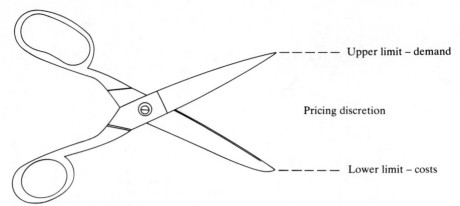

Figure 9.5 Upper and lower limits to price:pricing discretion

Demand and costs, then, can be likened to the two blades of a pair of scissors as shown in Fig. 9.5.

This notion of demand and costs as determinants of upper and lower limits is important in a wider context than that of simply pricing decisions. You will note that the gap between the blades in Fig. 9.5 gives the marketing decision-maker some discretion on pricing decisions. If there is no gap, then there is no profit and hence no discretion. A company can widen the gap between the blades in two ways:

1. It can reduce its costs, through improved manufacturing, greater efficiency, etc.
2. It can increase the perceived value of the benefits of its market offerings to the buyer.

The greater part of a company's marketing efforts is, or should be, aimed at the second of these. As far as is possible, effective marketing should 'desensitize' the customer to price. Unless the company is able and prepared to weather losses, price competition is the lowest form of competition. In order to be effective, competing primarily on price requires that rather stringent conditions be met:

—Sales volume must be much more sensitive to price changes than to changes in other elements of the marketing mix, e.g. advertising, salesforce, products, etc.
—Price advantages should be based on definite cost advantages that will not be easily lost over a period of time—for example when based on new and superior (patented) technology, or where barriers to entry are high.

In addition to cost and demand considerations, the marketing manager must consider the other elements of the marketing mix and the company's generic marketing strategy when considering pricing decisions. Similarly, the marketer's approach to pricing is characterized by a recognition of the need to consider a wide range of factors that will affect the pricing discretion and the eventual choice of a price level. Some of the more important of these factors are summarized below.

Input to, and considerations in, marketing pricing decisions

—Costs
—Demand
—Company and marketing objectives/resources
—Competition/market structure
—Social/legal aspects

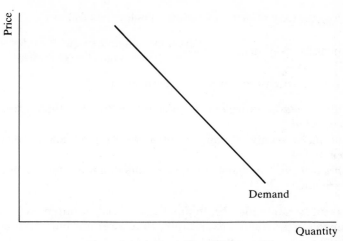

Figure 9.6 A simple demand curve

—Distribution/trade
—Other factors

Each of these is considered in turn.

Costs We have already seen how costs play an important role in pricing decisions. In addition, we have counselled against using costs alone to set prices. Nevertheless, costs do constitute the lower blade of the pricing decision, and the cost structure of the firm must be considered when setting prices. With respect to pricing generally, it is useful to consider three measures of the cost structure of the firm: the ratio of fixed to variable costs; the relationship between costs and volume, including, of course, cumulative volume of experience curves; and the costs of a firm relative to its competitors. Techniques such as break-even analysis, outlined earlier, and accurate and relevant cost information are extremely useful in the delineation and evaluation of price decisions.

Demand We have stressed that demand constitutes the upper blade of the scissors of pricing decisions. We cannot charge prices higher than the market will bear. Ideally, the price-maker would like information bearing in mind the following two interrelated questions:

—What will be the quantity demanded at any given price?
—What will be the effect on sales volume of changes in price?

What we are discussing here can perhaps best be explained with the help of a simple diagram. Figure 9.6 shows a simple demand curve. Even this simple curve contains a substantial amount of information which is extremely useful for pricing decisions. In particular, it allows the company to ascertain the relation between the price charged and the resulting level of demand. As Kotler suggests,[5] normally demand and price are inversely related; i.e., the lower the price, the greater the demand.

The slope of the curve in Fig. 9.6 also indicates how sensitive demand is to price changes; i.e., it indicates what the effect on quantity demanded will be for any given change in price. We normally refer to this as *price elasticity* of demand. It is important to distinguish between the demand curve for the industry as a whole and that faced by the individual company. Ideally, we would like information on both.

Formally, price elasticity of demand can be calculated as follows:

$$\text{Price elasticity of demand} = \frac{\text{Percentage change in quantity demanded}}{\text{Percentage change in price}}$$

Measures of price elasticity commonly range through:

$e < 1$: *Relatively price-inelastic*—a change in price results in a less than proportionate change in quantity demanded.

$e = 1$: *Unit price elasticity*—a given change in price results in an equal proportionate change in quantity demanded.

$e > 1$: *Relatively price-elastic*—a change in price results in a more than proportionate change in quantity demanded.

Useful though this information may be, in practice the relationship between demand and price, and therefore estimates of price elasticity, are difficult to ascertain and interpret. In particular, you should note the following considerations.

In markets where suppliers are able to *differentiate* their products from those of competitors, sales volume for the individual company is a function of:

—The total marketing effort of that company, i.e. marketing mix
—The marketing efforts of competitors

It is difficult to appraise the impact of our price policy upon sales without analysing the entire marketing mix relative to the marketing mix of our competitors.

Price sensitivity may be expected to differ between individual customers and/or groups of customers.

Taken together, differentiated 'products' and differences in price sensitivity mean that the price sensitivity of demand confronting a company is influenced by the choice of market segment and the extent to which prices are congruent with the *total marketing effort* to these segments.

In analysing demand, it is necessary to examine the *buyer's perception of value* as the key to pricing decisions. Essentially, that involves appraising the benefits sought by customers, these benefits being reflected in their buying criteria.

This enables a company to select the most appropriate market targets and then to develop a marketing mix for those targets with a particular marketing positioning in mind with respect to price, quality, service, etc.

Company and marketing objectives/resources We have already stressed that all marketing decisions, including pricing decisions, need to reflect and be consistent with overall company and marketing objectives. A company with an objective of a minimum of 20 per cent return on investment based on rapid market penetration may well require a different pricing strategy from one that is seeking only a 10 per cent ROI and a relatively small rate of market growth. Effectively, therefore, the selection of company objectives, market targets and the formulation of a marketing mix serve to constrain or delimit the range of appropriate pricing strategies and specific price levels. A particularly good illustration of this delineating of price decisions is contained in Oxenfeldt's 'multi-stage' approach to pricing.[6] The essence of Oxenfeldt's approach is as follows:

1. *The selection of market targets* The company's size, location, existing distributional arrangements, contracts with suppliers, customers and creditors, its reputation and past history will influence to a large extent the type of product the company can make, the service it can offer and

its probable costs, and will determine the market that the company can command, and the segments of that market that it should attempt to cultivate. It must identify where its strengths and weaknesses lie.

2. *The selection of a brand image* The image of a company or brand can have considerable bearing on the price that the company can charge, and will influence the type of customer that the company can attract. Most companies will be constrained by the image they have already built up. Thus, to a large extent, steps 1 and 2 are totally interdependent.

3. *The formulation of a marketing mix* The marketing mix (of advertising, promotion, selling, distribution product, etc.) must be selected so as to help reinforce the desired brand image. The direction or emphasis of this marketing mix will be limited by the target market and the brand image.

4. *The selection of a pricing policy* Oxenfeldt uses the term 'policy' to refer to overall pricing strategy, and suggests that the company should establish in advance a policy for dealing with general pricing conditions, answering such questions as:

—Do we price above or below the market average?
—Who are our competitors on price?
—Should we change price to meet competitors' price changes, and how quickly?
—Do we vary prices or aim for stability?
—Do we run price promotions?

Thus, pricing policy deals with recurring pricing problems, and tries to anticipate answers in advance.

5. *Establish a pricing strategy* Oxenfeldt uses the term 'strategy' to refer to the tactics that would be used to cope with unusual or irregular market conditions, such as:

—A change in legislation.
—A massive price reduction by a competitor.
—A radical fall-off in demand.
—A new entrant to the market.

All of these might call for some pricing action as a counter-measure.

6. *The selection of a specific price* The previous five steps will have narrowed down the choice of a final price to a fairly small price zone. The cost and revenue implications of various prices within this restricted range can be compared, elasticity within the range studied, etc. If the five steps leave no freedom of choice, then break-even analysis can be used to determine whether or not the demand that could be generated by that price would be profitable.

Company resources too, and particularly cash resources, must be considered in setting prices. For example, a decision to undercut competitors' prices often leads to a substantial drain on cash resources and should only be considered if a company can afford to sustain such a pricing approach.

Competition/market structure Companies in differing product markets find themselves faced with varying degrees of competition. Some markets are characterized by large numbers of competitors, whereas others may comprise relatively few companies competing for the same customers. The number of competitors affects pricing decisions in the following ways:

—Where there are many competitors selling similar or identical products, competition on price will be severe.
—When there is only one supplier, that supplier can establish his own price, within the constraints of government legislation.

Between these two extremes are those market structures that more often characterize the market economy. The first of these is a market structure where there are relatively few competitors and where often one or two dominant firms emerge which set the lead in determining prices in the industry. In turn, smaller less dominant firms in the industry determine their price levels in relation to those determined by these price leaders. The second type of market structure frequently encountered is one in which, although there is a large number of competitors, firms in the industry attempt to escape from severe competition on price by differentiating their market offerings through advertising, quality and product features.

In addition to current competitors, the company must also consider the relative ease with which new competitors are able to enter the market.

Social/legal aspects Legal and social considerations are also inputs to the pricing decision. Much of the legislation that pertains to trading practices and consumer protection relates to price-setting and pricing practices. Very few marketing managers are legal experts in this area, nor indeed can they be expected to be. Nevertheless, the variety of legal and social issues confronting the marketing manger today means that they must be treated as an additional input in the pricing decision.

Distribution/trade We must not forget that most companies market their products via middlemen in the channels of distribution. For this reason marketing management must consider how this will affect pricing decisions. For example, do we set prices with the final consumer in mind, or do we set them with distributors in mind? What control, if any, do we have over the final price that our distributor, perhaps a retailer, will eventually put on our products? What quantity discounts and what credit terms are we willing to extend to our distributors? etc. Such considerations may serve to complicate what is already a difficult decision area, but they are considerations with which the price-setter must contend whenever he is dealing with distributors or the trade.

Other factors The above are some of the main considerations in pricing decisions. In addition, the decision-maker may have to consider many other factors in setting prices. Some of these factors might be company-specific. For example, a supplier of products to the National Health Service may be involved in a system of tendering prices and may need to consider the policies and procedures of local authorities. Other factors may become important to the pricing decision as a result of unexpected changes in the company's market environment. For example, a major supplier might suddenly increase the prices of his raw materials; political events may cause commodity or energy prices to change as currency exchange rates fluctuate.

Psychology can also play a part in pricing, particularly at retail levels. This accounts for prices like 99 pence, £1.99, £9.99 and so on, because one penny more represents a psychological barrier. There are also psychological price brackets at work in which consumers are 'conditioned' to realize that goods falling within such brackets represent 'value for money'. Prices outside such brackets may infer that the goods are inferior or over-priced. It is well known that pricing goods or services cheaply, perhaps through mechanistic cost-plus procedures, can often be as bad as pricing too expensively.

PRICING METHODS, PRICING POLICIES AND PROCEDURES

Because of the wide range of possible factors that need to be taken into account in pricing, and because of the fact that their relative importance will vary from company to company, the marketing manager needs to be wary of adopting admittedly much simpler but possibly less effective heuristic pricing methods. Full-cost, or cost-plus, pricing is one example of such a pricing method, but there are many others, for example 'going-rate' pricing or 'target pricing'. Whatever the specific method used to set prices, it helps reduce the complexity of pricing decisions considerably if a company establishes a framework of pricing policy and procedures after due consideration of some of the factors outlined above.

A policy framework for pricing decisions should include processes and procedures covering the following areas:

1. *Pricing and company objectives* This should cover the role of pricing in relation to company objectives viewed as a set of targets with respect to, e.g., return on investment, market share, etc.
2. *The role of price in marketing strategy* This should delineate the major policy objectives for pricing in terms of its role in marketing. The policy should cover the extent to which price will be used to compete in the marketplace *vis-à-vis* the other element of the mix and market targets.
3. *Procedures and methods for determining specific pricing levels* This should specify how specific prices shall be set on products and services and the considerations in such decisions, e.g. costs, demand, competition, etc. This part of pricing policy should also allocate responsibilities, i.e. who is to be involved in pricing decisions and on what basis.
4. *The administration of price changes* In addition to setting prices, a company must also consider its procedures and policies with respect to administering and implementing price changes. The need to change prices may, of course, result from a number of factors, including increased costs, changed demand, etc. It is important that a system be established such that price changes are implemented effectively and efficiently. Also, care needs to be taken that frequent, short-term, price changes do not detract from the long-run overall pricing objectives determined earlier.
5. *Policies and procedures on credit, discounts, etc.* In addition to pricing levels and price changes, we should not forget that credit policies and procedures for offering discounts for quantity and/ or early payments are important facets of pricing policy.

SPECIAL ISSUES IN PRICING DECISIONS

So far in this chapter we have outlined and discussed the factors that need to be considered in making any pricing decision. Having said this, some categories of pricing decisions do give rise to certain problems and issues which deserve special attention. Two of the more important of these categories are: 'product-line pricing', and pricing to account for stages in the product life cycle.

Product-line pricing

The majority of companies produce and market not one but a variety of products and services. Provided that neither the costs nor the demand for a range of products is interrelated, decisions on the price of each product may be made independently. Where, as is usual, this is not the case, we must, at the very least, consider the possible effect of these interrelationships on our pricing decisions. In particular, we must consider establishing product-line pricing strategies. The meaning of interrelated demand and costs plus an outline of possible alternative product-line pricing strategies are detailed below.

Interrelated demand Products are interrelated in demand when the price (or some other element of the marketing mix) of one affects the demand for the other, in either a positive or negative way.

Interrelated costs Two products are interrelated in cost when a change in the production of one affects the cost of the other.

Alternative product-line pricing strategies

1. Prices proportional to full cost, i.e. same net profit margin for all products.
2. Prices proportional to marginal cost, i.e. same percentage profit margin over marginal cost (contribution).
3. Prices proportional to conversion cost or 'value added'. Conversion cost is found by substracting purchased material costs from the allocated full costs.
4. Prices that produce the same degree of contribution margins dependent upon conditions of demand in differing segments.
5. Prices related to target market requirements such as to yield an overall required rate of return from the product mix.

Strategies 1, 2 and 3 are dependent upon cost and ignore demand; 4 and 5 are more adequate. These are based on the criterion that prices should reflect the demand relationships existing between products in the line to yield the required return on average assets employed.

Pricing and the product life cycle

As we have seen, pricing decisions are not once-and-for-all decisions; they need to reflect changing competitive and market factors.

One of the factors that is suggested to affect the pricing decision is the stage of a product in its life cycle. In Chapter 8 we classified these stages as:

—Introduction
—Growth
—Maturity
—Decline

The suggestion is that each stage may require, or be best fitted to, a particular set of marketing strategies and marketing mix combinations, including, of course, price. For example, in the case of pricing *new products* at the introduction stage of the life cycle, we may distinguish between, for example:

—*Selective penetration strategy* High price/low promotion, often referred to as market skimming, with the price being lowered at successive stages in time as the product achieves larger sales.
—*Pre-emptive penetration strategy* Low price/heavy promotion.

The strategy selected at this stage then has clear implications for pricing.

Similarly, research indicates that market response to the different elements of the marketing mix may change over the life cycle of a product.[7]

Clearly, then, we must reflect these considerations in a dynamic pricing policy.

CONCLUSIONS

In this chapter we have considered the role of pricing decisions in overall company and marketing strategies. We started by exploring a number of popular misconceptions about pricing: misconceptions that mitigate against effective strategic pricing.

Before considering how the marketing manager might approach pricing decisions, we looked at the approaches of the economist and the accountant. Despite limitations in each of their approaches, we saw that both contribute a number of useful concepts and techniques. In particular, the economist helps by stressing the importance of demand—the upper limit to pricing discretion, and the accountant contributes to our knowledge and recognition of the importance of cost—the lower limit. With these upper and lower limits in mind, we then examined a variety of other important inputs to the pricing decision, inputs which marketers must include if they are to arrive at sensible pricing strategies. In addition to demand and cost inputs, marketers must also consider, in particular, company and marketing objectives, company resources, competition and market structure, social and legal aspects, and middlemen, plus a number of other factors according to the circumstances.

The need to consider this number of factors makes it important that a company should establish a framework of pricing policies and procedures to include, for example, pricing and company objectives, pricing and marketing strategy, procedures and methods for setting specific prices, price changes, credit and discount policy.

Finally, we looked at special issues in pricing decisions, and in particular at the additional problems posed when pricing in a multi-product company and when considering setting prices for products in the different stages of their life cycle.

APPLICATION QUESTIONS

1. Why are pricing decisions strategic, and what misconceptions detract from this strategic role for pricing?
2. (a) What does the economist contribute to the pricing decision?
   (b) What does the accountant contribute to the pricing decision?
3. How does the marketer's approach to pricing differ from both that of the economist and the accountant?
4. What factors should be encompassed in a system of pricing policies and procedures?
5. What special pricing problems are posed
   (a) In product-line pricing?
   (b) In pricing to take account of the stage a product is at in its life cycle?

REFERENCES

1. B. Taylor and G. Wills, *Pricing Strategy*, Staples Press, 1969.
2. T. Watkins, *The Economics of the Brand*, McGraw-Hill, London, 1986, pp. 41–85.
3. R. G. Lipsey, *An Introduction to Positive Economics*, 8th edn, Weidenfeld & Nicolson, London, 1990.
4. G. Lancaster and L. Massingham, *Marketing Management*, McGraw-Hill, London, 1993, Chapter 8.
5. P. Kotler, *Marketing Management: Analysis, Planning, Implementation and Control*, 7th edn, Prentice-Hall, Englewood Cliffs, NJ, 1991, pp. 478–9.
6. A. R. Oxenfeldt, 'A decision making structure for price decisions', *Journal of Marketing*, **37,** January 1973.
7. Kotler, op cit., pp. 362–72.

TEN

CHANNELS OF DISTRIBUTION AND LOGISTICS

INTRODUCTION

In this chapter we shall be examining the routes by which marketers of products and services can ensure that these reach their intended market. We normally refer to these routes as *marketing channels*, which include those intermediaries through which products and services pass from the point of production to the point of intermediate and final use.

In the first part of the chapter we shall concentrate on the development and structure of marketing channels; we shall find that this area of marketing is in fact among the most dynamic, being characterized by increasingly rapid technological and market change. Within marketing channels in the United Kingdom this change is particularly marked in the area of retailing. Not only is the structure of retailing in the UK undergoing a period of rapid evolution, but increasingly this is being accompanied by innovations in technology which are changing the face of shopping as we know it. The modern marketer must adapt to and plan for these changes. Increasingly, the company that fails to take account of this changing structure will find itself at a disadvantage in the marketplace.

This first part of the chapter also explains the place of marketing channels in the marketing mix. The marketing manager needs to appreciate the various types of channel intermediaries, their role and function. Here, again, we shall find that these roles and functions are themselves changing. Against this background of evolving and changing channels of distribution, we shall examine the use of limitations of the once much vaunted 'wheel of retailing' hypothesis in order to assess the extent to which the hypothesis is relevant to marketing decision-making in this important area of the mix. With this as a background, the second part of the chapter looks at the management of channels from the point of view of the marketing decision-maker. Here we shall find that channel decisions are among the most important of the marketing decisions made by a company and are therefore strategic rather than tactical.

If channel design and choice are strategic considerations, the manager must also devote sufficient attention to the implementation and control of these strategies. Individual middlemen must be encouraged to act for the company, and their activities must be monitored and assessed. Thought needs to be given to the minimizing of possible channel conflict and the achievement of maximum cooperation both within and between the variety of channel members.

Finally, in this chapter we shall look at how the concept of what constitutes the 'place' element of marketing has widened in recent years to include the management of physical distribution and logistics.

THE DEVELOPMENT OF CHANNELS OF DISTRIBUTION

It is a fact that today most producers do not sell directly to the final users. Instead, the majority of goods and services move from producer to user through a series of intermediaries or 'middlemen' who perform a variety of functions. Collectively, these intermediaries and the institution of which they form a part are variously referred to as trade, marketing or, as we shall term them here, *distribution channels*. Bucklin[1] offers the following definition of a channel of distribution:

> A channel of distribution comprises a set of institutions which performs all of the activities utilized to move a product and its title from production to consumption.

In discussing the development of channels, a basic question must be, why are they used at all? Or, put another way, why don't all producers themselves sell directly to the consumer? Some, of course, do, but as we have seen the majority do not. There are a variety of reasons for this.

One reason is simply that many producers lack the necessary skills and resources to perform all the activities referred to in Bucklin's definition. Figures 10.1 and 10.2, together, illustrate this.

Figure 10.1 would seem to indicate that the exchange relationship between producer and user

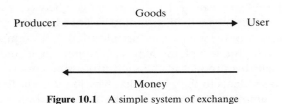

Producer ———————— Goods ————————▶ User

◀———————— Money ————————

Figure 10.1   A simple system of exchange

Producer

Goods ▶

Promotion ▶

Contact ▶

Negotiation ▶   User

Transporting and storing ▶

Financing ▶

Packaging/breaking bulk ▶

◀ Money

Figure 10.2   Today's system of exchange

is essentially very simple. Goods and services are provided to the final user, who in return for them passes back money to the provider. In fact, as shown in Fig. 10.2, today's business transactions are often characterized by a diverse range of complex and interacting activities which are required in order to facilitate the process of exchange. As McGarry[2] points out, a number of functions are necessary to bridge the time, place and possession gaps that separate producer and user. For example, a consumer may require to see the product before making a commitment to purchase. This may require that adequate display facilities are made available for the potential end-user. An individual producer may lack the necessary financial and skill resources to make such a facility available on a national basis.

Similarly, the end-user may require that a variety of products be made available to him at one geographical location. Imagine, for a moment, how much more complex, time-consuming and frustrating it would be if the shopper had to purchase sugar at one retail outlet, jam at another, soap at another and so on. It has long been a key function of middlemen to transform what Alderson[3] has referred to as 'heterogeneous mixtures' of products into 'meaningful assortments'.

A further, if connected, reason for the function of channels of distribution has been the increasing separation of the producer from his end-users. The households that purchase goods and services are not only separated geographically from producers, but are themselves often geographically dispersed. This dispersion, at both a national and an international level, has led to the growth of intermediaries who can bridge this spatial gap between producer and user.

Finally, the growth of channels of distribution is linked to the growth in complexity in industry itself, and in particular the increase in specialization. For example, the mining company extracts bauxite and from it produces aluminium. This aluminium is sold to a can manufacturer. The can manufacturer sells his product to the food processing company. The food processing company sells its canned products to the wholesaler, who in turn sells to the retailer. Finally, the retailer sells the food in aluminium cans made from the bauxite to the housewife. Industry today is comprised of a vertical chain of extractive, manufacturing and service companies, often each specializing in one part of the conversion process. This specialization gives rise to what might be referred to as 'breaks' in the industrial conversion process, and it is these break-points that the institutions and individuals that comprise channels of distribution have stepped in to bridge.

We can see from these reasons for the growth of channels of distribution that they play a very important role, not only in the marketing mix of the individual company, but in an economy as a whole. In fact at this second, macro level, channels of distribution can be said to form part of the marketing system of a country and, therefore, of the individual firm. As Howard points out,[4] a marketing system is for a total economy, it being the *means* by which all of the goods and services flow to the end-user from the different stages of manufacture and all of the funds flow in the reverse direction. An effective and efficient system of distribution, therefore, is essential to the well-being of an economy and the individual units that comprise it. Having said this, and notwithstanding the reason discussed for the development of distribution channels, there is no *a priori* reason why the functions performed by channels of distribution should not be performed by individual companies. In fact, the only economic justification for a company or a society entrusting these functions, or at least some of them, to middlemen is if they perform them more effectively and efficiently than would otherwise be achieved.

Figure 10.3 illustrates more specifically how using intermediaries can contribute in this respect. Without a middleman, each producer must contact all four customers. Therefore, 12 contacts are required for every producer's product to reach every customer. Including a retailer cuts the number of contacts down to only seven, and in fact each producer need only make one contact to the retailer in order to reach all the prospective customers. Even this much simplified example illustrates how channel intermediaries can bring economic benefits both to the individual

(a) No middleman

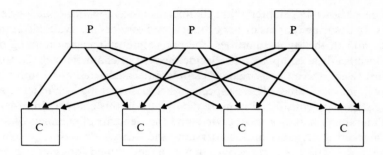

P = Producer
C = Customer
Number of contacts = 3 × 4 = 12

(b) With a middleman

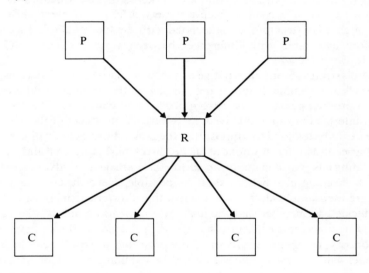

P = Producer
C = Customer
R = Retailer
Number of contacts = 3 + 4 = 7

Figure 10.3   How the middleman can contribute to efficiency

company and to the economic system as a whole. The example should also serve to dispel a widely held, but frequently misplaced, view that middlemen are economic 'parasites'. This view stems from the misconception that middlemen add nothing to benefit, but serve only to increase costs. Not only can middlemen substantially reduce the final cost to the consumer, but, in addition, they add to the utility the customer derives from products by means of, for example, variety, convenience, after-sales service, information, etc.

ELEMENTS OF CHANNELS OF DISTRIBUTION

It has already been shown in Chapter 4 that channel decisions constitute the 'place' element of the marketing mix. In ensuring that his or her products and services are available at the right time, in the right place and in the right quantities, the marketing manager is making decisions about distribution. Specifically, a company must decide the type of channel it will use to reach its target markets; it must select, recruit and organize channel intermediaries, and it must decide on stock levels, delivery modes and times. These aspects of decision-making—channel strategies, channel choice and logistics—are considered in more detail later in this chapter. In order to make these decisions, the marketing manager must understand the elements of channels of distribution. For example, the marketing manager must understand the various *dimensions* of channel structure, and, in particular, the *variety of channel types* to which these dimensions give rise. He or she should also be familiar with the *different sorts of channel intermediaries* or *middlemen*; their roles and relative advantages and disadvantages. Finally, the marketing manager must understand and appreciate the implication of the *dynamic and changing nature* of marketing channels.

Dimensions of channel structure

Channels of distribution are extremely complex marketing structures, and we can examine their components in a variety of ways and from a variety of angles. Nevertheless, one or two key characteristics of channel structure are associated with the 'personality' of a particular channel and are therefore associated with differences between various channels. One of these key characteristics is *channel length*.

Figure 10.4 illustrates several alternative channels of distribution distinguished primarily by channel length. Clearly channel length is determined by the number of different intermediaries through which a product passes *en route* from producer to consumer. The shortest channels are those where no intermediaries are involved, i.e. where the producer deals directly with the final consumer. One might be tempted to suppose that the most effective channels are those that involve fewer intermediaries and preferably none at all, i.e. direct marketing. Certainly, as we shall shortly see, direct marketing has grown in importance, and there are distinct advantages to both producer and consumer of keeping channels as short as possible. Nevertheless, our discussion of why intermediaries are used should alert one to the fact that shorter channels are not invariably more effective and efficient. Remember that the justification for using intermediaries is that they can perform certain functions more efficiently than can the producer. In the long run, and certainly in a free market economy, competitive forces and the profit incentive will tend to lead towards that length of channel which is most efficient under the circumstances. Circumstances here would include, for example, factors such as type of product, number of customers, geographical dispersion of customers, variety required by customer, type and range of services required, etc. Of course, this is not to say that the length of marketing channels for established product markets has arrived at the optimum: the optimum length is likely to change, and as we shall see, the role of some intermediaries has diminished considerably in marketing certain products. Nor should we assume that what is the appropriate length of channel for one company is identical for another company in

1. Producer → Consumer
2. Producer → Wholesaler → Customer
3. Producer → Wholesaler → Retailer → Consumer

Figure 10.4 Channel length

the same industry. As with all other marketing decisions, decisions about channel length are company-specific.

A second key aspect of channel structure concerns the *relationship between channel members* and, in particular, the relationships that pertain to the locus of power and decision-making in the channel structure. This, again, is an area of channel structure that has seen significant changes over the past few years. Today, three broad types of channel structure can be identified on the basis of different relationships: free flow or conventional marketing channels; single transaction channels; and vertical marketing systems.

The first of these, *free flow or conventional marketing channels*, is what many people have come to think of when they consider the relationship between different channel members. In this type of channel essentially each member in the channel—producer, wholesaler, retailer, etc.—operates as an autonomous business unit. Each level operates with its own aims and objectives in mind, and no one level of the channel has any degree of substantial control over the remaining levels. The primary force keeping the channel intact is a mutually beneficial trading arrangement which can be ended by either party should the arrangement become less beneficial. Although no formalized or contractual arrangement exists between the different levels in the channel (other, that is, than those pertaining to each business transaction), such channels do tend to establish trading practices with respect to the expected behaviour of each channel member. Such behaviour would include, for example, services or functions to be performed, consumers to be served, mark-ups and prices, etc.

The second type of channel based on this aspect of structure is what Bowersox *et al.* refer to as *single transaction channels*.[5] In fact, this type of channel is not really a channel at all in the sense of its duration, although a substantial amount of transactions are executed in this way. A single transaction channel is a channel that is brought into being or use specifically for each transaction. After the transaction is completed, the channel has fulfilled its role and the business arrangement in the channel ceases to exist. Examples of transactions that require and use this form of channel relationship would include financial stock and bond purchases, sales and purchases of houses, etc.

The third type of channel structure, based on different relationships between channel members, is what has come to be termed the *vertical marketing system* (VMS).[6] In a vertical marketing system each level in the distribution channel acts in a planned and unified way so as to achieve maximum efficiency for the channel as a whole. Unlike the conventional marketing channel, therefore, each level in the channel acknowledges and functions on the basis of interdependence.

The concept of vertical marketing may be split into three distinct approaches according to how and on what basis coordination and cooperation are achieved in the system. These three approaches to VMSs are: the corporate VMS; the administered VMS; and the contractual VMS.[7]

In a *corporate vertical marketing system*, one of the channel members *owns* preceding and/or subsequent levels in the channel. So, for example, a manufacturer who moves forward into retailing or a retailer acquiring production facilities would constitute a corporate VMS.

An *administered vertical marketing system* is one in which channel cooperation and co-ordination at the various levels are achieved through the dominance and power of one of the channel members. This has been perhaps one of the most significant developments in channel structure in the United Kingdom. Increasingly, power in channels has shifted to the retail end of the distribution network. As we shall see shortly, the trend in UK retailing has been towards larger and much more powerful retailing organizations. This concentration of power has meant that the larger retailing organizations are able to secure strong cooperation and support from suppliers. Retailers now play a very prominent role in determining, for example, pricing levels, product specifications and features, displays and promotional and branding policies on the part of their suppliers.

234 ESSENTIALS OF MARKETING: TEXT AND CASES

A *contractual vertical marketing system* is one in which coordination and cooperation in the channel are achieved through a formal contractual arrangement. There are many forms of such contractual channel arrangements including, for example, exclusive dealerships, cooperative and voluntary groups and the rapidly growing area of franchising. Again, some of these developments in contractual VMSs, and particularly franchising, are considered later in this chapter. At this stage, however, one should note that the key difference between contractual and corporate VMSs is the absence of ownership.

There are many reasons for the growth of vertical marketing systems, but the prime reason has been to improve overall effectiveness in the channel through increased cooperation and control. As we shall see, one of the important factors in channel design is the minimization of conflicting interests in the channel. Vertical marketing systems may not eliminate potential sources of conflict in channels; indeed, they can give rise to such conflict. Nevertheless, VMSs do bring with them a variety of tools and arrangements for dealing with conflicting interests.

Together, channel length and channel relationships constitute the most important elements of channel structure. A related aspect to structure, however, are the channel intermediaries themselves and, in particular, their role and functions in the channel. It is to these considerations that we now turn our attention.

Channel intermediaries

We have seen that the reason for using intermediaries to move products and services from producer to consumer rests on their superior efficiency in the performance of basic tasks. We have also seen that the range and nature of these tasks that an intermediary is required to perform would include, for example, providing an assortment, breaking down bulk, promoting and merchandising products, etc. As in other areas of industry and business, over time, specialization has arisen in the intermediaries' industry. Because of this, the range of functions that a particular type of intermediary is customarily expected to perform can be broadly delineated for each of the major categories or types of marketing channel members. Some examples of these major types are briefly outlined and discussed below, although one should note that the tasks and responsibilities of a particular type of intermediary can vary considerably from company to company. It should also be noted that, within each broad category of intermediary, a variety of specific or specialized formats can operate. For example, in whosale trading we can distinguish between wholesalers who deliver to their customers and often extend credit terms, and cash and carry wholesalers, where the purchaser selects and collects the goods from the wholesaler's warehouse with no credit being given.

Wholesalers The primary function of the wholesaler was, and still is, the breaking down of bulk. The wholesale trader buys in bulk from one or more producers and sells in smaller quantities to the *retailer*. In addition to performing this key function, however, the wholesaler often provides the following services:

—Provides storage facilities, thereby reducing the need for the retailer and producer to carry extensive stocks.
—Reduces the contact costs between manufacturers and retailers.
—Reduces marketing risks for the producer—the wholesaler shoulders some of the risks involved in interpreting and forecasting consumer demand.

Recent trends and patterns in the distribution system of the United Kingdom have led to a significant reduction in this type of channel intermediary.

Agents In many markets, particularly export markets, the agent is a widely used type of intermediary. Agents are of two basic types:

1. A *commission agent*, who secures orders from customers but does not, under normal circumstances, take title to the goods, and is not responsible for obtaining payment.
2. A *stockist agent*, who carries a stock of the manufacturer's products. They may either have purchased these stocks or may hold them on consignment. Often such agents will determine the mark-up on products and the discount that will be offered to dealers.

Retailers As Pitfield points out,[8] the traditional functions of the retailer in the channel of distribution stem from the personal relationship with the customer. Among the functions of the retailer in the channel can be included:

—The provision of variety (reducing shopping times and costs).
—Where appropriate, individual packing.
—Customer and credit facilities.
—Delivery and credit facilities.
—Promotion and merchandising.
—Final product pricing.

This relatively brief discussion of types of channel members and their functions illustrates that in channel decisions the marketer must not only consider the length and relationships of channel design, but must also be aware of the variety of channel intermediaries and the function they are best able to perform. In addition, the producer must take account of the trends and changes in channels and reflect these in channel decisions. It is to this dynamic aspect of channel management that we now turn our attention, with particular emphasis on one of the most rapidly evolving elements of channel structure in the United Kingdom—retailing.

Changing channels of distribution: the structure of retailing in the United Kingdom

Channels of distribution represent possibly one of the most rapidly evolving and dynamic areas of marketing. Nowhere is this more the case than in the area of retailing in the United Kingdom. Not only have these changes led to the growth of new types of intermediaries and the subsequent decline of more traditional ones; in addition, they have led to the growth of completely new channels for distributing products and services. Accompanying, and often under-pinning, these changes in overall structure have been equally important changes in the relationship between retailers and manufacturers and, in particular, in the locus of power channels.

Some of the more important of these changes and trends in UK retailing are as follows:

—Retailing has become, and is continuing to become, progressively more concentrated; i.e., a few very large retailers now account for a significant proportion of the retail market. Nowhere is this trend towards increased concentration in retailing more pronounced than in the area of grocery retailing, where the large multiples have grown to dominate this sector of the market. This growth has been achieved largely at the expense of the smaller independents and the co-operative societies. By the early 1990s large multiples accounted for some 70 per cent plus of all food samples in the United Kingdom, and over 40 per cent of sales of drink, confectionery and tobacco.
—The statistics illustrate that the number of retail outlets is declining.
—The trend has been towards much larger retail stores.
—Employment has fallen in retailing but productivity has increased.

—Competition in UK retailing is severe, with a large number of retailing companies competing for a share of consumer expenditure.

Some of the statistics on which these conclusions are based are shown in Tables 10.1 and 10.2.

These broad structural changes in retailing are the result of a number of factors. For example, as car ownership has increased, more and more consumers have begun to require 'one-stop' shopping, i.e. stores with adequate car parking facilities and with a range of merchandise which allows the customer to purchase all or most of the household needs from the one store. Overall, the changes have occurred as a result of retailers, in search of higher profits, having adapted themselves to changing circumstances.

This description of broad changes, too, tends to mask some quite significant and more specific developments in retailing which will continue to affect the producer's marketing policies. Some of the more important of these are:

—A continuing growth in the tradeshare held by large multiples.
—A continuing trend towards edge-of-town, one-stop shopping in larger stores, for example superstores and hypermarkets.

Table 10.1 Percentage shares of components of consumers' expenditure (current prices), 1961–1991

| Year | Total | Durable goods | Non-durable goods | | | | | Services | |
			Food	Alcoholic drink and tobacco	Clothing and footwear	Energy products	Other non-durable goods	Rent, rates, etc.	Other services
1961	100	8	24	13	10	6	10	8	22
1971	100	9	20	12	8	7	10	11	23
1979	100	11	17	11	8	7	11	11	24
1984	100	10	14	11	7	9	10	13	26
1991	100	10	12	12	7	10	9	14	26

Sources: CSO, *Economic Trends*; CSO, *Annual Abstract of Statistics*, London, 1992.

Table 10.2 Sales, outlets and employment for all retailing, 1966–1990 (1980 = 100)

	1966	1971	1976	1980	1982	1990
Retail sales volume (at 1980 prices)	80	88	93	100	102	108
Number of outlets	139	130	112	100	96	90
Total engaged (employees and self-employed)	119	118	105	100	93	87
Total manpower (full-time equivalents)	131	124	111	100	93	87
Sales volume per outlet	57	68	83	100	106	110
Sales volume per full-time equivalent	61	71	84	100	109	115

Source: Based on NEDO estimates from *Annual Retail Enquiries*; CSO, *Annual Abstract of Statistics*, London, 1992.

—A continuing shift of power from the producer to the retailing end of the distribution channel.

—Linked to the above factors, an increase in administered vertical marketing systems, with implications in particular for own-branding and specification buying.

—A continuing decline in both the numbers of independents and cooperatives, and the proportion of retail sales for which these types of outlets account.

—The continued growth of contractual vertical marketing systems, e.g. franchising.

—An increased internationalization of retailing within Europe.

These factors represent changes that have taken place in UK retailing over the past 10–15 years, and they are trends that are likely to continue. They are also changes that are of considerable marketing significance to the various levels of the marketing channel, from producers to the retailers themselves. Some of these are discussed in more detail below.

The growth and success of the multiples A multiple is a retail company that operates a number of retail branches with common ownership and a high degree of centralized control. It could be said that any retail organization that owns and operates more than one branch is a multiple. In fact, initially the term was applied only to retail organizations with five or more branches. The success of the multiples in UK retailing (and the relative lack of success of independents and co-operatives) is indicated in Table 10.3.

In recent years it has become common to distinguish between small multiples (operating between two and nine branches) and large multiples (operating 10 or more branches). It is the second of these, the large multiples, that have dominated UK retailing in recent years.

The success of the large multiples is due to a number of factors, in particular:

—Their very marketing-oriented approach, based on responding to changes in consumer shopping and spending habits.

—Their willingness and ability to introduce new innovations in retailing.

—As they have grown in size, their ability and power to bulk-buy from manufacturers, coupled with centralized control, has made them very cost-competitive. They are in a position to specify precisely what they want in the products supplied to them by manufacturers and will often have products produced for them by a manufacturer and will market those products using the multiple's own brand name.

The growth of supermarkets/hypermarkets and superstores The trend towards larger, one-step, retail outlets in the UK began in the early 1960s with the supermarket. Supermarkets began the trend for one-stop shopping. Previously this had involved visiting a small number of small specialist shops often located in different areas. This trend towards larger, one-shop outlets has continued with hypermarkets and superstores.

Table 10.3   The multiples in UK retailing: share of retail trade, 1966–1992 (%)

	1966	1971	1978	1986	1992*
Cooperatives	9.1	7.1	6.8	6.5	(6.0)
Multiples	34.5	38.5	46.5	55.0	(60.0)
Independents	56.4	54.4	46.7	38.5	(34.0)

* 1992 results estimated.
Sources: Census of Distribution; Retail Inquiry. November 1992.

Definitions vary, but a *hypermarket* is said to be a retail outlet having over 50 000 sq. feet (4645 sq. metres) of selling space with at least 15 checkouts. The number of hypermarkets in the United Kingdom continues to grow. More recently we have seen the growth of *superstores*, which have in excess of 60 000 sq. feet (5574 sq. metres) of selling space.

Both hypermarkets and superstores are likely to take an increased proportion of retail business in the UK based on the competitive advantages of economy and convenience.

A study by Sanghari and Treadgold[9] on European retailing underlines the fact that the growth of hypermarkets and superstores is not exclusively a UK phenomenon. France, West Germany, The Netherlands and Belgium have all experienced a growth in this type of retail outlet, facilitated by increased ownership of cars, refrigerators and freezers. The exception to this trend appears to be Italy, where, because the population remains concentrated in city centres, the growth of both supermarkets and hypermarkets has been restricted.

The decline of the independents and cooperatives Accompanying these trends towards multiples and superstores, and in fact as a direct result of these, the independent and cooperative sectors of UK retailing have declined (see Table 10.3). Again, this trend is likely to continue. A knock-on effect of this decline has been the reduced importance of the trade wholesaler, whose principal customers are the independents. Independents, cooperatives and wholesalers have each fought against this decline by, for example, forming voluntary groups (sometimes called 'symbol' shops), improving marketing and merchandising and switching to cash-and-carry.

The growth of franchising One of the fastest-growing types of retailing in the United Kingdom in recent years has been franchising. Introduced into the UK in the early 1950s, the original image of the typical franchise operation was one of high risk and dubious trading practices. However, since those early days franchising has become respectable and often very profitable with, as a result, an explosion in the number and range of franchises being operated. The rapid growth of this type of retailing in Britain is shown in Table 10.4. Today, franchising encompasses products from pipes to pastries and includes such well known names as the Body Shop, Prontaprint and Spud-U-Like.

This surge in franchising has been underpinned by the efforts of the British Franchising Association, which has developed codes of practice for franchising[10] and in doing so has greatly helped to reduce the risks to both franchiser and franchisee alike.

The internationalization of retailing A further important development in retailing has been the way in which European retailers, including those of the United Kingdom, have sought to expand

Table 10.4   The growth of franchising in the UK, 1984–1991

Year	Annual sales (£ bn)	Number of units	Jobs created
1984	0.8	7 900	72 000
1985	1.3	9 000	93 000
1986	1.9	10 900	126 000
1987	3.1	15 000	169 000
1988	3.8	16 000	181 500
1989	4.7	16 600	185 000
1990	5.2	18 260	184 000
1991	4.8	18 600	189 500

Source: 'Franchising in the United Kingdom', British Franchising Association/ National Westminster Bank, London, November 1991.

their retailing operations abroad. There are many reasons for this, not the least of course being the growth of the European Community and the continued moves towards free trade between member countries. These developments in trade are discussed more fully in Chapter 14, but at this stage it is sufficient to note that European retailers have been in the forefront of expansion across international boundaries. In the United Kingdom we have seen the establishment of retailers such as IKEA, originally a flat-pack furniture manufacturer of Swedish origin, Aldi, the largest West German food retailer, and Benetton, the Italian clothing group. Successful international forays from the UK include retailers such as Marks & Spencer, Body Shop, Safeway, Laura Ashley and John Menzies' Early Learning Centre. This trend towards the internationalization of retailing across the globe is one that is likely to continue as retailers seek out new profit opportunities.

Technology and retailing; the wheel of retailing There is little doubt that the broad structural changes that have occurred in retailing, and the more specific events on which these are based, have resulted in changes in the marketing and distribution policies of channel members. Technology, too, is now beginning to change the face of UK retailing and, in particular, the application of the ubiquitous microchip. Computerized stock control and order processing, often linked through computerized, laser-aided checkouts, are becoming commonplace in retailing. Similarly, a number of schemes are currently in operation which enable the 'shopper' to order products directly from the home via a computer terminal/television link. Such schemes will probably become more widespread in the future as the technology improves and the banking system becomes able to cope with electronic funds transfer. These and other developments pose questions as to the future shape of retailing in the United Kingdom.

In the 1960s McNair[11] suggested a hypothesis to explain and help predict changes in retailing structure—the so-called '*wheel of retailing*' hypothesis. Essentially, this hypothesis suggests that new forms of retailing operation begin as low-price, utility operations, established to challenge the higher margin and, by comparison, luxurious established outlets. These low-cost, low-margin operations attract price-conscious customers. Their success leads to expansion, with an upgrading of facilities, services and eventually prices. They, in turn, become susceptible to newer low-cost/low-price operations. The 'wheel' has turned full circle.

There is no doubt that at least some of the structural changes that have taken place in UK retailing do in fact accord with this hypothesis. More recently, however, McNair himself has concluded that the term is too narrow and limited to explain adequately the changes that have taken place. Nevertheless, what McNair's hypothesis does point to is the fact that retailing institutions, much like products, have life cycles. Moreover, a marked trend in retailing is the shortening of the life cycle for a particular type of institution and for each successive retailing innovation. It took, say, 50 years for department stores to achieve maturity, only 25 years for supermarkets, and hypermarkets will probably reach it in 10. Only one thing is certain about the shape of UK retailing in 10 years' time, and that is that it will be different from that which exists today.

These, then, are some of the major facets of channels and intermediaries, together with some of the major structural changes that are taking place in this important area of marketing. In the next part of this chapter we turn our attention to the design of channels and the important aspects of channel strategy.

CHANNEL STRATEGY

It is now recognized that channel decisions are strategic decisions in a company. There are two major reasons for this:

1. Channel decisions generally involve a company in long-term commitments—often to other organizations. Once established, a company's channels of distribution can be difficult to change, at least in the short run. Of course, as we have seen, the dynamic nature of marketing channels inevitably means that at some stage a company will need to re-assess the extent to which its channel strategy is optimum, and perhaps to make changes. Few companies, however, change channels at the same frequency, or with the same relative degree of ease, with which they might and can change their advertising or their prices.
2. Channel decisions intimately affect, and are affected by, virtually all of a company's marketing and operating activities. For example, the selection of target markets is affected by, and in turn affects, channel design and choice. Similarly, decisions about the individual marketing mix elements—for example, pricing, product and promotion—must reflect a company's channel choice.

The four major strategic elements of channel choice and design are as follows:

—*The delineation and selection of basic channel structure* Included under this element would be considerations as to channel length, types of intermediaries and functions of intermediaries.
—*The determination of required market exposure* Included under this element would be the decisions concerning the number of intermediaries to be used and their geographical dispersion.
—*Systems and procedures for ensuring maximum cooperation in the channel and the minimum of channel conflict* This would include, for example, the specification of territorial rights, franchising conditions, etc.
—*Marketing and channel support strategies* In particular, under this heading would be the relative emphasis and focus for marketing efforts in the channel.

These key elements are considered in more detail below.

Basic channel structure

We saw earlier that one of the principal differences between channel types is in the number and types of intermediaries used. At one extreme, the manufacturer may opt for the shortest channel available, i.e. direct distribution with no intermediaries being used. On the other hand, some channel structures incorporate several distinct levels, with a variety of intermediaries being involved in many products from producer to final user. Because of the variety of basic channel alternatives in this respect, we should be careful not to suggest what Stanton[12] refers to as an 'orthodoxy which does not exist'. Nevertheless, some of the basic channel structures, ranging from the most direct and shortest channel to one involving several levels, are illustrated in Fig. 10.5.

It should also be noted that channels with the same degree of directness (or indirectness), i.e. number of intermediaries, may differ in terms of the types of intermediaries used. An example of this is shown in Fig. 10.6.

To reiterate, the choice of basic channel structure involves both the choice of number and types of intermediaries that will be used. Very many factors will influence the basic range of channel alternatives and the choice between them by the marketer. At this stage, one should recall why channel intermediaries are used at all—i.e. that their use is justified when they perform functions more effectively and efficiently than would be the case if they were not used. Both the number and types of intermediaries that will be used depend upon the range and nature of the tasks involved in moving products and services from producer to final consumer, and upon the extent to which one particular channel alternative is superior to another. Against this general consideration, and again at the risk of oversimplifying this aspect of strategic channel choice, some of the factors influencing the choice between direct and more indirect channels of distribution are as follows:

Figure 10.5 Some basic channel alternatives

Figure 10.6 Channel valuations based on different intermediaries

More direct (shorter)		*Less direct* (larger)
Indirect products	→	Consumer products
Services	→	Tangible products
Few, more-concentrated customer groupings	→	Larger numbers of customers; geographically dispersed
More control required, e.g. quality, aftersales service, etc.	→	Control less important
Customer purchase in large amounts at infrequent intervals	→	Customers purchase frequently but in small amounts
Products that are bulky/expensive to handle, custom-built, have a high unit value, or are perishable	→	Less bulky, cheaper, standardized, non-perishable products

One is counselled to treat these facts affecting choice of channel length and types of intermediaries with caution. For example, many tangible consumer products of a non-perishable, low-value, standardized nature are distributed very effectively direct from producer to final consumer through mail order.

Required market exposure

A second key element of strategic channel decision-making is the decision concerning the required degree of market exposure. This is underpinned by decisions about the number of intermediaries that will be used at each level and their degree of geographical dispersion.

If a company wishes to have its product available through as many intermediaries as possible, then it must design an *intensive* system of distribution. For example, it will seek to recruit or encourage as many different types of retailers as possible to stock and sell its products. Further, it may seek as wide a geographical dispersion of these stockists as it can. Again, many factors would affect choice of channel strategy, including the marketing objectives and particularly the target markets envisaged by the company. One of the most influential factors in determining this element of distribution strategy is the extent to which the customer is likely to require a place and/or convenience utility from the distributor. For example, few buyers of razor blades would welcome having to travel long distances to purchase this relatively simple, inexpensive and frequently purchased product from one of a relatively few specialist retailers of this product.

In contrast to this form of intensive distribution, the marketer may instead opt for a system of *selective* or *exclusive* distribution. Whereas intensive distribution involves the sale of company products or services through as many outlets as possible, selective and exclusive distribution refer to the distribution of those products and services through a deliberately restricted number of intermediaries.

In fact, there are two dimensions to the 'selective'/'exclusive' decision. The first relates to the earlier decision as to the type of intermediaries to be used. For example, the marketer may determine that its products will be made available only through multiple retail outlets and not, say, through mail order. The second dimension relates to the possible choice of certain intermediaries within a particular type. For example, the marketer may determine that only a few selected multiples, or dealers or agents, will be encouraged to handle its products. The extreme form of this aspect of channel strategy is exclusive distribution, where only a few, or possibly only one, intermediary is given exclusive rights to distribute the company's products.

Since, by implication, a selective or exclusive system of distribution provides less 'convenience' and 'place utility' than an intensive distribution system, there must be other reasons for selecting those systems. Some of the factors that would incline a company towards selecting a more exclusive system of distribution would include:

—Where the product and/or service is such that the customer expects and/or requires specialist advice, service facilities, etc.
—Where the marketer and distribution would benefit from the possibly enhanced image associated with more selective distribution.
—Where the potential volume of market/territorial sales would not warrant more intensive distribution.
—Where the marketer wishes to retain more control of the intermediaries' marketing of the product, including, for example, pricing, promotion, credit, etc.
—Where more intensive distribution may give rise to problems associated with channel conflict between intermediaries at the same level in the channel, e.g. between different agents, different retailers, etc.

This last aspect of this element of channel strategy illustrates an important consideration in our discussion so far on this topic: namely, that the elements themselves overlap. Decisions between intensive and selective or exclusive distribution have implications for the third element of channel strategy, i.e. channel cooperation and conflict.

Channel cooperation and conflict

Earlier in this chapter vertical marketing systems were outlined and discussed. We saw that channel relationships constitute an important dimension of channel structure. We also saw that the growth of various types of VMSs is explained in part by the need to achieve coordination throughout the full length of the channel. An important strategic element of channel decisions, therefore, are those decisions that relate to channel cooperation and conflict.

Essentially, it is in the interests of all the members of a channel for there to be a substantial degree of cooperation. After all, a marketing channel is, or should be, a set of interlocking and mutually dependent elements which combine with a complete system for achieving a given set of tasks. Having said this, an almost inevitable feature of marketing channels is the potential for conflict between channel members. This should be considered by the marketer in the strategic design of his channels.

Stern and El-Ansary[13] point to two distinct types of conflict in channels based on the level in a channel at which such conflict may arise. The first of these is *horizontal channel conflict*. This is conflict that occurs between intermediaries at the same level in the channel. This type of conflict is primarily competitive and may occur between similar intermediaries (e.g. multiple *v*. multiple) or between dissimilar intermediaries (e.g. discount store *v*. multiple). Horizontal conflict may also arise between the members of a company's own channel. An example would be where conflict arises, say, between two of a company's own distributors, possibly concerning trading rights and practices.

The second, and much more prevalent, type of conflict is *vertical channel conflict*. This is conflict that occurs between different levels of the same channel e.g. between producer, wholesaler and retailer. This type of conflict is primarily power conflict between channel members.

Clearly, some types of channel conflict are natural and healthy. For example, it is to be expected that, in a competitive market environment, channel intermediaries at the same level will lock in competitive conflict. As we have seen, at the retailing level in the United Kingdom, the multiples appear to have emerged victorious from this competitive struggle. Nevertheless, we can expect both more traditional and newer forms of retailing institutions to continue to challenge this supremacy.

If this type of conflict is healthy and even functional, then, potentially at least, conflict between channel members may be very damaging indeed to one side and/or the other. For example, the producer may come into conflict with his retailers about the way they are merchandising and promoting his product. Retailers, on the other hand, may come into conflict with their suppliers about, say, the issue of own-label brands. The issue is not so much of totally eliminating such conflict, but rather of designing channel structures and relationships in such a way that the potential for conflict is reduced; and, where some conflict is inevitable, it should be better managed. Examples of mechanisms for achieving this, and thereby increasing cooperation in the channel, would include clear and enforceable dealer and franchising policies, arbitration procedures, producer/distributor councils and, as we have seen, the use of vertical marketing systems. Regardless of the mechanisms, or administrative and contractual procedures, for improving cooperation in the channel, one issue will be as to which level or type of organization should act as channel leader and exercise control over the channel. In practice, the resolution of this issue comes down to where the power lies in the channel. Various views have been put forward as to where this power is, or should be, concentrated in the channel. For example, some argue that the power, and therefore the leadership, in a channel should rest with the manufacturer who is best suited to translate consumer needs and wants, and scarce economic resources, into marketable products and services.

Others argue that this type of argument is 'vague' and 'subjective',[14] or that today the retailer is uniquely placed in the channel system to interpret end-user or consumer needs.[15] Again, as we have seen, there is no doubt that the developments in UK retailing have, in fact, led to channel power increasingly being vested at this end of the distribution system, and this fact must be taken into account in strategic channel decision-making. But why should any one channel level or intermediary exercise channel power? The hypothesis appears to be that without channel leadership there is a substantial possibility of conflicting dynamics destroying the channel; if leadership exists, on whatever basis and however it is exercised, there is less chance of this occurring. An alternative hypothesis is that the exercise of channel leadership in fact creates increased instability in the channel, since controlled cooperation is in effect only subdued conflict.

These contrary arguments illustrate that the study of the cooperation and conflict aspects of distribution decisions, and the concepts of leadership and power on which they are based, is still very much in its infancy. The decision-maker will need to exercise his knowledge, experience and simple common sense. Simply to suggest or argue for a particular arrangement of channel leadership and power ignores the complexity of markets, products and channel relationships. In general terms, in order to fulfil the primary objective of the marketing channel, channel leadership and power should devolve, or preferably should be arranged to devolve, to the channel members who are best able to fulfil this objective.

Marketing and channel support strategies

The fourth major element of strategic channel decisions concerns the relative emphasis and focus for marketing efforts in the channel. Of particular importance in this respect would be the choice between '*push*' and '*pull*' marketing strategies.

In some companies, marketing efforts and tactics are aimed primarily at 'the trade', i.e. at wholesalers, distributors, retailers, etc. For example, advertising and sales promotion, selling effort and pricing strategies are aimed at generating trade interest and demand for the company's products. This focus of company marketing effort is designed to '*push*' a product or service into the distribution pipeline by increasing salesforce and/or dealer interest and motivation to stock and sell the products.

A '*pull*' marketing strategy, on the other hand, is one where the primary focus of company marketing efforts is concentrated on the final consumer. The objective with this strategy is to generate sufficient consumer interest and demand for the company's products to be 'pulled' through the distribution pipeline. The distinction between 'push' and 'pull' strategies in relation to channels of distribution is shown in Fig. 10.7.

Examples of marketing efforts within each category of channel strategy include:

1. 'Push' strategies

   (a) Cash discounts and increased margins for dealers.
   (b) Direct mail shots to dealers.
   (c) Dealers competitions, free gifts or premiums.
   (d) Merchandising and dealer points of sale display material.
   (e) Salespeople's incentive schemes: competitions, bonuses, sales rallies, etc.

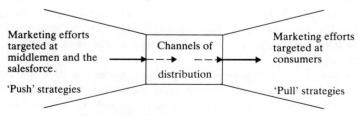

Figure 10.7 'Push' versus 'pull' strategies

(f) Trade advertising.

(g) Trade exhibitions.

2. 'Pull' strategies

(a) Consumer advertising.

(b) Reduced price offers to consumers.

(c) Consumer sales promotion.

In fact, as we shall see in Chapter 11, there are many more tools available to a company to implement 'push' or 'pull' activities. However, it is usually not a case of deciding between one or other of these strategies, but more one of determining where the balance should lie—towards push or towards pull.

Again, many factors will influence the choice of an appropriate balance, for example types of product, target market, marketing objectives, etc. What is important, in terms of strategic channel decisions, is that this relative balance should be determined in advance of, or at least in conjunction with, the strategic channel decisions that it so intimately affects.

In summary, we have looked at some of the key elements of strategic channel decision-making. In doing so we have also touched on some of the factors that will affect what would be an appropriate choice of channels for a company and their design. In the next section we will consider further some of the major factors that will serve to constrain and affect the channel decision. We shall also examine some of the specific criteria against which the variety of channel alternatives may be evaluated.

IDENTIFYING AND EVALUATING CHANNEL ALTERNATIVES

Bearing in mind the four key elements of channel strategy outlined earlier, the marketing decision-maker will need to delineate the major alternatives available to him or her in channel choice and design. In delineating these alternatives, he or she needs to consider a number of factors which effectively serve to constrain the channel choice. Some of the more important of these considerations are as follows.

Company and marketing objectives and resources

A key factor in delineating options for channel decisions is the company itself and, in particular, overall company and marketing objectives and company resources. For example, a company with long-run growth objectives based on increasing market share may have to look towards extending the breadth and depth of its distribution channels. Similarly, companies wishing to become market leaders in the grocery market have little option but to consider distributing through the multiples. The smaller company with fewer financial and staff resources may be forced into using more indirect channels for its products and will certainly have little power in the administration of the channel as a whole. Remember, as with other marketing mix decisions, distribution decisions should be consistent with and reflect overall company objectives and marketing strategy.

Target markets/customers

The design of channels of distribution is greatly influenced by the choice of target markets and the nature of customer characteristics within this market.

Before a company begins to consider the alternatives for channel choice and design, it should, ideally, have determined its target markets. In particular, the choice of target markets and channel alternatives may be interdependent. A company may discover that it cannot reach its preferred target market with the channel alternatives available, or it may find that this target market can be served profitably only with a particular system of distribution. In either case, target market selection and channel decisions must be made together. In addition, the company must take account of customer characteristics, in the target market(s). Examples of possibly important customer characteristics would include:

1. *The number of customers* As we saw earlier, large numbers of customers for a product tend to favour a more indirect channel of distribution, particularly where this is associated with a second key customer characteristic (see point 2 below).
2. *Their geographical dispersion.*
3. *Customer needs, habits and preferences* Together, these probably represent one of the most important considerations in channel design. It is pointless selecting a particular channel design which satisfies the company but does not satisfy the needs of the customer. For example, customers in the target market may have a preference for a particular type of channel intermediary, or they may have particular needs in purchasing the product which certain channel arrangements cannot provide. Sometimes consumer preferences may be based on custom and habit. Although it does not pay to ignore such preferences, where they are based only on habit a company should consider the possibility of developing other and possibly innovative channels of distribution for its products.

Product

The influence of product characteristics on channel decisions was outlined earlier in this chapter. For example, it was suggested that, generally, bulkier perishable, non-standard products will tend towards a more direct system of distribution. It must also be remembered that there are no rules here. We often find that essentially the same types of product are distributed in very different ways by different companies.

Competition

Channel decisions must, like other aspects of marketing, reflect competitive considerations. Again, one should be careful to note that we are not suggesting that a company should utilize the same or even similar channels to those used by its competitors. Indeed, a company may seek to examine the practices of its competitors in order to devise alternative methods.

Together, these considerations will constrain the range of appropriate channels and systems available to a company. It is likely that the decision-maker will still be faced with a range of channel alternatives including a range of possible intermediaries for which he or she must make the final choice. At this point, each of the remaining alternatives needs to be assessed against a set of additional and more specific criteria. Kotler[16] suggests that among the more important of these criteria are those that relate to *control*, *adaptive* and *economic* factors; to these we would add an additional element—that of *coverage*.

In terms of control criteria and channel choice, a company must consider carefully the extent to which its channel design will allow the company to exercise control over the marketing effort. As a general rule, a company has more control where it uses more direct channels for its products. Of course, it is often the case that the producer determines to relinquish some degree of control over how its products are marketed. After all, it may not have the necessary resources to, say, promote the product extensively. There is no 'recipe' as to what constitutes an appropriate degree of control, but it is important that this aspect be considered in the channel decision.

Adaptability in channel choice relates to the extent to which a company is able to change its distribution policy to accord with changed conditions. We know that today's marketer operates in a dynamic environment. Further, we have seen that channels themselves represent one of the most turbulent components of this environment. In this context, adaptability in channels relates to two important factors. First, the marketer must consider how easily he or she can change to an entirely new system of distribution, although it must be remembered that often channel decisions commit the marketer to long-term contractual relationships with channel intermediaries. A company can find itself at a serious disadvantage in the market if a long-term channel arrangement becomes inappropriate. A second aspect of channel adaptability relates to the relative ease with which a company can adapt its marketing effort *within* existing channels. This aspect is related to the control issue discussed earlier. For example, selling through multiples may afford the producer little option as to how his products are marketed to the final customer so as to take account of changed market and competitive conditions.

In terms of coverage criteria, again there are two related aspects. The first relates to the extent to which a particular channel arrangement affords the marketer access to sufficient numbers of customers and/or market segments. The second relates to the extent to which the channel alternatives will lead to the required degree of coverage for the entire product range. For example, it is often the case that intermediaries will stock only the more profitable (for them) product lines and will refuse to have, or will neglect, other, less profitable products in the product range.

The final criterion for assessing specific channel alternatives is possibly the most important. After all, controllability, adaptability and coverage are important only in that they affect long-term profits. Economic criteria, then, are predominant in the assessment procedure. Selection of channel structures and individual middlemen should be based on a careful assessment of the costs and revenues associated with each. On the basis of this assessment, the marketer should choose those channel arrangements that meet both the company's requirements—including that of profit—and customer requirements at the lowest possible cost.

FURTHER CONSIDERATIONS IN CHANNEL DECISIONS

So far we have outlined the key elements of strategic channel decisions and some of the considerations and constraints that will affect these. Having arrived at a strategic channel choice, a company must act to implement, evaluate and control this strategy. Individual intermediaries must be encouraged and/or recruited to suggest the channel choice. Marketing efforts and resources must be swung into operation—sales teams organized, merchandising and promotional material developed, delivery and warehousing systems developed, etc. Further, channels, and the intermediaries that comprise them, should be subjected to continuous and rigorous evaluation and control procedures with regard to both effectiveness and efficiency. These additional considerations point to the fact that the management of distribution in a company involves wider issues than those associated only with overall channel design. Increasingly, this is being recognized and has given rise to the growth of a total systems approach to distribution. We shall conclude this chapter by examining this systems approach. Before we do so, two further considerations about channel decisions should be noted.

Throughout this chapter we have discussed channel design and choice from the point of view of the producer. Remember, intermediaries themselves, from wholesalers to agents, distributors and retailers, are marketers too, and have their own marketing decisions to make including distribution. Finally, you should note that increasingly the question for the producer in channel decisions is not so much: 'What channels should we choose?' as 'Which channels will choose us?'

THE TOTAL SYSTEMS APPROACH TO DISTRIBUTION: LOGISTICS

In recent years, views on what constitute the elements of distribution management have increasingly taken into account additional elements over and above those associated only with the channel itself. It is now recognized that the effective management of the total system of distribution can contribute significantly to overall company success and profits. This total systems approach is variously referred to as *physical distribution* or *logistics* management. The more encompassing nature of the total systems approach to distribution is illustrated in the following definition of physical distribution offered by Arbury[17] as long ago as 1967:

> By 'physical distribution' we mean the interrelationship of all the factors which affect the flow of both goods and orders necessary to fill orders. This flow starts when the customer decides to place an order and ends when the order is delivered to the customer. Physical distribution involves not only the action required to fill a particular order, but also the action necessary to prepare oneself to meet customer needs.

The term 'logistics' is essentially a military one and was applied originally to the science and practice of moving, lodging and supplying troops. Some authors in fact make a distinction between marketing logistics and physical distribution, suggesting for example that the management of physical distribution is more concerned with the planning and control of distribution activities in order to minimize costs, whereas logistics broadens this to include the notion of customer and market needs. For our purpose, the terms 'physical distribution', 'logistics' and 'total distribution' systems are used interchangeably. Two vital considerations, however, will guide our discussion of this aspect of distribution:

1. The design of the total distribution should begin with customer needs and wants.
2. The total system should be designed so as to provide the required level of customer service or utility at the minimum system cost.

Before we discuss these considerations further, it is useful to explain the reasons for the growth in importance of this area of company operations and also some of the more important elements in the system. We shall start by examining the background to marketing logistics.

Two related factors explain the growth of marketing logistics. The first of these is the increasing awareness of the potential cost savings to be derived from the more effective management of physical distribution. In some companies the total cost of all the activities implied in Arbury's definition can represent the most significant simple element of cost on the organization. Important though this may be, it does not ask itself why companies have only comparatively recently turned their attention to these costs. A clue to this recent interest is given by Drucker,[18] when in an article in *Fortune* magazine he referred to physical distribution as 'The economy's dark continent'. What he was highlighting in the use of this colourful phrase was the fact that, unlike so many other areas of company activity with well-developed systems of monitoring effectiveness and well-established costs, physical distribution activities represent a broadly uncharted area in this respect. Together, high costs and relatively underdeveloped cost control mean that in many companies physical distribution represents one of the last remaining areas for potentially substantial cost savings.

The second factor that has given rise to growth in the application of marketing logistics is the recognition that properly managed, effective marketing logistics represents a powerful competitive tool in the marketplace. We shall now give further consideration to this potential for competitive advantage.

Logistics and competitive advantage

Perhaps the most important reason for the growth in importance and interest in physical distribution and logistics is the fact that the logistics system offers substantial potential for achieving a competitive edge and hence for winning and keeping customers. Particularly in industrial markets, where products may be relatively undifferentiated and prices and margins cut to the bone, companies may find that they can gain a competitive edge by using their logistics system to improve customer service levels. This in turn may allow a company to increase the volume of sales and/or to increase prices. Because of this, identifying appropriate levels of and types of customer service to be achieved by the logistics management system is a key aspect of planning in this area.

In the same vein, a number of developments and trends in industrial purchasing and materials management have heightened the importance attached by many customers to the service elements of the logistics systems of their suppliers and potential suppliers. Some of these were touched on in Chapter 3, when we looked at organizational buyer behaviour. But, for example, with modern continuous flow and large-batch manufacturing systems, a stock-out situation of even a relatively minor and inexpensive component may incur substantial costs in down-time. This potential problem is heightened where, as is increasingly the case, a firm's customers are using just-in-time (JIT) inventory principles. Clearly, where a manufacturer is using a JIT system, delivery, and hence the logistics performance of the supplier, is crucial and its importance heightened. A company that can perform well on its delivery performance, therefore, has a strong competitive edge over those suppliers who cannot. In fact, for many companies these days, an inability to supply JIT deliveries means that a supplier would simply not be considered.

Similarly, the trend in industrial purchasing towards materials management systems has put an increased emphasis on the logistics performance of a firm's potential suppliers.

These trends towards JIT and materials management are themselves, of course, indicative of the recognition on the part of the customers of the substantial costs, and hence potential cost savings, associated with elements of their own logistics systems, including stocks of raw materials, work-in-progress, the consequences of stock-outs, and defective raw materials and components from suppliers.

As a result, logistics service is now a key factor in supplier choice in industrial markets. Suppliers with poor logistics service, evidenced in late deliveries or stock-outs, are quickly dropped by industrial purchasers in today's competitive conditions. By improving the design and execution of marketing logistics, a marketer can develop a substantial competitive edge over other suppliers. Product availability, prompt delivery and efficient and accurate order processing are just a few of the services that can help capture and keep customers. Hence determination of the nature and level of logistics service elements is crucial to the effective planning of this area of marketing if it is to be used as a demand-generating marketing tool. In this way, physical distribution and logistics can be considered in just the same way as the product, price and promotional elements of the mix.[19] This concept is shown in Fig. 10.8. Some of the elements that comprise logistics can be used, through service levels, to influence demand, as shown.

The components and related activities of a company's total system of distribution will vary from company to company, but will broadly encompass some of the following factors:

Figure 10.8 The demand-creating role of physical distribution efforts
Source: *Adapted from* E. H. Ballou, *Basic Business Logistics*, 2nd edn, Prentice-Hall, Englewood Cliffs, NJ, 1987

—Materials procurement.
—Raw material inventories.
—Sales forecasting and production planning.
—Packaging.
—Warehousing and delivery.
—Order processing.
—Customer service.

You will note from this list that marketing logistics involves the total system of inputting, transferring and outputting materials, goods and services in a company. The idea is that the system as a whole be designed to provide the required level of customer service at minimum total cost. In planning the logistics system, therefore, the starting-point is customer needs and service requirements. We shall now briefly outline the steps in planning marketing logistics.

Planning marketing logistics

Planning marketing logistics is a complex process, requiring many elements to be coordinated and controlled. A fuller description is given in one of the many excellent specialist texts available on this area of marketing,[20] but the following represents an outline of the key steps offered by Lancaster and Massingham.[21]

Step 1: Establishing customer service needs We have already stated that the design of the logistics system should start with customer needs with respect to the service elements provided by the system. Because of this, therefore, it is important to establish what these are. For example, do customers require speedy delivery, or is reliability of delivery more important? Do customers require flexibility in dealing with, say, special orders, or do they require only standard products? And so on. It is essential to establish not only the customer's service needs, but also the relative importance attached to each need. Both needs and relative importance, of course, may vary between different industries, different customers, and even for different products supplied to the same customer. For example, on this last point we may find that certain components are more critical to a customer's production process than others, with a consequent increased importance attached by the customer to the reliability of delivery of these particular components. Similarly, if we take order cycle or lead times, in some industries—the motor car industry for example—order lead times must be kept to a minimum. In fact, this is an industry where most suppliers must increasingly supply on a just-in-time basis. These differences in the degree of importance attached to logistics service elements by different customers or industries have the potential to be used to segment and target markets by a supplier, where the basis of segmentation is differences in sensitivity to different service levels. What is important throughout this process is the need to establish the importance of the various elements from the customer's perspective.

Elements of customer service that are a direct result of the marketer's logistics system are:

—Order cycle time (time from order placement to delivery).
—Consistency of order cycle time (reliability).
—Information on order status.
—Flexibility in dealing with special requests.
—Returns—damaged and surplus goods.
—Response to emergencies.
—Freedom from errors in delivery, paperwork, etc.
—Quality of delivered products.

Step 2: Establishing current company and competitor performance with regard to service elements The second step of designing the business logistics system is to establish how well (or badly) the company and its competitors are performing in areas of logistics services seen as important by customers. In general terms, we need to be performing as well in these areas as our competitors. Any significant underperformance is likely to result in lost sales and market share. However, even if we are performing as well as our competitors, this is not to say that customers will be happy with current levels. Indeed, they may be distinctly unhappy about the service they are receiving from current suppliers. In other words, there may be significant marketing opportunities available to the company that is able and willing to improve its service performance. On the other hand, in assessing competitor performance we also need to look carefully at areas where we are significantly outperforming our competitors in order to assess whether or not our extra performance is justifying the additional cost of providing it. This brings us to the third and most difficult step in designing the business logistics system.

Step 3: Determining cost and benefits of making changes to current company performance in levels of logistics service: profit maximization Before we can make decisions about specific objectives for service elements and the design of the logistics system to achieve them, we need to assess carefully the likely costs and benefits, and hence profit potential, associated with different service levels. This brings us to a very important point about the overall design of the logistics system. You will recall that earlier we stressed the fact that logistics services can be important demand-generators. However, improvements in these services are also likely to be costly to the firm providing them. Therefore, in determining the appropriateness, or otherwise, of current company logistics services

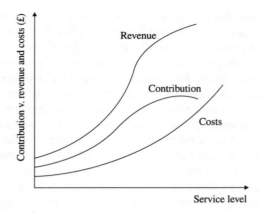

Figure 10.9   Costs, revenues and contribution *v.* service levels

and any proposed changes in these, we need to assess the likely impact on company profits. In other words, the optimal logistics system is not likely to be one that operates at lowest cost, as we may be losing too many sales. On the other hand, nor is the optimal system likely to be one that generates the greatest demand, as these sales will probably be generated at too great a cost. Put simply, the optimal business logistics system is one that generates the maximum profit. In turn, this requires that the company understands the relationships between service levels and demand, and between service levels and costs. We can then determine whether to increase or decrease service levels to generate maximum contribution. This notion of optimizing the profit contribution of the logistics system is shown in Fig. 10.9. We can see from the figure that maximum contribution is obtained at neither the lowest cost nor the highest service levels. Too low a level of service and we are losing revenue; too high, and we incur too high costs for the extra revenue generated. In theory, maximum contribution is obtained where the marginal cost of additional service levels is equal to the marginal revenue generated by these additional service levels. Needless to say, in practice, actually deriving the demand response functional (revenue) curve with respect to different levels of service can be difficult. Nevertheless, our earlier steps of identifying customer service requirements and current company and competitor performance in this area should at least give some indication of the likely response to increases or decreases in service levels.

As mentioned earlier, having established what types and levels of customer service the logistics system is to provide in order to support our competitive market strategy, the task of the logistics manager is to provide this service at minimum cost. It is not our intention to discuss the details of operating the logistics system, but it is important for the marketer to understand and recognize the existence of 'trade-offs' between costs and revenue.

In practice, therefore, as we stressed earlier, the system should be designed from a demand perspective. Essentially, based on our earlier analysis of customer needs, we should define our service level objectives based on the role we have determined for logistics services in our overall competitive strategy. The design of the total logistics systems should then be aimed at delivering this predetermined level of logistics services at minimum cost.

Step 4: Establishing specific objectives for areas and levels of logistics services   Overall objectives for logistics service levels will need to be translated to specific objectives for the various areas of such service. The variety of possible customer service elements were outlined earlier, but, for example, we will need to set quantified objectives for order cycle times, response to emergencies, consistency of order cycle time and so on.

Step 5: Planning, implementing and controlling the logistics system From a marketer's perspective, at this stage we can now pass the responsibility for the detailed planning, implementation and control of the logistics system over to the logistics experts. Their task is to design the system to give the desired level of service support in each of the elements of our prescribed customer service strategy. This will involve the planning, implementation and control of factors such as purchasing, inbound transport, production planning, inventory control, warehousing, order processing, outbound transport and so on.

We should be careful not to seem to be suggesting that it is only at this stage that the logistics experts should be involved. Even though customer and market needs must be paramount throughout the design of the logistics system, this can be achieved only through the cooperation and expertise of functions such as materials management, production planning and control and so on. In addition, we will need the help and cooperation of the channel members and suppliers, who must therefore be consulted. We should also note that the continued operation of an effective logistics system requires on-going information from sales and marketing, including sales forecasting, customer feedback and competitor information. Of all the elements of the marketing mix, perhaps the 'place' element requires more inter- and intra-firm communication and coordination than any other.

We have already come across the notion of a trade-off, but in this case we are applying it to the system as a whole, where the costs of the total system are traded off against revenue. In planning and operating the system, however, the logistics manager must also make trade-offs between the individual elements of the system in order to achieve the desired levels of customer service at minimum cost. This in turn, will require what logistics planners refer to as a *total cost approach* to distribution, and it recognizes the interdependence between the demands of logistics activities. So, for example, minimizing costs in one area, say inventory, may lead to more than proportional increases in another, say transport. To achieve this, a total systems approach to logistics is required.

Effective planning, implementation and control of the business logistics system is greatly enhanced by the introduction of a service policy and quantified service standards. Again, these need to be determined on the basis of customer and market needs.

The service policy should include written statements concerning the level of customer service in the form of promises to customers which the company will fulfil. These can represent a powerful promotional tool in helping to secure and keep customers, and can also inform staff as to the role and value of a logistics service in overall company and marketing strategy. Policy statements may be relatively simple, such as 'all orders received by noon will be shipped the same day', or more elaborate, covering in detail factors such as time, condition of goods, order communication, service contingencies and so on. The policy statement may then be translated into detailed operating standards for the logistics system. In turn, these standards form the basis of the logistics control system, against which logistics inefficiencies and out-of-line service situations can be quickly addressed.

CONCLUSIONS

In this chapter we have looked at the means by which products and services are channelled from producer to final customer. A channel of distribution is made up of institutions and middlemen where activities centre on the activities required to achieve this. The question is not, should we perform these activities? It is more, who should perform them? The reason for utilizing the services of intermediaries is that often they perform these activities much more effectively and efficiently than can the producer alone.

In order to make decisions about channels, the marketing manager must understand the elements of these channels. In particular, he or she must understand the key dimensions of channel structure: length, and relationships; the role, function, and types of intermediaries; and finally, the dynamic and changing nature of marketing channels.

Against this background, we looked briefly at the changing nature of retailing in the United Kingdom. We have seen that the face of retailing is changing, with recent trends being towards larger, more concentrated retail institutions. The multiples, in particular, have dominated UK retailing over the past 10 years. Finally, we have looked at the wheel of retailing hypothesis in order to gauge the extent to which this explains the changes we have seen; it does not. What we have noted, however, is that the pace of retail change is increasing, a factor which the marketing manager will undoubtedly need to take account of in planning for the future.

In addition, we have seen that channel decisions and management are among the most important decisions a company faces. In fact, channel design and selection is a strategic consideration. Among the key elements of this strategic decision are the delineation and selection of the basic channel structure, the determination of required market exposure, systems and procedures for ensuring maximum cooperation and minimum conflict, and marketing and channel support efforts.

Channel design and operating decisions are company and situation-specific—in short, there is no one superior method for distributing products and services. Important considerations in identifying channel alternatives in a company would include; company and marketing objectives and resources, target markets and customers, products and competitive factors. The final choice of specific channel(s) needs to be assessed against control, adaptive, economic and coverage criteria.

Finally, we have seen that, increasingly, companies are assessing their distribution activities from a marketing logistics or total systems viewpoint. Not only does this approach offer potentially large cost savings in the often high-cost area of distribution, but in addition, it can help a company become more marketing-oriented in the design of its system of physical distribution, and hence increase its competitiveness.

APPLICATION QUESTIONS

1. What reasons account for the development of channels of distribution?
2. Explain the importance of 'channel length' and 'channel relationships' in channel structure.
3. Outline some of the more significant changes in UK retailing over the past 10 years. To what extent are these changes indicative of a life cycle for retailing institutions?
4. (a) Outline the major strategic elements of channel choice indicating the significance of each to channel design.
   (b) Outline and discuss the criteria you would use in selecting a particular channel structure.
5. What are the key concepts in marketing logistics, and what do these mean in terms of designing the total distribution system in a company?

REFERENCES

1. L. P. Bucklin, *A Theory of Distribution Channel Structure*, Institute of Business and Economic Research, University of California, Berkeley, 1966, p. 5.
2. E. D. McGarry, 'Some functions of marketing reconsidered', in *Theory in Marketing*, R. Cox and W. Alderson (eds), R. D. Irwin, Homewood, IL, 1950.
3. W. Alderson, *Marketing Behaviour and Executive Action: A Functionalist Approach to Marketing Theory*, R. D. Irwin, Homewood, IL, 1957.
4. J. A. Howard, *Marketing Management: Operating, Strategic, and Administrative*, 3rd edn, R. D. Irwin, Homewood, IL, 1973, pp. 4–5.

5. D. J. Bowersox, *et al. Management in Marketing Channels*, Macmillan, London, 1968, p. 69.

6. L. P. Bucklin, (ed.), *Vertical Marketing Systems*, Scott, Foresman, Glenview, IL, 1970.

7. P. Kotler, *Marketing Management, Analysis, Planning, Implementation and Control*, 7th edn, Prentice-Hall, Englewood Cliffs, NJ, 1991, pp. 525–8.

8. R. Pitfield, *Business Organization*, Macdonald and Evans, London, 1982.

9. N. Sanghari and A. Treadgold, *Developments in European Retailing*. Dower House Publications, Taunton, Somerset, 1990.

10. British Franchising Association and National Westminster Bank, 'Franchising in the United Kingdom', London, November 1991.

11. M. P. McNair and E. G. May, 'The Evolution of Retail Institutions in the United States', Report 76–100, Marketing Science Institute, Cambridge, MA, April 1976.

12. W. J. Stanton, *Fundamentals of Marketing*, 5th edn, McGraw-Hill, London, 1978, pp. 364–5.

13. L. W. Stern and A. I. El-Ansary, *Marketing Channels*, 2nd edn, Prentice-Hall, Englewood Cliffs, NJ, 1982, Chapter 7.

14. I. F. Wilkinson, 'Power and influence structures in distribution channels', *European Journal of Marketing*, **7**(2), 1973.

15. B. Mallen, 'Conflict and co-operation in marketing channels', in *Reflections on Progress in Marketing*, L. G. Smith (ed.), American Marketing Association, Chicago, IL, 1965, pp. 74–7.

16. Kotler, op. cit., pp. 516–18.

17. J. N. Arbury, *A New Approach to Physical Distribution*, Dryden Press, Hinsdale, IL, 1967.

18. P. Drucker, 'The economy's dark continent', *Fortune*, April 1962, p. 103.

19. E. H. Ballou, *Basic Business Logistics*, 2nd edn, Prentice-Hall, Englewood Cliffs, NJ, 1987.

20. M. Christopher, *Total Distribution: A Framework for Analysis, Costing and Control*, Gower Press, London, 1971.

21. G. Lancaster and L. Massingham, *Marketing management*. McGraw-Hill Book Company, London, 1992, Chapter 11.

CHAPTER
ELEVEN
MARKETING COMMUNICATIONS

INTRODUCTION

Marketing communications is one of the most rapidly changing elements within the marketing mix, although many companies continue to ignore its importance. Despite the fact that above-the-line (direct) advertising currently accounts for expenditure running into billions of pounds per annum in the UK, with below-the-line (indirect promotional) expenditure at equally high levels, the application of management in these areas is subject to much criticism.

The purpose of this chapter and Chapter 12 is to examine the scope of the marketing communications mix in some detail—advertising, sales promotion, public relations and personal selling—and to discuss the nature, role and principles of these communication tools. The basic purpose of such tools is to communicate with consumers in order to persuade them to buy the company's products. As we shall see, this is by no means the only objective of this type of communication method open to marketing practitioners. To view it as being only sales-oriented is to underestimate the complexity of modern marketing communications.

COMMUNICATIONS EXPLAINED

H. Lasswell[1] puts forward the proposition that five basic questions form the basis of analysis in communications:

1. Who is the communicator? In this, the *control analysis*, the main task is to discover the purpose of the sender so that his or her message can be correctly interpreted.
2. What is the content of the message? *Content analysis* very often revolves around the question of informative and persuasive messages—while D. Ogilvy[2] claims that informative advertising is the most profitable, quoting the example of how effective it would be at emptying a building simply to tell people that there was a fire; to try to *persuade* them to leave could lead to arguments and delays.
3. Who is the audience for which the message is intended? *Audience analysis* is concerned with the identifying of prospects, the target audiences and the segmentation of markets.
4. What information media or means of transmitting the message are employed? *Media analysis* can be viewed as discovering where audiences are located and selecting the media and media vehicles that will reach them most effectively.

5. What behaviour follows the receipt of the message? *Effect analysis* is concerned with the relationship between message content and the subsequent behaviour of the audience.

These five basic analyses will be a recurring theme in this chapter and in Chapter 12.

A communication process can thus be summarized as who says what, in what channel, to whom, and with what effect. The four basic components of the process are:

1. The communicator (the encoder)
2. The message (the symbols)
3. The channel (method of communication)
4. The audience (the decoder)

Figure 11.1 is a very simplistic analysis, and the process of marketing communications calls for countless problems to be considered. For the communications to be effective, these problems must be researched and then overcome.

One of the major problem areas is *channel noise*. This is a term used to describe anything that interferes with the message during its time in the selected channel. We may view it as a variety of distractions between the communicator and his or her audience. With reference to marketing communications, the advertisement might be subjected to poor reproduction in the mass media in some way, or the salesperson might have to put up with a variety of interruptions while in the middle of his or her presentation. Not all of these can be planned for in advance, but some ways in which channel noise might be overcome are:

—*The use of attention-getting devices*—highlighting the need for good, effective creative ideas, and using methods of communication that secure the attention of the audience. This applies in all areas of marketing communications, whether it is the memorable jingle used in the advertising campaign or the tactics employed in below-the-line and personal selling efforts.
—*Repetition of the key part of the message*—in an effort to try to ensure that this is received and remembered by the audience, even if other parts of the message are lost.

Another interference which presents problems for the communicator is that of *semantic noise*; even though the message is received exactly as it was transmitted by the encoder, for some reason it is misunderstood. Each person in the decoder group aimed at by the marketing communicator will have his or her own frame of reference. Any words, for example, that are unknown to the audience, or that mean different things to the audience from what the communicator intended, may very well result in misinterpretation. A need for the perceptions of the encoder and decoder to be common is thus highlighted, since any disparity between what the communicator perceives and what the audience perceives can result in severe problems, and ineffective communications. Advertisers are

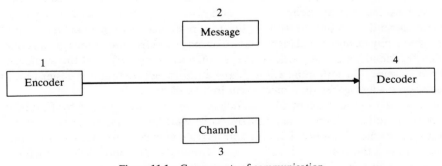

Figure 11.1 Components of communication

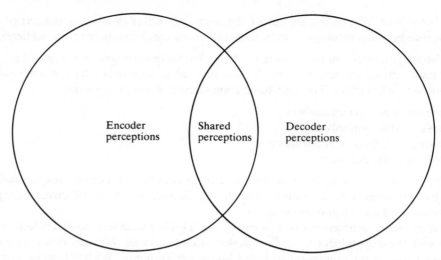

Figure 11.2 Encoder/decoder perceptions

often criticized for being out of touch with their audiences' tastes and attitudes, while salespeople may not possess the technical know-how and expertise to be able to relate to prospects.

Frye[3] argues that this problem, while being a key one for marketing management to contend with, may be less harmful in the early stages of the product life cycle, when the target audience (the innovators) may tend to be on a similar social and economic scale as the marketing communicator. This may be true in some instances, but it is equally untrue in many others. For example, in industrial markets there may be little difference between the various decision-making units in potential buying companies; or at least the differences may exist among groups of buyers at all stages.

The need for commonality of perceptions between communicator and audience is illustrated by Frye as a Venn diagram (see Fig. 11.2).

The marketing communications management team must, therefore, identify the possible problem areas. Where perceptions are not shared, they must try to reduce the problem areas by careful definition of terms used and by adjustment of the vocabulary used.

It must also be realized that the context in which words appear may affect interpretation, and also that material that is deemed to be too complex or too simplistic by the audience may then be dismissed. Audiences might then turn to competitors' communications in their search for more rewarding material.

A further problem area that the marketing communicator may face is a result of the *beliefs* and *attitudes* held by the various people in his audience. As already stated, interpretation of the message may depend upon the terms of the frame of reference. Each person has certain beliefs and attitudes, which may be individual (ego-related) or may stem from reference groups that affect him or her (family, friends, etc.). A message that challenges these may lead the audience to distort, misinterpret or reject the communication. Many authors believe that it is easier to try to redirect attitudes in some way, rather than meet them in a head-on clash.

Related to this is the concept of *cognitive dissonance*, put forward by Festinger.[4] When a person takes an action which is inconsistent with what he or she believes, then the cognitive elements are in conflict. This provides the marketing communicator with a most useful analysis framework, in both the pre- and post-purchase situations. The underlying principle is that new information must be in harmony with existing knowledge if dissonance is to be avoided. This also has implications for personal selling, which is discussed in Chapter 12. Suffice it to say here that marketing communicators must realize that audiences will attempt to reduce dissonance by exposing themselves to further messages in order to reduce the conflict. They will turn again to the advertisements, the sales literature and the salespeople in their attempts to seek reassurance.

The final problem area facing the marketing communicator is that of *feedback*. These are the reactions that take place along the communication process, but which are transmitted backwards—from audience to communicator. This flow might, of course, not be a direct one, but rather could pass through a number of intermediary stages before it is received by the communicator. The obtaining of feedback is vital to communications management, if campaigns are to be correctly evaluated and controlled and the question, 'why were we successful or otherwise?' answered. Within the area of marketing communications, feedback is one of the principal differences between the various activities. For example, in personal selling it can be instantaneous, whereas in advertising it is often slow, difficult and expensive to obtain.

COMMUNICATIONS STRATEGIES

All of these problems mean that the tasks facing marketing communications management are not as simple as the process initially outlined in Fig. 11.1. There are many potential problems that may have to be surmounted, but at least the recognition of these problems provides a useful starting-point in the formulation of communication strategies. Marketers must recognize that even the most effective communication strategy is unlikely to lead to effective communication with all the consumers at which it is aimed.

Once the scope and limitations of various communication strategies have been recognized, a strategy adapted to particular needs may be formulated.

Questions that should now be asked are as follows:

1. To which consumer group should the communications be directed?
2. What information will these consumer groups seek from our communications when deciding whether or not to buy?
3. What objectives should be set in order to communicate effectively with these groups?
4. How much will it cost to achieve these objectives? What size should the total budget be?
5. How should this total budget be apportioned among the various marketing communications activities available?
6. How much responsibility is to be assumed by the manufacturers and by the channel intermediaries?
7. How might the effectiveness of the campaign be evaluated and controlled?

CAMPAIGN PLANNING

This campaign planning process highlights the major decision areas faced by management. In order to provide insights into these, the rest of this chapter and Chapter 12 are devoted to close examination of many of the more important aspects of promotional planning. A marketing communications campaign planning process is put forward in Fig. 11.3.

By planning and implementing their communications campaigns in this structured way, it is suggested that a more professional approach can be adopted by communications management teams. Many authors have criticized the lack of management application in the area of marketing communications. Wills[5] asserts that it is not surprising that not many companies can truthfully answer the question of how good or bad their marketing communication efforts are. Wills puts forward the following reasons for this being the case:

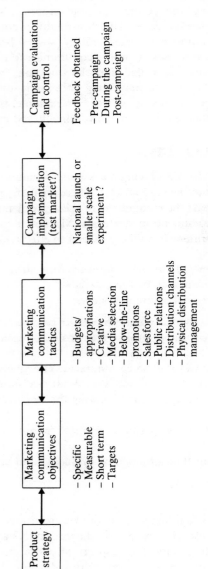

Figure 11.3 A marketing communications campaign planning framework

—The inertia of existing organizational structures.

—The lack of realization about the potential benefits of adopting a more professional approach to marketing communications.

There appears to be far more attention paid to other areas of the marketing mix, most notably product and pricing policies, while marketing communications tend to be ignored.

The organizational solution proposed is, as Wills points out, relatively simple. In Fig. 11.4, we see the need to raise marketing communications in the hierarchy of management thinking. Referring back to Fig. 11.3, we find that the prime need in the planning and implementation of marketing communication campaigns is for management to be objective-oriented.

Product strategy, as has been pointed out in Chapter 8, is seen as providing the initial sense of direction for the campaign. It acts as the key between the consumer, the product and market analysis, which form the basis of strategy formulation and the determination of the marketing communication programmes. The purpose of product strategy is to provide a single, unified direction for *all* of an organization's marketing programmes—including marketing communications. In this way, all the efforts are coordinated, and the product is moved towards the same goal by all of the organization's marketing efforts.

Product strategy receives inputs, and in turn provides guidance not just for marketing efforts. All of the organization's functional areas—production, financial, legal, personnel, etc.—are likewise coordinated by means of the overall product strategy, so that all of these efforts are directed towards a single, unified goal. There should only be one direction for a product, and the marketing communication activities should be coordinated with all of the other efforts in this way.

The strategy decision is long-term, first decided upon before the product is even produced or marketed; it will be adjusted only when major events happen—such as changes in the product itself or a change in consumer tastes.

Figure 11.4   Marketing communications coordination

Marketing communications objectives have now to be determined. These are, of course, more specific and short-term, and must be in line with the overall product strategy. The determination of these objectives is a key area in the planning of campaigns, and forms the cornerstone of the analysis. If good objectives are developed and clearly stated at the beginning of the process, then all the planners involved in the marketing communications process can attack their particular problem areas with good purpose and with their tasks having been eased. Copy specialists can prepare messages which are directed at achieving a specific purpose; personal selling, advertising and below-the-line promotional activities can all be coordinated; and the experts in media planning can use their expertise more effectively.

As Majoro[6] points out, the setting of clear, precise and measurable objectives can help in the following ways:

1. To integrate the marketing communications campaign with other marketing activities.
2. To improve the liaison with external agencies.
3. To determine communications budgets and appropriations.
4. To secure appraisal of the plans by top management.
5. To measure the results of communications efforts.

Too often, communications objectives are set which are too general, are confused with overall marketing objectives, or are non-existent. In a major survey of campaigns planned and implemented by advertising agencies in the United States, Britt[7] examined two major aspects of each campaign:

1. Were specific objectives set well enough for subsequent measurement to be made?
2. Did the agency attempt to measure effectiveness by clearly stating how the campaign fulfilled any previously stated objectives?

Only two of the campaigns met Britt's criteria for adequate objective setting, and most failed to specificy what criteria were to be used for evaluation.

Under the circumstances discovered by Majaro and Britt, everyone concerned with the campaign building process lacks direction, with the inevitable reduction in the utilization of skills. Unless valid objectives are set, then the tendency will be for each manager in sales, advertising, sales promotions and public relations to set his or her own targets. These might be good objectives viewed individually, but because they are not coordinated they must be sub-optimal. Optimization can only be sought when there is a common goal, with all of the marketing communications activities being coordinated in the pursuit of this.

Communications objectives

It may prove useful to list here some of the common objectives of communications campaigns:

1. Consumer communications

    (a) To inform about a new product.
    (b) To correct misconceptions about a product.
    (c) To increase frequency of use.
    (d) To remind.
    (e) To present special offers.
    (f) To educate consumers in how to use a product.
    (g) To build an image for the product/company.
    (h) To build up consumer loyalty.

2. Trade communications

   (a) To provide information.
   (b) To inform about promotional programmes.
   (c) To present special trade offers.
   (d) To avoid stockpiling.
   (e) To educate the trade on product usage.
   (f) To build patronage motives.

These are not, however, all-inclusive, and when used as the basis of a specific campaign they must be expressed in precise, measurable terms. The fact, however, that consumers and trade will receive not only commercial information via the organization's communication campaigns, but also information from non-commercial sources, presents major problems to the communications manager. Editorial comments from the various media, and word of mouth, are both examples of communications that are not under the control of the marketer, and may contradict the messages he or she is conveying. Marketers must, therefore, recognize that even the most effective communications strategy is unlikely to lead to effective communications with all of the prospects all of the time. The recognition of these limitations puts marketers in a position to formulate a strategy adapted to their own needs. The identification of problems to be surmounted is the first vital step in the formulation of any strategy.

    Having specified the objectives of the campaign, the next step facing the marketer is the selection of tools to disseminate the necessary information to the target audience. The nature of the programme objectives will obviously play a large part in establishing some guidelines for the overall communications budget. For example, the task of creating awareness for a product may require a smaller budget than, say, the task of instilling consumer loyalty for the product. Here communications management must try to achieve the following:

1. Identify and satisfy the target audience's interests in information.
2. Optimize the expenditure, so that the marginal cost of disseminating the information does not exceed the marginal revenue that is brought about.
3. Identify the extent to which the informational needs of the prospects can be resolved by promotional elements of the marketing mix, or by non-promotional elements.

There are many considerations to be taken into account:

—Overall marketing objectives and strategy.
—The level of competitive promotional spending in the target markets. Here, smaller producers tend to take their cue from larger manufacturers and adjust their budgets in line with the market leader.
—The level of sales generated by promotional activities.
—The objectives sought (called the 'objective and task' method). This calls for an ascertainment of advertising expenditure needed to reach marketing objectives that have been laid down in the marketing plan.
—the affordability of the proposals. Here the philosophy is that, after other cost centres have received their budgets, what is left over goes to advertising.

Each of these may be used as the basis for determining the budget. On an individual level, they may provide only limited insights. For example, if competitive spending is the only variable that is taken into account, then one major problem may be that the budget fails to consider the fact that the problems/opportunities faced by the company may be very different from those of its competitors.

Equally, if sales is the sole determinant of the budget total (whether this is a last year's, per unit or an adjusted sales figure), then a major criticism of this approach is that it regards the sales as the stimulus with communications as the response. It is obvious that this is wrong, and that the stimulus should be communications—leading to the response of sales. Taken further, the notion of sales determining the promotional budget implies that falling sales means a decreased budget and, conversely, increasing sales generates a larger budget. Logic must dictate that the opposite should be the case!

The whole area of budget determination within the field of marketing communication is full of controversy and criticism. A paper presented by Roberts[8] warns management of what he calls planning blight, and points out that advertising budgets are some of the last budgets to be set and the first to be slashed! The danger is one of the spiral decay.

An asset based method of budget allocation is one of the most logical ones. It assumes that advertising is a tangible item that extends beyond the budget period, looks at it as a long-term investment and attempts to ascertain the return on such expenditures. The 'incremental method' is its corollary, and this assumes that the least unit of money spent on advertising should bring in an equal amount of revenue.

Much support from many academic sources comes for the 'task approach'. This involves the marketer, once an objective has been specified, in costing out the various promotional tasks that are necessary to achieve this objective. Once again, we see the need for valid objective setting within the area of marketing communications. The best guideline to management must be to realize the importance of all these factors—sales, competitors, objectives and affordability, etc.— and to take account of them all when determining the budget. Adequate returns on investment will enable the marketer to command the resources necessary to continue satisfying consumers' interests.

Communications practice

The marketer, when deciding which promotional tools to use, is faced with a wide range of alternatives. Sometimes it is mistakenly assumed that advertising and personal selling are the only marketing tools through which to disseminate information. This view is far too narrow, since, through publicity and public relations activities, short- and long-term promotions and by means such as packaging, information can be conveyed most effectively by the marketer.

Determining which combination of these tools to use in particular situations is a very complex operation involving many considerations. One of the most important of these is determining how many and which decisions are made at the possible locations. For example, is the decision made chiefly in the home, at the office or in the store? When decision-making occurs mainly in the store, for example, the emphasis should be placed on point-of-sale and personal selling activities.

The nature of the product is also important in this respect. Although there are many dangers in putting forward rigid guidelines here, it would appear that advertising may be most effective when the information needs are not overly complex, as may be the case with convenience goods. Personal selling, on the other hand, with its obvious advantages of face-to-face exchanges, may be most suitable in disseminating information about more technical, specialist goods where the individual needs of particular customers have to be taken into account. The kinds of information to be disseminated must have a bearing on the selection of the marketing communication tools. It is the function of the creative programme to specify what message is to be communicated to the audience. The creative programme provides direction for the creative people, who will implement the campaign when the plan is completed and approved.

The basic direction for creative ideas is provided by the product strategy, since the market position that is to be aimed for must be the starting-point. The more specific communications objectives specify the steps to be taken to solve immediate problems facing the product, and the consumer, product and market analyses will have provided information upon which the creative programme should be based. In particular, the nature of the target audience and the problems that consumers are trying to solve will form the basis of the creative programme.

The three essential steps in building this programme for a product are:

1. The determination of the content of the message, aiming for consistency of information from various sources.
2. The presentation of the message; identifying a central idea and the way in which it is to be expressed and creating the advertisements and sales approaches.
3. Determining how the communications effort will be produced—for example, estimates of the production costs and production time schedules of advertisements, point-of-sale material and sales literature.

Communications management delegates much of the work involved in this process, since it involves very specialized skills. In most instances there is clearly a need to employ the services of the creative specialists to be found in the agencies. Responsibilities remain for providing information and directions to the creative team and for evaluating the output in terms of specific, predetermined criteria.

Advertising agencies are examined in more detail later in the chapter, together with other detailed examinations of various aspects of advertising. Personal selling is considered in Chapter 12. The next sections are devoted to the remaining aspects of the communications campaign plan—below-the-line promotions and public relations—in order to assess their applications in campaign planning and implementation.

Below-the-line promotions

Below-the-line promotions have been defined by Christopher[9] as 'all non-media promotion'. Engel et al.[10] define it as 'the supplementary selling activity which coordinates personal selling and advertising into an effective persuasive force'. There are, however, many problems of definition, since the 'line' is an artificial concept, used originally by advertising agencies to distinguish between promotional expenditures that were commissionable and those that were not. 'The implication of the line is that there is some radical difference between the purpose and effect of expenditures above and below the line.'[11] To some extent, any definition of below the line asssumed a false dichotomy, since many promotions are dependent on media advertising—for example when reduced offers are backed by national press advertising.

Within the context of communications planning, the marketer should be more concerned with adopting a total approach, whereby above the line and below the line are integrated to complement and support each other in the total communications process. A useful distinction has been drawn between those promotions that aim to move products from the marketing channel intermediary, and those aimed at moving the product from the manufacturers into the channels of distribution. These have been referred to as 'pull' and 'push' promotional techniques, which have already been detailed in Chapter 10.

The methods employed in promotional efforts must depend upon the objectives sought, the nature of the product, the type of distribution channel employed and the target audience.

The range of 'pull' (consumer incentives) includes the following:

—Price reductions—by the manufacturer, or by the retailer in the form of store price cuts.
—Coupons—a form of price reduction.

—Self-liquidators—where profits made on the merchandise offered (in return for money and 'box tops') cover the cost of the promotional effort.
—Premiums given free in/on/off the pack.
—Personality promotions.
—Consumer competitions.
—Free samples—offered either by post or through in-store demonstrations.
—Merchandising and point-of-sale displays, and advertising in the stores.
—Packaging.
—Sponsorship.
—Purchase privilege plans (buy one, get one free).
—Container premiums—where the container can be used after the contents have been consumed.
—Trade-in facilities.
—Credit facilities.
—Training schemes.
—Guarantees.
—Direct mail 'shots'.
—Saving schemes.
—Banded and twin packs.

Over the past 20 years, there has been tremendous growth in expenditure on these consumer incentives, to such an extent that it is estimated that the level of expenditure in the UK today exceeds that of above the line. Several factors have contributed to this growth in the use of sales promotion in consumer markets. The main ones are as follows.

—*Internal factors*

1. Promotion is now more accepted by senior management as an effective sales tool.
2. More brand/marketing managers are qualified and have experience of using sales promotions.
3. The store managers are under increasing pressure to increase (or at least maintain) their sales in what has been a difficult economic and marketing environment.

—*External factors* These include the following:

1. The number of brands has increased.
2. Competitors have become more promotion-minded.
3. Inflation and recession have made consumers more 'deal'-oriented.
4. The changing trade structure in many markets has meant greater competition between retailers.
5. The threat from retailers' own brands has increased.

The range of 'push' (trade and salesforce incentives) includes the following:

—Cash discounts.
—Increased margins.
—Competitions—trade and salesforce.
—Dealer premiums.
—Salesforce cash incentives.
—Exhibitions.
—Demonstrations.
—Direct mail 'shots'.
—Training schemes.
—Credit facilities.

The marketer may be faced with a number of problems, which offer him the opportunity to utilize some of these 'push' and 'pull' techniques. Spillard[12] states that the main advantages of these below-the-line techniques stem from their being:

—Very flexible and adaptable.
—Capable of specific action.
—Wide-ranging in applicability.
—Economical and cost-saving.
—Swift in action.

The marketing situations in which sales promotion may make a valuable contribution can range from payment problems to the need for advertising to have more 'punch', from consumer purchase to dealers not stocking the product, from the need to motivate the salesforce to blockages in the distribution channel, from the need for expert advice to the need for additional market information.

The decision whether or not to use sales promotion, and which particular techniques, is summed up by Ann Morgan,[13] who suggests the following:

1. Determine, in order of priority, the problems faced by the product/brand.
2. Determine the money available to solve these problems.
3. List and cost all the possible alternative solutions to the problems, e.g. theme advertising, pricing or product strategy, consumer promotions, etc.
4. Estimate the effectiveness of each solution.
5. If the answers to 3 and 4 suggest that a promotion is the most efficient answer to the problem, and if there is enough money available in 2, then a promotion is indicated. The marketer then needs to plan, implement and control the promotional campaign.

Managing sales promotion For effective sales promotion, the marketer must establish the objectives, select the appropriate promotional tool, develop and implement the programme, and evaluate the results.

Establishing the sales promotion objective As you would expect, the starting-point in planning sales promotion is the identification of the target audience and the specific objectives that the sales promotion is intended to achieve. Sales promotion can be aimed at one or more of the following:

—Consumers
—The 'trade' (retailers, wholesalers, distributors, etc.)
—The salesforce

Basically, sales promotion objectives derive from the basic marketing communication objectives for the brand. The specific objectives will vary depending on the type of market and the position of the product. For consumers, objectives might include:

—Announce a new product.
—Encourage product trial.
—Encourage greater use.
—Stimulate purchase of larger sizes.
—Attract non-users.
—Encourage brand-switching.

For retailers:

—Encourage stocking.
—Increase inventory levels.
—Encourage off-peak buying.
—Promote related products.
—Offset competitive marketing.
—Open up new outlets.
—Build retailer loyalty.

For the salesforce, the aim would be essentially to support retailer objectives, e.g.:

—Build display.
—Increase order size.
—Increase shelf space utilization.

Obviously, it is important to set realistic objectives for any sales promotion; and, although objectives should be simple and clear, it is possible to include both consumer trade and salesforce objectives; e.g.:

> To increase sales by X% during a sweepstake promotion period by obtaining special promotion related off-shelf displays of the brand in Y% of large retail stores and Z% in medium retail stores.

This type of objective has the advantage of stating how the goal is to be achieved and of identifying the outside support that will be needed.

Choosing the promotional tools Having established what the sales promotion is intended to achieve and with whom, the next step is to select the most appropriate and cost-effective sales promotion tools. Again, with such a variety of tools available, this is not easy. Each of the tools tends to have its relative advantages and disadvantages, and there is little consistent empirical evidence to suggest which tools work best in which situation and why. In most circumstances, it is advisable to make use of a specialist sales promotion agency when devising sales promotion programmes.

As an indication of the types of sales promotion tools available for each target audience, we now briefly outline some of the major tools used for consumers, for trade and for the salesforce.

Bargain packages There are two main forms of this promotional technique. One is where the product is advertised at a particular price but the pack is marked '5p off', which means that the purchase price will be reduced by that amount, but only on the products so marked, which is another way of saying 'while stocks last'. Many people take advantage of this type of offer, but they include all the regular purchasers of the product, many of whom just stock up with the product at the bargain price but then do not purchase the product again until their own stocks have been run down, by which time there might be another 'offer' on the same product. Packs marked for such a discount are often known as 'flash' packs.

The second form of this technique is where the offer is advertised as 'two for the price of one', or where, attached to the large size—of toothpaste, for example—is a smaller-sized pack. This method does not help the retailer so much as the manufacturer, who is able to increase the turnover of the large packs, sales of which may have been sluggish, and at the same time maintain his turnover of the smaller pack. At the same time, it means that less of the competitors' toothpaste will be purchased by the same customer during the following few weeks. This technique, whereby one pack is attached to another (often larger) pack, is known as the 'limpet' method. The title is self-explanatory.

Give-aways This is aimed at the younger end of the various market segments, and has been used extensively by the breakfast cereal companies. Into every packet of cereal is put a small toy or gift in an attempt to use the influencing power of children in this market.

Trade promotions Some of the more frequently used trade promotions include *discounts/cash allowances*, whereby a percentage discount or cash allowance is given for each case purchased.

Consumer sales promotions The following paragraphs cite some examples of techniques used in the promotion of consumer products.

Coupons The consumer must be in possession of a coupon or voucher of a particular value, which can then be 'redeemed' at the local store in exchange for the product or products named on the voucher at the usual price less the value of the voucher. There is usually a deadline, and the offer often applies to a particular size in the range of products, which usually means that the consumer, in order to take advantage of the offer, must purchase the product within a shorter space of time than he or she would normally have done. The effect of this is to increase the rate of stock-turn for both the retailer and the manufacturer.

One problem is, of course, that the majority of redemptions are made by people who would have bought the product anyway, and so to that extent the value of the scheme is doubtful. But where the voucher constitutes an introductory offer on a relatively new product, the 'bargain' element often persuades consumers to switch brand loyalties, perhaps (it is hoped) more than temporarily.

Self-liquidating offers An example of this would be where a manufacturer of tinned food purchases a quantity of kitchen knives from a supplier at a price of £1 per knife. The food manufacturer than 'offers' to sell the knives to the consuming public at the cost price of £1 or thereabouts, plus five labels from a particular size of the tinned food.

Again, the advantage to the retailer and the manufacturer is that the rate of stock-turn is increased, and the consumer also benefits by being able to purchase the knives at trade price. This type of operation is termed 'self-liquidating' because all the capital used by the manufacturer in purchasing the knives is returned by the consumer.

Sampling Many manufacturers—again, particularly in the areas of fast-moving consumer goods—give away free samples of their products. The sample is very often of a smaller size than the normal pack size, and it is hoped that customers will try the product, like it, and purchase the product in future. Once again, this operation is usually reserved for new entrants to a market. It has the added advantage that, if consumers are given a tablet of soap, for example, they are less likely to buy their usual brand that week, or until they have used up the free gift.

Additional products with order Extra products are sometimes given with each unit ordered; e.g., if a case of 12 is purchased, two extra products are given free.

Merchandising allowances A merchandising allowance compensates the retailer for featuring the manufacturer's products.

Advertising allowance/cooperative advertising An advertising allowance compensates the retailer for featuring the manufacturer's products in newspaper advertisements; alternatively, the supplier may organize collaborative advertising with the trade.

Exhibitions Exhibitions are, in some trades, almost obligatory. A well-known example in the UK is the Ideal Home Exhibition, which is held annually. It features all possible goods that can be used in a home and exhibits 'model homes' which are fully furnished and can be visited and inspected.

The bulk of exhibitions are industrial, however, and they include examples such as the Motor Show, the Office Equipment Exhibition, the Hardware Trades Fair and a number of others appropriate to various industries. Many of the exhibitions are mounted solely for the trade and the public are not allowed admittance.

Sales force promotion This is a growing area for the application of sales promotional techniques. Some of the more frequently used techniques are:

—Sales contests
—Bonus prizes
—Sales incentives and gifts

With such a wide variety of sales promotion tools to choose from, it is important that the most cost-effective ones are selected. The most appropriate tools in this respect will vary according to a number of factors, including type of product market, specific sales promotion objectives, target audience and the emphasis of the marketing strategy, e.g. 'push' versus 'pull' strategies. It is also important to recall that very often all three areas, i.e. consumers, trade and salesforce, will be targeted; such multifaceted campaigns must therefore be coordinated.

Developing the sales promotion programme The marketer, in addition to selecting the promotion type, needs to consider some additional decisions:

—*The size of the incentive* For example, how much should be offered—5p off or 20p off? A certain minimum incentive is necessary, but too high an incentive may be counter-productive.
—*Conditions for participation* Is everyone invited to be involved? What do consumers need to do in return, e.g. collect X packs tops?
—*Distribution vehicle* On-pack, in-pack, door-to-door, in-store (etc.)? The decisions here might be crucial.
—*Duration of promotion* How long should it run? Too short may mean missing many consumers; too long loses 'immediacy/impact'.
—*Quantity of promotion* How many packs, prizes (etc.) are there?
—*Timing and coordination* Here, seasonality in market, other retailer activities, production (etc.) must be considered.
—*Budget* Promotions should be properly thought out and costed in the light of their objectives (see against the background of the complete and coordinated marketing effort). It is easy to make mistakes.
—*Pre-testing* Whenever possible, the promotion should be pre-tested so that objectives and budgets can be properly tuned.
—*Legality* It is important to ensure that the proposed promotion is legal.
—*Responding to unforeseen events* Examples would be the launch of competitor, or a major crisis in the marketplace. Here the marketer must respond quickly and tactically.

The importance of the right theme It is now almost universally accepted that a brand is a complex assimilation of ideas, attitudes, values and beliefs on the part of its consumers. It is not just a physical, tangible and functional entity, but a reflection of aspirations and self-actualizations. It stands to reason, therefore, that promotions can and should encourage favourable attitudes to the brand. They must not demote the brand in consumers' estimations. This poses problems for a money-off deal, banded pack (etc.) which might be construed as devaluing the brand. Conversely, a 'value' or budget brand might be harmed by some up-market offer or appeal.

We know from research that the relationship between the functional, evaluative and psychological components of a brand are subtle.

Functional   = What does the product do?
Evaluative   = How well does it do it?
Psychological = Which of the consumers' basic motivational needs or roles does the brand
                imagery deliver?

In sales promotional terms, it is very important not to disturb the psychological beliefs built up via brand advertising. Here are some examples:

Domestos   = 'Impregnable security'
Comfort   = 'Loving softness'
Fairy Liquid = 'Gentle relationships'
Persil   = 'Caring whiteness'

Sales promotional themes for these brands should therefore aim to reinforce the beliefs.

Implementation and evaluation   As each promotion needs to be planned at the outset as an integral part of the overall marketing communications plan, proper lead times should be established. Production, the salesforce, the advertising agency and the trade will all be actively involved in the successful implementation (with the one concern of trade security *vis-à-vis* competition).

A further major consideration is whether the promotion should be backed by advertising. There is evidence that sales promotions are most effective when used together with advertising.

In terms of evaluation, a checklist should be produced and the promotion evaluated under the following headings:

1. Salesforce
2. Trade
3. Consumer
4. Achievement of objectives
5. Budget
6. Handling
7. Supplier service
8. Outside influences

Before the full-scale sales promotion is launched, it is advisable to pre-test the promotional vehicles selected. This can be done relatively quickly by using, for example, focus groups, selected in-store tests, or full-scale test marketing. If the testing is successful—indicating that the sales promotion will achieve the required objectives—the full-scale campaign can then be implemented.

The final stage, of course, is evaluation and control. Often the formal evaluation of sales promotion campaigns is overlooked by marketers. The chief factor in assessing the success of a sales promotion campaign is usually the effect on sales. However, this should also be compared with both the costs of the campaign and alternative ways of spending these monies, e.g. on other elements of the promotional mix.

In measuring the sales effectiveness of sales promotion, it is important to monitor sales over a longer period than the duration of the campaign itself. The explanation for this is given by P. Spillard and is shown in Fig. 11.5. The area $A + B$ in the diagram represents the additional sales volume generated by the sales promotion. Area A represents extra sales during the time the promotion is in effect, and B is the carry-over effect. Area C, however, represents future lost sales as a result of such sales being brought forward to take advantage of the promotion. For example, customers may stock up on the product concerned, causing a lagged effect. In addition, Doyle and Saunders[14] have pointed to a possible 'lead' effect; this is where, in anticipation of the sales promotion, customers delay the purchases they would otherwise have made. Similarly,

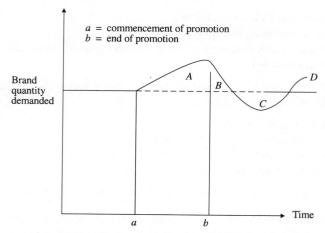

Figure 11.5   Sales promotion in its marketing strategy
Source: P. Spillard, *Sales promotion; its place in marketing strategy*. Business Publications, Plano, Texas, 1966, p. 112

salespersons may hold back on selling effort if they expect a sales contest with prizes to be introduced in the future.

These complications do not detract from the need to evaluate and control sales promotion; indeed, they add to it.

Planned and managed effectively, there is little doubt that sales promotion is one of the most effective of the promotional tools.

Public relations

Defined by the Institute of Public Relations[15] as 'the deliberate, planned and sustained effort to establish and maintain mutual understanding between an organisation and its public', this is a key element in the discussion of communication tools. Public relations is concerned with the behaviour of the organization, its products, services and individuals which give rise to publicity. Unlike publicity, which is a result of information being made known, the results of public relations are controllable.

Control will result from public relations activities only if, as F. Jenkins[16] states, 'the communications with various publics are planned with the purpose of achieving specific objectives'. Here again, we see the need for providing our marketing communications activities with a clear meaning and purpose.

The 'publics' that should provide the direction for an organization's public relations activities are as follows:

1. *The community* This is where the clear need is for the organization to act as if it were a member—just like a private citizen. Involvement in community activities and the development of a community relations programme are ways to achieve this goal.
2. *Employees* This internal aspect of public relations is often a neglected area in many organizations, but there are obvious benefits in involving the workforce in organizational goals and establishing mutual understanding.
3. *Government* Both local and national politicians are important sources of information for an organization, for example concerning proposed legislative changes affecting the business. The lobbying of politicians is not without criticism, but it should be recognized as an acceptable procedure in industrial/government relations.

4. *The financial community* Commercial and merchant banks, investors and share analysts, and city journalists provide a 'public' with whom an organization should communicate if it is to be seen as financially credible. The recent spate of mergers in the UK has highlighted the need to establish consistent relations over a period of time.

5. *Distributors* All types of middlemen in a company's channel of distribution—wholesalers, retailers, brokers, agents and dealerships, etc.—need information about products and services if they are to have the knowledge and confidence necessary to become effective re-sellers.

6. *Consumers* Often thought to be the only 'public' that concerns public relations. Here, as with distributors, there is a need for a company's public relations activities to be coordinated with other areas of marketing communications: advertising, sales promotion and personal selling. Educating, consumers and creating and maintaining interest among target audiences can lead to favourable attitudes being generated towards a company's products and services.

7. *Opinion leaders* These include trade associations and pressure groups. Public relations must attempt to understand the position of all important external groups—even if the group is opposed to them—if effective communications with them are to take place. It is far better for factual information to be the basis of discussion, not hearsay and exaggeration.

8. *Media* Public relations has a role to play in the development of relationships with the press. By aiming to achieve maximum publication and broadcasting of information, a company may create understanding in many target markets. Press relations is, therefore, seen as part of a well-organized public relations campaign.

There is a variety of techniques available to secure effective communications with the above 'publics'. These are discussed in detail by Haywood,[17] who also discusses the specific tactics to be employed. Such techniques include:

—Visits to the workplace
—Open days
—Sponsorship
—Community projects
—In-house publications
—Annual reports
—Video films
—Training courses
—Press releases

Public relations has come a long way from its origins. No longer should it be viewed as merely 'free advertising', 'propaganda' or 'publicity'. It has a key role to play in the planning and implementation of marketing communications campaigns. A 'personality' must be developed by an organization with a clear need for true and full information.

ADVERTISING

The dictionary defines 'advertise' as 'make known: to inform'. All advertisements can be seen to offer information, and can be regarded as communications about products, services and organizations. Viewed in this way, advertising's purpose can be seen as communication, but since all advertisements contain persuasive elements directed at the ultimate purpose of a sale, advertising must also provide motives. Consumers must be moved towards purchase; ideas must be communicated. These ideas might be generated by the creative people; at other times the ideas might be in the product, the service or the organization itself. A business definition of advertising would include this origination of ideas and the subsequent communication of such ideas with the purpose of motivating consumers along the path to purchase.

Advertising is concerned with the identification and presentation of desirable and believable benefits to the target audience in the most cost-effective manner. Most advertising expenditure is devoted to the promotion of brands by manufacturers. Currently, in the UK this area of advertising accounts for approximately 40 per cent of the total advertising 'spend'.

Advertising thrives on product differentiation, and an essential element here is the strategy of *branding*. Brand names are the vehicles through which manufacturers can establish an identity for their product; consumers relate to brands and form images of them. Whether the company aims for the same brand name for all its products or brands each of its products separately is a question of policy, and there are many promotional advantages available for each alternative. 'Family' brands might make the introduction of new products into the marketplace a comparatively easy task. Of course, there is always the danger that if the new product fails then damage might have been done to the whole of the product range; consumers might begin to perceive all of the company's products as being inferior. Individual branding of various products produced by a company, where different brand names are used for each, might offer more segmentation possibilities. Different varieties of a fast-moving consumer good might be individually branded and aimed at different segments of the market.

The defensive role of advertising should not be ignored, and it is often the case in situations of heavy branding that manufacturers advertise merely to preserve the *status quo*, knowing that their advertising efforts will be cancelled out by competitors.

It is not only with consumers that we find advantages of branding. Promotional effectiveness might also be increased in the case of trade advertising. Channel intermediaries might want to take on new brands from a manufacturer whose previous successes indicate that the new brand will also succeed. Indeed, in many cases where the middlemen find that they cannot refuse a new brand, the power within the distribution channel is often in the hands of manufacturers—strong, effective branding having put them in this powerful position.

In the case of private branding by retailers, not only does a manufacturer stand to increase output with possible resultant economies of scale, but also, the promotional onus is on the retailer. These possible advantages must be carefully weighted against any possible disadvantages that may accrue from distributional power having been sacrificed.

Imagery is concerned with personality. Brand image is what consumers will see and feel when the brand name is called to their attention by means of advertising. The task of the advertiser is to ensure that consumer reactions are favourable when the brand name is mentioned. Advertising is seen as being an important determinant of brand image, along with the physical characteristics of the brand, the price charged, the satisfaction it provides and the retailers who stock it.

Consumer knowledge about a brand is often quite high, particularly when the decision-making process has involved a lot of fact-finding and comparisons between alternatives—often the case when purchasing a speciality good. But such consumers do not always know so much about the company itself.

Corporate image

To establish, maintain and improve a corporate image, institutional advertising can be utilized. Corporate advertising, as practised today, is a relatively new phenomenon, but is very often misunderstood. Critics accuse it of being:

—Self-indulgent.
—A waste of money.
—Too general, since it has no specific targets.

Companies should, however, regard it as being a valuable public relations tool which may be directed at consumers, middlemen, financiers, employees, pressure groups, etc., in order to build up goodwill and confidence in the firm, create identity and publicize the firm's strengths. It is a long-term activity, requiring careful planning in order that the company is not faced with sudden crises which threaten its perceived standing. Not all events can be catered for, but corporate advertising—although it does involve the costs of buying the media time and space—is more controllable than public relations. The timing and content of the messages are no longer subject to the whims of editors, sub-editors and journalists.

Generic advertising

Advertising may be used to stimulate primary demand for a type of product or service, for example, the promotion of wool by the International Wool Secretariat and the promotion of milk deliveries by the Milk Marketing Board. The aims of generic advertising are to increase primary demand by promoting new uses, securing new users and persuading current users to buy more. A *group* of sellers often sponsor these programmes, these sellers being an association of manufacturers, service firms, agricultural producers, etc., all with a similar product to sell.

Seldom does a single producer use generic appeals in advertising, but an interesting example was the 'Put Mustard On It' campaign run by Colman's. A dominant market position and research findings indicated that the problem was one of frequency of usage, and this led Colman's to put forward this generic appeal rather than use a specific brand message. Primary demand determines the total market, with the commodity being pitched against a competing commodity (e.g., tea versus coffee) compared with brand competition, which is the basis of selective demand.

Sales effects

The ultimate purpose of all advertising is to generate sales. Direct, immediate responses are sometimes the objectives of advertising campaigns, as in the case of mail-order firms which aim for consumers to buy at once through the post. For instance, producers of records use television to generate as many sales as possible in the minimum amount of time. The objectives here are usually short-term in nature, and consumers are urged to act upon needs of which they are already aware.

To view sales as being the only valid objective of advertising is, however, too narrow a viewpoint. Modern advertising is far more complex than this. Indirect actions are also aimed for, although the ultimate purpose remains that of sales. In order that sales might eventually be brought about, the advertiser might direct the advertising campaign at other objectives, for example:

—Influencing attitudes
—Creating awareness about products and services.
—Increasing knowledge of brands and companies.
—Acting as a reminder.
—Motivating enquiries.
—Providing leads for the salesforce.

Here, advertising is often used to make buyers aware of needs they feel.

Sequential models

In order to determine *what* to say in advertisements, the advertiser must understand the advertising process in his target markets. Advertising works in a myriad of different ways: it varies according to many factors, including:

—The product of service being advertised.
—The organization doing the advertising.
—The target markets aimed at.
—The competitive environment.
—The time period in which the advertising is done.
—The media being used.
—The message content of the advertisement.
—The level of advertising being employed.

In order that specific, measurable objectives may be set for the advertising campaign, marketing must familiarize itself with current knowledge about how advertising works. Theories can only put forward general perspectives; the task for marketing is to analyse how these may be applied in the specific task under consideration.

The behavioural scientists have formulated a number of sequential models, attempting to shed light on the process consumers pass through on their way to action (purchase). In the 1920s the AIDA approach was put forward, stating that consumers pass through the successive stages of: Attention–Interest–Desire–Action. Criticism of this approach mainly centres around the fact that there is no allowance for 'build-up' and that the emphasis is far too much on the message, with little consideration of the role of the prospect.[18]

Daniel Starch[19] wrote in 1925:

An advertisement, to be successful:

(a) must be seen;
(b) must be read;
(c) must be believed;
(d) must be remembered;
(e) must be acted upon.

Again, the assumptions are focused on the advertisement itself, rather than the consumer, and there is far too much emphasis on the stimulus. There is too little analysis of the responses of the potential customer. There is also no allowance for 'build-up' in the model, with the implication being that successive exposures to the same advertisement will not interact. In practice, it is far more likely that there will be increasing (or diminishing) returns from additional advertising efforts.

In 1961 Colley[20] put forward the DAGMAR treatise—Defining Advertising Goals for Measured Advertising Results.

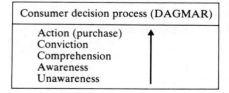

Figure 11.6 Consumer decision process (DAGMAR)

This is an attempt to identify the steps in the consumer decision-making process in order to allow for more precise definitions of advertising objectives and their measurement. Goals should be set in order to move prospects through the various levels; progression through the sequence increasing the likelihood of purchase (see Fig. 11.6). Colley drew attention to the fact that often the people concerned with implementing the advertising decisions may not have a common understanding of the purpose of the advertising effort: a point also commented on by D. Bernstein.[21]

In 1961, Lavidge and Steiner[22] proposed that consumers pass through the sequence shown in Fig. 11.7. As consumers perceive advertisements, they move along the hierarchical sequence of effects towards purchase.

Evaluation of the sequential models These sequential models have been used extensively by advertising researchers, but they are put forward not on the basis of empirical evidence but on the basis of common sense. In fact, Colley, when putting forward the DAGMAR model, stated: 'The concept of the Marketing Communications Spectrum is applied common sense.' The implications of these models are that the objectives of advertising are to get the consumer to learn something; to present persuasive messages which appeal to rational decision-making; and to turn non-buyers into buyers.

Palda,[23] in a critique of the models, draws attention to the following:

—Consumers may not always have favourable attitudes before purchasing a product.
—The models may be operationally weak because of the lack of dependable measurement devices.
—Consumers may not move through the sequence in a forward manner: they may also move backwards (from, say, 'conviction' back to 'liking' a product).

Sequential models are thus more theoretical than practical, and clearly work needs to be done in this area before actionable models can be put forward as active advertising tools.

Practical theories

Reeves[24] states: 'the consumer tends to remember just one thing from an advertisement—one strong claim, or one strong concept'. This theory of the unique selling prosposition (USP) proposes that, because of the problems of memory and credibility, if an advertisement tries to tell consumers too much it may fail. Effective advertising is secured by making a single, strong and motivating proposition to 'pull over new customers to your product'.

An alternative approach to the USP theory is that of 'brand image', often associated with David Ogilvy.[25] The claim here is that the purpose of advertising is 'to give a brand a first-class

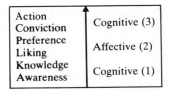

Stage (1) is concerned with knowledge and the process of thinking.

Stage (2) is concerned with attitudes, feeling or emotion.

Stage (3) is concerned with motives and the desire for action.

Figure 11.7 Hierarchy of effects

ticket through life'. This approach seems to be concerned with non-verbal methods of communication. By the evocation of moods, it is proposed that emotions will be generated which will lead to effective advertising. If consumers purchase on an emotional basis, then this approach may well prove to be effective, and rationality may not be necessary. Consider for a moment how the Martini advertisements successfully put forward the 'jet set image' and how the consumers would react if the 'voice over' finished by saying 'and only £2.89 a bottle'!

Emotion is also proposed by Martineau.[26] His opinion is that all human behaviour is a form of self-expression and that 'user images' are important. However, since people need to think of themselves as being rational, a rationalization is required by the consumer to justify his or her decision. The ideal advertisement proposed here is a combination of emotion and rationality, in line with the needs, perceptions and attitudes of the target audiences.

Joyce[27] states that the advertising/purchasing system is a rather complex system of interacting variables. The question of *what* to say is a key question for all advertisers, and it is proposed that the discussion of the various theories has shed some light on the question of how advertising works. The general perspectives provide insights. Joyce states 'the model itself is tentative' but this general conclusion seems unlikely to be overthrown'.

MANAGING ADVERTISING

Planning, implementing and controlling advertising is a complex and difficult process which often requires specialist skills. For example, media selection and scheduling is often conducted by trained specialists whose sole task is to ensure that this part of the advertising process is carried out effectively. We cannot look at all of the facets of managing advertising in great detail, but it is important to understand and appreciate the basic elements of managing the advertising effort before considering some of them in more detail.

The six basic elements of managing the advertising effort are:

1. Identification of the target audience.
2. Determination of clear, realistic and measurable objectives for advertising.
3. Determination of the advertising budget.
4. Message selection/creative platform.
5. Media selection and media scheduling.
6. Control and evaluation of advertising effectiveness.

Before considering each of these separately, it is important to stress once again that the planning and implementation of advertising, as with all the promotional elements, need to be set against the rest of the marketing mix and to be consistent with overall marketing objectives and strategy. In addition, external factors will also need to be taken into account including, for example, social and legal constraints, the choice of advertising agencies, competitors, and, of course, customers, and particularly their needs and motives. Finally, the overall role and emphasis given to advertising, together with some indication of the preliminary budget for advertising, should be set in the overall context of the promotional mix. This wider framework for advertising decisions is shown in Fig. 11.8.[28]

Identifying and analysing the target audience

> Generally, the more advertisers know about the advertising target, the more likely they are to develop an effective advertising campaign.

This quote from Dibb *et al.*[29] captures the importance of starting the management of an advertising campaign by understanding the target audience. The target audience will stem from

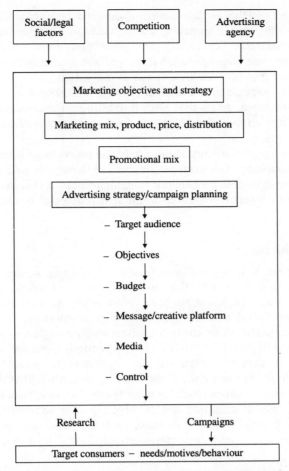

Figure 11.8   Managing advertising: a systematic approach

Source: Adapted from D. Aaker and J. G. Myers, *Advertising Management,* 2nd edn, Prentice-Hall, Englewood Cliffs, NJ, 1982, p. 30

broader marketing objectives and strategies—particularly, of course, segmentation strategies. Details of the target audience should include not only demographic data, e.g. age, sex, etc., but also location, ACORN group and so on.

It is not sufficient simply to *delineate* target audiences; the marketing communicator must also *understand* the target audience. There are many pertinent factors here, but, to take an example, in planning effective marketing communications the marketer needs to understand the buying decision process, i.e. how customers buy. The importance, in more general terms, of understanding this process was discussed in Chapter 3. In the context of communications decisions, the stage at which the target audience is in the buying decision process begins to provide important information for planning communications. For example, in the case of a new product, communications will have to stimulate the start of the buying process by encouraging problem or need recognition. Alternatively, if the target audience includes mainly those who are already regular purchasers of the product in question, our marketing communications might be aimed at minimizing post-purchase dissonance.

In addition to understanding how the target market buys and the stage of the buying process it has reached, it is also important to understand who is involved in the purchase process. For example, in Chapter 3 we saw that we can usefully distinguish between different roles in the buying process. So if, for example, we are launching a new brand of breakfast cereal, it is important to distinguish between 'influencers', 'deciders', 'purchasers' and 'users'. Of course, all of these roles might be embodied in the one target group, but, as we have seen in both consumer and industrial markets, these roles may also be filled by a range of individuals.

Sometimes it is also important to establish existing preferences, attitudes and so on of our target audience. For example, given that with marketing communications we are very often concerned with image, it might be important to establish our target audience's current image of the company and/or its products.

The analysis of the target audience should help the marketing communicator to assess the information needs of customers. For example, analysis of the search, and alternative stages of the buying process, will help to establish where our target market looks for information, the degree of reliance on word-of-mouth versus marketer-dominated sources of information, and the type of information sought.

Setting advertising objectives

Once we have determined the target audience for our advertising, we need to determine what we intend our advertising to achieve with that audience. In broad terms, it might be intended to inform, persuade or remind. While this might be useful in beginning to delineate the reasons and role of advertising in the overall marketing and communications mix, these broad classifications are not a sufficient guide to the next steps in the advertising management and campaign planning process. Ideally, we need to prescribe specific communications goals for advertising. Needless to say, this is where our earlier models of the sequences in buyer behaviour related to communications are useful. For example, Colley's earlier described DAGMAR model translates into some 52 possible communication goals for advertising. Notwithstanding the controversy over these models, they are helpful in setting specific objectives for advertising couched in terms of objectives for communications designed to move customers through the buying stages. These objectives should, whenever possible, be defined in quantitative terms and specify a time scale.

Determining advertising budgets

Earlier we briefly discussed some of the approaches to determining the overall budget for marketing communications. Having gone through the process of broadly determining the thrust or emphasis of promotional strategy between the different promotional tools, we should have at least a preliminary idea as to how much of the total budget will be allocated to advertising. However, at this stage, and taking into account our first two steps of advertising management, we now need to refine this process to arrive at a precise budget for advertising. In fact, the advertising budget can be arrived at on the same variety of bases as the overall budget for communications; i.e., it can be based on percentages of sales and/or profits, on competitors' spend, or on the objective and task method. Once again, the only justifiable method is the objective and task approach. Indeed, this is a distinct advantage if setting clear and quantified communications objectives for advertising in the preceding stage.

Deciding on the message/creative platform

The creative element of advertising is an area that can have the greatest impact on the success or failure of an advertising campaign. Unfortunately, it is also an area that, despite much research, generates considerable controversy as to what makes a successful creative advertisement.

The creative plan is normally based upon research that provides answers about:

1. The key unique features of the brand.
2. The criteria used by consumers in evaluating brands.
3. The brand image in relation to competition.

This platform for the creative plan should feature the basic promise to consumers and should provide substantiation first.

There are three essential steps in developing a creative programme. The first is to determine the content of the message. The advertising content serves the advertiser by carrying out the strategy and objectives set for the product. It serves the consumer by providing useful information about solving problems. Second, in addition to deciding what is to be said, the programme must consider how it is to be said. Finally, the creative programme must determine how the advertising will be produced (i.e. the creative execution).

The advertiser also faces numerous difficult choices in weighing up the promise or appeal. It has been suggested that advertisers should use rational appeals when their prospects face utilitarian problems and emotional appeals when problems are social or psychological! Research evidence indicates that 'fear appeals' raise consumer defences if the problem is a vital or unavoidable one, but they may be effective with less important problems.

Determining media selection and scheduling

This element of advertising management should be prepared concurrently with the budget decision. A wide variety of media vehicles are available to the advertiser, especially in the developed economies. Media planning, however, is made easier by adherence to the preceding steps in our advertising management programme. Overall marketing strategy, advertising objectives, budgets and creative strategy all serve to delineate and point to the required media strategy. Above all, media strategy is determined by the target audience.

This extremely important element of managing advertising is considered in more detail later in this chapter.

Evaluating and controlling advertising

Given the importance and expense of advertising, it is vital to assess how effective it is. Again, this is where the importance of the previous stage of setting clear and quantified objectives comes in. You will recall that when we discussed objectives for communication it was suggested that, although sales and profits may be the ultimate reasons for advertising (at least in the profit-making organization), there are distinct difficulties in relating these to advertising. Furthermore, because of this, it was suggested that advertising objectives be set in communications terms, e.g. increasing recognition and brand awareness. It is also important to recognize that advertising, and particularly the creative/copy content of advertising, must be evaluated before actually implementing the campaign as well as after the campaign. In the next part of this chapter we give an overview of the range of research techniques available for both pre-testing and post-testing advertisements. Briefly, though, the overall approach to evaluating and controlling advertising is set out below.

The evaluation programme begins by defining the elements and decisions to be evaluated, including elements from the budget programme, the media programme and the creative programme. Next, an *effectiveness evaluation procedure* is designed for each element. This must include specification of a standard as a base for comparison; when actual performance is measured it will be compared with the standard to determine whether or not performance is satisfactory.

Table 11.1 Marketing communications research

Turnover of research agency	Advertising research (%)	Sales promotion research (%)	Other marketing research (%)
£500 000+	$9\frac{1}{2}$	$1\frac{1}{2}$	89
£150 000–499 000	$16\frac{1}{2}$	$1\frac{1}{2}$	82
Under £150 000	23	3	74
Total average	13	2	85

Based on 28 UK agencies, including 18 of the 23 major UK research companies represented in the Association of Market Survey Organizations (AMSO)

For each programme element to be evaluated, the evaluation programme should specify the measurement technique to be used. For example, the *media audience measurement* evaluates the effectiveness of media programmes, the *recognition and recall tests* measure the effectiveness of individual advertisements, and techniques such as *consumer and retail audits* measure the effectiveness of overall campaigns.

Clearly, evaluating advertising requires research. We now turn our attention to some of the techniques of advertising research.

ADVERTISING RESEARCH

Claims that advertising efforts have been successful must often be viewed with a good deal of uncertainty. There are many variables over which the advertiser cannot hope to have complete control (e.g. competitors' actions, economic factors and prices), all of which may affect the advertising–sales relationship. The sequential models of the advertising process are used extensively in practice as a means to establish objectives for the measurement of advertising success or failure.

The amount of marketing communications research carried out is a frequent source of criticism—including the level of advertising research (see Table 11.1). It appears that research into advertising and other marketing communication efforts is far less extensive than research into other areas of marketing. P. Hodgson[30] surveyed the types of marketing research undertaken in the UK, and discovered that research into marketing communications was only a minor part of the total.

One reason often given to explain the lack of advertising research activity is the amount of confidence that marketing managers have in the available techniques.

Advertising research techniques

Although marketing research has already been covered in Chapter 5, this discussion centres more specifically upon research into advertising. A fuller discussion of this subject is also provided by Chisnall.[31] Generally, the tools of advertising research are referred to as 'pre-measurement' or 'pre-testing' and 'post-measurement' or 'post-testing'. In other words, the probable effectiveness of advertising may be assessed before the campaign is implemented, and evaluation of an advertising effort, once it has been run, may also take place. The measurements provided by both types of advertising research are potentially of immense value to advertising management. Indications of the ability of advertising to communicate messages effectively to target audiences will enable operational principles and guidelines to be developed.

Pre-testing advertisements

Advertising management may feel that an advertisement appears to be promising, but it is vital that the likely reactions of the potential buyers are first assessed. Advertisers must decide what responses will constitute effectiveness in line with pre-stated objectives, and then set out to see how likely it is that consumers will react accordingly to proposed advertisements. The effectiveness of the creative elements of individual advertisements—headlines, body copy, illustrations, slogans, etc.—may be tested, or the entire advertisement may be tested.

The major techniques employed in pre-testing are as follows.

1. *Checklists* This is a form of internal assessment by the advertiser, who picks the elements that he or she considers should be in an advertisement, to enable the systematic review of proposed advertisements to take place, point by point, against this list. The weakness of this approach is that a company is dependent upon the validity of the points that are contained in the list, and some important ones may also be omitted or overlooked when the checklist is compiled.
2. *Consumer juries* A sample of prospects independently visited or contacted by mail, or interviewed on a group basis, is used to test advertisements. Simple or complex responses from jury members are sought in order to gain insights into how well an audience has understood an advertisement just seen or heard by them. The major weakness of this technique is that assessment is on the basis of what people *say*, and this may not always reflect their behaviour in the market.
3. *Enquiry tests*: Alternative advertisements, published independently or together on a split-run basis (where different advertisements appear in the same issue of a magazine), are coded and the levels of enquiries generated are measured. In order to elicit enquiries, the advertiser must offer some reason for the audience to reply (e.g., a free sample of the product or an information brochure). The major weakness of this technique is that the advertiser has to assess the quality of the enquiry (some people write in just to receive mail!) and to assess further how effective the advertisement would be in communicating messages of a less direct nature (when offers are not made).
4. *Laboratory measurement devices* Sample consumers are placed in a controlled setting and shown proposed advertisements, and their physical responses are then measured. Sweat gland activity is measured by means of the psycho-galvonometer; pupil dilation can be recorded by a perceptoscope; images are flashed on a screen for a fraction of a second by the tachistoscope; the movement of an individual's eyes across the printed page is traced by an eye movement camera. These devices have the advantage of being apparently objective and conceptually simple, and distortion is limited since involuntary responses are measured (except in the case of the tachistoscope). Major shortcomings are that the laboratory setting may affect responses, and the relative sales effectiveness is not being measured.
5. *Experimentation* This is where representative areas are chosen to test advertising ideas. Different advertisements may be evaluated in this way, by publishing them in different parts of the market, and sales data obtained to enable measurement to take place.

There are many managerial problems in conducting these experiments. These are summarized under three main headings:

—The setting of valid objectives.
—The control aspects when designing and running the test.
—The interpretation of the data.

Post-testing advertisements

1. *Enquiry tests* These may be used to post-evaluate advertising efforts, when offers are made to which the potential buyer can be expected to reply. In the case of mail-order selling, the yardstick used to measure the level of effectiveness may consist of sales generated as well as enquiries for further information.

   By varying the advertisements used over time, and by maintaining detailed records, the advertiser is able to discover significant variations which can then be attributed to the differences in the advertisements.

2. *Recall/recognition tests* These are attempts to measure the number of people who have actually read a particular advertisement. The readership levels of various magazines are measured on a regular basis by the Starch Message Report Service, whereby readers 'recognize' advertisements or parts of them. A more rigorous version of recall testing does not involve showing advertisements to respondents, and advertisements must be recalled from memory (e.g. Gallup and Robinson's Impact Service).

   Recall testing may also involve 'dummy' magazines, where the respondent has advertisements in a scrapbook left for a few days. He or she is then test by being asked questions about the various advertisements contained in the portfolio.

   Recognition studies may be subject to biased or distorted responses by consumers, in that sample members may tend to exaggerate their actual readership. Recall tests attempt to control this by more vigorous screening of sample members and by counting only recall. A major criticism is that simple ideas and facts are favoured. The communication of complex ideas—which may be necessary for technical or novel products—may score low in recall tests.

3. *Consumer audits* A random group of consumers are asked if they have bought a product, how often they have bought it and what they have on hand—prior to the advertising being launched. Re-interviewing of these consumers then takes place after the advertising has been conducted in order to assess the percentage increase or decrease in the sales of the advertiser's product.

4. *Retail audits*: These are similar to consumer audits except that the retailer's stocks are measured before and after the advertising. The major problems with measuring the sales effects of advertising in these ways is that it is difficult to conclude that advertising has been responsible for the sales.

The pre-testing and post-testing of individual advertisements in the above ways can provide some insight into the overall effectiveness of advertising, but one is seldom able to measure all of its effects. At times, because the results of advertising may not happen immediately, it is difficult to relate the response to a particular stimulus. A lot depends on what other selling efforts are employed by the company and its competitors, how fast the turnover of the product is and how important advertising is to the sale of the product. Specific, measurable goals must be clearly defined in line with the DAGMAR treatise.

MEDIA SELECTION

In using media, the objective of management is to plan a media schedule which consists of the combination of media, and media vehicles, which most efficiently reach the target audience while still meeting various constraints (e.g. creative and budget). The first task for marketing is to identify and define the prospects (i.e. buyers and potential buyers of the product or service). In this way, various media alternatives will be seen to have more potential than others and the range of choice will become narrower. For example, if the campaign is to be directed to a group of potential female buyers, then magazines that are read predominantly by males are clearly ruled out.

More specific requirements of the media programme may be obtained by analysing the following:

1. *Budget constraints* The aim should be for audience requirements to be fulfilled in the most cost-effective manner. The usual measure used here is 'cost per thousand', provided by the formula:

$$\frac{\text{Cost of the insertion of the advertisement}}{\text{Number of prospects}} \times 1000$$

$$\text{e.g.,} \frac{\text{£30 000 for TV spot}}{\text{15 million audience}} \times 1000 = \text{£2 to reach every 1000 viewers}$$

The major weaknesses of this approach are:

—It assumes that *all* of the audience are prospects.
—It makes no allowances for effectiveness; i.e., to evaluate on a purely cost basis overlooks the fact that an alternative medium that has a more expensive 'cost per 1000' could be far more effective in getting the message across.

2. *Creative constraints* The media must also comply with creative requirements, and various messages may lend themselves to words/pictures, colour/black-and-white, prestigious/dominating medium, etc. The media planner must analyse these features of the various media alternative closely.

   Each of the various mass media has its attributes and shortcomings, as shown in Table 11.2.

3. *'Reach' v. 'frequency'* It must be decided whether the message should be distributed very widely among the prospects (termed 'reach') or concentrated on a smaller number of prospects ('frequency'). Where all potential buyers are estimated to be of equal value, it may be better for the advertiser to reach as many of them as possible; in cases where there are better prospects (heavier users of the product, for example) it may be better to build up frequency by providing them with many opportunities to see (OTS).

4. *Other constraints* These may be important depending upon the product, its strategy and objectives. For example, there may be a need for the quick production and insertion of advertisements in dynamic markets.

Matching prospects with media

A profile of the prospects should already have been obtained. The remaining alternatives still under consideration should now be profiled in more detail. The audience characteristics (the total size of audiences; the demographic, geographical and psychographic details of the audience); the production requirements of the medium/vehicle; the size of insertions and potential effects on salesforce and trade must now be analysed.

A decision must also be taken on the number of media to be used. Many larger advertisers do use a single medium, and television is used particularly because it is so dominating. In cases where the advertiser dominates a medium relative to competitors, it may be expected that the audience is more familiar with the advertiser's brand and preference may result. There are, however, many

Table 11.2 Media comparisons for advertisers

Media	Advantages/disadvantages
Television	Large audiences; demonstration of product in use (sound and vision); compulsiveness; viewed at home in a relaxed manner. Commercial breaks may be seen as irritating; a transient medium.
Cinema	Has many of the above advantages, but problem is the size of the audiences, which do, however, still retain segmentation possibilities.
Newspapers	Great flexibility in terms of timing—booked at short notice; illustrations can be used; regularly purchased by large numbers of people. Do have short life spans; may be difficult to get people to notice the advertising content.
Magazines	Have 'editorial' facilities with which to integrate advertising content; advertisements are expected by readers; magazines have long life spans; read at leisure; high 'readership, compared with circulation May have 'desert' areas which are seldom noted by readers, e.g., front and back pages.
Commercial radio	May be perceived as an 'intimate companion'; use of sound; segmentation possibilities. Has disadvantages of small audience size; transient medium—how well are the messages perceived or retained?
Outdoor and transportation	Many people have an OTS (opportunity to see)—most of the population spend some time outdoors; relatively low costs; short- and long-term possibilities; national campaigns are possible; segmentation possibilities May be subject to effects of the weather; how eye-catching and noticeable are they? Sites are subject to environmental criticism.
Newspaper supplements	Offer vast circulations at relatively low cost; opportunity to expose message at concentrated times; Sundays are a day of rest and family gatherings. Not passed around as much as magazines; have 'desert' areas.

advertisers who spread their budgets among the media. The potential advantages of this strategy are:

—Synergism—the '2+2 = 5' idea of media working in combination to product a greater output than the sum of the individual parts. Primary media may be chosen by the advertiser, with supportive media being used to back these up.
—Coverage may be extended beyond what could be achieved via a single medium.
—Greater segmentation capabilities—different messages attracting different market segments through different media.

Timing of campaigns

The two decisions to be taken now are:

1. The duration of the media schedule (i.e., when the campaign is to start and when it is to stop). Concentration should be placed when prospects feel most need for the product, or when they feel the particular need that is the key part of the message.
2. The spread of activity over this time period.

Advertisers may choose between spreading the messages fairly evenly over the time period, and alternating between heavy and light periods of activity within the time period (see Fig. 11.9).

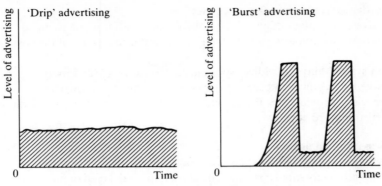

Figure 11.9 Advertising expenditure strategies

The media schedule

The media requirements, and the reasoning that leads to the selection of final media choices, should now be stated in full. This has meant that the advertiser has reached this stage by a gradual process of elimination, and the listing of the purchases to be made. Such purchases include: the size/length of insertion; insertion dates and times; the anticipated costs; and the projected reach. Frequency and cost efficiency of the insertions provide the benchmark against which actual performance may be compared.

ADVERTISING AGENCIES

Most advertisers use the services of an advertising agency for major parts of their advertising programmes. The selection of the agency is a key decision area, since the success of the advertising depends to a large extent upon the contribution of these specialists. The 'full service' agency offers a wide range of services—creative, media planning, marketing research; sales promotions and public relations; account planning and customer contact. It should be noted that a client may use such an agency over some or all of this wide range. Perhaps because of a feeling that the temptation exists to use more services than originally anticipated, or because of a feeling that the 'specialists' are better, there has been a growth of specialist 'hot shops'. These media and creative specialists offer their specialism and nothing more.

Using an agency

The first question to be asked is: 'Do we need to use an agency at all?' A major consideration here is the likely costs of the deal—in financial terms, agencies derive most of their incomes from the *commission system*. This tripartite arrangement is the subject of much criticism (i.e., who is the agency working for?) but it continues, despite various threats that it should be modified.

Under this system, agencies pay the media owner for mass media time/space purchases, minus a commission, usually in the 10–15 per cent range, and then collect the full amount from the client. In the UK income from commission currently accounts for 70 per cent of all advertising agency incomes. In addition, 'service fees' are charged by advertising agencies and account for the remaining 30 per cent of income.

Advantages for the advertiser in using an agency

1. Administrative economies—high salaries of full-time staff may be avoided.
2. Provision of monthly invoices—no 'hidden' costs; better recording of the costs and monitoring of budgets.
3. Commission system may 'subsidize' specialized services provided by the agency.
4. Agencies have more power in cases of disputes with the media owners.
5. Specialist services provided by the agency—particularly creative and media expertise—may make advertising more effective.

Disadvantages in using an agency

1. Service fees may make the work expensive—particularly if a lot of creative work is undertaken.
2. If the client is a relatively small customer, its work may be delayed or handled by agency juniors.
3. Possible security leaks—agency personnel, particularly account executives (the agency contact men) must work very closely with and within the client's organization.

Advantages to the media owner

1. Contact with fewer people—costs reduced and operations simplified.
2. Agency acts as a 'salesforce', getting orders for the media owner.
3. Agencies act as a 'principal' in law; i.e., the media owner collects from the agencies, who in turn stand any bad debts from clients.
4. Agencies possess specialist knowledge which may be of use to the media owner in improving the quality of reproduction of the advertisement and other content of the media.
5. The specialist skills provided by agencies may improve the effectiveness of advertising, and indirectly help to bring in more clients and advertising revenue.

Client/agency relations

Corkindale and Kennedy[32] put forward the following recommendations:

—Client and agency should agree a written advertising brief specifically on advertising objectives.
—Someone in the company must be responsible for coordinating the activities undertaken in the agency.
—Someone in the company must be able to justify the work being done in the agency.

The client must develop selection criteria once it has decided to use an advertising agency. The initial screening process will narrow down the range of alternatives, and hopefully lead to a more effective relationship. Factors to be taken account of here are:

—Size of proposed agency.
—Specialist skills offered by the agency.
—Range of services to be used.
—Skills of existing marketing/advertising personnel in the company.
—Agencies used by competitors.
—'Track record' of agencies.
—Location of agencies.
—The need for establishing *rapport*, and the likelihood of a long-term working relationship.

CONCLUSIONS

This chapter has shown the place of communications in the marketing mix. Communication strategies have been examined. Sales promotion (below-the-line) was discussed, as was the role of public relations. This was followed by an explanation of the purpose of advertising from the viewpoint of a company marketing its products or services. It further explored brand image and corporate image. Generic advertising was then discussed and the potential effect of advertising was summarized in terms of its effect on sales.

Theoretical models of advertising were considered and their usefulness assessed, followed by a practical assessment of advertising effectiveness through the medium of advertising research.

The selection of agencies and media is an important consideration in communication strategy, and criteria surrounding such selection were considered.

Chapter 12 considers the more personal elements of promotion in the form of selling and sales management.

APPLICATION QUESTIONS

1. With examples of your choice, show the usefulness of the following:
   (a) Brand advertising.
   (b) Corporate advertising.
   (c) Generic advertising.
2. Outline some of the major sales promotion tools available to the marketer.
3. Which 'publics' might a public relations campaign be aimed at?
4. Why are the sequential models of the advertising process so called? What insights may be gained by studying these?
5. Give three examples of each of the following:
   (a) Advertisements using the USP.
   (b) Advertisements based on 'imagery'.
   (c) Advertisements using rationality as the main motivator.
6. To what extent do you believe that below-the-line promotions are particularly useful in encouraging impulse purchases?
7. What do you understand by the terms 'internal' and 'external publics' in the context of public relations?

REFERENCES

1. H. Lasswell, in *Communcation of Ideas*, L. Bryson (ed.), Institute for Religious and Social Studies, 1975.
2. D. Ogilvy, *Confessions of an Advertising Man*, Atheneum, New York, 1963.
3. J. Frye, *Introduction to the Marketing Systems*, Stanford University Press, Stanford, CA, 1973.
4. L. Festinger, *A Theory of Cognitive Dissonance*, Row, Peterson & Co., Evanston, IL, 1957.
5. G. Wills, How Good or Bad are Your Marketing Communications? MEG Conference, 1976.
6. S. Majaro, 'Advertising by objectives', *Management Today,* January 1970.
7. S. H. Britt, *Marketing Management and Administrative Action*, McGraw-Hill, London, 1973.
8. A. Roberts, *Selling Advertising Budgets*, Advertising Association, London, 1986.
9. M. Christopher, *Marketing Below-the-Line*, George Allen & Unwin, London, 1969.
10. J. F. Engel, H. G. Wales and M. R. Warshaw, *Promotional Strategy,* R. D. Irwin, Homewood, IL, 1975.
11. W. Schlackman, *Some Psychological Aspects of Dealing*. MRS Papers, 1964.
12. P. Spillard, *Sales Promotion—Its Place in Marketing Strategy*, Business Publications, Plano, TX, 1966.
13. A. Morgan, *A Guide to Consumer Promotions*, Ogilvy and Mather, 1980.
14. P. Doyle and J. Saunders, 'The lead effect of marketing decisions', *Journal of Marketing*, February 1985, pp. 54–65.
15. Institute of Public Relations London, Public Relations Definition, 1986.
16. F. Jenkins, *Public Relations*, 2nd edn, International Ideas, Philadelphia, PA, 1983, pp. 1–11.
17. R. Haywood, *All about PR*, McGraw-Hill, London, 1984, pp. 141–244.
18. D. Corkindale and S. H. Kennedy, *Process of Advertising,* MCB Publications, Bradford, 1978.

19. D. Starch, *Principles of Advertising,* McGraw-Hill, New York, 1925.
20. R. H. Colley, *Defining Advertising Goals for Measured Advertising Results*, Association of National Advertisers, New York, 1961 and 1983.
21. D. Bernstein, 'Advertising: inexact science—bastard art', *Business Graduate*, Summer 1975.
22. R. T. Lavidge and G. A. Steiner, 'A model for predictive measurement of advertising effectiveness', *Journal of Marketing*, October 1962.
23. K. S. Palda, 'The hypothesis of a hierarchy of effects—a partial evaluation', *Journal of Marketing Research*, 3 (1), February 1966.
24. R. Reeves, *Reality of Advertising*, A. A. Knopf, New York, 1961.
25. Ogilvy, op. cit.
26. P. Martineau, *Reality in Advertising*, McGraw-Hill, London, 1961.
27. T. Joyce, 'What do we know about how advertising works', *Advertising Age*, 1967.
28. D. Aaker and J. G. Myers, *Advertising Management*, 2nd edn, Prentice-Hall, Englewood Cliffs, NJ, 1982, p. 30.
29. S. Dibb, with L. Simkin, W. M. Pride and O. C. Ferrell, *Marketing Concepts and Strategies*, Houghton Mifflin, Boston, Mass., 1991, p. 423.
30. P. Hodgson, 'What happened to sales promotion research?' *Marketing*, April 1977, pp. 71–4.
31. P. Chisnall, *Marketing Research*, McGraw-Hill, London, 1986, pp. 204–40.
32. Corkindale and Kennedy, op. cit.

SELLING AND SALES MANAGEMENT

INTRODUCTION

Personal selling is one element in a company's marketing mix. It is in fact classed within the 'promotion' (or communications) element of the '4 Ps', but it warrants a separate treatment in its own right. In industrial marketing, personal selling is likely to be the main communications tool, with expenditure in this area very much higher than for non-personal communications such as advertising or public relations. Highly technical products require a talk to prospective customers to put across their merits and to answer questions about their use. Consumer goods companies also use salespersons, primarily to sell into the trade, but in this area expenditure is likely to be higher for advertising than personal selling.

Personal selling must, therefore, be integrated with the whole marketing programme and should not be seen as a distinct activity divorced from the other elements of the communications and marketing mixes. Selling and sales management within a marketing-oriented firm are concerned with the analysis of customers' needs and wants and, through the company's total marketing efforts, with the provision of benefits to satisfy these needs and wants. Although the selling process might seem to be simple at first sight, a body of theory surrounds the subject; this has been documented by Saunders et al.[1]

SELLING AND MARKETING

Marketing is a strategic function and has a number of tactical activities, of which selling is one. Each has its part to play, but it is important that the various activities be coordinated so that the marketing policy can be carried through effectively. There is often controversy over which of the tactical activities is the most important. Such a controversy is generally meaningless, because the relative importance will vary between industries and between companies within a single industry. Selling generally, but not always, entails a personal meeting between seller and buyer. For a sale to be made successfully, it is usually necessary for the product to be of a satisfactory quality (i.e. value for money), to be available when required, to be packaged adequately, and to be competitive. It is the salesperson's task to present this information persuasively to the customers. When there is no salesforce, the information may have to be presented by means of a catalogue or brochure.

Relationship with marketing research

The function of marketing research is that of fact-finding. From the facts obtained, policies may be changed and products amended. Much of the information obtained from marketing research is fed to the sales department and can be used by the salesforce to counter competition. On other occasions, the salesforce can be used to provide information for the marketing research department. In this case, however, the kind of information that is obtained is usually of a limited nature. Salespeople do not make good researchers. It is common practice in most companies that use marketing research for the findings to be passed to the sales department for comment and sometimes for verification.

The marketing research department should never be thought of as *reporting on* the salesforce, but rather should be considered as a source of information that can be put to good use.

Relationship with other elements of the promotional programme

The relationship between the salesforce and other aspects of promotion should be a cooperative one. The sales department can be helped by *and* can help the advertising manager. Typical examples are where the salesforce obtains the agreement of customers either to donate window space for displays or to distribute display material themselves. Similarly, the promotional department helps the salesforce by 'softening up' customers through the pressure of advertising. Everyone is to some extent susceptible to advertising.

Both personal selling and various kind of publicity activity such as advertising are forms of marketing communications. All forms of marketing communications are interrelated, and all elements in the organization's marketing communications mix have a specific part to play in the overall scheme of things. Non-personal communications, in the form of advertising, public relations and sales promotion, should 'push' the customer, previously ignorant of the firm's products, towards them. It is then the role of personal selling to capitalize on the preceding communications and to actually close the sale. Hence, personal selling and other forms of publicity should all contribute to an overall marketing communications strategy.

THE SELLING PROCESS

Although no sales interview follows a rigid pattern, it is useful to distinguish seven elements in the sales process:

1. The opening
2. Need identification and stimulation
3. The presentation
4. Dealing with objections
5. Negotiation
6. Closing the sale
7. The follow-up

The fragmentation of the selling process into these phases is helpful when training salespeople, since development of skills within each area can be worked upon until proficiency is achieved.

The opening

Experienced salespeople know the importance of initial impressions. Consequently, they pay great attention to their appearance, manner and opening remarks. Buyers expect salespeople to be businesslike in their personal appearance and behaviour. Untidy hair and unbuttoned shirts with loose ties can create a lack of confidence in a salesman. Further, the salesperson who does not respect the fact that the buyer is likely to be a busy person, with many demands on his or her time, may cause irritation on the part of the prospective buyer.

Opening remarks are important since they set the tone for the rest of the sales interview. Normally they should be business-related since this is the purpose of the visit; they should show the buyer that the salesperson is not about to waste time. Where the buyer is well known to the salesperson and where, by his or her own remarks, the buyer indices a willingness to talk about a more social matter, the salesperson will obviously follow. This can generate close *rapport* with the buyers; but the salesperson must be aware of the reason for being there, and not be excessively diverted from talking business.

Need identification and stimulation

Customers buy products to meet needs and solve problems. Consequently, key factors in sales success are the identification of customer needs and problems, and in certain circumstances the recognition of a need or problem on the part of the buyer.

This 'needs analysis' approach suggests that early in the sales process the salesperson should adopt a question-and-listen posture. In order to encourage the buyer to discuss his or her problems and needs, salespeople tend to use 'open' rather than 'closed' questions. An open question is one that requires more than a one-word or one-phrase answer.

—'Why do you believe that a computer system is inappropriate for your business?'
—'What were the main reasons for buying the XYZ photocopier?'

A closed question, on the other hand, invites a one-word or one-phrase answer. These can be used to obtain purely factual information, but excessive use can hinder *rapport* and lead to an abrupt type of conversation which lacks flow. Examples of closed questions are:

—'Would you tell me the name of the equipment you currently use?'
—'Does your company manufacture 1000 cc marine engines?'

Salespeople should avoid the temptation of making a sales presentation without finding out the needs of their customers. It is all too easy to start a presentation in the same rigid way, perhaps by highlighting the current bargain of the week, without first enquiring about the customer's needs.

Need and problem stimulation are necessary when a prospect is happy with the *status quo* and does not recognize that the purchase of the salesperson's product or service could, for example, improve productivity, lower costs, or give greater financial security. In these cases, the sales task may involve the process of 'disturbing', whereby the salesperson *disturbs* the buyer's perception of life by showing, for example, how present methods are inefficient, or costly, or how present insurance cover is inadequate.

The presentation

The advantages conferred by carrying out a 'needs analysis' are realized during the presentation. The salesperson knows which product or brand, from the range of products or brands he or she is selling, best fits the customer's requirements, and is also aware of which benefits to stress.

The key to this task is to recognize that buyers purchase benefits and are only interested in product features inasmuch as they provide the benefits that the customer is looking for. Training programmes and personal preparation of salespeople should pay particular attention to deriving the customer benefits their products bestow.

Benefits should be analysed at two levels: those benefits that can be obtained by purchase of a particular type of product, and those that can be obtained by purchasing that product from a particular supplier. For example, automatic washing machine salespeople need to consider the benefits of an automatic washing machine compared with a twin-tub, as well as the benefits that their company's automatic washing machines have over competitors' models. This proffers maximum flexibility for the salesperson in meeting various sales situations.

Dealing with objections

Objections should not always be viewed with dismay by salespeople. Many objections are simply expressions of interest by the buyer. What the buyer is asking for is further information because he or she is interested in what the salesperson is saying. The problem is that he or she is not, as yet, convinced. Objections highlight the issues that are important to the buyer.

An example will illustrate these points. Suppose an industrial salesperson working for an adhesives manufacturer is faced with the following objection: 'Why should I buy your new adhesive gun when my present method of applying adhesive—direct from the tube—is perfectly satisfactory?' This type of objection is clearly an expression of a desire for additional information. The salesperson's task is to provide it in a manner that does not antagonize the buyer and, yet, is convincing. It is a fact of human personality that the argument which is supported by the greater weight of evidence does not always win the day; people do not like to be proved wrong. The very act of changing a supplier may be resisted because it may imply criticism of a past decision on the part of the buyer. For a salesperson to disregard the emotional aspects of dealing with objections is to court disaster. The situation to be avoided is where the buyer 'digs his heels in' on principle, because of the attitude of the salesperson.

The effective approach for dealing with objections involves two courses of action: the preparation of convincing answers, and the development of a range of techniques for answering objections in a manner which permits the acceptance of these answers without loss of face on the part of the buyer. Two commonly used methods for dealing with objections are the 'agree and counter' and the 'forestalling' techniques.

Agree and counter This approach maintains the respect the salesperson shows to the buyer. The salesperson first agrees that what the buyer is saying is sensible and reasonable, before putting forward an alternative point of view. It takes the edge off the objection and creates a climate of agreement rather than conflict. For example:

Buyer: The problem with your tractor is that it costs more than your competition.
Salesperson: Yes, the initial cost of the tractor is a little higher than competitors' models, but I should like to show you how, over the lifetime of the machine, ours works out to be far more economical.

Forestall the objection Perhaps buyers are continually raising the objection that the salesperson is working for one of the smallest companies in the industry. One way of dealing with this objection is to forestall, by raising the objection as part of the sales presentation. This allows it to be dealt with effectively by changing the objection into a benefit. Thus, the salesperson may say, 'My company is smaller than most in the industry which means that we respond more quickly to our customers' needs and try that bit harder to make sure our customers are happy.'

Negotiation

Many salespeople are given some discretion regarding the terms of the sale. They may negotiate price, credit terms, trade-in values and delivery times. It is a fact of much commercial life that the profit realized from a transaction will be dependent upon the outcome of negotiations. Success in negotiating derives from two factors: preparation, and the application of negotiating skills.

Preparation Before the parties to the negotiation meet, each should make careful preparations. This involves four factors: (1) assessment of the balance of power; (2) determination of objectives; (3) concession analysis; and (4) proposal analysis.

A seller's position will be strengthened if the buyer has very few options available to him or her, if the salesperson's products offer better solutions to the buyer's problems than the competition, and if the problem is of high importance and visibility to the buying organization. The salesperson should assess his or her position so that objectives can be set and the level of concessions to be given can be planned.

When setting objectives it is useful to consider two types: 'must have' and 'would like'. 'Must have' objectives are the minimum requirements of the deal, e.g. the lowest price at which a seller is willing to trade. 'Would like' objectives are the maximum a negotiator can realistically achieve. They define the opening positions of buyers and sellers.

Concessions analysis is vital to negotiating success as it allows calm consideration at what can be traded. A skilful negotiator will attempt to trade concession for concession so that ultimately an agreement which satisfies both parties is reached.

Proposal analysis involves determining the likely demands of the buyer, and the reactions to them. By this kind of anticipation, the seller can plan the kinds of counter-proposals he or she wishes to make, and thus avoid making mistakes in the heat of the negotiating battle.

Application at negotiating skills Two basic principles of negotiation are: to start high but be realistic, and to trade concession for concession. Making the opening stance high has two benefits. First, the buyer might agree to it. Second, it provides room for negotiation if he or she does not agree. Indeed, a buyer may have become accustomed to concessions from the seller in return for purchasing. Trading concession for concession can be achieved by means of the 'if . . . then' technique.[2] For example, the seller might say, 'If you are willing to collect these goods at our premises, then I am prepared to reduce the price by £10.' This is a valuable tool at the disposal of the negotiator since it promotes movement towards agreement and yet ensures that proposals to give the buyer something are matched by proposals for a concession in return.

Closing the sale

Some salespeople are reluctant to close the sale because they fear rejection. Yet in many sales situations failure to close will mean the order being placed with a competitor. In other situations, often industrial, it is inappropriate to attempt to close the sale since the buying process is lengthy. However, when the time has come for the close to be made there are a number of techniques available. Two methods are: the summary close, and the concession close.

Summarize and then ask for order This technique allows the salesperson to remind the buyer of the main points in the sales argument in a manner which implies that the moment for decision has come and that buying is the natural extension of the proceedings.

> Well, Mr Smith, we have agreed that the ZDXL4 model meets your requirements of low noise, high productivity and driver comfort at a cost that you can afford. May I go ahead and place an order for this model?

The concession close This involves keeping one concession in reserve to use as the final push towards agreement: 'If you are willing to place an order now, I'm willing to offer an extra $2\frac{1}{2}$ per cent discount.'

Follow up

Immediately after closing the sale, the salesperson should 'tie up' any loose ends (e.g. delivery times). In addition, the salesperson should make an appointment for a follow-up call after the initial order has been received to make sure that everything is going according to plan and to deal with any unexpected problems.

Many products also require the provision of after-sales service. Some manufacturers rely on their dealers to provide after-sales service (e.g. the motor trade); the manufacturer in such cases should be satisfied that dealers are capable of providing the required level of service. For many products, after-sales service is an important element in the marketing mix and needs to be costed into the final selling price of the product.

SALES MANAGEMENT

The sales manager's job is particularly difficult because subordinates are usually geographically separated from him or her. This can produce problems of communication and control not experienced by a purchasing or financial manager whose staff are located within the same building. However, the key responsibilities of sales management are similar to other managerial positions:

1. Setting of sales objectives and strategies
2. Recruitment and selection of salespeople
3. Motivation
4. Organization
5. Training
6. Control

Setting sales objectives and strategies

The sales manager is unlikely to be the only person involved in setting corporate sales objectives. Top management, marketing personnel and statisticians as well as sales managers may influence the level of the sales target for the forthcoming year. Once agreed, the performance targets for individual salespeople are likely to be set by sales management after consultation with the salespeople themselves. Performance targets may be set in terms of sales volume, call rates, profit margin achieved, numbers of new customers, etc. Sales strategy is the method by which objectives are achieved. For example, an increase in target sales may be achieved by the strategy of increasing calls to new customers, spending more time with existing customers or setting up a telesales team to give increased service to small customers. Sales management plays a key role in determining the most effective strategy to achieve corporate sales objectives.

Recruitment and selection of salespeople

The selection of salespeople, while of obvious importance to the long-term future of the business, is a task that does not always receive the attention it should from sales managers. All too often, the 'man profile' is ill-defined and the selection procedure designed for maximum convenience rather than optimal choice. The assumption is that the right person should emerge whatever procedure is used. Consequently, the interview is poorly handled, the smooth talker gets the job, and another mediocre salesperson emerges.

Two key aspects of recruitment and selection are the preparation of the job description, and personal specification and interviewing. A job description usually covers the following factors:

—The title of the job.
—Duties and responsibilities—the tasks that will be expected of the new recruit, e.g. selling, after-sales service, information feedback, and the range of products/markets/type of consumer with which he or she will be associated.
—The person to whom he or she will report.
—Technical requirements, e.g. the degree to which the salesperson needs to understand the technical aspects of the products to be sold.
—Location and geographical area to be covered.
—Degree of autonomy—the degree to which the salesperson will be able to control his or her own work programme.

Once generated, the job description will act as the blueprint for the personnel specification which outlines the type of applicant the company is seeking. The technical requirements of the job, for example, and the nature of the customers the salespeople will meet, will be factors that will influence the level of education and, possibly, the age of the required salesperson. A personnel specification may contain all or some of the following factors:

—Physical requirements, e.g. speech, appearance.
—Attainments, e.g. standard of education and qualifications; experience and successes.
—Aptitudes and qualities, e.g. ability to communicate; self-motivation.
—Disposition, e.g. maturity, sense of responsibility.
—Interests, e.g. degree to which interests are social; active or inactive.
—Personal circumstances, e.g. married, single, etc.

The factors chosen to define the personnel specification will be used as criteria of selection in the interview itself.

The objective of the interview is to enable interviewers to form a clear impression of the strengths and weaknesses of the candidates with respect to the selection criteria. Candidates should be encouraged to talk openly about themselves, but interviewers should take care to control the interview so that all relevant areas are covered. Otherwise a candidate may be allowed to talk about his strengths without due consideration of his weaknesses.

What happens at the beginning of the interview is crucial to subsequent events. The objective at this stage is to set the candidate at ease. Most interviewees are naturally anxious before the interview and when they first enter the interview setting. They may feel embarrassed or be worried about exposing weaknesses; they may feel inadequate and lack confidence; and above all, they may feel worried about rejection. This anxiety is compounded by the fact that the candidate may never have met the interviewers before and may thus be uncertain about how aggressive they will be, the degree of pressure that will be applied and the type of questions likely to be asked. Some sales managers may argue that the salesperson is likely to meet this situation out in the field and therefore needs to be able to deal with it without the use of anxiety-reducing techniques on the part of the interviewers. A valid response to this viewpoint is that the objective of the interview is to get to know the candidate in terms of the criteria laid down in the personnel specification, or 'man profile' as it is sometimes called. In order to do this, the interviewee must be encouraged to talk about him- or herself. If sales ability under stress is to be tested, role playing can be employed as part of the selection procedure.

Motivation

Motivation in theory   Although motivation is dependent on each salesperson's individual needs and desires, a sales manager can influence motivation both positively and negatively by his or her actions and policies. Some people have the opinion that salespeople are motivated solely by money; and indeed, the type of compensation plan a firm adopts can be a factor in achieving enhanced performance. However, there are other job-related factors which can influence motivation. A major contribution in this area was made by Herzberg et al.[3]

Herzberg distinguished between factors that can cause dissatisfaction but cannot motivate (hygiene factors) and factors that can cause positive motivation. Hygiene factors included physical working conditions, security and interpersonal relationships. Directing managerial attention to these factors, postulated Herzberg, would bring motivation up to a 'theoretical zero' but would not result in positive motivation. If this was to be achieved, attention would have to be given to true motivators. These included the nature of the work itself, which allows the person to make some concrete achievement; the recognition of achievement; the responsibility exercised by the person; and the interest value of the work itself.

The inclusion of salary as a hygiene factor rather than as a motivator was subject to criticisms from sales managers whose experience led them to believe that commission paid to their salespeople was a powerful motivator in practice. Herzberg accommodated their view to some extent by arguing that increased salary through higher commission was a motivator through the automatic recognition it gave to sales achievement.

The salesperson is fortunate in that achievement is directly observable in terms of higher sales (except in 'missionary' selling, where orders are not taken—e.g. pharmaceuticals, beer and selling to specifiers). However, the degree of responsibility afforded to salespeople varies a great deal. Opportunities for giving a greater degree of responsibility to (and hence motivating) salespersons include giving authority to grant credit (up to a certain value), discretion to offer discounts, and handing over responsibility for calling frequencies to the salespeople.

Herzberg's theory has been well received, in general, by practitioners, although academics, especially Dessler,[4] have criticized it in terms of methodology and oversimplification. The theory has undoubtedly made a substantial contribution to the understanding of motivation at work, particularly in highlighting the importance of job content factors which had hitherto been badly neglected.

Other theorists, such as Maslow,[5] Vroom[6] and Likert,[7] have worked within the area of motivation. For an evaluation of their contribution, see Lancaster and Jobber,[8] who have given a detailed review.

Motivation in practice   Three key elements in motivating salespeople in practice are the type of compensation plan adopted, the setting of sales targets, and manager–salesperson relationships.

Type of compensation plan   There are, basically, three types of compensation plan:

—Fixed salary
—Commission only
—Salary plus commission

Each will now be evaluated in terms of benefits and drawbacks to management and salespeople, with particular reference to motivation.

Fixed salary   This method of payment encourages sales personnel to consider all aspects of the selling function rather than just those that lead to a quick sales return. Salespeople who are paid on fixed salary are likely to be more willing to provide technical service and complete information feedback reports and to carry out prospecting than if they were paid solely by commission. The system provides security to the salesperson, who knows how much income he or she will receive each month, and it is relatively cheap to administer, since calculation of commissions and bonuses is not required.

The system also overcomes the problem of deciding how much commission to give to each salesperson when a complex buying decision is made by a number of DMU members who have been influenced by different salespeople, perhaps in different parts of the country. Wilson[9] cites the case of a sale of building materials to a local authority in Lancashire being the result of one salesman influencing an architect in London, another calling on the contractor in Norwich, and a third persuading the local authority itself.

However, the method does have a number of drawbacks. First, no direct financial incentive is provided for increasing sales (no profits). Second, high-performing salespeople may not be attracted, and holding on to them may be different using fixed salary since they may perceive the system as being unfair and may be tempted to apply for jobs where financial rewards are high for outstanding performers. Third, selling costs remain static in the short term when sales decrease; thus, the system does not provide the in-built flexibility provided by the other compensation systems.

Because of its inherent characteristics, this system is used primarily in industrial selling, where technical service is an important element in the selling task and the time necessary to conclude a sale may be long. It is particularly appropriate when the salesperson sells very high-value products at very low volumes. Under these conditions, a commission-based compensation scheme would lead to widely varying monthly income levels depending on when orders were placed.

Commission-only The commission-only system of payment provides an obvious incentive to sell. However, since income is dependent on sales results, salespeople will be reluctant to spend time on tasks which they do not perceive as being directly related to sales. The result is that salespeople may pursue short-term goals, to the detriment of activities that may have an effect in the longer term; salespeople may be reluctant to write reports providing market information to management and to spend time out of the field attending sales training courses, for example.

The system provides little security for salespeople whose earnings may suffer through no fault of their own, and the pressure to sell may damage customer–salesperson relationships. This is particularly relevant to industrial selling, where the decision-making process may be long and where pressure applied by the salesperson to close the sale prematurely may be detrimental.

From management's perspective, the system not only has the advantage of directly financing costs automatically, but also allows some control over salespeople's activities through the use of higher commission rates on products and accounts in which management is particularly interested.

It is most often used in situations where there are a large number of potential customers, the buying process is relatively short, and technical assistance and service are not required. Insurance selling is an example where commission-only payments are often used.

Salary-plus-commission This system attempts to combine the benefits of both the previous methods in order to provide financial incentives with a level of security. Since income is not solely dependent upon commission, management gains a greater degree of control over the salesperson's time than under the commission only system, and sales costs are, to some extent, related to revenue generated. The method is attractive to ambitious salespeople who wish to combine security with the capability of earning more by greater effort and ability. According to Donaldson,[10] 65 per cent of salesforces are remunerated on such a combination plan basis.

Clearly, managers who wish to use the incentive of extra money for good performance are going to choose commission-only or salary-plus-commission as their method of compensation. However, fixed salary schemes may be used where it is difficult to tie performance to individual salespeople's achievements, and where to do so may cause resentment and feelings of unfairness which may lead to demotivation.

Setting sales targets A key feature of the commission-only or salary-plus-commission payment plan may be the determination of each salesperson's sales target or quota. If a sales target or quota is to be effective in motivating a salesperson, it must be regarded as fair and attainable and yet offer a challenge. Because the salesperson should regard the quota as fair, it is usually sensible to allow him or her to participate in the setting of the quota. However, the establishment of the quotas is ultimately the sales manager's responsibility, and he or she will inevitably be constrained by overall company objectives. If sales are planned to increase by 10 per cent, then salespeople's quotas must be consistent with this. Variations around this average figure will arise through the sales manager's knowledge of individual salespeople and changes in commercial activity within each territory; for example, the liquidation of a key customer in a territory may be reflected in a reduced quota. The attainment of a sales target usually results in some form of extra payment to the salesperson.

Sales manager–salesperson meetings There are a number of ways in which meetings between the sales manager and his salespeople can lead to better motivation. First, they allow the sales manager to understand the personality, needs and problems of each salesperson. The manager can then better understand the causes of demotivation in individual salespeople and respond in a manner that takes into account the needs, problems and personality of the salesperson. Second, meetings in the field, which may form part of an evaluation and training programme, can also provide an opportunity to motivate. Sales technique can be improved and confidence boosted, both of which may motivate by restoring in the salesperson the belief that performance will improve through extra effort. Third, group meetings can motivate, according to Likert, when the sales manager encourages an 'open' style of meeting. Salespeople are encouraged to discuss their sales problems and opportunities so that the entire sales team benefits from the experience of each salesperson. This leads to a greater sense of group loyalty and improved performance. Finally, meetings between manager and salespeople provide the opportunity for performance feedback where weaknesses are identified and recognition for good work is given.

Organization

A major aspect of organizing a sales team is the decision regarding organizational structure. There are three basic alternatives: geographical, product-based and customer-based structures.

Geographical structure An advantage of this form or organization is its simplicity. Each salesperson is assigned a territory over which he or she has sole responsibility for sales achievement. Their close geographical proximity to customers encourages the development of personal friendships which aids sales effectiveness. Also, compared with other organization forms, for example product or market specialization, travelling expenses are likely to be lower.

A potential weakness of the geographical structure is that the salesperson is required to sell the full range of the company's products. These may be very different technically and may sell into a number of diverse markets. In such a situation it may be unreasonable to expect the salesperson to have the required depth of technical knowledge for each product and to be conversant with the full range of potential applications within each market. This expertise can be developed only if the salesperson is given a more specialized role.

Product-based structure One method of specialization is along product lines. Conditions that are conducive to this form of organization are where the company sells a wide range of technically complex and diverse products, and where key members of the decision-making unit of the buying organizations are different for each product group. However, if the company's products sell essentially to the same customers, problems of route duplication (and hence higher travel costs) and customer annoyance can arise. Inappropriate use of this method can lead to a customer being called upon by different salespersons representing the same company on the same day. When a company contemplates a move from the geographically based to a product-based structure, some customer overlap is inevitable; but, if only of a limited extent, the problem should be manageable.

Customer-based structures Three customer-based methods of organization are the market-centred, the account size and the new/existing account structures.

Market-centred structure Another method of specialization is by the type of market served. Often, in industrial selling, the market is defined by industry type. Thus, although the range of products sold is essentially the same, it might be sensible for a computer firm to allocate its salespeople on the basis of the industry served, e.g., banking, manufacturing companies, retailers, given that different industry groups have widely varying needs, problems and potential applications. Specialization by market served allows a salesperson to gain greater insights into these factors for his or her particular industry, as well as to monitor changes and trends within the industry which might affect demand for his or her products. The cost of increased customer knowledge is increased travel expenses compared with geographically determined territories.

Account size structure Some companies structure their salesforce by account size. The importance of a few large customers in many trade and industrial markets has given rise to the establishment of a 'key account' salesforce. The team comprises senior salespeople who specialize in dealing with large customers who may have different buying habits and may demand more sophisticated sales arguments than smaller companies. The team will be conversant with negotiation skills since they are likely to be given a certain amount of discretion in terms of discounts, credit terms, etc., in order to secure large orders. The range of selling skills required is, therefore, wider than for the rest of the salesforce, who deal with the smaller accounts. Some organizations adopt a three-tier system with senior salespeople negotiating with national accounts, ordinary salespeople selling to medium-sized accounts, and a telephone sales team dealing with small accounts.

New/existing account structure A further method of sales organization is to create two teams of salespeople. The first team services existing accounts, while the second concentrates upon seeking new accounts. This structure recognizes that gaining new customers is a specialized activity, demanding prospecting skills, patience, the ability to accept higher rejection rates than when calling upon existing customers, and the time to cultivate new relationships. Placing this function in the hands of the regular salesforce may result in its neglect, since the salespeople may view it as time which could be better spent with existing customers. Pioneer salespeople were used successfully by trading stamp companies to prospect new customers. Once an account was obtained, it was handled over to a maintenance salesperson who serviced the account.

Training

Training should not be confined to new salespeople. Experienced salespeople require refresher training, which has the benefit of sharpening skills and stimulating thought on new ways of selling. A training programme usually has five components:

1. The company—objectives, policies and organization
2. Its products
3. Its competitors and their products
4. Selling procedure and techniques
5. Work organization and report preparation

The first three components are essentially communicating the required level of knowledge to the salesperson. The first component will probably include a brief history of the company, how it has grown and where it intends to go in the future. Policies relevant to the selling function, for example, how salespeople are evaluated, and the nature of the compensation system will be explained. The way in which the company is organized will be described and the relationship between sales and the marketing function, including advertising and market research, will be described so that the salesperson has an appreciation of the support he or she is receiving from headquarters.

The second component, product knowledge, will include a description of how the products are made and the implications for product quality and reliability, the features of the product and the benefits they confer on the consumer. Salespeople will be encouraged to carry out their own product analysis so that they will be able to identify key features and benefits of new products as they are launched. Competitors will be identified and competitors' products will also be analysed to spotlight differences between them and the company's products.

Some training programmes, particularly within the industrial selling area, stop here, neglecting a major component of a training programme—selling procedures and techniques. This component will include practical sessions where trainees develop skills through role-playing exercises. For experienced salespeople, sales skills will be developed by on-the-job training. They will be accompanied on sales visits by their sales manager who will highlight strengths and weakness and provide guidance as to improved performance.

The final component of the programme—work organization and report writing—will endeavour to establish good habits among the trainees in areas which, because of day-to-day pressures, may be neglected. The importance of these activities on a salesperson's performance, and hence earnings, will be stressed.

For new recruits to the salesforce, it is important that they are given a thorough programme of training before operating in the field on their own. It goes without saying that, if successful recruitment has taken place, the salesperson who gets the job will understand the role of selling in the economy in general and the company in particular. The salesperson should also possess communication skills, such as asking appropriate questions, listening and talking in the same 'language' as the customer.

In addition to these areas, formal training will be needed as follows:

—*Preparation* The salesperson will have to know what aids will be needed prior to meeting the customer.
—*Prospecting* The importance of new business should be emphasized and the salesperson should be given guidance on how it might be obtained.
—*Opening the sale* On meeting the customer, it is important that the salesperson conveys the right initial impression.
—*Making sales presentations* Effective persuasion resulting in a sale is the hallmark of a good salesperson. This will require skill in verbal presentation, handling of visual aids and demonstration of the product. It is suggested by Winkler[11] that this skill is best developed by use of video and video playback techniques.
—*Dealing with objections* Customers can complain about a variety of issues, e.g. price, delivery. The salesperson should be trained in what to say and how to reply.

—*Closing the sale* This is the most crucial and highly skilled part of a salesperson's job. Knowing how and when to close a sale is what differentiates a really good salesperson from an average one. The salesperson needs to be trained to recognize, when leading up to a close, both verbal and non-verbal cues from the potential buyer. If the salesperson attempts to close the sale too early, he or she may face an objection that has not been covered and may not have been prepared for. This can create a difficult situation to handle. If, however, the salesperson leaves the close of sale too late, he or she may well go on talking and may tell the buyer something unnecessary, and hence give reasons for a changing of mind. Learning how and when to close a sale is an art. Closing techniques can be taught, but experience has a large part to play also. The good salesperson needs the qualities of a diplomat, a negotiator and a psychologist.

—*Work organization* The salesperson must be trained in the effective use of time through the use of journey planning and day planning.

After the initial training, field training is then conducted, and it is part of the role of the field sales manager to accompany the salesperson on a normal day's work to observe and offer sales back-up, but not to interfere. The field sales manager should afterwards advise the salesperson of their selling strengths and weaknesses. Once the new salesperson is deemed to be 'competent', there will be no need for the field sales manager to go along on every visit, and as the salesperson becomes still more experienced, so the need to accompany will diminish.

Evaluation and control

The prime reason for evaluation is to attempt to attain company objectives. By measuring actual performance against objectives, shortfalls can be identified and appropriate action taken to improve performance. However, evaluation has other benefits. Evaluation can help improve individual salespeople's motivation and skills. Motivation is affected, since an evaluation programme will identify what is expected of the individual, and what is considered good performance. Second, it provides the opportunity for the recognition of above-average standards of work performance, which improves confidence and motivation. Skills are affected since carefully constructed evaluation allows areas of weakness to be identified, and effort to be directed to the improvement of skills in those areas.

Although sales managers are interested in sales primarily as a percentage of quota or target, in practice a whole range of measures may be used—often for diagnostic purposes. Table 12.1 gives a summary of the more common quantitative measures.

In addition, salespeople may be evaluated on a number of qualitative dimensions. The most usual ones are:

—Sales skills
—Customer relationships
—Self-organization
—Product knowledge
—Cooperation and attitudes

For an evaluation and control system to work efficiently, it is important for the sales team to understand its purpose. To view it simply as a means for management to catch them out and criticize performance is likely to breed resentment. It should be used, and be perceived, as a means for assisting salespeople to improve performance, through integration with the company's sales training programme. Indeed, the quantitative output measures themselves can be used as a basis for rewarding performance when targets are met. This chapter has provided a checklist of measurements from which individual sales managers can select the most appropriate one for their

Table 12.1   Quantitative measures of performance

Sales	*Orders*
Sales revenue	Number of orders taken
Sales revenue as a percentage of quota	Order per call ratio
Sales revenue per order	Average order value
Sales revenue per call	Average profit contribution per order
Sales revenue from new accounts	
Accounts	*Calls*
Number of new accounts	Number of calls per period
Number of accounts lost	Calls on potential new accounts
Total number of accounts	Call on existing accounts
Profit	*Expenses*
Gross profit	Sales expenses to sales revenue ratio
Net profit	Average expenses per call
Return on investment	Expenses per square mile of territory
Profit per call ratio	

particular situation. They are summarized in Table 12.1. Such improvements in the sales evaluation and control system should result in enhanced effectiveness in the marketplace.

TERRITORY MANAGEMENT

Territories should be designed first of all with one basic principle in mind:

> The most effective form of contact

Perhaps five or six different salespersons from the same firm could be calling upon five or six different customers who are all located in the same area. They might even be calling at the same time. It may seem to be a wasteful use of manpower and expenses, but if the same contact is likely to be more effective by following such a policy, then it could be a profitable one.

The 'sales engineer'

Formulating or designing territories has developed into a highly complicated task. It is rarely sufficient to 'count the heads' and allocate according to population. Even with consumer goods, which may be consumed evenly throughout the country, such a technique is no longer valid. The factors that need to be taken into account are now so complex that some companies employ 'sales engineers'. These executives have nothing to do with engineering in the normally accepted sense of the word. Their task is to build territories and to make adjustments to them as situations change.

It is no accident that specialist organizations have developed which offer a service of designing territories by using sales 'bricks'. The sales brick is a geographical unit in which all the known buyers are listed. The bricks are generally roughly equal in sales potential. For example, one brick may contain 10 buyers of furniture and another brick may have 15. In such an example, the brick would have been calculated on the basis that the 10 buyers are, on average, slightly more important that the 15, but the total purchasing capacities are about the same.

Sales bricks can be constructed for almost every kind of industry. As the bricks are built up, they can be transferred in units from one territory to another. However, to design territories using the brick principle is a long and painstaking task, and not many companies can afford the time or expense to use this method.

Factors that determine territory design

There is an infinite number of factors, some of which are pragmatic and others of which may be personal. A salesperson may be allowed to visit another salesperson's territory and deal with a customer simply because it is known that they get on well together. Individual factors such as these cannot be legislated for but must be dealt with as they arise. Many companies encounter some such problems and try to meet them in the most practical way.

Some of the more practical factors are as follows:

—*Potential business* An estimate needs to be made of the amount of business that is available in the territory. The estimate should be in two parts. The first should be total business and the second, the share which the company may expect to obtain.

—*Number of active customers* Assuming the company is already doing business in the area, it should be possible to count the customers or to make an estimate of them. If the company only deals direct, then it will be a simple matter of counting them. If the goods are sold through wholesalers, an estimate or some research may be necessary. As well as the number of customers, it is also necessary to assess or calculate the amount of business they do.

—*Number of potential customers* There will be potential buyers with whom the company is not yet dealing. The estimate should be realistic and it may be necessary to grade them; sometimes customers are 'registered' agents. If they are registered with competitors, it may not be possible to convert them. If they are 'free' agents, then they are, of course, open to offers. As with the known customers, an estimate should be made of the amount of business they handle.

—*Location of customers* It is necessary to know not only how many and how important the customers and potential customers are, but also where they are located. The distribution of customers can provide headaches for territory planners.

—*Method of distribution* Some goods are, by their nature, tied to distribution depots, and territories have to be engineered around these depots.

—*Sales situation* A run-down area may require a salesperson to build it up; a well-developed area may require splitting because the existing salesperson has too much to do.

—*Frequency of call* How often should the salesperson call? Much depends upon the buyer, the size of the territory and the ordering frequency. This needs to be associated with the acceptable stock levels that customers are prepared to carry.

—*Mixtures of trade* When companies sell to several different trades, they may regard it as desirable for each salesperson to have a balanced mixture.

—*Identifiable boundaries* The characteristics of the territory, whether delineated geographically or by trade classification, must be clearly defined so that each is recognizable by its salesperson and by his or her neighbouring colleagues. Disputes about territory boundaries are unneccessary and can lead to discord.

—*Economics of representation* The most important factor in delineating territories is whether or not they will be economically viable. It is a common practice for the territory boundaries to be calculated roughly and for an estimate to be made of the likely business that will materialize. The salesperson's expenses are estimated, and the total cost of working the territory is then related to the anticipated turnover. Next, the profitability is calculated. Only then can a realistic assessment be made as to whether or not the new territory is likely to be worth while.

In making such calculations, attention must be paid to the possible future growth of the territory. Most companies are prepared to tolerate a low level of profitability, or even a loss in the short term, if there is the possibility of long-term profits.

Because of the high total costs of employing a sales representative, some companies, in the food trade in particular, use brokers to do their selling for them.

CONCLUSIONS

This chapter has reviewed the selling and managerial skills necessary for efficient personal selling. The modern marketplace requires sales teams who can not only sell but also negotiate terms and conditions that result in profitable orders. Sales managers must recognize the full extent of their managerial responsibilities, which include setting objectives and strategy recruitment and selection, motivation, organization, training and control.

The chapter has been written from the viewpoint of a company selling to customers, rather than buyers seeking out sellers. Particularly in industrial markets, the latter is often the case. Chapter 3 was concerned with 'Marketing and customers', and buyer behaviour (consumer and organizational) was discussed there in some depth. It can, therefore, be appreciated that a study of buyer behaviour is an essential prerequisite to good selling, because the seller can then focus appropriate selling points on to the avowed and unavowed needs of buyers.

APPLICATION QUESTIONS

1. Discuss the importance of 'needs analysis' within personal selling.
2. Outline the main stages in personal selling and discuss the techniques that can be used to achieve a sale.
3. What are the major functions of sales management? Discuss how the achievement of any *two* functions can be accomplished.
4. How can the links between motivation, training and evaluation lead to better sales performance?
5. It is not possible to motivate, only to demotivate. Discuss.

REFERENCES

1. J. Saunders, T. Hong-Chung and G. Lancaster, 'Traditional and modern views of personal selling', *Journal of Sales Management* (Monograph), **2**(1), 1985.
2. G. Kennedy, J. Benson and J. MacMillan, *Managing Negotiations*, Business Books, London, 1980.
3. F. Herzberg, B. Mausner and B. Block Snydeman, *The Motivation to Work*, John Wiley, New York, 1959.
4. G. Dessler, *Human Behaviour: Improving Performance at Work*, Prentice-Hall, Englewood Cliffs, NJ, 1979.
5. A. H. Maslow, 'A theory of human motivation', *Psychological Review*, July 1943.
6. V. H. Vroom, *Work and Motivation*, John Wiley, New York, 1964.
7. R. Likert, *New Patterns of Sales Management*, McGraw-Hill, London, 1961.
8. G. Lancaster and D. Jobber, *Sales Technique and Management*, Pitman, London, 1990.
9. M. Wilson, *Managing a Sales Force*, Gower Publishing, Aldershot, 1983.
10. B. Donaldson, *Sales Management: Theory and Practice*, Macmillan, London, 1990, p. 240.
11. J. Winkler, *Winning Sales and Marketing Tactics*, Heinemann, London, 1989, p. 242.

THIRTEEN
MANAGING THE MARKETING MIX

INTRODUCTION

In this chapter we shall examine the functions of marketing personnel in their role as managers.

All managers, irrespective of the functional specialism in which they spend their working lives, share common duties and activities. In particular, managers, including marketing managers, are responsible for planning, organizing, directing and controlling within their own function. Underpinning these control tasks is the manager's role as a maker of decisions. In Chapter 4 we examined the key decision areas of marketing management, including those that were referred to, collectively, as the marketing mix decisions. We also examined how marketing management relates to, and interacts with, the other functional areas in the business, and in particular its role in the overall planning and decision-making process.

With this as a background, this chapter traces the planning, organizing, directing and controlling aspects of marketing management. We shall start with the formulation of marketing plans and the strategies and tactics that accompany them. We shall then examine how scarce marketing and company resources need to be allocated and organized to support these marketing plans, and the need for marketing efforts to be evaluated and controlled.

The chapter concludes with a necessarily brief account of the important 'people-managing' aspects of marketing management. Marketing managers, like other managers, normally rely on 'getting things done through people'. To be effective, the marketing manager must be aware of the importance of managing the human assets under his or her control. This involves careful selection, training, motivation and, above all, leadership of marketing personnel.

THE NATURE OF MANAGEMENT

Most people have a notion of what managers do. In fact, it has proved extremely difficult to define what a manager is or does. There are many so-called 'theories of management', often offering different and personalized views on the nature of management. Before examining some of the most practical of these views, it is useful to explain briefly why the form and content of managerial work has attracted so much attention.

Since the early 1900s, attention has focused on the nature and function of managerial work. The prime concern of this attention has been to analyse the necessary managerial skills and behaviour with a view to improving effective managerial performance. A substantial part of the early attention in this field was in fact aimed at developing a 'science' of management or at least a set of prescriptive guidelines or principles that could be applied in all managerial functions. This desire to establish a body of management theory and principles was in turn prompted by the increasingly rapid industrialization which many countries experienced at the turn of the century, with its accompanying growth of large-scale organizations and mass production on a factory system. As industrialization progressed, scientific principles and practice were applied increasingly to the manufacturing and production processes. No such body of knowledge was available, however, to the practising manager of the time. Most managers learned how to manage the hard way; through a process of trial and error built upon experience. Not only was this felt by many to be an unsatisfactory situation, but the separation of ownership from control, which the growth of large-scale organization prompted, gave rise, for the first time, to the professional manager: a 'professional manager' none the less unsupported by the underpinning body of knowledge or learning necessary to any profession. Thus, management tended to be 'hunch' or 'rule of thumb'.

Some of the easiest attempts to professionalize the management function came from practising managers, who, on the basis of their experience, suggested basic principles of management in order to aid others in their work. For the purposes of this book, we do not need to be concerned with the variety of principles that were suggested, nor indeed with the controversy surrounding which of the individual viewpoints is most appropriate; there are many excellent texts available for the reader who is interested in an in-depth discussion of these issues, including that of Albors.[1] For our purposes, it is sufficient to note that, despite the 'unscientific' nature of many of these early approaches, the fact that they represent the collective wisdom extant some eighty or more years ago and the differences between the viewpoints offered, a picture did emerge of what comprised the essential elements of the management process. Moreover, the same basic elements are still propounded as being relevant to the manager of today: they are *planning, organizing, directing* and *controlling*. We shall examine how each of these relates to the task of marketing management.

PLANNING AND MARKETING MANAGEMENT

Planning is now recognized as being an essential feature of the manager's job. We have seen in Chapter 4 how planning applies at the corporate or overall business level, and the interrelationships that this gives rise to between strategic planners and marketing management. In addition to the marketers' input to development of corporate plans, marketing managers must, in the light of these plans, prepare plans for their own functional activities. As in corporate planning, marketing planning involves a series of iterative steps which require marketing management to *set objectives* ('where do we want to go?'), *formulate strategies and tactics* ('how do we intend to get there?'), and *prescribe time scales* for the implementation and achievement of these plans ('when do we want to get there?'). This 'where', 'how' and 'when' content of all plans is encompassed in our definition of the planning role of marketing management, which can be summarized as follows:

> The planning role of marketing management comprises the determination of marketing objectives together with the choice of strategies and tactics to achieve these objectives and a time scale for their implementation and achievement.

Some of the important elements in this planning role are now considered.

Setting marketing objectives

The determination of marketing objectives involves much the same procedure as that outlined for the setting of those at the corporate level. The process begins with an analysis of current and past performance in existing product markets together with a review of potential marketing opportunities and threats. Together with overall corporate objectives and strategies, this analysis provides the backcloth against which marketing objectives are set. Given that planning is concerned with the future, it might seem to suggest that setting marketing objectives should start with the past. In fact, historical data are essential if marketing objectives are to have that necessary characteristic of all objectives—realism. To set marketing objectives without regard to past performance is akin to planning a journey into unknown territory without consulting a map. For this reason, the start of the planning elements—setting objectives—is limited to the first basic element of all management: controlling. In fact, as we shall see, all four basic elements of marketing management are interlinked one with another.

In addition to the analysis of current and past performance, it was suggested that the determination of marketing objectives requires a review of potential marketing opportunities and threats. This stage of the objective-setting process requires a careful analysis of the marketing environment of the company. Of particular concern here will be those opportunities and threats posed by trends and changes related to *markets, customers, competitors* and *distributors*. At best, failure to consider these factors is likely to result, again, in unrealistic objectives; at worst it can lead to company failure.

The outcome of these analyses should be clearly defined, preferably in quantitative terms, and realistic objectives should be set for the marketing function. Multiple objectives for marketing should be consistent one with another and with overall corporate objectives and strategies. Finally, marketing objectives should be communicated to, and agreed by, those responsible for achieving them.

Determining and selecting marketing strategies and tactics

Having determined our marketing objectives, another key element is marketing management's planning role in the determination and selection of the routes by which these objectives will be achieved.

Increasingly, planning texts have drawn from the ideas and terminology of the military strategists, with terms such as 'encirclement', 'flanking' and 'bypass' strategies being used. Irrespective of the term chosen to describe a particular strategy, it is important to understand what the term 'strategy' means and the distinction between marketing strategies and marketing tactics.

Marketing strategies relate to the overall, broad patterns of marketing actions which a company might take to achieve marketing objectives. For example, a company with a marketing objective of increasing sales revenue by X per cent must select from a variety of different routes to achieve this objective. Among the marketing decisions that might be involved in this selection process, Kotler[2] identifies the following:

—Selection of market targets.
—Choice of market positioning strategies.
—Selection of an appropriate marketing mix.

A statement of the company's overall marketing objectives and strategy in our example, therefore, might run as follows:

> To increase sales revenue X per cent in the business microcomputer market, based on increased sales to the small business user via product improvement and penetration pricing.

Once again, the choice of marketing strategies must reflect both company strengths and weaknesses and a careful analysis of customer/market needs.

Within this broad framework of marketing strategies, marketing management must also specify *marketing tactics*. If strategies represent the 'grand plan'—the overall route to achieving marketing objectives—then tactics represent the 'fine-tuning': the details necessary to undertake and complete the journey successfully.

The importance of marketing tactics to the successful achievement of objectives should not be underestimated. Many excellent strategies have failed because of lack of attention, or an inappropriate tactic. On the other hand, although it happens rarely, even ill-conceived strategies can succeed because of clever tactical decisions.

Both conceptually and in practice, the lines of demarcation between marketing strategies and tactics are blurred. Tactics are derived from strategies, but these tactics in turn may be considered as sub-strategies which themselves require further tactics for execution. One principal factor which gives rise to this blurring between strategies and tactics, is the existence of a *hierarchy of different planning levels* within a company. What at one level in the planning hierarchy is considered tactics is, at another level, considered strategy. For example, what can be considered tactical decisions at the corporate or overall business planning level become strategies at the functional level. Furthermore, within a function, what is one manager's strategy may, for another manager, represent tactics. For example, the sales manager may have a strategy of opening a given number of new accounts, and will proceed to develop the appropriate tactics for his or her salesforce in order to achieve this; however, the strategy of opening new accounts may itself represent a tactical move as part of an overall marketing strategy. Having said this, we may broadly distinguish marketing tactics from marketing strategies in terms of the following general characteristics.

1. As stated previously, generally, tactics are *more detailed* than strategies.
2. Tactics generally encompass a *shorter period of time* than do strategies.
3. Tactics are *more flexible* than strategies and can be more readily changed to accommodate to new or changed circumstances. This element of flexibility is one of the most important aspects in the imaginative use of tactics in marketing and can add substantially to the effectiveness of marketing efforts. However, great care needs to be exercised in the use of tactics in this way. For example, it is possible that, in using tactics to meet changing markets and competitive conditions, a company will gradually drift off-course with respect to planned marketing strategies.
4. Finally, tactics differ from strategies in that the *range* of tactics available to the marketer is normally far wider than the range of strategies at the disposal of marketing management.

Collectively, these characteristics of marketing tactics mean that the imaginative use of them is particularly beneficial when a firm is faced with particular marketing problems. Some examples from the wide range of possible situations favouring the use of effective marketing tactics are as follows:

—When it is necessary to increase stock levels in channels of distribution.
—When competitive activity becomes particularly marked in certain products and/or geographical areas.
—When a company has to quickly establish demand for a new product.
—When the motivation of the salesforce is waning.

The overall relationship between marketing objectives, strategies and tactics is shown in Fig. 13.1. The final issue in the marketing manager's role as planner is the determination of time scales for marketing activities.

Figure 13.1 The relationship between marketing objectives, strategies and tactics

Prescribing time scales for marketing plans

Another key element of marketing planning is specifying time scales for marketing activities. This involves prescribing not only a time scale for the achievement of objectives, but also the timing and scheduling of activities required to meet them.

Time scales for the achievement of marketing objectives may vary to encompass anything from one month to 10 years ahead and more. It is conventional to refer to marketing objectives and plans as being either short, medium, or long-range in nature. For example, a company may have a long-range marketing objective to become market leader which might involve a sequence of marketing activities covering some five years or more. On the other hand, the same company might have short-term marketing objectives and plans covering, say, the next six months. What constitutes an appropriate time span for marketing activities, and, therefore, the distinction between long-, medium- and short-term plans, will vary from company to company. Steiner[3] suggests that what constitutes an appropriate 'planning horizon' for a company is related to the length of time to which the planning decision commits the resources of the company. In terms of marketing management, however, one of the most important planning tasks is the preparation of the annual marketing plan.

Preparing the annual marketing plan

Although the precise format of the annual marketing plan and its contents will vary between companies, the steps involved in its preparation will be broadly similar for any marketing manager.

At this stage it is helpful to trace through the format of a 'typical' annual marketing plan. This not only helps to illustrate the steps and analyses involved but also enables us to see how the various elements and the concepts and techniques discussed in this and the preceding chapters combine in an integrated way. This format is as follows.

1. BUSINESS DEFINITION/MARKET ANALYSIS
   1.1 *Business definition statement* Categorization of customer and users served and their needs.
   1.2 *Quantification of market size and trends* Current market size, forecast of market potential and rate of growth.
   1.3 *Segmentation analysis* Description of market segments, including bases of segmentation size and trends in each segment.

2. SITUATION ANALYSIS

    2.1 *Analysis of macro-environment* Economic, political, social/cultural, technological—review of key trends and changes.

    2.2 *Competitor analysis* Ranking, market share, strategies, capabilities, potential new entrants.

    2.3 *Company analysis* Company profit and sales performance, margins, market share, trends in performance; company resources, including financial, plant and buildings, personal, marketing, research and development.

    2.4 *Distributive analysis* Trends in channels, margins, trade terms, etc.

3. ANALYSIS OF KEY ISSUES/SWOT

Analysis of key issues from analysis in steps 1 and 2 summarized in the form of a Strengths, Weaknesses, Opportunities and Threats statement.

4. MARKETING OBJECTIVES

Statement of marketing objectives to include:

    4.1 *Market position* Sales, market share, image.

    4.2 *Financial position* Profits, margins, ROI. N.B. All the above to be quantified and time scales specified.

5. MARKETING STRATEGY

Statement of marketing strategy to include:

    5.1 *Target market(s)*

    5.2 *Positioning/competitive advantage*

    5.3 *Marketing mix strategy and tactics*

        —Product strategy and tactics

        —Pricing strategy and tactics

        —Distribution strategy and tactics

        —Promotional strategy and tactics

    Service products

    Additional elements of mix as appropriate, e.g. physical evidence, etc.

N.B. All the above to include scheduling of activities and time scales.

6. FINANCIAL PROJECTIONS AND BUDGETS

    6.1 *Cash and budgets*

    6.2 *Sales and profit forecasts*

7. CONTROLS AND CONTINGENCY PLANS

As this is the current marketing plan, objectives, strategies and tactics, together with the schedules of action in the plan, will encompass one year of marketing activities. However, again we should remember that the circumstances of the particular company and the markets in which it operates may dictate the need for both shorter-term planning horizons, including the need for immediate action, and/or longer-term marketing programmes, such as those needed for new product development.

The detailed marketing mix strategies and tactics are the heart of the annual marketing plan and may need to be developed around, say, separate products or possibly different geographical markets, according to how the company is structured and the range of markets in which it operates. In other words, we would have separate annual marketing plans for, say, the industrial products and consumer products divisions in the company, or for home and export markets.

As a guide to the range of decisions involved in the strategies and tactics for the marketing mix, Lancaster and Massingham[4] suggest some of the factors that the detailed marketing mix plans might consider for what in Chapter 4 were referred to as the 'conventional' four Ps as follows:

1. Products
   —Quality
   —Features
   —Options
   —Style
   —Services, installation, warranty
   —Packaging
   —Ranging, width and depth
   —New product development
2. Price
   —Pricing strategies, e.g. 'skimming *v.* penetration'
   —Price changes
   —List prices
   —Discounts
   —Allowances
   —Payment and credit terms
3. Promotion
   —Overall emphasis in promotional mix
   —Objectives, strategies and plans for:
     (a) Personal selling
     (b) Advertising
     (c) Sales promotion
     (d) Public relations and publicity
4. Place
   —Channel configuration/coverage/levels
   —Specific types of intermediaries
   —Terms and responsibilities of channel members
   —Order processing systems
   —Warehousing, storage, stocking and delivery policies

As we saw in Chapter 8, for service products this range of marketing mix decisions may be extended even further. This complexity is added to if we consider that we also need to develop detailed plans for each of the sub-elements of the marketing mix. For example, under the promotional element of the mix, we need to develop detailed plans for the advertising element of the promotion mix, which may include:

—Objectives
—Copy content/message
—Media decisions
—Timings/frequency
—Measurement of effectiveness/control

The essentials of a system of evaluation and control are shown in Fig. 13.2. Once again, it should be noted how this, the third basic function of marketing management, is related to the functions of planning and organizing. In fact, this control sequence is applicable at any level and for any management function in a company. Its essentials are:

—Setting standards for performance.
—Evaluating performance against these standards.
—Taking action to correct any deviations from standards.

Figure 13.2   The control sequence in marketing

As we have already covered the importance of setting specific and preferably quantifiable standards of performance for marketing, we shall concentrate here on the important evaluative and corrective elements of this process.

Essentially, in evaluating the department's marketing efforts the marketing manager needs to consider the following questions:

—What has happened?
—How does this compare with the standards of performance?
—What explains any differences between standards and actual performance?
—What action needs to be taken and by whom?

In fact, although the control process and the questions that relate to it are common to any control problem, as Kotler[5] points out, four types of marketing control may be distinguished:

—Control of the annual marketing plan.
—Control of profitability
—Control of efficiency.
—Strategic control.

The marketing manager is interested in all four types of control, but the prime concern is with the first and last of these, namely control of the annual plan, and strategic control. We shall examine both the purpose of these two control areas and some of the control techniques or approaches that are associated with each.

Annual plan control

The purpose of annual plan control is to determine the extent to which marketing efforts over the year have been successful. Among the most frequently used control techniques in this evaluation are likely to be sales analysis and analysis of market share.

Sales analysis   Despite exhortations to be marketing rather than sales-oriented in our approach to

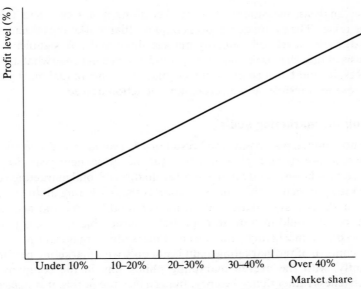

Figure 13.3   Generalized relationship between market share and profitability

customers, overall marketing standards of performance, and therefore techniques of evaluation and control, are often geared to the analysis of sales.

Normally sales analysis will commence with a comparison of budgeted sales revenue against actual sales revenue. Any variations may be due to volume and/or price variances. For example, an unfavourable sales variance may be due to having had to cut prices. The manager must now examine closely the possible reasons for this. Further detailed analysis may be by individual products, territories, customers, etc., in order to determine more precise information on the nature and extent of price cutting. It should be recognized that these analyses may not lead directly to action. Frequently, data from sales analysis will be used to formulate hypotheses that will form the basis for experimentation. The results of these experiments are actionable. Sevin[6] has referred to the combination of analysis and experiment as *productivity analysis*.

Analysis of market share   Of all the approaches to controlling annual marketing operations, analysis of market share represents one of the most useful and, therefore, widely used techniques. The principal reason for measuring and evaluating market share performance is that it allows a company to assess how well it is doing *vis-à-vis* competitors. For example, a company might find that, while its sales volume has declined over the year, its market share has increased. Clearly, declining sales volume would still represent a cause for concern; nevertheless, an increase in market share would indicate that a company is faring better than competitors in a market that has declined overall. The importance of this conclusion would suggest a very different course of action on the part of marketing management than that suggested by a simple analysis of sales.

A second reason for using market share analysis in marketing control stems from the fact that often overall marketing objectives are couched in terms of market share. Certainly, to some extent market share does indeed represent an overall indication of the efficiency of total marketing efforts compared with competitors. However, as we have seen in Chapter 5 with portfolio analysis, perhaps a more pressing reason for stating objectives in terms of market share is the newly recognized strong link between relative market share and profitability. The general nature of this relationship is shown in Fig. 13.3.

As with sales analysis, measurement of market alone is not sufficient to determine what actions should be taken. The evaluation process requires that marketing management determines the reasons for observed levels of company market share and any significant differences and trends. On the basis of this, the marketing manager must then determine what actions are required and by whom. Results and conclusions of the evaluation of the annual marketing plan must be discussed with those responsible, and a future plan of action agreed.

Strategic control: the marketing audit

More often than not, annual plan control will result in a re-evaluation of objectives, strategies and tactics with a view to preparing a plan of action for the subsequent year. From time to time, however, a more comprehensive and far-reaching evaluation of total marketing activities needs to be undertaken. One approach to such an evaluation is the marketing audit.

A marketing audit is a systematic, critical and preferably impartial appraisal of the total marketing operation: it would include an appraisal of basic objectives and policies, marketing methods and procedures, marketing personnel and marketing organization.

The primary concern of the marketing audit is not only with marketing performance but also, equally importantly, with the overall marketing philosophy in the company. It is more an appraisal of effectiveness rather than efficiency. In part, because of this, it is suggested that the full marketing audit be conducted not by marketing management but by an 'outsider', if not to the company then at least to the marketing function. The use of the full marketing audit is at present rather restricted—only a handful of UK companies have this as part of marketing control. Nevertheless, the usefulness of the marketing audit in a rapidly changing environment will no doubt lead to an increase in the number of companies incorporating this procedure.

DIRECTING AND MARKETING MANAGEMENT

The final, basic, and therefore essential, function of marketing management relates to the marketing department's human element. The marketing manager, like any other manager, relies upon people to get things done. Sophisticated marketing techniques, effective marketing plans and substantial financial resources in a company do not in themselves guarantee success. In the final analysis, a key factor in the determining of success or failure is the effective management of people. This is as true in marketing as in any other functional area of business. To some extent this aspect of marketing management is sadly neglected in marketing tests: perhaps surprising when one considers just how many 'failures' in marketing can be traced to the ineffective management of the human asset. The marketing manager must, therefore, give careful thought to the direction of these assets such that they contribute as much as possible towards desired results. Effective direction of marketing staff involves recruiting and selecting, training and developing, and leading and motivating, marketing personnel. The relationship between these elements and effective performance is shown in Fig. 13.4. In addition, it must also be realized that managerial influences will subjectively affect the planning process—a topic explored in detail by Greenley.[7]

Figure 13.4 Effective performance and aspects of directing

Abilities

Every manager will find it difficult to secure maximum performance from the staff if they lack the necessary abilities to function effectively in their duties. Ability, however, is in turn a function of a combination of effective recruitment and selection, plus effective training and development of marketing staff. Normally these aspects of human asset management are seen as being the prerogative of the personnel manager. The marketing manager, however, must not abrogate his duties in this area. The personnel department must be kept informed of the essential qualities and skills that they must look for in job applicants for sales and marketing posts. This, in turn, will require a careful job analysis and the preparation of job descriptions. Marketing managers need to be involved in this process; indeed, there is a greater value to a company in conducting regular job analyses and preparing up-to-date job descriptions. This enhanced value lies in the fact that determining manpower requirements makes it necessary for the marketing manager to think carefully about the tasks the marketing staff is required to perform and the extent to which these tasks are still relevant to the effective performance of the manager's function. Job analyses and descriptions also form the basis for assessing performance and organizing development and training programmes.

Having selected the best available staff for the marketing function, individual potential must be developed and refined; this applies equally to both new entrants and existing staff. The marketing manager should ensure that all members of staff are adequately trained. In the case of new staff this may involve induction training and the development of the basic skills required to do the job. Existing staff, too, may from time to time be required to acquire new skills and patterns of behaviour. The marketing manager should ensure that there is an adequate system of career planning for the human assets in his or her department. Once again, it is recognized that training and development are specialist areas requiring specialist staff, specialist knowledge, and a specialist text.[8] Every marketing manager, however, is directly responsible for ensuring that his or her staff members are given adequate leadership and are motivated.

Effort

Motivation and leadership together constitute the second major element of human asset performance. Surprisingly, the first of these—motivation of marketing staff—is given very little attention in conventional texts on marketing management. 'Surprisingly' because, as we have seen in Chapter 3, an understanding of human motivation is essential for effective marketing decision-making. This understanding should be applied to the motivation of marketing staff. Marketing management should look beyond the simplistic view that what motivates individuals at work is financial inducement: money. In the same way that consumers may be motivated by a variety of complex and often hierarchical factors, so too has research shown that many of the higher-order needs in Maslow's hierarchy[9] can be fulfilled if the work is designed so as to give marketing staff a real feeling of responsibility and achievement.

Finally, in the role of managing the human asset, the marketer must fulfil his or her leadership function. As Handy points out,[10] the 'leadership problem' has attracted countless theories and spawned endless research. The evidence and the theories remain ambiguous and inconclusive. In practice, effective leadership in marketing management requires that the manager achieve a balance between supporting and encouraging members of staff, and ensuring that objectives are successfully met. Above all, the effective leader must constantly strive to win the trust and respect of subordinates.

CONCLUSIONS

All managers, regardless of their functional specialism, have certain basic tasks to perform. Key among these tasks are the managerial elements of planning, organizing, directing and controlling. We have seen how each of these tasks applied to marketing management, from the planning of annual marketing activities through to their evaluation and control. Finally, we have examined briefly the often neglected but vitally important area of managing marketing personnel. If marketing management is to be effective, careful consideration should be given to the selection, training, leadership and motivation of staff.

APPLICATION QUESTIONS

1. Outline the key steps in the development of the annual marketing plan.
2. Distinguish between marketing strategies and marketing tactics. Under what circumstances is the effective use of marketing tactics particularly beneficial.
3. What is involved in the organizing element of marketing management?
4. Discuss the use of 'annual plan control' and the 'marketing audit' in the evaluation of marketing activities.
5. Why is it important for marketing management to make the most effective use of its human assets?

REFERENCES

1. H. H. Albors, *Principles of Management: A Modern Approach*, 4th edn, John Wiley, New York, 1974.
2. P. Kotler, *Marketing Management: Analysis, Planning Implementation and Control*, 7th edn, Prentice-Hall, Englewood Cliffs, NJ, 1991, Chapter 3.
3. G. A. Steiner, *Top Management Planning*, Collier Macmillan, London, 1969, p. 24.
4. G. A. Lancaster and L. Massingham, *Marketing Management*, McGraw-Hill, London, 1993, Chapter 17.
5. Kotler, op. cit., Chapter 26.
6. C. H. Sevin, *Marketing Productivity Analysis*, McGraw-Hill, New York, 1965.
7. G. E. Greenley, *The Strategic and Operational Planning of Marketing*, McGraw-Hill, London, 1986, pp. 143–64.
8. D. S. Markwell and T. J. Roberts, *Organisation of Management Development Programmes*, Gower Press, Aldershot, 1970.
9. A. H. Maslow, 'A theory of human motivation', *Psychological Review*, **50**, 1943, pp. 370–96.
10. C. B. Handy, *Understanding Organisations*, Penguin, Harmondsworth, 1976, pp. 87–104.

PART
FOUR

MARKETING'S WIDER ISSUES

FOURTEEN

INTERNATIONAL MARKETING

INTRODUCTION

The aim of this chapter is to give an insight into the complex area of international marketing. There is no suggestion that, having read this, you will have become an expert in marketing overseas or in export procedures, but you should at least be aware of some of the additional implications.

INTERNATIONAL MARKETING DEFINED

Marketers are not agreed that international marketing can be considered a subject separate from marketing on a domestic scale, and this is perhaps one reason why it has been difficult to arrive at a comprehensive yet succinct definition. For the purposes of this chapter, it is proposed to accept the definition put forward by Walsh.[1] International marketing is:

(a) the marketing of goods and services across national frontiers
(b) the marketing operations of an organisation that sells and/or produces within a given country when:
    (i) that organisation is part of, or associated with, an enterprise which also operates in other countries; *and*
    (ii) there is some degree of influence on or control of that organisation's marketing activities from outside the country in which it sells and/or produces.

In other words, the term 'international marketing' can be applied to the activities of the exporter and of any organization that has some international concern. A small manufacturing company can be an international marketer to a limited degree simply by distributing its products in foreign markets. Companies with overseas sales subsidiaries or overseas manufacturing plant (whether wholly or partly owned, or operating independently and manufacturing under licence) and the multinational corporation are all included in the definition.

From the point of view of the United Kingdom, export activity continues to be a significant factor in international marketing activities. As an industrialized nation lacking valuable raw materials, the UK is particularly dependent on international trade. It differs, therefore, from the USA, for example, from whose viewpoint many texts on international marketing have been written, since the latter's domestic market is large enough to absorb its production. Succeeding sections reflect the importance of engaging in international marketing.

MULTINATIONAL CORPORATIONS

The term 'multinational corporation' is widely used and has been variously defined. Once again, Walsh[2] provides a useful working definition. The multinational corporation is a company:

(a) which has a direct investment base in several countries;
(b) which generally derives 20–50 per cent or more of its net profits from foreign operations; and
(c) whose management makes policy decisions based on the alternatives available anywhere in the world.

The key factor is that the company should have a global outlook, making its business decisions with regard to the options available worldwide. It is not, therefore, a domestically based US or Swiss or Dutch company (although many multinational corporations have their origins in single domestic markets), but is a company whose operations span the globe. Manufacturing occurs simultaneously in several different countries and goods are sold worldwide.

The concept of global marketing includes a number of advantages for multinationals:

—*Programme transfers* They can draw upon strategies, products, advertising appeals, sales management practices, promotional ideas and so on that have been tested in actual markets and can apply them in comparable markets.
—*Systems transfers* They can introduce planning, budgeting, new product introduction and other successful systems developed and tested in the company into new markets.
—*People transfers* They can assign skilled people across national boundaries, thus drawing upon a manpower pool of international rather than merely national dimensions.
—*Scale economies in manufacturing* Multinational firms, in addition to obtaining traditional single-plant-scale economies, can combine components manufactured in scale-efficient plants in different countries into finished products.
—*Economies of centralisation of functional activities* Instead of duplicating and dispersing its functional staff, multinationals can concentrate activities at single locations and thereby develop greater competence and at the same time reduce costs.
—*Resource utilization* A major strength of multinational companies is their ability to scan the entire world to identify sources of manpower, money and materials that will enable them most effectively to compete in world markets.
—*Global strategy* They can scan the world for markets that provide opportunities to apply their skills, match the markets with their resources, and where necessary exploit opportunities, create and shift resources to tap identified opportunities.

Multinational corporations have become increasingly large over time, several having annual sales that equal the GNP of smaller European nations. They are, therefore, an extremely significant force. For a more detailed discussion, the reader is directed to Tugendhat's work.[3]

It is useful at this point to distinguish between international marketing and international trade. While trade between nations will inevitably impinge on the activities of international marketing, the terms are not synonymous. World trade is often a simple exchange of goods. In the Eastern bloc, for example, goods are seen as methods of payment rather than as a means of meeting market needs, and hence much trade is by barter.

While some of the activities of marketing may be involved in the exporting process (for example distribution activities), there may well be no marketing management. Terpstra[4] suggests a useful table of comparison (Table 14.1).

STAGES OF ECONOMIC DEVELOPMENT OF EXPORT MARKETS

The environment within which marketing operates is continually dynamic and largely uncontroll-

Table 14.1   Comparison of international trade and international marketing

Dimension	International trade	International marketing
Actors	Nations	Firms
Goods move across frontiers	Yes	Not necessarily
Impetus	Comparative advantage	Company decisions (usualy profit motivated)
Information source	Nation's balance of payments	Company records
Marketing activities:		
Buy and sell	Yes	Yes
Physical distribution	Yes	Yes
Pricing	Yes	Yes
Market research	Generally not	Yes
Product development	Generally not	Yes
Promotion	Generally not	Yes
Distribution channel management	No	Yes

Source: V. Terpstra, *International Marketing*, 3rd edn, Dryden Press, Hinsdale, IL, 1983.

able. For international marketing this difficulty is magnified; not only are the uncontrollable elements of the environment different from country to country, but the controllable elements of the marketing mix must be adapted to these differing environments. Particularly significant is the diversity that exists between levels of economic activity among nations.

W. W. Rostow[5] has provided a description of economies which suggests that all nations are in or are passing through one of the following stages:

—Traditional society
—Preconditions for take-off
—Take-off
—Drive to maturity
—Age of high mass consumption

More common terms are now in use, and while these may change over time (for example, the term 'less developed country' has given way to 'developing country'), they provide a more current classification.

1. *Subsistence economies* This category consists of those nations dependent on primitive agriculture, with a limited infrastructure and high dependence on foreign aid. Examples include much of Africa (Ethiopia, Burkina Faso) and parts of Asia (Bangladesh).
2. *Developing countries* There is increasing industrialization and a developing infrastructure in these. Such economies are usually reliant on raw material exports, often based on the extractive industries, including oil (Nigeria, Mexico and the Middle East).
3. *Industrializing countries* The rapidly industrializing economies of many South American countries (e.g. Brazil) and countries such as Portugal and Greece can be considered under this heading.
4. *Industrialized countries* This includes the major Western industrial countries of Europe, North America and Japan.

An additional sub-grouping, *affluent countries*, usually includes the United States, Sweden and West Germany, with their demand for high-quality, sophisticated consumer goods.

Note While the oil-exporting countries of the Middle East have a high GNP *per capita*, the development of their infrastructure is still limited and there is a wide disparity between rich and poor. Consequently, they cannot be considered as being truly affluent countries, but perhaps merit a separate category for the purposes of international marketing.

While the above classification is useful, it must be remembered that, as with all environmental factors, it is constantly subject to change. Equally, it may be difficult to place a nation in a particular category.

For the marketer, therefore, the stage in economic development may be a starting-point for researching opportunities overseas, but in itself will provide limited guidance.

IDENTIFYING EXPORT OPPORTUNITIES

Information for marketing decisions was considered in some detail in Part Two of this text. Quantitative and qualitative techniques previously discussed are equally relevant when attempting to identify overseas opportunities. In general, however, the backcloth against which these opportunities are seen is broader.

The number of possible markets is large—over 240 political states are listed in the *United States Statistical Yearbook*; of these over 150 are members of the United Nations. The number of nations that will provide viable market opportunities will, of course, differ from firm to firm and from product to product, and the arguments for concentrating marketing activity within a small group of markets versus spreading to a large number of overseas markets can also be seen to follow this pattern. Be that as it may, a framework for analysing overseas markets is a useful starting-point in a programme of marketing research. The aim of such a programme is to produce a ranked list of overseas markets for future marketing research in depth on the basis of likely potential for the company and its product(s), and to do it in the most cost-effective way. A suggested step-by-step approach is reproduced in Fig. 14.1.

A key factor to consider is market accessibility. This is more than determining how close a country is to the UK or other domestic market. It will include an assessment of both tariff and non-tariff barriers to trade.

A *tariff* can be simply defined as a tax on products crossing a frontier. Tariffs are often imposed by governments to protect local industry from overseas competition. The General Agreement on Tariffs and Trade (GATT) is an institution established to provide a worldwide forum for discussion in an attempt to reduce the need for tariffs.

Non-tariff barriers include other forms of government action to restrict imports, for example quotas. A *quota* places a specific limit, by volume or value, on the amount of goods exported to a specific market and is usually applied to a specific nation or group of nations. For example, the Multi-Fibre Arrangement (MFA) limits exports of textile products from developing countries to the UK and other European nations. Other non-tariff barriers include discriminatory exchange rate policies, restrictive customs procedures and restrictive administrative and technical regulations. For example, the technical regulations for electrical appliances differ between the UK and West Germany, despite common membership of the European Community (EC). France introduced a regulation whereby all video-cassette recorders imported from Japan were cleared through customs in a limited number of inland towns, effectively reducing the number of imports since only a relatively small number of products could be cleared per day. Non-tariff barriers also include geographic and climatic barriers.

Despite these problems, finding information about accessibility is relatively easy when using government sources such as the British Overseas Trade Board (BOTB). This first stage will reduce the number of potential markets literally from three figures to two, at least as far as direct export is

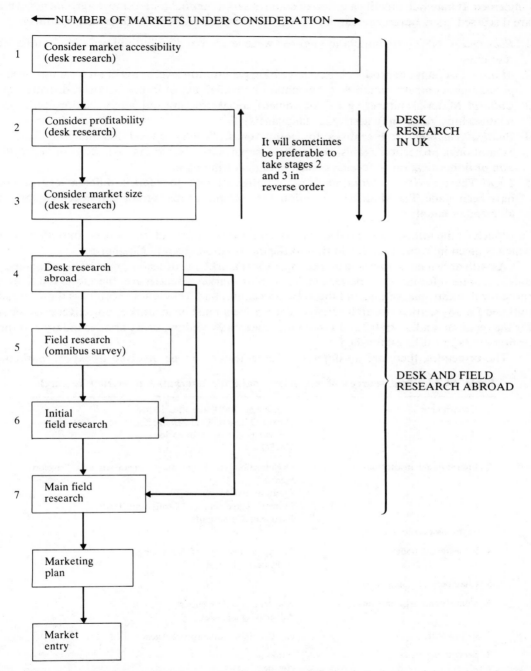

Figure 14.1   International research strategy: a stage-by-stage approach aimed at selection of the markets of greatest potential at the lowest possible research cost
Source: L. S. Walsh, *International Marketing*, Macdonald and Evans, London, 1981, p. 18

concerned. It may well identify a group of countries for potential joint venture agreements, which are discussed later. Further research can then be considered under the following headings:

1. *Economic* GNP/GDP; population figures; wage levels and distribution; price levels; inflation; resources.
2. *Market* Size; stage in product life cycle; market penetration level or average consumption level per annum; competition; market segmentation; availability of media, services, distribution.
3. *Cultural* Material culture (e.g. role of women); social structure and family relationships; social relationships; religion(s); aesthetics; language(s).
4. *Political environment* Incentives for joint venture/wholly owned manufacture (e.g. tax exemptions); protection against competitive imports (tariffs and quotas). *Risks* of appropriation or domestication of foreign owned manufacturing plant.
5. *Legal* There is no true international law, although attempts to reconcile different legal practice have been made. The Madrid Convention, for example, protects trade marks of signatories in all member countries.

Much of the information needed can be obtained from secondary sources, an outline list of which is given in Table 14.2 in addition to the information given in Chapter 5.

As with decisions in domestic marketing, export marketing decisions must be based on up-to-date, accurate information. The reasons for export market research are, therefore, the same as those for domestic marketing, and the basic procedures and techniques encompass those already outlined for any market research activity. The problem must be identified, objectives must be set for the research, and a careful and systematic research procedure, using first secondary and then primary data, must be established.

The principles, then, are no different. Nevertheless, anyone involved in export marketing

Table 14.2   Some sources of secondary data for international market research

1. Government	Department of Trade and Industry
	British Overseas Trade Board
	Central Office of Information
	HMSO
2. International institutions	Organization for Economic Cooperation and Development
	International Monetary Fund
	General Agreement on Tariffs and Trade
	European Community
3. Trade associations	
4. Professional bodies	Chartered Institute of Marketing
	Institute of Export
5. Chambers of commerce	
6. Commercial organizations	Market research agencies
	Advertising agencies
7. Consultants	e.g. Economist Intelligence Agency
8. Service industries	Banks
	Airlines
	Freight forwarders
9. European Society for Opinion and Market Research (ESOMAR)	
10. Other published sources, e.g. Axel Springer Publishing Group (W. Germany)	

research will tell you that there are added complexities in researching across international frontiers. Let us examine some of these problems.

Obtaining secondary data

Differences in the availability and quality of secondary data are important considerations in export market research. Although exporting is recognized as vital to the economic well-being of a country, not all countries—or, more specifically, not all the would-be exporters to them—are equally well served when it comes to published statistical data.

It is a fact that great care should be taken in using any market research information that is derived from secondary sources. In the case of market and statistical information published outside the country of the exporter, great care should be taken in attempting to verify the accuracy of the data.

Differences between countries

Differences between countries are generally much greater than those experienced within a country with respect to social and marketing practices, political and commercial institutions and, of course, language.

In researching export markets, it is important to remember that conditions may vary so much from country to country that each country has to be looked at individually. Above all, it is important not to assume that, because a product or service is a commercial success in one country, it will automatically be so in another. This is true even of countries which, for political or historical reasons, share similar customs, life styles and, indeed, languages.

There are many examples where, because some basic—if apparently small—difference has been overlooked, a great deal of money and effort on the part of the exporter has been wasted. Even within a country, regional variations may be sufficient to require different marketing strategies. These variations add to the complexity of research in export markets and should be considered at a very early stage in research design.

Defining boundaries

Definition of the boundaries of potential export markets adds a further complication to export market research. There is an obvious need to define the boundaries of potential export markets before we being to research them. But are frontiers the best way of doing this? We can define potential export markets as follows:

—Geographically.
—Administratively—say, according to the location of the international divisions of the company.
—By trading blocs, e.g. EC, EFTA, LAFTA, ASEAN.
—Politically.

Clearly, the approach adopted will affect the research procedure and should be defined at the outset.

Cost of research

Managers often flinch at the complexity and cost of export market research, and admittedly, market research, whether in-company or agency-commissioned, can be very expensive. However, if care is taken at the early stages of market assessment, the costs—particularly in relation to the benefits—need not be onerous.

The essence of keeping down market research costs is to approach the assessment of export potential in a step-by-step way.

Preliminary screening of markets The first step is to conduct a preliminary screening of export markets and to discard those that offer little or no potential. Information provided at this stage may also provide a basis for the decision as to whether or not to export.

Much of the information collected at this stage may be the result of *desk research* using secondary (published) data.

It is difficult and dangerous to list the factors that every company should consider at this preliminary screening stage. Each company must select those criteria for assessment that are relevant to its own particular product markets, objectives and resources. Examples of factors that might be considered are:

—*Accessibility*: distance, freight and similar charges, import duties, quotas, prohibitions, licence requirements, exchange problems—other non-tariff barriers.
—*Market size*: present total size, local production; imports and exports, past trends, future trends.
—*Profitability*: present market price levels in relation to landed costs.

Information sources Again, it must be stressed that at this stage in market assessment much of the information can be obtained at relatively little cost from published sources. If anything, the potential exporter is rather better served with marketing information than for domestic markets. This again reflects the acknowledgement of the importance of exporting by governments.

Of all the general reference sources available, among the most comprehensive and informative are those produced by government agencies and the commercial banks. For example, in the United Kingdom the government's British Overseas Trade Board (BOTB) will provide information on: foreign import regulations and tariffs; agents and business contacts; export market research, etc. Similarly, many of the major banks provide basic market information on developments in the world's major trading nations.

Detailed investigation of export markets

The potential export markets that remain after the screening process should now be subjected to a more detailed analysis based on information obtained from first hand investigations in the remaining market(s). This information may be collected:

—By visits to the overseas market by company personnel.
—By commissioning market research.
—By both.

It is important at this stage to remember the following points:

—Field research should be carried out only in markets shown to be promising.
—Market research is unlikely to indicate market entry for all markets; i.e., inevitably there will be some wastage.
—The research terms of reference should be designed right from the start as input to the marketing plan. Details of the plan or brief will, of course, vary according to company, product range and marketing situation.

In order to qualify as a potential export market, it is likely that the following conditions will have to be met:

1. There must be enough potential customers who need the benefits of the product or service.
2. Enough potential customers must recognize these benefits, or it must be possible to persuade them.
3. Potential customers must have the resources to purchase the product/service.
4. It must be possible to reach them via distribution channels efficiently and economically.
5. Total demand at a price must enable the manufacturer to cover costs and make a profit.

Using the press

In many countries there is no national press, regional newspapers being dominant. When trying to assess the value of an advertising campaign, one has to consider at least half a dozen newspapers which have different readerships.

Examination of tastes and customs

On top of all this, there are the varying customs, likes, dislikes and prejudices in each country which have to be examined before any research is undertaken, so that no time is wasted because some basic fact has been overlooked. For instance, if one considers the pet food industry, it must be remembered that in many foreign cities people live in flats where they are precluded by rules from keeping pets. With regard to the do-it-yourself trade in Switzerland, one must take into account the fact that most townspeople again live in flats, where they are forbidden by the terms of the lease to make any alterations to their apartments, or even, in some cases, to use electric drills or similar tools.

Because of all the above variations, a questionnaire prepared for an English market would be quite meaningless, as many of the questions would not apply, and the factors affecting the customer's decision to buy would be different.

Research overseas must be tailored to the country in question, and in this it is essential not to generalize. Many people are inclined to look upon South America or the Far East as a whole, which is quite wrong; each country is different, and in many cases there is a huge difference between the capital and the rest of the country.

Desk research must be carried out very carefully and very thoroughly. The researchers must endeavour to obtain as much relevant information as they can, and be prepared to have summaries of reports, or even complete reports, translated. When this has been done, it is possible to assess the worth of a visit to the market in question in order to gather more information. In many cases, the best method is to discuss the question in depth with the export department staff dealing with the region in question, as they will be able to fill many of the gaps left by desk research. Once this has been done, the export sales staff will be briefed exactly as to the information that is required, and a selling visit to the overseas country can be coupled with a market research investigation, which will then be relatively inexpensive.

The market research department should by this time have a good idea of the market in question, its distribution channels and its likes and dislikes, and should be in a position to assess roughly the types of product or methods of selling that will be suitable. If the potential appears to be sufficiently large, a market research visit can then be arranged, to go further into the points that have to be settled before the marketing operation starts.

The aim of a marketing research programme is to arrive at a group of markets that offer potential for export and where similarities with the domestic market, rather than differences from it, can be emphasized and exploited.

THE MARKETING MIX APPLIED TO INTERNATIONAL MARKETING

The term 'marketing mix' was introduced in Chapter 4 and its major elements discussed in some detail in Part Three of this text. Again, it must be said that the issues raised are as important to marketing internationally as they are to marketing in the domestic environment. Certain aspects of the mix hold special significance for international marketing.

Distribution

A detailed discussion on channels of distribution has already been provided in Chapter 10, but distribution for international marketing not only includes the structure of channels within a range of overseas markets, but, perhaps more fundamentally, must also address the strategic problem of market entry.

The options available fall into the following broad categories:

—Indirect export.
—Direct export.
—Manufacture abroad through joint ventures.
—Manufacture abroad through independent production.

These can be further subdivided as shown in Figs 14.2 and 14.3.

Any or all of these alternatives may be in use in one company, and for a full discussion of all

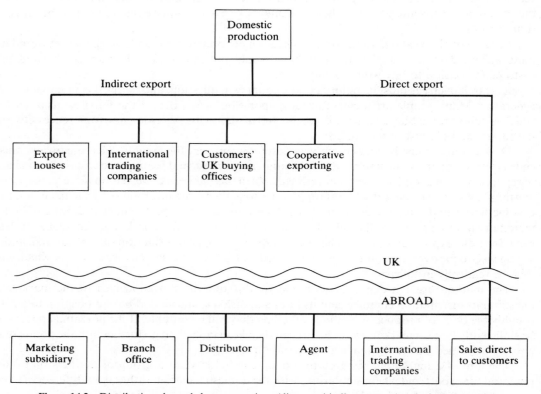

Figure 14.2   Distribution channels between nations (direct and indirect export): principal alternatives

Figure 14.3   Distribution channels (manufacture abroad): principal alternative channels
Source: L. S. Walsh, *International Marketing*, Macdonald and Evans, 1982

the options listed the reader is directed again to Walsh's[6] work. Certain alternatives have been selected for brief consideration here.

Agency   This may be defined as the legal relationship that exists when one person or company (the agent) is employed by another person or company (the principal) to bring that principal into a contractual relationship with third parties. A sales agent is thus employed to bring about a sales contract between his principal and the third party. The legal title to goods never passes to an agent; it passes, as a result of the agent's efforts, directly from principal to customer, the agent receiving a commission as payment. In marketing practice, however, the expression is loosely used to include distributors.

Distributors   These have been defined as customers who have been granted exclusive or preferential rights to purchase and re-sell a specific range of products in specified geographical areas or markets. Distributors are, therefore, wholesalers, who are 'paid' by the difference between purchase price and resale price (and *not* from any commission from the suppliers). As such, their role is as defined for similar channel intermediaries in domestic operations.

Agents and distributors offer similar advantages to the would-be exporter. They have local experience of market conditions and business practice, valuable to the new exporter, and they involve little or no investment costs. Such advantages should be carefully weighed against the disadvantages. Agents, in particular, are often unable to take a long-term view, which is essential for effective marketing management. Agents have a living to make and are understandably interested in those products that earn commission from the outset. They usually represent various companies and offer a wide range of products. A new product thus might not receive as much attention as a proven successful product.

Agents and distributors are only two options available to exporters, and, while often successful, they should be viewed against the alternatives. A branch office, and company-employed local salesforce, while involving considerable investment, can offer long-term potential for development.

As far as *overseas assembly and manufacture* are concerned, joint ventures require some attention. It would be impossible to consider all the alternatives in a chapter of this length, but the major advantage common to all options is that of market access (where this may be impossible as a result of tariff or quota restrictions). The degree of risk varies—it is relatively low where licensing is concerned and substantial in the case of jointly owned manufacturing facilities, where the possibility of expropriation by the national government adds to the problem of financial outlay.

For purposes of clarification, some attention is now given to two joint-venture options, licensing and franchising.

Licensing This is the term used to cover a wide range of agreements relating to the sale or leasing of industrial or commercial expertise. This may include a patent covering a product or process, manufacturing 'know-how', and the use of a trade mark or brand name. In return, the licensee pays a sum, often a minimum amount annually, or an agreed percentage of turnover annually. Licensing can, therefore, be said to involve the sale of intangibles.

Franchising This is a *form* of licensing, but the franchiser provides a standard package of components or ingredients together with management and marketing services and advice. Since franchising involves the transfer of tangibles, it can enable greater control of the operation for the originating manufacturer than licensing. Examples of successful franchising operations include Pepsi Cola, which sells its concentrate to franchises who own bottling plants, employ local staff and control their own promotional budgets; other examples are Benetton, the Italian knitwear manufacturer, whose franchised shops are now a common feature of European high streets, and the Body Shop.

The selection of a channel for market entry is vital to the success of distribution within each overseas market. The shorter the overall channel of distribution, the greater the control. In terms of international marketing, a greater cost is the financial involvement. For smaller firms, some sacrifice of control is thus inevitable in many instances and a balance between these two issues must be achieved.

Finally as in domestic markets, no section on distribution can ignore physical distribution or logistics. The importance of physical distribution for exporting in particular is such that a short section is devoted to this topic at the end of the chapter.

Product

Perhaps the most significant decisions for international marketing are those of product standardization and variety reduction. Examples of the need to meet individual national requirements, in particular where consumer goods are concerned, abound. One particularly descriptive example of the modifications needed to the Leyland (now Rover) Mini for successful exporting to Japan is given by Whymant.[7] In addition to overcoming the emission requirements, a wide range of other specifications had to be met:

1. The tyre must not protrude, so on Minis 'eye-brows' have to be fastened on the two front wings.

2. An audible warning device at 110 kph.
3. A red band on the speedometer to show when this speed is reached.
4. A heat shield above the catalyst to stop occupants of the car cooking, and a grass shield underneath so that what grass you do see in Tokyo doesn't catch fire!
5. Special low wattage headlamps.
6. Overheat catalyst warning.
7. Special regulation number plate bracket.
8. Torch for use in breakdown.
9. Modification of emergency parking system for use in breakdown.
10. Side-wing repeater flashers to show when back indicator is on.
11. Reflectors on rear a different size and at a different angle.

While a standard product to meet a global need is attractive to the marketer, not least in terms of economies of scale, it may be impossible in practice. Legal, technical or climatic requirements may make modification mandatory. In addition, local tastes may make it desirable. Certainly, in view of the differing stages of economic development reached by different nations discussed earlier, a similar need may be met by a variety of products. The following section on a product life cycle for international trade highlights this problem.

The eventual result of product modification can lead to an over-full range of products; and, while the review and elimination procedures presented in Chapter 8 remain valid for international marketing, the scale of the problem is often much greater. International product elimination is, therefore, an area of great importance. In certain circumstances where domestic production costs or small-scale production runs make a product unprofitable, alternative options such as licensing (see above) may enable the marketer to improve profits while retaining market position.

Keegan[8] has identified five possible strategies (Fig. 14.4) for international marketing which encompass the mix elements of product and promotion. These are discussed in brief before considering the promotional element in the next section:

1. *Straight extension* This is the introduction of the product in the same form and with the same communications in use at home. This is a tempting strategy, as it involves no additional manufacturing or marketing costs. Examples of successful products include Pepsi Cola.
2. *Communications adaptation* This is where a company modifies its promotional theme but retains an unchanged product. This strategy has a relatively low cost of implementation since major manufacturing costs are not incurred. The example quoted by Keegan is that of bicycles, which are a product designed to meet leisure needs in the United States and other developed countries, but are a basic mode of transport in many developing nations.

		Products		
		No change	Adapted	New product
Marketing communications	No change	Straight extension	Product adaptation	
	Adapt	Communication adaptation	Dual adaptation	Product invention

Figure 14.4 Keegan's strategies for international marketing

3. *Product adaptation* This involves the modification of a product for reasons discussed earlier, e.g. preferences, while retaining the communications theme. Products that are particularly susceptible to taste, e.g. food and clothing, are such examples.

4. *Dual adaptation* This involves modifying both product and communications to meet the needs of specific markets. Keegan cites the introduction of instant coffee into the United Kingdom, where tastes differed from other European nations in which there is a longer coffee-drinking tradition, and where the initial launch was to a different market segment—the young, who were less traditional and for whom a specific communications message was required.

5. *Product inventions* Where product needs and market conditions are similar to those in the home market, the first four strategies are effective options. In other countries, such as the developing nations, this may not be the case. Product invention, or the development of a new product to meet consumer needs at an affordable price, may be the only alternative. The invention 'backwards' from modern technology of a better manual washing machine for those countries where washing is still done by hand is a good example.

There is no best strategy for a firm—the optimum choice will depend on the specific product–market–company mix.

Promotion

The elements of the communications mix discussed in Chapter 11 are as relevant for international marketing as they are for domestic marketing. For an established company marketing its products overseas, the decisions to be taken hinge on whether a standardized promotional campaign can be contemplated or whether promotion should be adapted to individual national needs.

Complete standardization of all aspects of a campaign is rarely possible—language differences alone ensure this. It is possible, however, for a *common creative idea and message* to be adopted—the Esso Tiger is a classic example—using similar media and a common advertising strategy.

The organization of advertising on an international scale is modelled on the US pattern, with branches of many US advertising agencies throughout the world. The environmental differences, discussed above in relation to international marketing research, play a very significant role in international advertising decisions: cultural differences, government attitudes to advertising and, in particular, availability of advertising media are of particular relevance. Even among industrialized nations, commercial television is not always available to the advertiser. Where it is offered, advertising flexibility (by channels in the UK, for example) can be lacking, with lead times of a year being common.

In addition to the national media available within each overseas market, an additional category, international media, can be added to the list of means of promotion for the international marketer. These are publications that aim, as a matter of policy, at coverage in several different countries. They include consumer magazines, such as *Readers' Digest*, *Time*, the various airline publications, trade and technical magazines, international commercial radio and international commercial television which is becoming increasingly significant with the growth of cable and satellite television. Such developments make the prospect of a standardized campaign attractive, particularly in view of cost savings in the production of creative promotional material.

Exhibitions, often considered as an element of below-the-line advertising, are probably of more importance to the international marketer than they are in domestic business. They allow buyer, intermediary and seller to come together, minimizing the costs and time involved for each. Exhibitions range from the giant international trade fairs covering all products and industries, such as Leipzig and Hanover, to the highly specialized international exhibitions specific to a particular product category, for example Pret-à-Porter and the London Boat Show. For a detailed list of international exhibitions, the reader is advised to consult the DTI's *Trade Promotions Guide*.

Agents and distributors have been considered above as intermediaries in the distribution channel. They should also be viewed as an integral part of a company's promotional activities. The representative overseas (and this will include a company employee, whether based locally or in the domestic market) is the first point of contact for the potential buyer. The representative's attitude to the buyer, his or her knowledge of the company and its products, and freedom to negotiate terms have an important (and sometimes adverse) influence. The position of the overseas sales representative is one of isolation from head office, and it is essential to foster two-way communication links.

Note The Central Office of Information (COI) offers a substantial public relations/publicity service to exporters of new or improved products or services. A professional news release is prepared and distributed to media in a variety of countries, including radio and television in certain countries where the COI has regular spots. The service is *entirely free* and is, according to the COI, often little known to would-be exporters.

Pricing

The methods of pricing detailed in Chapter 9 should be used as a basis for any pricing decision in international marketing. However, additional factors must be taken into consideration. Not least of these are the relationship between domestic and overseas pricing and the issue of transfer pricing.

The true marketer will expect to price the product or service according to the needs and requirements of the market. This may or may not be a price similar to that at which goods are sold at home. In practice, various constraints may prevent this, such as inadequate market information (which may not always be the fault of the marketing researcher, but rather a result of the market's stage of development as a whole), a prevailing world price, or the proximity of other markets where the same product is sold. Legal reasons may also be of relevance; the recent decision of the European Court to ban price differentials for motor cars sold in different member states of the EC was such an example.

The terms of payment under which goods are sold to export markets will add a further dimension to the price. Costs of packing, insurance and freight between buyer and seller all have to be borne and will determine the real selling price of goods. It is beyond the scope of this chapter to consider terms of trade in detail, but your attention is drawn to Walker's work[9] which includes definitions of accepted terms of trade (Incoterms).

Finally, the question of which currency is to be used as a basis for quoting prices overseas is significant. Following the marketing view, the aim of meeting consumers' or industrial buyers' needs would suggest that goods sold in the local currency to intermediaries would be more acceptable. Clearly, such a policy would simplify the buyer's position and would provide a significant competitive advantage in many instances. It must be stated, however, that pricing in the currency of the market may be inappropriate or impossible where developing or Eastern bloc countries are concerned. Since these currencies may not be freely convertible on the international money market, the decision is then to trade in either the domestic market currency or the currency of a third country (for example US dollars or Swiss francs).

Two final comments will be made before leaving this topic. First, although a price to meet the needs of the market must be desirable to achieve an optimum level of sales, it is undoubtedly simpler to base overseas prices on one of the techniques of cost-based pricing. In some instances, however, this may lose a market for the company, since the initial price may be too high for any significant sales to result; in others, it may cause the company concerned to price a product too low in relation to the established competition, thereby reducing potential profit and perhaps adversely affecting the image of the product in the eyes of the consumer.

Second, there have been allegations of 'dumping' products overseas by a variety of nations. Dumping can be described as the sale of goods in foreign markets at a price lower than the production cost. This appears to contradict the theory of market pricing, but it is true that industrialized countries tend to penalize such imports. To what extent setting a price to meet market demands can, or should, be viewed as dumping is open to debate. It is a question of degree and will, in many instances, depend on the product or industry concerned. In any event, the practice of true dumping, often at marginal prices, can be a high-risk strategy in international marketing. Goods sold at artificially low prices to an overseas buyer can (and often do) return to compete as competitively priced imports in the domestic market.

A second important issue in pricing for international markets is that of transfer pricing. The meaning of, approaches to, and issues involved in transfer pricing are outlined below.

When a company operates in several international markets, with different divisions or units operating as profit centres in each of these markets, it will often find itself transferring components or finished products between the different international divisions. To enable the profit performance of each unit to be evaluated, a price must be established for each inter-unit transaction. This is known as the *transfer price*.

Transfer prices may be established on a number of bases, such as cost, cost plus a standard margin, or arm's-length transfer, i.e. the same price as would be quoted to an independent customer. Central corporate management will usually establish the basis of the transfer price, with the aim of ensuring both a realistic assessment of the contribution of any one unit and the maximization of the profit of the enterprise as a whole.

The transfer price between operating units in different countries can be manipulated to minimize tax or import duty liability or (in effect) to transfer funds. For example:

1. Products may be transferred into high-duty countries at an artificially low transfer price so that, assuming duty is charged *ad valorem*, the duty paid will be low.
2. Products may be transferred into high-tax countries at high transfer prices so that profits in the high-tax country are virtually eliminated and, in effect, are transferred to low-tax countries.
3. Products may be transferred at high prices into a country from which dividend repatriation is restricted or subject to government taxes—in effect, invisible income replaces a formal dividend.
4. Similarly, it is possible to avoid an accumulation of funds in a country with high inflation rates, or where an early devaluation is thought to be a probability, or where expropriation is feared.

For these reasons, national governments are particularly interested in the uses (and abuses) of international transfer pricing. This is a complex area, but essentially we can summarize the attitudes of governments to transfer pricing as follows:

—The government of the *exporting* country has an interest in seeing that the transfer price is not artificially low, and it will endeavour to ensure that appropriate profits are made and taxes paid within its jurisdiction.
—In the *importing* country, the tax authorities are usually on the look-out for unreasonably high transfer prices, which will reduce local profits and, consequently, liability to income tax; while the customs authorities will, in contrast, be watching for low transfer prices designed to minimize duty liability.

As a final comment on this aspect of pricing, we should note that international transfer pricing can also be used as a weapon in the overall marketing strategy: profits can be concentrated, by vertically integrated corporations, at the stage of production where there is least competition. Competitors operating at other stages of production can thus be discouraged by the relatively low profits to be earned.

Pricing is a complex area that, in common with the other elements of the marketing mix, cannot be viewed in isolation. An integrated approach to all '4Ps' is as essential for international marketing as it is for domestic marketing.

PRODUCT LIFE CYCLE FOR INTERNATIONAL TRADE

The product life cycle theory, as discussed in Chapter 8, has proved useful in identifying future strategies for products and services. By applying it to international trade, Wells[10] has shown the relevance of the theory to importing and exporting a product.

It is contended that exporters would be helped if they had methods of analysing the export potential of their products and had predictors of which products were most likely to be threatened by import competition.

Exporters have traditionally relied upon economic theories which conclude that each country will export those products that use the country's most abundant production factors. However, when such theories are applied to the detailed problems facing business people, they become of limited value.

The trade cycle model has been proposed as an aid to exporters, and this is closely related to the product life cycle concept in marketing. Wells first proposed a theory that combined both, and in order that we might attempt to modify his model, a summary of his proposal is given below.

According to the trade cycle concept, many products follow a pattern that can be divided into four stages:

1. US export strength.
2. Start of foreign production.
3. Foreign production competitive in export markets.
4. Import competition begins.

A brief look at the reasoning underlying each of these stages will give some clues that might help the business person to identify the stage at which a particular product may be. The concept can then be of assistance in predicting the future product trade performance, and in understanding what actions the manager can take to modify the pattern for certain products and to profit from different stages of the cycle.

Phase 1: US export strength

The US market is special because it has a large body of very high-income consumers; for this reason, products that satisfy the special demands of such consumers are likely to be introduced in the United States. Moreover, owing to the monopolistic position of the United States as a supplier of new products that satisfy these special demands, they offer the best opportunities for export.

There is no simple relationship between demand and invention, but nevertheless, there can be little doubt that certain products are simply more likely to be developed initially in America. Although labour is cheaper abroad and production costs would be lower, it is more sensible to manufacture in the United States because production is closer to the market and near to specialist supplies. This is because at the early stages of a product's life design is often in a constant state of flux, and demands for design changes must be rapidly translated into more suitable products which require the availability of close communication with specialized suppliers. The existence of a monopoly, or of significant product differentiation at the early stages of the product life cycle, reduces the importance of costs to the manufacturer.

At this point, the American manufacturer has a virtual monopoly for the new product in the world market. US exports start as a trickle and develop into a steady stream as active export programmes are established by the American firms.

Phase 2: Start of foreign production

Product familiarity abroad increases, causing overseas markets to become so large that the product which once appealed primarily to the US consumer comes to have a broad appeal in more prosperous foreign countries. Not only does a potential foreign producer now have a market close at hand, but also, some of his costs will be lower than those of the US producer. Imports from America have to bear duty and overseas freight charges—costs that local products will not carry. Moreover, the potential foreign producer may have to invest less in product development, the US manufacturer having done part of this for him. Some measure of the size of his potential market has been demonstrated by the successful sale of imports. Favourable profit projections based upon a demonstrated market and an ability to underprice imports will eventually induce an entrepreneur in a more prosperous foreign market to commence manufacture.

During this second stage, American exports will still supply most of the world's markets. However, as foreign producers begin to manufacture, US exports to certain markets will decline. The pattern will probably be manifested in a slow-down in the rate of growth of US exports.

Phase 3: Foreign production competitive in export markets

As the early foreign manufacturers become larger and more experienced, their costs should fall. They will begin to reap the advantages of scale economies previously available only to US manufacturers—but, in addition, they will have lower labour costs. Hence their costs may be such that foreign products become competitive with American goods in third markets where goods from both countries have to carry similar freight and duty charges.

During this stage, US producers will be protected from imports in their domestic market where they are not faced with duty and overseas transportation costs. However, foreign goods will gradually take over the markets abroad which were previously held by American exports. The rate of growth of US exports will continue to decline.

Phase 4: Import competition begins

As the foreign manufacturer reaches mass production based on domestic and export markets, the lower labour rates and perhaps new plant may enable it to produce at lower costs than an American manufacturer. The cost savings may be sufficient to pay freight and US duty and still compete with Americans in their own market. This stage will be reached earlier if the foreign producer begins to think in terms of marginal costs for export pricing. If the firm believes that selling can be done above full costs in the home market and excess capacity can be used up by 'dumping' abroad, US producers, who are pricing on full costs, may very quickly be undercut. During this final stage, US exports will be reduced to almost zero, while import competition becomes severe.

Thus the cycle is complete, from the United States as a strong producer and exporter, to the stage where imports may capture a significant share of the American market.

The early foreign producers (usually Western Europeans) will face a cycle similar to that of the US manufacturer. As still lower-income markets become large enough, producers in these countries will eventually become competitive, displacing the dominance of the early foreign manufacturers. The manufacture of products moves from country to country in what Hufbauer[11] has called a 'pecking order'.

Clearly, no simple model can explain the behaviour of all products in international trade. However, this model does appear to be useful for understanding trade patterns in manufactured goods. Although no such model should be used by the business person without careful examination of individual products, it does provide some useful hints as to which products might be exportable and which might suffer import competition. The concept can also give clues as to the potential success of various product policies.

To extend the market for a product at home and abroad, the business person may practise a strategy of market segmentation, making design changes in the product to appeal to different types of consumers, but there comes a point where design changes can no longer make a product competitive abroad or safe from imports. Firms may follow two strategies for survival: a continual product roll-over, shifting resources to new products more suited to the unique demands of the market; and/or manufacturing abroad, to take advantage of lower production costs and to save tariffs and transportation charges.

LANCASTER'S MODIFICATION AND EXTENSION TO THE THEORY[12]

According to Wells's theory, as a product moves down the 'pecking order' over time, a series of curves with similar amplitudes will result. However, Lancaster suggests that, the further down the pecking order a product goes, the higher will be its consumption over time. Thus, each product life-cycle curve will have a progressively higher amplitude. This is explained diagrammatically in Fig. 14.5.

Curve (1) represents band 1, and we can see that (a) represents (band 1) production of a product for the (band 1) market. It is appropriate that the first curve should be the United States, as most new products commence their life there. As this market becomes saturated, the American producers seek export opportunities in developed European markets (band 2), shown in (b). The American production of the product continues to supply one market in decline in (c) as European producers begin to market the same product in their home market (d). At this stage European production grows as rapidly as American production declines, and eventually European producers are meeting their home market demand by themselves (e). In stage (f) the developed European producers have reached the pinnacle of production, providing their home market, the American market and next band developing countries, (band 3) with the product. However, in section (g) sales of the product decline in the European and developing country markets now being supplied, as the developing countries themselves begin to produce the product (h). Now developing country production grows as rapidly as European production declines, and eventually developing country producers are meeting their home market demand by themselves (i). Now the developing countries have reached the height of their production (j), supplying America, Europe, their home market and less developed countries (band 4), and then they move into decline (k) as less developed country production increases (l). This cycle of trade from one group of countries to another can continue as long as there are countries less developed than the previous ones.

It should be noticed that each curve is higher than the previous one because production increases in relation to the increased demand. This is because the movement of the product from one curve to the next creates active consumers who did not exist before, primarily as a result of product development and experience gained in production, but also because of increased demand as less-developed countries become more affluent.

To give examples of the type of countries involved in the above model, 'Europe' denotes

Stage	Production	Consumption
a	①	①
b	①	① + ②
c	①	① + ②
d	① + ②	① + ②
e	②	① + ②
f	②	① + ② + ③
g	②	① + ② + ③
h	② + ③	① + ② + ③
i	③	① + ② + ③
j	③	① + ② + ③ + ④
k	③	① + ② + ③ + ④
l	③ + ④	① + ② + ③ + ④
m	④	① + ② + ③ + ④
n	④	① + ② + ③ + ④
o	④	① + ② + ③ + ④

Figure 14.5 Lancaster's modification to Wells's theory

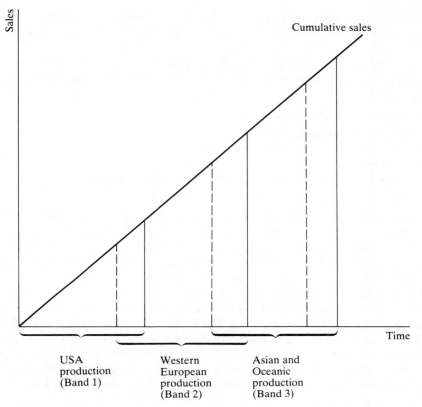

Figure 14.6 Cumulative sales, per Lancaster's modification to Wells's theory

Western Europe—those countries that are technically advanced second only to the United States. Such countries would typically be Britain, West Germany or France. By developing countries, we mean some European countries and some Far Eastern countries—Portugal, Greece, Hong Kong and South Korea would be good examples. Less-developed countries would follow economically and technically after these developing countries, but may be split into various degrees of development. Such countries would typically be The Philippines, Indonesia, Sri Lanka and Nigeria.

Looking at the model cumulatively, we can see a gradual progression in sales of the product. By adding the total consumption levels at each point in time (i.e., by inverting sections *d*, *h* and *l*), we find a straight line of cumulative consumption (see Fig. 14.6). The different stages in each curve can still be identified on this straight line.

In fact, the descriptions given more or less neatly match the definitions given earlier in this chapter, with the United States being an example of an 'affluent country' and so on down the scale to 'subsistence economies'.

LOGISTICS OF EXPORTING

Physical distribution of logistics is an activity often neglected in texts on international marketing. However, as we saw in Chapter 10, it is an extremely important subject, particularly for the export marketer; it is one of the major cost elements in international marketing and has been identified as a crucial factor in non-price competitiveness. Research by Steuer *et al.*[13] showed that in the case of machine tools a rise in waiting time of one month will reduce export orders by approximately 10 per cent.

Logistics includes the three areas of warehousing, inventory control and transport (and, in the case of export marketing, the associated documentation). As far as consumers are concerned, these factors are represented by:

—The speed with which orders are filled.
—The ability to meet emergency orders.
—The delivery of goods in acceptable condition.
—The policy on returned goods.
—The options offered on minimum order sizes and transport modes.
—The charges for services (if any).

The concept of total distribution cost has been discussed in Chapter 10. Nowhere is this concept of more importance than in international marketing. The methods of transport potentially available to the export marketer are varied—seafreight, road, rail, canal and airfreight—and it is well known that, on a unit weight or volume rate, the costs of airfreight, for example, are significantly greater than seafreight. This simplistic comparison ignores cost saving in other areas of logistics that can be achieved by airfreight. Greater speed of delivery has a positive effect on cash flow—a company's money is tied up in goods for a shorter period of time; lower safety stock levels reduce the costs of stockholding: cost of insurance, handling and customs clearance can be significantly reduced. This is not to say that airfreight should be the preferred mode of transport—bulk items are clearly excluded—but it serves to indicate that it is unrealistic to consider the freight rate alone in physical distribution decisions. In general terms, however, it can be said that on a regular basis, low-bulk, high-value items are carried by air, while high-bulk, low-value products (e.g., coal) are more effectively moved by sea.

This generalization tends to ignore the other modes of transport already mentioned. Road transport as a means of conveying goods from place of manufacture to place of consumption is highly developed throughout Western Europe, and the use of roll-on/roll-off (ro-ro) ferries is extremely important in trade between the UK and her EC partners. On mainland Europe the canal and river system is commercially viable. The important factor to consider, therefore, is just what is available to reach a specific overseas destination, and how this relates to total distribution costs.

Few export marketers have the knowledge or experience to make all logistics decisions. Traditionally, a freight forwarder has been used to bridge the gap between seller and shipper, whose role has included booking the space on a particular transport mode, documentation and customs procedures and, in many cases, export packaging. Control of logistics was, therefore, fragmented. Most companies have now replaced at least a part of the international freight forwarder's role by an in-house function. Developments in aligned documentation under the auspices of the Simplification of International Trade Procedures Board (SITPRO) mean that international documents can be produced as easily as companies' commercial invoices.

The management of international logistics has all the problems of domestic physical distribution, but is complicated by its needs to operate across a wider spectrum of transport modes and accepted practice in differing countries. For a full discussion of this topic you are recommended to consult Davies's text on export distribution.[14]

TRENDS AND DEVELOPMENTS IN INTERNATIONAL MARKETING

As we might expect, the international marketer is faced with one of the most dynamic and complex of marketing environments. Trade across national frontiers has been one of the fastest growing areas of economic activity over the past twenty years and has witnessed many changes and developments. In fact, the past five years have witnessed some of the most far-reaching trends and developments for international marketers seen during this century. Successful international marketers have been those who have adapted to these trends and developments by seizing the opportunities presented. The next decade, however, is likely to be no different with respect to the speed of change; and to remain successful the international marketer needs to be aware of and respond to these future developments. Three of the most significant of these recent developments affecting international marketing, together with an indication of their implications, are outlined in the following paragraphs.

The single European market

The advent of a single European market at the end of 1992 was an important event for businesses both inside and outside the European Community (EC). A number of social, political and economic adjustments will now have to be made within each of the member countries. To complicate matters further, the amount and pace of change are likely to differ from country to country. For example, the United Kingdom has only recently begun to regard itself as part of 'Europe' and is therefore likely to experience a greater amount of change in adjusting to the conditions needed to make the single market a success.

The new 320 million-strong market (which will eventually become the largest in the industrialized world) offers significant business opportunities to firms within the member countries. A barrier-free Europe will also give firms the opportunity to improve their global competitive standing. The new opportunities presented by '1992' will accrue not only to firms within Europe but also to businesses outside the European Community, which are also looking to take advantage of the new single, expanded unified market.

Many firms are already taking a proactive stand in pushing ahead with their plans and strategies to create and exploit the new market opportunities presented within the European Community after '1992'.

Certainly, progress towards a single market will not be trouble-free and there remain many problems to be resolved. As Colchester[15] points out, 1992 was more a symbolic than a definitive date for the creation of a single market. Whatever the problems, however, it is certain that progress towards the single market and perhaps eventually a single currency, will continue.

The newly industrialized countries (NICs)

The pattern of world trade is changing. In recent years we have seen the impact of countries such as North and South Korea, Singapore and some of the African countries in world markets as they progress to full industrialization.

These countries are likely to present themselves as formidable competitors in world markets in the next decade and beyond. As their economies develop, they will be capable of producing ever more sophisticated goods and services and also will benefit from the relatively low labour costs in these countries. Countries such as Korea are already posing a competitive threat in relatively high-technology products. The whole of the Far East, as well as countries in Africa (e.g. Nigeria), will become important markets and also formidable competitors. Obviously, marketing strategies of the future—particularly in those companies planning to adopt a global marketing stance—must take the emergence of NICs into account.

Changes in Eastern Europe and the former Soviet Union

Mr Gorbachev's policies of *glasnost* and *perestroika*, which began in the mid-1980s, have resulted in the democratization of the (now former) Soviet Union and an adoption of a more free-market economic philosophy. Other Warsaw Pact countries (for example, both Poland and Hungary) are now pledged to becoming fully fledged democracies and intend to run their economies more along free-market capitalist lines. The latter half of 1989 saw the destruction of the Berlin wall and the move towards a reunified Germany.

These developments present both opportunities and threats to firms in the established Western democracies.[16] It is likely that new markets will open up for existing Western goods and services, particularly high-technology products and financial services. On the other hand, the more marketing-oriented development of these economies will eventually mean greater competition in world markets.

CONCLUSIONS

Any chapter of this length on a topic as wide as international marketing must by its very nature be selective. An attempt has been made to concentrate on those aspects of international marketing that are different from similar areas of activity in domestic marketing by posing additional issues and problems faced by the international marketer.

The chapter has, therefore, covered the international economic environment, the identification of export opportunities and international physical distribution. A large portion of the chapter has been devoted to the elements of the marketing mix on an international scale, in particular, strategies for entering the overseas market, product and communication alternatives, the concept of the international product life cycle and aspects of pricing as related to overseas marketing.

The principles of marketing are as true for international as for home markets. Customers' needs have to be analysed and understood, objectives must be set and performance must be controlled and measured. Special knowledge is, however, required and special training is necessary, both in the practicalities of export marketing and in the linguistic sense.

Finally, the dynamic nature of international markets means that, more than ever, the international markets must be constantly aware of trends and changes, which give rise to opportunities and threats.

APPLICATION QUESTIONS

1. How does the international marketing environment differ from the environment in the domestic market?
2. What are the major difficulties likely to be encountered in carrying out research (both desk and field) for international marketing?
3. What alternative product and communication strategies are open to the international marketer?
4. What are the additional issues to be considered in pricing a product for overseas markets?
5. What are the major alternative market entry strategies, and what benefits and disadvantages do they have?

REFERENCES

1. L. S. Walsh, *International Marketing*, Macdonald and Evans, London, 1981, p. 4.
2. Walsh, op. cit., pp. 5–6.

3. C. Tugendhat, *The Multinationals*, Penguin, Harmondsworth, 1984.

4. V. Terpstra, *International Marketing*, 3rd edn, Dryden Press, Hinsdale, IL, 1983.

5. W. W. Rostow, *The Stage of Economic Growth*, Cambridge University Press, Cambridge, 1960.

6. Walsh, op. cit.

7. R. Whymant, 'Why Britain is bamboozled by a bamboo curtain', *Guardian*, 21 October 1980, p. 19.

8. W. J. Keegan, 'Multinational product planning: strategic alternatives', *Journal of Marketing*, **33**, January 1969, pp. 58–62.

9. A. G. Walker, *Export Practice Documentation*, Newnes-Butterworth, London, 1977, pp. 22–6.

10. L. T. Wells, Jr, 'A product life cycle for international trade', *Journal of Marketing*, **32**, 1968, pp. 1–6.

11. G. C. Hufbauer, *Synthetic Materials and the Theory of International Trade*, Harvard University Press, Cambridge, MA, 1966.

12. G. A. Lancaster and I. Wesenlund, 'A product life cycle theory for international trade: an empirical investigation', *European Journal of Marketing*, **18** (6/7), 1984, pp. 72–89.

13. M. D. Steuer, R. J. Ball and J. R. Eaton, 'The effect of waiting time on foreign orders for machine tools', *Economica*, **33**, pp. 387–403, 1984.

14. G. Davies, *Managaing Export Distribution*, Heinemann, London, 1984.

15. N. Colchester, '1992 = 1990 + 2 or Thereabouts', in *The World in 1990*, Economist Publications, London, 1990, pp. 49–60.

16. P. Meller, 'Back to the USSR', *Marketing*, August 1990, pp. 22–3.

FIFTEEN

SOCIAL, LEGAL AND ENVIRONMENTAL ASPECTS OF MARKETING

INTRODUCTION

Much of marketing literature is concerned with the functional activities of marketing management, this being applied to the concept or philosophy of marketing, which holds that its basic purpose is the satisfaction of consumers' wants and needs. This chapter examines marketing from a wider 'social' perspective and suggests that management responsibilities involve more than the company/consumer interface. A recognition is, therefore, made of the increasing complexity of marketing. The satisfaction of one consumer group may create considerable conflict in another group. The existence of the consumer movement is evidence of this conflict; and on a broader scale, ecological and social issues must also be incorporated into a marketing equation whose original variables were restricted to sales, growth and profit.

In an increasingly competitive business environment, it is not suggested that the need for profit should in any way be relegated. Similarly, this chapter does not criticize the basic tenets of the marketing concept. Rather, the objective is to make the reader aware of marketing's obligations to society as well as to specific consumer groups. Society is made up of individual consumers; a marketing approach that considers society will, therefore, ultimately fulfil the requirements of the marketing concept.

Finally, in this chapter we shall turn our attention to the issues involved in applying marketing to what are now often termed 'not-for-profit' organizations. Marketing concepts and techniques are increasingly being applied in organizations outside the 'conventional' commercial profit-oriented type. Not-for-profit organizations encompass organizations as diverse as charities, political parties and public-sector organizations such as hospitals, the police and museums. Just as we did in Chapter 8 for services, we need to consider the 'special' issues that arise when implementing marketing in this type of organization.

MAJOR CRITICISMS OF MARKETING

Micro dimensions

As consumer markets have become more complex and marketing more sophisticated, its practice has become the subject of increasing controversy and criticism. This is due, to some extent, to media and organized consumer misuse and misunderstanding of the word 'marketing' itself. 'Marketing' as discussed today in the media often becomes the generic term which describes a multitude of malpractices ranging from actual dishonest trading to over-exaggerated advertising claims. A company that describes itself as 'marketing-oriented' can run the risk of being grouped with those firms that do not practise marketing at all in the real sense. This is one explanation for the poor image which marketing has in the minds of many consumers and media controllers.

However, it must be recognized that, even among those companies that adhere to the marketing concept, some criticism as to its functions is justified. Typical criticisms are outlined in the following list:

—Many products are at least wasteful of resources and in some cases dangerous to health.
—Much packaging and labelling is unnecessary or deceptive.
—Advertising is misleading.
—Advertising exploits children and makes people dissatisfied.
—Delivery is unreliable.
—After-sales service is inefficient.
—Market research invades privacy.

There are no excuses for such (valid) criticisms, and there is obviously much room for improvement. It must be remembered that in a competitive environment firms do not set out to antagonize customers if they wish to remain in business. Moreover, consumers usually have the sanction of spending their money where levels of service are more acceptable. The onus here is on marketing practitioners to recognize and remedy their areas of weakness and to promote themselves and their activities so as to be distinguished from the less savoury and often purely sales-oriented approaches that some companies employ.

Macro dimensions

There is a more intellectual and more fundamental basis from which marketing can be criticized. This concerns marketing's economic and ethical role in the way in which needs are satisfied and resources are allocated. The fundamental debate as to the validity of respective political systems and their approach to resource allocation is beyond the scope of this text; the intention is to consider the problem within the context of 'market' economies. Within such a framework, it is perhaps inevitable that the marketing manager has, in his or her professional role, typically viewed the problems of society from a different viewpoint from that of the external or public observer. The former has tended to emphasize the success and contribution which business in general has made to society, while the latter looks beyond the individual firm and highlights the negative aspects of marketing in society. A subsequent section of this chapter examines how differing ideals in the way marketing is viewed can be reconciled. This section deals with criticisms that call into question marketing's impact on society and are, therefore, 'macro' in nature.

Although it is difficult to classify such criticisms conveniently because of their wide variety, they can be roughly divided into 'economic' and 'ethical' sub-groups. Economic criticism centres around the theme that marketing is inefficient and chiefly concerns the following proposals.

Marketing creates monopoly and limits consumer choice The possibility of a company becoming so powerful that it will decide what the consumer will buy and at what price is a denial of the marketing concept and one of the chief fears of the consumer movement. In the private sectors of the developed world, although the development of even larger and more powerful companies is recognized, true monopolies rarely exist. As well as government regulation (in the form of the Monoplies and Mergers Commission in the UK and Anti-trust Legislation in the USA) the buying public is rarely sufficiently homogeneous to permit exclusive control by a monopolistic power.

Part of the opposition to monopoly is rooted in the economist's notion that perfect competition among sellers is the fairest way in which business can serve society and that a state of monopoly will allow the worst fears of marketing critics to materialize. It is true that monopoly is the antithesis of perfect competition, but these represent extremes of economic theory: the reality lies somewhat between the two. Marketing is in fact characterized by many economic business conditions. Some markets are supplied by numerous small- to medium-sized companies, while others are represented by the state of oligopoly.

We should remember that good marketing strategy should centre around a distinctive competence of the firm.[1] In this way the most successful companies become something like monopolists in their fields. For the consumer, the most important factor is that such a firm's competitors will continually strive to emulate this success. Thus, the current leader has little room for complacency. Such competition acknowledges the idea of consumer sovereignty and is the best safeguard that consumers have against exploitation by powerful companies.

The reality that increased market share leads to a disproportionate increase in market advantages, profits and thus power has led many markets to a state of oligopoly.[2] The existence of such power has caused marketing's critics to prophesy that such firms will eventually dictate what, where and when consumers will buy. Certainly there are instances of the abuse of power, most notably among some multinational companies in the Third World, and such activities must be deplored. In Western markets such power is tempered by competition as well as the ability of the consumer to remove his or her custom. In the UK in the early 1970s, genuine fears were expressed about the power of large bakeries and breweries to 'impose' white sliced bread and gas-filled beer upon the nation. Although these markets were in fact oligopolistic, it seemed that they were in possession of monopoly-like powers, supplying only what was profitable and convenient for them to produce. The resurgence of more traditional products was testimony to consumer power and a timely reminder to those firms that had neglected the marketing concept. Britain's largest bankers have had to shake off any complacency that they may have had in the 1970s. Not only has competition increased between them, but also they are realizing that they have no 'divine right' to exclusivity in the marketing of their services, as evidenced by the ending of their power through legislation which has opened up their traditional market to other financial institutions like building societies.

Similar examples are not difficult to find; they usually reveal that successful companies gain power so long as they efficiently satisfy demand, while at the same time, the standards of other companies are raised in their efforts to emulate the leader. Such a leader is constantly under threat from potential competition, differentiated and substitute products, and changes in the nature of consumer demand. Critics of marketing play a valuable social role—it would be naive to bestow complete altruism on all the business world, or indeed to overlook genuine mistakes. It is proposed that the nature of markets themselves will militate against monopoly, and that if situations approaching monopoly exist, these will remain only so long as they efficiently satisfy consumer needs and wants.

Marketing involves too much competitive promotion The major criticisms of competitive promotion are directed at the advertising industry. Indeed, advertising is criticized by business itself because of the notorious difficulties involved in evaluating its effectiveness. Our main concern is with external critics who contend that purely competitive advertising is wasteful and that the consumers' real need is for advertising to be informative. If advertising were reduced or did not exist (so the argument runs) manufacturers' overheads would decrease and this would result in cheaper goods. The argument is extended to question the need for the multiplicity of apparently similar products which advertising is engaged in promoting.

The desire of consumers to have brand choice is well known, but marketers should not reject such criticism out of hand. When the US government banned cigarette advertising, it was interesting to note that sales did not fall significantly and that the relative market share of the cigarette manufacturers (all of whom were heavy advertising spenders) did not change. Cigarettes may, of course, present a special case, but the event certainly caused large spenders of advertising money to stop and think.

More usually, marketers are able to provide economic justification for their promotional expenditure. So as to maintain profitability, manufacturers place great reliance on their ability to achieve an optimum production–overhead ratio. Advertising can help to achieve and maintain such a position, but it must be remembered that, if sales that exceed the optimum are induced, such effort may become counter-productive.

Marketing is wasteful The 'middleman' is often the butt of marketing criticism. A long and complicated channel system is seen as wasteful and unnecessary. Students of channel structure should be able to present cogent reasons justifying the need for middlemen—that is, from the manufacturer's point of view. There is no doubt that some channel systems are less than efficient. In the macro sense, critics bemoan the transportation around the country of apparently identical goods which are produced by different manufacturers. Frequently these goods are in fact highly differentiated with respect to style, design and brand name. There is, moreover, an important movement towards the simplification of channel systems which is discernible in the rise of discount stores and hypermarkets.

Despite the inefficiencies of marketing, it is logical to assume that companies will endeavour to reduce costs whenever possible. Efficiency is, of course, necessary for profit, and profit is essential for survival, but the implication for the consumer is that it allows the company to increase competitiveness and so reduce prices or improve service.

From the social perspective, critics question social values which it is claimed marketing is largely responsible for creating.

Marketing promotes materialism and creates artificial needs and values The economist and social philosopher J. K. Galbraith described, as early as 1952, the creation of wants as the 'dependence effect'. He criticized the process of production and marketing for satisfying wants that were not 'original' within the consumer, but which were actually created by marketing in the first place.[3] Much of the blame for so-called stimulation of wants is laid at the door of advertising. Whether the source of our desire to acquire products and life styles which we could physically live without is inherent in ourselves, or is imposed upon us by phenomena such as advertising, is the subject of major philosophical debate. Some psychologists maintain that our wants are not really concerned with the acquisition of, say, an expensive hi-fi system, but rather that such an act realizes an inner psychological need. If this is the case, then marketing plays the valuable social role of want fulfilment, satisfying wants that otherwise, it could be argued, the consumer would search to fulfil in some other way. To this extent, if blame is to be attached, it must be shared by the buyer and the seller.

Questions as to the power of marketing and advertising to distort values and create artificial wants cannot be easily resolved. Is marketing to be blamed for the general rise in living standards which has facilitated the style of spending, which is itself the source of so much criticism? It may be that some critics underestimate the ability of consumers to discriminate and choose for themselves. The existence of social inequality has led to the comment that advertising dissatisfies the poor by portraying a world that is beyond their means. This is a socio-political comment as much as a direct criticism of marketing.

Advertising is offensive and deceptive Fraudulent and deliberately deceptive advertising is infrequent as it is controlled by legislation. It is relatively rare because it is the advertiser's job to gain confidence among the target market and not to destroy it.

Much of the advertising deemed 'questionable' involves sins of omission as well as commission. The existence of advertising control is testimony to the fact that some advertising has presented half truths which, although not necessarily making blatantly false claims, have in reality set out to deceive. The socially responsible advertiser aims to communicate genuine product features to the public, and, while the need for regulatory bodies to control the less ethical is reprehensible, its existence appears to have raised the standards of advertising in general. In the United States, the Federal Trade Commission now reports that 97 per cent of advertisements checked each year satisfactorily adhere to its code of conduct.[4]

Marketing is unethical Often the individual marketer's own personal standards may be compromised in the business situation. This problem of ethics is aggravated by the confusion that exists as to what the ethical obligations of marketing are. In recent years we have witnessed numerous examples of 'leaks' and revelations from individual employees of large organizations. If, for example, in detriment of his or her own career and financial security, an executive publicly discloses that the company has deceived or endangered its customers, the employee's corporate allegiance has then been overruled by his or her personal ethical code. For the average individual, the dilemma is unlikely to reach such critical proportions, but an ethical problem nevertheless remains.

Clearly, the solution lies with higher management, who could obviate the causes of ethical conflict. The power of the media and of consumerism has developed to such an extent that management is in any case under considerable pressure to adopt an increasingly responsible stance. Major initiatives have indeed been taken by enlightened companies that see valid marketing opportunities in such an approach. The question of social responsibility in marketing will be dealt with in a later section of this chapter. When we are discussing marketing ethics, though, we should be careful to note that the term 'ethics', and in particular what constitutes 'ethical' versus 'unethical' behaviour in the context of marketing, is very difficult to define. Dibb[5] suggests that ethics may be one of the most misunderstood and controversial concepts in marketing.

THE CONSUMER MOVEMENT

The phenomenon of consumerism is central to the theme of this chapter. Its existence is testimony to the failures of marketing, while, at the same time, consumerism has been responsible for marketing's increasingly important social dimension. Much of this process of change is due to legal and governmental action which has obliged companies to pay heed to consumerist activity. A potentially more important outcome is that responsible companies view consumerism not as coercive or threatening, but as a definite opportunity to serve their markets better.

Development of the consumer movement

The origins of the consumer movement are firmly based in the USA. This is not to say that the need for consumerism did not exist in Europe and the UK. Rather, factors such as mass production and mass marketing were quicker to develop in the USA. Here, organized consumers successfully achieved their aims both at the turn of the century and in the 1930s. However, these were isolated movements which were directed at specific targets. Once successful, there appeared to be no need to continue with further organized action. It was not until the late 1950s and early 1960s that the consumer movement as we know it today began to materialize. Social commentators such as J. K. Galbraith, Vance Packard and Rachel Carson began to alert the American nation, not only to specific cases, but to the whole philosophy and social rationale on which society (as it related to the business world) was based. The Second World War probably developed the birth of such a movement, because the austerity of the immediate post-war environment made consumers more likely to be grateful for the luxury of being able to acquire goods that had previously been scarce than to complain about their quality or the marketing methods associated with them. Moreover, during the war period itself, organized groups of dissatisfied consumers were not conducive to the spirit of patriotism which prevailed. By the early 1960s, however, definite challenges to the *status quo* that business had enjoyed were emerging.

The Second World War notwithstanding, it is likely that consumerism was an inevitable development of our economic system, and it is equally likely that the movement will not only endure, but will continue to to grow.[6] In America the 'champion' of consumerism was Ralph Nader, whose book *Unsafe at Any Speed* was a challenge to, and a formidable indictment of, the American automobile industry—and in particular General Motors. Nader was an influential figure of the 1960s who was responsible for a number of federal laws such as the Meat Inspection Bill and the Fire Research and Safety Law, but his influence was far wider than in these specific spheres. His greatest impact was that he engendered in the public the idea that monolithic business institutions could in fact be challenged and that those who were at fault could no longer act with impunity. This notion spread through the USA via the mass media and was transferred (albeit more slowly) to the UK.

Within the UK itself, an important parallel to Ralph Nader (in terms of influence on the public attitude) was the development of the consumer magazine *Which?* From very humble beginnings in a garage in South London, circulation experienced a dramatic rise, such that within a very short time *Which?* became a household name. *Which?* selects a series of consumer goods for each publication, objectively tests them on a variety of counts and then publishes its conclusions. The result is that products and their companies are classified according to their relative performance. Such a concept was hitherto undreamed of. Like Nader, *Which?* has not only achieved a specific task, but has also contributed to the feeling, or notion, that consumers need no longer accept the offerings of big and small businesses alike without voicing their opinions.

The meaning of consumerism

Consumerism is well defined as 'a social movement seeking to augment the rights and power of buyers in relation to sellers'.

To understand the full implications of such a definition, it is worth while examining what these rights have traditionally been held to be.

Sellers have the following rights:

1. To introduce any product in any style or size, provided that it is not injurious to health and safety and provided that potentially hazardous products are supplied together with appropriate warnings.
2. To price products at any level, provided that there is no discrimination among similar classes of buyers.
3. To say what they like in promotion of their products, provided that any message is not dishonest or misleading in content or execution.
4. To spend any amount of money they wish, to promote their product and to introduce any buying incentive schemes, provided that these cannot be defined as unfair competition.

Buyers in their turn have their own rights and the right to expect certain things from sellers and their products:

1. Not to buy products offered to them.
2. To expect the product to be safe.
3. To expect that the product is in fact essentially the same as the seller has represented.

An appreciation and a knowledge of the respective rights of the buyer and seller help to put the consumer problem into perspective.

The biggest weapon of the consumer has traditionally been held to be that of the 'silent vote', that is, the right not to buy unsatisfactory goods; this is the concept of consumer sovereignty. Logically, therefore, companies who mis-serve the market will usually run out of customers. This is indeed a powerful sanction and has been cited earlier when discussing major criticisms of marketing. Consumerists argue that the onus is not on the consumer to veto unsatisfactory goods after having first been disappointed; rather, it is up to the sellers of goods to take all reasonable steps to ensure satisfaction before offering goods for sale. They further argue that such a step will be greatly facilitated if certain basic consumer 'rights' are recognized.

What should consumer rights be?

In 1962 President John F. Kennedy clearly delineated four basic consumer rights. His declaration was probably the most important single step in the advancement of consumerism. He proposed the following:

1. *The right to safety* Consumers have the right to expect that products do not possess hidden dangers. This was the basis of Nader's campaign against the automobile industry. In the UK, the aftermath of the thalidomide affair forced attention to turn on food and drugs. Occasionally, such attention has led to allegations of alarmist activity by consumerists. In the USA, the use of cyclamates in artificial sweeteners was alleged to have a carcinogenic effect. Subsequent investigations held that such products were harmless in the quantities normally consumed by human beings.
2. *The right to be informed* Consumers should be protected from inadequate and misleading product information and from deceptions in advertising, guarantees and product labelling. Possibly the most extreme example is that of cigarette advertising and the introduction of government health warnings. Other examples are less controversial, but the idea remains the same: consumers should be responsible for their purchase decisions only after having been in receipt of adequate product information.
3. *The right to choose* Consumers have the right to real competition among sellers and should not be subjected to confusing promotion and product labelling. An experiment in California showed that such was the variety and complexity of labelling, that supermarket shoppers were incapable of relating quantity to cost when making purchases.[7]
4. *The right to be heard* Consumers have the right to express their dissatisfactions in a manner that will attract attention and so achieve positive results. Consumerists argue that individual consumers, apart from having no 'voice', do not necessarily have the time or the skills to make complex choice decisions or to absorb product information when it is preferred. Organized bodies should, therefore, be established to speak for them. A further argument is that modern shopping methods have distanced the seller from the buyer so that dissatisfactions are difficult to voice with any degree of success.

Consumerism today

A great deal of the demands which the consumer movement originally made have now been met. This is not to say that the need for consumer protection has diminished, or that it is likely to do so. There is also the danger that, after several years of success, those responsible for administering and improving consumer protection will become complacent, less dynamic and less responsive to change. Consumerists are also becoming involved with protection at the macro level. The progress already made must not be allowed to slide, but it is likely that future consumerist interest will focus more on macro price levels (such as lobbying the EEC on food prices) and on multinational business, than on the day-to-day problems of the high street. However, one issue that continues to grow in importance for marketers is the attention paid to environmental and ecological issues, the so-called 'green' movement.

Green issues and marketing In 1989 a Market Intelligence Report[8] published the results of a UK survey in which respondents were asked to list the issues they considered to be among the most serious problems facing the country. Pollution of the environment ranked second on the list only to the then much disliked poll tax. In the same report, the following is a sample of some of the views expressed:

—90 per cent of respondents considered our sea and river pollution as fairly or very serious;
—80 per cent were aware of the problems of acid rain, nuclear waste and leaded petrol;
—65 per cent were concerned about the use of chemicals in farming.

These examples of consumer attitudes are indicative of the increased awareness, and in some cases alarm, about the state of the environment. Moreover, rightly or wrongly, marketers and marketing practices are seen as being at the heart of many of these and other environmental issues. The result has been the emergence of what is now often referred to as the 'green' consumer. Put simply, an increasing number of consumers are interested in, and in some cases will only buy, environmentally friendly products. Only a few short years ago such green consumers were considered an oddity, and the numbers involved meant that only a few, usually small and specialized, companies catered for their needs. With the increased awareness of environmental issues referred to earlier, however, green consumers are no longer a fringe group, and as a result marketers have had to respond to changing customer needs in this area. There is little doubt that the impact of this greening of the customer is significant and far-reaching. Moreover, the number of green customers continues to grow.

Although there are many ways in which the impact of the green consumer has made itself felt on marketing practice, perhaps the most obvious impact has been the recognition by marketers of the marketing opportunities for green products. Ozone-friendly aerosols, CFC-free fridges and freezers and lead-free petrol have perhaps been the subject of the best known marketing compaigns, but other products include batteries (e.g. Varta), disposable nappies (e.g. Peaudeuce), cars (e.g. Volkswagen) and biodegradable washing powders (e.g. Unilever). Moreover, the impact is not restricted to the physical products themselves but also affects their packaging and labelling, their development and testing (e.g. non-animal-based testing of cosmetics) and their promotion.

Only one thing is certain, and that is that green issues in marketing are here to stay. As with the broader issue of consumerism, of which green issues are only a part, the greening of consumers represents both an opportunity and a threat.

Companies that are prepared to identify opportunities for more environmentally friendly products and practices, and which can produce genuinely green products and practices to meet these, will find a growing market. Companies that continue to ignore the green consumer and/or to address green issues only in a superficial way will increasingly find their sales threatened by a more environmentally aware consumer.

The undoubted success of the consumer movement cannot be wholly ascribed to a positive response on behalf of the business world. During the 1960s and 1970s in particular, mistrust, misunderstanding and complacency were typical corporate responses to the consumerist phenomenon. Just as few motorists are likely to consider themselves as being bad drivers, few firms are able to appreciate or be willing to admit that the consumer movement has been aimed against them. It is not suggested that companies have decided to persevere with a policy of deception or poor service; the real answer is that, until consumer issues began to take on national importance, most companies genuinely believed that they were fulfilling their consumer responsibilities.

Despite the initial reluctance of firms to respond to the consumer movement, the 1980s witnessed definite progress in the attitudes and actions of business organizations. That this was due to enlightenment and altruism is the subject of debate. What is more certain is that governmental and legal action has not only obliged companies to initiate change but has also permitted the realization that consumerism has become a fixture of society which, if properly approached, can provide positive opportunities for marketing management. The creation of a Ministry for Consumer Affairs testifies to the government's commitment to consumer protection. The following section details the extent of remedies in law and sources of advice that are available to consumers. It is, therefore, perhaps lamentable that statutes and official bodies have had to be the instrument of change, but what is important for the consumer is the fact that change has taken place. It is significant that major companies in the retail sector have adopted unit pricing voluntarily or have insisted on explicit labelling details. Other businesses have published true rates of interest (annual percentage rates) for credit deals or have used the fact that their products adhere to the respective regulations as a major theme of their promotional campaigns. As we have seen, yet others have responded to green issues by producing more environmentally friendly products. Whether this is altruism or a response to legislation is not really relevant; the important thing is that these initiatives have been taken.

MARKETING AND CONSUMERISM

Marketing's ethical issues are, of course, inextricably bound up with consumerism, and the implications for both reach beyond the boundaries of 'marketing management' in the commonly accepted sense of the term. The response of marketing to consumerism presents us with philosophical as well as practical questions. Kotler's call for a 'revised marketing concept'[8] would take into account the long-term moral and social issues with which marketing should now concern itself. Before examining further such a concept, we should recognize certain practicalities which complicate the issue.

The essence of marketing strategy is to think and plan for the long term. This strategic approach is also essential if a firm wishes to adopt an increased social orientation and to respond positively to consumerism. The economies of business life, on the other hand, tend to invoke short-term concern, and while the evidence of successful long-term strategy is all around us, this is never easily achieved. It is likely that such difficulties will be accentuated by the addition of a consumerist/social dimension to long-range planning.

The second important consideration is that of the social/economic environment itself. Consumerism, taken to its logical and ultimate conclusion, implies a major redistribution of wealth and power. By how much the business world is willing, or able, to subscribe to such a movement is an important subject of debate. This in turn is closely linked to the attitudes of government, which may vary according to the social and economic conditions that prevail. In theory, pro-consumer government action should benefit the government (in terms of popularity) plus business; if a positive response is made, then consumers themselves will react favourably. Major initiatives have already been taken by various governments, and such a sequence of benefits has already occurred. However, it is important that we do not underestimate the complexity of this process.

Having taken into account the above considerations, we can examine how marketing should react to consumerism. It is apparent that the consumer movement has graduated beyond the realms of 'micro' issues, although it has been suggested that the need for vigilance in this resepct will continue. The future concerns of marketing should involve the long-term and broader issues of consumerism. This is the theme of the following 'Social marketing' section. The immediate realization must be that consumerism must be seen as an opportunity, and that the suspicion previously associated with it should be abandoned. Many firms have already proved this to be a viable and profitable approach. In many respects, consumerism has done the work of the marketer by identifying a whole range of previously unsatisfied needs and wants. These opportunities concern such items as unit pricing, honesty in labelling and credit agreements, and new green products. They extend into the satisfaction of psychological needs. The manufacturer who, for example, produces a product and includes and conceals a hazardous component in order to save costs, will suffer in the long term at the hands of a competitor who treats safety as a 'feature' and builds this into marketing strategy and tactics. Consumerism, properly viewed, does not challenge the marketing concept, but is a major reinforcement of it.

CONSUMER LAW AND PROTECTION

The consumer movement has had a profound effect upon the British legal system. The rate of change in consumer marketing since the early 1960s has brought with it equivalent change in the law, which has been considerably modified to protect the consumer from unfair practices. The law relating to consumer protection is not a clearly defined code; it is made up of extensions and amendments to contract law. Its basis is in legislation (such as the Factors Act 1889),[10] which was designed to define the law as to contractual relationships between traders. In Britain there is no such thing as a 'consumer law' as a single entity, nor is there a comprehensive code of consumer protection. There is, nevertheless, a wealth of statutory instruments which have been introduced during the last 20 years designed to effect specific control over potential injustices and to exploit actions of the consumer. There is also the existing contract law, which has a high degree of relevance to current situations in which the consumer may be at a disadvantage.

The following examples of statutes illustrate the potential for consumer legislation. The list is not meant to be exhaustive, but is included so as to provide an insight into the wide range of consumer protection.

1. Aerosol Dispensers (EEC Requirements) Regulations 1977.
2. Babies Dummies (Safety) Regulations 1978.
3. Business Advertisements (Disclosure) Order 1977.
4. Consumer Credit (Credit Reference Agency) Regulations 1977.
5. Cooking Utensils (Safety) Regulations 1972.
6. Cosmetic Products Regulations 1978.
7. Electric Blankets (Safety) Regulations 1971.
8. Mail Order Transactions (Information) Order 1976.
9. Price Marking (Bargain Offers) Order 1979.
10. Pyramid Selling Schemes Regulations 1973.
11. Toys (Safety) Regulations 1974.

Further legal remedies for the consumer are to be found in contract law. Although it has already been stated that there is no such thing as 'consumer law', and although existing legislation is somewhat hybrid in nature, it is possible to place the law as it relates to the consumer into two broad categories. First, remedies exist under private law and second, remedies have been created by administrative and governmental action. These latter remedies are backed up by criminal law and come under the jurisdiction of the Director General of Fair Trading.

Before continuing, it is important that one should understand the nature of a 'contract'. To be binding in law, a contract need not necessarily be formally drawn up by solicitors and signed by both parties. All that is necessary is that an 'offer' be made which is 'accepted' and that the exchange take place for some 'consideration': in most cases this is financial. The implication for consumers is that such a contract takes place every time a purchase is made.

Remedies available under private law: the Sale of Goods Act 1979

The original Sale of Goods Act was passed in 1893 and has been constantly amended since then. The Act defines the statutory rights of the buyer (and seller) with respect to the transfer of property in goods for a money consideration (the price). The 'inalienable' rights of the consumer are set out by the Act. These concern the transference of title from the seller to the buyer, and the description and quality of the goods.

An important component of the Act concerns the question of 'merchantable quality'. The definition of merchantable quality is the cause of some debate. The question is covered by the implied terms of the Act and should not be equated with mere 'description' of the goods. The definition that currently applies is found in Section 14(2) of the Act and provides that:

> Where the seller sells goods in the course of a business, there is an implied condition that the goods supplied under the contract are of merchantable quality.

By section 14(6), 'merchantable' means 'as fit for the purpose or purposes for which goods of that kind are commonly bought as it is reasonable to expect having regard to any description applied to them, the price (if relevant) and all the other relevant circumstances'.

Linked to the idea of merchantable quality is the 'fitness for purpose' for which goods are bought and the 'availability' of those goods, which are also implied terms of the Act.

The supply of services

As marketing is concerned with the provision of both goods and services, we should also consider consumer rights when the product is a service rather than a tangible good. Separate, and perhaps less exhaustive, legislation covers this area, but there are well-established precedents which refer to contracts for services. The Unfair Contract Terms Act 1977 was particularly concerned with the application of exemption clauses by the supplier of services. The 'reasonableness test' afforded protection for both buyer and seller when such clauses were included in a contract.

The more recent Supply of Goods and Services Act 1982 furnished the consumer with further specific attention. Services must be carried out with 'reasonable care and skill', 'within a reasonable time' and at 'a reasonable charge'. Of course, what is 'reasonable' is dependent on the facts and circumstances of the case and how these are interpreted by the judge.

Misrepresentation and false trade descriptions of goods

Perhaps the most often quoted piece of consumer legislation is the Trade Descriptions Act of 1968 and 1972 (TDA). It is also likely that, while the seller should be aware of all consumer legislation, the TDA has the widest scope of application. The Act overlaps to some extent with other legal remedies, but it is specific in that it applies only where a trader has made a claim about the goods offered for sale. This is of particular relevance to the consumer nowadays when advertising, promotion and direct mail campaigns have reached an intensive level. Test cases in the courts have tended to concern malpractices in second-hand car trading, but the precedents that have been set have equal applications in all manner of consumer transactions.

The TDA is clearly of particular relevance to advertising practice. While the Act does not specifically deal with claims as to 'value' and 'worth', the creative jargon of the advertiser's copy may lead to the making of intentional or unintentional false claims about a good or service. This leads us to an important legal point on the subject of advertising—that of the traders' 'puff'. Claims made about a brand of perfume or beer, or the hackneyed 'desirable residence' of the estate agent's jargon, are not likely to be construed as being legally binding. If, however, the advertiser uses a phrase such as 'results guaranteed', such a promise *is* sufficiently definite as to be legally enforceable. If a company makes a claim about its product, it is up to the courts to decide whether the statement is legally enforceable or merely a 'puff' of creative imagination.

The subject of false trade descriptions is linked to that of misrepresentation, which is dealt with separately under the Misrepresentation Act 1967. The easiest way to understand misrepresentation is to remember that is must relate to a question of fact and that any representation becomes legally significant only if it turns out to be false. The categories of misrepresentation should also be appreciated. These are: fraudulent, negligent or innocent. In the latter case, damages are not usually available to the consumer, although costs and expenses arising from the trader's action may be awarded.

Consumer credit

The Consumer Credit Act 1974 is an example of direct response to consumer protection as the purchase transaction becomes more complicated and open to abuse.

The Act controls the advertising of credit and canvassing where dishonesty is concerned, and it requires the company offering credit to disclose fully all information about the agreement, including the rights of cancellation. The consumer also has the 'right to a remedy' if a so-called 'credit bargain' is subsequently found to be extortionate. More recently, a 'cooling off' period has been introduced during which the consumer may reflect on a purchase, and decide whether or not to go ahead with the responsibilities of a credit agreement.

The proliferation of credit facilities that now exist has led to a whole series of legislation on the subject. The principal intention here is to bring attention to the significance of this legislation, rather than to expand upon the individual statutes.

Product liability

The consumer usually makes a contract of sale with a retailer. Under the terms of the Sale of Goods Act, the usual recourse to justice in the event of complaint is made to the retailer and not to the manufacturer. There are, however, occasions when the consumer has the right to bring a case against the manufacturer of defective goods. Such liability with respect to safety is set out in the Consumer Safety Act 1978 and the Consumer Protection Act 1987. Similarly, where a guarantee is offered by the manufacturer, the offer for sale is deemed to have been made by that party and not the retailer.

In civil law, a consumer has the right to sue in the 'tort' of negligence, because a manufacturer has the legal duty of care to ensure that his goods are not dangerous (this being subject to a series of limitations). Although remedies in fact existed long before the consumer movement, such an action is nevertheless a powerful weapon in the modern consumer's armoury in cases of negligence.

Remedies available due to administrative and governmental action

The failure of traders and manufacturers to comply with government regulations may result in civil or criminal action being taken against them. The rationale behind the establishment of the various consumer bodies is not to facilitate a flood of legal actions. The principal idea is to create a system whereby the existence of such bodies performs a self-regulatory function on behalf of manufacturers, advertisers and similar business practitioners. Before 'going to law', the consumer has (in the event of complaint) various sources of advice, plus the opportunity to take advantage of official assistance which will bring pressure to bear upon the offending party. The regulatory bodies established to oversee some of the recently privatized industries, such as OFGAS in the gas industry, are good examples of this.

In addition to, and in conjunction with, legal remedies, the consumer is protected by the following bodies that 'supervise' the law.

The Director-General of Fair Trading The post of Director-General of Fair Trading was created by the Fair Trading Act 1973. This Act was also responsible for setting up the Consumer Protection Advisory Committee. The role of director-general is essentially supervisory. He must monitor the activities of the business world and investigate potential causes for concern and publish the findings if necessary. Such information is available from the Government Office of Fair Trading. He should also encourage trade associations to prepare codes of practice and thus encourage self-regulatory activities. An example of the influence of the director-general was in the creation of the Price Marking (Bargain Offers) Order 1979. This was introduced after recommendations for action against misleading bargain offers were made.

Self-regulation by manufacturers The setting up of voluntary codes of practice by various industries is valuable for consumer protection in that it is beneficial for companies to be seen to be adhering to the code. Moreover, a company will usually support the elements of the code because miscreants will damage the image of the industry as a whole. Voluntary codes will not, however, protect consumers from companies that are determined not to take part in such schemes. Such industry codes do, in many cases, obviate the need for legislative action. The Office of Fair Trading is a useful arbitrator in consumer/trade disputes. The duties of the office are also to approve, monitor and revise codes that are not functioning satisfactorily.

The advertising industry set up the British Code of Advertising Practice as early as 1962. Consumer complaints are brought before the Advertising Standards Authority, whose duty it is to see that advertisements are 'legal, decent, honest and truthful' and that they are prepared with 'a sense of responsibility to the consumer'.

Sources of advice and assistance for the consumer Consumer activism has identified the fact that, for a large proportion of the population, legal remedies, however comprehensive, are beyond their financial reach. Similarly, many consumers are not able to articulate their complaints in the manner which the law often requires. To compensate for this, a conscious effort has been made by volunteers (often from within the legal profession) and by local authorities, to establish advice centres. With one exception, these centres do not deal exclusively with consumer problems, but provide a wide range of legal advice and consumer information. Legal Advice Centres provide an advice service in the largest UK cities. In the latter case this extends to representation in courts, although normally this is available only to those who could qualify under the Legal Aid Scheme.

All local authorities have a Trading Standards Department which exists expressly for the protection of the consumer. This was originally established to ensure the proper execution of the Weights and Measures and Food and Drugs Acts. While this is still the case, the remit of the department now encompasses an advisory role in the event of consumer disputes. Since 1972, such assistance has been augmented by the creation of Consumer Advice Centres. These also publish a wide range of informative leaflets which help consumers to know what is available and what their rights are.

Finally, Citizens Advice Bureaux are run on a volunteer basis in most UK cities. As with law centres, the work of the bureaux is not exclusively concerned with 'consumer affairs'. They are particularly involved with social issues such as housing and payment of social security.

Although the range of legal remedies, and the scope of advice sources, may seem daunting to a prospective business person, it must be remembered that they are merely designed to uphold the law and ensure fair treatment of the consumer. A business that is seriously engaged in satisfying consumer 'wants' and 'needs' need not feel threatened or led to treat the protectors of consumers as adversaries. Indeed, as has already been suggested, consumerism should be viewed as a marketing opportunity rather than a threat.

SOCIAL MARKETING

The term 'social marketing' has yet to acquire a universal definition as to its nature, and the extent of its boundaries has yet to be agreed. However, it is clear that the satisfaction of business management needs is no longer an exclusive sphere for marketing. It is also accepted that marketing should act in conjunction with the public interest by serving the goals of society as well as those of business. Social marketing is, therefore, a broader concept than that expressed by the management system's definition. Social marketing 'refers to the study of markets and marketing activities within a total social system'.[11]

Development of social marketing

Marketing management has been exceptionally efficient in satisfying the material wants and needs of consumers. With this in mind, many economists and sociologists alike believe that, for large sections of the Western world, the needs of consumers now centre on the 'quality' rather than the quantity of life, and that this shift of attention is a feature of the post-industrial society. Of course, the high demand for consumer goods and services is unlikely to abate, but a change in the priority of needs is likely to accelerate. A. H. Maslow has called these new priorities the 'meta-needs' of society. This change is undoubtedly the result of affluence. Related to this, but not as easily explained, are marked value changes. These have also contributed to the emergence of the social marketing concept.

Certainly, consumerism has shifted its emphasis from what might be termed 'micro' to societal issues, these being social costs, social values, social products and social benefits. Some progressive companies have been quick to recognize this, and they in turn have heightened this level of social awareness.

As we saw earlier, a further feature of 'post-industrial' values[12] concerns the issue of environmentalism. Marketing's success in providing for our material needs and wants has also created widespread pollution (both cultural and physical), congestion, waste and ecological imbalance. Marketing is in fact only partly responsible for these phenomena, but it must share the burden of finding products and methods that reduce or eliminate their harmful effects.

Whatever the precise reasons for the development of a social marketing system, it is clear that there remains vast scope for further development, and that, like consumerism, this movement will endure.

Boundaries of social marketing

The traditional viewpoint of marketing would hold that the principal responsibility of marketing is to provide products that satisfy consumers' needs efficiently and profitably. Provided that this is done in a socially responsible way (so runs the argument), the socio-economic *status quo* will be maintained to the mutual benefit of consumers and producers. The difficult question is in the definition of social responsibility. Is this fulfilled by the production of safe products, the publication of honest advertising, or the reduction of pollution?

Proponents of 'social marketing' would greatly extend this responsibility. They see marketing as a social force which not only transmits a standard of living but also serves as a force that reflects and influences cultural values and norms. Thus, the boundaries of marketing extend far beyond purely economic criteria. This would concern those areas where there are clearly recognizable links between marketing and its social effects; e.g. cars—pollution and congestion; foodstuffs—pesticides and preservatives; manufacturing—atmospheric pollution, noise and safety. If business is so efficient in satisfying the most detailed wants of consumers, surely this expertise could, and should, be used to find ways of providing this satisfaction at a reduced social cost. This would have the effect of creating markets as well as making individual firms and whole industries more attractive to the consumer.

Some regard marketing as being so powerful and intrinsic to society that it should concern itself with welfare issues such as poverty, education and health care. It is not in fact uncommon for businesses, both large and small, to involve themselves with such issues. The cynical may regard this as sophisticated image-building. Whatever the motives may be, the fact remains that business and marketing expertise is beginning to develop and exhibit social as well as economic roles.

It is not clear where the boundaries of social marketing should be erected, but it does appear that there are clear advantages both to society and to business if a social orientation were to be incorporated into marketing strategy.

The transition from 'managerial' to 'social' marketing does not imply a replacement of the traditional marketing concept, but rather its extension so as to recognize and encompass the wider needs of society. This added dimension suggests that profit need no longer be marketing's sole goal. However, the need for profit undoubtedly remains the most essential element of a company's survival, and even the most enlightened firm cannot begin to implement a social programme without sufficient funds to initiate and perpetuate its actions.

The role of the government

Early moves towards consumer awareness were more the results of consumerist pressure than action initiated by business. This pressure was in turn supported and strengthened by government in the form of legislation and advisory bodies. The issues raised by social marketing in the 1980s required solutions by business, by government or by both. Social progress is likely to be more successful and beneficial for all concerned if business initiates social change rather than having this enforced upon it by an external agent.

Already, the decision whether or not to adopt socially oriented measures is in some cases no longer an option, but a question of legislative enforcement. It is vital, therefore, that marketing becomes a socially oriented method of management as a result of its own efforts. Governments and their policies change quickly relative to the life-span of companies. Moreover, they are not necessarily the best equipped to ensure that changing social needs are met. Marketing is already a social activity, and changes that it is involved in are likely to be enduring and closely related to society. This is not to say that governments have enacted bad legislation, or that they do not have an important role to play in social development. There obviously exist many companies that would have ignored their social responsibilities had not government forced them to recognize them. The important factor is that marketing executives and corporate bodies react before coercion takes place, and that this reaction has a beneficial effect.

Social orientation

By how far government will be instrumental in social development is unclear. The pragmatic view is that consumers would benefit from, say, pollution control no matter who the initiator is to be. It is suggested that consumers will receive better long-term benefits if the greater part of this responsibility is adopted by marketing.

A positive response to the requirements of fair trading or product reliability is relatively simple. Here the actions of the firm have a direct and immediate effect on its customers. The results of social marketing may have little immediate benefit for the individual, but profound significance for society as a whole. If a company re-formulated its packaging so that it was less wasteful and did not pollute, the immediate customers might prefer the original formula of packaging and the company would lose custom. Similarly, added safety features in cars and modified engines that reduced pollution would inevitably cost more and thus be unpopular with car buyers. In the long term, however, such moves would be beneficial to society. There is, therefore, a severe conflict between the long- and short-run interests of consumers and business. The social marketing concept holds that, if non-consumers suffer in the course of immediate user satisfaction, then the marketing concept is not ultimately being fulfilled.

This is a difficult, ambitious and long-term proposal which will require re-education on behalf of consumers, the business community and society as a whole. The role of marketing is to adopt a social orientation which, while generating long-term profitability for the firm, satisfies immediate consumers and those parts of society that are affected by the firm's activities.

MARKETING AND NOT-FOR-PROFIT ORGANIZATIONS

The previous section has traced the development of a broader-based societal approach to marketing. In order to evolve from purely business-oriented to the social concept of marketing, companies will have to undergo substantial changes in their approach to strategy. This transition has a mirror image when one considers the role of organizations whose function it is to cater for needs other than the commercial needs of society. Just as the business world has in the past tended to ignore the social dimension, not-for-profit organizations have tended not to apply a marketing management approach to their activities.

Such an attitude towards the management of not-for-profit organizations has been fostered by the 'market economy' common to most Western countries, which suggests that 'marketing' is the exclusive domain of the profit-oriented organizations. For example, public bodies, because they have been in the business not of attracting customers, but of providing services that consumers have considered as their right, have often not thought it necessary either to make themselves attractive, or to be sensitive to the needs of those whom it is their duty to serve. This section presents the marketing concept as equally applicable to not-for-profit as well as commercial organizations. This is true because not-for-profit organizations also have 'products' and 'consumers', but in particular because marketing should be seen as a social activity which goes 'beyond the selling of toothpaste, soap and steel'.[13]

Not-for-profit organizations have 'marketing' problems

Not-for-profit organizations, whether inside or outside the mainstream of the public service, are frequently the subject of criticism for having top-heavy bureaucratic structures, an apathetic attitude to their consumers, and poor and wasteful management which is characterized by a reluctance to innovate. Such criticisms can be summed up as unresponsiveness and lack of communication. These are classic marketing problems, and it is not, therefore, unreasonable to assume that marketing can contribute to their solution. This view can be supported if we examine some of the marketing issues in what constitutes a large proportion of not-for-profit organizations, namely public-sector organizations.

Due to the fact that many public services are (a) virtual monopolies and (b) funded by government, it is not possible to draw significant parallels between such organizations and the commercial sector other than to recognize that both groups have 'marketing' problems. The essential difference is that for many public-sector organizations the principle of consumer sovereignty has a reduced significance. For the most part it has not been possible for consumers to exercise the ultimate sanction—the withdrawal of patronage. This is not to say that all public bodies have failed to respond effectively to their consumers. It is, however, true that, where such failure has taken place, had the rules of the commercial sector been applicable, the guilty organizations would probably have been forced to change or go out of existence.

Since the period immediately after the Second World War, the UK has witnessed a dramatic growth in the number of not-for-profit organizations dedicated to the service of the public. At the outset, the level of altruism and the immediate job in hand were probably such that a conscious marketing effort was not thought necessary. Over time, the same changes that have necessitated changes in commercial marketing have also affected the public sector. Changes in life style, levels of affluence and the economy have altered attitudes to institutions which were once considered to be major social benefits. These changes have not been restricted to amenities such as libraries and other public recreational facilities, but have also extended to charities, the police force and the health authorities. It could be argued that the public has little choice but to accept the public services with which they are provided. To accede to such a proposition would, however, be to deny the fundamentals of the marketing concept. While a city library may lose custom because it is not a pleasant place to visit, the only equivalent to such a sanction with respect to more immediately essential services is an unresponsiveness which engenders apathy and eventually hostility. When such a situation occurs, an organization becomes inefficient, not only from an internal viewpoint, but quite clearly from the viewpoint of consumer satisfaction.

The missing element in organizations that have had experiences as described above is 'communication'. Quite simply, the organization has lost touch with its consumers. During the last decade not-for-profit organizations have begun to adopt a 'marketing orientation' which is designed to remedy this, not only in what is physically being offered, but also in terms of image and customer impressions. Like the business sector, there has been a transitional period during which organizations have moved from a 'selling' to a 'marketing' orientation. The providers of public amenities, for example, have recognized that it is not sufficient merely to offer short-term incentives and promotional campaigns; rather they have come to terms with deciding 'what business they are in'! Libraries or public swimming baths are more than what they seem to be if one considers them as satisfying the 'leisure' needs of the community, rather than providing a lending service or a pool of water in which to swim.

That not-for-profit organizations can have marketing problems has not always been recognized. This recognition is the first and principal step of readjustment to the changing needs of society and to better serving those needs that have always existed. The second step is to adopt a marketing approach to management. This can be achieved by viewing the not-for-profit organization as the marketer views the firm and its markets.

Not-for-profit organizations and marketing principles

The principles of marketing are no different for not-for-profit organizations than they are for any commercial enterprise. The concept of the marketing mix has equal application: just as different companies employ a mix that is appropriate to their markets, the optimum marketing mix for public bodies will depend on the type of organization and the market conditions that prevail.

Applying marketing to not-for-profit organizations is made easier by regarding their marketing structures first as one would regard that of any commercial enterprise. Not-for-profit organizations are made up of the following components:

1. *Production* This may seem unusual at first sight, but it makes sense if one considers production as an input/output system, whatever the 'product' might be. Input may simply involve the generation of ideas or the acquisition of the means to produce a service. However, this should be subject to the same degree of impetus and control that is applied to any production line of physical goods.
2. *Personnel* The labour force is an integral part of the total marketing system; the appointment, training and reward structure should be implemented with this 'total' system in mind.
3. *Purchasing* Just as in business, this should be conducted with cost and finished product in mind.
4. *Marketing* Marketing is responsible for thinking in terms of the 'product', whether this be a good or a service. Marketing's role should also concern image, the environment and the optimization of the individual components that make up the organization. An actual marketing director is an increasingly evident feature of progressive organizations.
5. *Consumers* Whatever the degree of choice that consumers have as to their usage of an organization, it should be uppermost in the minds of managers that, although custom may not be lost by inefficiency and poor communication (as in the case of a hospital), these defects imply that the marketing concept is not being successfully implemented. All the factors listed above should, therefore, be focused on the consumers.
6. *Publics* In addition to the immediate consumer/supplier interface, the list of miscellaneous publics common to any organization should be considered so as to measure are improve goodwill and to afford a monitor on the changing environment.

Although there may need to be some modification to their application, most of the central concepts and techniques of marketing discussed in earlier chapters of this text, such as target marketing, market research and forecasting, analysing consumers, and so on, are equally relevant and useful to the not-for-profit organization. Just as in the profit-oriented organization, the basic aim of not-for-profit organizations is to obtain a desired response from a target market. The desired response may be, for example, a visit to a health centre or increased support for a police force, rather than the exchange of money for products and services, but the principles of marketing remain the same.

In fact, there is evidence to support that, after a slow start, not-for-profit organizations are increasingly applying market principles and techniques. For example, Mercer[14] cites the research of Cousins[15] in the UK. Cousins found that 62 per cent of the UK not-for-profit organizations she surveyed claimed to produce a written annual marketing plan, compared with only 57 per cent of the for-profit organizations in her sample.

This is an extended view which takes us beyond the limited definition of marketing as being solely a profit-making activity. The extended view is that marketing is a socially useful activity essentially concerned with the satisfaction of human needs. This is the 'customer' rather than the 'marketing' concept; it embodies the real meaning of marketing and as such is ideally suited to the management of not-for-profit organizations.

CONCLUSIONS

This chapter has looked at marketing from a wider social viewpoint and has discussed how this is sometimes at odds with, and sometimes complementary to, the managerial view. More to the point, it has demonstrated that the social view can have positive connotations in terms of marketing.

Major criticisms of marketing have been cited together with a discussion of the causes of these criticisms. The consumer movement has been charted from its roots in the USA to the up-to-date situation as it now pertains in the UK. The legal situation has also been discussed from the viewpoint of consumers, and a discussion has been undertaken as to how this can have beneficial effects for marketing. Social marketing has been considered together with the need for modern not-for-profit organizations to adopt the marketing concept.

APPLICATION QUESTIONS

1. By how much do you feel that management has failed to fulfil the marketing concept? What arguments would you offer in defence of marketing?
2. Why should management consider consumerism to be more of an opportunity than a threat?
3. Discuss the role of government activity in the consumer–marketing interface.
4. What do you consider to be the realistic boundaries of social marketing? List ways in which a social orientation came to be evident in the marketing activities of companies in the 1980s.
5. In what way do you think that marketing management and the marketing concept has relevance for not-for-profit organizations? Illustrate your answer with actual examples of not-for-profit organizations that have adopted a marketing approach.

REFERENCES

1. C. W. Hofer and D. Schendel, *Strategy Formulation: Analytical Concepts*, Southwest American Publishing, Edmond, OK, 1978, p. 151.
2. R. D. Buzzel *et al.*, 'Market share—a key to profitability', *Harvard Business Review*, January/February 1975.
3. J. K. Galbraith, *The Affluent Society*, Houghton-Mifflin, Boston, 1952, pp. 124–5.
4. S. W. Dunn and A. W. Barban, *Advertising—Its Role in Modern Marketing*, Dryden Press, Hinsdale, IL, 1978.
5. S. Dibb, L. Simkin, W. M. Pride and O. C. Ferrell, *Marketing Concepts and Strategies*, Houghton-Mifflin, Boston, 1991, p. 620.
6. P. Kotler, 'What consumerism means for marketers', *Harvard Business Review*, May–June 1972, pp. 48–57.
7. M. L. Bell, *Marketing Concepts and Strategy*, 2nd edn, Houghton-Mifflin, Boston, 1972.
8. *Market Intelligence*, MINTEL, July 1989.
9. P. Kotler, 'What consumerism means for marketers', *Harvard Business Review*, **50,** May–June 1972, pp. 48–57.
10. For those students who seek precise information as to the law relating to consumer protection, see: *Consumer Law Statutes*, 4th edn, Monitor Press, Sudbury, Suffolk, 1984.
11. W. Lazer and E. J. Kelley, *Social Marketing—Perspectives and Viewpoints*, R. D. Irwin, Homewood, IL, 1973, p. 4.

12. W. Lazer and E. J. Kelley, 'Redeploying market resources towards new priorities: the new "consumer demand"', reprinted in: *Social Marketing*, **8,** pp. 246–8.
13. P. Kotler and S. L. Levy, 'Broadening the concept of marketing', *Journal of Marketing*, **33,** January 1969, pp. 10–15.
14. D. Mercer, *Marketing*, Basil Blackwell, Oxford, 1992, p. 22.
15. L. Cousins, 'Marketing planning in the public and non-profit sectors', *European Journal of Marketing*, **24**(7), 1990, 29–40.

SIXTEEN
AN INTRODUCTION TO CASE STUDIES

INTRODUCTION

Case studies deal with real situations and, by providing an opportunity for the student to make decisions under similar constraints as the actual decision later in the real world, have real significance in marketing and business education.

It is to be recognized and appreciated that the organizations that served as the basis for case study scenarios may be disguised to prevent company identification.

The implicit question to be answered in every marketing case is: What is wrong, and what should be done to put things right? This does *not* mean that there is necessarily any known or uniquely correct solution to the marketing situation under consideration. In many case studies the outcome of the situation is not known, and even if it were, it does not prove that the action taken was the optimum.

The essential task in all case study work is to analyse the situation presented in depth. A first reading is not sufficient to grasp the total dimensions of any case; very often, the significance of the facts, data and information embedded in the case does not emerge until detailed qualitative and quantitative analysis is undertaken.

The significance of the extracted information can then be weighed and evaluated, and decisions can then be made as to the most appropriate course of action.

Good decisions depend not just upon logic and facts, but also upon sound judgement and imagination. Decisions should be translated, in terms of the underlying set or sets of problems to be developed, into a positive plan of action.

This brief introduction to case studies indicates that this approach to education training and personal development has the following key benefits:

1. It uses real-life business situations to work on, but without the risks associated with the real world.
2. It applies a global view to a business setting—so often, the individual perspectives of members of a team within an organization are narrowed owing to the limitations and responsibilities of the job and the time available.
3. It creates personal detachment from the problem setting, so enabling a more objective understanding to be achieved.
4. It facilitates learning from complexity. Real-life business situations are rarely ordered; managers must learn to cope and understand the complexity of problem areas. Using the case

method helps to develop individual capacity to tackle complex business issues.

5. Using different roles in the context of the case study scenario develops wider perspectives. Evaluating the position from a number of different viewpoints assists the building of one vital managerial quality: sound judgement.

6. Applying 'in-depth analysis' provides a strong information base from which decisions can be taken. Opportunities are created for applying new techniques in a 'safe' situation before using these in the real world.

7. Identifying and prioritizing problems builds the powers of evaluation required for rational decision-making.

8. It enables actionable decisions to be made by applying logic, facts, judgement and imagination.

9. Designing strategic plans and the related controls stimulates creativity, which encourages the individual to experiment and thereby to become conditioned to the dynamics of change.

10. Achieving group interaction to test out ideas and to learn from the experience of others helps the individual to develop interpersonal skills which are vital for success in marketing and business management.

Discrete skills can be learned by using case studies, and these include basic analytical skills, skills of application, creativity, written and oral communication and, through awareness of one's self, social skills.

A MODELS APPROACH TO CASE STUDY ANALYSIS

Many students experiencing a case study for the first time face a conceptual barrier:

1. What am I expected to do?
2. How do I make a start?
3. I have read the case study thoroughly but it appears too complex to tackle.

The most basic question to ask is, What is wrong? Then, What can I do to put it right? Then, Do my suggestions overcome the difficulties I have identified in the case? Figure 16.1 explains in diagrammatic terms.

The dimensions of analysing difficulties in organizations have to be considered in relation to the complexities involved. It is useful, and indeed essential, to attempt to discover and define the boundaries to the difficulties facing the organization, i.e. to view the company in the case study as an 'analysis and decision system' (Fig. 16.2).

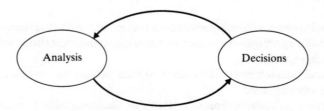

Figure 16.1 A simple model of approach to case analysis

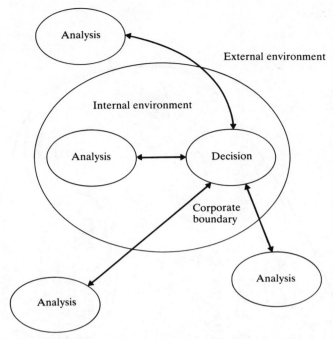

Figure 16.2   A sophisticated model of approach to case analysis

Two environments need to be examined:

—The internal organizational environment.
—The external organizational environment.

Analysis must be conducted both within the defined boundaries of the organization and beyond, in the external corporate environment.

Analysis conducted both internally and externally will then lead to decision proposals which relate to the internal organizational environment in the context of the wider external company environment.

Therefore, the analysis process must span and bridge the defined boundary to enable the company to be viewed as an 'open system' which interacts with its environment, both taking from and adding to the dynamic status of the 'world' beyond the immediate boundaries of the company.

To jump across the hurdle from analysis to decisions in the context of marketing case studies, a closer look is required at the essential components that comprise the analysis and decision system (see Fig. 16.3).

The components within this analysis and decision system are interrelated in many ways, the main relationships being demonstrated by arrows in Fig. 16.4. These relationships are the processes that cause the system to function. The relationship diagram in Fig. 16.4 demonstrates the dynamic qualities of the analysis and decision system, showing how the parts relate to the whole system.

To tackle marketing case studies, the relationships conveyed may be broken down into a set of systematic processes or procedures, as shown in Fig. 16.5, to (a) prepare a case study, and (b) present the case for examination purposes.

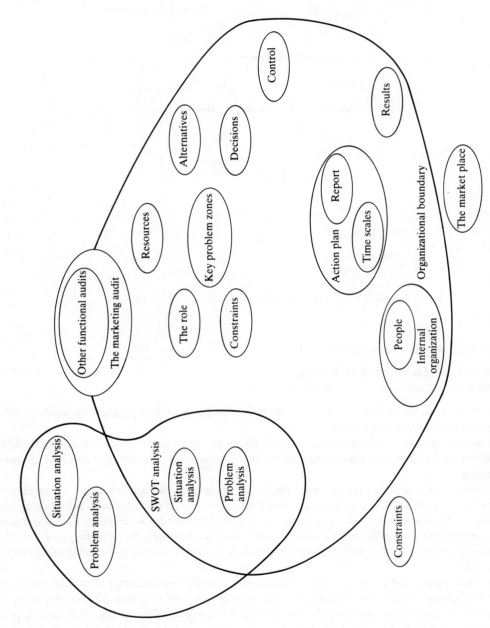

Figure 16.3 A marketing case study analysis and decision system

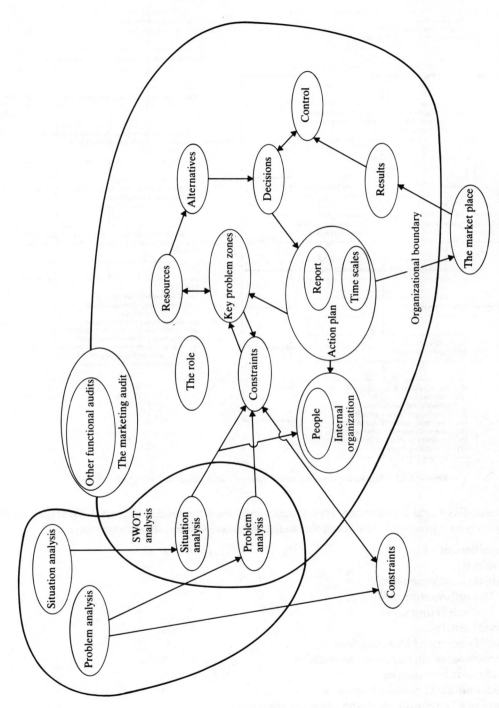

Figure 16.4 A marketing case study analysis and decision relationship diagram

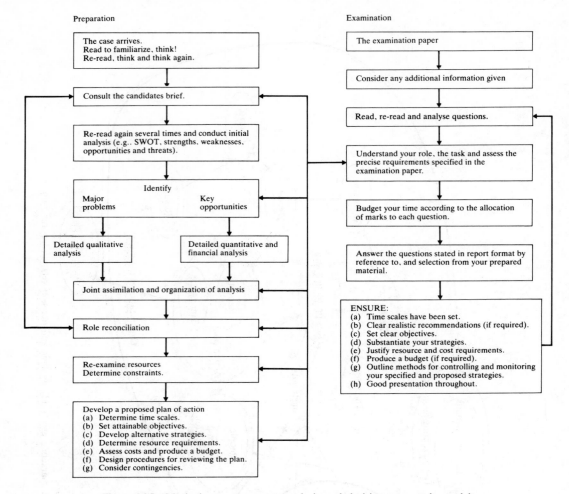

Figure 16.5 Marketing management: analysis and decision case study model

The analysis and decision case study model can now be extended to a set of 20 stages for the preparation and presentation of complex marketing case studies. These stages are:

1. Familiarization.
2. The brief.
3. Initial situation analysis:
   —The information audit.
   —The marketing audit.
4. SWOT analysis.
5. Initial constraint identification.
6. Problem identification and analysis:
   —Quantitative analysis.
7. Redefinition of problem zones.
8. Review of environmental and resource constraints.
9. Statement of assumptions.

10. The business mission.
11. Alternative courses of action.
12. Setting time scales.
13. Setting objectives.
14. Developing strategies.
15. Tactics.
16. Staffing and organizational responsibility.
17. Contingency planning.
18. Results.
19. Control.
20. Report presentation.

USING THE ANALYSIS AND DECISION MODEL

Stage 1 Familiarization

Read through the case study quickly several times to familiarize yourself with the case study scenario.

Read through again, this time more slowly to determine more about the organizational setting, the products/services, and people involved in the environmental context in which the case study scenario is set. Consider the facts presented and the information that can be gleaned from them. Consider how the information presented in the case can best be organized to help you refer back to it for more detailed analysis. At this stage do not discard any of the case material as being invalid.

This is not the time to identify problems or to suggest solutions.

If possible, it is advisable to leave the case for a few hours to help to digest the material to which you have been exposed for the first time.

Above all, remain global in the thoughts you may have marshalled.

At this initial stage avoid all temptation to tackle the detailed aspects with which you have been confronted.

Stage 2 The brief

In certain marketing case studies, as a potential candidate for assessment or examination, you will be given a brief which specifies the role you will be required to take with reference to the case study scenario. Consider your position carefully. In particular:

1. Are you to be a member of the organization? If so:
   (a) In what capacity?
   (b) Is this a staff or line capacity?
   (c) What will be the boundaries of your responsibility?
2. If you are an external consultant to the organization:
   (a) What is your position?
   (b) What is your brief—actual or anticipated?
   (c) Who will be affected by your actions, where, when and how, both within your own consulting organization and in the client company?

Now reconsider the case study material with which you are familiar, in the light of the position in which you are placed.

Stage 3 Initial situation analysis

The information audit It is time now to transfer your review of the case study into a more detailed description and clearer understanding of the situation and the role you have to perform with respect to the total scenario.

To develop your understanding, it is necessary that you interpret the case facts and data to build up an information bank to establish the actual information you have, assumptions about it and the additional information you may need in the real-life situation.

An assessment, therefore, must be made and the following questions should be posed:

—How reliable are the facts, figures and stated opinions?
—To what extent can the information presented be accepted as precise and valid?
—Are there gaps in the information presented?
—Are these gaps designed purposely by the case study writer for identification and explanation by students?
—Is the information presented likely to be subject to change as a result of the dynamic conditions presented, or to be provided at the examination stage?
—Where are the weak links in the information?
—Are the sources of information given valid?

Students may find it helpful to structure the audit under a series of headings before asking these questions. The structuring will depend upon the case being studied, although functional business areas, issues presented, processes in the organization, time dimensions, personal relationships, and financial and statistical issues are suggested for the beginner.

To complete the information audit, it must be remembered that case studies are rarely written to provide clear facts but rather to encourage the student to use deductive logic to infer or even speculate, to stimulate ideas.

It is necessary, therefore, at the end of the audit to provide a set of assumptions from which to build.

The marketing audit Having determined the status of the information presented in the case study, it now becomes necessary to conduct a marketing audit on the total case scenario in preparation for a SWOT analysis that will, in turn, lead to the design of a strategic marketing plan.

The marketing audit of the case study must build up an information base to check the validity and reliability of all facts and stated opinions that relate to marketing issues arising in the case study scenario.

A checklist of points needs to be examined. Although no checklist is completely comprehensive and hence foolproof in application, the following major headings distinguish the internal and external audit.

External company environmental factors
1. Macro-economic environment
    (a) Political/legal/fiscal
    (b) Economic
    (c) Social/cultural
    (d) Technical
2. The market environment
    (a) Market profiles
    (b) Customer profiles

(c) Product profiles
(d) Pricing profiles
(e) Communication profile
(f) Channel and physical distribution profile
(g) Industry structural profile
(h) Competitor profiles and profitability

It would be quite impossible to compile a complete list of factors under each heading. The student to complete a 'profile' under each section, should answer the following: Who? What? Where? When? How? Why? and summarize the difficulties arising.

Internal company environmental factors The internal audit is a complete examination of the situation that currently exists. The internal marketing audit should examine every element that should be contained in an idealized marketing plan, together with the systems and procedures used to design, develop, implement, control, and review the plan (see Table 16.1).

The marketing audit contributes to the student's SWOT analysis in the following way:

Internal audit → Strengths and weaknesses
External audit → Opportunities and threats

During the process of auditing the case study, where information presented conflicts, as often it does in the real world, candidates must apply common sense, make assessments and state their assumptions before proceeding.

Table 16.1   The marketing audit

Internal audit elements	Current position		
	Design systems	Implementation systems	Control systems
1. Corporate and market analysis			
2. Constraints			
3. Apparent and stated assumptions			
4. Key problems and potential problem resolution			
5. Resource evaluation			
6. Time dimensions for planning marketing			
7. Objective setting and achievement			
8. Strategic marketing planning			
9. Tactics employed			
10. Organization for marketing			
11. Forecasting			
12. Budgeting systems			
13. Sales analysis			
14. Sales achievement			
15. Market share(s)			
16. Profit performance			
17. Total marketing mix variables			
18. The marketing information system			

Stage 4 SWOT analysis

The evaluation of the information and marketing audits can now be organized into a SWOT analysis.

Strengths and weaknesses → Historic internal review to date
Opportunities and threats → External current review, forecast over a future time period

The SWOT analysis provides the basis upon which later stages in the model depend. It should aim to condense the case information in an ordered form for easy subsequent reference.

By committing the SWOT to a written presentation, a better understanding of the total case study emerges. In turn, this assists the student to focus on particular issues to help achieve clear problem definition.

The SWOT analysis should be conducted rigorously and is usually best achieved by syndicates working in groups, which often produce creative insights which can be developed to produce distinguished marketing planning proposals.

The content of the SWOT analysis should not appear just as a set of concise, static statements in the pro forma provided in Fig. 16.6, but be *used* to generate *thoughts* for clear problem definition. The real value of a SWOT analysis is to consider the implications that arise from it at corporate and marketing levels. A critical assessment can then be made of the main problem themes facing the company and priorities set for tackling them, and in this way the student can ensure that the key result areas of the business have been appraised.

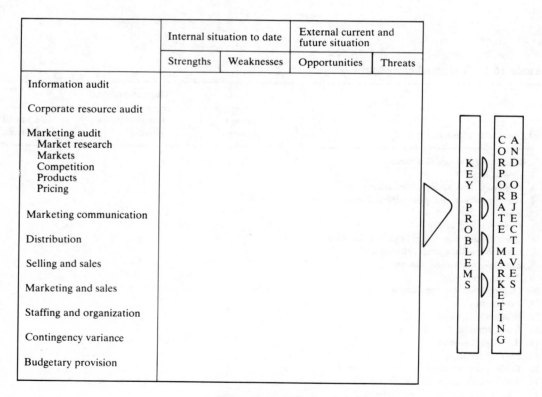

Figure 16.6 'SWOT'

Stage 5 Constraints

Constraints may impose problems upon an organization. They may also provide the limits within which problems can be both identified and researched.

The audits conducted—i.e. the case information audit, the corporate audit and marketing audit—and analysed in the SWOT analysis will highlight the constraints, both internal and external, which provide limits to organizational performance.

Internal resource constraints and external market constraints provide a framework within which objectives can be set, maximized and achieved.

Stage 6 Problem zone identification and problem analysis

The next extension to the SWOT analysis is to interpret it in terms of key problem areas for attention.

The definition of, and distinction between, problem areas will depend upon the role the student adopts. With a specific role brief, the boundaries of responsibility can be clearly drawn and provide the basis from which an actual perspective can be taken. Where the brief is vague, the case study student must take a variety of perspectives and hence will view the organization from different angles in order to identify a variety of problem areas.

The initial step must be individual or group brainstorming on problem areas to ensure that nothing is discounted at this initial stage.

The definition of problems is quite difficult, because the nature of problems often means that they actually comprise sets of problems, which become problem zones; in turn, there are often related difficulties which are hard to isolate for analysis and action. Complex sets of problems are known as *messes*. The task of the candidate, therefore, is to separate out those problem zones that are containable.

Handling problem zones is a matter of scale. Small-scale problems or difficulties:

—Have an interdefinable boundary.
—Involve a limited number of people.
—Can be treated as a separate matter.
—Have limited applications.
—Are capable of being clearly prioritized.
—Operate over a limited time scale.
—Require information that is known.
—Have a known problem.
—Possess a known solution.

'Messy' problem zones are much larger and poorly defined:

—They have no readily defined boundary.
—They involve more people.
—They cannot be treated individually and disentangled from the context.
—They may have far-reaching implications.
—The time scale is uncertain.
—They are difficult to prioritize.
—Information needed is not specified and is difficult to specify.
—It is not sure what the problem really is.
—No immediate solution is known.

Within marketing case studies simple problems may be posed, but often the problem zone lies between the two extremes above.

One way in which problem zones can be detected is to distinguish between what commonly exists and the desired state for the future.

The tension which exists between the SW area and the OT area in SWOT analysis is a rich source for problem area detection.

Students often consider problems in isolation, where in effect there is usually a causal relationship, which can be quite complex and hence multicausal in origin.

Distinction must be drawn between symptoms and fundamental problems to ensure that the outcomes expected and planned for actually occur.

Students can usefully distinguish between existing problem zones and anticipated problem zones. In the latter area, using the SWOT analysis, this classification can be further divided into problem areas for opportunity exploitation and problem areas to avert the risk of impending threats.

Problem areas defined should be capable of action and hence they need to be prioritized with reference to the scale of the problem area specified and the time scale for overcoming them. Hence the use of a time scale running from the immediate term to the long term over specified years and months is useful.

In many case studies problems may be difficult to define. The student should distinguish between the following problem zones:

—Actual explicit problem zones.
—Concealed problem zones.
—Potential problem zones.

The student should realize that in the first two zones some may be historic or recurrent problems.

The analysis of problem settings in case study scenarios must ultimately be assessed in terms of who and what is affected and to what extent the problem is zone-controllable and by whom.

Problem zones can often be highlighted by the imposition of criteria for organizational assessment. It is against such standards that problems which previously had not been identified become revealed.

Detailed problem analysis—quantitative The identification of problem zones from the SWOT analysis may require, in certain case studies, the application of financial and statistical techniques to assist the depth of analysis required accurately to specificy the level of problem(s) facing the company.

Within the space of this text, we cannot provide a comprehensive résumé of such techniques. However, one set of financial assessment techniques often of immediate use is financial ratio analysis.

Financial ratios The subject area of financial analysis is underpinned by ratio analysis. Financial ratios in use are numerous. The marketing student should not need to become a financial analyst to use them but rather should be selective and know the implications of the main categories.

Ratios are not a standard formula for judging the performance of a business. Many ratios are in common use and express standard relationships, but these are only a guide since management cannot be reduced to a formula. What the standard relationships do convey is a logical and important operational sequence of related key control figures. The absolute figures by themselves are of limited value to management.

Ratios are not a substitute for judgement. Management is not provided with answers to its problems by ratios. Judgements must be used not only in the selection of key ratios to suit the business but also in the evaluation of these ratios. Ratios calculated on an industrial basis or for a group of companies operating in a similar type of business, where there is a common basis of calculation, also enable the student to compare company performance with industry performance.

Ratio analysis is a useful financial technique to assist management in the control of the business, provided its limitations are understood.

The marketing student in the analysis of case study profit and loss accounts and balance sheets should be aware of the importance of the following basic ratio types.

1. *Liquidity ratios*
   These are used to assess the company's ability to meet its current financial obligations.
   (a) *The current ratio*
       Formula: Current assets divided by current liabilities.
       Interpretation: The number of times current liabilities are covered by current assets. This is a fairly crude measure expressing the company's ability to meet current obligations with a margin of safety, which may arise from the varying quality of the current assets, particularly with reference to stocks and the status of debtors. A more critical measure of the company's solvency is the 'quick ratio', known also as the 'acid test'.
   (b) *The acid test*
       Formula: Quick assets divided by current liabilities.
       Interpretation: The number of times current liablities are covered by quick assets. Quick assets are cash and 'near cash' items, but *not* stock because it may not be quickly convertible to cash. Quick assets are often considered as current assets minus stocks. In most cases this is cash plus debtors, a critical measure which should be in 1:1.

2. *Profitability ratios*
   These are used to assess the company's profit performance with reference to the direct costs and indirect costs of the business and the associated control of both in relation to sales performance.
   (a) *Gross profit %*
       Formula: Gross profit divided by sales multiplied by 100.
       Interpretation: As a percentage of sales revenue, gross profit is the margin created from absolute sales for the period minus the direct costs represented by the cost of sales.
   (b) *Net profit %*
       Formula: Net profit before tax and depreciation divided by sales multiplied by 100.
       Interpretation: Net profit or loss is the result of charging the indirect costs as revenue expenses of the business against the gross profit margin. To present an objective picture, the net profit figure is taken before depreciation has been charged and corporation tax deducted.
   (c) *Return on total assets*
       Formula: Net profit divided by total assets multiplied by 100.
       Interpretation: The ratio measures the rate of profitability achieved on the total assets of the business. Much will depend upon the accuracy of the assets valuation in the company's balance sheet. There is frequent debate over which profit figure to use. The key is to be consistent throughout the analysis. Options include:

                         —The figure used in the net profit per cent ratio.
                         —Net profit after tax.

In either case, it is considered appropriate to add back the interest charged on long-term debt to demonstrate objectively the company's capacity to produce profits from total asset utilization.

(d) *Return on capital employed*

Formula: Net profit before tax and long-term interest divided by total capital employed multiplied by 100.

Interpretation: This is considered to be the primary ratio from which family trees of ratios can be extended to form a pyramid. It expresses the efficiency of management and measures its performance to generate a *rate* of return on the total capital and reserves of the business.

(e) *Return on owner's equity*

Formula: Pre-tax profits divided by equity capital multiplied by 100.

Interpretation: This ratio measures the rate of return on the owner's investment in the business. As a percentage, absolute return can also be measured for every £100 invested.

3. *Funds management*

These ratios are used to assess how efficiently the company uses the available working capital, particularly with reference to inventory holding, debt collection and payment.

(a) *Debtors collection period*

Formula: Debtors divided by sales multiplied by 365 (days).

Interpretation: The ratio determines the time taken by the company to collect debts. It provides a clear indication of the efficiency of credit control.

(b) *Average payment period*

Formula: Creditors divided by purchase multiplied by 365 (days).

Interpretation: This ratio determines the average time taken for the company to pay its bills. The relationship between 3(a) and 3(b) gives an indication of how the company manages cash flow.

(c) *Stock turnover*

Formula: Sales divided by closing stock.

Interpretation: This ratio measures the rate at which stock moves through the business. A more critical measure can be made by taking the cost of sales figure. The ratio is expressed as the 'number of times' stock is turned. If this is then divided into 365 days, one can assess the number of days' or months' stock that is tied up on the company shelves. Often less dynamic companies tie up a considerable amount of working capital through poor inventory control.

4. *Ability to borrow*

These ratios demonstrate the position of the company in relation to the level of indebtedness and the management of the capital structures.

(a) *Debt ratio*

Formula: Current liabilities divided by total assets multiplied by 100.

Interpretation: This ratio measures the percentage value of the current liabilities in relation to the total asset value of the business. This demonstrates the amount of current short-term indebtedness which is covered by the company's assets and hence the company's ability to pay off current liabilities from the sale of total assets.

(b) *Capital gearing ratio*

Formula: Fixed interest capital divided by shareholders' funds multiplied by 100.

Interpretation: The ratio reflects the percentage of fixed interest capital and business commitments in relation to the shareholders' funds. It shows the relative position of creditors to the business owner's stake in the company. The fixed interest capital figure is also called net debt and is calculated by adding long-term debt to debentures to overdraft and short-term loans less the cash the company has as a current asset.

Stage 7 Redefinition of problem zones

Owing to the length and associated complexity of some case studies, it is necessary to conduct further financial and statistical analysis to gain a more complete understanding of the material presented.

The results of the quantitative analysis must now be set against the backcloth and market setting of the organization to provide a balanced view. Hence it is the consideration of further quantitative and qualitative analysis that may force the student to redefine the problem zones before proceeding to the next stage of the model.

This provides a natural break, a time to sit back and reflect on the analysis progress to date before adopting a more focused view of the situation. Once the finishing process starts, it is very difficult to revert to take a holistic view again. Therefore, allowing for the time constraints imposed, the longer one can take in problem analysis to provide a global situation summary, the better will be the design of the proposed action plan.

It is at this stage, therefore, before confirming the problem zones for attention, that the candidate should finally reconcile the role(s) in relation to the case study scenario.

Stage 8 Review environmental and resource constraints

Before proceeding to the action plan, students should check that the environmental and corporate resource constraints have been fully appraised and stated so that progress can be planned within these limitations.

In particular, modifications to the design and implementation of resource management can be considered, so that slack or wasted resources can be manipulated to maximize efficient resource utilization.

Stage 9 Statement of assumptions

Based upon the analysis conducted so far, students must state all assumptions before proceeding with the development of objectives and the strategic marketing plan.

Stage 10 The business mission

The corporate plan comprises a statement of the global business mission for the company. This direction is laid out as a set of corporate objectives, corporate strategies with the main tasks for the time period defined, plus corporate financial projections as a set of budgets.

The corporate plan should dictate the changes required for the period. These changes are operated by each strategic business unit in the organization.

The business mission must precede the setting of marketing objectives and the development of marketing strategy, and therefore it provides the foundation for marketing planning.

Simple but demanding questions must be answered:

—What business is the company in now?
—What business is the company *really* in?

—How well is the company doing?

—What assumptions can be made about the future?

—Where should the company be, say, in five years' time, and why?

—What routes can be taken to get there?

—What will be the market reaction?

—What is the level of corporate risk?

—Which direction should the company actually take?

—What resources does the company have, and what will it need?

—How can it be ensured that the company will arrive at the intended destination?

—What action needs to be taken to achieve the business mission, and what will be the total cost?

The answers to these questions should be summarized on a corporate statement which specifies the future business mission for the organization.

Stage 11 Alternative course of action

Students are now required to take a substantial conceptual leap from problem definition to suggesting alternative solutions.

Creativity is the key! Enjoy the process of generating ideas; have fun; be experimental. So far the process has been quite rigid, yet turgid courses of action are not really required, and rarely do they provide the best solutions for strategic planning.

In some cases, alternatives may be explicit in the case study; the student is merely required to set up criteria by which to weigh the alternatives. Often, though, alternative courses of action are required to embrace, contain and resolve the key problems prescribed.

Students in these case situations must have an overall appreciation of the global alternatives which are feasible and provide a basis upon which to assess these alternatives to make a firm judgement.

Good solutions are often as good as the ability to define and separate problems for attention.

Problem zones may be too wide to handle in one attempt and hence students must aim to tailor the chosen course of action to lower-level problems.

In all case study work there is no *one* solution, but rather defensible and justifiable courses of action which jointly attempt to resolve the difficulties the organization faces. Owing to the 'soft' nature of many problem settings, solutions may be partial at one end of the continuum and a whole set of problems may be resolved at the other. Rarely will independent courses of action achieve an all-embracing solution to the complexities of a defined problem zone. Rather, it is a set of related and hence integrated combined solutions which serve to make real progress towards overcoming or containing organizational problems.

Courses of action will normally achieve systemic effects both within the organization and beyond, into the environment of the marketplace, and hence alternatives must be assessed objectively to ensure optimization within the previously defined constraints.

Basic cost–benefit analysis of the proposed alterations is suggested. Students should consider the negative outcomes of their proposals as well as the positive effects.

Above all, the selected course of action must be feasible and achievable within the defined limitations of the company scenario posed.

Stage 12 Setting time scales

Problem analysis and the selected course or courses of action must be set in the context of time. Realistic time scales must be set for the development of a strategic plan.

Plans are usually devised on a rolling planning basis, and hence a one-year plan can be so rolled over, for example, a three- to five-year period with reviews scheduled at regular intervals.

Students should develop the time horizon for action both within a 12-month period and beyond. Even within the one-year plan there are events that require immediate action—say, within three months. These also should be clearly distinguished.

The complexity of a problem zone may require, for example, a series of sequential actions over a specified time scale ranging from three months to three years—in which case, students should demonstrate clearly the use of appropriate action phased over the specified time period.

Stage 13 Setting objectives

Having chosen and justified the best course of action to resolve the problems presented, this decision must be implemented in the form of a formally presented plan.

Many marketing case students do not know the questions with which they may be faced in an examination, and hence the most appropriate form of preparation is to draw up a comprehensive marketing plan from which sections can be selected on the day of the examination.

Objectives provide the basis for the plan and should be specified at corporate and marketing levels and then at marketing-scale plan levels so that strategies are designed to relate to the specified objectives at the various levels of the plan.

Marketing objectives should be specified for the prescribed time periods in both quantitative and qualitative terms and should be capable of action, measurement and achievement within the selected periods. They should be both consistent and attainable.

It is vital that objectives are specified clearly so that you can communicate precisely what it is that you wish to do.

The SWOT analysis provides the stimulus from which objectives should be set. Objectives should be designed to overcome the key problems and problem zones that were determined from the SWOT analysis.

A useful technique is to develop an objective tree which starts at global higher-level objectives and obtains a clearer focus for action at the lower marketing-scale plan levels, i.e. a hierarchy of objectives. This hierarchy should specify what is to be achieved at each level.

The setting of marketing objectives should aim to achieve balance within the marketing mix and allow for a degree of flexibility.

Marketing objectives should embrace the company philosphy and encourage the development of revised policy.

Essentially, the following areas cannot be ignored in the design of marketing objectives:

—Market position
—Change
—Output
—Resource utilization
—Staff performance and attitude
—Social responsibility
—Profitability
—Cost control

Stage 14 Developing strategies

Marketing objectives specify *what* is to be achieved. Marketing strategies should outline *how* the objectives are to be achieved.

Marketing strategies are determined from objectives, not the other way round; but the student must ensure that the proposed strategy is not over-embracing and does not go beyond the requirements of the specified objective. This is a common fault in student presentations, which in many cases extends to a total reorganization of the company both internally and with reference to its position in the marketplace—albeit to achieve a very modest objective.

Strategy is the route to the achievement of objectives over the specified time intervals for which the objectives have been set.

Balance is a keynote; the internal consistency of the plan must be checked to ensure that the marketing elements for which strategy is designed are integrated and not competitive. When presented, the designed marketing strategy should demonstrate where the emphasis has been placed in order to achieve marketing objectives and the wider business mission.

As a mechanism for marshalling the impact of the developed strategies, financial resource deployment must be specified clearly in the form of a total marketing budget illustrating capital sources, revenues and expenditure.

The strategic marketing plan should demonstrate the utilization of existing resources and those additional resources to be procured to implement the designed strategy.

Stage 15 Tactics

The detailed implementation of the strategic plan is conveyed as an action plan which specifies the actual individual activities to be undertaken with due dates for their achievement.

Stage 16 Staffing and organizational responsibility

People have problems, not organizations; and people design, implement, administer and review plans to overcome problems. Students preparing case studies often demonstrate a total detachment from the human activity system of the organization.

Human resource management is a key factor in the management of the marketing function. Therefore, attention to this critical area is essential in preparing marketing management case studies.

Case material will have varying levels of information about key personnel involved, but where it is provided students must analyse the staff profile, consider the existing position and detect areas where change is required.

Change may mean not simply hiring and firing—even if this is within the remit given in the student brief—but also staff development, training, instruction and progression within the organizational structure.

In particular, the deployment of staff to take responsibility for the implementation of the marketing plan is an essential part of case study preparation.

Staffing should be viewed in a global context to include the appointment and appraisal of external agencies and consultants.

Stage 17 Contingency planning

Strategic planning in the relatively safe internal corporate case environment is one thing. Implementing the plan to achieve the designed strategy is quite another!

The purpose of contingency planning is to enable and even force management to think ahead to answer the question, 'What if our expectations are not realized in the real world?'

Contingency thinking is designed to create answers to the 'What if?' questions so that management will have the answers ready ahead of time if the designed strategy goes wrong. In case study preparation, the vital section on contingencies forces the student to think about a wider range of situations that might occur than when strategies were first designed to meet corporate and marketing objectives.

The student should consider how flexible the designed plan is if conditions should change. Answers to the following questions are needed:

—What is the capability of the organization to adapt to changed conditions?
—How quickly can the organization respond and with what internal and external effects?
—In what way must the organization respond to avert a crisis or the partial achievement of objectives?
—What options are open to the company in the light of anticipated change? How should these options be evaluated and what action should be taken?

At an earlier stage in this case study analysis and decision model the student had to generate ideas and decide between alternative courses of action. Reference back may provide a source for idea generation when designing the contingency plan.

Stage 18 Results

The case study student is often required to produce a strategic and tactical plan in a vacuum where the input is simply the case study material and the output is a well-presented strategic marketing plan. It is assumed that the results of the plan are the achievement of the specified plan objectives. If the objectives have been carefully and clearly communicated in a hierarchy and allocated to responsibility centres for action, monitoring, evaluation and adjustment, the task is usually deemed complete. Often answers to the following questions are overlooked:

—When implemented, what will be the tangible results of the proposed action?
—Can these results be quantified?

Therefore, the projected outcomes should be considered not only in terms of qualitative contribution, but also in financial terms, with reference to anticipated profits and profit contribution.

Stage 19 Control

The management process has been described as planning, organizing, directing, controlling, communicating, coordinating and evaluating organizations and individuals to achieve effective decisions.

The control function needs careful attention in the preparation of a marketing plan.

The control function should monitor feedback and assess performance so that appropriate adjustments can be made to achieve the desired goals and objectives of the organization.

A system of controls should be specified in both qualitative and quantitative terms in accordance with the time dimensions of the designed plan.

By designing a control system to review regularly actual performance against forecasted performance, management should be in a position of *knowing* what may go wrong.

The control system, efficiently administered, should avoid surprise, avert crisis and prevent the plan getting out of control.

To measure progress towards the achievement of goals and objectives, responsibility centres should be designated. No student must consider these without reference to the culture of the organization and the ability to adopt controls.

Despite the stage of organizational development or size of the organization, all managers should be in a position to highlight impending problems that will require immediate attention. This ability produces time in which to diagnose and analyse problem areas, then to design a strategy to resolve the difficulty. Levels of control to be designated should link with the management structure and organizational levels of the company.

To design a control system for the marketing plan, every element in the plan should have a set of specified controls tailored to fit the plan and the organization. Students must be aware that there is not one ubiquitous control model that can be applied to all plans.

The control system should facilitate situational analysis, problem diagnosis and the setting of priorities for feedback, and should specify the form and frequency of controls.

The main aim is for the designed marketing plan to succeed. The control system assists the progression towards success.

In the real world, plans fail frequently owing to a number of often interrelated factors. Typical factors are shown in Fig. 16.7 and should be provided for by the structure in the design of the marketing plan control system.

To assist the control of the marketing plan, the company must have a marketing information system. The complexity of the system will vary considerably depending upon the size of company and style of company management.

The system is a structured, interacting complex of staff, machines and procedures which should be designed to generate an orderly flow of pertinent information. Information is needed

Figure 16.7 Marketing plan control system

from the external and internal organizational environment for use as a basis for decision-making in specified areas of responsibility.

Therefore, the information system lies between the environment and the marketing executive user.

The student must consider what the marketing planning system needs, in what form, and what is economically feasible within the financial resource constraints of the organization.

Budgetary control The most vital ingredient in business is planning for profit. Without profit, rarely can business survive and grow. An essential activity is profit planning and control, and budgeting is probably the widest-ranging control technique used because it percolates the entire organization.

Budgetary control in the context of the marketing plan is generally designed and adopted to coincide with the financial year of the company.

Correctly applied, the process of budgetary control makes a penetrating, critical and almost uncompromising evaluation of the performance of the marketing plan.

Students must recognize that budgeting and the associated information system provide a major contribution to achieving the objectives of the marketing plan.

The system must be inspired at senior management level and used to set operational standards with accountability for performance. The budgetary control system must be set up to allow for measurement against planned and forecasted performance.

When compiling case study marketing plans, students must realize that budgeting involves more than just forecasting. It provides a framework for evaluating performance.

In the context of case study examinations, students are often required only to list the appropriation of a total budget under relevant cost/profit centres. This is usually the final stage of an exhausting examination. Students must realize that this is only the beginning, and that the budget headings with forecasted income and expenditure have real organizational implications.

Stage 20 Case study report presentation

Written reports must be planned to achieve maximum impact on the reader.

The planning stage starts with the purpose of the report, to whom it is to be presented, what is to be included and how it is to be presented.

The purpose of a written case study report for students of marketing may be for course assessment or formal examinations. The function is to inform the reader of the facts, to explain the proposed course of action and to convince the reader that the recommendations and plans proposed are justifiable in the hope that a favourable reading/assessment is awarded.

A report must be written with a clear understanding of who the readers are and what they know of the situation, so that communication can take place at their knowledge level. For examination case reports, assume that the reader, your examiner, has a low knowledge level; do not overestimate his or her ability. You must be able to *demonstrate* your knowledge and understanding of the situation. The reader's attitude under conditions of assessment should be objective, but in the real world the writer must be aware of prevailing attitudes so as not to offend the reader.

In both the real world and for course assessment, you must have vision about what the reader wants to receive in terms of content, style and presentation.

Remember that reports are not extended essays but concise statements setting out your thoughts and proposals simply and clearly.

All recommendations should be justified to support your proposed plan of action, but do not bore the reader with in-depth analysis—this is in your working papers for subsequent reference if required.

It is important that the report is so structured that:

—The report is read.
—It is understood.
—It follows a logical sequence leading the reader along a particular path.

Planning the structure of your report before writing is absolutely essential.

For examination candidates, questions posed under examination conditions should be broken down into their component parts and a structure designed to ensure that all component parts have been handled. This structure then forms the headings for your report. Remember to commit to paper the most important points first, just in case your time budget has been exceeded for that particular section of the examination paper. Ensure that conclusions and recommendations are labelled clearly to receive maximum attention by the reader.

The conventions for structuring a report vary considerably. One format used personally is as follows:

1. *Title page* This contains the report title, to whom it is addressed, the date, author's name and company and the list to whom the report is to be distributed.
2. *Summary* This is a résumé of the terms of reference of the report with a short statement containing key functions, conclusions and recommendations. (This may also serve as a 'short report' for senior executives not wishing to indulge in the complete work.)
3. *Detailed contents list* This should show clearly the structure of the report with a numbering system which is used throughout the report. Major headings and sub-headings should be shown and indexed by page number for easy reference.
4. *The main report* This section contains the detailed facts and plans to support the summary given above. The main report should substantiate the recommendations made to the company in the summary section.
5. *Appendices* This section should comprise three sub-sections:
   (a) Supporting data to back up the main body of the report but which are too detailed for inclusion in the main section and would otherwise disrupt the flow of the report.
   (b) Sources of reference, itemizing the bibliography and external sources consulted in the preparation of the report.
   (c) Glossary of terms, to assist readers not totally conversant with the more technical aspects of the report.

For examination candidates, this structure may be appropriate only where the one global question has been asked. Where questions are issue-specific, the report must be tailored to the actual examination questions asked. This can be seen clearly in the worked examples included in later chapters of this book.

One alternative structure that may be applied by examination candidates is as follows:

1. *The problem statement* This is an interpretation of the specific examination questions stated in terms of a problem for solution.
2. *The implications of the problem* This section contains a concise résumé of the causes and effects of the problem.
3. *Alternative courses of action* This is a succinct statement of the options that could be taken to solve the problem area.

4. *Conclusions and recommendations* This is a statement of the selected course of action, justifying it and explaining in detail the recommended action to be taken.

Presentation is crucial for a report to be well received. Each page must appear interesting to the reader's eye. The use of white space, headings, indentations and report numbering systems should be applied to create maximum impact.

Remember the reader's attention span may be quite short, so sections and paragraphs should reflect this. In short, write simply, write briefly, write positively, and avoid cluttering the main text with elaborate diagrams, charts and tables.

Finally, to complete what has been a comprehensive overview of case study analyses and how they should be approached, an appendix is provided giving some useful concepts and definitions. It is unlikely that you will ever need all of these definitions in the context of marketing case studies, but the list is as comprehensive as possible in terms of modern business policy cases analysis. The next chapter concentrates upon marketing case study analyses.

APPENDIX TO CHAPTER SIXTEEN: Some Useful Concepts and Definitions

(Reproduced from material kindly supplied by Professor E. C. Lea and Dr B. Kenny, University of Huddersfield.)

Accounts payable   Amounts owned by the firm to creditors (US).

Accounts receivable   Amounts owing to the firm by its debtors (US).

Accumulation depreciation   The cumulative amount of depreciation written off a fixed asset.

Acid test   *see* Quick ratio.

Amortization   The writing off, over a period, of an asset or a liability.

Asset   Any property, tangible or intangible, that can be expressed in monetary terms and that brings benefit to the firm, e.g. plant and equipment, stocks, goodwill.

Asset turnover   Ratio of sales to net tangible assets.

Authorized share capital   The maximum share capital that a company can issue at any given time. The amount, which can be altered by the shareholders in general meeting, is stated in the Memorandum of Association and must be disclosed in the balance sheet. Also called *Nominal share capital* or *Registered share capital*.

Average collection period   The frequency with which a company collects its debts:

$$\frac{\text{Debtors} \times 365}{\text{Credit sales}} \text{ days}$$

Bonus shares   Shares issued to existing shareholders without further payment on their part. Also referred to as a *Scrip issue* or a *Capitalization issue*.

Book value   The monetary amount of an asset as stated in the balance sheet. Usually represents acquisition cost less accumulated depreciation.

Business planning   Involves the process of establishing objectives and the development and implementation of strategy, extending down to the development of sales forecasts, establishment of budgets, anticipation of needs for capital and facilities and equipment.

'Cash cows'   Low-growth products that usually generate more cash than is required to maintain market share. Generally regarded as the foundation of the firm.

Convertible loan stock   Loan stock which may be converted at the option of the holder at a future date or dates into ordinary shares at given price ratios.

Cost of capital   The cost to a company's ordinary shareholders of issuing shares or debentures, of retaining profits, or of other sources of funds.

Creditors   Amounts owing by a company resulting from, say, the purchase of materials.

Cumulative preference shares   Preference shares entitled to be paid the arrears of their dividend before any dividend is paid on the ordinary shares. Any arrears must be disclosed as a note to the balance sheet.

Current assets   Those assets that are either already cash or can reasonably be expected to become cash within one year from the date of the balance sheet, e.g. debtors, stock-in-trade. If the directors believe that any of the current assets will not realize their balance sheet values in the ordinary course of business, this fact must be disclosed.

Current liabilities   Liabilities that are expected to have been paid within one year from the date of the balance sheet, e.g. trade creditors, proposed final dividend, current taxation.

Current ratio   Ratio of current assets to current liabilities. A measure of liquidity.

Debentures   Loans that are usually, but not necessarily, secured on the assets of the company. Usually redeemable but may be irredeemable.

Debtors   Amount owing to the company, e.g. from the sale of goods. Usually shown in balance sheets net of provision for debts unlikely to be recovered.

Deferred taxation   Tax that is due beyond one year from the date of the balance sheet.

Depreciation   Expense recording the using up of fixed assets through operations. Usually measured by allocating the historical cost less disposable value of the asset on a straight-line or reducing-balance basis.

Discounted cash flow   The present value of future cash receipts and payment, i.e. their value after taking into account the delay in receiving or paying them.

Diversification   A strategy by which the firm's growth objectives are achieved by adding products or services to the existing lines. Concentric diversification takes place when the products added are similar to existing types, from a production, marketing channel, customer or technology point of view. *Conglomerate diversification* refers to growth into areas unrelated to the company's present product/market scope (often associated with acquisitions).

Divestment   Refers to retrenchment strategy. The selling off or liquidation of a division or unit of an organization.

Dividend   That part of the profits of a company which is distributed to the shareholders. May be interim (paid during the financial year) or final (recommended by the directors for approval by the shareholders at the annual general meeting). Both must be disclosed gross of tax in the profit and loss account. The proposed final dividend is shown gross in the balance sheet as a current liability.

Dividend cover   The ratio between earnings per share and the ordinary dividend per share.

Dividend yield   The relationship between the ordinary dividend and the market price per ordinary share.

'Dodos'   Term for describing low-share–negative-growth products. Used in context of product life cycle/product portfolio analysis.

'Dogs'   Products that are at a cost disadvantage and have few opportunities for growth at a reasonable cost. Generally low market share product needing cash to survive and, consequently, not profitable.

Earnings per share   Net profit after tax attributable to the ordinary shareholders, divided by the number of ordinary shares.

Earnings yield   The relationship between the earnings per ordinary share and the market price per ordinary share. The reciprocal of the price–earning ratio multiplied by 100.

Environment   Generally refers to *external* forces affecting the organization. These may be classified under legal, social, political, economic, technological and market forces.

Equity share capital   Defined by the Companies Act as any issued share capital that has unlimited rights to participate in either the distribution of dividends or capital. Often more narrowly defined to mean ordinary shares only.

Experience curve   A postulate that suggests that, as the firm grows in size and experience, it is able to reduce costs and improve productivity for a given activity.

Financial ratios   Relationships among items in financial statements.

Fixed assets   Assets held for use in the business rather than for re-sale.

Fixed overheads   Those overheads whose amount remains constant over the usual range of activity.

Gearing   The relationship between the funds provided to a company by its ordinary shareholders and the long-term sources of funds carrying a fixed interest charge or dividend.

Goodwill   The difference between the 'value' of a company as a whole and the sum of the values of the tangible assets and liabilities taken separately. Usually recorded only when the company is being evaluated for, say, potential purchase.

Historical cost   The usual basis of valuation in published financial statements. Favoured because it is more objective and more easily verifiable by an auditor. Its use is contentious, especially in times or inflation.

Holding company   A company that controls another company, called its *Subsidiary*. Balance sheet of holding company must show separately amounts owing to and owed by subsidiaries.

Intangible assets   Assets such as goodwill, patents and trade marks.

Integration   Growth strategy characterized by the extension of the firm's business definition, i.e. vertical (forward and backward) integration. In this case the firm may integrate forwards to assure control of distribution, or backwards to safeguard supplies of raw materials.

Issued expenses   Expenses of making an issue of shares or debentures.

Issued share capital   The amount of the authorized share capital that has been issued; the remainder is the unissued share capital. The amount of the issued capital must be disclosed in the published balance sheet. Not necessarily equal to called-up or paid-up share capital.

Issue price   The price at which a share is issued. Since the issue may be at a premium or a discount, the issue price is not necessarily equal to the par value.

Liabilities   Amounts owing by a company, which must be disclosed in the published balance sheet. For example:

—Aggregate amount of bank loans and overdrafts
—Aggregate amount of other loans
—Amounts owing to subsidiary companies
—Recommended dividend
—Redeemed debentures
—Debtors

Liquid assets   *see* Quick assets.

Loan capital   Funds acquired by non-short-term borrowing from sources other than the shareholders of the company.

Long-term debt   Long-term sources of funds other than equity (share capital and reserves).

MBO (management by objectives)   A technique that establishes a formal approach requiring top, middle and lower management to operate by a system of objectives.

Market price   The price at which a company's securities can be bought or sold on a stock exchange. Not necessarily equal to the par value or the issue price.

Minority interest   That part of a subsidiary company's shareholders' funds that is not held by the holding company. Usually shown as a separate item on the net worth and liabilities side of a consolidated balance sheet.

MIS (management information system)   A formal system of gathering intelligence—information to be used by the strategist. For example, economic data, market reports, technological development, etc., plus data on internal operations.

Net current assets   Another name for working capital.

Net profit ratio   Ratio of net profit to sales.

Net tangible assets   Assets except for intangible assets (goodwill, patents and trade marks), less liabilities.

Net working capital   Another name for working capital.

Net worth   Assets less liabilities. The proprietorship section of a balance sheet, usually referred to in the case of a company as shareholders' funds or share capital and reserves.

Nominal share capital   *see* Authorized share capital.

Non-voting shares   Shares with no voting rights. Non-voting ordinary shares are usually cheaper to buy than those carrying votes.

Objectives   Desired targets or results which at the basic level may be expressed in financial, product/mission or social–psychological terms; at the fulfilling level, objectives may be defined in more directed fashion, such as relationships with customers or continuous improvement of resources.

Ordinary shares   Shares entitled to share in the profits after payment of debenture interest and preference dividends. Often referred to as the *Equity capital*.

Paid-up share capital   The amount of the called-up share capital which has been paid up by the shareholders.

Par value   The face or nominal value of a share or debenture. Not necessarily equal to the issue price or the current market price. Dividend and interest percentages refer to the par value; yields, to the current market price.

PIMS (profit impact of marked strategies)   UK study relating to profitability analysis (see Schoeffler, Buzzell and Heany, 'Impact of Strategic Planning on Profit Performance', *Harvard Business Review*, **52,** March–April 1974, pp. 137–45).

Policies   Broad guidelines to pursuing objectives, and designed to clarify or sharpen up those objectives.

Preference shares   Shares that usually are entitled to a fixed rate of dividend before a dividend is paid on the ordinary shares, and to priority of repayment if the company is wound up.

Participating preference shares are also entitled to a further dividend if profits are available. If a preference dividend is not paid, the arrears must be disclosed as a footnote to the balance sheet. Arrears can arise only if the shares are cumulative as distinct from non-cumulative.

Price–earnings ratio   The multiple of the last reported earnings that the market is willing to pay for a company's ordinary shares; the reciprocal of the earnings yield multiplied by 100.

Product portfolio (analysis)   Relates to specific marketing strategies to achieve a balanced mix of products that will produce the maximum long-run effects from scarce cash and management resources.

'Question marks'   Sometimes known as *'Problem children'*. High-growth/low-market-share products. Cash generation is low and cash needs high.

Quick assets   Current assets less stock-in-trade.

Quick ratio   The relationship between quick assets and current liabilities. Also known as *Liquid ratio*, or the *Acid test*. A measure of liquidity.

Quoted investments   Investments for which there is a quotation or permission to deal on a recognized stock exchange or on any reputable stock exchange outside the UK. Must be shown separately in the balance sheet.

Reserves   Reserves arise either from the retention of profits or from specific capital transactions such as the issue of shares at a premium or the revaluation of assets. Must not include provisions—unless the directors consider they are excessive—or the taxation equalization account. Not a charge against profits; not necessarily represented by cash on the other side of the balance sheet. Movements in reserves during the financial year must be disclosed.

Reserve fund   A reserve that is represented by specially earmarked cash or investments on the other side of the balance sheet.

Retained profits   Profits not distributed to shareholders but reinvested in the company. Their cost is less than a new issue of shares, because of the issue costs of the latter.

Return on investments   Ratio of profit (usually before interest and tax) to net tangible assets. A measure of profitability.

Revaluation   The writing-up of an asset to its current market value.

Revenue reserves   Reserves regarded by the directors as being normally available for dividend.

Rights issue   An issue of shares in which the existing shareholders have a right to subscribe for the new shares at a stated price. The right can be sold if the shareholder does not wish to subscribe.

Share capital   Unless limited by guarantee, a company registered under the Companies Act must have a share capital divided into a fixed amount. The ownership of a share gives the shareholder a proportionate ownership of the company. The share capital is stated in the balance sheet at its part (nominal) value.

Shareholder   Member of a company whose part ownership of (share in) the company is evidenced by a share certificate.

Shareholders' funds   The proprietorship section of a company balance sheet. Includes the share capital and the reserves (sometimes called *Net worth*).

Share premium   Results from issuing shares at a price higher than their par value. Must be disclosed in the balance sheet as a reserve. Cannot be used to pay dividends, but can be used to make an issue of bonus shares.

'*Stars*'   Products that are market leaders and also growing at a fast rate. They represent the best opportunity for growth and investment.

Stock-in-trade   For a manufacturing company consists of raw materials, work-in-progress and finished goods. Usually valued at the lower of cost or market value.

Stock turnover   Ratio of sales (sometimes, cost of sales) to stock-in-trade.

SBU (strategic business unit)   An operating division of a firm which serves a distinct product–market segment or well-defined set of customers. Generally it has the authority to make its own strategic decisions as long as they meet corporate objectives.

Strategy   As a concept, refers to the total system incorporating the firm's objectives, policies and the planning required to achieve objectives. In the managerial sense, strategy relates to the continuous process of effectively relating the organization's objectives and resources to opportunities in the environment.

Synergy   Exists when the strengths of two companies or units, when put together, more than offset their joint weaknesses:

—Many products resulting in higher utilization of facilities, personnel and overheads (operating synergy).
—Many products using same plant and equipment (investment synergy).
—Management experience in one industry helping to solve problems in another industry (management synergy).

Synergy can thus be gained through application of production, marketing or financial expertise.

Time interest earned   The number of times that a company's interest is covered or earned by its profit before interest and tax.

Turnover   Sales. The profit and loss account must disclose the amount and basis of turnover for the financial year. The directors' report must disclose group turnover and profit (or loss) before the tax is divided among classes of business that differ substantially.

Unquoted investments   Investments for which there is not a quotation or permission to deal on a recognized stock exchange or on any reputable stock exchange outside the UK. If they consist of equity of other companies, directors must give either an estimate of their value or information about income received, profits, etc.

Unsecured loan   Money borrowed by a company without security.

'*War horses*'   Term used to describe high-share/negative-growth products. Used in context of product life cycle/product portfolio analysis.

Working capital   Current assets less current liabilities.

Work-in-progress   Partly completed manufactured goods.

Yield   The rate of return relating cash invested to cash received (or expected to be received).

MARKETING CASE STUDY EXAMINATIONS

A marketing case study examination requires candidates to apply themselves in a managerial capacity to a simulated practical marketing situation.

The examination is often 'open book', meaning that candidates may bring into the examination hall material which they have prepared in advance of the examination. This approach enables the candidates to produce a more comprehensive answer within the examination period, provided that time is not lost in the sifting and searching of the prepared material. An efficient filing system is crucial to achieve effective management of examination time.

The candidate must be completely familiar with every aspect of the case to be able to approach the examination with confidence. Effective preparation for this examination depends upon effective training. Candidates must build up stamina for their final performance, and hence practise up to and including a 'mock examination' is most advisable.

BEFORE THE EXAMINATION

While mini case scenarios may be presented at the examination, major case studies arrive in a time period before the examination. The candidate must plan, organize, coordinate, direct, control and evaluate the preparation of the case study in the context of the role specified in the candidate's brief.

The candidate must consider the following simple questions in depth:

1. What are the major problems and key opportunities?
2. Then, in order to resolve and exploit them:
   (a) What has to be done, to whom and by whom, for what reason?
   (b) How should this be done?
   (c) When should this action take place and over what period?
   (d) Can these actions be justified?
   (e) How much will it cost the organization?
   (f) Can the expenditure be justified and are funds/resources available?
   (g) How can a check be made on what is to be achieved?
   (h) What should be done if circumstances change?

The candidate must reconcile the specified role(s) and understand fully the boundaries of power, influence, authority and responsibility. It is strongly recommended that the case study preparation includes the duties and responsibilities of key managerial positions within a variety of marketing and sales organizations and that a distinction be drawn between the position of executive directors, non-executive directors and external consultants. Candidates must realize that preparation involves preparing *themselves*, as well as preparing the analysis and decision-making for a major marketing case study. Candidates may benefit from role-playing exercises to assist the learning process of identifying with roles—this process is central to answering questions in the case study examination.

Consult the case study instructions to determine and understand instructions on information sourcing.

Much has to be achieved in a short time, so do not waste a moment by researching beyond the boundaries of the case material unless there is stipulation. Case studies are designed to be self-contained exercises. Searching for additional material will undoubtedly lead to confusion and frustration. Credit will not be given for external information introduced into your examination answers unless this is part of the candidate's brief.

On a practical note, make sure you have a 'good night's sleep' the night before the exam. Burning the midnight oil until the dawn chorus breaks will drain both your physical and your mental energy.

Set out for the exam with a full kit of well documented notes, pens, pencils, ruler, calculator, etc.—candidates still rush out on the day of the examination and arrive late having forgotten their kit.

AT THE EXAMINATION HALL

Arrive in time, avoid having a *heavy* meal, bring a watch, and try to have a calm, cool, clear and collected mind. Sitting examinations can be a traumatic experience for many, but do not forget that the examiners are human, are on your side and are trying to pass you.

Arrange your prepared material and kit so that it can be easily accessed. Remember, the more that you bring into the examination hall, the more time may be lost sifting through it.

THE EXAMINATION PAPER

Credit can only be given for what is written in the examination answer book, not for what has been previously prepared. Read the rubric and make sure you understand and follow the instructions it contains. Determine how many questions are required to be answered and judge the amount of time to be given to each based upon the allocation of marks. The effective management of time within the three-hour time scale is critical to a candidate's performance.

Read all the questions and make sure that you understand precisely what is required. Carefully consider any additional information given.

ANSWERING THE QUESTIONS

1. *Your role* The role specified in the candidate's brief may be expanded and thereby clarified on the examination paper, which means that candidates may need to restructure their thinking to respond to the situation stated and to answer fully the questions posed.
2. *Layout, style and presentation* Management report format is recommended. Essay style is inappropriate and too inefficient to convey fully the level and complexity of answer required within the three-hour period. Candidates should conceive headings and adopt a numbering system in a fashion similar to that used in the specimen answers in this textbook. A good

examination paper will use the facing page of the examination book to outline the contents of the report showing appropriate sections as dictated by the examination questions.

Presentation is the keynote in most reports. Candidates should create 'white space' to present their reports legibly and in a way which attracts the examiner's eye.

3. *Questions* Questions do not have a standardized format. They may vary in number but usually will be action-oriented and inevitably will require strategic marketing plans.

Make certain that you answer the question stated, and not that which you would have liked to answer.

4. *Answers to questions* There is no 'right' answer to case study questions. In the case of marketing analysis and decision cases, the examination paper should present clear, well-substantiated decisions. In open-book examinations, the time for analysis has been provided with the issue of the case well before the examination. This analysis should enable the candidate to be completely familiar with the on-going situation. From this position, appropriate action can be recommended in the examination room. Do not re-state the situation or give a lengthy, detailed analysis—the examiners are fully aware and attuned to the case situation! In a real-life marketing situation, problems have to be solved and opportunities seized by taking action, not by dwelling on a situation, doing nothing and losing out. Such is the emphasis required in the examination room!

Answers are to be succinct, to the point, and with clearly outlined proposed courses of action; avoid a muddled list of alternatives.

Candidates are advised to follow the procedure outlined in the case study model illustrated in this textbook and to observe the necessity for reiteration as indicated by the loops.

Pre-prepared answers rarely succeed in fitting the requirements of open-book examination questions. A lack of imagination by the majority of candidates is a major weakness. Creativity is highly rewarded. It is the candidate's individual ideas that the examiner is looking for, not a batch of identical scripts carefully dictated or rehearsed before the day!

CANDIDATES WHO FAIL—'THE MAGNIFICENT SEVEN'

The waffler

The candidate who produces a large volume of written material which normally starts 'Before answering the questions I will review the company situation . . .' Some 14 or 20 pages later, having strayed up many a blind alley, the candidate starts question 1 only to leave a hurried note, 'Sorry, ran out of time.'

The backroom boy

All analysis and no action. Granted, there is a need for this type of person in certain avenues of marketing, but the examination requires a strategic plan of action. Examination day is 'D-DAY'—a day for decisions.

The waster

Produces little of anything remotely relevant to the subject being examined.

The non-conformist

Likes to sit for an examination paper that has not been set, has blatant disregard for the actual questions and produces a marathon marketing plan, probably directly copied from pre-prepared material.

The syndicate member

Regurgitates answers that have been produced on a group basis without integrating the answers to the precise questions set, so relates poorly with what is required.

The dreamer

Fails to understand the role, and usually reorganizes the entire company, including firing key executives outside his orbit. The dreamer plans beyond the wildest hopes of the company.

The marginal failure

Tried hard but not hard enough to satisfy the examiners. May succeed next time.

EIGHTEEN

CASE STUDY WITH SPECIMEN ANSWER: FISHER PLC (HANDTOOLS MARKETING)

Fisher, based in Swansea, Wales, is a public limited company (plc). The 'Fisher Works' in Swansea opened at the turn of the century to provide tools for Welsh industries.

The Welsh steel industry provided many of the raw materials needed in the manufacturing process, and despite the recession in the steel industry, both nationwide and in the Western world, demand for Fisher products today remains active.

Fisher plc (hereafter referred to as Fisher), currently has an estimated 15 per cent share by value of the UK non-power hand tool market. Significant export trade has developed over the past 15 years to secure brand recognition in different countries. Certain Fisher products also are manufactured under licence in Germany and France and are sold throughout Europe. Similar trade has developed in eastern coast states of the USA. Direct exports from the UK to worldwide customers outstrip domestic sales within the UK.

The UK market for Fisher hand tools can be classified as:

—Domestic purchasers
—Professional users (i.e. tradesmen)
—Industrial buyers

Recent research among distribution channels has revealed that approximately 40 per cent by value fall into the first of these categories, with industrial buyers taking 20 per cent.

The Fisher brand has penetrated each of these market segments with considerable success to achieve its overall market position.

A variety of trading agreements on price and volume are used to secure a stable position within the distribution channels. The wholesale trade accounts for 47 per cent of UK turnover; retail trade some 35 per cent; 12 per cent to mail order houses, with the residual sales to direct accounts.

These various channels reach a variety of end users. The company, to quote its marketing manager, has yet to achieve a *complete* picture of 'which type of purchaser and/or end user buys which type of tool from which source of supply—internal estimates rarely agree'.

Market segmentation by end user provides a variety of profiles, ranging from the owner of a screwdriver to the owner and frequent user of a complete range of tools. The end user can be classified on a continuum ranging from the 'non-user' through to the 'semi-skilled/do-it-yourself enthusiast' to the 'skilled non-professional' and on to the 'tradesman'.

Among the market classified as 'domestic purchasers' above, 50 per cent are considered 'skilled' users, 40 per cent 'non-skilled' users and the rest 'very occasional users'. The term 'skilled' can be variously defined, but refers to the frequency of use rather than the real ability of the end user.

Market development has been achieved through the trade user to the domestic user over time. This accounts for a wide discrepancy of market shares achieved by type of tool within the defined domestic, professional and industrial markets. To complicate the total market profile further, different types of tools are supplied to each market sector, although many of the tools in the Fisher range are purchased in each sector.

Despite market research findings which have revealed variations in brand quality perception, among end users, of the different types of tools, the Fisher brand is among the leaders in terms of brand recall and brand image when the market is considered as a whole. Furthermore, for specific tools, the Fisher brand has a consistently higher image rating than other market suppliers.

Overall, the company considers itself, and is considered by the markets it serves, to have a good image. Favourable attitudes have been revealed by wholesale and retail distributors as well as tool users. The major attributes cited in recent in-depth research with distributors included 'Products in the range are distinctive'; 'Good reliable tools'; 'Good range of tools'; 'Good variety in different sizes of tools'; 'Effective support and good display materials'; 'The terms of trade are fair—although we never keep pace with demand on certain items.'

Periodic market research is a feature in which the company takes pride. A survey covering the total market for Fisher tools completed in March 1990 revealed the following key findings:

—The major factors influencing all forms of household do-it-yourself (DIY) activity were:

    (a) Number of years married.
    (b) Age and income of the end user.
    (c) Age and type of house.
    (d) Period of time in residence.

—Readership was confined to the popular national daily press, and DIY magazines.
—All types of consumers recalled a variety of brand names.
—There was an insignificant difference in the 'DIY habit' among the male, 25–55, B, C1, C2, and D socio-economic groups.
—Domestic purchasers appear more brand-loyal than their trade counterparts, who tend to purchase a wide variety of brands and furthermore are more fully aware of suitable substitutes.
—A significant number of domestic purchasers will not accept a substitute for certain Fisher tools.
—Manufacturers' delivery from leading market suppliers appeared to be a general problem associated with this market.
—The need for DIY tools to be sold by specialist retailers is reducing substantially.
—Traditional tool retailers adhere to the manufacturers' recommended prices.
—All retailers offer a cash discount to tradespersons.
—Growth in tool discounting for domestic purchasers is developing at retail 'discount outlets'.
—Many cheap, foreign tools are available on the market.
—A significant number of purchases of low priced tools are for replacement purposes.
—Quality perception is *the* prime brand purchase motivator among all types of buyers.
—Quality and durability are the key factors considered by the trade users.
—All groups considered the 'effect of advertising as minimal' in influencing the purchase decision.

Within Fisher plc, strategic marketing decisions have depended upon the internal management information system—a fully computerized system totally integrated throughout production, sales and distribution operations.

The board takes pride in the system, which is considered by key users at middle management and executive levels to provide regular up-to-date information at the required level to assist decision-making.

The recently conducted market research now forms part of the marketing information system.

Detailed analysis has revealed the need to review and adjust the marketing plan in the following areas:

1. Pricing
2. Distribution, stock control and ordering procedures
3. New product development
4. Marketing communications

Initial internal discussions have taken place; the preliminary debates have considered:

—The market control that can be secured through a differential pricing policy throughout the various distribution channels and between channel members.
—A revision of minimum order levels to increase order size and thereby reduce the frequency of deliveries.
—More effective product screening and wider use of test marketing prior to the national launch of new products.
—The choice between a generic campaign to promote the Fisher brand across all market segments and product-oriented advertising.
—More effective control of current international business operations and the alternatives for the future.

Each area is considered to be a priority for future marketing operations.

Fisher's London-based advertising agency, Bowland Furness and Lonsdale (BFL), strongly favours a campaign to build the Fisher brand *per se*. Bill Bowland, the accounts director, has a clear vision for the next 12-month period. At a recent internal agency meeting, Bill proclaimed:

> We've got to get right through to the end-user—this means promoting Fisher with a big push. The Fisher brand has a good image; we have to build this further to enhance credibility and awareness among non-users to create more sales and yet retain the brand-loyal customers.
>
> The Fisher account is a key plc account; we cannot risk their dissatisfaction—my hunch is that they may ask other agencies to pitch for this campaign if we cannot convince them that the brand image is more important than the product.

Lisa Furness, BFL creative head, claimed:

> The Fisher brand represents a set of consumer-type products, their hand tools are not in any way industrial. Therefore, we are selling to people with competing demands for their cash. We must persuade them that Fisher is best. Above all, the dimensions of the Fisher brand must represent not only quality, durability and good value for money, but also the 'human' dimensions.

Within the London advertising agency circuit Lisa's work was often considered distinctive and above all memorable. BFL accounts were mainly consumer; awards for creativity and poster design are among the accolades achieved. The current range of key accounts covers men's cosmetics, two government accounts, a confectionery manufacturer, a brand of toothpaste, hi-fi equipment, carpets and home computers.

Lisa continued:

> Fisher have a complex understanding, or misunderstanding, of their market. I believe that market segmentation has a place in their marketing strategy, but the bottom line is that tools are tools and

people buy brands. The concentration for the campaign must be on media advertising; the integration required is around the Fisher brand so we should capitalize on this—use just one theme throughout the campaign and create maximum impact. We need a concept now to embody the Fisher brand; the copylines will follow. I will arrange for a brainstorming session—above all, we must be bold, distinctive and simple. We must ensure that Fisher favours Furness—well, BFL—hey?

Within the Fisher marketing department at the quarterly review, sales were down on forecast and some concern was raised about current advertising effectiveness.

Ken Slater, as marketing manager, had recently quarrelled with Lisa Furness over some non-business matters and this may have coloured his comments to the marketing team:

> I wonder if BFL really understand our market; we have been with them for three years now and we have only just remained on target. I think that the salesforce need more help to promote our range of products. We must put the product first and, our trade relationship cannot be overlooked. Less advertising, more sales promotion and beef up the public relations activities may be the formula for the future. We must be ever mindful of the contribution of market research—we have defined clearly our market segments–each requires special and separate marketing communications activity.

Ken Slater, as a member of the Chartered Institute of Marketing, had attended an open-day event at Moor Hall in April and met a number of advertising personnel. Two individuals left favourable impressions; Lynne Barker and Colin Webb from the Barker Webb agency based in central London. Lynne and Colin had left a large international agency some 18 months previously to form a new outfit with three other young advertising staff from other London-based agencies. With luck, good judgement and the dedication to hard work, the new agency was billing £3.5 million. Good contacts throughout the advertising industry enabled Barker Webb (BW) to offer a full range of services from creative design, market research, sales promotion, display materials, exhibition work, direct mailing apart from the regular business of campaign planning and execution.

Ken Slater, without reference to BFL, had briefed BW. The accounts held by BW covered a broad spectrum of products and services, although its collective experience was wider still. Naturally BW was keen to pitch for the new account. Prior to setting up BW, Colin Webb, in his previous employment, was accounts director for one of Fisher's main competitors.

APPENDICES TO CHAPTER 18

18.1 Company Organization Chart and Personnel Profiles
18.2 Report on the UK Market for Hand Tools
18.3 Memorandum—Profit and Sales Performance
18.4 Sales Analysis—Years Ending 1 April 1988–1993
18.5 Selected Abstracts from Market Research Report, April 1993
18.6 Memorandum—BFL Advertising Agency
18.7 Memorandum—New Product Development
18.8 Memorandum—Profitability
18.9 Memorandum—Profit to Sales Position

APPENDIX 18.1   Company Organization Chart

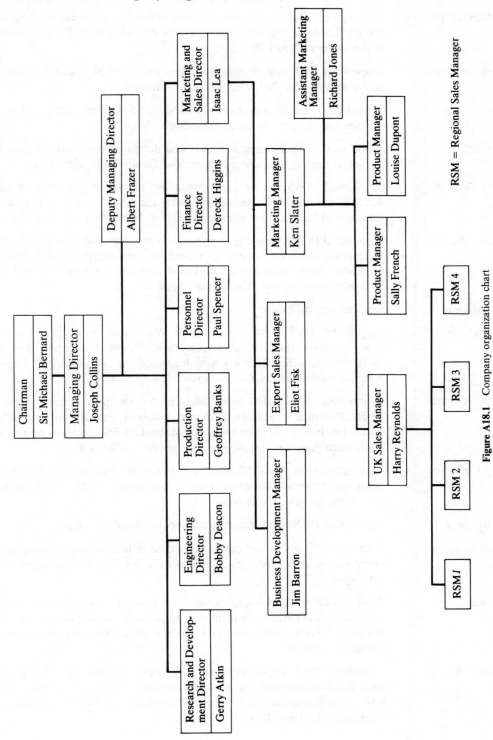

Figure A18.1 Company organization chart

RSM = Regional Sales Manager

Notes to Fisher plc organization chart

Sir Michael Bernard	Appointed 1984. Chairman of three other large manufacturing companies. Serves on a number of government committees. Former Member of Parliament. Aged 70.
Joseph Collins	Appointed 1985. A former finance director. Aged 58, plans to retire at 60 to home in Spain. No other business interests.
Albert Frazer	Appointed 1988 by merchant bankers for a four-year period. Chartered accountant, former business consultant. Aged 46.
Gerry Atkin	Appointed 1975. Former research and development manager. Aged 45. Joined company as a school-leaver. All family links with Wales.
Bobby Deacon	Appointed 1988 on the retirement of former engineering director. American national. Process engineer by training. Previously engineering manager of Kansas Extruder Corporation. Wife born in Wales. Aged 43.
Geoffrey Banks	Appointed 1984. Former group product manager of six years' experience. Five years' sales experience in household furnishing industry. Business graduate from Manchester Business School. Diploma holder from Chartered Institute of Marketing. Aged 38.
Richard Jones	See candidates' brief.
Sally French	Appointed 1988 from Fisher salesforce. Aged 26, single. Currently studying part-time for Chartered Institute of Marketing Diploma. Ambitious to achieve a marketing management position by 30. Recently rejected a job offer by BFL. Handles new products.
Louise Dupont	Appointed 1990. MBA from Manchester Business School. Aged 27, single. Previous experience in market research. French national. Higher education in UK. Father owns an established French tools and tooling equipment company employing 120 people, based in Paris.
Harry Reynolds	Appointed 1974. Aged 55, with 20 years' experience with Fisher in sales positions. Controls 16 representatives across four sales regions through four regional sales managers.
Paul Spencer	Appointed 1988 from Welsh Steel Works. Aged 37, single.
Dereck Higgins	Appointed 1986. Former chief cost accountant, now finance director and company secretary (designate). Works closely with the managing director. Aged 41.
Isaac Lea	Appointed 1986 by Joseph Collins from a major competitor with a brief to achieve marketing integration at board and subordinate levels. Task has yet to be completely achieved—further organizational development is planned. Aged 45.
Jim Barron	Appointed 1974. Previous Fisher UK sales manager. Aged 61. Responsible for international business development. Key role in maintaining links with European and American licensing agreements. Tasks quite separate from Eliot Fisk.

Eliot Fisk	Appointed 1988 from Kansas Extruder Corporation. Aged 39. Role confined to direct export sales from the UK to worldwide customers. May absorb Jim Barron's job in three years' time as export director.
Ken Slater	Appointed 1988 from fast-moving consumer food products manufacturer.

APPENDIX 18.2   Report on The UK Market for Hand Tools

To: Ken Slater—Marketing Manager
From: Louise Dupont
Date: 10 May 1993

1. Secondary data

The market for hand tools is poorly documented. The problem, typical of most published statistics, is that figures never conform and estimates vary considerably. Therefore, the figures in this report are to be considered as a guide only because they are very approximate indications. One major reason for this statement is the complex distribution system and the various sources of supply to the end purchaser/user.

2. Market trends

Overall there is a marked decline in the market for traditional hand tools. In volume terms this has amounted to some 35 per cent over the past three years—as a conservative estimate.

Approximately 75 per cent of the UK market is supplied by imported products, which normally are much cheaper at retail selling prices than the British manufactured product.

3. Industry sales (£ million)

	1988	1989	1990	1991	1992
UK manufacturers' sales at ex-factory prices	132	135	112	104	95^E
Exports	82	81	87	89	n/a
UK manufacturers' sales to home market	49	54	25	22	n/a
Imports	63	82	82	83	n/a
Total UK sales	112	136	107	105	n/a

E = Estimate
Source: Government statistics.

Market sizes of selected hand tools, 1991	Sales at manufacturer's ex-factory prices
Spanners,* socket sets* and wrenches*	35
Saws and blades	11
Pliers,* pincers* and rippers*	10
Measuring and marking tools	10
Screwdrivers	9
Files and rasps	6
Hammers	4
Wood chisels	2
Planes	2
Carpenters bits and braces	1
Other hand tools	15

*Products not produced by Fisher.
Source: Government statistics.

4. Market behaviour

There is a distinct tendency towards the purchase of cheaper tools. The DIY sector appears, during times of recession and high unemployment, to be more price-sensitive and less quality-conscious. The concern appears to be for 'everyday tools', and not 'lifetime tools'. It is estimated that the DIY sector accounts for 35 per cent of the market by value at manufacturer's ex-factory prices (i.e. manufacturer's selling prices).

5. Changing pattern of distribution

Large supermarkets, superstores and DIY discount retailers are increasing in importance.

Specialist tool shops are a very important sector of the retail trade, where the consumer can obtain advice, but they are losing sales to the DIY supermarkets. Manufacturers who had ventured into the retail trade through vertical integration are now reversing this trend.

Builders merchants, a traditional channel, retain their position, although the majority of sales are to professional users.

The decline in the volume trade to the UK market has led to considerable de-stocking at the retail end, and although this process has now ceased to a great extent, considerable selling effort is required to bring sales back to former levels. As a result, most manufacturers are working at far below production capacity. Increased import penetration means that UK manufacturers must fight harder for domestic market sales.

6. Marketing implications

The implications for Fisher are wide-reaching. A revised marketing plan must be drawn up to select the best strategy for the next three-year period in the hope that the market will be restored to former levels of buoyancy.

Over recent years there has been a marked tendency towards power tools to replace hand tools—further research should be conducted in this area.

APPENDIX 18.3   Memorandum—Profit and Sales Performance

To: Ken Slater   Date: 1 May 1993.
From: Isaac Lea

I have just received preliminary year-end figures from Dereck Higgins. Our performance for the past four years has not improved in real terms.

The increase in total sales value is between 3 and 4 per cent per year and our ratio of profit before taxation to sales hovers at approximately 2 per cent. It has been made quite clear to me that, for a company of our size and reputation, this is just not good enough—we would be better employed on the money market than in the sale of hand tools. Our shareholders are becoming restless after the recent years of apparent stagnation. We must give active consideration to a revised marketing strategy for the forthcoming year.

Our increased dependence upon overseas trade may necessitate the appointment of an international advertising agency to supplement, or replace, BFL. I would suggest an annual advertisement budget of £250 000 to cover home and export markets.

I would welcome your urgent attention to this matter.

APPENDIX 18.4   Sales Analysis—Years Ending 1 April 1988–1993

Home and export sales—year ending 1 April

	1988		1989		1990		1991		1992		1993	
	H (%)	E (%)	H (%)	E (%)	H (%)	E (%)	H (%)	E (%)	H (%)	E (%)	H (%)	E (%)
Breakdown by product group												
Saws	81	19	55	45	50	50	48	52	45	55	45	55
Measuring tapes	90	10	83	17	82	18	80	20	76	24	75	25
Screwdrivers	78	22	70	30	62	38	61	37	60	40	57	43
Files and rasps	40	60	40	60	41	59	37	63	35	65	30	70
Hammers	41	59	43	57	39	61	34	66	32	68	31	69
Wood chisels	36	64	31	69	30	70	27	73	27	73	22	78
Planes	45	55	39	61	37	63	35	65	31	69	30	70
Carpenters bits	45	55	38	62	36	64	34	66	31	69	26	74
Vices	40	60	41	59	40	60	36	64	32	68	33	67
Hand drills	45	55	37	63	35	65	34	66	32	68	30	70
Total Fisher products	74	26	53	47	49	51	44	56	40	60	38	62

H = Home.
E = Export.

Overseas markets for Fisher hand tools*—year ending 1 April

	1984	1989	1991	1993
Western Europe	2	5	8	10
Eastern Europe	2	4	5	7
Asia	3	4	5	7
Middle East	14	15	16	18
Africa	3	12	14	15
South America	2	2	3	1
USA	—	5	5	4
Total % sales	26	47	56	62

* All export sales are through Fisher appointed agents in the respective markets.

Direct home sales analysis—year ending 1 April

	1984 (%)	1989 (%)	1990 (%)	1991 (%)	1992 (%)	1993 (%)
Wholesale	42	23	21	19	17	16
Retail	20	18	17	15	14	13
Mail order	6	6	5	5	4	4
Institutional/industrial	6	6	6	5	5	5
Total % of Fisher sales revenue	74	53	49	44	40	38

Retail sales by type of outlet

	1984 (%)	1989 (%)	1990 (%)	1991 (%)	1992 (%)	1993 (%)
Builders merchants	1	1	1	1	1	1
Discount stores	1	1	1	2	3	3
Supermarkets	2	2	2	2	2	1
Department/chain stores	2	2	2	2	1	1
Specialist tool shops	4	4	4	3	2	2
Ironmonger/hardware stores	6	4	3	2	2	2
DIY shops	4	4	4	3	3	3
Total sales %	20	18	17	15	14	13

APPENDIX 18.5   Selected Abstracts from Market Research Report, April 1993

Hand tool market—competitor profile*

Conducted by Jackson Market Research
Project Leader: Richard Jones
Date of Report: April 1993
Research Commissioned: November 1992

1. Sample composition:
   Tradesmen   200
   Domestic users   500
   Institutional/
      industrial buyers   15
   Mail order   10
   Wholesalers   10
   Retailers   50

2. Sampling frames:
   Selected without regional bias to provide national representation.

3. Sampling methods and data collection method:

   —*Tradesmen* Quota sampling—quota controls age and type of trade/profession: personal interviews, on and off the job.
   —*Domestic users* Random sampling—street interviews: post-survey stratification into levels of skill by usage rate.
   —*Mail order companies* 100 per cent of all registered: telephone interviews—for initial screenings followed by personal interviews at company premises.
   —*Institutional* * *industrial buyers* A 25 per cent sample of Fisher key accounts: personal interviews.
   —*Wholesalers and retailers* A 10 per cent sample of Fisher accounts stratified by size of account to provide a representative sample nationally: personal interviews.

Structured interviews were used throughout the survey using recorded questionnaires.

* Abstract from full report.

Competitor analysis—year ending April 1993

Company code	UK (%)	Export (%)	UK hand tool market share (%)	Import (%)	UK manufacturer	Hand tool product range code	UK media advertising expenditure (£000)	Size of sales force	Year of market entry
A	65	35	3	nil	✓	Sp, Pl, F, H, C, Wr	10	5	1937
B	42	58	8	10	✓	Sa, H, Wo, Me, C, V, Spi, O	80	10	1951
C	90	10	2	nil	✓	Sa, Me	5	4	1939
D	45	55	4	nil	✓	Me, H, W, C	—	6	1928
E	20	80	4	5	✓	Wo, V, C, F, Wr, Sc, Pla	10	5	1946
F	38	62	15	35	✓	Sa, Me, Sc, F, H, Wo, Pla, C, O	120	16	1919
G	100	—	20	100	no	Sp, Sa, Pl, Me, Spi, F, H, Wo, Pl, O, Ps	100	12	1972
H	100	—	15	100	no	Sp, Pl, F, H, Wo, O	120	8	1980
I	100	—	29	100	no	Sp, Sa, Pl, V, Me, Spi, F, H, Wo, Pl, O	250	n/a	1970 onwards

NB: Assume UK hand tool market=£100 million at manufacturer's selling prices.

Company code: F = Fisher plc
I = Other importers

Other codes = Independent organizations

Product range codes
Sp	Spanners	Wo	Wood chisels
Wr	Wrenches	Me	Measuring tools
Pl	Pliers, pincers, rippers	Spi	Spirit levels
F	Files and rasps	V	Vices
H	Hammers	Sc	Screwdrivers
C	Carpenters' bits and braces	Pla	Planes
Sa	Saws and blades	O	Others

Competitor rating by tradesmen—Rating scale −5 to +5

	Company codes								
	A	B	C	D	E	F	G	H	I
Value for money	+3	+2	+3	+2	+2	+3	+1	+2	+2
Durability	+4	+2	+5	+2	+5	+3	−2	−1	−2
Appearance	+3	+2	+4	+2	−1	+3	+1	+1	−1
Design	+3	+2	+4	+2	+1	+3	−1	−1	−1
Reliability	+4	+3	+5	+3	+5	+3	−3	−2	−2
Range of products	+3	+3	−4	+2	+2	+4	+4	+4	+5
Advertising	−4	−2	−4	−4	−4	+1	+3	+3	+2
Quality	+4	+3	+5	+3	+4	+3	−1	−1	−1
Guarantees	+3	+1	+4	+2	+3	+3	−1	−1	−1
Packaging	−2	+1	+1	+1	+1	+2	+2	+2	+1
Availability	+1	+4	+1	+4	+3	+4	+3	+3	+5

Competitor rating by institutional/industrial buyers—Rating scale −5 to +5

	Company codes								
	A	B	C	D	E	F	G	H	I
Value for money	+4	+2	+2	+2	+2	+4	−1	−1	−1
Durability	+5	+2	+5	+3	+5	+3	−3	−2	−3
Appearance	+3	+3	+3	+1	−1	+4	−1	−1	−1
Design	+3	+3	+4	+2	+1	+3	+1	+1	+1
Reliability	+5	+3	+4	+4	+5	+3	−2	−2	−2
Range of products	+3	+4	−4	+2	+2	+4	+3	+2	+4
Advertising	−4	+1	−3	−4	−4	+2	+2	+2	+1
Quality	+5	+3	+5	+4	+4	+3	−1	−1	−1
Guarantees	+4	+3	+3	+2	+2	+3	−1	−1	−1
Packaging	−1	+3	+1	−1	−1	+4	+2	+2	+1
Availability	+2	+1	−1	+3	+3	+4	+4	+3	+5

Competitor rating by domestic purchasers—Rating scale −5 to +5

	Company codes								
	A*	B	C*	D	E†	F	G	H	I
Value for money	+3	+3	+1	+2	+1	+4	+4	+3	+3
Durability	+4	+4	+5	+2	+5	+3	+3	+3	+2
Appearance	+2	+3	+2	+2	−1	+4	+2	+3	+1
Design	+2	+3	+4	+2	−1	+3	+2	+3	+2
Reliability	+4	+4	+5	+2	+5	+4	+3	+3	+2
Range of products	+1	+2	−4	+3	+1	+4	+4	+3	+5
Advertising	−5	+1	−5	−5	−5	+2	+2	+3	+1
Quality	+4	+3	+5	+3	+3	+3	+2	+3	+2
Guarantees	+3	+2	+4	+3	+2	+3	+1	+1	−2
Packaging	−2	+1	+1	+1	+1	+4	+1	+2	−1
Availability	−4	+4	−3	+4	−2	+4	+4	+3	+5

* Small sample response (less than 15%).

† Limited brand recognition (35% response).

Competitor rating by wholesale, retail and mail-order channels*—Rating scale −5 to +5

	Company codes								
	A†	B	C‡	D	E§	F	G	H	I
Value for money	+2	+3	+2	+2	−1	+3	+3	+3	+2
Reliability	+4	+3	+5	+4	+5	+3	−2	+1	+1
Design	+2	+3	+4	+3	−1	+4	+1	+1	+1
Range	+2	+3	−5	+2	+2	+4	+4	+3	+5
Advertising	−5	+2	−5	−5	−4	+2	+2	+2	+1
Guarantees	+2	+2	+2	+2	+3	+3	−2	+1	+1
After-sales service	+2	+2	+1	+2	+3	+3	−2	+1	+2
Customer satisfaction	+4	+3	+5	+3	+2	+3	−1	+1	+1
Trade discount	−1	+1	−2	−3	−3	+1	+4	+4	+5
Delivery service	−1	+1	−3	−1	+1	−1	+3	+4	+5
Packaging	−2	+2	+1	+1	−2	+3	+2	+2	+2
Protit potential	−1	+1	−1	−1	+1	+2	+5	+5	+5

* Results of surveys were very close, hence the mean scores have been applied in this table.
† Small sample response.
‡ Restricted distribution.
§ Not mail order.

APPENDIX 18.6   Memorandum—BFL Advertising Agency

To: Ken Slater
From: Richard Jones
Date: 10 May 1993

I realise that I am a very new member of the marketing team, but feel that I have a small contribution to make on the above subject, I hope, therefore, that you will treat this memo in the spirit in which it is written. I am not trying to 'teach my grandmother to suck eggs'.

Naturally you are concerned with BFL's performance, and an immediate reaction may be to request another agency to provide a presentation—I would suggest two other agencies. This would keep BFL 'on its toes'. The agency I worked for, Bard, Klein and Mason, would be worth considering; there may have been changes since I left but the man to contact is Colin Webb, my former boss. I can also recommend one of my former market research clients, an advertising agency based here in Swansea, Fortnam and Golde.

Before any decision is taken, it is fair to consider what BFL has achieved; I have a checklist for agency evaluation which you may find helpful.

Should you wish to proceed with other agencies, we should offer BFL the chance to retain the account and notify the company of our intentions. We must not overlook BFL's 10 years' experience as an agency and the billing size of £27 million.

APPENDIX 18.7 Memorandum—New Product Development

To: Richard Jones
From: Ken Slater
Date: 15 May 1993

I have been aware for some time of the need to diversify beyond hand tools and yet remain within the DIY market.

An opportunity has arisen for Fisher to act as distributors for a Swedish company manufacturing paint applicators. The product range comprises paint brushes, paint rollers and a more recent innovation, paint pads. The latter I have no interest in whatsoever.

How do you suggest we proceed?

This is your assignment with the company; please advise me of your progress. I would hope to receive your report by the middle of June.

On the subject of your memo of 10 May, I thank you for your comments and would ask you to supply the checklist you mentioned with your report.

APPENDIX 18.8 Memorandum—Profitability

To: Dereck Higgins
From: Ken Slater
Date: 16 May 1993

I refer to our conversation of some two weeks ago concerning our profit to sales position.

I have now had time to reflect upon the situation; appropriate attention is being given to the matter but this is under Mr Lea's direct authority. However, at present our information system does not carry financial trend information over the past five years; would you, therefore, provide an outline analysis of the cost impact areas which have a direct influence upon our net profit before tax position? Kindly send a copy also to Mr Lea for information.

My new assistant manager is keen to develop his interest in the financial control area. I am encouraging this and have asked him to talk with you directly.

I understand that Mr Lea approves fully of staff development initiatives.

APPENDIX 18.9 Memorandum—Profit to Sales Position

To: Ken Slater
          c.c. Isaac Lea
From: Dereck Higgins
Date: 17 May 1993

I understand that during Isaac Lea's vacation to the Middle East you have to deal with the running of the department.

The issue of profitability is a number one priority at board level.

I have appended a brief outline of cost trends which contribute to profitability. In marketing you really influence all these areas—including the reduction in numbers of the workforce through poor sales performance.

However, you may feel that additional ratio analysis and financial analysis would be helpful; kindly telephone my secretary to arrange a meeting and bring along your new assistant.

Analysis of Fisher plc profit to sales—year ending 1 April (%)

	1989		1990		1991		1992		1993	
	M	F	M	F	M	F	M	F	M	F
Pre-tax profits Sales	4.5	2.2	4.5	2.1	4.0	2.2	3.5	2.1	3.5	1.9
Production cost Cost of output	82.1	76.0	81.5	73.3	80.1	72.1	78.3	72.5	78.0	72.5
Distribution cost Cost of output	6.1	9.6	6.3	12.3	6.8	12.9	7.3	12.9	7.5	13.0
Selling cost Cost of output	2.0	4.5	2.5	5.9	3.0	6.3	3.3	6.1	3.5	6.3
Administration cost Cost of output	9.8	7.7	9.7	8.5	10.1	8.7	11.1	8.5	11.0	8.2

M = Median of UK manufacturers A, B, C, D, E.
F = Fisher performance.

QUESTIONS

As Richard Jones, you are forming a close working relationship with Ken Slater.

Your first report is now due for presentation and should comprise the following sections:

Section 1 Justified recommendations for proceeding with diversification into paint applicators together with a comprehensive specification of the information required at this early stage of new product development.

(20 marks)

Section 2 A checklist for advertising agency evaluation and your judgement of how best to evaluate the alternatives now open to Fisher advertising account.

(20 marks)

Section 3 What you expect from BW at their forthcoming presentation.

(20 marks)

Section 4 An assessment of the current market position of Fisher plc both at home and overseas, with justified options for development to 1986.

(40 marks)

GENERAL APPROACH

The candidate must have adopted the role of Richard Jones, the newly appointed assistant marketing manager.

The examination required the candidate to produce a report for Ken Slater, the marketing manager. It was expected that all candidates would use management report format.

It was expected that all sections of the report would be answered.

The importance of questions has been shown, and candidates should have observed the differential allocation of marks.

It is expected that time should be allocated to match this distribution of examination marks. A good tip is to allow 1½ minutes per mark; i.e., a 20-mark question should be given 30 minutes' writing time. This tactic should leave time for answer planning and reading through the final script before the end of the examination.

THE APPROACH TO EACH SECTION

Section 1—Diversification

(20 marks)

Practical insights were required. No student was expected to make a 'go decision' on the basis of the case information. It was too early to make firm recommendations in this direction without a feasibility study. Half of the marks were allocated to the first part of the question; the second part was straightforward and required a simple listing of the required information before further interest was to be taken by the company.

Students should have adopted the role of Richard Jones with his background experience in market research, and acted accordingly.

Section 2—Advertising agency evaluation

(20 marks)

The first part of the question was to be fully anticipated by the student—40 per cent of the mark allocation was given for the advertising agency checklist.

Part two required a method for evaluation of the advertising agency options:

—The international advertising agency
—The local agency in Swansea, Wales
—The existing account holders, BFL
—The new agency, BW

Section 3—Forthcoming BW presentation

(20 marks)

Each analysis and decision case study attempts to explore the varied dimensions of marketing. This case has featured advertising agency dynamics.

At a superficial level, the candidate was required merely to state what would be expected at an advertising agency presentation.

To pass and attain higher grades, a consideration of the size of the budget and the importance of the marketing factors was expected. In the context of the case, the issue of segmentation, market position, distribution penetration and the export markets could not be overlooked. The debate between brand and product advertising could have been explored.

Section 4—Current market position

(40 marks)

This question was deliberately open-ended, giving both the strong and the weak candidate the opportunity to develop a theme within the context of the question.

The case study was broadly based, stimulated interest in several directions, with sufficient material to fire the diligent student to prepare thoroughly in advance of the examination. The candidate was expected, therefore, to answer the following *implicit* questions:
1. Where is Fisher now, both at home and overseas?
2. What are the problems associated with the current state?
3. How can we best proceed to exploit these markets for the future?

ANSWERS

REPORT

To: Ken Slater, Marketing Manager
From: Richard Jones, Assistant Marketing Manager
Subject: First report on diversification, advertising agencies, Fisher's current position and short-term development
Date: 18 June 1993

Introduction

I have been with the company for just a short while and have, therefore, much to learn about the organization, the market and the internal and external corporate environment. This report is a first attempt. I would welcome the opportunity to discuss the content, format and appropriateness of the document so that it may be amended before circulation and subsequent filing.

Section 1—Diversification into paint applicators

Fisher plc is a multi-product company facing changing demand patterns for tools the company manufactures. Diversification is just one route to retain profitability. However, I feel that the company's product strategy should be subjected to a thorough scrutiny. A company product audit would enable the marketing department to match the current provision with market demand. Perhaps it is time to 'put our house in order' before considering yet new ventures.

At this stage I would recommend most strongly that we *do not* proceed with an adoption decision until a feasibility study is conducted, completed and given full management consideration. There is simply not enough information currently available upon which to make a sound decision.

Before undertaking a feasibility study, initial corporate considerations must be given. These may save considerable management time on what may turn out to be a fruitless and costly exercise.

A few simple, yet penetrating, questions must be asked:

—Where is Fisher plc now?
—Where do the company and the shareholders want it to be, say, within five years?
—How do we get there?
—How does diversification into paint applicators contribute—if at all?
—What will be the effect on the Fisher brand name if the new product range does not receive trade, professional and/or consumer acceptance?
—Can the company afford failure?
—What is the real opportunity cost, i.e. the cost of other development options that are forgone should the company adopt the Swedish company's proposals?
—The proposed diversification is within the DIY market, but is this really the business the company is in? Painting and decorating is beyond the current sphere of company knowledge and outside the current technology orbit, which is based upon steel (not wood and bristles).

At this early stage I would advise a cautious approach. I would advise, assuming the above questions have been answered to management's satisfaction, that the following information is obtained.

Market information

—What is the size of the UK market, by volume and value?
—What are the secular, cyclical and seasonal trends?
—What is the rate, if any, of the real growth in the market?
—Who are the competitors?
—How well established are they?
—How are market shares distributed?
—What changes have taken place in market shares over the last five years?
—How brand-loyal is the market at trade, professional and consumer levels?
—What are the main purchase motivations, and how have these changed in recent years?
—Can market gaps be identified?
—What will be the real cost of market entry and what are the potential financial gains and over what period of time?
—When could Fisher expect to achieve break-even?

Product information How does the Swedish product compare on:
—Product specification?
—Appearance?
—Actual quality?
—Perceived quality?
—Performance?
—Raw material costs and hence price to the trade and final markets?
—Supply and maintenance of supply?
—Image (and brand image)?

Price information
—What are the unit costs?
—How price-competitive will the product be on the UK market assuming import and transportation on costs?
—What are the trends in Swedish raw material costs?
—How price-sensitive is the market at trade, professional and consumer levels?
—What return does the company require from this investment, and how does this affect price–volume relationships over specified periods of time?

Product information
—What is the level and form of support that we can expect from the Swedish company? Can it be used to sell the product in?
—What is the cost of selling in and subsequently selling the product out in the final end-user markets?
—Does the Swedish brand have a marketable USP or will Fisher have to inject artificial product plus points?
—What is the likely response from competition?
—Will Fisher achieve trade acceptance, and if so under which brand—Fisher or the Swedish brand?
—Can Fisher trade on existing brand image at all? As overseas distributor for a Swedish manufacturer, it is unlikely unless the Swedish company adopts the Fisher brand name.
—How can we promote/merchandise the product effectively at the point of sale?

Distribution information
—Can existing channels be used—and to what extent?
—Will new channels be required?
—What is the real cost of distribution? What percentage can be absorbed within existing capacity?
—How will the introduction of the product affect trade relationships?
—Can we give the trade sufficient margin to fend off competition?

Sales information
—Can the product simply be added to the existing product portfolio?
—What is the level of additional selling effort required and the coincident need for training?
—What level of priority should be given to selling paint applicators? For how long? What will the effect be on other products?

The above sections are not exhaustive but are intended, within the time available, to raise a number of key questions, which must be answered before we can proceed further.

Communication with the Swedish company is advised as a 'holding operation' while we consider our opinions in this direction further.

Section 2—Advertising agency evaluation

The checklist for advertising agency evaluation previously discussed is as follows. Some of the points may require clarification or de-jargonizing. May I suggest this can be achieved at our review meeting.

Checklist From personal experience, after visiting and meeting the agencies and discussing their services and client profile, short-listing agencies involves full consideration of the following points:

1. Creativity
2. Experience
3. Absence of internal conflict
4. Reputation
5. The size in terms of employees and billings
6. International structures
7. Management style and ability

However, the appointment decision has hinged on the following criteria:

1. The understanding and interpretation of client marketing problems
2. Creativity
3. Management experience and style
4. The real ability of the agency
5. Compatibility between agent and client teams
6. The presentation and agency track record
7. The size of the agency

In evaluating the existing agency and in making an assessment of the alternatives available, the following points should be considered in detail:

1. Agency management structure
2. Internal procedures
3. Basis of remuneration
4. Internal method of costing, plussing-up and charging; allocation of overheads
5. Legal and financial status: major shareholders; issued capital; turnover
6. Clients—names, industry groups, billings, number of years with named contacts for references
7. Experience in relevant industries and markets
8. Quality of advertisements in relation to brief of:
   (a) Copywriting
   (b) Creativity
   (c) Visuals
   (d) Campaign continuity
   (e) Measurement of results
9. Campaign assessment in relation to:
   (a) Campaign plan
   (b) Copy platform
   (c) Visual mix
   (d) Visual continuity
   (e) Measurement of results

10. Media services and expertise in:
    (a) Press
    (b) TV
    (c) Direct mail
    (d) Merchandising
    (e) Packaging
    (f) Point of sale
    (g) Sales literature
    (h) Technical publications
    (i) Exhibitions
    (j) Photography
    (k) Press relations
    (l) Public relations
11. Research:
    (a) Advertising
    (b) Media
    (c) Campaign
    (d) Market
    (e) Product
12. Overseas connections
13. Provincial branches
14. Personal compatibility with and professional capability of:
    (a) Account executive
    (b) Account director
    (c) Creative head
    (d) Media manager
    (e) Research and/or marketing head
    (f) Managing director

Evaluation of alternatives The options open to Fisher at this time are:

1. The international advertising agency
2. The local agency in Swansea, Wales
3. The existing account holders, BFL
4. The new agency, BW

The choice may be subjective but the extent of subjectivity should be minimized. One method is to take the checklists above and to appraise each alternative on a rating scale from 1 to 5 as shown below.

Agency options

Checklist criteria	International agency	Local agency	BFL	BW
A	5	4	2	1
B	3	3	3	3
C	4	2	1	1
D	1	2	3	5
'N'				
Totals	xxx	xxx	xxx	xxx

At this level the analysis is too simplistic. Differential weights should be applied to each criterion so that a priority rating is determined. The total scores can then be assessed to rank the agencies accordingly. This is merely a simple technique to help the selection process but does not replace management judgement.

In my position as assistant marketing manager with limited knowledge of some options and more knowledge of others, I feel my assessment would be biased. Had I considered myself to be in a more objective position I would have completed the task outlined above. Perhaps we could fill in the matrix together and as a result of joint discussion complete the exercise. Having completed such in the past, I found from personal experience the act and discipline of using the checklist in this way was more useful as a framework for evaluation than the actual achievement of a mathematical solution. In the same way, the rigour and thought that are required in any planning process are often more beneficial than the published and agreed document. In short, the *process* of evaluation is often *the* most important factor.

Section 3—The BW presentation

Advertising agency presentations vary considerably. This can be attributed to differences between agencies and how hungry they may be for the account. Differences as applied to the aforementioned criteria are diverse and hence the style, quality, time, *rapport* and content of the presentation will vary. Equally, what I expect from an agency presentation, and the interpretation I will give to the presentation, will be different from other members of the client team. Once again, we enter the realms, to an extent, of subjectivity.

My evaluation must depend, therefore, on what *we* actually expect of the agency. Until we have agreed our terms of reference, then, we can only assess the presentation on the interpretation of the brief the agency has received from us. Since I have not been closely involved at the process level, it is difficult for me to comment on the expected content of the presentation. Having stated the above caveats, I would in this situation expect to consider the agency on the criteria previously specified. However, there are some central points that BW should not overlook.

Apart from the creativity, a full consideration of the size of the Fisher budget must be given. I would be particularly keen to consider how the budget has been appropriated between media and non-media activity. The scheduling of advertising activity in relation to market demand is vital, as is the placement of advertising in relation to market weights. I would expect some consideration of the likely response in relation to the projected levels of exposure. The importance of market factors must be set in perspective—the agency must not consider the exercise in isolation from the market, but rather as a means of bridging a communications gap.

Answers to the issue concerning product/brand advertising must be resolved.

The fundamental issues of segmentation, distribution penetration and export markets must be given full treatment against a prescribed market position for Fisher.

The above points must be considered by BW. How they are handled will depend upon the style of presentation—but answers must be forthcoming. If not, the agency should be probed to test its level of understanding of our brief.

On a more formal note, I would expect a clear statement of:

—Our marketing objectives.
—BW marketing communications, advertising, sales promotion and public relations objectives.
—BW creative strategy and media strategy to achieve the objectives.
—A research programme to pre-test and post-test the campaign.
—Budget appropriation and designation of responsibility.

Much will hang upon the effectiveness of the presentation. The level of detail is a matter of judgement and how BW has judged the requirements and level of understanding of the client team.

Above all, a good level of agency confidence and commitment is vital. Agencies must convey that they know their business and what they believe is best for us. In so doing, they should be able to impart a willingness for effective agency–client communication. *Rapport*, therefore, is a keynote, and this is often difficult to achieve at the initial presentation stage.

Section 4—Current market position

The market position of Fisher plc must be set in the context of prevailing market factors. The following factors are considered relevant.

1. Despite a multi-million pound market, maturity has been reached and there is little doubt that market decline has started. Within this overall position, there is little evidence of growth sectors within the mass market.
2. Important consumer trends are in evidence. There is an apparent preference and hence significant trend towards power tools.

    A weakening in brand preference at trade level exists, although the DIY sector is very brand-conscious despite increasing consumer patronage of low-price functional hand tools.
3. At industry level there is apparent over-capacity, which will further threaten the domestic market even in the short term.
4. A very significant percentage of industry production is exported, although companies cannot compete effectively with foreign imports. It appears that export markets remain an attractive target for further development and hence will offer survival opportunities for UK hand tool manufacturers—especially with the weakening position of sterling.
5. Owing to stagnant home sales, the effect of import penetration, declining markets and excess capacity, price flexibility is very limited in this very competitive domestic market.
6. There has been, and will continue to be, a shift in channels of distribution. Direct sales to retailers have increased at the expense of the wholesale trade.
7. As yet there appears to be only moderate promotional support to create a pull effect on the channel.
8. *Fisher's domestic market position: strengths* The company is:
   (a) The largest in total sales value of all UK manufacturers.
   (b) The largest exporter of all UK manufacturers.
   (c) The largest in terms of domestic sales of all UK manufacturers.
   Despite the industry position outlined above, and with the very real threat from imported products, Fisher has a confirmed market position which has not, as yet, been seriously affected. The company enjoys a dominant market position with a formal marketing organization to support and defend and furthermore protect this position.

   Fisher enjoys good trade/distributor relationships with good brand images at industrial, trade and consumer levels. The Fisher brand and associated quality image are maintained across a well-established product range.
9. *Fisher's overseas market position: strengths* In addition to the extended Fisher organization structure overseas, there is good potential to increase sales further in existing countries and to penetrate others—albeit from a position of strength and experience.
10. *Fisher's domestic market position: weaknesses*
    (a) Despite Fisher's market stature, profitability is very low.
    (b) In comparison with the industry, Fisher has high selling and distribution costs.

(c) The opportunity to diversify into power tools to consolidate the domestic market position has been lost.

(d) Capacity is under-utilized.

(e) Service levels may be too high, as reflected in high distribution costs.

(f) The company is in a poor position to undertake cost effective innovation—and yet, it cannot face further decline in pre-tax profits.

(g) Selling costs far exceed industry average and these have considerable impact on the profit to sales position.

11. *Fisher's overseas market position: weaknesses*

(a) From our knowledge, the exclusive use of agents until now implies that little initiative has been taken for the further development of international organization or export structure. With the dependence of the company on exports, planning is needed now in this direction.

(b) Comment (a) is, however, undermined by the widespread export activity—showing little real evidence of concentration.

12. *Fisher plc: short-term plan to 1995* It is vital to realize that, while much exists for attention, priorities must be given to defined problems and plans developed for those areas that are agreed priorities. Further discussion is needed to secure agreement and commitment to the key result areas for the immediate and short term.

I consider the following to be short-term priorities:

(a) *Market research*

   (i) As an independent exercise, the power tool market should be explored to confirm or otherwise market gaps that may exist for Fisher to exploit—provided that this does not contravene company policy.

   (ii) A feasibility study for paint applicators should be given full consideration, subject to board approval.

   (iii) A segmented end-user purchase profile is required to assist in the future development of sales and promotional strategy. Fisher knows who the buyers are but has insufficient knowledge of their purchase habits and restrictions. Adjust-

Potential development areas to 1995

	Home market rating	Overseas market rating	Immediate action	Short-term action
Corporate research	5	5	✓	
Corporate objectives	2	2		✓
Marketing objectives	3	3		✓
Marketing research	3	2	✓	
Product development plans	2	2		✓
Pricing planning	5	5	✓	✓
Distribution planning	3	3		✓
Advertising and promotion plans	4	4	✓	✓
Sales plans	5	3	✓	✓
Staffing plans	2	3		✓
Controls on the marketing plan	4	4		✓
Budgeting	2	2		✓

Rating scale 1 to 5, where 1 indicates low adjustment levels and 5 indicates high adjustment levels.

ments to distribution/strategy should follow, especially with the degree of change occurring in the retail distribution of hand tools.

Market and sales forecasts should be produced to assist with the interpretation of the internal company research proposed below.

(b) *Internal company research*

    (i) To assist in the management of future company profitability and hence to cultivate better relationships with Fisher plc shareholders, an independent study should be conducted as an immediate priority.

    (ii) Profit contribution analysis by product group, product item and by market segment should be undertaken to determine the high cost impact areas and those that make a contribution to corporate profitability.

    (iii) Accurate costing information is required together with accurate sales data.

    (iv) A combined effort between the marketing and finance sections is needed to ensure that organizational commitment is given to the task and that it is conducted thoroughly and professionally.

    (v) The implications of the findings should have a direct impact on marketing and sales planning.

    (vi) It is anticipated that product policy may be reviewed, pricing policy may be adjusted and new sales strategies implemented to ensure that every possible avenue is explored to maintain *and* improve pre-tax profitability.

    (vii) The findings of the study will assist in the revised targeting of overseas markets to help achieve further geographic expansion.

    (viii) It is anticipated that these developments will be fully documented in the company's export market development plan.

(c) *Staffing*

The findings of the research may have staffing implications. Notwithstanding this, manpower development and linked succession planning is required as a result of the positions of Geoffrey Banks, Jim Barron, Harry Reynolds and the ambitious product managers, Sally French and Louise Dupont.

    (i) The company must be aware of the staffing situation and not wait until a crisis occurs. The research programme will act as a stimulus to consider staff before new strategic plans are drawn up and agreed.

    (ii) Until the above work is undertaken, it is inappropriate to outline specific development plans.

    (iii) The findings of the research will strongly influence the future direction of the company, which, of necessity, must change course.

    (iv) The probable areas for change are shown in the table.

13. *Review*

I look forward to discussing this report with you in the near future.
Signed: Richard Jones.

NINETEEN

CASE STUDY WITH SPECIMEN ANSWER: A. & C. WATSON LTD (INDUSTRIAL MARKETING)

A. & C. Watson Ltd, was founded at Coventry in 1954 by two brothers, Alan, an industrial chemist, and Christopher, a mechanical engineer. The brothers were inspired by their father, who held a family tradition in managing Watson Steel Works Ltd. The 'works' has changed operations during its 100-year history from a sheet metal works to a firm specializing in the precision engineering of machine tools which today is managed by Michael Watson, the third and eldest son.

The 'Watson Brothers', as they were known locally, used customized business as their path to growth and business development, and operated successfully by making metal washers and shims* for special applications—albeit largely as a result of trade 'passed on by father'.

Today A. & C. Watson (UK) Ltd (ACW), one of some thirty gasket manufacturers in the UK, is a successful international company owned by an international conglomerate, the Neal Sanders Corporation, whose worldwide consolidated turnover far exceeds £200 million (see Appendix 19.1).

The 1970s saw a major development to the ACW product range; further differentiation of the basic washer and shim types led to considerable product depth by type, size and specification. Fibre washers were introduced made from both asbestos and simple plastic polymers.

Gaskets were developed for a wide range of end-use industries using various materials ranging from mild steel to special metal hardenings, laminated brass and metal-asbestos combinations.

In addition to the development of woven asbestos for insulation end use and special gasketing for 'ring joints', there came the development of the Helitex gasket, which was a completely new concept in industrial sealing (see Appendix 19.2).

This new type of gasket is based upon a series of spirally wound concentric interfacings which combine stainless steel with an asbestos packing. The new gasket withstands much higher stress tolerances and extreme variations in temperature. It also produces a watertight seal and is highly resistant to vibration, corrosion and fire. The uses in the industrial and engineering sectors have consequently appeared almost limitless and are still developing on a worldwide scale.

The late 1970s saw further product development and the first stage of international business development. Export trade to the United States had been growing steadily, and to exploit the market further a new company, A. C. Watson (US), was set up in 1979 to handle East Coast

---

† Thin metal packings used to make mechanical parts fit.

business. Some seven years later, a sister organization was formed in Chicago to supply West Coast industry. Both factories have ensured a firm foothold in the US and Canadian markets and recently have acquired a majority shareholding in the Evans Corporation, which manufactures automobile gaskets.

During 1983 and 1985 two sales subsidiaries were set up by A. C. Watson (US), in Nigeria and Singapore respectively, to supply Africa and the Far East. Currently no plans exist to commence manufacture in these countries, but they will continue to be 'far-off field storage depots'.

The latest factory, which operates as an independent manufacturing subsidiary of ACW (UK), was opened in June 1986 in Holland to exploit opportunities within the Dutch petrochemical refining industries. Over a further three-year period ACW (UK) appointed sales agents in Sweden, Venezuela and Mexico.

Coincident with this international expansion, a new depot was built in 1982 at Aberdeen to serve the North Sea oil industry.

Diversification into a range of industrial sealants and pneumatic sealing equipment has been achieved and a new sealants salesforce was appointed in 1984 to supplement the existing UK and European sales teams.

Just nine months have passed since the establishment of a special trouble-shooting team which offers technical specialism. Apart from routine maintenance of industrial installations, they have the range of equipment and products to handle most customer requirements in the petrochemical refining industries. This team of seven highly trained engineers has been named 'Force 10'.

Expansion has been at the cost of heavy research and development, re-equipping the manufacturing plant and ensuring the highest standards of precision for Helitex with the installation of micro-computer technology for application to micro-engineering and other production operations. The research and development team, which enjoys the opportunity for speculative research, has a reputation for innovative product designs, many of which are far ahead of the rest of the industry. Extensive tests of existing products, undertaken in the laboratory testing station, are supplemented by yet further research which is in response to technical and scientific leads. Currently, plastics and new polymer compounds are being tested for stress, tolerance, vibration, etc., in the hope that new product ideas will emerge.

Production, although operating at 70 per cent capacity, has not been without setbacks. All production machinery is imported from the USA and delays in delivery times have been a constant source of frustration. The environmentalist lobby on the use of asbestos, and subsequent legislation, has caused an accelerated programme of research and development to produce substitute materials. A close watch is now kept on the market environment to keep the factory alerted to any future threats.

The company enjoys good working relationships at all levels and one worker representative from the trade union attends the monthly board meetings.

ACW enjoys a very low staff turnover, and, despite the recent redundancy of 35 production operatives and early retirement agreed with 15 others at junior administrative levels, employees have remained loyal to the company.

The culture of the ACW organization is one of a high regard for the management hierarchy. The small board of five directors has a separate suite of offices, a separate dining room and kitchen on the first floor and car parking designated by name plates. A high sense of achievement and self-sufficiency is part of the charisma created by the Watson brothers.

Middle management, defined by those with the title 'manager', have a separate dining room adjoining the works canteen. ACW managers share an open-plan office on the ground floor of the main two-storey office building.

Corporate planning is a matter of basic group policy, with the emphasis on setting objectives which match company resources to production requirements.

While lunchtime discussions are dominated invariably by internal influences and priorities, formal board meetings occur monthly with quarterly presentations made to the Neal Sanders board. Budgetary control, sales target achievement and technical considerations receive particular attention, while a positive zest for new innovation permeates every meeting.

Christopher Watson firmly believes that it is the responsibility of his sales and marketing director, Stephen Sutcliffe, merely to sell what ACW produces, an opinion that is also voiced by Mark Sutton, his research and development manager.

A memo sent to Sutcliffe on his appointment gives a clear indication of the MD's convictions (see Appendix 19.3).

Following Stephen Sutcliffe's appointment, the seals salesforce was reorganized into three regions to increase the accountability of individual representatives. A new 'Midlands' region (Area B) was designated under Bob Pearce, a former ACW representative of some 10 years' standing. Further appointments to the salesforce were made in 1988 when two engineering graduates were taken on to replace David Clarke and Andrew Smith, who had been promoted from the seals salesforce to regional sales management of the newly created sealants salesforce (see Appendix 19.4).

In all, eight new representatives were appointed and placed on an intensive six-month training programme organized by external sales training consultants. These eight representatives still remain at ACW and two have recently obtained the CIM Diploma by part-time evening study.

Sutcliffe has, on several occasions, consulted the mature salesmen about further training, but the force resents the 'need for re-schooling'. They consider that technical representatives or sales engineers, as they are known, do not require high-pressure selling techniques in this industry, and that the firm's success to date proves this.

All salesmen are paid on a 'salary-only' basis, with a Christmas bonus usually amounting to a further month's money paid at the discretion of Stephen Sutcliffe. This discretionary bonus is on the basis of Sutcliffe's assessment of an individual's performance throughout the year. It is a system that Sutcliffe believes in and one that he considers works best after his 30 years' experience as a technical representative. However, his sales managers do not share the same view. Frank White firmly believes in the need for a commission system, but does not wish to press too hard for this, having been with the company for only two years, and having taken over the job previously handled by Sutcliffe himself!

Advice from Terry Porter has been heeded. 'Frank, don't rock the boat if you want to get on, I say the same to my regional managers and they appear content. Neal Johnson and Max Bennett have been with me for 12 years now and the company looks after them well. Bob Pearce, who has an ambitious wife, is my only potential mutineer.'

André Pascalle, the international member of the sales management team, is a major asset to ACW. Of French and Austrian parents, he speaks French, German, English and Spanish fluently and has local working knowledge of the countries and operational areas of his sales agents, where he spends some 40 per cent of his time. He works closely with Stanley Reed on international contracts, and has four representatives in Germany who return to the UK after a six-week journey cycle. His sphere of influence throughout the company is considerable and he spends more time with the Watson brothers than with his immediate boss. He was offered the board appointment of marketing and sales director before Sutcliffe but turned it down on the basis that it would constrain his movements and stunt his job satisfaction.

Monitoring the movements of the salesforce is achieved by a mandatory 'Friday phone-in'.

The German reps are expected to call in each Friday between 10.00 a.m. and 12 noon to the Coventry office. In the event of André Pascalle's absence, they report direct to Stephen Sutcliffe. The UK sales representatives telephone their regional managers, who, in turn, report in to Terry Porter and Frank White. Sutcliffe expects a report phoned to him at home by 10.30 each Saturday morning.

A monthly UK sales meeting is held at Head Office, and this is supplemented by an annual weekend sales conference held in a London hotel each June after the publication of the annual accounts.

Internal sales office administration and ordering are handled by the customer service department, where complaints and after-sales service enquiries are dealt with swiftly and efficiently. Alan Humphreys, a former sales manager, has spent his entire working life with the company and after an unfortunate road accident decided to stay with paperwork and an office job, rather than be out on the road. As customer service manager, he is a highly valued member of the management team.

The dispatch and onward distribution of products takes place from the main warehouse at Coventry, but the recent downturn in business during the recession in European trade has, despite computerized stock control, produced unusually high stock levels.

ACW has a conscious policy of maintaining high customer service levels and prides itself on providing good delivery times irrespective of cost. Production is often disrupted by urgent orders for Helitex specials, and this is a frequent source of conflict between Len Roberts and Alan Humphreys.

ACW vehicles and sales fleet are maintained to the highest standards and renewed regardless of mileage every two years.

All export orders are air-freighted using the services of a local freight forwarding agency to handle the documentation requirements.

One distinguishing feature at the works is a helicopter pad, itself an attraction and source of newsworthy items. It was built in 1979 to handle the booming business with the oil exploration and refining industries in the North Sea, where a broken pipeline seal or flange can cause a considerable loss in production and delivery times must be kept to a minimum.

In accordance with the board policy 'marketing' activities are kept low-key. No funds are consciously appropriated for media advertising, although trade press coverage is enjoyed from the regular editorial coverage of new applications of Helitex. The majority of the small promotions budget is allocated to sales aids, samples, sales kits and technical data sheets. Being conscious of the firm's corporate image, Christopher Watson commissioned a new 12-page, four-colour brochure and found this to be well received by both actual and potential customers who were largely unaware of the total range of products manufactured by ACW. The success of this brochure has led to further work on the development of a new company logo, new house colours and new letter headings for stationery, etc., to make sure that a new dynamic image is effectively communicated on all company instruments.

Stephen Sutcliffe has read this new move as either a 'change of heart' or as a direct remit from the Neal Sanders Corporation, and, to make sure he is fully aware of market reactions to ACW and the range of products, he has commissioned a small market research survey—of which some desk research is detailed (see Appendix 19.5).

A lecturer at a local college, a personal friend, has also produced a short statement on the public relations image presented by ACW and its salesforce (see Appendix 19.6).

Meanwhile, John Mills's team has also been working on a detailed analysis of sales activities and market trends (see Appendix 19.7).

To complete the 'audit', detailed discussions have been held on pricing policy, pricing strategy and tactics—all previously the realm of Mark Taylor.

Sutcliffe believes that it is now time to take stock of his operations, and make significant changes to meet the challenge of the next five years so that he may be able to hand over the reins of a successful and well-managed operation upon his retirement. He is now giving careful consideration to the final accounts and profit contribution trends (see Appendix 19.8).

APPENDICES TO CHAPTER 19

APPENDIX 19.1   The Neal Sanders Corporation

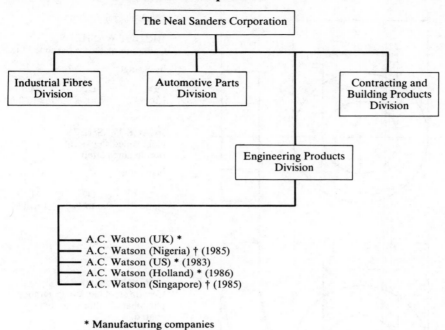

* Manufacturing companies
† Sales subsidiaries

Figure A19.1   The Neal Sander Corporation

APPENDIX 19.2 Typical Washers, Shims and Helitex Gaskets

(ALL sizes in millimetres)

BRIGHT WASHERS
Cadmium plated or hardened brass:

Size range

D1	D2	T
1 to 40	2 to 77	0.2 to 6.6

BLACK WASHERS
Cold rolled steel strip-
option zinc plated.

Size range

D1	D2	T
5.5 to 75	9.2 to 120	1 to 11

SPRING WASHERS
Carbon steel hardened, tempered
phosphated oil or lanolin
coated.

Size range

D1	D2	T
3.1 to 50	5.5 to 66.5	1 to 8

CRINKLE WASHERS

Size range

D1	D2	T
1.7 to 21.2	3.5 to 34.7	0.2 to 2.6

(continued)

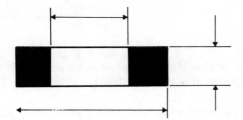

SHIMS

Laminum shim stock, also half
hardened brass aluminium and
stainless steel.

D	D1	T
10 to 150	15 to 190	0.15 to 3.20

OTHER TYPES PRODUCED

Tablock washers, tapered washers
with or without shaft keyways.

TABLOCK   TAPERED   WITH SHAFT KEYWAY

HELITEX GASKETS

Built to customer requirements.
Current D limit 12 feet and
T not less than 3 millimetres.

Figure A19.2   Typical washers, shims and helitex gaskets

APPENDIX 19.3   Memorandum—Appointment of Stephen Sutcliffe

To: Stephen Sutcliffe   Date: 18.9.85
From: C. Watson, Managing Director
Subject: Appointment

Welcome to the board, and to the new job of Marketing and Sales Director. It is a grand title, and 'marketing' is included to be fashionable with the international scene. Frankly, you are my *Sales* Director, I hope you will never forget it!

You have a Marketing Services Manager and a small team—do not let them interfere too much; their job is to generate more sales volume by discovering new potential for our products.

My view is that marketing is a luxury; it costs money, and you can't measure the results of the achievement—all far too woolly. Given a free hand, I would rather have another four reps on the road. Sales are all that matter; they get the orders—or at least it's your job to make sure they do. Our success to date has proven that good sales service is all that is required to run a business effectively and I don't want to be found wrong. I'm fully aware of the problems ahead, but our research and development team are second to none.

Good luck; it is good to have a man of mature years on the board.

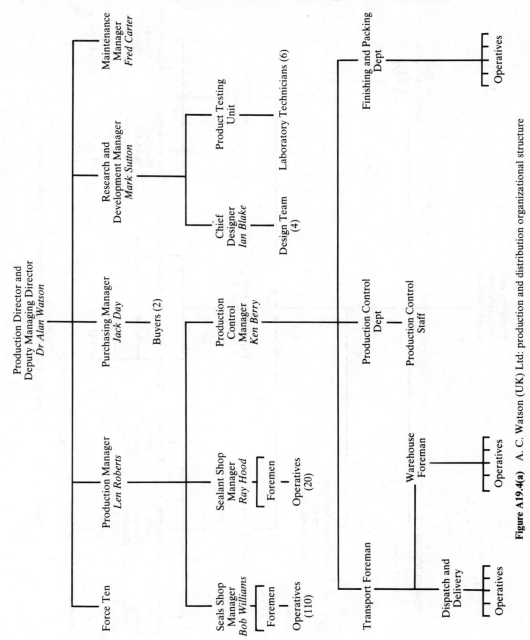

Figure A19.4(a) A. C. Watson (UK) Ltd: production and distribution organizational structure

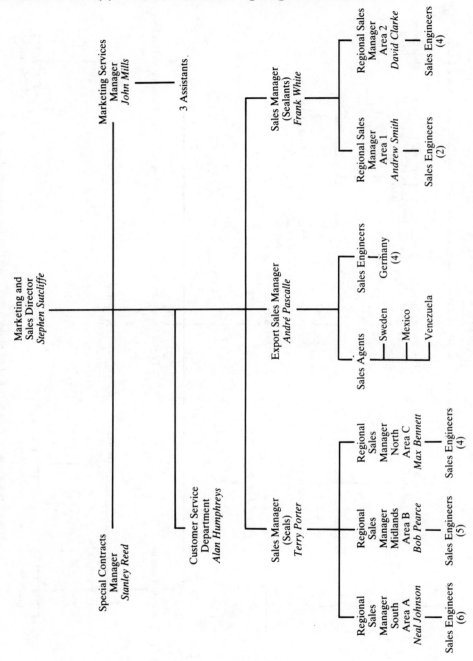

Figure A19.4(b)   A. C. Watson (UK) Ltd: sales and marketing organizational structure

APPENDIX 19.4(c)   Sales Areas

Sealants area I   = Seals area A +
                    Seals area B

Sealants area II = Seals area C
                    as far as
                    dotted line

Figure A19.4(c)   Sales areas

APPENDIX 19.5(a)   UK Market Trends by Value (Index 1986 = 100)

	1988	1989	1990	1991	1992	1993*
SEALS						
Washers, shims and metal packings	114	114	132	139	143	145
Helitex-type gaskets	129	142	180	201	211	223
Other gaskets for mechanical engineering end use	131	141	174	193	209	237
Fibre washers and jointings	125	146	150	129	141	172
Automotive gaskets	136	147	167	174	179	189
Laminated brass sheeting and foils	112	132	146	169	185	208
SEALANTS						
Mastics	112	123	156	167	189	203
Ring joint sealants	108	117	131	142	153	167
Compound sealant	118	132	147	167	197	213
Waterproof sealant	107	110	133	143	155	160
INDUSTRY						
Natural gas	124	167	208	239	272	301
Natural gas liquids	130	145	179	250	600	700
Crude oil production	150	352	444	903	1396	1514

* Estimate

Source: ACW Marketing Services Department.

APPENDIX 19.5(b)   Initial Appraisal of Market—1990

Major market segments	Washers	Other gaskets	Helitex gaskets	Compound sealants	Ring joint sealants	Fibre washers	Mastics
Oil refineries and petrochemical refining		✓	✓				
Original equipment manufacturing (pumps, compressors and valves)	✓		✓		✓	✓	
Building contractors							✓
Heat exchange and exhaust manufacturing		✓					
The gas industry			✓	✓		✓	
The electrical industry	✓		✓				
Oil exploration companies	✓	✓					
The automotive industry (prime movers)	✓	✓	✓				
Engineering contractors			✓	✓	✓		✓
Specialist end use			✓		✓	✓	
Our competitors			✓				

Major product groups

443

APPENDIX 19.6   Memorandum—Public Relations Perspective

Dear Stephen,

My observations are as follows:

1. On first arriving the company's name was only visible from one direction when approaching the ACW complex.
2. The reception area and visitors' waiting room do not convey a welcoming atmosphere, despite a most efficient receptionist whose telephone manner was commendable.
3. The office staff speak well of the company, are happy in their work and operate with an air of efficiency, and all appear most courteous to visitors.
4. The company has a positive sense of identity, but it is poorly conveyed. The company headed notepaper is old, inappropriate to an international image and does not represent the best possible impression.
5. Little use is made of the Neal Sanders centralized publicity facility in London.
6. The salesforce are motivated by goodwill and a positive sense of corporate identity but receive insufficient information and direction from Head Office. Particular weaknesses appeared to be no guidance for cold calling, no sales targets for product groups, an absence of profit contribution knowledge and infrequent individual assessments by their regional managers.

Yours truly,

Peter

APPENDIX 19.7   Sales Analysis—Years Ending 1987–93

Total ACW sales by product group—years ending April 1987–93 (£000s)

Product Group	1987	1988	1989	1990	1991	1992	1993
SEALS							
Washers and shims/metal packings	572	652	647	866	936	1017	850
Helitex	920	1276	1430	1882	2018	2310	2 544
Other gaskets	370	415	497	642	678	688	791
Fibre washers	74	131	230	96	55	72	152
Automotive gaskets	303	474	535	651	704	624	560
Insulation materials	149	193	219	255	94	84	89
Laminated brass sheeting	99	131	153	170	209	123	103
SEALANTS							
Mastics	—	—	—	60	152	332	606
Ring joint sealants	—	—	87	167	180	198	190
Compound sealants	—	—	28	105	195	314	507
Waterproof sealants	—	—	—	11	53	93	132
Total UK sales	2487	3272	3826	4905	5274	5855	6 524
Total exports	925	1241	1601	2416	3164	3759	4 349
Total sales	3412	4513	5427	7321	8438	9614	10 873

Export sales by product group—years ending April 1989–93 (percentages)

Exports to	1989				1990				1991				1992				1993			
	A	B	C	D	A	B	C	D	A	B	C	D	A	B	C	D	A	B	C	D
Germany	1.3	7.5	5.6	—	0.9	8.1	4.9	—	0.9	9.2	4.9	—	0.7	9.3	4.5	—	0.5	9.6	3.6	0.3
Sweden	—	1.9	0.8	—	—	2.3	1.3	—	—	3.7	1.5	—	0.3	4.6	2.1	—	0.4	4.8	2.2	0.2
Mexico	—	—	—	—	—	0.3	—	—	0.2	0.6	—	—	0.2	0.9	—	—	0.3	1.7	—	—
Venezuela	—	3.2	5.1	—	—	5.4	6.2	—	0.6	7.3	5.6	—	0.7	9.6	5.0	0.4	0.9	9.9	4.9	0.3
Others*	0.7	2.7	0.7	—	0.4	2.6	0.6	—	0.2	2.4	0.4	—	—	0.8	—	—	—	0.4	—	—
Total export % of ACW sales revenue	29.5%				33.0%				37.5%				39.1%				40%			
Representing (£000's)	£1601				£2416				£3164				£3759				£4349			

A: Washers and shims.

B: Helitex.

C: Other gaskets for mechanical engineering end use.

D: Fibre washers.

* Others to: Iran, Libya, United States, Nigeria, Singapore.

UK salesforce analysis for year ending April 1993

	Call rate		New prospects			
Salesforce	No. per week $\bar{X}$	Coefficient of variation† (%)	Each journey cycle	Number converted this year	Journey cycle (days)	Value of orders achieved (£)*
SEALS						
Area A						
B. Anstey	12	16.7	4	6	20	331 197
A. Majors	10	30.0	5	2	20	380 667
C. Whiffin	14	7.1	3	4	20	403 991
D. Allen	9	22.2	2	1	20	350 123
S. Lawrence	8	12.5	1	2	20	420 871
M. Aldred	13	23.1	3	3	20	397 151
Area B						
E. Lees	15	13.3	7	10	25	156 600
P. Fisher	19	15.8	9	6	25	171 417
C. Smith	20	15.0	6	2	25	233 921
S. Hudson	17	17.6	4	5	25	133 089
W. Tyler	13	15.4	3	3	25	87 089
Area C						
H. Brown	9	22.2	3	2	20	589 416
D. Young	11	18.2	3	2	20	617 032
N. Watson	8	12.5	2	3	20	505 473
K. Fletcher	7	28.6	1	0	20	310 079
SEALANTS						
Area 1						
J. Hood	23	21.7	14	11	30	212 327
K. Neal	25	20.0	16	13	30	246 921
A. Summers	19	10.5	12	9	30	202 427
J. Mason	21	14.3	9	6	30	186 325
Area 2						
T. Old	17	17.6	12	5	30	265 200
L. Raven	15	20.0	10	7	30	321 793

* A percentage of orders are placed and the sales accredited to the appropriate territory.

† Coefficient of variation $= \dfrac{\text{Standard deviation}}{\text{Mean } \bar{X}} \times 100.$

NB: André Pascalle could not offer comparative data.

UK sales revenue analysis by region—years ending April 1988–93 (percentages)

	Seals							Sealants				
	1988	1989	1990	1991	1992	1993		1989	1990	1991	1992	1993
Area A	n/a	40	37	37	35	35	Area 1	2	4	7	10	13
Area B	n/a	23	24	20	18	12						
Area C	n/a	34	32	32	31	31	Area 2	1	3	4	6	9
Totals	100	97	93	89	84	78	Totals	3	7	11	16	22

SEALS

			%
Factors	15%	Oil refineries and petrochemical refineries	37
		Engineering contractors	6
End-user industries	79%	Automotive industry	10
		Gas industry	7
		Electrical industries	4
		Oil exploration	9
Competitors	6%	Original equipment manufacturers (pumps and valves and compressors)	6

SEALANTS

			%
Factors	28%	Automotive body builders	19
End-user industries	59%	Building/construction and engineering contracting industries	16
		Marine users	7
DIY sector (do-it-yourself)	13%	Specialist end-users including original equipment manufacturers	17

Figure A19.7   Home sales breakdown by customer groups

APPENDIX 19.8(a) Profit Contribution by Product Group—Years Ending April 1987–93 (percentages)

Product group	1987 H	1987 E	1988 H	1988 E	1989 H	1989 E	1990 H	1990 E	1991 H	1991 E	1992 H	1992 E	1993 H	1993 E
SEALS														
Washers and shims	16.3	0.8	15.1	1.1	12.2	1.1	12.1	0.7	11.8	1.2	11.1	1.2	10.7	1.3
Helitex	41.1	5.3	37.1	9.4	39.2	10.6	38.0	12.9	37.6	13.0	37.9	17.1	37.8	19.4
Other gaskets	14.1	5.1	12.1	4.9	11.8	4.6	11.1	5.1	10.3	7.1	9.9	7.6	8.4	7.4
Fibre washers	0.3	—	0.6	—	1.1	—	0.2	—	0.1	—	0.2	—	0.7	0.2
Automotive gaskets	12.2	—	14.2	—	13.7	—	12.3	—	11.7	—	8.4	—	6.4	—
Insulation materials	3.2	—	3.7	—	3.7	—	3.9	—	1.8	—	1.0	—	0.7	—
Laminated brass sheeting	1.6	—	1.8	—	1.9	—	1.9	—	2.1	—	1.3	—	0.9	—
	88.8	11.2	84.6	15.4	83.5	16.3	79.5	18.7	75.4	21.3	69.8	25.9	65.6	28.3
SEALANTS														
Mastics	—	—	—	—	—	—	0.2	—	1.2	—	1.9	—	3.3	—
Ring joint sealants	—	—	—	—	0.2	—	1.0	—	0.9	—	0.9	—	0.8	—
Compound sealants	—	—	—	—	*	—	0.6	—	1.0	—	1.1	—	1.5	—
Waterproof sealants	—	—	—	—	—	—	*	—	0.2	—	0.4	—	0.5	—
	—	—	—	—	0.2	—	1.8	—	3.3	—	4.3	—	6.1	—

H: Home trade.
E: Export trade.
* Insignificant amount.

APPENDIX 19.8(b)   Profit and Loss Accounts

A. & C. Watson (UK) Ltd* profit and loss accounts, years ending April 1987–93 (£000s)

	1987	1988	1989	1990	1991	1992	1993
Sales*	3412	4513	5427	7321	8438	9614	10873
Cost of sales	2146	2880	3526	4705	5218	6042	6904
Gross profit	1266	1633	1901	2616	3220	3572	3969
Expenses	921	1173	1315	1767	2309	2870	3230
Profit before tax	345	460	586	849	911	702	739
Tax	170	225	291	420	460	360	381
Net profit	175	235	295	429	451	342	358

* Note final accounts for ACW (UK) only (ACW sales revenue worldwide currently exceeds £25 million).

APPENDIX 19.9   Summary Balance Sheets

A. & C. Watson (UK) Ltd summary balance sheets, years ending April 1987–93

	1987	1988	1989	1990	1991	1992	1993
Fixed assets							
Freehold land and buildings (at cost)	110	250	311	427	530	530	530
Plant, equipment and vehicles (depreciated)	220	320	460	710	779	800	840
Total fixed assets	330	570	771	1137	1309	1330	1370
Current assets							
Stock and WIP	259	315	472	553	687	842	1064
Debtors	287	395	511	732	914	960	1087
Bank	72	89	121	185	472	585	635
Total current assets	618	799	1104	1470	2073	2387	2786
Current liabilities							
Creditors	300	441	597	783	912	1025	1120
Dividends	10	11	12	20	20	35	27
Taxation	170	225	291	420	460	360	381
Total current liabilities	480	677	900	1223	1392	1420	1528
Current assets *less* current liabilities	138	122	204	247	681	967	1258
Total net assets	468	692	975	1384	1990	2297	2628
Financed by:							
Share capital	175	175	175	175	350	350	350
General reserve—retained profit	293	517	800	1209	1640	1947	2278
	468	692	975	1384	1990	2297	2628

QUESTIONS

Stephen Sutcliffe retired on 1 May 1993 and has emigrated to live with his son and daughter-in-law in Australia.

As Duncan Morris, you have been appointed at the request of the Neal Sanders Corporation to replace Stephen Sutcliffe.

Previously you were a divisional marketing manager at the Evans Corporation, where your track record was regarded highly: much had been achieved during your five years with the company. Now you have returned home to Coventry, where you were employed in sales and sales management positions in the automotive industries.

You have been given a clear brief to review the sales and marketing operations at A. & C. Watson Ltd, where there is now a desire at board level for the company to become more marketing oriented!

You are required to prepare a report for Christopher Watson, your managing director, for subsequent discussion at a special meeting of the Neal Sanders board which you will be required to attend.

Your report should comprise the following sections:

Section 1 Home and export sales and profit forecasts by product group for the next three years, i.e. until April 1996.

(25 marks)

Section 2 A strategy for the achievement of these forecasts to include the following:

(a) Internal reorganization of the sales and marketing functions.
(b) Management and control of field sales operations.
(c) Your marketing mix plans.

(60 marks)

Section 3 An outline budget itemizing expenditure levels for the achievement of Sections 1 and 2 over the specified period.

(15 marks)

REQUIRED APPROACH TO EACH QUESTION

Section 1—Home and export sales and profit forecasts by product group for the next three years

The *total* question must be answered, *and* in sufficient depth, because this section 'provides the foundation' for the rest of the paper.

Candidates should have prepared, well in advance, much of the requirement for this question.

Section 2—Strategy to achieve Section 1

(a) *Internal reorganizations* The candidate is given an open brief. The important ingredient is *rationale*—change alone will not gain full credit without the *justification* for it. This section can easily take much more examination time than you intend! Remember that a well-balanced answer to all three parts of Section 2 is required to achieve a reasonable proportion of the allocated marks.

(b) *Management and control of field sales operations* The distinction required here was between *internal* operations and *field* operations.

Again, with a wealth of data the danger is to overshoot the time allocation for the section. Therefore, a focus is required on key issues rather than a full dissertation on sales management and the control of field force operations.

(c) *Marketing mix plans* The essense is on the *mix* and not on producing a full marketing plan, which alone would absorb the total three examination hours.

Again, a focus on key points is essential. The marketing mix plan *must* be designed to achieve the sales and profit forecasts outlined in Section 1.

Section 3 Budgets

There are various ways to tackle this section but I suggest that a reference back to Section 1 is necessary and the additional expenditures incurred should be itemized.

ANSWERS

Section 1—Sales and profit forecasts, UK and exports to 1996

Total sales Total sales for ACW are expected to increase at between 10 and 12 per cent per annum, taking the revenues to approximately £15.5 million by the year ending April 1996. The total forecast is based upon a straight-line extrapolation of historic data and applying the forecast factors stated above.

Product group sales The method of forecasting *total* sales is considered legitimate in the light of known data on ACW overall performance.

This overall position is not, however, achieved by proportionate increases within each product group. Each group has different rates of increase and decline in accordance with the changes in market demand, the respective product life cycles and future marketing/sales policy.

Export sales Growth in total export performance is expected to continue and is forecasted to achieve a 45 per cent status on total ACW sales revenue, by year ending April 1996. This projected trend should achieve total export sales of approximately £7 million during this time period.

Sales forecasts These forecasts have been produced in the same format as the core data provided in Appendix 19.7.

Profit forecasts The decline in the profit-to-sales position must be arrested. A 10 per cent profit-to-sales ratio should be achieved by the year ending April 1996 which will yield a projected net profit before taxation of £1.5 million.

The profit contribution projections have been extended in the format provided in Appendix 19.8 of the case.

In percentage terms, a growth in contribution is expected from exports in accordance with the increase in sales revenue.

On the home market, sealants are expected also to increase profit contribution.

Jointly, the increase in contribution in these two areas will reduce the dependence on profits from home market seals sales, i.e. in *percentage* terms. Volume profits in *value* terms will naturally increase in accordance with profit projections. A percentage decline does not represent a decline in financial terms.

Profit contribution and profit forecasts are shown in the tables on page 453. Profit to sales ratios have been modified from the case data to account for the economics/diseconomics of scale and the associated 'on-costs' adjustments of each.

Total ACW sales forecast by product group—years ending April 1994–96 (£000s)

Product group	1994	1995	1996
SEALS			
Washers and shims/metal packings	800	725	650
Helitex	2652	3400	3900
Other gaskets	850	1000	750
Fibre washers	180	200	200
Automotive gaskets	500	400	300
Insulation materials	50	25	—
Laminated brass	70	50	—
SEALANTS			
Mastics	995	1200	1550
Ring joint sealants	190	190	190
Compound sealants	600	700	800
Waterproof sealants	150	160	185
Total UK sales	7227	8050	8525
Total exports	5023	5950	6975
Total sales	12250	14000	15500

Export sales forecast by product group—years ending April 1994–96 (percentages)

Exports to	1994				1995				1996			
	A	B	C	D	A	B	C	D	A	B	C	D
Germany	0.4	9.9	3.0	0.3	0.3	10.2	3.0	0.2	0.3	10.5	2.5	0.2
Sweden	0.5	5.4	2.5	0.2	0.6	5.9	2.7	0.2	0.6	6.5	3.0	0.1
Mexico	0.5	2.1			0.6	2.7			0.6	4.0	0.3	—
Venezuela	1.0	10.6	4.1	0.3	1.1	11.0	3.5	0.3	1.2	11.8	3.0	0.2
Others*		0.2				0.2				0.2	—	—
Total export % of ACW sales revenue	41%				42.5%				45%			
Representing (£000's)	£5023				£5950				£6975			

A Washers and shims.
B Helitex.
C Other gaskets for mechanical engineering end use.
D Fibre washers.
* Others to: Iran, Libya, United States of America, Nigeria, Singapore.

Profit contribution by product group—years ending April 1994–96 (percentages)

Product group	1994		1995		1996	
	H	E	H	E	H	E
SEALS						
Washers and shims	10.0	1.2	9.5	1.0	9.0	0.8
Helitex	37.5	21.6	37.5	24.8	37.5	28.2
Other gaskets	7.4	7.0	6.0	6.5	4.5	6.0
Fibre washers	1.0	0.2	1.0	0.2	1.0	0.2
Automotive gaskets	5.0	—	4.0	—	3.0	—
Insulation materials	0.3	—	—	—	—	—
Laminated brass sheeting	0.8	—	0.5	—	—	—
	62.0	30.0	58.5	32.5	55.0	35.0
SEALANTS						
Mastics	5.0	—	5.7	—	6.5	—
Ring joint sealants	0.8	—	0.8	—	0.8	—
Compound sealants	1.7	—	1.9	—	2.0	—
Waterproof sealants	0.5	—	0.6	—	0.7	—
	8.0	—	9.0	—	10.0	—
Profit forecasts*	£857 000		£1 190 000		£1 500 000	

* Before tax.
H—Home trade.
E—Export trade.

Profit forecasts by product group—years ending April 1994–96 (£000s)

	1994		1995		1996	
	H	E	H	E	H	E
SEALS	531	257	696	387	825	525
SEALANTS	69	—	107	—	150	—
TOTAL	857		1190		1500	

H—Home trade.
E—Export trade.

Section 2(a)—Internal re-organization of sales and marketing

The need The ACW sales and marketing organization has developed over time with the expansion of the company. The task that has now to be achieved is to attain the sales and profit targets outlined in Section 1 over the specified three-year period. As Duncan Morris, the newly appointed sales and marketing director, my first duty is to the ACW organization, my peers and my subordinate staff.

Reorganization is disruptive and is conflict-generating in its very nature. My objective will be to introduce change effectively, with the minimum amount of upheaval and to ensure that the change secures the full participation of all involved. This means that timing is vital; the 'new broom sweeps clean' syndrome may serve to alienate rather than to secure additional commitment.

To become known, accepted, involved and trusted is a first priority before the climate is right for further organizational development. Then it is a matter of personal judgement on when to initiate organizational change.

Before the plan is drawn up, a series of formal meetings and more informal gatherings will be necessary to assess staff reaction and solicit views on a wide range of company-oriented issues.

Administration, sales records and the marketing information systems To achieve the forecasted growth, the internal organizational efficiency must be considered as a major priority—'first put one's house in order!'

The need for two separate sets of sales territories, i.e. sealants and seals, appears largely historical. These should be rationalized into a new common format that is suitable and agreeable to all concerned, and also improves the internal efficiency of data search, administration and performance appraisal.

With the growth potential of sealants, these should be absorbed into the seals regions and be known geographically as Northern, Southern and Midland regions. The short-term effect would mean that Andrew Smith is Sealants regional sales manager for the Midlands and Southern regions instead of Sealants Area 1.

Sales management A distinction must be drawn between sales management, marketing management and the joint direction of both functions. As Duncan Morris, my existing span of control is too wide, I do not need to be involved in 'day-to-day' operations, but more with the strategic and longer-term plans for the future. Sufficient operational pressure will exist at board level; therefore, a new position of UK sales manager should be created and filled within the next nine-month period. This may present a promotion opportunity for one of the existing sales managers and create internal promotion opportunities for others—also stimulating additional motivation from within the sales organization.

The new sales structure would, therefore, be as follows:

Figure A19.7 Sales management structure

The marketing function For the immediate term in my role of marketing director, I would plan and direct marketing operations. A careful assessment of the role, function and contribution of the marketing services *staff* function would be undertaken with a view to the assessment of the value of such a unit.

By the end of the three-year period, the marketing function should have *line* authority over sales at middle management level. The need for a special contracts manager, a customer services manager and a marketing services manager reporting to me directly is questionable.

This could be overcome by introducing a marketing manager into the structure and leaving these as subordinate functions to the new marketing manager. The medium-term plan must wait until I can assess the abilities of existing sales managers and determine their strengths and weaknesses, their likely response to retraining and their reaction to another new executive. My objective is to ensure the ACW company becomes marketing-oriented, but this cannot be at the expense of alienating the sales function.

Promotion and training *into* a marketing management position may be a more desirable alternative than bringing in yet more 'new blood'.

A career path for those CIM Diploma holders within the sales staff could then be secured, and this may encourage others into training for these most worthy professional qualifications.

Marketing orientation As the director with profit responsibility, marketing planning is an essential process. A high priority must be placed on the integration of the marketing plan into the company's planning and budgetary control cycles. Liaison and agreement must be secured across the board; once top-level commitment to marketing principles can be ensured, then organizational development and restructuring can follow smoothly with the minimum of top-level resistance.

Section 2(b)—Management and control of field sales operations

The following problems are apparent:

—Resistance to sales training among older reps.
—No commission system.
—Current method of payment not considered suitable.
—André Pascalle, the export sales manager, appears 'a law unto himself'.
—Within the UK, journey cycles are not standardized.
—Journey cycles are not coordinated between the UK and export sales teams.
—The 'phone-in feedback system' may have operational difficulties.
—UK and export reps meet only at the annual sales conference.
—An apparent lack of sales planning and control manifest by the variation of performance of reps and call rates, prospects, and order value between the two salesforces at national and regional level. To ensure that the company is 'geared up' to achieve the sales forecasted, the above problems must be considered as immediate, and therefore carry a high priority for action.

The following action is recommended for implementation with the next six-month period.

Training External sales training consultants should be appointed to design and implement a sales training programme based upon the training needs of the company and the individual needs of the representatives.

A simple sales training course is *not* envisaged but a consultative period, spent in the field, as a diagnostic exercise to determine accurately the specific needs and then design the most appropriate cost effective programme with periodic reviews, *is*.

Payment A new payment structure should be negotiated, with a commission element that:

(a) Satisfies present complaints.
(b) Stimulates more sales.

Export sales Sales targets must be set for André Pascalle's team. While his 'power base' may be difficult to influence in the short term, he can still be made accountable for the achievement of targets. The operation must not only be tightened up but must also be communicated effectively to ensure that projected sales performance is attained. The German market must be considered as a first priority for increased accountability.

Journey cycles All UK and export journey cycles should be standardized and the most suitable period accepted. The four-week cycle, i.e., 20 working days, is recommended.

Phone-ins The operational difficulties must be investigated and remedied. If problems are insurmountable, a new system should be implemented.

Sales conferences Two conferences should be held annually—one three-day *planned* event, one two-day meeting with a social agenda for reps' wives.

'Special orders' Higher stock levels should be kept, if practicable, to avoid disruption to production and improve customer service.

Sales planning and control A *system* must be designed, implemented and maintained so that accountability starts with the representative and ends at my office as sales and marketing director. The current system is weak at all levels throughout the organization.

Standards must be set and agreed in joint consultation with the regional sales managers. Once agreed, they will be responsible for the implementation of the sales control system.

A full investigation followed by a written report on regional performance, followed by a set of reports on individual representatives, will be necessary to evaluate current performance *before* imposing new standards.

Reasons for the differences between salesforces and reps within regions must be pursued.

Standards must be set for:

—Call rates.
—Variation in call rates per week.
—Number of new prospects each week.
—Targets set for new prospect conversion.
—Sales quotas set for each region.
—Sales targets set for each representative.

A new sales-maintaining feedback system must be designed and implemented to provide Head Office with regular current information on field activity and also to inform reps of their performance against standards and targets set.

Regular reviews, i.e. monthly, must be made with reps by regional sales managers (RSMs) and in turn between the RSMs and the sales managers.

The newly appointed UK sales manager will take overall responsibility for sales performance.

Section 2(c)—Marketing mix plans to year ending April 1996

Within the constraints of this paper, these plans will be outline plans only and will be designed to achieve the quantitative forecasts set in Section 1.

Corporate objectives

—Achieve continued development of ACW company operations both at home and overseas.
—Improve the rate of return on capital employed in the current climate of industrial recession.
—Re-establish ACW profitability through company-wide marketing orientation and action.

Marketing objectives Within the framework of ACW corporate policy and the agreed corporate plan:

—Achieve sales of £15.5 million and a net profit before tax of £1.5 million by year ending April 1996.
—Achieve export sales contribution of 45 per cent of total ACW sales revenue.
—Exploit profitable segments of the home and overseas markets.
—Rationalize the existing product range to eliminate cheap unprofitable products.
—Reorganize the sales and marketing functions.
—Maintain and expand the market dominance in the field of spirally wound gaskets (Helitex).
—Develop the market for sealants and further penetrate the mastics market.
—Provide a sound basis for marketing planning activities.

Market research To ensure that the company's marketing strategy is planned to achieve maximum profitability, in-house desk research should be conducted by the marketing services team. This research would comprise an in-depth Pareto exercise to measure the profit contribution *vis-à-vis* sales volume by the end-use market and customer classification. This would determine with some accuracy the 'real' importance of the identified market segments and offer direction for future action.

The internal information system should be fully conversant with all sources of marketing information relating to the markets which the company services. A close watch must be maintained on uncontrollable variables and the future effects of further environmentalist lobbies.

Field research should be undertaken to determine the attitude towards ACW among customer groups and suppliers and to test the reaction towards the new promotional material.

As Duncan Morris, it is my impression that much has yet to be achieved in terms of corporate image.

For my benefit as the new sales and marketing director, I would require a full environmental review of the market to be conducted internally. This would include:

—Market(s) profiles.
—Customer/end-user profiles.
—Competitor profile.
—Product/service profile.
—Market segment analysis.
—Target market identification.

The product plan Upon joining the company, it was apparent to me that efficiency can be increased and profitability improved if we produce that for which there is a substantial market. Some products carried do not yield sufficient return and result in company working capital being tied up in 'dead stock'.

It is proposed that pending a more detailed analysis the following ranges are dropped:

—Laminated brass sheeting.
—Insulation materials.

Sealants Sealant sales should be restricted to the UK market to allow for a period of consolidation. The company cannot stretch the sales resource too wide; exploitation and further penetration potential exists on the home market.

The mastics market should be considered as a 'number one priority' for the sealants salesforce for the next three-year period.

Seals Helitex must remain the 'number one' product and be pushed hard to meet sales and profit targets both at home and overseas.

Sales of Helitex produce sales of 'other gaskets' and 'washers and shims' and the trade should not be overlooked.

Further product development in terms of speculation, tolerances, etc., should be aimed for to attain further market development for this product. New market applications should be explained through product differentiation.

Products for export markets The major product groups should continue to be pushed, i.e. washers and shims, Helitex, other gaskets and fibre washers.

Helitex will remain the 'number one export' with further market penetration in all cited countries, Venezuela and Germany will remain the most important markets in sales volume terms. Mexico and Sweden are expected to achieve increased significance over the next three-year period.

It is not planned to extend 'width' of the export range at this stage but to search for development within the existing range, to improve 'depth' of products offered to actual and potential industrial buyers.

Increased production capacity utilization must be aimed for at this stage by increasing output from the existing production resource and thereby to increase company profitability.

Product development For the medium term the company must ensure that the sealants market is given substantial support to allow mastics to become the number two company product to reduce ACW dependence on Helitex for sales and profits.

The pricing plan It is apparent from the case that different pricing methods are being used for the different product ranges. This is shown by the variation in the profit contribution to sales situation. The figures below (all percentages) are for sales (S) and profit (P):

	1991		1993		1995*	
	S	P	S	P	S	P
Washers and shims	19.6	13.0	15.1	12.0	11.6	10.5
Helitex	61.5	50.6	65.4	57.2	72.2	62.3
Other gaskets	25.3	11.1	22.8	15.8	21.6	12.5
Automotive	13.3	11.7	8.6	6.4	5.0	4.0

* = Forecast

The position is clouded further by the different apparent pricing structure in export markets.

The projections for 1995 indicate the pricing strategies to be applied. 'Cost-plus' is not appropriate owing to the price sensitivity in certain competitive market sectors.

Sales of washers and shims are expected to assume less importance, but none the less a price increase will yield higher pro rata profit contribution.

The sales of Helitex dominate and the product USPs allow the company to change premium prices to maximize the profit margin from this product range. Price increases in the medium term for Helitex must be considered carefully; to achieve increased penetration in the 'multi-markets' prices will need to be softened accordingly, and hence the profit margin per unit reduced in real terms. Longer-term pricing considerations must be given attention because ACW is heading into a situation where sales and profits are too heavily dependent upon the performance of Helitex.

It is assumed that the range of 'other gaskets' is various in nature, but also that a competitive market for these exists. It is also assumed that a significant percentage of other gasket sales is derived from Helitex sales, because the two key market segments of oil exploration and oil refining are serviced by Helitex and 'other gaskets'.

To retain market position, the margin on other gaskets will be reduced, and by adopting this stance competition may be held at bay.

These markets represent 46 per cent of home end-user industry seals sales and should be handled with care. To substantiate further this recommendation, there can be little brand loyalty for other gaskets, whereas Helitex, for the immediate term at least, remains unique.

Promotion

Above the line Above-the-line activity in the past has been limited to editorial coverage for Helitex. It is proposed to introduce advertising in the trade press to support the selling effort of the two field forces. In turn this will assist the re-motivation of the force brought about by retraining and the new payment structure.

Target audiences Advertising will be directed at the trade to 'push' additional products into the distribution pipeline.

The target audiences, therefore, will be factors, industrial specifiers and purchasing officers in end-user industries for both seals and sealants. This will take up 80 per cent of the press advertising budget.

The DIY sector should also be developed to create awareness and stimulate interest in ACW Sealants.

Budget A budget of £25 000 should be appropriated for 1994 and reviewed annually thereafter. This modest budget will not only be the first expenditure on advertising, but also will overcome a threshold problem at board level of appropriating company funds to such a purpose.

All above-the-line activity will be restricted to press.

Impact To obtain additional mileage from editorial coverage, 'feature ads' should be used, and, in addition, advertising support to the editorial that is offered to publications which are read by the identified target audiences.

The prime objective is to maximize exposure (OTS) among the target groups; therefore, matching readership profiles of the trade publications to the specified target audiences will be essential.

Below the line In accordance with the total review of sales planning, and the use of external sales training consultants, existing sales support materials must be appraised and modified/supplemented where necessary. This includes sales aids, samples, sales kits and technical data sheets.

Keeping the ACW and Helitex names in the forefront of the market is vital.

In this market it is considered inappropriate to offer promotional gimmicks, but selective 'give-aways' including pens, diaries, calendars and phone note pads, are considered appropriate.

Budget It is considered that below-the-line activity is more important in this market and, furthermore, direct sales support is required now! A budget of £75 000 is proposed for below-the-line activity, which will total £100 000 with the proposed above-the-line activity.

Impact The combined effect of new sales incentives and sales planning, plus a *planned* programme of advertising and sales promotion, will not only achieve an element of surprise in the market, but also stimulate sales because this is the first major promotional push in the company's stated history.

Feedback The effectiveness of advertising and sales promotion activities must be monitored closely to measure, as far as is possible, the effect in terms of changed attitudes and sales response. This will help me, as Duncan Morris, to press for an increased budget for the following and succeeding years.

Public relations A climate of uniformed opinion should be maintained between ACW and the identified publics.

Public relations activities should not be haphazard acts of public spiritedness which are aimed at securing maximum exposure through the exploitation of the press and other media, but planned events, integrated with the total ACW marketing communications activity.

Distribution It is assumed from Appendix 19.7 that the following main channels exist:

1.	ACW (UK)	UK seals and sealant factors	Indirect
2.	ACW (UK)	UK seals and sealant end-user industries	Direct
3.	ACW (UK)	Export through sales agents	Sweden Mexico Venezuela
4.	ACW (UK)	Export through sales engineering	Germany

To achieve the forecasted sales revenues in home and export markets, the volumes of products flowing down these channels will all increase.

With the increase in projected export business, and taking into account company UK sales projections and the trend analysis by *value* in Appendix 19.5, priorities between and within these channels will change.

The maintenance of trade channel alliances is vital to ensure that the company retains a balanced perspective with reference to these channels.

This may require a shift in selling emphasis to ensure equitable work loads and returns to gain maximum advantage from the existing channels.

The German market, in particular, must be reviewed to consider the cost/benefit of the attention currently given to this single market.

The development of German sales agents as used in Sweden, Mexico and Venezuela should be investigated.

A feasibility study should be conducted within the next 12 months to evaluate this alternative. Channel efficiency must be the prime consideration at all times.

Section 3—Budgets

For Section 1—Sales and profit forecasts for year ending April (£000s)

	1994	1995	1996
Total sales	12 250	14 000	15 500
Cost of sales	7 750	8 820	9 750
Gross profit	4 500	5 180	5 750
Profit before tax	857	1 190	1 500

For Section 2—Sales and marketing expenditure levels during the period to April 1996

The following items are areas of *additional* expenditure, which would not otherwise have been incurred. These items have been absorbed within the cost of sales figures above.

	£
MARKET RESEARCH	
Desk and field research	7 000*
Feasibility study (distribution)	2 500*
SALES	
Sales training and consulting services	10 000*
Administration and MIS changes	8 000*
Sales planning system design and implementation	5 000
New UK sales manager (incl. on-costs and car)	20 000
Sales conference	5 500
MARKETING	
New marketing manager (incl. on-costs and car)	25 000
Marketing planning administration	5 500
Advertising	25 000
Sales promotion	75 000
Public relations	5 000
CONTINGENCY	16 500
	210 000

* A substantial proportion considered as non-recurring charges.
NB: Should the feasibility study result in a sales agency decision for Germany, savings may be made by the reduction/redeployment of the representatives involved.

CASE STUDY WITH SPECIMEN ANSWER: APEX LEISURE LTD

'A new company with a new concept in total fitness', claimed Alan Brooks back in July 1988. Alan Brooks was then the new managing director of Apex Leisure Ltd, based in Bracknell, Berkshire. His statement was made with a vision focused on a five-year time horizon. Initially the new private limited company was the sole importer and distributor of multi-gym equipment for use in sports clubs and gymnasiums around the United Kingdom. Its overnight success led to a much bolder move just two years later, when a 20-year lease was signed for a new property with vacant possession in the heart of the City of London.

The lease was granted by Wates Estates, who owned the new freehold site—an ambitious complex of residential, office and commercial units which, in architectural terms, could only be described as tastefully futuristic.

The trustees of Wates Estates at first were reluctant to grant the lease to Apex Leisure Ltd, because the latter's relatively short history was insufficient grounds for a solid covenant. None the less, Apex's plans for the site were heartening, and with solid trade and bank references, plus a good personal projection on the part of Alan Brooks, his ambition of 1988 was realized.

On the signing of the fully repairing and insurance lease with agreed five-yearly rent reviews, the 'concept' of the Brooks Health and Fitness Centre was off the ground. A full 12 months of renovation led in July 1991 to the opening of the Brooks Club, the largest and best equipped fitness centre in the City of London.

Pride, ambition and achievement, however, had to be tempered with the realities of financing the business. Alan Brooks had had little financial training; in 1988 this 42-year-old entrepreneur, father of two, had had seven years' relevant experience in retail selling and sales management in the health foods products industry.

The 'easy fortunes' of the multi-gym business were soon eroded in the financing of a much larger project.

The financial difficulties facing Alan Brooks were typical of those of the small businessman whose ambition far exceeds an ability to plan and control business operations:

1. The business was under-capitalized.
2. Insufficient working capital needs had been projected.
3. Cash flow forecasting was far too ambitious in the over-estimation of revenue and the under-estimation of expenditure.
4. There had been unrealistic planning for break-even and profit volume considerations.
5. Insufficient professional advice had been sought before embarking upon the project.

The supporting banks were very concerned with the trading progress and threatened to foreclose on the business.

With the pending bankruptcy of its owner, the Brooks Club seemed scheduled for premature closure. However, the freeholders of the site, Wates Estates, were still committed to the concept of the club, and furthermore had successfully completed leases on other units in the complex based upon the fact that these facilities would be available.

In December 1991 Wates Estates acquired an 80 per cent shareholding in Apex Leisure Ltd and injected substantial venture capital to rescue the situation. Alan Brooks was retained as managing director but Clare Hepburn was appointed as director of the club, which then was renamed 'Crispins' to reflect, she explained, the fitness image that should accord with the club.

Clare was a natural choice for the position as she had operated a similar club in Miami, Florida, for four years and had only recently returned to the UK.

With a somewhat chequered history, Crispins opened officially for business on 1 February 1992 and today is managed soundly under Clare's direction, with membership building in numbers and the club growing in stature and local recognition.

At a presentation to prospective corporate club members, Clare gives her well rehearsed introduction:

Why do we focus attention upon corporate financial accounts to assess performance? Why are we preoccupied with the bottom line? The answer may be, simply, survival!

If we take a more creative view, then the minefield of human asset accounting leads us to realize that corporate financial health depends upon the well-being of company staff.

In short, it is time that companies took a keen look at investment in employees as well as at a return on investment in future and current capital projects!

Yes, it is time for British companies to consider American-style corporate fitness programmes, because the evidence is building that business enterprises are gaining profitable growth from giving health a high priority.

Recent surveys have revealed that over 35 million working days are lost every year in Britain owing to employee heart conditions. The coincident loss of revenue is estimated at £1.5 billion!

How can we continue to ignore these facts of commercial life? Take, for example, the threat of Japanese competition and the challenge of the true post-1992 Common Market. . . . The British are nine times more likely to die from heart disease. . . . Why should we assess the marketplace as the only field to do battle, when diet and exercise should be the training ground on which effective and sustained business strategy depends? Do you realize that over 20 people die every hour from coronary failure here in Britain?

So what is to be done?

Well, the evidence relating to successful fitness initiatives are not Japanese in origin, but American!

Corporate health programmes have been in operation for some years there and their effectiveness is beyond doubt. Health care programmes have achieved remarkable results: absenteeism arising from sickness—down 15 per cent in one major multinational after 18 months and down 40 per cent over five years in a major American oil company. Even insurance companies that had a better-than-average position in the stress ratings of executives claim marked improvements in the number of working days lost after the introduction of health care programmes for male and female staff.

The 'heart' of any corporation is its people; corporations must look after their people's hearts.

A good example has been set by the British government's Department of Employment with its initiatives relating to smoking, drinking, exercise, health screening and so on; but it's time now for your companies to look after their employees' hearts. Yes, it's time now to wake up to the problem! There are simply too many excuses that cause corporate health and fitness to be a low priority on the corporate agenda—usually, lack of executive time and the fallacious assumption that staff have to be superfit and hyperhealthy before starting a fitness programme. Maybe the weakest but most frequently cited excuse is 'Well, we like the way we are!'

A survey recently completed shows a marked difference in attitude between US and UK companies, the former considering the issue as one of corporate and social responsibility, the latter dispensing with the issue lightly.

Surely, to change attitudes, to change behaviour, to overcome complacence, corporate fitness must be packaged to make it attractive—that is where we can help. Welcome to Crispins!

Following Clare's introduction, the group is then shown the comprehensive facilities. The short tour is also a well rehearsed routine to show the club 'in use', working rather than empty. Visits are timed tactically to project the best possible impression to the first-time visitor.

The impression created is usually most favourable.

After the visit, the group is normally handed over to the membership secretary, who, in a well rehearsed professional manner, concludes the visit with a brief statement of the benefits derived from joining Crispins. The script has been carefully prepared by Clare Hepburn and reads:

At Crispins a free full health screening is offered to all members, involving a confidential interview and the completion of a computerized questionnaire with one of our medical staff.

The survey enquires about eating habits, exercise taken, levels of perceived stress and the areas to which it relates, and life style. A comprehensive medical examination is then given so that an individual assessment is made of each club member. Exercise programmes are then prescribed, after consultation with the club member's local general practitioner/doctor should there be a specified problem.

A variety of activities will be combined to build up stamina and improve members' fitness. These include aerobics activities, swimming, weight training and use of exercise equipment in our gymnasium. Following this initiation into the world of enhanced fitness, many members make fuller use of the comprehensive range of facilities that are offered.

Members soon become addicted to the benefits that are directly derived from getting into good physical and hence good mental shape.

The social atmosphere at Crispins spurs people on to adopt a healthier approach to life.

At the end of this typical routine, Clare normally reappears to make a concluding statement:

It is common practice for our staff to give presentations to companies or to invite them to visit the club and inspect our facilities; but sooner or later companies may take the initiative and come to us, and not wait for an invitation. Then we will know we have a successful concept—it is only a matter of time!

Thank you for visiting Crispins today. Our brochure contains comprehensive details of the terms and conditions of club membership.

We look forward to receiving your applications in due course, but in the meantime please do not hesitate to contact me or Fiona, our membership secretary, should you have any further questions.

It is company policy *not* to sign up new members on the day of the visit. The selling activity is conceived as 'deliberately low-profile' to avoid the impression that the 'club needs new members'. Seven days are allowed to elapse before Fiona will make a follow-up telephone call to those who have visited the club as potential corporate or individual members.

Wates Estates are delighted with the progress that has been achieved with Crispins and have now realized the potential of diversification beyond the business of estate management, in which they have a 90-year history.

As a trust body, Wates Estates have substantial funds, backed with an equally substantial fixed assets portfolio of freehold property around London and the surrounding counties. One such property is Acotts Manor, a stately home in Berkshire, purchased for an undisclosed sum from the previous owners in 1987. Until recently the property had been leased to and occupied by an American film producer, but now it is empty and destined to serve a new function.

The appointment of Adrian Scott as business development manager led Sir Douglas Reed, chairman of Wates Estates, to explain their intention:

At Acotts Manor we need to meet the challenge of the 1990s and beyond; we need to build also in new directions. Stately homes, unless open to the public, are a drain on any owner's financial resources, and hence the Board of Trustees have decided to take a new challenge, one of substance, we think.

We have commissioned Leonard Grey & Partners for the development, which has already started and will take place over three to four years in two stages: firstly, to open Acotts Manor as a model life style centre for getting into good physical and mental shape; and secondly, to extend the planned facilities and capacity by building more residential facilities within the surrounding parkland.

APPENDICES TO CHAPTER 20

APPENDIX 20.1   Crispins—An Outline of Club Facilities

Club opening hours

—6.30 am until 10.30 pm, Monday to Friday
—10.00 am until 5.30 pm, Saturday

Days closed

Sundays and public holidays

Sports facilities

—Swimming pool
—Squash courts
—Fully equipped gymnasium with state-of-the-art machines, including multi-station gyms, vertical chest benches, exercise bikes, treadmills, rowing machines, weights and all standard equipment

Health facilities

—Sauna baths, male and female (separate)
—Steam baths, male and female (separate)
—Hydro pool and jacuzzi

Group exercise sessions

—Low-intensity aerobics
—Water exercise classes*

* To be introduced.

Treatments

—Solarium
—Therapeutic massage

Low-calorie restaurant serving lunch and dinner

Closed Saturday

Bar serving soft drinks and alcoholic beverages

Other activities/facilities

—Periodic lectures on health, heart care and stress management
—Quarterly club magazine outlining past and future events
—Organizing of sports activity holidays
—Doctor in attendance for consultation each weekday evening

Note: At Crispins, individualized exercise programmes are given to all members by qualified and trained instructors.

APPENDIX 20.2   Crispins—Organization Chart, March 1990

Figure A 20.2 Crispins—Organization Chart, 1990

Note: Crispins have geared up staff in anticipation of reaching the membership target of 850 members, so currently there is ample capacity to manage and operate the club.
* See Appendix 20.1.

APPENDIX 20.3   Crispins—Club Membership Status, March 1993

	Current	Target for December 1993
Total number of members	540	850
Female members (%)	30	50
Male members (%)	70	50
Individual members (%)	80	60
Corporate members* (%)	20	40
Membership joining fee (£)	350	425
Annual fees per member (£)	1150	1375
% payable by credit card (%)	15	25
% payable by montly direct debit (%)	80	25
% cash or cheque in advance (%)	5	50
Active membership (at least three attendances weekly) (%)	45	80
Passive membership (at least three attendances monthly) (%)	35	20
Inactive membership (less than one attendance in three months) (%)	5	—
Subscriptions cancelled (%)	15	—

* Corporate members pay one membership joining fee of £350 but are required to pay a £10 000 annual fee in return for 10 corporate membership cards. All members must be designated by the company. Memberships are not transferable to other employees unless at the express written request of the company. Memberships cannot be bought or sold on the open market.

APPENDIX 20.4   Crispins—Current Membership Profile, March 1993

Age/sex breakdown

	No. of members	
Age group*	Male	Female
18–24	19	20
25–34	81	97
35–44	212	40
45–54	60	5
55–64	6	—
	378	162

* Persons under 18 years of age are not eligible to attend the club.

Socio-economic groupings

	No. of members			
	AB	C1	C2	DE
Male	313	53	12	—
Female	85	69	8	—

Exercise activity at time of joining

	No. of members		
	No regular exercise	Some exercise	Using a planned exercise routine
Male	213	90	75
Female	45	80	37

Age:weight:height ratio at time of joining

	% overweight for height within age band	
Age band	Male	Female
18–24	10	15
25–34	40	45
35–44	70	40
45–54	50	50
55–64	33	—

Family status

	No. of members		
	Single	Married	Married with children
Male	65	40	273
Female	70	36	56

Salary levels per annum

	No. of members	
£ sterling	Male	Female
Less than 10 000	—	—
10 000–13 999	—	8
14 000–17 999	26	29
18 000–22 999	38	26
23 000–26 999	42	43
27 000 and above	272	56

Main mode of getting to work

	No. of members					
	British Rail	London Underground (tube)	Car	Walk	Taxi	Bicycle
Male	212	65	53	3	37	8
Female	70	48	19	12	11	2

Time taken to arrive at the club from home

	No. of members	
Minutes	Male	Female
Less than 10	—	—
10 but less than 20	—	2
20 but less than 30	10	4
30 but less than 40	20	19
40 but less than 50	36	26
50 but less than 60	77	30
60 and over	235	81

Time taken to arrive at the club from the place of employment

	No. of members	
Minutes	Male	Female
Less than 10	59	20
10 but less than 20	90	36
20 but less than 30	173	80
30 but less than 40	37	26
40 but less than 50	19	—
50 but less than 60	—	—
60 and over	—	—

Membership of other clubs/associations*

	No. of members	
Purpose	Male	Female
For general health and fitness	19	26
Business	57	5
Social and entertainment	6	5
For dedicated sports activities	52	11
Others	7	12

* Certain members have more than one other membership.

Attendance at any health farm

		No. of members		
	Never	Once only	Once per year	More than once per year
Male	345	27	6	—
Female	90	47	20	5

Main motivations stated for joining Crispins

	No. of members	
	Male	Female
To lose weight	113	83
To learn to swim	17	26
To keep fit	270	162
To take regular exercise	143	102
As a preventative health care activity	216	90
To balance executive stress with bodily exercise	247	71
To regain personal vitality	42	15
To remedy a health weakness	36	12
To recover from a long-time illness	6	2
To help to regain total fitness	137	72

Averaged personal priority rankings of members at time of joining

	18–24		25–34		35–44		45–54		55–64	
	M	F	M	F	M	F	M	F	M	F
1. Work	1	1	1	1	1	1	1	2	2	4
2. An active social life with friends	2	3	3	4	10	8	3	4	6	3
3. In-home entertaining	11	11	2	5	5	4	4	5	3	7
4. Watching television as a form of relaxation	6	6	9	7	6	5	5	6	5	5
5. Eating out	7	5	8	8	4	6	7	7	11	12
6. Family life in general	8	7	4	3	2	2	2	1	1	1
7. Keeping fit	4	4	7	6	11	7	12	10	8	6
8. Visiting relatives	9	9	10	9	9	10	6	8	7	8
9. Taking overseas holidays	5	8	6	10	7	9	10	9	12	10
10. Attention to personal grooming and attire	3	2	5	2	3	3	9	3	9	2
11. Maintenance of home and garden	12	12	11	12	8	12	8	12	4	9
12. Hobbies not involving physical exercise	10	10	12	11	12	11	11	11	10	11

M = male; F = female

APPENDIX 20.5 Transcript of Interview Conducted by Adrian Scott with Clare Hepburn, March 1993

Question

How would you describe the nature of your business at Crispins?

Reply

If you are asking for a mission statement, I have this already prepared for our new brochure. It reads:

> The Crispins Club is in the business of providing a wide range of facilities and treatments to assist in the enhancement of people's personal health and fitness and thereby to improve their duration and quality of life.
>
> Through our collective experience, we aim to give the highest levels of caring individual attention to our members in the areas of health and fitness training and planned exercise programmes.
>
> At Crispins our members' health is a first priority.

Question

Within the current resources, what are your expectations for the club?

Reply

Firstly, to build membership to the levels targeted; secondly to achieve a balanced use of the facilities we provide for our members; and finally, to achieve the financial performance budgeted and agreed with our parent company, Wates Estates.

Question

What are the main constraints which restrict the achievement of these expectations?

Reply

1. There is a limit to the amount of time I am able to devote to the personalized promotion to individuals and companies as potential members.
2. Members' disposable time and the availability of club time are difficult to harmonize.

Question

With what degree of efficiency or effectiveness is the club operating?

Reply

Well above expectations as this point in time, but well below maximum capacity.

Question

Where do you see the club in, say, five years' time?

Reply

By that time, operating effectively at maximum capacity, with a sound financial and market standing; productive and continuing to innovate in the fields of personal health and fitness.

Question

What do you consider to be the main strengths of Crispins?

Reply

Well, there are many, so I'll give them to you off the top of my head. Location, catchment area, accessibility to the London Underground network; Crispins is 'new', with up-to-date facilities; there is total care for members from fitness assessment to individual coaching; easy payment terms; highly qualified staff recruited from the top physical education colleges in the UK; support from major companies; high profile in the locality; Olympic-standard swimming pool; excellent security; good-quality clientèle. I suppose also we have become a lunch-time and evening oasis for the gathering of office-weary executives.

Question

How about weaknesses? What do you consider these to be?

Reply

Well, we are only just finding these out as a result of experience. There is a substantial variation in the patterns of club attendance and usage. There are no car parking facilities nearby. Our inactive accounts suggest something is wrong but I don't know what—yet!

We have a company policy of taking no outside bookings of club facilities. I am not happy with this because it frustrates financial performance. This may become acute because our business is seasonal—July, August, December, January and Easter are all low periods. We need the ability to attract more members of the right calibre without appearing too exclusive, yet I do not want to open the floodgates to all comers.

Question

How would you assess the future of the club in terms of unexploited opportunities?

Reply

Well, this is difficult because my main concern is reaching our membership targets. Then it is time to plan ahead, and I may need your help.

Question

I will be only too happy to help, provided you don't view me as someone from head office spying on what you are up to.

To turn to business, what do you see as the main threats facing Crispins in the future?

Reply

Crispins, as you know, had a shaky start. I have not met Alan Brooks so it is unfair to comment further. However, we are saddled with a five-year rent review, and estimates from friends in the property business have considered an increase of 150 per cent to be realistic. This will put considerable pressure on club financing, membership fees and who knows what else. Even though Wates Estates own the freehold, we are expected to bear market-level rents. We are an independent profit centre even within Apex Leisure Ltd. I have heard rumours that another club is to be opened in a nearby four-star hotel within the next nine months. This places even more pressure on us to get new members signed up now!

Question

Where do you see the key areas of future business potential?

Reply

In the area of corporate health and fitness, and we have the ability to exploit it.

Question

I would like to ask you an open question about Acotts Manor. What are your feelings?

Reply

Well, this *is* a catch-all question. Where were you trained? OK, here goes. My initial reaction to your question is that Acotts is simply fabulous. I would love to have the reins and make it really big in the residential health, beauty and fitness market.

The history, location and ambience of the Manor are all in its favour; many of the rooms have been restored in the traditions of the seventeenth century. The business concept is difficult to position. It is a hotel on the one hand, a gourmet restaurant on the other, a health farm for the rich and famous, a sports and fitness centre for the locals. The picture will become even more complex if the time-sharing venture is launched.

I can see that our parent company seeks maximum flexibility in the usage of the facilities and at the same time, to use your jargon, it needs maximum capacity utilization—I just hope it works. On the other hand—and now I have run out of hands—from Wates Estates' viewpoint, the site was a burden. Now, after investing, I guess, a very substantial sum indeed, they will get capital appreciation from the site and in time cash flow from the business to cover the fixed and variable costs. Clearly, profit is a much longer-term goal. I have not been involved in planning. I made one suggestion to build repeat business—that was the 'Acotts Gold Card', giving credit facilities to holders and preferential discounts on beauty treatments. This has been adopted, and with 365 days' trading on site it may be a substantial benefit.

I would imagine that there has been adverse reaction from local people, for as time goes on it will increase the traffic to an otherwise quite rural area.

If the pressure becomes too great the entire site could be disposed of as a going concern. This is typical of the acquisitions strategy that is hitting the hotel and leisure market generally.

I hope this is helpful. These are random thoughts only, and not what I would call a professional, considered opinion.

APPENDIX 20.6   Crispins—Club Usage Analysis, March 1993

Codes: M = Monday; T = Tuesday; W = Wednesday; TH = Thursday; F = Friday; S = Saturday. L = light occasional usage; M = moderate regular usage; H = heavy usage.
** Free use to members.
  † Additional charge to members.
†† Prices at competitive market rates.

Sports facilities

Hours													
6.30–8.30		8.30–10.30		10.30–12.30		12.20–2.30		2.30–4.30		4.30–6.30		6.30–10.30	
Day	Use	Day	Use	Day	Use	Day	Use	Day	Use	Day	Use	Day	Use
Swimming pool**													
M	L	M	L	M	L	M	M	M	L	M	M	M	M
T	L	T	L	T	L	T	M	T	L	T	M	T	M
W	M	W	L	W	L	W	M	W	L	W	M	W	H
TH	M	TH	L	TH	L	TH	M	TH	L	TH	M	TH	M
F	M	F	M	F	L	F	L	F	L	F	L	F	M
S	—	S	—	S	L	S	L	S	L	—	—	—	—

Squash courts†

Moderate use	Light use	Light use	Moderate use	Moderate use	Heavy use	Heavy use
M to F	M to F	M to F	M to F	M to F	M to F	M to F
		Light use S	Light use S	Light use S	Light use S	

Gymnasium**

Weekdays 6.30–8.30 am light usage; 8.30 am–4.30 pm very light usage
        4.30–6.30 pm light usage; 6.30–10.30 p.m. moderate usage

Saturdays Negligible use

Group exercise sessions

Low-intensity aerobics†   Two one-hour sessions held Tuesdays, Wednesdays and Thursdays, 6.30–8.30 pm. Well attended by ladies.

Health facilities

Sauna baths**   No daytime usage; moderate usage 6.30–10.30 pm
Steam baths**   No daytime usage; moderate usage 6.30–10.30 pm
Hydropool** }
Jacuzzi**   }   The pattern of usage is very similar to that of the swimming pool.

Treatments

Solarium†   Heavily booked Monday–Friday, 10.30 am–4.30 pm
(30 minute sessions)   Light use only 6.30–10.30 pm
Hours 10.30 am– 10.30 pm;
closed Saturdays

Therapeutic   Light usage until 6.30 pm; then moderate usage until 10.30 pm
massage†
Hours 4.30– 10.30 pm;
closed Saturdays

Other facilities

Hours									
10.30–12.30		12.30–2.30		2.30–4.30		4.30–6.30		6.30–10.30	
Day	Use	Day	Use	Day	Use	Day	Use	Day	Use
Restaurant ††									
M	L	M	M	M	M		—	M	L
T	L	T	M	T	M		—	T	L
W	L	W	H	W	M		—	W	M
TH	L	TH	H	TH	M		—	TH	M
F	L	F	H	F	H		—	F	L
Bar ††									
M	L	M	L	M	L	M	L	M	M
T	L	T	M	T	L	T	L	T	M
W	M	W	H	W	M	W	L	W	M
TH	M	TH	H	TH	M	TH	L	TH	M
F	M	F	H	F	H	F	M	F	H

APPENDIX 20.7   Acotts Manor—History and Location

Acotts Manor, set in 315 acres of peaceful private parkland, has been described as a stately home. In fact, it dates back to the seventeeth century, and, like many such manorial residences, has been extended over succeeding years to provide substantial accommodation.

This lakeside Berkshire manor house has 42 bedrooms, a range of reception rooms and an historic library, all steeped in English history. The outbuildings are of especial interest, in particular two huge barns which are claimed to be even older than the original house. In former times owners used the barns for banqueting, and more recently, they have occasionally been open to the general public on public holidays as a revenue-earning activity for the owner.

With the comprehensive motorway network that now dissects the country, the manor is within relatively easy reach by car. It is within $1\frac{1}{2}$ hours' driving time of central London and somewhat less from the major airports of Gatwick and London Heathrow. Major population centres are hence within easy reach. The nearest British Rail station is a 33-minute drive by car or taxi.

Few places in Britain offer such potential for tasteful development, to enable more people to experience part of our English heritage and to enjoy the environment of the English countryside.

APPENDIX 20.8   Acotts Manor—Stage 1 Development: Target Date to Open June 1994

Statement elicited by Adrian Scott from Leonard Grey, senior partner and architect of Leonard Grey & Partners, March 1993.

Acotts is to be transformed, with local planning authority already granted, from a country manor of slow but certain decay into one of the top six residential fitness and leisure centres in Britain, complete with conference facilities to seat 80 persons theatre style.

The lakeside location provides for a host of leisure and enthusiastic water activities ranging from sailing, windsurfing, canoeing and fishing to beautiful parkland walks and riding. Areas have been designated for clay pigeon shooting, archery and even falconry. To complete the outdoor provision are six grass tennis courts and a nine-hole golf course which is to be extended to 18 holes in the future.

The vagaries of English weather have been anticipated; hence a balanced range of indoor facilities include swimming pool, heated spa pools, separate male and female saunas, a solarium and eight squash courts. A small gymnasium will be equipped with exercise machines similar to those at the Crispins club for use under the expert guidance of highly trained instructors. Aerobics will be featured as a regular daily activity.

The range of beauty treatments, beauty therapy and beauty culture is planned to be extensive, encompassing personal skin care, body and facial massage, skin analysis and consultation, deep cleansing facials, manicures, nail sculpture, pedicures, aromatherapy, herbal baths, eyebrow trimming, eyelash tinting and perming and associated cosmetology.

The hairdressing salon will provide not only traditional cut, style and trim, but also hair examination to determine the strength of hair roots so that appropriate hair treatments can be recommended.

To assist guests attending Acotts, a small shop will be opened within the manor to retail products for skin, body and hair care, biocosmetics and shampoos, natural food supplements for sports people, a limited range of natural dietary foods, vitamins and mineral supplements and homeopathic medicines. For the more studious, a range of health books will be on offer.

Acotts as a centre of excellence will be committed to total health care and in particular will emphasize the gains from alternative medicine. Acupuncture treatment and reflexology will be arranged by special appointment.

All this means that Acotts Manor is to be a health farm of distinction. Plans are even made to run professional beauty training courses leading to international diplomas with the aim of producing top beauticians and using the manor as a means of getting expert exposure under the guidance of the Acotts professional team.

Two restaurants will be opened to cater for distinct but different needs. 'Bites', with a low-calorie menu for weight-watchers, will also provide hot and cold non-alcoholic beverages between 9 am and 7 pm. 'Acotts', a refined licensed dining room, will serve classic English cuisine to both residents and non-residents.

You may be amazed at the detail I have given you, but I have worked with Sir Douglas for many years; we are close family friends. His wife, Doreen, is a qualified beautician who frequents the top health farms. Her interest and help have been simply tremendous.

Stage 2 Development: Tentative Date for Completion, July 1997

(Statement issued by Leonard Grey, cont.)

As you will understand, Stage 2 is even more ambitious.

Planning permission has been applied for and granted for 30 fully equipped timber framed lodges, purpose-built, individually sited in the grounds, each to sleep four to six persons. This will develop the current concept of Acotts Manor into a luxury time share complex. By buying into the time share scheme, lodge time owners can become members of Acotts and thereby use the facilities, not just for the period of the time share, but each day for the 40-year period of the time share agreement.

With an awareness of the negative publicity that has been given to the characteristic high-pressure salesmanship associated with time share ventures, Acotts plans to complete these new leisure facilities first so that prospective purchasers can view before deciding to buy. Furthermore, a full 30-day period for cancellation has been determined to avoid bad publicity.

The time share lodges are to be fully equipped to a high specification for self-catering, including microwave ovens, dishwashers, waste disposal units, etc. As a touch of Acotts class, Sir Douglas has suggested that the cutlery is to be silver and the crockery, high-quality china.

Again, the corporate market will be a prime target. A time share week then will be not only a holiday but a venue for meetings, client entertainment or even an incentive for a company's high achievers.

Clearly, an additional benefit is the opportunity to exchange for an equivalent site and time availability worldwide under the time share exchange scheme, to which Acotts Manor will be affiliated.

This project is, however, in its infancy. Our priorities are with Stage 1.

QUESTIONS

In your capacity as Adrian Scott, you have been in post for over four months and are required to report to the office of Sir Douglas Reed, chairman of Wates Estates, on the following:

1. The advice you would give to Clare Hepburn to:
   (a) Build membership levels to those targeted for December 1993.
   (b) Achieve a more balanced use of the club facilities.
   Then state how this advice, when implemented, would further improve the financial and market position of Crispins.
2. The steps that need to be taken to achieve an effective launch plan to promote the opening of Acotts Manor in July 1994.
3. The form and content of a feasibility study to assess the Stage 2 development plans for Acotts Manor.

ANSWERS

Report to: Sir Douglas Reed
Chairman
Wates Estates
From: Adrian Scott
Date: June 1993
Subject: Key areas of concern for Apex Leisure Ltd

Contents

Section 1 Crispins
(a) Membership
(b) Club utilization
Section 2 Promotional launch of Acotts Manor
Section 3 Stage 2 development of proposals at Acotts Manor

Section 1(a)—Achieving membership levels to December 1993 target

Target membership profile
Target: 850 members
Comprising: 510 (60%) individual members
340 (40%) corporate members
in a balanced male/female ratio

This represents a 57.4 per cent increase in membership in just nine months and requires, according to Crispins' membership status (Appendix 20.3), new members to modify their mode of payment away from monthly direct debits to cash and credit card settlements.

Realization of target membership profile into qualitative targets to be achieved

—78 additional individual members (i.e. approximately 2 per week)
—23 additional corporate members, each holding 10 membership cards (i.e. approximately 1 per week)

This will achieve the desired position from that declared in March 1993.

Assumption It is assumed that membership recruitment has continued through April, May and June 1993.

Scale of operation to achieve targets As a new venture, the task of securing two additional individual members per week plus one corporate member is modest.

Focus Concentration should be given to corporate accounts.

Action to be taken to build targets to levels set

First priority: target market—corporate members Senior executives with sports club membership and decision-making responsibility who are employed by profitable, medium to large-size companies in high-stress industries located within the immediate catchment of the Crispins club.

Second priority: target market—individual members 25–34-year-old C1 females and 35–44-year-old AB males working within 30 minutes' travelling time of the club who wish to become *active* members of London's latest state-of-the-art fitness centre.

Time scale The next six months.

Emphasis A promotional and supporting personal selling programme.

Message and creative appeal

—*Individual members* Crispins is a prestigious health club. Membership alone enhances social status, but the prime reason for joining is the maintenance of a healthy life through physical fitness in today's stress-ridden executive life.
—*Corporate accounts* (i) Protect the human asset value of the enterprise through a corporate fitness programme, managed for your company's executives by Crispins. (ii) Profitability and financial health depend upon a fit, active, healthy management.

Communications mix
　Rationale The nature of the task in hand is modest. The target number of members will yield the following revenue through membership fees for the club:

Individual accounts	£
78 @ £1150 per annum at current rates	89 700
@ £350 joining fee	27 300
Corporate accounts	
23 @ £10 000 per annum	230 000
@ £350 joining fee	8 050
	355 050

A budget level should be set of approximately 5 per cent of targeted income, i.e. £20 000.

Communications mix strategy Above-the-line media activity would create heightened awareness levels for Crispins, but the amount of wastage in terms of target audience coverage renders this approach inappropriate. Accurate targeting and the most cost-effective means of reaching these targets must be borne in mind at all times. Therefore media activity would be used only as a contingency measure should target membership not be attained.
　The focus for this 'Crispins membership drive' must therefore be below-the-line. Within the options available, a direct mail campaign with a supporting in-house telephone marketing initiative is proposed because it provides the opportunity to:

—Control the promotional impact.
—Monitor response levels.
—Target precisely the desired market segments.
—Personalize the promotion.
—Schedule the exposure to meet organizational response constraints.

Approach

Individual membership target audience From a quick survey of existing members of Crispins, it is possible to identify job position, functional responsibility and industry. Target profiles can then be built for both male and female membership.

Many executives will be in professional grades, e.g. accountants, lawyers, bankers, marketers, etc. The services of a direct mail house could be employed to target these potential customers through a highly selective mailing list secured from existing sources. It would be wise to consider professional membership bodies such as the Chartered Institute of Marketing which have an active membership in the London region.

It is suggested that the mailing is grossed up to 1000 initially, aiming for approximately a 1 per cent 'sales conversion' to membership.

This task is quickly and easily accomplished.

Corporate membership A highly selective direct mailing campaign should be designed based upon existing corporate account profits aimed at matching existing business to potential business. The pay-off from these corporate membership accounts at a later stage may be substantial!

The location of potential corporate clients is captive. Again, the direct mailing house should personalize these mailings and restrict the rate of mailings to a controlled number per week to prevent the membership staff at Crispins from being inundated with enquiries.

Anticipating a lower conversion ratio, it would be wise to target 1000 companies, and roll out the mailing in four shots of 250.

The direct mailing piece This should comprise, both individuals and companies:

1. An invitation letter, personalized to a designated recipient and signed by Clare Hepburn, inviting the person concerned to view the facilities at a mutually convenient time to see the club 'at work'.
2. A brochure—'Crispins'. This is the main communications instrument. Design, layout, style, presentation, colour, weight and quality of paper/board need careful consideration to ensure that the corporate image conveyed meets with the expectations of potential clients. The services of a design house are essential—this must be a very professional job. It is suggested that a clear brief is given to three design houses and proposals be viewed within a three-week period. This stage is critical. It will either make or break the club—this *must* go well—it will provide the foundation for future communications activities.

Budget implications The design, artistic production, print, mailing operation and follow-up will absorb the majority of the budget, leaving a 15 per cent margin for contingencies.

The follow-up personal selling operation Administrative coordination is vital. The workload should be handled internally. However, provision should be made for one or two telesales staff on short-term contract to handle enquiries and to make follow-up contact with prospective corporate accounts.

Existing membership The essence of successful marketing is to 'win new customers and keep them'. Action must be taken to reduce the attrition rate of members through a well conceived customer relations programme in which club staff are actively involved. Regular communications through newsletters and personal contact are vital to build up and maintain a club culture where membership is something of real value—and not just another personal expense or company overhead. The value chain concept to gain and retain competitive advantage should be introduced. (A further report on this concept could be provided with Clare Hepburn's agreement.)

Section 1(b)—Achieving a more balanced use of club facilities

Existing position There is not an effective utilization of club facilities during club opening hours. Usage rates vary from day to day and during each day.

In specific terms, selected weaknesses are as follows:

1. *Swimming pool*
   Fact: Light usage during office hours until lunch time and again 2.30–4.30 pm.

   Proposed action

   (a) Target members on the desirability of the use of personal flexitime in order for the club to provide a more balanced usage of this facility.
   (b) Offer swimming instruction and water aerobics during off-peak times.
   (c) Consider offering out the facility to athletic club non-members who are training for competition swimming events—at an appropriate fee!
   (d) Encourage water sport activities in off-peak hours.

   Note: This weakness may not be overcome completely. However, to build some activity in off-peak times is vital to club culture—also important to club visitors as potential members.

2. *Squash courts*
   Fact: Light usage between 8.30 am and 12.30 pm Monday to Friday and all day Saturday.

   Proposed action

   (a) Offer squash coaching lessons and exhibition games at these times.
   (b) For established club members, offer off-peak squash court rates.
   (c) Offer the facilities to selected four-star hotels nearby for use by hotel guests—at a premium court rate.

   Note: This may only be a short-term position; as club membership builds, so will squash court usage. The problem may be lack of courts in two years' time!

3. *Gymnasium*
   Fact: Evening-only effective usage on weekdays.

   Proposed action

   (a) Plan and implement a schedule of individualized and group training sessions.
   (b) Promote lunch-time workouts followed by a salad luncheon at the club.
   (c) Promote the idea of 'space' in the gymnasium in light periods—with individual coaching.
   (d) Offer ladies-only and gents-only sessions in the gymnasium for those who are traditionally embarrassed about mixed exercise routines in the gym.
   (e) Link gym to motivation to join the club—reduce weight, stay fitter; actively promote this within the club.
   (f) Develop and monitor individual exercise routines; get involved with club members in their exercise programmes.

Note: A high level of investment is made in gymnasium equipment. This is to be utilized and should not simply remain on display. It is not good for the club image. It is important for *all* club members to realize that 'the gym' is there for *all* to use to *become* fitter, and not just for those who, having obtained super fitness standards, may parade in the gym. The club must promote the real health benefits of regular exercise taken in the gym.

4. *Low-intensity aerobics*
   Fact: Popular for ladies, although only six sessions per week.

   Proposed action

   1. Increase number of classes and move into light-usage periods.
   2. Encourage males to attend.
   3. Introduce high-intensity aerobics for the keen aerobics enthusiasts.

   Note: It is important to build on identified strengths, as this is one that will certainly win and keep women members loyal to the club—and, through word of mouth, may bring in more individual members.

5. *Sauna and steam bath*
   Fact: Evening-only activity.

   Proposed action

   (a) Promote the benefits of these facilities through a series of short talks for members.
   (b) Offer family sauna or steambath facilities.
   (c) Link the use of sauna to therapeutic massage to increase usage of both.

   Note: This also may be a seasonal factor—these facilities will not be used during summer months. Fluctuations in usage may be a fact of life that the club will have to accept. Power can be saved if there is no daytime use.

6. *Treatments—solarium and therapeutic massage*
   Fact: Little evening use of solarium; little daytime use of massage.

   Proposed action

   (a) Offer a 'price promotion' for each to include off-peak times.
   (b) Design and circulate an educational leaflet on types and benefits of massage.
   (c) Introduce reflexology during light usage periods, following a promotion and educational programme on such to members.

   Note: These treatments would appeal to both male and female members. The growing awareness of the health benefits of traditional massage should be exploited; then other fitness and beauty related treatment may follow in time.

7. *Restaurant and bar*
   Fact: Overall, with a few exceptions, the club restaurant and bar are well attended between 12.30 and 4.30 pm and in the evenings on weekdays.

Proposed action

(a) Research is needed to determine the motive for joining/using the club. Is Crispins a fashionable up-market, health-conscious club for members who treat the club more as a social (or business) venue during the five-day working week?

(b) Is the club appealing to those who wish to be club members *per se*?

(c) Is there a syndrome akin to the golf club member who never leaves the club house to play a round of golf?

(d) Answers are needed so that the image to be presented features customer needs and not a concept of Crispins that has been determined by management.

(e) Fundamental questions need to be answered to determine 'social members' from active users of club fitness and health improvement facilities.

(f) Fundamental segmentation of club membership profiles are now necessary—especially with the new membership drive about to break.

Note: The intended purpose of the club and existing club usage appear not to be in balance at this point in the club's history. Marketing strategy may need to be pursued carefully around usage 'strengths'.

Impact on financial and market position

1. *Market position* A market communications programme to attract new members will:

   (a) Position Crispins in the context of other fitness venues in the catchment area.

   (b) Convey exclusivity.

   (c) Convey a value chain to potential members to achieve competitive advantage.

   (d) Build awareness among professional managers and their companies of the importance and need for fitness among key, if not all, employees.

   (e) Place Crispins ahead of the field—at least for the short term.

2. *Financial position* At this stage in the development of any new business, there are certain key areas of concern:

   (a) When will we break even?

   (b) When will we produce profits?

   (c) How do we survive until then?

   (d) What are our working capital needs?

   (e) How do we avoid a liquidity crisis?

   (f) How do we retain the confidence of our financial bankers?

   (g) How do we ensure that we stay in business?

   (h) When will it be possible to get capital recovery?

   (i) If the venture fails, what are our options to limit the level of financial risk?

Therefore, the key issues of cash flow, profitability, liquidity, solvency, working capital tensions and corporate funds management cannot be ignored.

If the above plans are implemented and membership targets achieved, answers to the nine questions may become clearer and confidence will be built for handling the key issues above.

Section 2—Promotional launch of Acotts Manor in 12 months' time: July 1994

The pre-launch period: July 1993–May 1994

Step 1: *Research* Fundamental marketing questions need to be answered in depth to provide an understanding of the market(s) to be served.

1. Who are the 'real' buyers?
2. Where are they located?
3. What motive(s) will induce purchase?

A market profile will hence be provided so that discrete segments can be prescribed for attention and market potential can then be established.

Acotts Manor has a complexity of 'product offerings'. It is vital to establish precisely the target groups to which this 'array' will appeal.

Step 2: *Assumption-setting* Assumptions must be set for the determinants of demand and macro-environmental factors, and for the nature of competition.

It is also to be assumed that the launch date is now confirmed and that local resistance will be overcome from the neighbourhood in which Acotts Manor is situated.

Finally, it is to be assumed that the financial and manpower resources are in place and committed in time for commencement of operations.

Step 3: *Reference to corporate objectives* It is important that the launch and subsequent official opening of Acotts Manor are part of the corporate development plans for Wates Estates. Therefore it is necessary to refer to corporate-level intentions to ensure that this programme is in line with the company's business mission and its determined corporate finance and new financial goals.

This is not a lengthy procedure. It places Acotts Manor in the context of the Wates business entity as a whole.

Step 4: *Determination of marketing objectives for Acotts Manor as a new strategic business unit* The corporate objectives now need to be set in both qualitative and quantitative terms.

Image, stance and positioning must be conveyed with refinement for Acotts Manor and the markets it is designed to serve.

Fundamentally, this is a new 'product' for a series of existing market segments. Objectives must therefore be set for market penetration within the short term. This means that quantitative objectives are needed in order to set targets for the total membership profile by corporate and individual accounts.

These quantitative objectives present a clear perspective for the external agency and internal staff who will have direct responsibility for their attainment.

Step 5: *Budget determination* Policy is needed for the level of expenditure to be allocated:

1. To the launch.
2. To the follow-through period, including the official opening scheduled for October 1994.

A rationale is needed for the determination of the budget which will also be of assistance before communication plans are laid down for year 2.

It would be wise to consider the 'task approach' for the launch and year 1 on the assumption that Wates Estates will be treating communications expenditure as an investment for future returns rather than an item of tax-deductible revenue expenditure. Therefore it may be wise to adopt a percentage of membership fees as a means of controlling the level of communications expenditure.

A cautionary note is essential. A contingency budget of at least 25 per cent needs to be set aside for unforeseen expenditure and for adjustments to communications activities in year 1 that may be necessary to attain the previously determined marketing objectives.

Step 6: *Setting marketing communications objectives* From the marketing objectives above, it is necessary to obtain a clear sense of focus for this launch campaign.

The scale and purpose of this communications plan must be included in these objectives, so that an external agency will have a clear grasp of the nature of the communications task to be accomplished.

Essentially, it is necessary to maximize the communications impact among the identified target audiences within the time and budget constraints imposed.

Step 7: *Prescribing the target audiences* This stage is critical. The success of any communications plan hinges upon the ability to prescribe clearly the target audiences to be reached.

The communications mix elements can then be modelled to fit, and thereby match, the profiles of target market segments. The research (Stage 1) previously undertaken will have determined:

1. Who the buyers are.
2. Where they are located.
3. The motives that will induce purchase.

Priorities now need to be set so that the communications plan has a clear sense of purpose. Subsequently, it will be easier to determine the effectiveness of the campaign in terms of the percentage of the target audiences actually reached and subsequently converted to 'membership' of Acotts Manor.

Step 8: *Agency selection* It is assumed that the level of investment in the development of the Acotts Manor complex will be matched with a realization that this plan cannot be conceived 'in-house'. Professional guidance, planning and implementation are vital to convert this complex into a commercial reality.

Options available must be selected based upon the company needs for agency services. It is essential to determine 'what' is needed, both now and in the future, from a communications agency so that a brief can be carefully conceived for those who will be invited to 'pitch' for the Acotts Manor account.

It is to be realized that the size of the account will not be large enough to entice an agency on a media commission-only basis. Therefore the agency appointed will be paid on a fee-plus-commission basis and may in the future provide a communications consultancy service rather than simply advertising design and placement.

The wider organization of Wates Estates could benefit also in the future from these services. Therefore, this step should concern future communications needs as well as the needs to accomplish the task in hand.

Step 9: *Agency presentations* From those selected and invited to pitch for our account—three to five in total—we will view and consider the presentations for:

1. Creative appeal and execution.

2. Media choice and usage.
3. Use of budget.
4. The human dynamics, i.e. whether the agency has understood our brief, our organization and whether we can work together with them effectively in the future.

Step 10: *Agency appointment* From the presentations, one agency will be selected.

Step 11: *Appraising the agency communications plan for the Acotts Manor launch and follow-through campaign to include the official opening* A series of reviews will be undertaken with the agency to refine and agree on the creative interpretation and the communications mix to be used to ensure that the right atmosphere has been achieved in the visual work and the best exposure has been planned for the key messages about 'Acotts'.

The structure of the plan should be considered carefully for exposure, impact to be created and timing.

The element of the plan, including media activity (above-the-line), promotion (below-the-line) and publicity, needs to be balanced to achieve the marketing communications objectives. The roles to be fulfilled by (a) the agency and (b) the client (ourselves) need to be clearly understood. The place of, and purpose to be fulfilled by, internal and external corporate public relations needs to be clearly ascertained, both for the communications launch and in client handling. This area is of critical importance in the service industries and is an essential component of customer care strategy.

The appraisal, review, modification and refinement of the plan will lead eventually to its agreement for implementation.

The launch period: June 1994–September 1994 The launch period shows a span of four months, i.e. one month before the opening of Acotts Manor for business and three subsequent months up to the official opening in Ocober 1994.

During this time, the agency's responsibility will be for the communications mix execution and review. Internally, Acotts must be equipped for handling enquiries and converting sales. Records should be kept to monitor and evaluate the source of enquiries with regard to how these subsequently convert to business.

The promotional launch period should be sustained to give Acotts the level of activity needed to get the complex moving. After a long period of refurbishment, Wates Estates will expect good activity levels at Acotts quickly, so that by the time of the official opening in October Acotts is firmly in business.

The follow-through period: October 1994–May 1995 In addition to the official opening, an effective launch plan must provide for the follow-through period of communications activity among existing and potential customers.

The official opening Fundamentally, this is a public relations activity to:

—Announce Acotts Manor to the identified publics.
—Create a climate of informed opinion between the organizations and the many publics it serves.

The importance of this event should not be underestimated. A great deal of communications mileage can be obtained if the event is well conceived, planned, executed and reviewed.

Within the overall communications plan, this PR event will also have three key elements:

1. The pre-official opening period to announce the event.

2. The official opening day.
3. The follow-through period of PR communications activity.

The follow-through period: November 1994–May 1995 Through the regular monitoring and review of the achievement of the quantitative communications targets, the level of media exposure during the follow-through period can be determined. Also, the approach and message to target audiences can be modified to accomplish the specified communications tasks.

After the first four months, the level of actual business attained should be assessed for variance against targets and the appropriate promotional stand taken to win and retain business for Acotts Manor.

It is vital to realize that existing customers too must receive regular communications and to ensure that this plan is not only focused upon attaining new accounts.

Section 3—Stage 2 development proposals at Acotts Manor for July 1997: the form and content of a feasibility study to assess this development

Corporate-level audit Projections for four years are required. Therefore the company needs to know where it is now in order to establish how it will arrive where it wants to be in four years' time.

Clearly stated corporate objectives need to be derived from a well determined corporate mission statement. This is of utmost importance. The proposed development must harmonize with the company's intended business purpose, otherwise the focus for the enterprise will be lost.

To take this development step at a time when Acotts has yet to be opened means that this feasibility study will be conducted over a distinct time period in the future.

It is proposed that the conduct of this study be realistic to the time scale for implementation of Stage 2 of this development.

With this medium-term time scale in perspective, the company needs to maintain a continuous surveillance of the market situation with reference to time share style developments in the UK and indeed within Europe. On-going analysis of corporate strengths and resources needs to be undertaken to ensure that the development can proceed with confidence.

Key criteria need to be determined by which this development can be appraised and evaluated. These criteria need to be both financial and non-financial so that the level of total risk can be properly evaluated and periodically reviewed. Once these criteria have been laid down and agreed, it is appropriate to relate the development project to these criteria to determine the feasibility or not of progressing with Stage 2 at Acotts Manor.

Fundamentally, the company must be able to determine clearly whether or not it has or will have the capacity to meet its ambitions in accordance with the planned scale of operations.

The scenario Thirty fully equipped timber-framed, purpose-built lodges are to be constructed within the grounds of Acotts Manor and marketed as a time share complex during July 1997.

Assumptions It is assumed that Acotts Manor Stage 1 will have been successfully launched and target membership achieved, and that this will provide the essential foundations for Stage 2 of the development.

Feasibility research This comprises three fundamental stages:

1. Experimental and technical research.
2. Market research.

3. An analysis and integration of findings in terms of time, cost, human resource needs and the commercial potential.

Stage 1: *Experimental and technical research* To convert the concept into a feasible proposition, the company will need to conduct design studies of the basic technical alternatives, lay down performance specifications, and examine the feasibility of construction. Within the real estate business, it would have the contacts and capacity to fulfil this requirement. An estimate will then be needed for project development time and costs.

Stage 2: *Market research* Demand analysis is vital to this feasibility study.

Research must be commissioned to examine the characteristics of the market, its size and prevailing trends.

The nature of competition must be carefully evaluated. This involves not only an identification of the key areas of future competitive threat, but also an examination of potential purchasers' motivation to establish the real psychological triggers to (a) initiate and (b) complete a purchase. It is then that the real nature of potential competition can be discovered.

The value system of potential buyers is the keynote to success. Motivational research through focus groups may provide some revealing evidence upon which to pursue this line of enquiry.

An examination of needs is necessary to make the match between product/service requirements and customer requirements. Segmentation here will be vital in order to discover, carefully, the prescribed target markets.

This essential market research will provide the foundation for the positioning of Acotts Stage 2 among defined, targeted, prioritized market segments. From there, demand analysis can be achieved with a clear sense of focus.

It should be noted that this research programme should feature quality and psychological variables and not just price and availability.

Stage 3: *Commercial potential* The commercial potential will now need to be assessed in light of Stage 1 and Stage 2 findings in terms of time, cost and manpower requirements. Stage 3 provides the basis of a first management review to give this development project authorization.

Financial analysis to be undertaken at this stage of the feasibility study Outline income and expenditure analysis needs to be conducted to ascertain the financial viability of the project. Costs and revenues will need to be projected using discounted cash flow (DCF) techniques over a five-year period (to the end of year 1 of the development, assuming the time scale is actually realized for July 1997).

Thereafter, price analysis can be undertaken to exploit seasonal peaks and troughs, and break-even analysis completed with cost–price–volume–profit projections forecasted well into the life of the project.

Estimates will be required for expenditure to include:

1. Venture capital needed to design, build and equip the lodges.
2. Cost of capital for the duration (currently 16 per cent per annum).
3. Working capital requirements to cover all items of revenue expenditure to launch and operate Stage 2.
4. Short-term loans/overdraft requirements.

Cash flow projections will be needed to determine the time period of negative cash flows and the level of short-term funding required. These will depend upon projected sales revenue forecasts for, say, at least three years into the project.

Allowances for contingencies ± 25 per cent should be given to both income and expenditure so as to account for the level of potential financial risk arising from the 'worst possible' scenario as well as the 'best possible' outcome. The feasibility of the project now needs to be considered against its desirability. Projects with a projected return on capital employed of less than the cost of capital would be unwise—unless capital appreciation of the site can be assured.

Payback periods and net gains from the project need careful analysis. The opportunity cost of the capital and time invested in this development should also be evaluated against its desirability.

At a time when market conditions are turbulent, financial analysis for this feasibility study should err on the side of caution.

Purpose of the feasibility assessment The fundamental purpose is to reduce or avert risk under conditions of incomplete knowledge and thereby to assist in confident forward planning.

The marketing implications arising from the feasibility study would be the setting of time-dependent marketing objectives with outline strategic marketing mix plan alternatives to be proposed for consideration.

Cautionary note It would be wise to track the success of Stage 1 before embarking on this feasibility study.

INDEX